Cities of God

The history of archaeology is generally told as the making of a secular discipline. In nineteenth-century Britain, however, archaeology was entangled with questions of biblical authority and so with religious as well as narrowly scholarly concerns. In unearthing the cities of the Mediterranean and Near East, travellers, archaeologists and their popularisers transformed thinking on the truth of Christianity and its place in modern cities. This happened at a time when anxieties over the unprecedented rate of urbanisation in Britain coincided with critical challenges to biblical truth. In this context, cities from Jerusalem to Rome became contested models for the adaptation of Christianity to modern urban life. Using sites from across the biblical world, this book evokes the appeal of the ancient city to diverse groups of British Protestants in their arguments with one another and with their secular and Catholic rivals about the vitality of their faith in urban Britain.

DAVID GANGE is Lecturer in History at the University of Birmingham. He is author of *Dialogues with the Dead: Egyptology in British Culture and Religion* (2013).

MICHAEL LEDGER-LOMAS is Lecturer in the History of Christianity at King's College London. He is editor, with Scott Mandelbrote, of *Dissent and the Bible in Britain, c. 1650–1950* (2013).

Cities of God

The Bible and Archaeology in Nineteenth-Century Britain

DAVID GANGE
AND
MICHAEL LEDGER-LOMAS

CAMBRIDGE
UNIVERSITY PRESS

University Printing House, Cambridge CB2 8BS, United Kingdom

Published in the United States of America by Cambridge University Press, New York

Cambridge University Press is part of the University of Cambridge.

It furthers the University's mission by disseminating knowledge in the pursuit of education, learning, and research at the highest international levels of excellence.

www.cambridge.org
Information on this title: www.cambridge.org/9781107004245

© Cambridge University Press 2013

This publication is in copyright. Subject to statutory exception and to the provisions of relevant collective licensing agreements, no reproduction of any part may take place without the written permission of Cambridge University Press.

First published 2013

Printing in the United Kingdom by TJ International Ltd. Padstow Cornwall

A catalogue record for this publication is available from the British Library

Library of Congress Cataloguing in Publication data
Cities of God : the Bible and archaeology in nineteenth-century Britain / edited by David Gange, Michael Ledger-Lomas.
    pages cm
ISBN 978-1-107-00424-5 (Hardback)
1. Bible – Antiquities   2. Middle East – Antiquities.   3. Archaeology – Great Britain – History – 19th century.   I. Gange, David, author, editor of compilation.   II. Ledger-Lomas, Michael, author, editor of compilation.
BS620.C53   2013
220.9′3094109034–dc23

2013013363

ISBN 978-1-107-00424-5 Hardback

Cambridge University Press has no responsibility for the persistence or accuracy of URLs for external or third-party internet websites referred to in this publication, and does not guarantee that any content on such websites is, or will remain, accurate or appropriate.

Contents

Illustrations   [*page* vi]
Notes on contributors   [xi]
Acknowledgments   [xii]

Introduction   [1]
MICHAEL LEDGER-LOMAS AND DAVID GANGE

1. Troy   [39]
   DAVID GANGE AND RACHEL BRYANT DAVIES

2. Jerusalem   [71]
   SIMON GOLDHILL

3. Nineveh   [111]
   TIMOTHY LARSEN

4. Pithom   [136]
   DAVID GANGE

5. Babylon   [164]
   MICHAEL SEYMOUR

6. Sodom   [197]
   ASTRID SWENSON

7. Bethlehem   [228]
   EITAN BAR-YOSEF

8. Ephesus   [254]
   MICHAEL LEDGER-LOMAS

9. Rome   [285]
   JANE GARNETT AND ANNE BUSH

Bibliography   [315]
Index   [355]

Illustrations

Troy

1.1 Heinrich Schliemann, *The Double Scaean Gate*   [*page* 54]
   Source: Heinrich Schliemann, *Troy and its Remains* (London, 1875), facing p. 303.
1.2 *Schliemann's Excavations at Mycenae*   [66]
   Source: *Illustrated London News* (3 February 1877), p. 1.

Jerusalem

2.1 James Fergusson, *Perspective View of Herod's Temple as Restored*   [83]
   Source: James Fergusson, *The Temples of the Jews and the Other Buildings in the Haram Area at Jerusalem* (London, 1878), frontispiece.
2.2 View of Capharnaum, photograph   [89]
   Source: Yeshayahu Nir, *The Bible and the Image: The History of Photography in the Holy Land, 1839–1899* (Philadelphia, PA, 1985), p. 104.
2.3 *Ruth and Boaz*, photograph   [90]
   Source: Nir, *Bible and the Image*, pp. 144–5.
2.4 Palestinian scene, photograph   [92]
   Source: American Colony, Jerusalem.
2.5 C. R. Ashbee, Sketch for the Redevelopment of Jerusalem   [96]
   Source: King's College, Cambridge, Modern Archives Centre.
2.6 *From a Drawing by Major General C. J. Gordon*   [99]
   Source: Charles Wilson, *Golgotha and the Holy Sepulchre* (London, 1906), p. 206.

Nineveh

3.1 *Lowering the Great Winged Bull*   [112]
   Source: Austen Henry Layard, *Nineveh and its Remains: With an Account of a Visit to the Chaldaean Christians of Kurdistan, and the*

Yezidis, or Devil-Worshippers; and an Enquiry into the Manner and Arts of the Ancient Assyrians (2 vols., London, 1849), I, frontispiece.

3.2 Sculpted relief   [119]
Source: Joseph Bonomi, *Nineveh and its Palaces: The Discoveries of Botta and Layard, Applied to the Elucidation of Holy Writ* (London, 1852), p. 1.

3.3 Henry Phillips, *Austen Henry Layard in Albanian Dress*   [122]
Source: William Bruce, ed., *Sir A. Henry Layard, GCB, DCL, Autobiography and Letters from his Childhood until his Appointment as HM Ambassador at Madrid* (2 vols., London, 1903).

Pithom

4.1 Edward Poynter, *Israel in Egypt*, engraving [detail]   [153]
Source: *Illustrated London News* (30 January 1868), pp. 84–5.

4.2 The brick store-chambers of Hebrew bondsmen   [155]
Source: J. H. Breasted, *Egypt through the Stereoscope* (Washington, DC, 1904), position 32.

4.3 *A Buried City of the Exodus*   [156]
Source: *Illustrated London News* (4 August 1883), p. 124.

Babylon

5.1 Plan of Babylon's ruins   [168]
Source: Claudius Rich, *Memoir on the Ruins of Babylon* (London, 1815), frontispiece.

5.2 Dalziel brothers after Edward John Poynter, *By the Waters of Babylon*, woodcut   [174]
Source: *Dalziels' Bible Gallery: Illustrations from the Old Testament: From Original Drawings by Sir F. Leighton* [etc.] (London, 1881), no pagination.

5.3 John Martin (1789–1854), *Belshazzar's Feast*   [177]
Private Collection, photo © Christie's Images, The Bridgeman Art Library.

5.4 Edwin Long, *The Babylonian Marriage Market* (1875)   [181]
Source: Royal Holloway College, The Bridgeman Art Library.

5.5 Hormuzd Rassam   [185]
Source: British Museum.

5.6 The reconstructed Ishtar Gate in Berlin   [192]
Source: Author's photograph.

Sodom

6.1 *Itinéraire du Pourtour de la Mer Morte* [204]
Source: Louis Félicien Joseph Caignart de Saulcy, *Voyages Autour de la Mer Morte et Dans les Terres Bibliques* (2 vols., Paris, 1853), I, leaf 5.

6.2 *Map of the Dead Sea and Surrounds* [206]
Source: Albert Augustus Isaacs, *The Dead Sea: Or, Notes and Observations made during a Journey to Palestine in 1856–7, on M. de Saulcy's Supposed Discovery of the Cities of the Plain* (London, 1857), facing p. 74.

6.3 John Martin, *The Destruction of Sodom and Gomorrah* (1852) [218]
Source: Laing Art Gallery, Newcastle-upon-Tyne, UK, The Bridgeman Art Library.

6.4 William Holman Hunt, *The Scapegoat* (1854–6) [221]
Reproduced in A. G. Temple, *Sacred Art: The Bible Story Pictured by Eminent Modern Painters* (1903), frontispiece.

6.5 *Looking South, on West Side of Dead Sea, from Am Jiddy (Engedi) with Jebul Usdum in the Far Distance* [223]
Source: Jacob. E. Spafford, 'Around the Dead Sea by Motor Boat', *The Geographical Journal*, 39 (1912), 37–40.

Bethlehem

7.1 J. M. W. Turner, *Bethlehem* [234]
Source: *Landscape Illustrations of the Bible ... from Original Sketches Taken on the Spot Engraved by W. and E. Finden* (2 vols., London, 1836), II, plate 25.

7.2 *Bethlehem* [235]
Source: Henry Baker Tristram, *Scenes in the East: Consisting of 12 Views of Places Mentioned in the Bible* (London, 1884), facing p. 1.

7.3 *The Plains of Bethlehem* [241]
Source: Helen B. Harris, *Pictures of the East: Sketches of Biblical Scenes in Palestine and Greece* (London, 1897), facing p. 45.

7.4 *Mother-of-pearl Workers of Bethlehem* [250]
Source: Charles Wilson, ed., *Picturesque Palestine, Sinai and Egypt* (2 vols., New York: D. Appleton, 1880), I, p. 133.

Ephesus

8.1 Thomas Allom, *Ephesus* [260]

Source: Thamas Allom, *Constantinople and the Scenery of the Seven Churches of Asia Minor* (London, 1838), facing p. 63.

8.2 *Ephesus*, photographic plate   [261]
Source: Alexander Svoboda, *The Seven Churches of Asia* (London, 1869), no pagination.

8.3 *Ephesus*   [266]
Source: Edward Falkener, *Ephesus and the Temple of Diana* (London, 1863), frontispiece.

8.4 *View of Excavation on the Site of the Temple, looking East, December 1871*   [268]
Source: John Turtle Wood, *Discoveries at Ephesus: Including the Site and Remains of the Great Temple of Diana* (1877), first plate following p. 192.

8.5 *The Ephesus Room*   [272]
Source: Ada Habershon, *The Bible and the British Museum* (London, 1909), facing p. 9.

8.6 Gustave Doré, *St Paul at Ephesus*   [279]
Source: *The Holy Bible: Containing the Old and New Testaments, According to the Authorised Version, With Illustrations by Gustave Doré* (3 vols., London, 1889–91), III, facing p. 200.

Rome

9.1 Robert Macpherson, *Portion of the Interior Wall of the Coliseum, c. 1860*, albumen print from collodian negative   [288]
Source: The Trout Gallery at Dickinson College, Carlisle, PA.

9.2 Unknown photographer, *Recent Excavations – Chamber of the House of Pudens of the First Century, Excavated in March 1870, in front of the Church of S. Pudentiana, West Side*, 1870, Parker catalogue no. 1733, albumen print from collodian negative   [296]
Source: Parker Collection of Historical Photographs, Oxford: Ashmolean Museum (on loan to Department of the History of Art).

9.3 Unknown photographer, *Excavations 1871 – View of the Ruins of the Porta Capena, with the Gardener's Cottage, to Shew the Exact Site of It*, 1871, Parker catalogue no. 2222, albumen print from collodian negative   [297]
Source: Parker Collection of Historical Photographs, Oxford: Ashmolean Museum (on loan to Department of the History of Art).

9.4 *Palace of the Caesars* [304]
Source: W. J. Conybeare and J. S. Howson, *The Life and Epistles of St Paul* (2 vols., London, 1856), II, p. 512.

9.5 *The Mamertine Prison, Rome*. Drawn by W. Linton on the spot. Engraved by E. Finden [305]
Source: J. M. Wilson, *Landscapes of Interesting Localities Mentioned in the Holy Scriptures* (2 vols., Edinburgh, London and Dublin, 1852), II, facing p. 280.

9.6 Charles Smeaton, *Catacomb of S. Domitilla – Brickwork at the Entrance, c. AD 100, Taken with Magnesian Light*, c. 1864–6, Parker catalogue no. 620, albumen print from collodian negative [306]
Source: Parker Collection of Historical Photographs, Oxford: Ashmolean Museum.

9.7 *Interior of Colosseum* [307]
Source: Richard Deakin, *Flora of the Colosseum of Rome; or, Illustrations and Descriptions of Four Hundred and Twenty Plants Growing Spontaneously upon the Ruins of the Colosseum of Rome* (London, 1855; 1873 edn), facing p. 48.

Notes on contributors

DAVID GANGE is a lecturer in the Department of History at the University of Birmingham.

MICHAEL LEDGER-LOMAS is Lecturer in the History of Christianity at King's College, London.

RACHEL BRYANT-DAVIES recently completed a Ph.D. in Classics at the University of Cambridge.

SIMON GOLDHILL is Professor of Greek and the Director of CRASSH, University of Cambridge.

TIMOTHY LARSEN is Carolyn and Fred McManis Professor of Christian Thought, Wheaton College, Illinois.

MICHAEL SEYMOUR works at the Metropolitan Museum of Art, New York.

ASTRID SWENSON is a lecturer in the Department of Politics and History, Brunel University.

EITAN BAR-YOSEF is a senior lecturer in the Department of Foreign Literatures and Linguistics, Ben-Gurion University of the Negev.

ANNE BUSH is Professor and Chair of Design in the Department of Art and Art History at the University of Hawai`i.

JANE GARNETT is a fellow and tutor in History at Wadham College, Oxford.

Acknowledgments

This book is the outcome of work undertaken by the Cambridge Victorian Studies Group, which was generously funded by the Leverhulme Trust. Alongside the Trust, the editors would also like to thank King's College, Cambridge which hosted the two-day workshop at which drafts of this book's chapters were discussed. They are grateful to the directors of the Cambridge Victorian Studies Group – Mary Beard, Simon Goldhill, Peter Mandler, Clare Pettitt and James Secord – for their support during their three years as postdoctoral fellows on the project. They also owe a great deal to the contributions of their colleagues: Jos Betts, Helen Brookman, Adelene Buckland, Rachel Bryant Davies, Sadiah Qureshi, Astrid Swenson and Anna Vaninskaya. As well as the contributors to the collection and members of the Cambridge Victorian Studies Group, several other scholars made important contributions to the workshop, notably Scott Mandelbrote, Jonathan Parry, Eleanor Robson and William St Clair. Michael Sharp, Liz Hanlon and Gillian Dadd at Cambridge University Press have demonstrated superhuman patience and supportiveness in shepherding the volume into print, while the text has been much improved by the comments of anonymous readers for the Press. Ruth Long and the other members of the Imaging Department at Cambridge University Library were extremely helpful in procuring the majority of the images for this volume, as too was John Moelwyn-Hughes at the Bridgeman Art Library. Both editors would like to thank their current institutions for their support: the School of History and Cultures, University of Birmingham and the Department of Theology and Religious Studies, King's College, London, respectively.

Introduction

MICHAEL LEDGER-LOMAS AND DAVID GANGE

> Glorious things are spoken of thee, O city of God (Psalm 87: 3)

At the turn of the twentieth century, Sir William Willcocks (1852–1932), one of Britain's leading engineers, proposed a scheme for the economic regeneration of the Near East. He aimed to export the urban growth of Victorian Britain to regions which he saw as key arenas in the imperial mission. Willcocks had recently designed the Aswan dam, which revolutionised agriculture in the Nile valley, when he published *The Restoration of the Ancient Irrigation Works on the Tigris: Or, the Recreation of Chaldea* (1903). He argued that the cities of the Old Testament had declined and disappeared because of geographical change, specifically alterations in the courses of the great rivers. By reversing this change, British industry could lead cities such as Ur, the birthplace of Abraham, to spring up again in all their ancient glory; the prosperity of the Bible lands could be restored. His biblical schemes for the rejuvenation of the rivers of the Old Testament world were raised in the House of Commons, presented at the solemn proceedings of the leading learned societies and discussed at length in the British and American press. Politicians professed their sympathy, but eventually baulked at the funds that would need to be raised to carry them out.[1] It was a quixotic campaign, proposed by a fervent Protestant who also wished to use the evidence of ancient waterways to locate the vanished Garden of Eden – his aim being not just to restore Ur, but paradise. Yet it encapsulates the theme of this book, which explores the presence of the biblical city in nineteenth-century British culture.[2] Its chapters show that it was in cities that archaeology, the study of the Bible and contemporary experiences of urbanisation intersected throughout the long nineteenth century.

---

[1] See, e.g., 'Egypt: The Storage of the Nile Waters – the Raian Basin', 2 August 1888, *Hansard*, 329, 1216–17; Colonel Ardagh and Conyers Surtees in *Proceedings of the Royal Geographical Society*, 9 (1887).

[2] 'The Garden of Eden and its Restoration: Discussion', *The Geographical Journal*, 40 (1912), 145–8; William Willcocks, *From the Garden of Eden to the Crossing of the Jordan* (Cairo, 1919); William Willcocks, *Sixty Years in the East* (London, 1935); Alessandro Scafi, *Mapping Paradise: A History of Heaven on Earth* (Chicago, 2006), pp. 348–50.

In the decades before Willcocks dreamed of Chaldea, Great Britain had become perhaps the most densely urbanised nation on earth. Urbanisation had been a distinctive feature of England's eighteenth-century economic development. In the half-century before 1800, England had accounted for 70 per cent of urban growth in Europe, despite possessing only 7.7 per cent of its population. A striking feature of this urbanisation was the rapid growth of provincial cities. The combined population of Manchester, Birmingham, Liverpool and Leeds rose from around 30,000 inhabitants in 1700 to around 300,000 by 1800. This drift to towns became an unstoppable current in the nineteenth century. By mid-century, the majority of Britons lived in towns, while several cities had experienced staggering rates of growth. From 1750 to 1850 for instance, the population of Liverpool leapt from 22,000 to 376,000 people.[3] By the early twentieth century, over 75 per cent of the population of England and Wales lived in towns; half a million people lived in large provincial cities and over 6 million in greater London, which symbolised the new age of the metropolis.[4]

While urbanisation became a global, even universal, phenomenon in the century after 1850, Britain was unusual in having to confront its problems and seize its potential from an early date. Urbanisation in this period was not simply a function of industrialisation, nor reducible to quantitative measures of productive activity or population density: what made cities was the creation of distinctively urban experiences and ways of life.[5] When nineteenth-century Britons sought to comprehend, celebrate, lament or direct the urbanisation of their society, they reached for idealised models of city life drawn from history, mythology and religion. It is the starting point for this volume both that the Bible was a vital, perhaps even the principal, source of such models and that urbanisation made British scholars, and their publics, unusually interested in them.

Britons interested in biblical cities were well poised to make new use of an ancient category. Not only were the pages of the Bible scattered with hundreds of cities, but for centuries some of them had been abiding symbols of vice or spiritual possibility. While Jerusalem stood alone as *the* city of God, the object of Jewish yearning and lament and Christian meditation, other cities had come to encapsulate the perils and opportunities facing all

---

[3] E. A. Wrigley, *Energy and the English Industrial Revolution* (Cambridge, 2010), pp. 60–7.
[4] Lynne Lees, 'Urban Networks', in Martin Daunton, ed., *The Cambridge Urban History of Britain: 1840–1950* (Cambridge, 2000), pp. 68–9.
[5] Jürgen Osterhammel, *Die Verwandlung der Welt: Eine Geschichte des 19 Jahrhundert* (Munich, 2009), pp. 366, 380.

Christians: Babylon, Sodom and Gomorrah, Rome.[6] The premise of this book is that what was new in the study and depiction of biblical cities in nineteenth-century Britain was not just the scale of the social problems that needed explaining in the present, but also the quantity of information that travellers and archaeologists could amass about them. Histories of archaeology in the Mediterranean and Near East have recognised its intimate dependence on imperial power and commercial clout, but its biblical preoccupations have often been seen as a quirky tangent or an embarrassing obstacle to scientific progress. By embedding the discoverers of ancient cities in the world of Protestant thought from which many of them emerged and to which they all contributed, this book makes an interlinked contribution to the histories of archaeology and Victorian religious cultures – showing what the former did for the Bible, but also what the Bible did for them.

The variety of cities in the Bible is overwhelming, ranging as it does from Memphis (Noph in the Old Testament) to Petra (Edom) and from Corinth to Ur; from obscure settlements whose location or very existence was long disputed to centres of immemorial power and prestige, such as Damascus and Rome. Rather than covering all of these cities, this volume offers a series of nine overlapping portraits, which suggest the range and depth of the preoccupation with biblical cities in nineteenth-century Britain. It also ranges outside the pages of the Bible itself to cover Troy, where nineteenth-century excavations suggested connections between an ancient city and an authoritative text that had a direct impact on thinking about the Bible. While the strength of these chapters lies in their variety, they feature a recurrent set of preoccupations, which the remainder of this introduction outlines in some detail, providing a map of the religious and institutional terrain onto which the chapters can then be plotted.

The first theme is the connection between the ancient city and understandings of biblical authority. The change from understanding the world as comprehended within Scripture to understanding Scripture as comprehended within the ancient world in which it was produced was a tectonic shift in the making of modern culture.[7] Yet the speed and extent of that shift are still not yet fully understood. It is often identified with the growing prestige of the natural sciences and the rise, predominantly in German

---

[6] There are 1,171 uses of the words 'city' and 'cities' in the Authorized Version of the Bible.
[7] Hans Frei, *The Eclipse of Biblical Narrative* (London, 1974); Henning Graf von Reventlow, *The Authority of the Bible and the Rise of the Modern World* (London, 1985); David Katz, *God's Last Words: Reading the English Bible from the Reformation to Fundamentalism* (London, 2004).

universities, of higher criticism as a discipline, which in combination suggested that the Scriptures could not be an authoritative record of what had really happened in the past because miracles did not happen.[8] This book suggests a more complicated picture, arguing that archaeology helped British apologists to perpetuate the legacy of their scholarly predecessors, insisting that the Bible could pass the most stringent empirical and scientific tests of its accuracy in matters of fact. The anxiety to see in the Bible the unique measure of truth provided a cause around which a position on the relationship between the Bible and archaeology assumed a powerful if unstable unity. To term this a 'Protestant' position is not of course to suggest that Protestant churches, parties and sects agreed on the proper weight to accord Scripture, empirical inquiry and the testimony of tradition. The chapters that follow survey attitudes and people that range from Anglican high churchmen who looked tenderly on traditions associated with sites such as the Holy Sepulchre to Protestant dissenters, both Trinitarian and Unitarian, whose spiky independence and aversion to hierarchy and ritual made them sceptical of sacralising places without the express authorisation of Scripture. Nor is it to deny that British writers remained heavily dependent on the contributions of foreign scholars, both Catholic and Protestant, and on the collaboration of local informants. It is, though, to explore a literature that was cross-denominational in its appeal and a rhetoric of exploration and authentication whose nationalist emphases obscured the inconvenient truths that British travellers in the Mediterranean and Near East were often intellectually dependent on Continental allies and confronted on all sides by the material traces of a Catholic piety of place that they ostentatiously rejected.

The second, related theme of the book is the crucial contribution made by scientific travellers and then archaeologists to this apologetic discourse. The fault lines of biblical authority ran through the biblical city. On the one side were German higher critics and their British epigones, who wanted to decompose books of the Bible into oral and documentary traditions and then to reassemble them into secularised histories of religious thought. On the other was a shifting alliance of religious thinkers who wished to defend the Bible as a fairly transparent set of narratives about the world and who found in urban archaeology convincing proofs of its accuracy. This book stresses the institutional developments that made such archaeology possible and its privileged connection with the religious sphere – public, but not

---

[8] Frederick Gregory, *Nature Lost? Natural Science and the German Theological Traditions of the Nineteenth Century* (Cambridge, MA, 1992), parts 1 and 2.

necessarily critical – in which debates about the authority of the Bible took place. It argues that archaeology not only belongs alongside geology, higher criticism and the comparative study of religion as a discipline of historical recovery that affected the reading of the Bible, but that it often worked to complicate and disrupt rather than to complement the impact of these other disciplines.

The final important theme, one which distinguishes this book from existing surveys of biblical archaeology, is its attention to the religious and urban context in which these debates took place. Not only did an ever growing number of British Protestants live in increasingly large towns and cities, but they were interested in turning cities to religious purposes. The churches, historians of Victorian religion now recognise, had not given up on the city.[9] When they thought about how to reform their own cities, Protestant ministers and laity turned to the cities of the Bible for encouragement and admonition. Archaeologists could rely on an appreciative hearing in a culture that increasingly defined Christianity as an urban religion. 'No other religion which has a Heaven ever had a Heaven like this,' wrote the fluent lay evangelist Henry Drummond (1851–97) about Saint John's dream of the New Jerusalem. 'Christianity is the religion of Cities.'[10] Duncan Bell has suggested that later Victorian thinkers were reluctant to concede that the histories of Greece and Rome offered patterns for the fate of their own imperial society and that they increasingly rejected parallels between their own imperial polity and Greco-Roman city states.[11] Yet Christian preoccupations bridged the widening gulf between ancient and modern. The chapters show that as new technologies brought nineteenth-century Protestants face to face with the ancient past – carrying them to the sites by railway and steamship, bringing photographs of them into their Bibles and homes – the effect could be estranging, with the imposing cities of their imagination fading to untenanted ruins or squalid hamlets. Yet at the same time they worked to rebuild their grandeur through colossal exhibitions, imagined reconstructions or even by rebuilding at the sites themselves. They recognised that city life was as much mental as material and worked to instantiate civic and religious ideals first worked out in biblical cities within their own culture.

---

[9] Simon Green, 'Church and City Revisited: New Evidence from the North of England, c.1815–1914', *Northern History*, 43 (2006), 345–60.
[10] Henry Drummond, *The City Without a Church* (London, 1893), p. 9.
[11] Duncan Bell, 'From Ancient to Modern in Victorian Imperial Thought', *Historical Journal*, 49 (2006), 735–59.

The foundations of the biblical city: text, exploration and belief

Christian interest in the cities of the Old and New Testament is almost as old as Christianity. Jerusalem and Rome had for instance been sites of pilgrimage from late antiquity onwards, when Christian devotion to the Holy Land and to the tombs of saints had created a new sacred topography which rivalled then supplanted that of the pagans: sacralising sites, amassing relics and erecting imposing shrines and churches on top of them and generating in due course a rich culture of antiquarianism, which would be both a resource and embarrassment to Protestant travellers.[12] The specific motive for nineteenth-century British interest in visiting, digging up and reconstructing these cities derived, though, from a transformation in the understanding of the Bible that had begun with early modern efforts to contextualise both the Old and New Testaments.[13] From the later sixteenth century, Protestant scholars had injected greater discipline into the study of Old Testament texts, insisting that before they were read typologically they must first be understood literally. This literal sense was a historical one, to be recovered through antiquarian and philological comparison of the language and customs of the Hebrews with those of neighbouring peoples. Prolonged strife between Protestants and Catholics over the origin and lineaments of the primitive church and the rebellion by pietists and latitudinarians against

---

[12] E. D. Hunt, *Holy Land Pilgrimage in the Later Roman Empire AD 312–460* (Oxford, 1982); R. A. Markus, *The End of Ancient Christianity* (Cambridge, 1991), pp. 139–57; Jas Elsner and Ian Rutherford, eds., *Pilgrimage in Greco-Roman and Early Christian Antiquity: Seeing the Gods* (Oxford, 2007).

[13] For the arguments in this paragraph see, from a huge literature, Peter Harrison, *'Religion' and the Religions in the English Enlightenment* (Cambridge, 1990), chapters 4 and 5; François Laplanche, *La Bible en France: entre mythe et critique, 16ème – 19ème siècles* (Paris, 1994); B. W. Young, *Religion and the Enlightenment in Eighteenth-Century England: Theological Debate from Locke to Burke* (Oxford, 1994); Debora Shuger, *The Renaissance Bible: Scholarship, Sacrifice and Subjectivity* (London, 1998); Jonathan Sheehan, *The Enlightenment Bible: Translation, Scholarship, Culture* (Princeton, NJ, 2005), chapter 4; David Sorkin, *The Religious Enlightenment: Protestants, Jews, and Catholics from London to Vienna* (Princeton, NJ, 2008); Suzanne Marchand, *German Orientalism in the Age of Empire: Religion, Race, and Scholarship* (Cambridge, 2009); Scott Mandelbrote, 'Biblical Hermeneutics and the Sciences, 1700–1900: An Overview', in Jiste van der Meer and Scott Mandelbrote, eds., *Nature and Scripture in the Abrahamic Religions: To 1700* (Leiden, 2009), pp. 1–37; J. G. A. Pocock, *Barbarism and Religion: Volume 5, Religion: The First Triumph* (Cambridge, 2011); Scott Mandelbrote, 'Early Modern Biblical Interpretation and the Emergence of Science', *Science and Christian Belief*, 23 (2011), 105–10. For a brilliant recent survey see Dmitri Levitin, 'From Sacred History to the History of Religion: Paganism, Judaism and Christianity in European Historiography from Reformation to "Enlightenment"', *Historical Journal*, 52 (2013).

Reformation scholasticism committed scholars with very different confessional allegiances to contextualising the actions and utterances of Christ and his apostles in the world of the ancient Mediterranean. Sacred history was therefore not so much secularised as hybridised, its story now supplemented and explained by insertion into and comparison with other civilisations. Insofar as this enterprise was an enlightened one, it formed part of a clerical or religious enlightenment centred on Britain and Protestant Germany. Aware that deists were making anti-clerical use of antiquarian researches to undermine faith in a written revelation, British and German scholars sought to show that the morals and learning of the Hebrews were appropriate to their time. They sought moreover to show that it was possible to treat large passages of Scripture as historical narratives or prophetic predictions, whose factual accuracy could be tested in minute detail. Alongside the internal evidences for the Bible's truth – correspondences between its different books or its agreement with the dictates of human conscience – they could adduce external coincidences between its narratives and the built, engraved and written remains of the world that it had described. Cities were storehouses of such evidence.

Not only was there ever greater reason to be interested in the cities of the Bible, but it was becoming easier to reach them. Most of them were located in an Ottoman Empire dwindling from a feared opponent of Christendom into a reluctant diplomatic and commercial partner that now had to accommodate European visitors. Chaplains and consuls in Smyrna from the later seventeenth century onwards were some of the first to seek out lost cities in Asia Minor, while the Society of Dilettanti sponsored investigations there and in the Aegean.[14] Such activities strengthened a reorientation of interest from the Grand Tour of Italy to new hunting grounds in the eastern Mediterranean. The wealth of publications on ruins that resulted brought a new lease of life to the venerable study of biblical antiquities. Scholars no longer had to rely on ancient authorities such as Josephus to supplement their Bibles but could draw on the direct testimony amassed by travellers. The potential use of travel literature was obvious to Johann David Michaelis (1717–91), a Göttingen professor who sponsored the expedition of Carsten Niebuhr (1733–1815) to the site of Babylon, as discussed in Michael Seymour's chapter below. Using Niebuhr's findings in the notes to his edition of the Bible, Michaelis developed a 'philology of things', which

---

[14] James Mather, *Pashas: Traders and Travellers in the Islamic World* (London, 2009); Richard Chandler, *Travels in Asia Minor and Greece: Or, An Account of a Tour Made at the Expense of the Society of Dilettanti* (London, 1776); Laplanche, *Bible*, p. 72; Bruce Redford, 'The Measure of Ruins: Dilettanti in the Levant, 1750–1770', *Harvard Library Bulletin*, 13 (2002), 5–36.

cross-referenced the text with an archive of extra-textual knowledge about people, cities and nature.[15] If his enterprise looks alluringly modern, then the discovery of cities also reinvigorated older methods of reading the Bible. Students of prophecy argued that travellers could test the warnings both of the Old Testament and the Book of Revelation against the evidence of things seen: cities menaced by God with destruction had been literally destroyed.[16]

The ties between text and city in British thought were disrupted, but finally much reinforced by the Revolutionary and Napoleonic Wars. The attempt to read the Bible on its own terms rather than through the creeds of the established church became suspect to many Anglicans while the British were fighting a state and a nation that the *philosophes* had made. The evangelical revival, whose religion was at once experiential and doctrinal, revived allegorical and typological readings of the Scriptures that had never been wholly displaced by the pursuit of the literal sense.[17] War encouraged many Britons to see themselves or at least their particular sect as a covenanted nation, the antitype of Israel.[18] In Ashton-under-Lyne, the 'Christian Israelites' who followed John Wroe (1782–1863) not only adopted Jewish dietary practices, but attempted to build a New Jerusalem in the Pennines, complete with gatehouses.[19] Raised on a diet of triumphs and disasters, a generation of writers on prophecy urged that theirs was not the historical study of things past but the decipherment of calamities still to come. For many British Protestants, the prophetic enemy would still be the Roman Catholic Church, lending a confessional emphasis to many of the investigations pursued in the volume. For evangelicals in particular Rome was more than ever the Beast of Revelation rather than a site of pilgrimage or the hunting ground for Christian antiquities.

---

[15] Sheehan, *Bible*, chapter 8; Michael Carhart, *The Science of Culture in Enlightenment Germany* (Cambridge, MA, 2005); Michael Legaspi, *The Death of Scripture and the Rise of Biblical Studies* (Oxford, 2010).

[16] Neil Hitchin, 'The Evidence of Things Seen: Georgian Churchmen and Biblical Prophecy', in Bertrand Taithe and Tim Thornton, eds., *Prophecy: The Power of Inspired Language in History 1300–2000* (Stroud, 1997), pp. 119–42.

[17] See Mandelbrote, 'Early Modern Biblical Interpretation' and Scott Mandelbrote, 'Early Modern Natural Theologies', in Russell Manning, ed., *Oxford Handbook to Natural Theology* (Oxford, 2013) for qualifications to the prioritisation of the literal reading by Protestant scholars.

[18] Nigel Aston, 'Horne and Heterodoxy: The Defence of Anglican Beliefs in Late Enlightenment', *English Historical Review*, 108 (1993), 895–919; John Gascoigne, *Cambridge in the Age of the Enlightenment: Science, Religion and Politics from the Restoration to the French Revolution* (Cambridge, 1986); John Gascoigne, 'Anglican Latitudinarianism, Rational Dissent and Political Radicalism in the Late Eighteenth Century', in Knud Haakonssen, ed., *Enlightenment and Religion: Rational Dissent in Eighteenth-Century Britain* (Cambridge, 1996), pp. 219–40.

[19] Philip Lockley, 'Millenarians in the Pennines, 1800–1830: Building and Believing in Jerusalem', *Northern History*, 47 (2010), 297–317.

At the same time, the radicalisation of 'higher criticism' imperilled the project from a different direction. German critics recognised that the effort to ascertain the literal meaning of Scripture caused religious difficulties when it asserted things that either could not have happened (miracles), or should not have happened (God's approval of massacres carried out by the Israelites). The anxiety to retain the Bible as a religious resource pushed many critics to explain that the stories in which miracle narratives were embedded did not pretend to historical truth. Instead they expressed the mythopoeia common to all early literatures. God's apparent endorsement of cruelty or immorality could similarly be explained by a theory of accommodation in which divine revelation was always tailored to the limited understanding of a primitive people. Both forms of rationalism spread to New Testament criticism, helping to explain Jesus Christ to a culture reluctant to accept either his miracles or his claims to messianic and superhuman status. The writings of David Friedrich Strauss (1808–74) and Ferdinand Christian Baur (1792–1860) were totemic examples of German historicism. Strauss had cast doubt on the possibility of sorting historical fact about the life of Jesus from myth and legend in the gospels while Baur recast most of the New Testament as the end product of struggles to shape the doctrine of the early church rather than an authentic portrait of Jesus and the apostles.[20]

Until the later nineteenth century, 'Germanism' occasioned splenetic reactions in both Britain and America. Yet as many of the chapters in this volume show, the dread of 'rationalism' and 'neology' strengthened commitment to finding concrete proofs of the veracity of biblical narrative. The religious world in Britain was hardly united in its reaction to German theology and biblical criticism and a fuller account than is possible here would trace a spectrum of reactions from panicked denial to calm acceptance. Yet until the later nineteenth century, a conviction that systematic collection and study of external evidences could help to ascertain and defend the literal meaning and the historical truth of Scripture was widespread among British Protestants. Evidential treatises by Nathaniel Lardner (1684–1768), William Paley (1743–1805), Thomas Chalmers (1780–1847) and others were never out of print and plenty of new ones were published.[21] Not the least attraction of the study of

---

[20] Among the many guides to this shift are Frei, *Eclipse*; Gregory, *Natural Science*, parts 1 and 2; Thomas Howard, *Religion and the Rise of Historicism: W. M. L. de Wette, Jacob Burckhardt, and the Theological Origins of Nineteenth-Century Historical Consciousness* (Cambridge, 2000).

[21] See Michael Ledger-Lomas, 'Shipwrecked: James Smith and the Defence of Biblical Narrative in Victorian Britain', *Angermion*, 1 (2008), 83–110.

evidence was that it allowed one to demolish the flying buttresses of extra-scriptural traditions with which the Roman Catholic Church had supported the text.

British evangelicals felt that providence had appointed them to find such evidences. The informal empire that Britain established in and around the Mediterranean served a religious mission in which a defence of Christian civilisation was superimposed onto an older anti-Catholicism. During the Napoleonic Wars, the Royal Navy not only wrecked Napoleon's expedition to Egypt – itself a stimulus to the scholarly investigation of biblical lands – but established its lasting dominance in the Mediterranean. Its officers knew their classics and Bible and in the course of their duties amassed much new information about the location and present condition of ancient cities.[22] The struggle to find and expropriate prestigious classical antiquities had been a pursuit of war by other means and it outlasted the war itself; after the peace, the fragmentation of the Ottoman Empire encouraged piratical consuls and adventurers to get their hands on whatever they could and to ship it back to the British Museum. The result was a shift away from such leisured, even hedonistic, collectors as the Catholics Charles Townley (1737–1805) and Henry Blundell (1724–1810) who had drawn on private means to collect Roman antiquities in Italy.[23] The new breed of collectors were often enabled or even funded by the British state, whose interest in culture was no less real than that of France or Prussia, albeit less generous.[24] Scientific journeys often enjoyed a direct or semi-detached relationship with European state power. Thomas Spratt (1811–88) and Edward Forbes (1815–54) had for instance explored Asia Minor as part of the expedition to seize the Xanthus marbles for the British Museum; the French state commissioned investigations of Asia Minor by Charles Texier (1802–72) and Léon de Laborde (1807–69). The foundation of an Anglo-Prussian bishopric at Jerusalem as part of manoeuvres designed to contain the influence of France and its ally Mehmet Ali (1827–78) in the

---

[22] See, e.g., Francis Beaufort, *Karamania: Or, a Brief Description of the South Coast of Asia-Minor* (London, 1817); Charles Leonard Irby and James Mangles, *Travels in Egypt and Nubia, Syria, and Asia Minor, During the Years 1817 and 1818* (London, 1823).

[23] See, e.g., Edmund Southworth, 'The Ince Blundell Collection: Collecting Behaviour in the Eighteenth Century', *Journal of the History of Collections*, 3 (1991), 219–34; Viccy Coltman, *Classical Sculpture and the Culture of Collecting in Britain since 1760* (Oxford, 2009).

[24] Debbie Challis, *From the Harpy Tomb to the Wonders of Ephesus: British Archaeologists in the Ottoman Empire 1840–1880* (London, 2008); Holger Hoock, *Empires of the Imagination: Politics, War, and the Arts in the British World, 1750–1850* (London, 2010).

Mediterranean basin is another indication of how the Protestant appropriation of the region benefited from the extension of informal empire.

The hunt for cities and their contents remained a scientific and a co-operative as well as an acquisitive and imperialist pursuit. Early nineteenth-century travellers were not just pocket Nelsons, intent on national aggrandisement, but were part of a transnational and increasingly a transatlantic republic of letters, a world made by words whose members evolved shared procedures to check and supplement the discoveries of their predecessors.[25] If there was 'co-operative emulation' between the British and French empires for much of this period, then the same holds true for relations between their scholars.[26] Thus although British public opinion alternately feared and mocked the adventuresome Napoleon III as a 'Tiberius of the Tuileries', he was admired for sponsoring expeditions to discover antiquities in Asia Minor, Syria and Palestine. British scholars who had to trim their ambitions to the stinginess of their 'great commercial nation' envied the well-funded expeditions undertaken in Asia Minor, Syria and Palestine by William Waddington (1826–94), the Comte de Vogüé (1848–1910) and Ernest Renan (1823–1902).[27]

Travellers who benefited financially or otherwise from the growing reach of the imperial state fostered a new approach to classical and biblical texts. Doyens of 'scientific travelling', such as Edward Daniel Clarke (1769–1822) and William Leake (1777–1860) methodically collected observations and local place names, which they then compared with Pausanias or Strabo, offering the prospect of stepping outside the circle of antiquarian commentary on authoritative texts and rigorously testing their accuracy for the first time.[28] This procedure applied equally to the classics of Greek and Roman literature or to the Old and New Testaments. Thus Major James Rennell (1742–1830), a retired surveyor-general to the East India Company, used his cartographic skills and the information of travellers to resolve problems as various as the location of Troy and Babylon, the death of the Gadarene

---

[25] See Anthony Grafton, *Worlds Made by Words: Scholarship and Community in the Modern West* (Cambridge, MA, 2009) on this community in an earlier era.

[26] David Todd, 'A French Imperial Meridian, 1814–1870', *Past and Present*, 210 (2011), 155–86.

[27] George T. Stokes, 'Recent Discoveries and the Christian Faith: I', *The Sunday at Home* (25 May 1889), 325–6; Jon Parry, 'The Impact of Napoleon III on British Politics, 1851–1880', *Transactions of the Royal Historical Society*, 11 (2001), 147–75.

[28] William Martin Leake, *Journal of a Tour in Asia Minor, with Comparative Remarks on the Ancient and Modern Geography of that Country* (London, 1824), p. v; Malcolm Wagstaff, 'Colonel Leake and the Historical Geography of Greece', in James Moore, Ian Morris and Andrew Bayliss, eds., *Reinventing History: The Enlightenment Origins of Ancient History* (London, 2008), pp. 169–83; Richard Stoneman, *Land of Lost Gods: The Search for Classical Greece* (London, 1987).

swine and Paul's shipwreck.[29] Antiquarian books, Reginald Stuart Poole (1832–95) later concluded in his guide to the *Cities of Egypt* (1882), could now be 'left to idle curiosity... We now know that it is worse than useless to speculate where we can observe, to theorise when we have only to reach out our hands and grasp the facts.'[30] This intimate connection between philology and exploration endured in both classical and Near Eastern archaeology. Philologists depended on explorers to find the written materials on which they worked, while explorers needed inscriptions to identify and date cities and their monuments in the age before stratigraphy.[31]

The study of cities quickly became integral to proving the authority of texts, not least because it was easier to authenticate the location of places than to prove a course of events. This turn was most evident in the Holy Land, where the American scholar Edward Robinson provided British investigators with a method and rhetoric in his *Biblical Researches in Palestine, Mount Sinai, and Arabia Petraea* (1841). German-trained, Robinson diligently collected place names and observed geographical features, comparing these data with the text of Scripture as a way of identifying biblical locations without needing to rely on dubious religious traditions.[32] Robinson's prestige is another example of how the British passions explored in this book were part of a wider Protestant pattern. His American public was just as eager as the British for news of biblical sites and the growing number of American missionaries in the region was well placed to provide it.[33] Robinson's co-author Eli Smith (1801–57) was a Presbyterian missionary, as was William McClure Thomson (1806–94), whose *The Land and the Book* (1859) soon rivalled Robinson with the British public.[34] Robinson inspired British

---

[29] James Rennell, *The Geographical System of Herodotus Examined and Explained, by a Comparison with Those of Other Ancient Authors, and with Modern Geography* (London, 1800); James Rennell, 'On the Topography of Ancient Babylon: Suggested by the Recent Observations and Discoveries of Claudius James Rich, Esq.', *Archaeologia*, 18 (1817), 244–62; James Rennell 'On the Voyage, and Place of Shipwreck, of Saint Paul, A.D. 62', *Archaeologia*, 21 (1827), 92–108; James Rennell, 'Concerning the Identity of the Architectural Remains at Jerash, and Whether They are Those of Gerasa, or of Pella', *Archaeologia*, 21 (Jan. 1827), 138–47.

[30] Reginald Stuart Poole, *The Cities of Egypt* (London, 1882), pp. 32–3.

[31] Eve Gran-Aymerich, *La Naissance de l'archaéologie moderne, 1798–1945* (Paris, 1998), chapter 2 and p. 130; Bruce Trigger, *A History of Archaeological Thought* (Cambridge, 1996), p. 165; Thomas Davis, *Shifting Sands: The Rise and Fall of Biblical Archaeology* (Oxford, 2004), p. 19.

[32] Ibid., pp. 6–10.

[33] Andrew Porter, *Religion Versus Empire? British Protestant Missionaries and Overseas Expansion, 1700–1914* (Manchester, 2004), pp. 120–5; John Davis, *The Landscape of Belief: Encountering the Holy Land in Nineteenth-Century American Art and Culture* (Princeton, NJ, 1996).

[34] Heleen Muree-van Den Berg, 'William McClure Thomson's *The Land and the Book* (1859): Pilgrimage and Mission in Palestine', in Muree-van Den Berg, ed., *New Faith in Ancient Lands:*

imitators. Arthur Penrhyn Stanley (1815–81) took Robinson's book with him on the tour that resulted in his *Sinai and Palestine, in Connexion with Their History* (1856). Like Robinson, Stanley felt that to stand within the remains of biblical cities was to feel an intuitive confidence in the reality of the texts that described them.[35] George Adam Smith (1856–1942), a Free Churchman trained in Germany and who owed his introduction to Palestine to a spell in Egypt with the American Mission, produced an enduring classic of the genre: the *Historical Geography of the Holy Land* (1894), whose popularity is noted in Simon Goldhill's chapter.

The assurances about the reality of scriptural narrative that 'sacred geography' provided became more important during the third quarter of the nineteenth century as higher criticism began to be more widely debated in Britain. Poole was representative in observing of biblical events that 'no sooner are they fixed than they become real'.[36] Both British and German higher critics often used geographical slips in the text of Scripture to destabilise its historical authority. Populisers of archaeology therefore loved nothing more than parables of death and resurrection in which cities whose very existence was pooh-poohed by the critics were suddenly found in their proper places by the discovery of 'some ancient monument, a tablet, a statue, or a coin'.[37] Thus the Rev. Josias Leslie Porter (1823–89), an Irish Presbyterian missionary in Syria, confessed he had suspected the Pentateuch of exaggeration when it described the Israelites conquering sixty walled cities and still more unwalled towns (Deuteronomy 3:4–5) in Bashan, a land no bigger than Kent. But it was the simple truth: he had counted them on his recent travels there and vindicated a three-thousand-year-old text.[38] This rhetoric spilled into adjacent fields. David Gange and Rachel Bryant Davies show below that, although the hunt for Troy was not new in the nineteenth century, the context for Heinrich Schliemann's celebrated finds was a desire to poke in the eye the critics who had butchered Livy and Homer before dismembering the Bible.

This apologetic discourse was popular. What we might term Higher Tourism benefited from the insatiable appetite for travel writing in the early Victorian period. The elite reading nation that bought new books set

---

Western Missions in the Middle East in the Nineteenth and Early Twentieth Centuries (Leiden, 2006), pp. 43–64.

[35] See Edward Aiken, *Scriptural Geography: Portraying the Holy Land* (London, 2010).
[36] Poole, *Cities*, p. 95. On the changing nature of scriptural geography see Aiken, *Scriptural Geography*.
[37] Poole, *Cities*, p. 30.
[38] Josias Leslie Porter, *The Giant Cities of Bashan: And Syria's Holy Places* (London, 1865), pp. 90–1.

a fashion for the genre and it became a staple of lending and mechanics libraries.[39] By closing the Continent for a generation, the Napoleonic Wars had diverted a tide of scribblers southwards. 'A visit to Athens or Constantinople [had] supplied the place of a dissipated winter passed in Paris, Vienna or Petersburgh,' wrote Thomas Legh in 1817, 'and the traveller was left to imagine and perhaps to regret, the pleasures of the modern cities of civilised Europe amid the monuments of the ruined capitals of antiquity.'[40] The tourists diverted southwards to Greece, Asia Minor and the Holy Land and the missionaries who followed in their wake treated their ruined cities as a palimpsest on which they could read both classical and biblical allusions. Sometimes there might be tension about which lay uppermost. When the Anglican missionary John British Hartley began his tour of Asia Minor at Corinth, his thoughts might have run on the classical sites of Parnassus, Helicon and Cithaeron. Yet on recollecting that it was in Corinth that Paul had written of his determination to know nothing but Christ crucified, he resolved that 'Parnassus was more interesting to me, from the reflection that the eye of St Paul had rested on it, than from any other cause: I was delighted, because I could hold a species of distant communion with him, by means of this classical mountain.'[41] Hartley's polite genuflection to Greece toppled into prostration before the Bible. More often than not, however, different kinds of geopiety fused easily, supersaturating even nondescript sites with recollection. Thus when François-René de Chateaubriand (1768–1848) came to Jaffa during his iconic narrative of a journey to Jerusalem, he offered it as an *amuse-bouche* to readers impatient for the Holy Land, summoning up associations that bridged prehistory and the Napoleonic Wars: Andromeda and the sea monster; Jonah, who had taken ship here; Judas Maccabeus, who had burned Jaffa; St Peter, who had resurrected Tabitha there; St Louis, whose queen had given birth to a son there during the Crusades; and even and inevitably Napoleon.[42]

The gentlemanly travelogues that mingled erudition and edification were plundered and emulated by authors and publishers of the annotated Bibles, commentaries, biblical dictionaries and popular journals produced throughout the long nineteenth century. These works catered to a 'people of one book', who had an unquenchable appetite for reading, circulating and studying Scripture. The British and Foreign Bible Society circulated

---

[39] Nigel Leask, *Curiosity and the Aesthetics of Travel Writing, 1770–1840* (Oxford, 2002); William St Clair, *The Reading Nation in the Romantic Period* (Cambridge, 2004), pp. 233–5.
[40] William Feaver, *The Art of John Martin* (Oxford, 1975), p. 43.
[41] John British Hartley, *Researches in Greece, and the Levant* (1831; London, 1833), pp. 4–5.
[42] François-René de Chateaubriand, *Itinéraire de Paris à Jérusalem* (1811; Paris, 2005), pp. 286–90.

27 million Bibles and New Testaments at home and abroad in its first fifty years, another 72 million in the following thirty years and a staggering 86 million in the last twenty years of the nineteenth century. The enormous numbers of Sunday school pupils formed a particularly important market for religious books: there were 3.5 million scholars in Britain in 1870 and 6 million in 1903.[43] By the mid-nineteenth century there was also a growing market in religious periodicals that exploited the interest of the middling classes in travel, adventure and useful knowledge. *The Sunday at Home*, *Good Words*, *The Quiver* and *The Leisure Hour* carried countless reviews of books of travel to Bible lands, gossipy tours through the region and summaries of historical and archaeological research on biblical cities. Lacking Chateaubriand's panache, they emulated him in treating ancient cities such as Athens or Damascus as layered with classical, biblical and modern memories. Ushering readers of *Good Words* around Athens in 1897, Mary Gardner grouped together the Parthenon, the Areopagus on which Paul had delivered his 'wonderful speech' and the 'modern cemetery' with the 'tall white monument to the memory of Henry Schliemann, the finder of Troy' – modern archaeology adding a site of memory to those it had disinterred.[44] To these occasional sketches should be added the numerous popular books in Britain and America that aspired to be comprehensive guides to biblical cities and their archaeology in the period.[45]

The increasing density and quality of illustration was crucial to such literature: as the printed image became central to popular culture, so it confronted readers with increasingly precise images of biblical cities in their current state.[46] Bible lands meant good business for landscape artists such as Thomas Allom (1804–72) and William Henry Bartlett (1809–54), engravings of whose paintings appeared in costly volumes with a pious letterpress

---

[43] See Michael Ledger-Lomas, 'Mass Markets: Religion', in David McKitterick, ed., *History of the Book in Nineteenth-Century Britain, 1830–1914* (Cambridge, 2009), pp. 324–58 for these figures and further bibliography; Tim Larsen, *A People of One Book: The Bible and the Victorians* (Oxford, 2011), is a spirited statement of the Bible's pervasiveness in nineteenth-century religion.

[44] M. Gardner, 'A Walk in Athens', *Good Words*, January 1897, 31–7.

[45] See, e.g., Theodore Buckley, *The Great Cities of the Ancient World: In Their Glory and in Their Desolation* (London, 1852); John R. Macduff, *In the Footsteps of Saint Paul* (London, 1855); John Stebbins Lee, *Sacred Cities. Narrative, Descriptive, Historical* (Cincinnati, OH, 1877); Stanley Leathes, *The Cities Visited by Saint Paul* (London, 1878); Frank DeHass, *Buried Cities Recovered, or, Explorations in Bible Lands* (1882; Philadelphia, PA, 1884); William B. Wright, *Ancient Cities from the Dawn to the Daylight* (New York, 1899); William B. Wright, *Cities of Saint Paul: Beacons of the Past Rekindled for the Present* (New York, 1905); Francis Clark, *In the Footsteps of St. Paul: His Life and Labors in the Light of a Personal Journey to the Cities Visited by the Apostle* (New York, 1917).

[46] Patricia Anderson, *The Printed Image and the Transformation of Popular Culture, 1790–1860* (Oxford, 1994).

and then in the pages of illustrated Bibles and biblical commentaries. Their art was soon supplemented by photography. From 1839, when Frédéric Goupil-Fesquet (1817–78) took his first daguerreotypes of Jerusalem, until the First World War, over one hundred photographers visited or were active in the Holy Land alone.[47] Because they were reproduced as engravings, the impact of photographs on the public was quick, while from the 1880s the advent of half-tone reproductions made them the dominant mode of representing biblical cities.[48] The 'Queen's Bible' produced for the 1862 International Exhibition and lavishly illustrated with fifty-six plates by Francis Frith (1822–98), was an early example of a trend in which photographs supplanted romanticised landscapes or reproductions of Old Masters in illustrated Bibles.[49] Photography and archaeology developed hand in hand. Photographers such as Auguste Salzmann (1824–72) and Frith – a Quaker – had a positivistic faith in their ability to render the facts and aspired to intervene in recording and dating archaeological discoveries, while the Palestine Exploration Fund (PEF) made extensive use of photography.[50] Yet there could still be sermons in photographs of stones. The Free Churchman Alexander Keith (1792–1880) commissioned his son George to take daguerreotypes of ruined cities to provide further and unquestionable illustrations of prophecy in later editions of his enormously popular treatise on Christian evidences.[51] Similarly, Jane Garnett and Anne Bush's chapter below shows how photography became a counter in heated arguments about how to read the traces of apostolic Christianity in Rome.

The large, predominantly urban, public of Bible readers and Sunday school pupils who pored over images of Damascus and Tyre explains why inquiry into biblical cities was important in Victorian culture. Of course, not everybody who roamed over city mounds or knocked about Jerusalem was haunted by a desire to prove the Bible true. Tim Larsen argues below that Austen Henry Layard (1817–94) was more interested in establishing the dignity of Assyrian art than in vindicating the Jewish prophets. Others

[47] Eyal Onne, *Photographic Heritage of the Holy Land, 1839–1914* (Manchester, 1980), p. 7.
[48] Eitan Bar-Yosef, *The Holy Land in English Culture 1799–1917: Palestine and the Question of Orientalism* (Oxford, 2005), chapters 1–3.
[49] *The Holy Bible, Containing the Old and New Testaments, With Introductory Remarks to Each Book, Parallel Passages, Critical, Explanatory, and Practical Notes, Illustrated with Photographs by Frith* (Glasgow, 1862); Yeshayahu Nir, *The Bible and the Image: The History of Photography in the Holy Land, 1839–1899* (Philadelphia, PA, 1985); Douglas Nickel, *Francis Frith in Egypt and Palestine: A Victorian Photographer Abroad* (Oxford, 2005).
[50] Kathleen Howe, ed., *Revealing the Holy Land: The Photographic Exploration of Palestine* (Berkeley, CA, 1997).
[51] Alexander Keith, *Evidence of the Truth of the Christian Religion: Derived from the Literal Fulfilment of Prophecy* (1823; Edinburgh, 1847). Keith's work was in its fortieth edition by 1873.

aimed at subverting not just some of the dominant modes of reading the Bible but at disrupting faith in Trinitarian orthodoxy. As David Gange argues in his chapter on Pithom, the lapsed Unitarian Harriet Martineau (1802–76) used her Egyptian travelogue to question the unique truth of Christianity. Even Stanley's emollient book disconcerted many evangelicals by scorning their vision of prophecy. Instead, it presented ruined cities as the natural consequence of the rise and fall of civilisations. Yet these quiet rebellions should not obscure the pious horizon of reception for the findings of travellers and archaeologists.[52] More revealing than Martineau's heterodoxy was the initial difficulty she had in finding a publisher. For every Stanley, who tried to inculcate a grown-up attitude to prophecy, there was a Josias Porter, for whom every deserted village was another proof of Isaiah.

This apologetic mode irritated university men and free thinkers who were conversant with higher criticism and intent on the 'free discussion of theological difficulties'.[53] Anonymously reviewing the Bampton lectures of George Rawlinson (1812–1902) in 1860, the Anglican theologian Rowland Williams (1817–70) snorted with contempt at their evasiveness. As the relative of the great Assyriologist Henry Rawlinson, the lecturer

comes laden with the spoils of antiquity. Buried cities have yielded up their treasure. The stones cry out from the wall in attestation of what he promises to prove. *Parturiunt montes*. We have perused his volume with anxious candour, and never knew, until we laid it down, how ... near an approach to nothing on the side of Revelation had been effected by all the Assyrian excavations.

For Williams, who was soon to be hauled before an ecclesiastical court for his contribution to *Essays and Reviews* (1860), it was trivial to prove the existence of Nineveh. What Rawlinson had conspicuously failed to provide was a 'hieroglyphical representation of the drowning of Pharaoh, or a sculptured record in Nineveh that the destruction of Sennacherib's army was miraculous'. Yet the point of departure for higher criticism was precisely this: questioning the 'supernatural claims of the Bible'. Those claims were to be settled by developing principles of historical verisimilitude and through close attention to the composition and transmission of biblical books, not by the 'disembowelling of buried cities'.[54] Liberal Anglicans and

---

[52] Frederick Bohrer, *Orientalism and Visual Culture: Imagining Mesopotamia in Nineteenth-Century Europe* (Cambridge, 2003), chapter 1.

[53] James Anthony Froude, 'A Plea for the Free Discussion of Theological Difficulties', in *Short Studies on Great Subjects* (1867–83; 4 vols., London, 1898), I, pp. 202–40.

[54] [Rowland Williams], 'Rawlinson's Bampton Lectures for 1859', *Westminster Review*, 18 (1860), 33–49.

broad churchmen such as Williams continued to grumble at the flat-footed literalism and canting tone of the archaeologists and their boosters. In 1871, Charles Kegan Paul (1828–1902), a clergyman and journalist who had experimented with Unitarianism and was soon to give up his orders, sniffed at the PEF's argument that identifying sites mentioned in Scripture verified its narratives. This was no more compelling than an argument for the truth of Sir Thomas Mallory's Morte d'Arthur because 'the Vale of Avalon (or Glastonbury) or Caerleon or Usk may still possibly be identified with well known spots'.[55] And yet the 'explorer' continued to meet with the 'naïve question ... "Do your discoveries go to prove that the Bible is true?"'[56]

The empire of archaeology: institutions and audiences

The development of access to the Bible lands into sustained activity by archaeological organisations such as the PEF and Egypt Exploration Fund (EEF) took decades. Most of the British figures remembered as early archaeologists were in the Near East for political or military purposes, for it was official postings in cities from Jerusalem to Baghdad that facilitated British archaeology. Layard conducted diplomatic missions for Stratford Canning (1786–1880) before beginning archaeological explorations from his base at Mosul. Sir Henry Rawlinson (1810–95) trained Persian troops before he became a political agent in Ottoman Arabia, where he was able to transcribe cuneiform inscriptions and eventually contribute to their decipherment. The initial exploration of the Dead Sea was facilitated by the search for a short cut to India. Later, in the 1860s, the loose alliance of military men and churchmen that made up the PEF functioned in the Holy Land by conducting topographical tasks for the British War Office.[57]

Officers and diplomats were among the most fluent authors of the literature of exploration discussed above. Such precursors to the excavation report as Layard's best-selling *Nineveh and its Remains* (1849) defined a market for archaeological research in Britain. But excavation continued to be associated with adventurers; it was treated contemptuously by much of the scholarly community, seen as grubby and unbecoming of a gentleman. Not just the

---

[55] Charles Kegan Paul, 'The Recovery of Jerusalem', *Theological Review*, 8 (1871), 412.
[56] Claude Reignier Conder, 'Ancient Palestine and Modern Exploration', *Contemporary Review*, 45 (1884), 856.
[57] John James Moscrop, *Measuring Jerusalem: The Palestine Exploration Fund and British Interests in the Holy Land* (Leicester, 1999), pp. 63–128; Haim Goren, *Dead Sea Level: Science, Exploration and Imperial Interests in the Near East* (London, 2011), part 2.

insalubrious conditions in the field, but the distinctly manual nature of the work were frowned upon by scholars such as Samuel Birch (1813–85), founder of the Society of Biblical Archaeology (1870–1919). Until the last third of the century, the bulk of study of the ancient past continued to be done from Britain, by scholars who had never left Europe, from the vantage point of learned societies and the universities. The initial membership of Birch's Society was dominated by an eclectic mixture of classicists, clerics, biblical critics, students of ancient languages and gentlemen scholars.[58] The aim of those sent to the field was thus often the acquisition of antiquities to be sent home for study.

Plunder may have offered the quickest route to the front page of the *Illustrated London News*, but some artists and architects became more concerned about recording and conserving monuments *in situ* as part of intelligible urban wholes. The exploration of Pompeii was one sign of a shift towards 'urbanism' in which archaeologists became more interested in recording the spatial organisation of whole cities. It was evident in the excavation of Antinoë by the French and of Pergamum and Olympia by the Germans; in the Pauline cities of Ephesus by the Austrians and Corinth by the Americans; and most remarkably in the stratigraphical exploration of Egyptian tells by Flinders Petrie (1853–1942).[59] This was the context for rows over the desirability of the restoration or relocation of the features of newly unearthed ancient cityscapes. Were they a source of colossal monuments for the museums that had often funded the expeditions or could excavations result in the revelation of a city as a whole, navigable object?

The British Museum exemplifies these complexities because although it was the premier showcase for antiquities in Britain it often did more to obstruct than support interest in cities. Far from dominating or even encouraging the study of Egypt for instance, the Museum initially engaged in a vain attempt to steer the public away from Egypt towards ancient Greece. Its marked bias towards the supposed golden age of Greek art was frustrating for those who wanted the prominent display of artefacts from Egypt, Assyria or from the later age of Greek civilisation.[60] Yet its archives

---

[58] Membership list in *Transactions of Society for Biblical Archaeology*, 1 (1872).

[59] On this theme, see Gran-Aymerich, *Naissance*, pp. 95–7, 105–7, chapters 5–6; Suzanne Marchand, *Down from Olympus: Archaeology and Philhellenism in Germany, 1750–1970* (London, 1996), chapter 3; Stephen Dyson, *In Pursuit of Ancient Pasts: A History of Classical Archaeology in the Nineteenth and Twentieth Centuries* (London, 2006), pp. 111–28; Davis, *Sands*, pp. 30–7; John R. Bartlett, 'What has Archaeology to Do with the Bible: or Vice Versa?' in John R. Bartlett, *Archaeology and Biblical Interpretation* (London, 1997), pp. 1–19.

[60] On these conflicts, see Ian Jenkins, *Archaeologists and Aesthetes in the Sculpture Galleries of the British Museum, 1800–1939* (London, 1992).

demonstrate that visitors to the museum were often church groups who brought their Bibles with them in search of explication. Their appetites were fuelled by such guidebooks as *The Bible and the British Museum* (1904) by Ada Habershon (1861–1918), an evangelical of Moody and Sankey's school and author of the hymn, 'Will the circle be unbroken?'[61] Print not only enabled visitors to the Museum to subvert its interpretative framework, but enabled archaeological findings to be mapped onto enduring structures of religious thought. While pioneers of Egyptology such as the very popular Gardner Wilkinson (1797–1875) tried to detach their work from Old Testament apologetics, many readers continued to subscribe to the providential readings of ancient civilisation offered in such works as Robert Wilberforce's *The Five Empires: An Outline of Ancient History* (1840), which presented human civilisation since the Fall as a series of efforts to recover 'the natural perfection which man had from God's image within, and of God's outward presence'.[62] They continued to believe that the main reason for reading the inscribed stones and built remains of ancient cities was to learn lessons about God's purposes for man.

The third quarter of the nineteenth century represented a key moment in this popularising shift, making it feasible for archaeological organisations to survive and prosper by subscription alone. The profile of archaeology was boosted by spectacular finds such as Layard's at Nineveh, George Smith's discovery of the Deluge tablets in the 1870s and the discovery of the mummies of pharaohs apparently mentioned in Genesis and Exodus in 1881. The fit between organisations such as the PEF and the imperial state remained close, but they were no longer reliant on organisations such as the War Office and were much more than a function of military or diplomatic activity. New editions of textbooks such as *Cory's Ancient Fragments* with more accessible introductions were one sign of the interest aroused by discoveries such as those made by Smith (1840–76). Archaeologists could now communicate directly with the broader public, with newspapers throwing open their columns to archaeological reports and developing their own specialised interests, the *Daily Telegraph* and *Times* becoming known for their Assyriological coverage, and the *Morning Post*, under the influence of Amelia Edwards (1831–92), developing an association with Egyptology.

Not only did the work of archaeologists reach the Protestant public, but affluent members of that public could increasingly go to see archaeologists at work. Prospecting the land of Gilead for possible Jewish settlement in

---

[61] Ada Habershon, *A Gatherer of Fresh Spoil: An Autobiography and Memoir* (London, 1918).
[62] R. J. Wilberforce, *The Five Empires: An Outline of Ancient History* (London, 1841), p. 1.

1879, the diplomatist and mystic Laurence Oliphant (1829–88) imagined the springs of Amatha as a popular resort for 'European valetudinarians' who could mix bathing with 'the more serious occupation of excavating the buried cities of the Decapolis', refreshing themselves from their 'archaeological labours with the excitement of wild boar, gazelle, and partridge shooting'.[63] The fantasy was justifiable, for Cook's tour of Palestine, Ephesus and Constantinople had begun in 1869 and quickly became routine.[64] By 1903, American tourists could embark at New York with Cook for a seventy-day cruise on the *Moltke*, taking in Madeira, Gibraltar, Algiers, Malta, Athens, Constantinople, Smyrna (for Ephesus), Beyrout (for Damascus), Haifa (for Galilee), Jaffa (for Jerusalem and Bethlehem), Alexandria, Cairo, the Nile, Naples, Nice and Monte Carlo. This was 'typical "Twentieth Century" travel, in that it renders accessible to the many what was for years the exclusive privilege of the wealthy few'.[65] These tourists were on a pilgrimage as well as a junket. In 1877, the Rev. Arthur Gore's whistle-stop tour of Athens began with an evening trip to 'the Areopagus, to listen, by St Luke's help, to St Paul addressing the "more than commonly religious" Athenians'.[66] Archaeology was integral to these emotions. The American tourist George Barton told how 'like Paul we then "departed from Athens and came to Corinth," only we did not, like him, go on foot or in a small boat, but in a railway train, which was comfortable, if not swift'. Once there, Barton pored over the diggings of the American School, which was exposing Paul's Corinth to view, before voyaging on to the Austrian excavation of Ephesus, where he feasted on blackberries and mused on the city's fallen greatness.[67]

The implications of the development and popularisation of archaeology for the study of the Bible and its cities were more problematic than this summary implies. Tensions emerged between popular concerns – which ensured income from subscriptions and gave archaeologists their public influence – and the demands of a developing discipline.[68] In 1880, pressure

---

[63] Laurence Oliphant, *The Land of Gilead: With Excursions in the Lebanon* (London, 1880), p. 137.
[64] E. H. Bunbury, 'Anatolica', *Academy*, 7 (1875), 2; Thomas Cook, 'Travelling Experiences', *Leisure Hour* (June 1878), 394; Tim Larsen, 'Thomas Cook, Holy Land Pilgrims and the Dawn of the Modern Tourist Industry', in R. N. Swanson, ed., *Holy Land, Holy Lands, and Christian History* (Woodbridge, 2000), pp. 459–73.
[65] *Cook's Cruise to the Mediterranean, the Orient and Bible Lands* (New York, 1903).
[66] Arthur Gore, 'A Walk through Athens', *Quiver*, 18 (1883), 735–8.
[67] George Aaron Barton, *A Year's Wandering in Bible Lands* (Philadelphia, PA, 1904), pp. 67–78.
[68] See David Gange, *Dialogues with the Dead: Egyptology in British Culture and Religion* (Oxford, 2013).

already existed for the removal of explicit apologetic concerns from the discipline: an end to what Samuel Birch called 'sentimental archaeology'.[69] Habituated as we are to understand the emergence of a scholarly discipline as emancipation from a prior agenda in favour of a pure quest for knowledge, it may look as if archaeology's biblical concerns were likely to wither away quickly. It is an impression likely to be strengthened by reading the excavation reports through which the history of archaeological practices is usually written, which gradually turned from evocative accounts of biblical explorations into sober records of archaeological process. To concentrate on them would, though, be misleading. One of this book's arguments is that in shining a light on the reports we risk neglecting the penumbra of other publications issued by archaeologists and their supporters, in which they recounted their religious experience or peddled theological and civilisational theories. Archaeologists such as Petrie, Percy Gardner (1846–1937) and Sir William Mitchell Ramsay (1851–1939) published much on such subjects and *Cities of God* insists on the relevance of such works in assessing their careers.

Archaeologists were hardly the only scholars to pronounce on the Bible in later nineteenth-century Britain. They had to reckon with theologians in the universities and the upper echelons of the church, who were reluctant to trust Assyriologists, Egyptologists or Holy Land archaeologists – who might be from dissenting backgrounds or inclined to the quiet heterodoxy of the laity. The founders of the PEF had to negotiate sectarian jealousies about their work, with the Archbishop of York declaring at its inaugural meeting that 'we are not a religious society, we are not about to launch into any controversy, we are about to apply the rules of science'. This was not good enough for Edward Bouverie Pusey (1800–82), the Regius Professor of Hebrew at Oxford, who refused to take a public part in it because it would have to moot theories that 'traditionalists could not espouse'.[70] Sayce experienced these suspicions when in 1882 he was passed over as Pusey's successor for the Regius professorship. Yet as his *Reminiscences* (1923) wryly recorded, the successful candidate, Samuel Driver (1846–1914), turned out to be even more of a handful. Biblical critics such as Driver were advancing their claims to represent a discipline at this time and fighting to establish their studies as a science of texts independent of dogmatic presuppositions.[71] While biblical criticism drew on anthropology and the

---

[69] Margaret Drower, *Flinders Petrie: A Life in Archaeology* (London, 1985), p. 65.
[70] Moscrop, *Jerusalem*, pp. 68–70.
[71] T. Willis Glover, *Evangelical Nonconformists and Higher Criticism in the Nineteenth Century* (London, 1954); John William Rogerson, *Old Testament Criticism in the Nineteenth*

comparative study of religion, it jealously guarded its own procedures and commitment to the minute dissection of texts. Leading critics such as Driver, T. K. Cheyne (1841–1915) and A. S. Peake (1865–1929) sniffed at apologists who brought the clumsy weapons of archaeology into the domain of textual criticism.[72]

The tension between professions informs *Cities of God* at several points. At Jerusalem, Goldhill shows how feuds over the location of the Holy Sepulchre were coloured by status anxiety as well as by national and confessional differences. At Pithom, Gange argues, Egyptologists and their public thought they were fighting the higher critics brick by brick. There was often more scope for collaboration in this period between critics and archaeologists on the ground of the New Testament. Prominent German scholars such as Adolf Harnack (1851–1930) were more generous in their assessment of the historical value of the synoptic gospels and Acts than the scholars of Tübingen and were interested in incorporating the evidence of monuments and inscriptions into their studies of apostolic Christianity.[73] The dialogue was closer still in Britain, where students of ancient cities such as William Ramsay collaborated with respected critics such as J. B. Lightfoot. Delivering the Hulsean Lectures in Cambridge's Great St Mary's Church, Frederick Henry Chase (1853–1925) noted in 1902 that in revealing the 'secrets of the cities of Asia Minor' the 'spade of the excavator' had bolstered the Acts of the Apostles.[74]

Chase would say this: he was an Anglican apologist for the Bible. Yet the complexity of the relationship between the city and the scientific study of Scripture belied such blithe statements. Many scholars, particularly those of a modernist bent, felt that cities did not so much prove Scripture as change the ways in which it was read. A case in point was the papyri found in the rubbish mounds of cities: 'light from the east' that illuminated the language and culture of Hellenistic town dwellers and therefore suggested that the Pauline epistles were written in the ordinary language of their day rather

---

Century: England and Germany (London, 1984); John William Rogerson, *The Bible and Criticism in Victorian Britain: Profiles of F. D. Maurice and William Robertson Smith* (Sheffield, 1995).

[72] T. K. Cheyne, 'Pressing Needs of the Old Testament Study', *Hibbert Journal*, 1 (1902–3), 747–62; A. S. Peake, *The Bible: Its Origin, its Significance and its Abiding Worth* (London, 1913), chapter 10.

[73] William Frend, *The Archaeology of Early Christianity: A History* (London, 1996); William Frend, *From Dogma to History: How our Understanding of the Early Church Developed* (London, 2003), chapters 1 and 2.

[74] Frederick Henry Chase, *The Credibility of the Acts of the Apostles* (London, 1902), pp. 8–9. See similarly George Stokes, 'Modern Discoveries and the Christian Faith: St Paul at Ephesus', *The Sunday at Home* (4 June 1892), 485–8.

than a theological argot.[75] Archaeology could threaten the purchase of Christianity itself. The *Babel und Bibel* controversy surveyed by Seymour below shows how proponents of a racialised archaeology could sneer at the worth of Hebrew civilisation and shake confidence in the primacy of Old Testament religion. Just as disconcerting was growing evidence from the study of inscriptions that mystery cults of resurrected and salvific deities had pullulated in the 'great cities' of the East. This suggested to archaeologists such as Percy Gardner and biblical critics such as Kirsopp Lake (1872–1946) that much of Paul and John's language about Christ might be derived from or at least expressed in the symbolism of 'Oriental' religions. Freethinking opponents of Christianity went further, suggesting that Jesus Christ himself was just another myth.[76]

Types of the city

'If any nation is to be lost or saved by the character of its great cities, our own is that nation,' wrote the Congregational divine and historian Robert Vaughan (1795–1868) in his primer on *The Age of Great Cities* (1842). It was the urban culture in which archaeological findings were received and the religious imaginary that it fostered which makes this a book about cities rather than just another addition to the scholarly literature on biblical archaeology. It could be argued that for most of those engaged in biblical study, cities mattered not as real entities but as heaps of words: inscribed 'monuments' that 'bear the name or recount the deeds of the heroes of Scripture' and so provide 'striking confirmations of the Bible narrative'.[77] Nor does the Bible necessarily dispose its students to study or idealise cities. Its readers could find in it validation for a hankering for rural well-being, which recent historians of Victorian culture have qualified but not entirely denied.[78] The Israelites had fled from or destroyed cities as well as founding

---

[75] Samuel R. Driver, *Modern Research as Illustrating the Bible* (London, 1909); James Hope Moulton, 'New Testament Greek in the Light of Modern Discovery', in Henry Barclay Swete, ed., *Essays on Some Biblical Questions of the Day* (London, 1909), pp. 461–500; Adolf Deissmann, *Light from the Ancient East* (London, 1910).
[76] See, e.g., Arthur Drews, *Die Christusmythe* (Jena, 1909).
[77] Archibald Sayce, *Fresh Light from the Ancient Monuments* (London, 1893), pp. 3–4. See too W. S. W. Vaux, *Ancient History from the Monuments: Greek Cities and Islands of Asia Minor* (London, 1877).
[78] Peter Mandler, 'Against "Englishness": English Culture and the Limits to Rural Nostalgia, 1850–1940', *Transactions of the Royal Historical Society*, 7 (1997), 155–75; Paul Readman, *Land and Nation in England: Patriotism, National Identity and the Politics of Land 1880–1914* (Woodbridge, 2008).

them, while Jesus was often imagined as roaming the Galilean hills and taking his metaphors from sparrows and lilies. William McClure Thomson wrote in *The Land and the Book* (1859) that the Bible had the 'air of country life' and that 'He who came from heaven to earth for man's redemption loved not cities'.[79] 'No doubt God has his way in great cities,' conceded Edwin Paxton Hood (1820–85), a Congregational minister, but He really 'care[d] for villages', not for those 'dreadful drifts of huge and seething populations,' those 'great seats of almost unweldable and unwieldable power'.[80] Even freethinkers fell under the pastoral spell, Anna Kingsford and Edward Maitland pronouncing that

> a Hierarch must not dwell in cities. He may begin his initiation in a city, but he cannot complete it there. For he must not breathe dead and burnt air, – air, that is, the vitality of which is quenched. He must be a wanderer, a dweller in the plain and the garden ... [in] direct contact with the ... unpaved grass and earth of the planet.

He must flee the 'abominations of Babylon'.[81]

Biblical cities nonetheless mattered to inhabitants of 'the age of great cities'.[82] Analysts of the culture of history in the nineteenth century have emphasised that it was engrossed by urban events and settings: Thomas Carlyle's revolutionary Paris, or the Tower of London. This interest in the urban past reflected the pride and perturbation with which nineteenth-century Britons viewed the rapid urbanisation of their society.[83] It was a trend that retained its power to the very end of the century: 'the main stream of the national life', stated the slum parson Hensley Henson (1863–1947) in 1898, 'is now running, with an ever increasing volume, in urban channels'.[84] The sanitary, economic and social problems created by city growth need no emphasis, subject as they are of a vast scholarly literature. Here we emphasise that urbanisation also created a slow-burning problem of imagination

---

[79] William McClure Thomson, *The Land and the Book* (1859; 2 vols., New York, 1874), I, pp. vi–vii.
[80] Edwin Paxton Hood, *The Villages of the Bible: Descriptive, Traditional, and Memorable: Sabbath Evening Lectures in Brighton* (London, 1874), p. 5. It was ironic that in 1885 Hood would die in Paris.
[81] Anna Kingsford and Edward Maitland, *The Perfect Way: Or, the Finding of Christ* (London, 1909), p. 244.
[82] Robert Vaughan, *The Age of Great Cities: Or, Modern Society Viewed in its Relation to Intelligence, Morals, and Religion* (London, 1843), p. 1.
[83] Billie Melman, *The Culture of History: English Uses of the Past 1800–1953* (Oxford, 2006), pp. 10–11. See too Osterhammel, *Die Verwandlung*, p. 364 for the primacy of the city in nineteenth-century theories of historical development.
[84] Hensley Henson, *Apostolic Christianity: Notes and Inferences Based Mostly on Saint Paul's Epistles to the Corinthians* (London, 1898), p. viii.

and representation, not least for devout Protestants.[85] How should cities be imagined and what in particular was their relationship with religion?

The question is all the more suggestive now that historians no longer portray Protestant ministers and thinkers as apathetic or helpless before the secularisation of their society. Indeed, historians have emphasised that in all but the most unpromising environments they reacted to city growth by creating a Christian and 'bourgeois civilisation'.[86] Their responses to cities demonstrated not so much terror at imminent catastrophe as fear of an unknown future, for which the feudal and early-modern past provided no obvious guidance.[87] The problem with 'large towns', fretted the renowned Scottish minister Thomas Chalmers, was that they lacked the thick web of social relationships that sustained religious observance in cosy places like Oxford or Bath. His solution was to break down the city into a conglomeration of godly villages, patrolled by zealous elders.[88] This was too Scottish and too pessimistic a solution for England. Much of the rich religious literature produced from his day until the early twentieth century instead emphasised the need for a specifically urban faith that set the evils and potential of cities into the widest historical context. Vaughan warned against rushing from undeniable 'scenes of depravity and wretchedness' to the conclusion that urban life was intrinsically harmful to morals or religion. After all, when the 'Almighty placed the Hebrew tribes in possession of the cities of Canaan, he recognised man as a citizen, as an improvement upon man as a wanderer'.[89] For Vaughan and others, the relationship between the Bible and the modern city was symbiotic: the Bible shaped the understanding of urbanisation; city life coloured how the Bible was read.

Writers reached for the biblical city to express their faith that for all the outward pomp and wealth of modern cities, they still lived under the reign of a materialised providence. Their prosperity depended on the faith and morality of their inhabitants, who were deeply conditioned by their

---

[85] Asa Briggs, *Victorian Cities* (London, 1963); Tristram Hunt, *Building Jerusalem: The Rise and Fall of the Victorian City* (London, 2004); Andrew Lees, *Cities Perceived: Urban Society in European and American Thought* (Manchester, 1985); Caroline Arscott, 'The Representation of the City in the Visual Arts', in Martin Daunton, ed., *Cambridge Urban History* (Cambridge, 2007), pp. 811–32.

[86] S. J. D. Green, 'In Search of Bourgeois Civilisation: Institutions and Ideals in Nineteenth-Century Britain', *Northern History*, 28 (1992), 228–47.

[87] See notably Callum Brown, 'Did Urbanization Secularize Britain?' *Urban History Yearbook* (1988), 1–14; Green, 'Church and City'.

[88] Thomas Chalmers, *On the Christian and Civic Economy of Large Towns* (3 vols., London, 1821); Stewart J. Brown, *Thomas Chalmers and the Godly Commonwealth in Scotland* (Oxford, 1982).

[89] Vaughan, *Great Cities*, pp. 6, 103.

surroundings. The buccaneering Christian Socialist Charles Kingsley (1819–75) made the point when he recalled seeing Bristol delivered to blood and fire during the 1831 Reform riots. He had learned that the 'social state of a city depends directly on its moral state, and – I fear dissenting voices, but I must say what I believe to be truth – that the moral state of a city depends – how far I know not, but frightfully, to an extent as yet uncalculated, and perhaps incalculable – on the physical state of the city; on the food, water, air, and lodging of its inhabitants'.[90]

The accretion of archaeological evidence did not so much displace as reinvigorate the typological use of Scripture to read backwards and forwards between present and past. The Old Testament abounded with cities whose downfall had long been seen as a judgment on their inhabitants. Exhibited as panoramas, John Martin's paintings of their collapse could admonish or at least excite those who were conscious of skirting the precipice of political disorder.[91] The same process gave Victorian cities their 'historicist' buildings and spaces. Town halls and art galleries reminiscent of Athenian temples or Florentine palaces expressed not so much a yearning for escape into the past as a desire for symbols to educate urban populations in discipline and freedom.[92] It is significant that John Ruskin's *The Stones of Venice* (1851), which inspired so many of these buildings, blurred biblical and historicist registers, warning England that it might share the fate of Venice – the very ruin with which Isaiah had threatened Tyre.[93] Britain had an advantage over such models: Vaughan wrote that it could avoid the fate of Babylon and Tyre because it was not just a Christian but also a Protestant society, which had in the gospel a means of avoiding the temptations that had destroyed pagan cities.[94]

London features in this volume as the city most frequently twinned with biblical predecessors. Typology could of course give any city its biblical double: Victorian preachers turned Saint Paul's Corinth into Liverpool or Brighton, while as Astrid Swenson demonstrates below not just London, but Oxford, Cambridge and Paris had their turn as Sodom. Yet even before public attention was drawn to the shock cities of the Industrial Revolution, the overgrown capital of the *ancien régime* had long been identified with

---

[90] Charles Kingsley, 'Great Cities and Their Influence for Good and Evil', *The Works of Charles Kingsley: Volume 13. Sanitary and Social Lectures and Essays* (London, 1880), p. 191.
[91] Ralph O'Connor, *The Earth on Show: Fossils and the Poetics of Popular Science, 1802–1856* (Chicago, 2008), pp. 300–3.
[92] Patrick Joyce, *Liberalism and the Rule of Freedom* (London, 2004), pp. 150–2.
[93] John Ruskin, *The Stones of Venice* (1851; 2 vols., London, 1880), I, p. 1.
[94] Vaughan, *Cities*, pp. 93, 315.

Babylon and Nineveh.[95] The more London forged ahead as the capital of the modern world – shining with plate glass and flaring with gas light, crossed by iron bridges and honeycombed by underground railroads – the more, paradoxically, it suggested parallels with such cities.[96] As Michael Seymour notes below, Babylon changed from a spiritual type of papal Rome to a symbol of the monstrous agglomerations doomed by their very wealth to be overthrown: London was the 'great Babylon' because it was the 'metropolis of the world'.[97] Even before they were pinpointed and excavated, Babylon and Nineveh were models of what London or Paris should avoid becoming, pure expressions of wealth and despotism, in which (said Vaughan) the 'darkest recesses of ignorance, and crime, and wretchedness' existed 'beneath the shadow of temples and palaces which have become the wonder of the world'.[98] While the awful sublimity of Regency and early-Victorian London therefore begged parallels with the Old Testament, the imposing forms of modern architecture crept into depictions of past cities. Martin's paintings of divine catastrophes overwhelming Old Testament cities drew on the neo-classical buildings of Edinburgh or Newcastle, while Ralph Waldo Emerson was reminded of Martin's Babylon on a gloomy trek through the stuccoed desolation of west London.[99]

The desire for city-dwellers to find parallels to their own experience therefore created a horizon of reception for the discoveries of the archaeologists. Londoners flocked to panoramas of Martin's paintings because despite their rhetoric of precise recreation they conveyed an overwhelming impression of massiveness. Some of the chapters in this book show how such expectations led the discoverers and popularisers of buried cities to inflate the proportions of what they had found. Larsen shows that, although what Layard had found at Nineveh was essentially a temple complex, he fudged his plans to bring them into agreement with Isaiah's measurements, at a stroke both confirming his accuracy and establishing Nineveh as the gigantic city familiar from Martin's works. The process went a stage further

---

[95] Lees, *Cities*, pp. 7–9; Mark Girouard, *Cities and People: A Social and Architectural Survey* (London, 1987), chapter 17.

[96] Lynda Nead, *Victorian Babylon: People, Streets and Images in Nineteenth-Century London* (London, 2005); Kate Flint, *The Victorians and the Visual Imagination* (Cambridge, 2000), chapter 6.

[97] Robert Mudie, *Babylon the Great: A Dissection and Demonstration of Men and Things in the British Capital* (2 vols., London, 1825), I, p. 33; Robert Mudie, *London and Londoners: Or, A Second Judgment of 'Babylon the Great'* (London, 1836).

[98] Vaughan, *Cities*, p. 21.

[99] Feaver, *John Martin*, p. 145; Morton Paley, *The Apocalyptic Sublime* (London, 1986); Nicholas Taylor, 'The Awful Sublimity of the Victorian City', in Jim Dyos and Michael Wolff, eds., *The Victorian City* (2 vols., London, 1973), II, pp. 431–48.

in the architectural court created at the Sydenham Crystal Palace in the early fifties – a venue whose attractions rivalled those of the more staid British Museum. Layard and James Fergusson (1808–76), the architectural historian and testy polymath who appears in several of this book's chapters, did not so much reconstruct Nineveh as produce a speculative stage set that emphasised the great scale of the city.[100] While visitors to Sydenham or to Charles Kean's 1853 production of Byron's *Sardanapalus* could enjoy the resurrected sublimity of Nineveh, they could also dream over vast cities in the pages of their Bibles, which filled up with Piranesian depictions of colossal temples, huge courtyards and endless colonnades. These speculations crossed the gulf between the ancients and the moderns, permitting for instance the off-hand description of Ephesus as the 'Liverpool of Asia'.[101] Gange emphasises in his chapter on Pithom that for many Egyptologists the question of whether pharaohs had matched or even surpassed modern engineering remained a live one.

This emphasis on the monumental made many encounters with the sites of biblical cities disappointing, even dismaying, to Victorian pilgrims. Many cities mentioned in the Bible had altogether disappeared or else been recycled into their modern successors, while by strange caprice some of the cities that boasted the most impressive remains were barely mentioned at all in Scripture, such as Palmyra (the Tadmor of 2 Chronicles 8:4), or were ignored altogether, such as Baalbec or Gerasa/Jerash.[102] This posed a public relations problem for the PEF, which could never emulate Layard's coups. Defending the Fund in the reviews, the explorer Claude Reignier Conder (1848–1910) noted that 'if the Palestine explorers have not brought back the Ark from Jerusalem, the golden calves from Bethel, Ahab's ivory palace, or Samson's coffin' then they had done the public the negative service of 'destroying error ... Huge libraries of controversy have been swept away when the spade of the excavator has dug up truth.'[103] Conder rightly grasped that Protestants were interested just as much in the obliteration of cities as in their survival. The chapters below show that students of prophecy took a gloomy pleasure in the near or total disappearance of Sodom and Gomorrah, Babylon and Ephesus. Untenanted ruins afforded

---

[100] Bohrer, *Orientalism*, pp. 212 ff.
[101] Edward Ziter, *The Orient on the Victorian Stage* (Cambridge, 2006), chapter 4; Wright, *Cities of Saint Paul*, p. 31.
[102] This did not prevent striking images of Baalbec by Frith and others being used to illustrate ancient heathenism, while for heroic attempts to identify Gerasa with Mahanaim in Gilead see Josias Porter, 'A Recent Journey East of the Jordan', *The Sunday at Home* (18 August 1877), 523.
[103] Conder, 'Ancient Palestine', pp. 857–9.

gratifying reflections on the distinction between the permanence of Scripture and the fragility of earthly things. Poole thus invited Christians to 'contrast the enduring spiritual work of Moses with the shattered material trophies of the great oppressor of his people'.[104]

The absence of many material remains could aid imaginative reconstruction. What pious travellers found harder to deal with were sites where life had carried on cheerfully since biblical times, turning noble cities of the mind into insignificant, even squalid places. Already disappointed by Antioch, the only thing William Henry Bartlett found to admire in decrepit Tarsus – St Paul's birthplace and described by him as 'no mean city' (Acts 21:39) – was his luxurious billet with M. Gillet the French consul, where 'one might have supposed oneself in the Chausée d'Antin'.[105] Norman Macleod (1812–72), a Church of Scotland minister and the founding editor of *Good Words*, was dismayed to find in Bethany only 'dust, confusion, children, dogs, and poverty. Everything is squalid as in Skibereen, Connemara, or, alas! some villages in the Hebrides.'[106] The shock was most acute at Jerusalem. Goldhill shows below that Protestant pilgrims struggled to accept that their shining city on the hill was just another grubby Levantine town that lived up neither to Scripture nor to their own expectations of decency and civility. Archaeology in Jerusalem was therefore linked to a disinclination to accept the identity of the two places. The real Jerusalem was fortunately many metres beneath the present city; while the site of Christ's tomb could not be found in that monument to fanaticism, the Church of the Holy Sepulchre.[107] Eitan Bar-Yosef shows in his chapter below the need for a similar adjustment at Bethlehem. It serves as a caution on the impact that travel and archaeology might have on the vernacular biblical imagination, for Bethlehem continued to matter to Victorians mainly as the 'little town' of Christmas hymns and nativity plays. The story of Rome is perhaps the most complex. Garnett and Bush's chapter shows that Protestant visitors were tempted to suspend credulity about the sites where the apostles had been martyred. At the same time, they were aware that Rome was the throne of the papacy: not an open book, but a ragged palimpsest of apocryphal traditions.

Archaeology therefore smoothed the ragged frontier between the ideal and the actual. British Protestants always reminded themselves of that

---

[104] Poole, *Cities*, p. 87.
[105] W. H. Bartlett, *Footsteps of our Lord and his Apostles* (1851; London, 1852), p. 82.
[106] Norman Macleod, *Eastward* (London, 1866), p. 174.
[107] Sara Kochav, 'The Search for a Protestant Holy Sepulchre: The Garden Tomb in Nineteenth-Century Jerusalem', *Journal of Ecclesiastical History*, 46 (1995), 278–301.

boundary: while drawn to the mystique of pilgrimage, they reminded themselves that Christ had established a universal and thus placeless religion. The novelist Elizabeth Rundle Charles (1828–96) introduced her journey to the Bible lands with the observation that

to our *faith* Hudson's Bay, of which apostles never heard, is as holy as the Sea of Galilee; and the streets of London, which Christians tread, as sacred as the streets of Jerusalem, 'where our Lord was crucified,' – because the tread of those blessed feet has consecrated the whole earth.[108]

The conviction that the kingdom of Christ was a spiritual entity rather than something to be identified with material remains gained from the late nineteenth-century perception that large cities were again growing faster than religious and civic ideals could keep up. Protestant thinkers emphasised once more that cities present or past were more than a congeries of houses and shops but religious and political entities passed on from the classical and biblical past, which enjoined particular duties and created spiritual possibilities. As Andrew Fairbairn (1838–1912), a Congregational divine, argued in *The City of God: A Series of Discussions in Religion* (1883), the city had not always been just a place

where narrow and unfragrant closes are crowded with the poor, and spacious yet hard and monotonous squares are occupied by the rich. The Latin *civitas*, the Greek *polis* had nobler meanings. Their cardinal and honourable sense was not the place, but the living community, – the men of kindred spirit and blood, who claimed the same parentage, shared the same past, lived under the same laws, possessed the same privileges, liberties and rights, followed the same customs, observed the same worship, believed the same religion.

Christianity had not replaced this conception of the city, but given it a 'high ideal sense, only enlarged, exalted, and transfigured by the relation in which it stands to God'.[109]

Size then was not everything. Macleod argued that the squalid villages of Palestine mattered more than Nineveh and Babylon. As George St Clair wryly noted in 1892, although Jerusalem could fit into Hyde Park, it had been the 'theatre of great events'.[110] Indeed, the many later nineteenth-century Protestants interested in the reform of their own cities cared less

---

[108] Elizabeth Rundle Charles, *Wanderings over Bible Lands and Seas* (1862; New York, 1866), p. 12.
[109] Andrew Fairbairn, *'The City of God': A Series of Discussions in Religion* (London, 1882), p. 357.
[110] George St Clair, *Buried Cities and Bible Countries* (London, 1892), chapter 3.

about the dimensions of the actual Jerusalem than the 'new Jerusalem' of the book of Revelation, which was best appreciated by a trip to Patmos, the site of St John's exile, rather than Palestine. The New Jerusalem was a consummation and epitome of civic ideals: Hebraism built with Hellenic bricks. They considered the recovery of this concept vital if they were to inspire their readers to redeem the chaotic, even soulless togetherness of those 'huge amorphous wens' in which 'ten thousand of us might disappear tomorrow, and the human tide would roll on as before ... if we are to secure the best ends of the common life we shall have to revise, and in the Greek direction, our whole doctrine of the city'.[111] John's New Jerusalem had awaited the faithful at the end of the world, but in the later nineteenth century it was the emblem of a kingdom to be realised on earth. For Henry Drummond, the church was not an isolated institution perched within an otherwise godless and immoral city. The ideal Protestants should put before themselves was that of the *City without a Church*. St John had taught Christians not to create ecclesiastical enclaves within an otherwise godless city but to make the whole city holy. This they must do patiently but systematically, converting street after street, for 'let a City be a Sodom and Gomorrah, but if there are ten righteous men in it, it will be saved'. Jerusalem was to be found not just in heaven but in cities of the present: 'It is London, Berlin, New York, Paris, Melbourne, Calcutta – these as they might be and in some infinitesimal degree as they have already begun to be.' In each of them could be realised the city that descended from heaven. 'The project is delirious?' asked Drummond. 'Yes – to atheism. To John it was the most obvious thing in the world.'[112]

These calls to activism reflect new confidence about the religious potential of the city, which was no longer just 'the citadel of the world's fever, [or] the ganglion of its unrest'.[113] Historians have long recognised that the 'civic gospel' behind municipal reform reflected profound changes in the religious culture of urban elites. Civic gospellers believed that the incarnation of Christ was a vote of confidence in the goodness not just of created nature but specifically of human nature and civic life.[114] The Platonic Christian Socialist Henry Scott Holland (1847–1918) thus argued that 'there should be, through the town, through humanity up gathered into towns, a finer and richer and deeper and more pregnant manifestation of what God actually is,

---

[111] Jonathan Brierley, *Our City of God* (London, 1907), p. 169.
[112] Drummond, *Church*, p. 18.   [113] Ibid., p. 7.
[114] E. P. Hennock, *Fit and Proper Persons: Ideal and Reality in Nineteenth Century Urban Government* (London, 1968); Cheryl Walsh, 'The Incarnation and the Christian Socialist Conscience in the Victorian Church of England', *Journal of British Studies*, 34 (1995), 351–74.

than in Nature alone'.[115] It is just as striking that this ideal reacted upon the historic cities of the Bible themselves. Simon Goldhill shows below that British philanthropists installed drains in Jerusalem and planned suburbs in an effort to create the sort of city that they yearned for at home, superimposing the New Jerusalem on the old. Jane Garnett and Anne Bush similarly note that British visitors were divided by the squalor of Rome. Those who wished to eradicate its smelly backwardness were met by others who valued it as a sign that the Holy City was largely exempt from thrusting materialism. In 1899, William Sharp reassured the readers of *Good Words* that Rome was still the 'eternal city', its traditions not yet wholly obscured by 'the second-rate Parisianism of the Via Nationale, the London-Suburbanism of the despoiled Gardens of Minerva, the Battersea-dreariness of the model dwellings in the Prati di Castello, the trams in the Corso and motor cars on the Flaminian Way'.[116]

Moreover, the later Victorian proliferation of civic gospels did not represent a secularising capitulation to a fashionable immanentism or the nostrums of social science. Many of those involved in attempts to civilise the inner cities continued to be ardent believers in sin and salvation and their struggle to keep a distinctively Christian piety alive maintained the biblical city as an ideal into the twentieth century.[117] Protesting in 1908 against the 'new wave of materialist altruism', the Oxford archaeologist and Anglican modernist Percy Gardner warned against an excessive preoccupation with remedying material poverty. After all, 'one must remember that Christianity grew to maturity in the slums of ancient cities, slums compared with which the worst districts of London and Liverpool are paradises'.[118] As his words implied, the fashionable slum settlement movement made intensive use of biblical models. Many of those who colonised the East End of London saw it through the spectacles of the Bible and the classics rather than the ostensibly clear lenses of sociology. Samuel Barnett (1844–1913), the moving force behind Toynbee Hall, knew little about the needs of the industrial economy; he divided up the world into heartless rich and godless

---

[115] Stephen Paget, *Henry Scott Holland: Memoir and Letters* (London, 1921), pp. 240 ff. See similarly John Clifford, *The New City of God: Or, The Primitive Christian Faith as a Social Gospel* (London, 1888), p. 13 and Robert William Dale, *The Laws of Christ for Common Life* (London, 1884), p. 8.

[116] William Sharp, 'The Eternal City', *Good Words*, 40 (1899), 268–9.

[117] David Bebbington, 'The City, the Countryside, and the Social Gospel in Late Victorian Nonconformity', in Derek Baker, ed., *The Church in Town and Countryside* (Oxford, 1979), pp. 415–26.

[118] Percy Gardner, 'Lay Liberalism', in *Anglican Liberalism by Twelve Churchmen* (London, 1908), pp. 161–2.

plebs, seeing class division as the product of greed.[119] The conception of London as another Rome in need of the simple apostolic gospel is still more pronounced if the gaze shifts from the muscular agnosticism of Toynbee Hall to settlements run by committed Anglicans and dissenters.[120] They envisaged themselves as repeating the work of the apostles, carrying out in London's slums the 'revival, as a real force for the guidance of human life, of the doctrines taught by Jesus Christ and practiced by the Christians of the first century'.[121] The parallel between London – or New York – and the cities of the Roman Empire was a common one: both were nodes of vast networks that cosmopolitan Christians could use to spread the gospel. Archaeology supported the parallel, for it not only demonstrated the complexity and in a sense the modernity of the imperial system but showed that the New Testament was a reliable account of how the apostles had mobilised that system for Christ.[122]

The fall of the biblical city

The world of biblical cities described in this volume is no longer ours. When and why did it disappear? The answer must emphasise the unravelling of the synthesis between archaeology, biblical apologetics and intense but fragile civic pride outlined in this introduction. To begin with archaeology, it is arguable that the First World War represented a genuine watershed in its relationship with the public. Organised excavation in the Bible lands had fallen back dramatically between 1914 and 1919. For archaeological organisations, this was a period of introspection and debate about what approaches and techniques entitled their disciplines to be seen as scientific. After the First World War, these organisations had to rebuild their support-base, extensively re-advertising for members. Many old subscribers rejected the appeals, some citing the declining devotion of the PEF and the EEF to shedding light on the Bible. The proportion of members whose interest in

---

[119] Standish Meacham, *Toynbee Hall and Social Reform, 1880–1914: The Search for Community* (New Haven, CT, 1987).

[120] Seth Koven, *Slumming: Sexual and Social Politics in Victorian London* (London, 2004), chapter 5; David Newsome, 'The Assault on Mammon: Charles Gore and John Neville Figgis', *Journal of Ecclesiastical History*, 17 (1966), 227–41.

[121] Robert Archey Woods, ed., *The City Wilderness: A Settlement Study* (New York, 1898); John Gorst, 'Introduction: Settlements in England and America', in Arthur Winnington Ingram, ed., *The Universities and the Social Problem: An Account of the University Settlements in East London* (London, 1895), p. 11.

[122] Henry Scott Holland, *God's City and the Coming of the Kingdom* (London, 1897), pp. 45, 159.

archaeology was overwhelmingly biblical thus fell appreciably. Near-Eastern archaeology's role in the academy was also changing. Assyriology had entered British universities much more easily than Egyptology or equivalent disciplines. This was simply because of the Assyrian language's close relationship to Hebrew: thanks to this mechanism it had been incorporated into the world of biblical scholarship relatively easily. The Egyptian language had no such felicitous affinity, so became a subject of university study much more slowly: when its institutionalisation began, haltingly, in the 1890s, it had no necessary institutional reliance on the study of biblical languages and archaeology, and it, in turn, provided a non-theological association for Assyriology.[123]

The meaning of biblical archaeology therefore gradually became less capacious, less permissive and more tightly controlled by a specific group of qualified practitioners. Perhaps the most obvious aspect of this was the tendency of biblical archaeology to become increasingly synonymous with the archaeology of Palestine. Again, the First World War was a key watershed. The collapse of the Ottoman Empire and the establishment of a British Mandate of Palestine provided the political context in which an international cast of scholars including John Garstang (1876–1956) and the influential William Foxwell Albright (1891–1971) developed a discipline with a strong academic identity, but decreasing concern for more popular interests. As Thomas Davis notes, 'Albright profoundly changed the nature of biblical archaeology. When he first arrived in Palestine it was a nebulous supradiscipline more interested in Assyrian texts than Palestinian pots.' Albright's influence guided it in the direction of a field-oriented discipline, centred on a fertile intellectual community in Jerusalem. The interwar period was undoubtedly the heyday of biblical archaeology, yet its technical manner meant that it had less call on the interest of the Sunday readers and Sunday school pupils who had been agog at the heroics of Layard or trouped obediently through the British Museum with Ada Habershon. The Bible continued to determine where archaeologists dug, but in Britain at least it no longer linked them to a community of readers who shared their assumptions.[124]

The Mandate's impact was not just confined to this tight-knit archaeological community: it altered the relationship of the British to the Holy City in ways that reduced the city's imaginative potential. The Mandate injected a powerful dose of reality. Dreams were no longer sufficient or

---

[123] See Gange, *Dialogues*.
[124] Davis, *Shifting Sands*, chapters 2 and 3; Roger Moorey, *A Century of Biblical Archaeology* (Louisville, KY, 1991), chapter 3.

even desirable in a twentieth century where the future Jerusalem had to be created not with spades and sermons, but by mundane administration. The real Jerusalem had long served as a check on visions of the city's divine character; as Goldhill shows, it now interposed itself in ways that could not be ignored.[125]

The declining interest in biblical archaeology also reflected the shrinking market for religious publishing. Religious titles as a proportion of all titles published in Britain had been in slow but inexorable decline during the nineteenth century. From the early twentieth century, societies such as the Religious Tract Society noted with concern that sales figures were now falling in real terms. Christ, complained one tract writer in the 1920s, was no longer popular. This reflected a series of interlinked developments: the decay of the 'British Sunday' and the consequent decline in the practice of Sunday reading and the stalling of the associational ideal that had given Britain its armies of Sunday school pupils and tract distributors.[126] Yet the increasingly technical thrust of archaeology and biblical criticism alike had made it harder to produce literature that was properly scholarly and powerfully edifying. Thus the limpid realism and the mild optimism of the later nineteenth-century 'lives' of Jesus that had made him into a genial social and moral reformer was endangered by the disintegrating impact of form criticism and a new appreciation of what had supposedly been his radical eschatology.[127] This was not to deny that biblical archaeology still did well when imaginatively marketed: Hodder and Stoughton sold 190,000 copies of Werner Keller's *The Bible as History* (1956).[128] Rather than appealing to a mainstream public, however, works such as Keller's now often draw a narrower if extensive constituency: the transatlantic community of conservative evangelicals, for whom archaeological evidence is a means of mounting a naively factual defence of scriptural inerrancy and whose rational, Baconian rhetoric disguises a counter-cultural pessimism about scientific progress and the prospects of modern civilisation.[129]

---

[125] Simon Goldhill, *Jerusalem: City of Longing* (Cambridge, MA, 2008), chapters 6–7.

[126] Ledger-Lomas, 'Mass Markets: Religion', p. 338; John Wigley, *The Rise and Fall of the Victorian Sunday* (Manchester, 1980); S. J. D. Green, *The Passing of Protestant England: Secularisation and Social Change, c.1920–1960* (Cambridge, 2011).

[127] Daniel Pals, *Victorian 'Lives' of Jesus* (San Antonio, TX, 1980); Mark Chapman, *The Coming Crisis: The Impact of Eschatology on Theology in Edwardian England* (Sheffield, 2001).

[128] John Attenborough, *A Living Memory: Hodder and Stoughton Publishers 1868–1975* (London, 1975), p. 169.

[129] James Barr, *Fundamentalism* (1978; London, 1981), p. 139; Harriet Harris, *Fundamentalism and Evangelicals* (Oxford, 1998), chapters 3 and 4; George Marsden, *Fundamentalism and American Culture* (1980; London, 2006).

While the intellectual and religious conditions became markedly less propitious to interest in biblical cities, so too did the evolving urban life of Britain. Historians have emphasised that the later nineteenth and early twentieth centuries were an optimistic period for the churches. Sunday schools and voluntary associations permeated the public culture of the industrial villages and commercial towns of provincial England with the language of Christianity. Yet in inner cities and above all in London these efforts did not bring higher levels of attendance and membership of churches.[130] The very zeal with which later Victorian Protestants 'number[ed] Babylon ... objectifying the moral crisis and rendering it in comfortingly tabular form' may have emptied their religion of its theological content and endowed it with a philistine hostility to pleasure that repelled the non-aligned.[131] These failures strengthened the hand of those who argued that the metropolitan civilisation of the early twentieth century created problems that could not be solved by the old Christian nostrums but required a hard-headed resort to such measures as emigration, internal colonisation, or even the sterilisation of the unfit.[132] A Protestant civic gospel faced competition from sociologists and municipal bureaucracies whose growth socially concerned church people had done much to encourage, from proponents of home colonisation or from the garden city movement. Some of these movements invoked the city of God, but to picture an escape from rather than the reform of the city.[133]

Suburbanisation had already weakened the Protestant civic gospel, as the bourgeoisie voted with their feet and made social segregation a reality for the first time. Dissenting churches that had expended their resources conquering cities now left them along with their congregations; the wealthy individuals who had run missions to the urban poor lost interest in the task.[134] Out in the suburbs, the biblical rhetoric that had underpinned parallels between London and Babylon looked overheated. As Astrid Swenson shows in her chapter, when Hensley Henson attacked Barking as another Sodom, he aroused laughter rather than anguish. The colour of suburban London was not the pitch black of sin and heathenism but the

---

[130] Green, *Passing*; Hugh McLeod, *Piety and Poverty: Working-Class Religion in Berlin, London and New York 1870–1914* (New York, 1996).
[131] Dominic Erdozain, 'The Secularization of Sin in the Nineteenth Century', *Journal of Ecclesiastical History*, 62 (2011), 81.
[132] Arnold White, *The Problems of a Great City* (London, 1886); Hunt, *Jerusalem*.
[133] Callum Brown, *Religion and Society in Scotland since 1707* (London, 1997), chapter 6; Frank Prochaska, *The Disinherited Spirit: Christianity and Social Service in Modern Britain* (London, 2006).
[134] For this argument see Brown, *Religion and Society*, chapter 6.

grey of monotonous employment and leisure; it was the home of Mr Pooter, rather than Pharaoh or Nero. Critics of suburban anomie such as Charles Masterman (1874–1927) noted that despite all the churches that dotted suburban London, 'the curtain of the horizon has descended around the material things and the pitiful duration of human life'. Masterman sighed not for a New Jerusalem, but for the vaguer hope of 'some background to life' to unite dispersed suburbanites.[135]

The biblical city did not collapse in the early twentieth century as suddenly as the walls of Jericho – which Charles Warren had, incidentally, prospected for the PEF in 1868. Rather it had slowly fallen apart, with many of its building blocks being cannibalised for use in other activities. The idealism of the New Jerusalem lived on in socialist thought; the trust that archaeology will literally authenticate Scripture still thrives today on the internet, the last and most secure recourse of evangelical Protestantism. The biblical cities that Willcocks wanted to erect by the Nile and Tigris and Henry Drummond by the Thames have, though, vanished from British culture for good.

---

[135] Charles Masterman, 'Realities at Home', in Charles Masterman, ed., *The Heart of the Empire: Discussions of Problems of Modern City Life in England, With an Essay on Imperialism* (London, 1901), pp. 30–1.

1 | Troy

DAVID GANGE AND RACHEL BRYANT DAVIES

Nineteenth-century Britons fought over the landmarks of Jerusalem and Troy with greater intensity than any others. One might ask, parodying Tertullian, 'what has Troy to do with Jerusalem?'[1] However, nineteenth-century archaeology and scholarship subverted this injunction to separate the church from the history and thought of Greece to such an extent that it would be difficult to capture the changing relationships between city and text without first discussing the city of the *Iliad*, that 'Bible of classical times'.[2] The famously besieged and destroyed city was, for decades, the proving-ground for techniques that were subsequently applied to Scripture, while travellers often visited the Troad *en route* to the Holy Land, or *vice versa*. This correlation between belief in Homer's veracity and faith in the Bible runs throughout British responses to the search for Troy, underpinned by connections between biblical criticism and classical scholarship. Homer's Troy – a city located at the crossroads between mythology, epic and history – highlights the contested authority of both classical and biblical texts. Such disputes reached fever-pitch with the claim of Heinrich Schliemann (1822–90) to have uncovered the city of Homeric epic because uncertainty about the authenticity of Homeric epic had become entwined with increased alarm about higher critical scepticism from the 1850s onward. Once located and excavated, the remains of Homer's Troy could symbolise the triumph of the literary imagination – both classical and biblical – over sceptical criticism.

The most sensational events in Troy's archaeological history, Schliemann's excavations at Hisarlik, occurred at the moment, in the 1870s, when controversies concerning the relationship between secular and sacred knowledge were most intense. Thanks to texts from Thomas Henry Huxley's 'On the Physical Basis of Life' (1868/9), Charles Darwin's *Descent of Man* (1871) and John Tyndall's 'Belfast Address' (1874) to Huxley's 'On the Method of Zadig' (1880) the idea that 'science' and 'religion' were in direct conflict was aired

---

[1] Tertullian, *De Praescriptione Haereticorum*, ed. Pierre de Labriolle (Paris, 1907), p. 16: '*Quid ergo Athenis et Hierosolymis?*' ('What does Athens have to do with Jerusalem?')

[2] Richard Engelmann and William Anderson, *Pictorial Atlas to Homer's Iliad and Odyssey* (London, 1892), p. iv.

with new confidence in the British press. Classical literature played crucial roles in the invective of the early 1870s. Tyndall's 'Belfast Address' famously invoked Lucretius and the 'atomism' of ancient Epicureans, while William Kingdon Clifford's vain attempt to subvert the quickly solidifying divide between rationalism and faith used the siege of Syracuse in the Peloponnesian War to demonstrate the 'universal duty of questioning all that we believe'; an imperative that 'no simplicity of mind, no obscurity of station, can escape'.[3]

Lucretius and Thucydides provided occasional historical illustrations and analogies in these debates; Homeric Troy was a constant presence. Readers soon understood that what was said of this city could pose nagging metaphysical questions. As early as 1857, Elizabeth Barrett Browning had presented the critical deconstruction of this single pagan text as a rebellion against the divine nature of the cosmos itself:

> Wolff's an atheist;
> And if the Iliad fell out, as he says,
> By mere fortuitous concourse of old songs,
> We'll guess as much, too, for the universe.[4]

Her husband Robert put it less snappily, but in terms more revealing of the complexes of enchantment and disillusionment that coalesced around this city-as-symbol which, in his words, enabled 'truth and falsehood [to be] known and named as such':

> And, after Wolf, a dozen of his like
> Proved there was never any Troy at all,
> Neither Besiegers nor Besieged, – nay, worse, –
> No actual Homer, no authentic text,
> No warrant for the fiction I, as fact,
> Had treasured in my heart and soul so long –
> ... though Wolf – ah, Wolf!
> Why must he needs come doubting, spoil a dream?[5]

The philologist Friedrich August Wolf's *Prolegomena ad Homerum* (1795) was by far the most frequently cited sceptical text on Troy. It was directly

---

[3] Helen Small, 'Science, Liberalism and the Ethics of Belief', in G. N. Cantor and S. Shuttleworth, eds., *Science Serialized: Representations of the Sciences in Nineteenth-Century Periodicals* (Cambridge, MA, 2004), p. 240; W. K. Clifford, 'The Ethics of Belief', *Contemporary Review* (January 1877), 307–8.

[4] Elizabeth Barrett Browning, *Aurora Leigh* (London, 1857), p. 226.

[5] Robert Browning, 'Development', in John Pettigrew, ed., *Poems* (2 vols., London, 1981), II, pp. 918–21.

modelled on one of the most controversial contemporary products of higher criticism, J. G. Eichhorn's *Einleitung in das Alte Testament* (1780/3), and asserted the oral composition of Homer's epic poems, raising questions over their authorship, dating and authenticity, and kick-starting the 'Homeric Question'.

The loss of imaginary, often 'childhood' Troys under the scrutiny of scholarship that aimed, in Robert Browning's words, to 'sift the grain from chaff' became a familiar lament of Romantic and post-Romantic poetry. Almost a century after the *Prolegomena*'s publication, its effects on those who believed in a single author of the *Iliad* was still vividly recalled by *The Examiner* as 'so very shattering … that their old firmness of faith is gone for ever, and doubt and distrust reign triumphant in its stead'.[6] When John Ruskin (1819–1900) had felt himself in this spiritual 'mess' in 1864, it was to the topographer of Troy, Henry Acland (1815–1900), that he turned to ask whether the Athenians were 'all wrong' in building the Parthenon, and if so, whether those who designed the spire of St Mary's in Hinksey could be equally misguided. By this time, the appetite for scholarship that might liberate Athens from the rationalism of the 'vulgar materialist' George Grote and Homer from the scepticism of Wolf was extensive.[7]

This parallel between Homeric and biblical narratives – which placed Troy in the same imaginative landscape as Jerusalem – was only strengthened when the same travellers and scholars contributed to debates over Troy's location and to arguments over sites such as that of Christ's Tomb. The Cambridge mineralogist Edward Daniel Clarke (1769–1822), for example, having 'found the situation where Ilium once stood', proceeded to Jerusalem, where he visited 'the possible site of our Saviour's tomb'.[8] He disputed both its location at the Church of the Holy Sepulchre and the site of the springs which supposedly identified Homer's Troy. Meanwhile, Philip Hunt (b. 1770) and Joseph Dacre Carlyle (1758–1804), who were attached to Elgin's embassy with a view to collecting New Testament manuscripts, visited the Troad both with him and subsequently in March 1801, when they were only three days behind Clarke and his student Cripps. The two cities were frequent subjects of comparison: the first modern topographer to

---

[6] 'Mr. Gladstone's Last Homeric Study', *Examiner* (8 April 1876), 407.
[7] E. T. Cook and A. Wedderburn, eds., *Works of John Ruskin* (31 vols., London, 1903–12), XXXIV, p. 18.
[8] 'Dr Clarke's Travels', *La Belle Assemblée* (1813), 306 ff.; Edward Daniel Clarke, *Travels in Various Countries of Europe, Asia and Africa: Part 1, Russia, Tartary, and Turkey* (Cambridge, 1810), pp. 342–6; J. M. Crook, *The Greek Revival: Neo-Classical Attitudes in British Architecture 1760–1870* (London, 1972), p. 27. See further Simon Goldhill, *Jerusalem: City of Longing* (Cambridge, MA, 2008), p. 21.

propose the site now accepted as Troy claimed that 'Hissarlik [*sic*], if proved to be the true site of Homer's Ilium, becomes consecrated ground [since] ... Ilium was for a considerable period to the Heathen world, what Jerusalem is now to the Christian'.[9]

The chapters of this book show different biblical cities rising to prominence at specific moments in the nineteenth century: Sodom, for instance, was found most useful in the angst-ridden, radicalised 1840s. The Romantic travels of Clarke, Hunt, Carlyle and Byron represent one such peak for discussion of Troy, but the city became most relevant to Protestant thought later, interest in it building through the 1860s until it exploded into full view after 1870. The reason was not just archaeological discoveries, but also changes in the questions asked of pre-classical history and literature, which were in turn brought about by developments in biblical interpretation. Ruskin's personal crisis came in the same year as the Oxford Declaration collected signatures of 10,906 churchmen denouncing all those who doubted that any part of the Bible was the Word of God. This was the same moment at which leading Church of England clerics stood trial at the Court of Arches for heresy: the culmination of the *Essays and Reviews* (1860) controversy. One of the 'seven against Christ' who contributed to the volume, Charles Wycliffe Goodwin (1817–78), was known primarily as an Egyptologist; another, Rowland Williams (1817–70), used his contribution to review Baron Christian Carl Josias von Bunsen's perspectives on pre-classical languages and chronology. Bunsen and his British followers insisted that secular history was the 'external shell' to which Scripture was the 'kernel': the two had grown together, were entirely symbiotic, and the former must provide the framework in which the latter was interpreted.[10] Over the following decade, Troy reappeared in every new crisis of biblical authority. W. R. Cassels (1826–1907), for instance, dismissed the *Iliad* as 'base anthropomorphic mythology' in *Supernatural Religion: An Inquiry into the Reality of the Divine Revelation* (1874), a text with the primary purpose of challenging the historicity of the gospels.[11]

From the opposite perspective, churchmen and public figures renegotiated the relationships between ancient history and Revelation, in terms that still favoured the latter, in works with titles such as *The Place of Ancient Greece in the Providential Order of the World* (William Ewart Gladstone's valedictory address of Rector of the University of Edinburgh, 1865). After

---

[9] Review of Charles Maclaren's *Dissertation*: 'The Plain of Troy Described', *Athenaeum* (9 May 1863), 616.

[10] C. C. J. von Bunsen, *Egypt's Place in Universal History* (5 vols., London, 1848–67), I, p. 176.

[11] [W.R. Cassels], *Supernatural Religion* (3 vols., London, 1874), I, p. 111.

1870, Heinrich Schliemann, the German businessman excavating at Troy, and George Smith (1840–76), the bank-note engraver deciphering Deluge Tablets in the bowels of the British Museum, provided fresh material for archaeological intervention in these debates. They consolidated and extended the role of pre-classical history in the theological soul-searching that accompanied both the rise of scientific naturalism and the popularisation of higher critical ideas.

Even before Schliemann, the imaginative capital of these tropes was enormous: the 'Homeric' poetry of the Brownings was the tip of a vast iceberg of verse. Large numbers of justifiably forgotten poets also used Troy to 'Get truth and falsehood known and named as such', often uncritically conjoining the classical and biblical in the process. From the dozens of instances that could be cited, two particularly earnest examples will suffice. John Box was master at Dorking Grammar School, author of several works of biblical literature and handbooks to arithmetic. His enormous epic poem, *The Deluge* (1881), began with the obligatory Miltonic appeal:

> Triune Lord of all! Whose spirit moved
> That giant of our English song to sing
> Of man's first disobedience

and 'the loss / Of Paradise and all its perfect bliss!'. This divine aid was petitioned for assistance in recounting

> Eden's happiness; its sin;
> And all the sorrow that with sin returned!

As soon as this biblical invocation is complete, however, Box embarks on a lengthy account of Homeric geography, recalling 'infantine navies of the ancient world' that accomplished heroic deeds 'twixt' the limits of the Mediterranean Sea. The prose preface to later editions of this multi-volume work set out the author's thesis: 'Eden and Paradise are now covered by the Mediterranean.'[12] Around this sea 'Each cape, each cove is monument that marks / Heroic deed'; but 'greater things' lie hidden beneath the waters. When Box recounts the journey of a bold ancient mariner, the rapid juxtaposition of Homeric and biblical vicinities such as Charybdis and Tarshish (the city Jonah reached on his biblical odyssey) hints at the dramatic affinities he wants to draw: Odysseus' route away from Troy carried him over a biblical landscape. Through such re-working of the long-standing equation between Eden and Troy the geographies of pre-classical

---

[12] John Box, *The Deluge* (3 vols., London, 1882), I, p. ix.

literature – Pentateuch, *Iliad* and *Odyssey* – become identical. This was an equation that had, until Schliemann, been the preserve of the sceptical – 'researches' concerning Troy were 'equally idle and hopeless with those ... respecting the position of the garden of Eden' – but which was now employed from new, more traditionalist, angles.[13] Another forgotten poet, William Watkins Old (Royal Society Fellow and Plantagenet historian) also published verse that refracted Homer through the Protestant lens of Milton. In his pastiche *Il Penseroso*, Old suggested that the original blind bard, aware of the true nature of creation, had spoken allegorically of biblical events. Penelope is Eve; Odysseus is Adam. Old's poem concludes with Penelope's vision of the tree of life: the 'mystery of Eden' is disclosed and 'Wisdom Divine' reveals that 'these two things' – Hellenic and Hebraic learning – 'were one, in truth'.[14]

Writing amidst the convulsions of the modern Eastern Question, Alexander Kinglake (1809-91) described Box and Old's palimpsestic Eastern Mediterranean as a 'grand, simple, violent world'.[15] Precisely because of the mass of overlaid Homeric and biblical traditions that these poets exploited, travellers could imbue almost any of the region's ruins with biblical *and* Homeric auras. As Ruskin's friend and correspondent, Henry Acland, had emphasised in *The Plains of Troy* (1839), the ruins of Alexandria Troas (built by Alexander to emulate Homer's city) were known as 'Priam's Palace' and 'it was from this Troas that St Paul sailed into Macedonia. Here also on his return he restored to life Eutychus' (Acts 20:9).[16]

These classical–biblical conflations were endowed with new and more problematic implications during the 1860s. Homeric–biblical parallels were tied to questions of identity that became increasingly divisive after Matthew Arnold's essays on *Culture and Anarchy* (1867-8).[17] Arnold's adapted Herderian categories – Hebraism and Hellenism – were not simply metaphors in the generation when Box wrote his *Deluge*: they were used until the early twentieth century as vital tools of social and historical analysis. 'The essential identity of European civilisation with the Greek' rubbed up against Ruskin's assumption that the English were the 'Israel of all the Earth'.[18] As this chapter will demonstrate, identities built on these legendary genealogies, which fused the classical and biblical into their supposed modern composite, the Victorian Briton, can be found throughout the British

---

[13] Charles Maclaren, *The Plain of Troy Described* (1822; Edinburgh, 1863), pp. v–vi.
[14] William Watkins Old, *New Readings of Homer* (London, 1860), pp. 139–42.
[15] Alexander Kinglake, *The Invasion of the Crimea* (8 vols., London, 1863–87), I, p. 37.
[16] Henry Acland, *The Plains of Troy* (Oxford, 1839), p. 14.
[17] David DeLaura, *Hebrew and Hellene in Victorian Britain* (Austin, TX, 1970).
[18] Cook and Wedderburn, eds., *Works of John Ruskin*, XXIX, p. 92.

press. Even as Troy's appearances in critical discourse threatened to consign these identities to the status of fanciful myth, mapping and digging Troy showed how myth could be restored to the status of scientifically verified fact. As we shall see, this conflict had been fought out by travellers and antiquarians for decades, but Arnold's categories placed it in particularly stark relief.

As this contest between text and topography caused Troy to stutter out of myth into material reality, and then back again, the city was discussed in the language of 'faith', 'revelation' and 'inspiration'. Nowhere did entanglement between Hellenism and Hebraism become more intractable than at this site; and no other site demonstrates how flimsy the partitions between the categories of sacred and secular remained. From Arnold and Carlyle to Gladstone and Ruskin, the great names of the age made heartfelt interventions in debates that interrogated the nature of archaeological knowledge itself. To such evangelistic apologists for Homer and the Bible, the disputed textual evidence lacked substance next to rivers and hills, walls and weapons, pots and palaces which all seemed to stand in the exact spots that 'Homer' or 'Moses' had said they would. The techniques of mapping and digging were tested here against textual analysis as tools for deciding where the character traits of Europeans had come from and what the British could know of their origins.

These heady debates involved, and encouraged, some unexpected assumptions about the social functions and literary genre of the *Iliad*. This included the widespread insistence that the *Iliad* was to the Greeks what Scripture was to Jews or Christians. This 'Greek's Bible', the fount of Hellenic 'theology', could easily become a modern secular Bible in the sense that Homer's 'genius' made it heretical to question his grasp of history or geography, while an 1892 *Illustrated Atlas to Homer* would literalise this analogy by describing itself as 'a Greek illustrated Bible'.[19] Kinglake's earlier description of his relationship with Homer captures a more playful version of this trope:

as an old woman deeply trustful sits reading her Bible because of the world to come, so, as though it would fit me for the coming strife of this temporal world, I read, and read the Iliad.[20]

---

[19] W. H. Mason, 'Homer and Dr. Schliemann', *Macmillan's Magazine* (September 1876), 448; Engelmann and Anderson, *Pictorial Atlas*, p. iv.
[20] Alexander Kinglake, *Eothen: Or, Traces of Travel Brought Home from the East* (London, 1844), p. 56.

The British press repeatedly scrutinised these trusting attitudes to classical literature, often in tandem with other cultural crises. Bunsen's ancient history was, according to the British Museum curator Samuel Birch, the 'most critical work yet published' on ancient Egypt; yet William Smith in the *Quarterly* (writing in that most resonant of years, 1859) excoriated the Baron for his failure to grasp the difference between human classics and divine Scripture.[21] 'A kind of halo', he wrote, rests on Greek and Roman texts, making it 'almost as presumptuous to question the tales of Livy as the statements of the Bible'. Ancient historians had proved incapable of developing 'laws respecting the value of evidence' or of examining 'the grounds upon which the ancients themselves believed in the stories which they related'.[22] Bunsen, Smith implied, had failed to appreciate the difference between human and divine in according too much credit to authors outside providential traditions. In 1864, the outgoing Home Secretary and editor of *The Edinburgh Review*, George Cornewall Lewis (1806–63) penned a satirical pamphlet in which he applied the outmoded 'credulity' of ancient historians like Bunsen to modern history and demonstrated that Charles I and Charles II were one and the same.[23]

The efforts of Smith and Cornewall Lewis had little impact on the generation that followed them and the reasons for their failure are among the core concerns of this chapter. Schliemann's comment in *Troja*, that he believed in the *Iliad* 'as in the Gospel itself' became one of his most quoted but least examined dicta.[24] It inspired one of the most prolific writers on Homer of the century, William Ewart Gladstone, and filtered into reviews of his work: Gladstone, *The Examiner* insisted, made the *Iliad* 'an object more of devotion than mere study, of reverence more than of dry enquiry'.[25]

Strikingly, in the hands of this four-times Prime Minister, analogies between Homer and Scripture were much more than self-conscious rhetorical devices. Gladstone considered it self-evident that as the two great texts of the early world, the Old Testament and the *Iliad* could be used to elucidate one another; the details of society left out of one could be filled in from the other. More striking still, Homer was raised unequivocally to the

---

[21] [William Smith], 'Bunsen's Egypt and the Chronology of the Bible', *Quarterly Review*, 55 (1859), 382.

[22] Ibid.

[23] George Cornewall Lewis, *Suggestions for the Application of the Egyptological Method to Modern History* (London, 1862).

[24] Anon., 'Troy and its Remains', *Morning Post* (18 September 1875), 3; Anon., 'Dr. Schliemann's Trojan Antiquities', *Edinburgh Review* (April 1874), 513: the passage in question is the *Edinburgh Review*'s translation of a phrase from Schliemann's *Einleitung*, p. xi.

[25] Anon., 'Mr. Gladstone's Last Homeric Study', *Examiner* (8 April 1876), 407.

status of sacred history with the argument that elements of divine revelation could be unpicked from the *Iliad* and *Odyssey*.[26] Gladstone's colossal *Studies on Homer and the Homeric Age* (3 vols., 1858) stands as the most sustained assertion that divine providence had been universally distributed in the early world, and that the Homeric poems contained the most complete recollection of this primordial golden age.

While this idea received short shrift on publication in 1858, it is significant that its influence (and the number of its imitators) grew substantively. This was in part because Gladstone's status as one of the century's greatest public figures meant that, amidst the archaeological enthusiasm of the 1870s, he was able to appoint himself as mediator between archaeologists and the public; but it was also a result of the mounting polemic – associated first with Darwin and *Essays and Reviews*, then with the more aggressive statements of Cassels, Huxley and Tyndall. In these decades, the debate over the relation of biblical and classical texts shifted significantly. In the 1850s, scholars such as William Smith had countenanced the deconstruction of ancient texts like Homer and Livy while assuming that the Bible stood apart and could remain intact. Tension was raised as churchmen such as Samuel Wilberforce (in the aftermath of *Essays and Reviews*) insisted that critical assaults on Livy were preparatory work for attacks on the Old Testament. Like Wilberforce in his riposte, Gladstone believed that all forms of pre-classical written authority stood or fell together. In 1858 this idea appeared eccentric and reactionary. The biblical and Homeric discoveries of archaeologists gradually altered the balance of power between these two perspectives. By 1880, statements concerning the authority of ancient texts that had once looked improbable and dogmatic could be presented, with confidence, as empirically true.

The reception history of German higher criticism in Britain provides one framework for this development. Classical texts and remains had been used to elaborate and elucidate Scripture for generations. The enlightened *Altertumswissenschaft*, developed notably in Göttingen and then applied to the Old Testament by scholars from Michaelis to Heyne, had done exactly this.[27] Mid-century German-influenced thinkers in Britain, particularly Unitarians such as John Kenrick (1788–1877) in his *Egypt of Herodotus* (1841), had taken up this Hanoverian mantle. The challenge to this mode

---

[26] For instance W.E. Gladstone, *Studies on Homer* (3 vols., London, 1858), II, p. 8: the poems of Homer 'afford a most valuable collateral support to the credit of the Holy Scripture, considered as a document of history'.

[27] Jonathan Sheehan, *The Enlightenment Bible: Translation, Scholarship, Culture* (Oxford, 2005); Michael Carhart, *The Science of Culture in Enlightenment Germany* (London, 2007).

came from more radical, and sceptical, criticism of the New Testament such as that championed by D. F. Strauss. British engagement with this criticism, which was essentially internalist and literary rather than archaeological or geographical, expanded only gradually; it began in radical circles but eventually infiltrated larger intellectual constituencies through works like George Eliot's translation of Strauss' *The Life of Jesus, Critically Examined* (1846) and heterodox statements such as Francis William Newman's *Phases of Faith* (1850). These ideas, which challenged the supernatural in all its forms, interpreting supernatural occurrences as evidence of the unreliability of a text, were more widely publicised in the 1870s than ever before. The growing concern of this criticism with the gospels as well as the Old Testament is key to the panic it increasingly engendered. Events of the 1860s showed that the law had no teeth against heresy, especially when, unlike the essayists, lay offenders such as Cassels were not subject to the jurisdiction of the Court of Arches. The Brownings' impassioned response to Wolf, when his work on Homer was already half a century old, shows the same process occurring in classical scholarship; it parallels the equally neurotic reception of Spinoza in the 1870s.[28] Archaeological popularisers, including Archibald Henry Sayce (1845–1933), now built their public identities around the defence of ancient texts from newly publicised critical attacks. In works that culminated with the best-selling of his many volumes – *The Higher Criticism and the Verdict of the Monuments* (1897) – Sayce gave a highly partial history of the higher criticism which observed that critical thought had taken decades to filter through to the public; he charged himself with the task of ensuring that archaeological counterarguments struck home with the instantaneous impact of lightning, not the distant, delayed rumbling of thunder.

As these debates indicate, where other cities in this volume allowed thinkers to negotiate ideas such as order and chaos; civilisation and wilderness; authority and liberty; or faith and doubt, investigations of Troy confronted the starkest such dichotomy. The contested ground that Troy occupied was that between truth and lie, reality and non-existence. Whereas few doubted the actual existence of biblical cities such as Sodom and Gomorrah (whatever their opinions as to events said to have occurred there, or where the cities' remains might be), a host of scholars doubted that Troy 'had any existence, except in the brain of Homer'.[29] Others, with

---

[28] David Katz, *God's Last Words: Reading the English Bible from the Reformation to Fundamentalism* (London, 2004), pp. 248–67.

[29] H. M. Westropp, *The Age of Homer* (London, 1884), p. 25.

the *Iliad* and *Odyssey* instilled in them from youth, retained a commitment to this literature that – like Schliemann's – could almost rival their faith in Scripture. Although much debate about Homer was actually about the Old Testament (as the writings of Gladstone demonstrate), attempts to draw parallels between the two could also work the other way. As the following section will show in more detail, they could serve to discredit those who impugned Homer's reliability: challenging the authenticity of Homer's *Iliad* and *Odyssey* – and therefore the existence of the city of Troy – was made comparable to denying the veracity of the Bible.

Topographical and archaeological endeavour at this ostensibly non-biblical city set the tone for much archaeology throughout the biblical world, in the same way as the controversy and then excitement over Schliemann's excavations set out the lines of interpretation that are pursued in many of the following chapters. By the time of Schliemann, Troy was a buttress for biblical archaeology. Advertisements for *Troy and its Remains* boasted that 'What Botta and Layard did for Khorsabad and Ninevah, Dr. Schliemann has done for the cities which rose in succession on [the] mound of Hissarlik'; a paper at the Church Congress in 1884 hoped that 'ere long Sayce may be able to do for Heth what Layard, Botta, and Rawlinson have done for Assyria, or Schliemann for Troy and Mycenae'.[30]

'The Battle of Bunarbashi': the search for Troy's location

Part of the impact of Schliemann's discoveries at Hisarlik came from the contrast with the failure of the theory which had placed Homer's Troy at Bunarbashi. This theory met great acclaim from its publication in 1791 but was finally abandoned in 1864.[31] Reviewers and critics of archaeological excavations in the 1870s reminded their readers of this topographical background, describing how 'the battles of Troy are once more fought by scholars bent on fishing historical truth out of the deep well of a poetical myth', and claiming that the first exposition of the 'Bunarbashi theory' had 'created all over the civilised world an intense sensation far greater than the

---

[30] For example in 'Dr. Schliemann's Great Work' (advertisement), *Pall Mall Gazette* (26 January 1876); reprinted in e.g. *Pall Mall Gazette* (19 April 1876) and *Examiner* (15 April 1876); Church Congress reported in 'Results of Recent Historical and Typographical Research upon the Old and New Testament', *John Bull* (11 October 1884), 671.

[31] A. C. Lascarides, *The Search for Troy, 1553–1874: An Exhibit* (Bloomington, IN, 1977), p. 37; cf. [Hartley Nelson Coleridge], 'Acland's *Plains of Troy*', *Quarterly Review*, 66 (1840), 356.

sensation produced in later times by the discovery and the excavation of Ninevah by Layard'.[32]

The location of Troy had long been 'vexed and much debated', but had escalated into a huge international debate after 1775.[33] Before this date, Troy's multiple identities as a mythical and historical location (or both) were not widely interrogated or seen as mutually exclusive: sixteenth-century travellers to Constantinople had followed Virgil in identifying Troy with the impressive ruins visible from Tenedos, until the traveller George Sandys (1578–1644) identified them as the Hellenistic town of Alexandria Troas in 1610. Later visitors to the Troad often travelled with Alexander Pope's whimsical drawing of the plain, which illustrated episodes from Homer's narrative and continued to be reproduced in editions of his translation of the *Iliad* well into the nineteenth century.[34] In 1775, however, a debate was sparked when Robert Wood (1716–71), who had captured public imagination with his folios on the ruins of Palmyra and Baalbec, refused to mark Troy on his map of the Troad. Such realism, and his suggestion that Homer's epics were originally oral, overshadowed the merits of his topography in the eyes of the learned public.[35]

In response, two Frenchmen soon set out 'to do what Mr. Wood could not'.[36] The ambassador to the Ottoman Empire, the Comte Choiseul-Gouffier (1752–1817), along with his assistant Jean-Baptiste Lechevalier (1752–1836), matched the landscape with Homer's description and claimed the 'true site' of Troy, on the Balli Dag hill above the Turkish village of Bunarbashi, for France.[37] As the classical scholar Sir Richard Jebb (1841–1905) would comment almost a century later, this theory 'originated the

---

[32] 'From our Constantinople Correspondent', *The Times* (5 June 1876), 12; Anon., 'Troy and Mycenae', *The Times* (12 April 1877), 8.

[33] Charles John Ellicott, 'Introduction', in *Story of the Trojan War: An Epitome (From Classic Writers) of Incidents, Actions and Events which Occurred Before, At and After the Siege of Troy* (London, 1875), p. i.

[34] For an account of earlier travellers, see Crook, *Revival*, pp. 16–21, Lascarides, *Troy*, pp. 9–29 and T. J. B. Spencer, 'Robert Wood and the Problem of Troy in the Eighteenth Century', *The Journal of the Courtauld and Warburg Institutes*, 20 (1957), 75–105. The best nineteenth-century accounts are those by P. W. Forchhammer, 'Observations on the Topography of Troy', *Journal of the Royal Geographical Society of London*, 12 (1845), 28–44, and Charles Maclaren, *The Plain of Troy Described: And the Identity of the Ilium of Homer with the New Ilium of Strabo Proved* (Edinburgh, 1863).

[35] Robert Wood, *An Essay on the Genius and Writings of Homer: With a Comparative View of the Ancient and Present State of the Troade* (London, 1775).

[36] Anon., 'Description of the Plain of Troy', *English Review* (21 May 1793), 322.

[37] For more details about their work see Crook, *Revival*, pp. 21–4 and Lascarides, *Troy*, pp. 29–35.

modern controversy as to the site of Troy'.[38] Moreover, in digging burial mounds popularly ascribed to Achaean heroes, Lechevalier claimed to have discovered the funerary urn of Achilles, a copy of which was displayed in Paris.[39] Much rhetoric concerning the French as the ancestors of the heroic tradition embodied by Achilles followed.[40] Lechevalier, like Wood, produced maps on which 'The Pergamus of Priam, ruins of temples, foundations of walls, the Scaean gate, the hot and cold sources of the Scamander, the station of the Greeks, the tombs of heroes, were ascertained, laid down, and irrevocably named'.[41] Once again, Troy seemed to have become a historical and geographical reality, a site of pilgrimage inhabiting the same conceptual space as biblical sites, and once more 'Homeric pilgrims ... tested their doubts or confirmed their faith on the plain of sacred Ilios'.[42]

As *The Times* would later insist, Lechevalier's *Discovery of Homeric Ilium*, which even fixed 'the site of Priam's garden ... ought to have been entitled "Visions of an Enthusiast"'.[43] Nonetheless, the theory, first expounded to the Royal Society of Edinburgh in 1791, became hugely popular. In the heat of the Napoleonic Wars, however, the eccentric British scholar Jacob Bryant (1717–1804) endeavoured to wrest the impetus from the hands of the French. Bryant subjected Lechevalier's maps to mathematical scrutiny, and found them wanting. He parodied Lechevalier's literalising approach and concluded that the Frenchman's facts

form an artificial system, designed to determine the times of ancient events, and reconcile the histories of the first years. But those histories are not to be reconciled, and they are rendered more and more contradictory by the very means used to make them agree.[44]

Bryant's criticisms, and his declaration that 'the city Troy of Homer never existed', provoked passionate defences and *ad hominem* vitriol in an astoundingly long and furious debate.[45] Ironically, this was credited with the popularisation of 'the Trojan Controversy' as those 'who had never heard of Troy before, heard of it now'.[46] The British argument on Troy now

---

[38] Richard Jebb, 'A Tour in the Troad', *Fortnightly Review*, 39 (1883), 514.
[39] For more on the excavation and 'finds', see Crook, *Revival*, pp. 24, 162.
[40] For some discussion of the nationalist aspect see Jennifer Wallace, 'Digging for Homer: Literary Authenticity and Romantic Archaeology', *Romanticism* 7 (2001), 82.
[41] John Cam Hobhouse, *A Journey Through Albania and other Provinces of Turkey in Europe and Asia* (2 vols., London, 1817), I, p. 134.
[42] Jebb, 'A Tour', 514.   [43] Anon., 'Troy and Mycenae', *The Times* (12 April 1877), 8.
[44] Jacob Bryant, *Dissertation Concerning the War of Troy* (1796; London, 1799), p. 23.
[45] Lascarides, *Troy*, p. 38.   [46] Coleridge, 'Plains of Troy', pp. 355 ff.

began to draw on the writings of German scholars such as Wolf, who questioned whether Homer himself had ever existed, never mind the city of his fictions. Bryant's views were divisive even in Britain, but were granted increasing authority by their compatibility with contemporary literary theories and their influence on leading Homeric scholars, such as the period's great historian of Greece, George Grote (1794–1871), who claimed that if there is any fact among these ancient legends 'it is there by accident'.[47]

If Bryant's theories were controversial with scholars such as William Gell (1777–1836), whose superbly illustrated 1804 travelogue supported Chevalier's 'Bunarbashi theory', they were attacked by those who resented the blasphemous connotations of his scepticism, and hated by those with a more overtly imaginative investment in the epics.[48] The first pamphlet to respond to Bryant likened his opinions to 'Tom Paine's most profligate, rash, audacious and ignorant attack on Revelation'.[49] In a less polemical vein, Kinglake would write, some half a century later, that when reading Homer as a child 'you form strange mystic friendships with the mere names of mountains, and seas, and continents, and mighty rivers' as well as with the heroic spirit of events that took place around them.[50] Bryant's scepticism endangered both these relationships. Perhaps the most famous response to this apparent negation of ancient heroism was that of Byron who visited Lechevalier and Choiseul-Gouffier's sites in the Troad to revel in the arena of Homeric glory:

I stood upon the plain daily, for more than a month, in 1810; and if anything diminished my pleasure, it was that the blackguard Bryant had impugned its veracity . . . I venerated the grand original as the truth of *history* (in the material *facts*) and of *place*. Otherwise, it would have given me no delight. Who will persuade me, when I reclined upon a mighty tomb, that it did not contain a hero? – its very magnitude proved this. Men should not labour over the ignoble and petty dead – and why should not the dead be Homer's dead?[51]

Byron had travelled with John Cam Hobhouse (1786–1869), who summed up the effects of this turn-of-the-century spate of interest in the site of Troy in a volume which remained aloof from any one theory, but whose original intention, the *Morning Post* later claimed, was 'to expose the monstrous

---

[47] A. Bain, ed., *George Grote: Minor Works* (London, 1873), p. 132.
[48] William Gell, *The Topography of Troy, and its Vicinity* (London, 1804).
[49] Gilbert Wakefield, *A Letter to Jacob Bryant, Esq: Concerning his Dissertation on the War of Troy* (London, 1797), p. 17; Spencer, 'Robert Wood', 98.
[50] Kinglake, *Eothen*, p. 59.
[51] Thomas Moore, *Letters and Journals of Lord Byron, with Notices of his Life* (London, 1830), p. 101.

forgeries of Chevalier and the credulity of those who put faith in him and his disciples'.[52]

Monsieur Le Chevalier determined upon the discovery of Troy and succeeded ... Even the sober scepticism of English scholars gave way before the torrent of asserted proofs ... Another traveller, however, apparently of a totally different complexion, restored to us our ancient uncertainty; and when we travelled, the village of Bournabashi was no longer Troy; the springs of the Scamander and Simois had disappeared, and the encampment of the Greeks had again sunk into the nonentity to which it was before reduced by the trident of Neptune.[53]

Over half a century later, Napoleonic fervour had died down: scepticism and interest in Bunarbashi as the possible site of Troy coexisted, as is evident from contemporary reactions in the press.[54] But Schliemann chose to distance himself from these debates by following the advice of Frank Calvert (1828–1908), which he later denied he had needed or received, to dig at the less popular, but increasingly likely, site of Hisarlik.[55] By mid 1874 he had echoed Lechevalier's extraordinary confidence, casting Bryant's concerns aside in claiming that 'the excavations I have made this year have sufficiently proved that the second nation which built a town on this hill ... are the Trojans of whom Homer sings'.[56] As Lechevalier had done at Bunarbashi, Schliemann identified specific ruins as the Scaean Gate, the Temple of Athena, the Tower of Ilium and the Palace of Priam described by Homer. However, Schliemann presented the public with plans and engravings of the walls of Troy (Fig. 1.1) and descriptions of the ruins of a city that had been destroyed by burning in ancient times. In addition, he labelled a large and diverse collection of bronze items 'Priam's Treasure', buried when Troy fell. This would be exhibited, free of charge, at the South Kensington Museum in London in 1877–8, and photographs of his wife Sophia dressed in excavated jewellery identified as the 'Gold of Helen' were widely circulated. As we shall see, the advancing technologies of archaeology and

---

[52] Anon., 'Travels in Albania', *Morning Post* (11 December 1855), 3.
[53] Hobhouse, *A Journey*, p. 134.
[54] See Rachel Bryant Davies, 'Imaginary Cities: Troy and Carthage in the Long Nineteenth Century' (unpublished thesis: University of Cambridge, 2011), pp. 10–52.
[55] Hisarlik had been considered the site of Troy by Charles Maclaren in *The Plain of Troy Described*; Calvert had bought part of the site in 1863 or 1864 to test the theory after excavating Bunarbashi and identifying it as Gergithe, but without the funds to excavate extensively he persuaded Schliemann of the claims of the site. See Lascarides, *Troy*, pp. 62–5 and for a full account of the complex wranglings over early excavations at Hisarlik, Susan Heuck Allan, *Finding the Walls of Troy* (Berkeley, CA, 1998).
[56] [Philip Smith and William Ewart Gladstone], 'Discoveries at Troy', *Quarterly Review*, 136 (1874), 545.

Figure 1.1 Heinrich Schliemann, *The Double Scaean Gate*

photography were transforming imaginative reconstructions of Homer's Troy from 'an unsuspected relic of the past' to 'the famed town, ruined, jarred, blackened', which 'Dr. Schliemann's spade has conjured up ... from its once apparently ghostly abode'.[57]

'Troy divine': reading Homer 'by the light of our Bibles'

In 1858, in between these two fits of interest in the site, the future Prime Minister William Gladstone published a three-volume work of Homeric scholarship that would be the most expansive product of his five-decade fascination with the poet. His work was assaulted by critics for amateurish scholarship and has been viewed by historians as an eccentric intervention in a slightly more measured scholarly debate.[58] Commentators assert that

---

[57] Anon., 'The Reader', *Graphic* (6 March 1875), 227; Karl Blind, 'Troy Found Again', *Antiquary* (May 1884), 202.

[58] For instance, *The Times* (12 August 1858), 7; [William Henry Smith], 'Gladstone's *Homer*', *Blackwood's Magazine*, 84 (1858), 127–48. Literature on Gladstone's Homeric interest is good on its status in the 1850s and 1860s, but offers less for later decades: David Bebbington, *The Mind of*

Gladstone was led by religious belief and a powerful antipathy to sceptical criticism to publish theories owing more to ideological and sentimental impulses than to research or considered analysis. Where his work has often been read as an isolated eccentricity or a throwback to an old tradition, it was in fact prescient of an attitude to the pre-classical world that was widespread in responses to Schliemann and gave Near Eastern archaeology and antiquarianism in the last third of the nineteenth century a decidedly new character and significance in cultural and religious life.

Three factors were at the heart of this character: literalism in interpretation of ancient texts; a heightened perception of the relevance of pre-classical texts to the modern world; and tendencies to look for the workings of providence in ancient literature and sites. These were exactly the inclinations that historians have seen as atavistic in Gladstone's works but which defined the quest for biblical sites, particularly in Egypt, after 1880 (explored in chapter 4). The development of a revived Christian earnestness in study of the ancient world was associated with an increasingly social and cultural, rather than chronological or political, focus in archaeology which treated sites primarily as sources of illumination for the cultural contexts of these two great bodies of literature.

In *Studies on Homer*, Gladstone revived a form of degenerationism that saw a sophisticated universal religion encompassing the globe in prehistory. Unlike many others who made this claim (ranging from Godfrey Higgins to Friedrich Max Müller) he contended that this primeval religion was specifically Christian, with knowledge not just of the events of Genesis, but of the coming Incarnation: the whole world had shared access to divine providence.[59] The breakdown of universal understanding of divine intent was a delayed consequence of the Fall; the mind of man had been impaired by the influence of the fruit of the tree of knowledge, so that over generations it lost its capacity for abstract thought.[60] Only when this limitation combined with the dangerously fertile imaginative faculty of archaic Greece did it become necessary for divine knowledge to be entrusted to a chosen people who would preserve it in their own, purely temporary, Hebrew religion.[61] Dating from the time of this disjunction of sacred and secular knowledge the Homeric texts were assumed to be the one non-Judaic indication of the nature of this pristine religious tradition. Since they contained more details than Scripture of daily life and of the working of the minds of the great men

---

Gladstone (Oxford, 2004); Richard Jenkyns, *The Victorians and Ancient Greece* (Oxford, 1980); Frank Turner, *The Greek Heritage in Victorian Britain* (New Haven, CT, 1981), pp. 135–86.
[59] Gladstone, *Studies on Homer*, II, pp. 3–6.   [60] Ibid., p. 19.   [61] Ibid., pp. 5 ff.

of that glittering age, the *Iliad* and *Odyssey* could often provide superior evidence about the ideal condition of man than could the Old Testament.[62]

This was a sweeping scheme of history in which divine knowledge had been replaced by the mere inventions of myth-making man. Deterioration was gradual at first because of the longevity of the patriarchs, but was rushed on in a whirlwind of destructive speculation as the classical era dawned.[63] Where Plato and Aristotle occasionally demonstrate glimpses of divine light, Euripides was but a parody, while later productions such as Virgil's *Aeneid* could have no hope of reflecting Homer's true meaning however much they imitated his epic form. Lucretius' *De Rerum Natura* eventually plumbed the depths of human error before Christianity began to be unleashed from Judaic bonds and divine wisdom reclaimed the human mind.[64] The most resilient non-scriptural embodiments of providence, Gladstone argued, were three Olympian deities too sophisticated to be human inventions: Jupiter, Minerva and Apollo (to maintain Gladstone's consistent Latinisation).[65] As the only universally worshipped gods of Olympus these represented respectively godhead, divine providence and Messiah.[66] Such analogies gave rise to similar questions: was the mother of Apollo – Latona – Eve or the Virgin Mary?[67] But Gladstone's understanding of the providential role of Homer related primarily to this Hellenic Holy Trinity whose characters he credited with maintaining the high moral tone of early Greek civilisation.

Two years later, Old produced his eccentric *New Readings of Homer* – one of the first publications to demonstrate Gladstone's influence – and pushed these ideas even further. He argued that:

Elucidatory and supporting the revealed scriptures, [Homer's] writings are themselves a very Bible of texts, from which the most instructive sermons might be preached . . . They show us the total inability of our race, even when at its maximum power, to solve for ourselves the problems of our destiny.[68]

Old claimed that if we are to read Homer accurately 'we must do so by the light of our Bibles, as well as by the observation of human society at large'.[69] He claimed two motivations in putting this work together. One was to restore poetry to its rightful social role, second only to Scripture. The other was even more ambitious: to confront 'the great problem of our age – to reconcile that strange antagonism and distance between faith and knowledge, philosophy and belief'.[70] Several others took up these ideas.

---

[62] Ibid., pp. 523–31. [63] Ibid., pp. 4–5. [64] Ibid., pp. 23–5. [65] Ibid., pp. 39–171.
[66] Ibid., p. 44. [67] Ibid., p. 153. [68] Old, *New Readings*, p. 32. [69] Ibid., p. 40.
[70] Ibid., p. 37.

Stopford A. Brooke (1832–1916), Chaplain in Ordinary to the Queen, argued for this universal providence in an essay on Milton published in *Theology in the English Poets* (1874). Brooke and his reviewers asserted that Milton demonstrated an inexplicable failure to grasp the Christian import of the earliest Greek poetry: *Paradise Regained*, in which Christ is made to disown classical tradition, was a fanatical denial of divine dispensation in the ancient world.[71] Even more than Old and Gladstone, Brooke and his reviewers extracted the pagan sting from Homeric epic, papering over the idea that any pre-modern Christians had ever regarded them as 'other' and making them an essential part of true Christian learning.

The views of Gladstone and Old were unusually elaborate for the mid-nineteenth century, and their influence was certainly narrow in the early 1860s. But, as publications such as Brooke's demonstrate, the authority of these ideas mounted gradually. Many of these unlikely insertions of Homer into a biblical context would be dedicated to Gladstone, including Old's *New Readings* and *The Homeric Birthday Book*, a leather-bound, gold-leafed presentation volume that featured a short Homeric 'verse' as 'guidance and encouragement' for each day in imitation of the scriptural diaries popular at the time.[72] Gladstone's first publication to sell in really large numbers was his pamphlet *The Place of Ancient Greece in the Providential Order of the World* (1865) which presented many of the theological arguments of *Studies on Homer* in condensed form. The toned-down *Juventus Mundi: The Gods and Men of the Heroic Age* (1869) would prove more palatable for many who objected to *Studies on Homer*'s providential claims. Gladstone's new theme in *Juventus Mundi* was the use of the revised chronologies of ancient Egypt (specifically those by François Lenormant) to justify early dating of the Homeric poems: Gladstone had begun to make use of archaeology.[73]

Returning to Kinglake can, however, serve as a reminder that these sentiments already had a pedigree. When writing of his visit to the Troad, Kinglake remembered the religious feeling engendered in youthful days spent reading Pope's translation of the *Iliad*. The introduction to the edition

---

[71] See especially [Stopford A. Brooke], 'Theology in the English Poets', *Dublin University Magazine*, 84 (1874), 89.

[72] V. E. G., *The Homeric Birthday Book* (London, 1890).

[73] Gladstone's first public advocacy of Schliemann was in articles entitled 'The Place of Homer in History and in Egyptian Chronology', in the first of these, *Contemporary Review*, 24 (1874), 1–22, he assured the public that 'a real objective Troy is thus, for the first time ... presented to our view'.

he owned had claimed that 'the Iliad was all in all to the human race – that it was history – poetry – revelation – that the works of men's hands were folly and vanity, and would pass away like the dreams of a child, but that the kingdom of Homer would endure for ever and ever'; Kinglake adds that 'I assented with all my soul'.[74] He depicts himself in the same vein as did the young Macaulay, who famously tormented his classmates by acting out the story of Achilles in the playground. Kinglake's evocations of childhood are telling. They evoke the enchantment embodied by this heroic literature; but they also hint at how nineteenth-century education brought Troy and the Holy City close together. Homer, just like the Bible, was the source of many educated Britons' 'earliest intellectual culture': Troy's reality, like that of Eden and the New Jerusalem was so deeply ingrained from childhood that in 1873 the editor of *The Times* could even claim that 'not long ago it was almost a capital offence at one of our greatest Public Schools to be ignorant of the supposed fact that Bunarbashi is the modern name of Troy'.[75] But it was not just the well-known classical and Christian content of the mid-Victorian grammar school that was at play: the finishing touches to Gladstone's relationship with the classics and the Bible were made at Oxford. Here the *Literae Humaniores* course famously pushed two great moral texts together: Aristotle's *Ethics* and Bishop Butler's *Analogy of Religion*. As Frank Turner has recognised, these two dominating centre-pieces of Oxford educations were rarely differentiated in terms of historical context.[76] They were read as dehistoricised textbooks that combined to produce a complete moral education. Gladstone read Homer and the Old Testament as parallel authorities on the human condition in precisely the same way as the Oxford system of the 1830s led students to see works of fifth-century Aristotelian philosophy and eighteenth-century apologetics as complementary texts. Aristotle and Butler, alongside Homer and Moses, remained powerful influences throughout Gladstone's life, resurfacing repeatedly in his works on church history. On a less intensive level, it seems likely that long-lasting perceptions of Homer and the Bible as dual authorities may have been combined in the minds of many from early in their intellectual lives.

---

[74] Kinglake, *Eothen*, p. 57.
[75] [Smith and Gladstone], 'Discoveries at Troy', 528; this article was written under Gladstone's guidance; see Ernst Meyer, *Heinrich Schliemann: Briefwechsel*, (2 vols., Berlin, 1953), I, p. 267; *The Times*, (27 March 1873), editorial.
[76] Turner, *Greek Heritage*, p. 160.

'A new era in the study of antiquity': Schliemann at Hisarlik

By the late 1870s, Gladstone's works formed 'the single most extensive body of Victorian Homeric commentary', and as their volume increased, so the fortune of his ideas rose considerably.[77] This upturn in influence was in large part due to the resurgence of popular interest in archaeology accompanying the Trojan excavations of Schliemann. Where Layard and his peers had negotiated paths between contemporary criticism and the literalising interests of much of their public, Schliemann bulldozed over the barrier of scepticism that had for decades problematised popular and scholarly reactions to archaeology. His finds reached the public shortly after George Smith's translations of cuneiform tablets that seemed to contain part of a Mesopotamian memory of the biblical flood. Smith's finds had been publicised widely and *The Daily Telegraph* had soon raised £1,000 to dispatch him to Mosul to find the other part of the narrative. Extraordinarily, he had succeeded almost immediately. To many writers on ancient history, this find was the most important archaeological discovery to date.[78] Coming so quickly after this, Schliemann's similarly remarkable luck, accompanied by a knack for presentation and penchant for exaggeration, led to uniquely high expectations being placed on archaeology: only after 1900 would British archaeologists widely admit (as many had in the 1850s) that their discipline did not possess the accuracy to retrieve details of specific ancient events such as the regency of Joseph or construction of Noah's Ark. For the intervening decades archaeology, even in the hands of celebrated pioneers such as Flinders Petrie (1853–1942), was accorded a phenomenal precision that led to an almost shopping-list-like degree of specificity in the aims of many excavations.[79]

Schliemann brushed aside developments in attitudes to Troy that had occurred between 1799 and the 1860s, reviving the confident Homeric literalism of Le Chevalier and Choiseul-Gouffier. As far as many British readers were concerned, Schliemann's excavations completed the revolution that Gladstone had prefigured in *Studies on Homer*; he seemed to demonstrate that critics such as Grote were misguided in dismissing the events of the *Iliad* and *Odyssey* as pure mythologies; he seemed to erase the

---

[77] Ibid.
[78] For instance Amelia Edwards, 'Was Ramases II the Pharaoh of the Exodus?', *Knowledge*, 2 (1882). For more on comic parodies of Schliemann's specificity, see Rachel Bryant Davies, 'Imaginary Cities'.
[79] See, for instance, David Gange, 'Religion and Science in Late Nineteenth-Century Egyptology', *Historical Journal*, 49 (2006), 1083–103; also Bryant Davies, 'Imaginary Cities', pp. 43–6.

'blackguard' Bryant from intellectual history. Like many commentators, Gladstone's enthusiastic response to Schliemann's endeavours made certain that these Trojan excavations were contextualised in terms of the higher criticism: Schliemann's vindication of Homeric narrative was eclipsed by the implication that the critical method in general had been discredited and that the Bible had emerged triumphant from the assaults of irreverent scholarship. When Schliemann lectured in Britain, he and Gladstone formed a potent double-act, with the statesman as vocal intermediary between the archaeologist and the public.[80] They were 'protagonist and deuteragonist', or, in the words of Arthur Evans (1851–1941), 'Gladstone became [Schliemann's] prophet'.[81] In his first major public advocacy of Schliemann, Gladstone assured the public that 'a real objective Troy is thus, for the first time ... presented to our view'; he celebrated the powerful confirmations of his own well-known theories 'from the progress of archaeology'.[82] Gladstone's Christianised mediation might go some way towards explaining why 'contrasted with the cold and even hostile reception that Schliemann met with in his own country ... his popularity with the educated British public was phenomenal'.[83] In Germany, Evans argues, Schliemann's lack of professional qualifications irritated the establishment; in Britain, where amateur scholarship such as that of Schliemann and Gladstone was much more welcome, his 'material results were regarded as a sufficient vindication of the means employed' and 'the literal belief of Schliemann in the Homeric poems found a responsive echo'.[84] Even the publicity-loving Schliemann, who kept papers such as *The Times* continually updated about his excavations, was taken aback by the intensity of his celebrity.[85] Inspired by this partnership, A. H. Sayce

[80] For instance 'Homeric Troy', *The Times*, (26 June 1875), 9, where Schliemann's paper 'The Discovery of Homeric Troy' (delivered to the Society of Antiquaries London, 24 June 1875) is given a synopsis, while Gladstone's laudatory comments on this paper are printed in full, taking up double the column inches accorded to Schliemann himself; other particularly notable evidence can be found in M. R. D. Foot and Colin Matthew, eds., *The Gladstone Diaries* (14 vols., Oxford, 1968–94), IX, pp. 250 ff; and *The Times*, (23 March 1877), 10.

[81] John Vaio, 'Gladstone and the Early Reception of Schliemann in England', in William M. Calder III and Justus Cobet, eds., *Heinrich Schliemann nach hundert Jahren* (Frankfurt, 1990), p. 426; Arthur Evans, introduction to Emil Ludwig, *Schliemann of Troy*, trans. D. F. Tait (London, 1931), p. 20.

[82] W. E. Gladstone, 'The Place of Homer in History and in Egyption Chronology', *Contemporary Review*, 24 (1874), 1–22. Gladstone later extended this article into a book, *Homeric Synchronism: An Enquiry into the Time and Place of Homer* (London, 1876) while 'reading Schliemann all the while'; Foot and Matthew, eds., *Gladstone Diaries*, IX (5 Nov. 1875).

[83] Evans in Ludwig, *Schliemann of Troy*, p. 20.   [84] Ibid.

[85] E.g., 'A minute account of his recent investigations in the Troad' was sent to German papers and published in, e.g., *The Manchester Times* ('The Site of Troy' (2 July 1870), 212; 'New Discoveries

heralded the beginning of an '"archaeological revolt" against the fantasies of subjective criticism'.[86] He celebrated Schliemann in the most effusive terms:

> With the excavations of Dr Schliemann a new era began in the study of antiquity. Criticism had either demolished the literary tradition or thrown such doubt on it as to make the scholar hesitate before he referred to it. The ages before the beginning of the so-called historical period in Greece had become a blank or almost a blank. They were like the maps of central Africa made some fifty years ago in which the one-eyed monsters or vast lakes which had occupied it in the maps of an earlier epoch were swept away and nothing was put in their place. It has been reserved for modern exploration to supply the vacant space, and to prove that, after all, the mountains of the moon and the lakes of the Portuguese map-makers had a foundation in fact.[87]

Public opinion had long awaited someone capable of discrediting Bryant's flat denial of the heroic spirit. Suddenly, identification of biblical and Homeric heroism and sophistication in the primeval world seemed to be all the rage. Over the course of the 1870s and 1880s, Gladstone's Christian degenerationism gained an influence that had seemed impossible before archaeological discoveries such as those of Smith and Schliemann had altered historical feeling. Of course, dissenters did not just vanish. *The Examiner*, no doubt piqued by the exclusive reports of these finds, was provoked by *The Times*' editorial – praising Schliemann's further proof of the Trojan War's reality at Mycenae – into criticising *The Daily Telegraph* for its 'tremendous outcry about two years ago because a tablet had been dug up in Babylonia with something or other on it about the Deluge'. Nonetheless, it is telling that even dismissive, sceptical commentators conflated these biblical and classical discoveries: *The Examiner* continued by labelling *The Times*' enthusiasm as 'hysterics of the same kind', which led it to 'talk nonsense about Clytemnestra, and Agamemnon and his heroes, and Cassandra and her lockets'.[88]

The renewed Christian degenerationism, which made the primeval world an idyll of perfect monotheism, was entwined with wide-ranging changes to

---

at Troy', *Pall Mall Gazette* (27 May 1874), 7 and others printed reports of the Turkish Government demanding 50 per cent of the treasure, and of the lower excavations; a letter announcing intention to display Priam's treasure was printed in the News Section of *The Times*: 'Troy' (16 August 1877), 3.

[86] A. H. Sayce, *The Higher Criticism and the Verdict of the Monuments* (London, 1894), p. xiv.
[87] Ibid.
[88] 'Editorial', *The Times* (18 December 1876), 9; '*The Times* in Hysterics', *Examiner* (23 December 1876), 1433.

the way in which the ancient world was studied.[89] No longer did Oxbridge-educated museum keepers and antiquarians control pre-classical scholarship. Practical men without traditional educations such as Petrie and Schliemann (whose biography was often held up as exemplary) now shared that mission and swept along a host of churchmen and popular writers who made ancient histories with biblical relevance a significant branch of the burgeoning literary market.[90] One dramatic illustration of this is the fate of the period's standard handbook of pre-classical history, *Cory's Ancient Fragments*. This had originally been published in 1828, and a revised 1832 edition was reprinted throughout the century. It was aimed at the trained antiquarian and made up of parallel texts of Greek remnants of ancient literature and English translations. It was universal in ambition, though small in scale. But in the midst of the archaeological enthusiasm aroused by Schliemann and George Smith, *Cory's Ancient Fragments* was rapidly overhauled. The Greek texts were removed, and explanatory introductions were added to each translation. The whole work was reformed as a popular book for a mass audience. As its editor wrote, *Cory's Ancient Fragments* is not now a complete text on the pre-classical world as it once aspired to be, but

a fitting supplement to the fragments which have been exhumed from the mounds of Nineveh, and rescued from the tombs and mummy-pits of Egypt. Having set aside the Greek text as a costly and useless encumbrance, [the book is now addressed] to the ordinary English student, who does not happen to have enjoyed the advantages of early classical training ... In carrying out my plan I shall explain Hebrew, Assyrian, Greek, Phoenician, and Egyptian words wherever they occur, and thus endeavour to place the English reader ... on a level with the best Oriental scholars of our day.[91]

Archaeology during these decades succeeded in involving the public in a way that the discipline has rarely done before or since.

---

[89] For the argument that ancient history was a narrative of decline from sophisticated monotheism to 'vulgar fetishism', see George Rawlinson, *History of Ancient Egypt* (2 vols., London, 1881), I, p. 315; John Macpherson, *Apologetics* (3 vols., London, 1888), III, p. 82; Sydney Herbert, *Egyptian Art and its Influence* (Cheltenham,1884), p. 9; Peter le Page Renouf, *Lectures on the Origin and Growth of Religion as Illustrated by the Religion of Ancient Egypt* (London, 1880); John Ward, *The Sacred Beetle* (London, 1902), p. 6.

[90] E.g., 'London', *Daily News* (24 April 1874); W. J. Stillman, 'Homer's Troy and Schliemann's', *Cornhill Magazine*, 29 (1874), 663–74; 'Dr. and Madame Schliemann', *Graphic* (20 January 1877).

[91] Richmond Hodges, ed., *Cory's Ancient Fragments: A Manual for the Chronologist and Mythological Antiquarian, Revised Edition* (London, 1876), pp. viii–ix.

'Imagination guided the spade': the archaeology of an imagined city

Among the most striking features of the responses to Schliemann's excavations was an intense debate over the nature of archaeology. Schliemann had claimed to have been guided by the poetry of Homer. Epic poems that many had identified as literary fictions seemed vindicated by the discovery of the historical facts they recounted. Schliemann's discoveries were wrangled over at great length, with one word cropping up again and again in discussion of whether Schliemann's methods were reliable or his results valid: 'imagination'.

Like innumerable 'Homeric pilgrims' before him, Schliemann had gone to the Troad with a fixed idea of Troy accreted from imaginative readings of the *Iliad*. He had vivid conceptions of Troy and its environs in his head from childhood, and when he excavated at Hisarlik it was exactly this imagined city that he claimed to have recovered. As W. J. Stillman put it, 'It was Homer's Troy he wanted, and Homer was his guide-book.'[92] Byron, too, had expected to find scenes fitting for ancient heroism in the Troad and had revelled in what he saw. Tellingly, Kinglake had been disappointed when he stood by the 'divine Scamander' in 1834, his feelings of 'half-expected rapture' 'chilled and borne down ... under all this load of real earth and water'; but later his imagination had reshaped the scene and he remembered the site as a truly heroic space: 'let these [scenes] once pass out of sight, and then again the old fanciful notions are restored, and the mere realities which you have just been looking at are thrown so far back into distance that the very event of your intrusion upon such scenes begins to look dim and uncertain, as though it belonged to mythology'.[93] Schliemann also expected an imposing city-site, but where Kinglake had needed to leave the site to imagine one, Schliemann could use his excavator's spade to shape a buried site that fitted his ideals. To Schliemann, imagination was an archaeologist's greatest asset: it was what fitted him uniquely to fill in the void between poetry and reality, 'to make us believe that no one ever doubted the *Iliad* or the existence of Troy'.[94] But to those schooled in the tradition of Bryant, Schliemann's imagination seemed to have been allowed to run free at the expense of any scholarly perspective or 'counterpoise of judgement'.[95] One reason Schliemann's excavations became so important in the late

---

[92] Stillman, 'Homer's Troy', 666.   [93] Kinglake, *Eothen*, p. 34.
[94] William Simpson, 'The Schliemannic Ilium', *Fraser's Magazine* (July 1877), 1.
[95] William Borlase, 'A Visit to Dr. Schliemann's Troy', *Fraser's Magazine*, 17 (1878), 228.

nineteenth century was that, through them, the role of imagination in archaeology was fought out.[96]

Schliemann had done enough to challenge assumptions that the Heroic Age was purely mythical, but much scholarly opinion was still against him.[97] Likewise, Stillman and Simpson, writers for the journals, complained in the mid-1870s 'that it is Troy he has discovered he establishes by asserting that it is so' and because 'The Doctor everywhere proves too little and assumes too much'.[98] Stillman even judged 'Priam's treasure ... an archaeological joke' and compared it to the biblical forgeries of Moses Shapira (1830–94), claiming that 'we must not be surprised that there are many who regard his treasures as another Shapira swindle'.[99] The big question that dogged Schliemann's supporters was whether the ruins he found really matched up to the sacred city of Homer: 'why should that city be Troy?'[100] To most classical scholars in the 1870s and early 1880s, Schliemann had found nothing to suggest grandeur on the scale of Homer's Troy. They argued that Homer, writing at a later time, had described his own more advanced civilisation rather than a pre-classical city. William Copeland Borlase (1848–99), who had travelled to Hisarlik, described in *Fraser's Magazine* how, like Simpson, he had experienced 'an irresistible inclination to regard the whole thing as a joke'. Tellingly, he too compared this feeling of being taken in to that experienced by travellers to the Holy Land, especially at 'their first sight of Jerusalem'; here, however, he blamed the experience on 'the gilding with which Herr Schliemann, in the exuberance of his almost poetic imagination, has overlaid his discoveries' of a 'primitive fort'.[101] H. M. Westropp (1820–85) in his *The Age of Homer* (1884) stated that 'Homer mentions the walls of the Palace of Priam as being built with polished stone', and asked 'are these descriptions confirmed by the rude remains of a prehistoric city discovered at Hisarlik by Dr Schliemann and identified by him with the Troy of Homer?'[102] For Borlase, the answer to this question had been a resounding 'no', despite his claim 'never [to have] believed that Troy had ever existed anywhere in all the size and splendour of the poet's rich fancy any more than I had supposed that Arthur's Camelot was all that is has been described to be'.[103]

---

[96] For more on invented evidence, the role of the imagination and disappointing visits to Troy, see Bryant Davies, 'Imaginary Cities', 24–48.
[97] Ian Morris, *Archaeology as Cultural History* (Oxford, 2000), is good on the efficacy of this challenge.
[98] Simpson, 'Schliemannic Ilium', 1.   [99] Stillman, 'Homer's Troy', 674.
[100] Review of *Trojanische Alterthumer*: 'German Literature', *Examiner* (14 March 1874), 265.
[101] Borlase, 'A Visit', 232 ff.   [102] Westropp, *Age of Homer*, p. 25.   [103] Borlase, 'A Visit', 232.

Effectively, the reputation of two imaginations was at stake: that of Schliemann and that of the poet himself. Westropp recounted the spacious streets, the lofty walls, wide gates and palace containing fifty rooms in Homer's Troy, and concluded that 'all this is a mirage, an unsubstantial pageant, which never had any existence, except in the brain of Homer'.[104] His city of splendid palaces and chiefs was, according to the parallel widespread in the 1870s, 'either as imaginary as the state of society in the times of King Arthur and the Knights of the Round Table as drawn by . . . Mr Tennyson, or it is the outcome of a knowledge of the civilisation of a quite later age'.[105] Westropp represented an orthodoxy that was quickly subsiding, but could draw on the authority of a host of scholars from the previous decade: Sir Richard Jebb (1841–1905) had stated that 'the poet's town of Troy . . . was a creation of his own fancy, influenced by handsome cities of his own time', while F. A. Paley (1815–88) stated that Troy was 'more or less a mythical city'.[106] An authority from even further back, Philostratus, could also be evoked with his statement that Troy 'would never have been had not Homer lived, he was really the founder of Troy'.[107] The spirit of Bryant was kept alive by the *Edinburgh Review*, which asserted that 'the old undoubting faith of former days, which has received the Trojan War as an event as historical and unquestionable as the Crusades [has] almost entirely passed away'. As Westropp summed up this article: 'any attempts at precise identification [of the site of Troy] are dreams', or as W. H. Mason put it for readers of *Macmillan's Magazine*, 'the reconciliation of . . . the city of the Muse and the city of the spade, is an impossibility'.[108]

Yet Schliemann was not finished. He excavated more Homeric sites, most famously Mycenae and Tiryns. At Mycenae – the Homeric seat of Agamemnon – he discovered grave shafts containing gold deposits, including the famous death masks that he ascribed to the family of Agamemnon. He also excavated the kind of grand monuments that had been absent from discoveries at Troy. The now familiar Lion Gate and Tholos-Tomb were among these: Figure 1.2 shows the former on its way to becoming a major tourist draw. Schliemann marketed these discoveries by persuading Gladstone (who was at first reluctant to claim archaeological expertise for himself) to write a preface for his excavation report: the archaeologist claimed to feel that so influential a statesman's input would make his

---

[104] Westropp, *Age of Homer*, p. 13.   [105] Ibid., pp. 26–7.   [106] Ibid., p. 13.   [107] Ibid.
[108] Edward Herbert Bunbury, 'Dr Schliemann's Trojan Antiquities', *Edinburgh Review*, 139 (1874), 507; Westropp, *Age of Homer*, p. 13; Mason, 'Homer and Dr. Schliemann', 454.

Figure 1.2 *Schliemann's Excavations at Mycenae*

work an 'immortal one'.[109] With his reputation much enhanced, the excavator returned to Hisarlik and banished the doubts even he had harboured about its identity as Troy. In his hands, and in those of Wilhelm Dörpfeld after Schliemann's death in 1890, excavations in different strata of the Hisarlik mound produced monuments that convinced an even broader audience than the earlier discoveries.

Schliemann had always commanded much greater support from the public and from non-classicists such as Gladstone and Sayce than from classical scholars; his support, Gladstone claimed in *The Times*, issued 'from the heart ... of the English people'. His free exhibition of the 'Trojan collection' in London was motivated by gratitude for this 'warm reception'. From the 1876 Mycenae finds onwards, the opinions of classicists also swung continually in his favour.[110] By the turn of the century, for the first time since Lechevalier, the Heroic Age was widely asserted by scholars and public alike to have been real. Walter Leaf (1852–1927), Fellow of Trinity College, Cambridge, and President of the Hellenic Society and the Classical Association, campaigned from the 1880s to the 1920s for the idea that 'the poems really do depict, as contemporaries, the Achaean age, as they profess'.[111] Troy was historical, Leaf later wrote, and the twentieth century would reject 'futile' and divisive denials of the Trojan War. Wolf's sceptical *Prolegomena* had been superseded by excavations at Hisarlik: criticism 'gave the nineteenth century to the philologist; the archaeologists have given the twentieth to the historian'.[112] To Leaf (as to Sayce) Schliemann was 'epoch making'.[113] Henry Browne, Professor of Greek at University College, Dublin, included a chapter entitled 'The Triumph of the Spade' in his *Handbook of Homeric Study* (1908). It surveyed the scholarship of the previous decades and concluded that 'as to Hisarlik, the world has long been convinced that Schliemann was right'.[114] Browne asserted that Schliemann's discoveries were among 'the most remarkable finds in history', and alterations to his theory by Dörpfeld in 1893 merely reinforced the earlier achievement: 'it does not follow that because some of his views have been since corrected our debt to the man is less'.[115] Thomas Day

---

[109] Meyer, *Heinrich Schliemann: Briefwechsel*, II, p. 68; *Mycenae* was dedicated to Gladstone 'for his kind assistance and encouragement'.

[110] 'The Architecture of Troy', *The Times* (1 May 1877), 6.

[111] Walter Leaf, 'Introduction', in Carl Schuchardt, *Schliemann's Excavations: An Archaeological and Historical Study*, trans. Eugenie Sellers (London, 1891), p. xxiii; this work is much less confident in these assertions than Leaf's later works, especially *Homer and History* (London, 1915), would be.

[112] Leaf, *Homer*, pp. 1–3.   [113] Leaf, 'Introduction', p. xxi.

[114] Henry Browne, *Handbook of Homeric Study* (London, 1908), p. 245.   [115] Ibid.

Seymour (1848–1907), Professor of Greek at Yale, was still blunter: 'at present no one doubts, at least openly, that Hisarlik is the site of Homeric Troy'.[116]

While the misgivings of the 1870s were being dispelled, many, including key archaeological populariloopularisers of the next decade such as the British Museum antiquarian Reginald Stuart Poole (1857–1939), made further, and sometimes even more explicit, attempts to draw historical connections between the great literary texts they saw being vindicated: biblical schemes as to the origin of the Homeric poems flourished. Some emphasised the similarities between Greek and Hebrew alphabets, or between Greek and Egyptian worship. One popular version of this argument even contended that only a portion of the Hebrews evacuating Egypt during the Exodus had reached the Promised Land while many others gradually straggled into Greece. With the early Greeks identified as Hebrews, 'the true secret of Homer and his *Iliad*' was revealed: the work was a series of patriotic historical songs written by God's elect to produce 'an alliance between Greece and Asia against the inroads of Egypt'.[117] This offered a more literal connection between Scripture and the Homeric epics than even Gladstone had allowed, and demonstrated more immediately why elaborations of the content of the Old Testament might be found in the *Iliad*. Another widely circulated idea was that Solomon had written the *Iliad* (resurrected from Joshua Barnes' famous treatise of 1710, which had supposedly been intended to persuade his wealthy wife to support the publication of his renderings of the *Iliad* and *Odyssey*), while novelists also elaborated the connection: Andrew Lang and H. Rider Haggard had the aged Odysseus sail to Egypt in search of Helen of Troy, only to become embroiled in the events of the Exodus.[118]

Even those who explicitly disagreed with Gladstone over the probability of shared knowledge between Greeks and Hebrews often now conceived Troy in biblical terms. One of the most dramatic examples comes from an 1875 prose retelling of *The Story of the Trojan War* with a preface by Charles John Ellicott (1819–1905), Bishop of Gloucester and Bristol. Ellicott had contributed to the response against *Essays and Reviews*, editing *Aids to Faith* (1862), and over a long career provided staunch defences of the historicity of the Old Testament. In *Christus Comprobator* (1891) he made his strongest case for the principle that Christ's acceptance of Old Testament authority

---

[116] Thomas Day Seymour, *Life in the Homeric Age* (London, 1907), p. 548.
[117] E.g., A. Bilderbeck to Samuel Birch, n.d.: Ancient Near East Department correspondence archives, British Museum, London, 1884/23–4.
[118] Andrew Lang and H. Rider Haggard, *The World's Desire* (London, 1892).

was a guarantee of its rigour. As a favourite of Benjamin Disraeli and a leading high-churchman, who played a leading role in many of the great theological questions of the age, Ellicott's entanglement in debates over the *Iliad* demonstrates their wide reach: it shows how they played out even in circles where Gladstone's enthusiasms were not embraced. His introduction to *The Story of the Trojan War* attempted to demonstrate that discoveries at Troy were illustrative of biblical life: the *Iliad* and *Odyssey* had entered more fully than 'any book, except the Holy Scriptures, into the foundation of modern thought and life' so that 'for the student of Scripture, the prince of heathen poets possesses a special interest'.[119] It is, he wrote, 'quite unnecessary to insist upon … the actual connection between the lays of the Greek bard and the inspired records of the chosen people':

Whether the Hebrew chronicles, in any form, could have reached the eye or ear of the poet in his many wanderings is, to say the least, extremely doubtful. But Homer bears an independent witness to the truth and accuracy of the sacred narrative, so far as its imagery and diction are to be taken into account, which is very remarkable. Allowing for the difference in the local scenery, the reader of the *Iliad* may well fancy that he is following the night-march of Abraham, the conquests of Joshua, or the wars of the Kings; while in the *Odyssey*, the same domestic interiors, the same primitive family life, the same patriarchal relations between the king or chief of the tribe and his people, remind us in every page of the fresh and living pictures of the Book of Genesis.[120]

Ellicott's work goes on to enumerate an enormous range of parallels between the two texts, arguing for instance that Priam in envisioning 'the miserable sight' of the fall of his city, is analogous to Isaiah, who voiced 'the prophetic burden of Babylon'.[121] The volume concludes with a supporting appendix constructed from lengthy extracts of the press coverage of Schliemann's finds.

Although long-term trends would see imaginative renderings of literary material lose almost all authority in archaeological methodology, the immediate effects of Schliemann's excavations worked in the opposite direction. An increasing number of writers, from 1873 until after the turn of the century, believed that Schliemann had found what he said he had. They drew the lesson that the literary text – whether the *Iliad* or the Bible – was a fruitful guide for the archaeologist. Equally, as an article about Troy in the *Girl's Own Paper* (a penny weekly published by the Religious Tract Society) claimed, archaeology was now regarded 'as a witness to historical truth, but more especially as a corroboration of the narratives contained in Holy Scriptures'.[122]

---

[119] 'E. M. G.' and Ellicott, *Story*, pp. xi, xx. [120] Ibid., pp. xx–xxi [121] Ibid., p. xxii.
[122] 'Archaeology for Girls', *Girl's Own Paper* (16 February 1895), 315.

For two decades, this ancient literature took a central place in the archaeological imagination. It was the reappraisal of the role of literature in archaeological scholarship – triggered by renewed belief in historical Troy – that made archaeology so attractive to the late nineteenth-century public, and it is in the context of these debates that the biblical excavations of the late nineteenth century need to be read. For the rest of the century, the twin colossi of Schliemann and Gladstone would symbolise the historical potency of archaeology. Leading organisations of biblical archaeology, from the Palestine Exploration Fund to the Egypt Exploration Fund and the Society of Biblical Literature would clamour for their support. Among these organisations, the city of Troy itself would be a symbol of the triumph of the literary imagination and the perceived defeat of a previously excessive scepticism.

This significance was often clearly articulated in the press. *The Monthly Packet of Evening Readings for Members of the English Church* included a description of 'A Day in the Troad' in 1881, because 'So determined an explorer deserves all the honour that is paid to his zeal and work'.[123] It emerges especially unmistakably in an article by Karl Blind (1826–1907), a German journalist and refugee in London, which welcomed Sayce's linking of Troy to the Hittite empire:

what a telling, what a crushing, argument this is against the paltry doubters who would fain have diminished the significance of Dr. Schliemann's discoveries, even after the earth had opened its mouth to tell of the existence of the fated town which had been consumed on a bed of flames![124]

Just as he rejoiced that 'The very stones have spoken – *saxa loquuntur* – to say that Ilion once was', so later travellers to Schliemann's Hisarlik could also place the 'evidence of the spade' above that of Homer's epic, describing how 'these charred and scattered ruins bear record that there was a Troy, and that it fell: then, too, we have its story in the greatest epic ever written'.[125] Thanks to Schliemann's self-professed Homeric faith, Troy could now be confidently marked on a map; because of his imagination and unflinching belief, spectacular finds had been made just where the *Iliad* suggested they should be. This all seemed to show that faith and archaeological success went hand in hand.

---

[123] George Washington, 'A Day in the Troad', *The Monthly Packet of Evening Readings for Members of the English Church* (1 July 1881), 83.
[124] Blind, 'Troy Found Again', 198.
[125] Ibid., 202; Mary Mason Poynter, 'A Day at Old Troy', *Athenaeum* (20 March 1915), 271.

2 | Jerusalem

SIMON GOLDHILL

'It is the guidebook': the Bible as Baedeker

The invention of the steamship was the making of Victorian Jerusalem. Unlike many of the sites discussed in this volume, there was no need to discover the physical location of this city; the history of longing for Jerusalem was deeply embedded in the Western imagination, with the biblical injunctions not to forget Zion and the concomitant desire to return from exile giving rise to centuries of literature and art that had represented the city as an endpoint of the journey of life or as a model for the perfection of heavenly or earthly existence. Jerusalem stood at the foundation of the Crusades, which made the Holy Sepulchre and the Temple of Solomon iconic aims of military striving and provided a model for the interaction of West and East that has not yet been fully worked through.[1] For any Victorian, there were different conceptual mappings of Jerusalem, depending on education, religious commitments and political aspirations. As we will see, a Sunday School pupil, an ardent Evangelical, an earnest Protestant, an engaged Restorationist all constructed changing, often conflicting historical and contemporary comprehensions of the city of David, the Temple and the site of the Passion. But for any Victorian, Jerusalem, as *the* city of the Bible, as a Graeco-Roman capital, lavishly created and destroyed in

---

[1] From a huge bibliography, for an indication of the relevant debates see Yehoshua Ben-Arieh and Moshe Davis, eds., *Jerusalem in the Mind of the Western World, 1800–1948* (Westport, CT, 1997); Eitan Bar-Yosef, *The Holy Land in English Culture 1799–1917: Palestine and the Question of Orientalism* (Oxford, 2005); Arnold Blumberg, *Zion before Zionism, 1838–1880* (Syracuse, NY, 1985); Eric Cline, *Jerusalem Besieged: From Ancient Canaan to Modern Israel* (Ann Arbor, MI, 2004); Jonathan Riley-Smith, ed., *The Oxford History of the Crusades* (Oxford, 1999); Carole Hillenbrand, *The Crusades: Islamic Perspectives* (Edinburgh, 1999); Guy Le Strange, *Palestine under the Moslems: A Description of Syria and the Holy Land from AD 650 to 1500* (1890; Beirut, 1965); Lee Levine, ed., *Jerusalem: Its Sanctity and Centrality to Judaism, Christianity, and Islam* (Philadelphia, PA, 1999); F. E. Peters, *Jerusalem: The Holy City in the Eyes of Chroniclers, Pilgrims and Prophets from the Days of Abraham to the Beginnings of Modern Times* (Princeton, NJ, 1985); Helen Rosenau, *Vision of the Temple: The Image of the Temple of Jerusalem in Judaism and Christianity* (London, 1979); Nitza Rosovsky, ed., *City of the Great King: Jerusalem from David to the Present* (Cambridge, MA, 1996); Simon Goldhill, *Jerusalem: City of Longing* (Cambridge, MA, 2008).

the classical text of Josephus, and as the centre of the medieval world, offered a repertoire for imagining the city as historical site and as ideal form. Jerusalem the city is a palimpsest of its Old and New Testament images, its Jewish, Greek, Roman, Christian and Muslim topographies – as perceived and debated in profoundly committed nineteenth-century engagements. It would be hard to find a more complex site to explore what – how – a biblical city could mean in the Victorian imagination.

A visit to Jerusalem was inevitably an encounter between these imaginings and a small, dirty, impoverished, Middle Eastern city. From the Renaissance to the middle of the nineteenth century, to make such a visit was dangerous, arduous and expensive. It was not a usual part of the grand tour, and both the journey itself and the political conditions of the Ottoman Empire discouraged extensive tourism. Entrance to key sites, such as the Temple Mount, was forbidden to all but Muslims. The extraordinary variety of visual and verbal pictures of Jerusalem throughout this period was necessarily constructed out of scraps of information, projections of biblical grandeur and idealistic schemata. The invention of the steamship, together with the weakening of the Ottoman Empire, alongside the expansion of Western imperialist projects, brought Jerusalem into the arena of nascent mass tourism – especially for religious visitors.[2] The clash between the long tradition of imaging Jerusalem and what these visitors saw is the first defining frame of Victorian Jerusalem.

This clash was instantiated in a flood of guidebooks and travel memoirs. More European descriptions of journeying in the Holy Land were published in the first three quarters of the nineteenth century than in the previous fifteen hundred years put together – at least 2,000 extended essays or books; or two a month for seventy-five years. Nor did the outpouring stop until well into the twentieth century, when books on the politics of the region took over as the dominant form.[3] This genre is fully self-conscious and creates a horizon of expectation. So, when Stephen Graham (1884–1975)

---

[2] See, in general, James Buzard, *The Beaten Track: European Tourism, Literature, and the Ways to Culture, 1800–1918* (Oxford, 1993); for changing conditions in Palestine see Blumberg, *Zion*; Yehoshua Ben-Arieh, *Jerusalem in the Nineteenth Century: The Old City* (Jerusalem, 1984); Yehoshua Ben-Arieh, *Jerusalem in the Nineteenth Century: Emergence of the New City* (Jerusalem, 1986); Timothy Larsen, 'Thomas Cook, Holy Land Pilgrims and the Dawn of the Modern Tourist Industry', in R. N. Swanson, ed., *Holy Land, Holy Lands, and Christian History* (Woodbridge, 2000). William Howard Russell, *A Diary in the East during the Tour of the Prince and Princess of Wales* (London, 1869), pp. 321–2 marks the change in tourism when he laments seeing 'his favourite valley filled up with a flood of "mere English whom no one knows"'.

[3] See Reinhold Röhricht, *Bibliotheca Geographica Palaestinae: chronologisches Verzeichnis der von 333 bis 1878 verfassten Literatur über das Heilige Land* (London, 1989); Yehoshua Ben-Arieh, *Painting the Holy Land in the Nineteenth Century* (Jerusalem, 1997).

made plans to visit Jerusalem in the years before the First World War, he writes that 'friends told me that I was sure to be disappointed, that everyone going there nursed high hopes which were destined to remain unfulfilled . . . the banality and sordidness of the everyday scenes would be a great shock to me'.[4] Disappointment at the gap between the wonderful image and the sordid reality of city life had by now become a commonplace, something 'everyone' knows to expect. Back in 1822, when Robert Richardson (1779–1847) made the pre-steamship journey, travelling as a physician to the Countess of Belmore, it was not yet a cliché: 'These plain embattled walls in the midst of a barren mountain track,' he wondered, 'do they enclose the city of Jerusalem?'[5] The forbidding landscape, the unimpressive walls, the smallness, dirtiness and confusion of the city surprised the first visitors, baffled many and became finally a cliché of the Jerusalem tour.

During the nineteenth century, the physical landscape of Jerusalem changed significantly, even if the phrases of response show considerable consistency. The size of Jerusalem was the first surprise to those from European or American cities: 'A fast walker could go outside the walls of Jerusalem and walk entirely round the city in an hour. I do not know how else to make one understand how small it is.'[6] At the beginning of the century, there were no more than 10,000 inhabitants, about the same size as Acre or Gaza. Of these, perhaps 4,000 were Muslim, 3,000 Christian and 2,000 Jews. At the eve of the First World War, the population had grown to at least 70,000, of which 45,000 were Jewish.[7] Jews were an absolute majority of the population of Jerusalem probably by the middle of the century, though these numbers are hard to collect (and bitterly contested today on political grounds).

The effect of this growth was intense overcrowding, especially in the Jewish quarter, exacerbated by poverty: most of the Jews were poor immigrants, few worked and many subsisted on charitable donations from Europe. Second, it led finally to the growth of housing outside the walls: a rich man's house here or there, followed by charitable foundations of housing for the poor, followed by a more general expansion: the new

---

[4] Stephen Graham, *With the Russian Pilgrims to Jerusalem* (London, 1913), p. 123.
[5] Robert Richardson, *Travels along the Mediterranean and Parts Adjacent: In Company with the Earl of Belmore* (2 vols., London, 1822), II, p. 236.
[6] Mark Twain, *The Innocents Abroad, or, the New Pilgrim's Progress: Being some Account of the Steamship Quaker City's Pleasure Excursion to Europe and the Holy Land* (Charlottesville, VI, 2002), p. 422.
[7] Yehoshua Ben-Arieh, *Jerusalem in the Nineteenth Century* (Tel Aviv, 1989), pp. 22–49. Tudor Parfitt, *The Jews in Palestine 1800–1882* (Woodbridge, 1987), pp. 33–8 lists population estimates from Western sources.

Jerusalem.[8] In 1881, it was still possible to count the developments outside the walls on the fingers of one hand. By 1919, there was an extensive and even more rapidly growing town surrounding the old walled city, despite the financial crisis of the 1890s. British town-planners were now needed.[9] But the Old City itself remained a byword for physical discomfort for the Western traveller. So, in 1807, François-René de Chateaubriand (1768–1848), with an eye back to Paris, sniffed: 'In this heap of rubbish, denominated a city, the people of the country have thought fit to give the appellation of streets to certain desert passages.'[10] In 1901, at the end of a century of growth, a standard guidebook noted, 'The streets are not drained – few are wide enough for wheeled traffic. Attempts at sanitation are of the most primitive order. There is no water supply – no gas – no European shops – no postal delivery (except through the hotels).' And it smelled foul. As Mark Twain (1835–1910) – from 1867, in the middle of our period – wrote, very much 'from abroad': 'Rags, wretchedness, poverty and dirt, those signs and symbols that indicate the presence of Muslim rule more surely than the crescent flag itself, abound. Jerusalem is mournful, and dreary and lifeless. I would not desire to live here.'

Jerusalem prompted a century of disappointment, even to those who found the inspiration they were looking for. 'Everyone is not strong enough to live in Jerusalem,' reflected Selma Lagerlöf (1858–1940) in her fictional account of the Christian community known as the American Colony, which did make a go of a life in the Holy City.[11] These doleful views of the city were not prompted solely by the lack of creature comforts, however. Many Western tourists were Protestants, and, unlike Twain, often earnest in their perspective. Jerusalem, and in particular the Church of the Holy Sepulchre, proved deeply shocking, even and especially after so many accounts had prepared the traveller to be shocked. The Church of the Holy Sepulchre was run by three major denominations, the Greek Orthodox Church, the Franciscans (Latins) and the Armenians. The Eastern or Roman rites, conjoined with the repeatedly violent dissension between the three groups, proved deeply offensive to the religious

---

[8] Ben-Arieh, *New City*.
[9] C. R. Ashbee was the first (see Alan Crawford, *C. R. Ashbee: Architect, Designer and Romantic Socialist* (London, 1985), pp. 151–95), but the later plans are discussed in Harry Kendall, *Jerusalem: The City Plan: Preservation and Development during the British Mandate, 1918–1948* (London, 1948).
[10] François-René de Chateaubriand, *Travels in Greece, Palestine, Egypt and Barbary: During the Years 1806 and 1807*, trans. Frederic Shoberl (London, 1812), p. 330.
[11] Selma Lagerlöf, *Jerusalem*, trans. Jessie Bröckner (London, 1903), p. 231. See also Bertha Vester, *Our Jerusalem: An American Family in the Holy City, 1881–1949* (Garden City, NY, 1951).

sensibilities of the Western Protestant tradition. The reaction of George Curtis (1812–94), an American political journalist who became one of the founders of the Republican Party, can stand for many: 'The Christianity peculiar to Jerusalem is unmitigatedly repulsive.'[12]

There were two strands of distaste, both of which masked the aggressive self-definition of Protestant and especially Anglican pilgrims against the older religious groups at a time of intense anxiety about the prospects of Protestant Christianity. The first commonplace is to dismiss the behaviour of the clergy of the Church of the Holy Sepulchre as vulgar, violent and, of course, unchristian. Edward Robinson (1794–1863), the American archaeologist, calmly observed of the Latin monks and clergy: 'There was hardly a face among all those before us, that could be called intelligent.'[13] Kaiser Wilhelm deplored the 'free fights and battles in the churches'.[14] Robert Curzon (1810–73), who was present at the murderous riot of 1834, described the rioters with the full panoply of Orientalist disgust: 'some, almost in a state of nudity, danced about with frantic gestures, yelling and screaming as if possessed'.[15] The British Consul, James Finn (d. 1872), at another such occasion, saw that 'In the gallery of the Syrians there were women dancing, clapping hands and shrieking the *tehihleel* of joy'.[16] This was not the Christianity of the Home Counties. The so-called Miracle of the Fire at Easter, as one might expect from contemporary controversy over miracles, attracted the most pointed criticism, not just for the riotous behaviour of the celebrants, but also for the fakery of the event. Harriet Martineau (1802–76), in her best-selling travelogue, called the occasion 'a holiday in Hell', and hated the 'mummeries done in the name of Christianity'.[17] Herman Melville bluntly commented: 'All is glitter and nothing is gold. A sickening cheat.'[18] It is 'a matter of common knowledge', comments one journalist, that the church shows nothing but 'monstrous

---

[12] George Curtis, *The Wanderer in Syria* (London, 1852), p. 189.
[13] Edward Robinson, *Biblical Researches in Palestine, and in the Adjacent Regions: A Journey of Travels in the Year 1838* (1841; 2 vols., London, 1856), I, p. 224.
[14] Neil Grant, ed., *The Kaiser's Letters to the Tsar: Copied from Government Archives in Petrograd* (London, 1921), p. 66.
[15] Robert Curzon, *Visits to the Monasteries of the Levant* (London, 1849), pp. 192–204.
[16] James Finn, *Stirring Times, Or: Records from Jerusalem Consular Chronicles of 1853 to 1856* (London, 1878), p. 459.
[17] Harriet Martineau, *Eastern Life, Present and Past* (3 vols., London, 1848), III, pp. 124, 125. The word 'mummery' became a leitmotif of such complaints. On miracles, see Bruce Mullin, *Miracles and the Modern Religious Imagination* (London, 1996).
[18] Herman Melville, *Clarel, A Poem and Pilgrimage in the Holy Land* (London, 1960), p. 88; Franklin Walker, *Irreverent Pilgrims: Melville, Browne, and Mark Twain in the Holy Land* (Seattle, 1974).

trivialities of ecclesiastical theatricality'.[19] Robinson in his masterpiece, *Biblical Researches in Palestine, Mount Sinai, and Arabia Petraea* (1841), a book which won the Royal Geographic Society gold medal, famously called Jerusalem a place 'of credulous superstition, not unmingled with pious fraud'.[20] 'Pious fraud' – an allegation with a long history in religious controversy – echoed through the next fifty years as a source of contention.[21] The rows and ceremonies of the Church of the Holy Sepulchre allowed good Protestant travellers to see in an extreme form – and thus rail against – the bugbears of ritualism, hypocrisy and emotional incontinence.

The second complaint was to challenge the identification of the site as the place of the Passion.[22] In the name of archaeological and historical science, scholars lined up to re-consider the evidence and to assert that the Church of the Holy Sepulchre could not be the real site of Golgotha. We will see shortly how General Gordon reacted to these doubts by discovering a new spot for the Crucifixion. But first the arguments against the Church of the Holy Sepulchre. The single most pressing problem was that Golgotha was said by the gospels to be outside the walls of the city, on a road, clearly visible, and with gardens nearby. The Church of the Holy Sepulchre is in the middle of the Old City. Modern archaeology has proved decisively that at the time of Jesus this site was outside the then walls; but throughout the nineteenth century this was far from clear. More scholarly debates centred on the criticism of the sources for the miraculous rediscovery of the site by Helena, the mother of Constantine, after the city had been flattened and re-built as Aelia Capitolina by Hadrian. Robinson was so sure that the

---

[19] Arthur E. Copping, *A Journalist in the Holy Land: Glimpses of Egypt and Palestine* (London, 1911), pp. 221, 228.
[20] Robinson, *Biblical Researches*, p. 251.
[21] See, e.g., Frederick Bliss, *The Development of Palestine Exploration* (London, 1906), p. 220.
[22] For this debate, see André Parrott, *The Temple of Jerusalem* (London, 1957); James Fergusson, *An Essay on the Ancient Topography of Jerusalem, with Restored Plans of the Temple* (London, 1847); George Williams, *The Holy City: Or, Historical and Topographical Notices of Jerusalem* (London, 1845); Robinson, *Biblical Researches*, I, pp. 407–18; Charles Wilson and Charles Warren, *The Recovery of Jerusalem: A Narrative of Exploration and Discovery in the City and the Holy Land* (London, 1871); Charles Warren, *The Temple or the Tomb, Giving Further Evidence in Favour of the Authenticity of the Present Site of the Holy Sepulchre* (London, 1880); Charles Wilson, *Golgotha and the Holy Sepulchre* (London, 1906); Claude Conder, *The City of Jerusalem* (London, 1909); Joachim Jeremias, *Jerusalem in the Time of Jesus* (London, 1969); and the apologists (still) for the Garden Tomb, Bill White, *A Special Place: A Wide Angle View of the Garden Tomb, Jerusalem* (Stanborough, 1989), William Steuart McBirnie, *The Search for the Authentic Tomb of Jesus* (London, 1975). Gordon, Merrill, Schick, Conder, Flinders Petrie and others published articles in the *PEFQ* from 1885 to 1894: *PFQS* 1892 80–91 collects the long debate from the *The Times* and lists the *PEFQS* articles on the Garden Tomb.

identification was false that he ostentatiously refused to enter the church. By 1892, the arguments over the authenticity of the church and thus the religious experience it offered are sufficiently *au courant* to appear even in the novel *Three Vassar Girls in the Holy Land*, a rather mawkish educational tome for older children: 'Emma acknowledged she had no desire to visit the so-called Church of the Holy Sepulchre, with its collection of legendary holy places; but Violet felt there would be an interest in standing in a place which had been held sacred for ages, and was consecrated by the faith and strong emotion of many loving and trusting souls.'[23] The novel schematically offers a choice for good religious tourists: recognise and dismiss the fraud, or recognise the interest – from the outside, as it were, as a tourist – in seeing a place where so many have worshipped. In either case, much as the novel triumphs by converting the Jewish love-interest to Christianity, so the Church of the Holy Sepulchre is divested of religious force for the Protestant abroad.

Three Vassar Girls in the Holy Land also provides the title for this section. Violet visits Gethsemane with her brother Frank, who is miserably in love with Bird (Zipporah), the Jewish girl. 'Frank threw himself upon a seat, and took a book from his pocket. "Is that a guidebook?", Violet asked. "It is *the* guidebook," he replied. "Wander about by yourself, please, there's a good sister; I feel as if I had lost my way, and I want to study it up"'.[24] Frank has his Bible, which for many was the only guide to Victorian Jerusalem. A trip to Jerusalem was precisely to tread the ground where Jesus had walked and David sung. So the Countess of Belmore is presented in Richardson's account as the paragon of the Christian tourist when she 'visited the memorable spots in and about Jerusalem with all the zeal and feeling of a pious Christian, taking the Holy Scriptures as her guide'.[25] But it is integral to the Victorian discovery of Jerusalem that this is not a simple tourist gaze. To stand in this laden landscape is not just to stare, but to meditate, not just on moral life (as Frank in *Three Vassar Girls* studies to find again his way), but on the relation between past and present, on the meaning of history for the Christian in the Holy Land. So Harriet Martineau writes in her three-volume *Eastern Life: Present and Past* (1848), a description of her eight-month trip, which was a successful publication although too freethinking for some tastes: 'With all this before my eyes, my mind was with the past. It seemed as if the past were more truly before me than what I saw. Here

---

[23] Elizabeth Champney, *Three Vassar Girls in the Holy Land* (Boston, MA, 1892), p. 158.
[24] Ibid., p. 172. [25] Richardson, *Belmore*, II, p. 250.

was the ground chosen by David, and levelled by Solomon to receive the Temple.'[26] And this leads into two pages of emotive description of 'these places [which] had been so familiar to my mind's eye from my youth up'. Martineau is a religious sceptic fully aware of the claims of modern science and the challenges of history to the Bible, and she is keen to anatomise her response. She is aware that she sees as much with her mind's eye – through the memories of her reading, her religious feelings – and in this way the past becomes present to her; her mind, in a striking phrase, is 'with the past'. Martineau leads her reader to see beyond the physical, material world to find a past, in and through which the present's significance is located. The traveller's task is to see, to experience – to discover – religious history.

Martineau, like so many travellers to Jerusalem, strives to overcome the distaste for the 'grovelling superstition' and unpleasant city life in front of her by discovering a disembodied, spiritual, historical experience of the sites. A. W. Kinglake (1809–91) had gently parodied this stance in the wonderful *Eothen* (1844), an account of his travels in the Middle East. Kinglake, who has already featured in Gange and Bryant Davies' chapter as an ardent believer in Homer's Troy, cultivates the persona of an intelligent but fey man-about-town, effortlessly superior to the troubles of city life. There are, he notes with amused detachment from the heated debates about archaeological truth and the Bible, 'many geographical surprises which puzzle the "Bible Christian"'.[27] But he cannot join Martineau in her emotiveness: 'there are people who can visit an interesting locality, and follow up continuously the exact train of thought that ought to be suggested by the historical associations of a place ... I am not thus docile: it is only by snatches, and for a few moments together, that I can really associate a place with its proper history'.[28] But even the sardonic Kinglake assumes that seeing Jerusalem sets at stake historical, and, inevitably, religious self-awareness. If Victorian historiography is marked by a consciousness of its own modernity in pursuit of the past, and Victorian Christianity is drawn into a specific contest over history, Jerusalem becomes the archetypal topos for the performance of this self-consciousness.

---

[26] Martineau, *Eastern Life*, III, pp. 110, 117.
[27] Alexander Kinglake, *Eothen: Or, Traces of Travel Brought Home from the East* (London, 1844), p. 219.
[28] Ibid., p. 169.

A map of discovery

Edward Robinson has a good claim to be the founder of biblical archaeology. He was born in 1793 in Southington, Connecticut and brought up in a strict Congregationalist household. He was very successful at school, and was quickly appointed to the faculty of the fledgling Hamilton College, in upstate New York, where he served for just one year. He married into a wealthy family, and when his wife died young, Robinson found himself rich and without ties. After some years of private study, concentrating more on the classics than the Bible, he moved to the Andover Theological Seminary in Massachusetts, a fiercely anti-liberal establishment, where he came under the influence of Rev. Moses Stuart (1780–1852), a conservative theologian and charismatic teacher. Under his guidance, Robinson trained for four years in Europe (marrying a German professor's daughter, a traditional route to academic preferment), and returned to become one of the foremost biblical scholars in America. He was appointed the first professor of Biblical Literature at the Union Theological Seminary in New York. It was from here that he set off to Palestine in the company of Eli Smith (1801–57), a missionary explorer with experience of the Middle East.[29]

They travelled together throughout 1838 in Spartan conditions across the whole of Palestine, recording nightly what they had found, which, to their minds, constituted no less than a systematic proof of the truth of the Bible's geography – the Old Testament as much as the New – and thus scientific support for the Scriptures, which had been challenged by German higher critics from Eichhorn to Strauss. Neither Robinson and Smith nor their readers seemingly felt that their claims of scientific objectivity were jeopardised by such conservative, Protestant apologetics.[30] *Biblical Researches*, published simultaneously in England, America and in Germany (in German translation), made Robinson famous. The book was even received

---

[29] Henry Smith and Roswell Hitchcock, *The Life, Writings and Character of Edward Robinson, DD, LL.D* (New York, 1863); Neil Asher Silberman, *Digging for God and Country: Exploration in the Holy Land, 1799–1917* (London, 1982), pp. 37–47. The lack of reference to Robinson is one of the many remarkable gaps in Edwin Aiken, *Scriptural Geography: Portraying the Holy Land* (London, 2010).

[30] It is hard wholly to support the rather pietistic judgement of Michael Oren, *Power, Faith, and Fantasy: America in the Middle East, 1776 to the Present* (London, 2007), p. 136 that 'he never let religious beliefs cloud his scientific judgement'. The combination of Protestantism and Orientalism is never far from the surface. Paradigmatically, Robinson wrote in *Later Biblical Researches in Palestine, and in the Adjacent Regions: A Journal of Travels in the Year 1852* (London, 1856), p. 162 on his second trip to the Holy City: 'Jerusalem is still in all its features an oriental city; in its closeness and filth, in its stagnation and moral darkness.'

as a sign of Divine Providence by one reviewer, with the archaeologist cast in the charged role of a witness to the truth of God: 'Little did they think that they were obeying an impulse from on High, and that Jehovah meant them to be witnesses of His truth to the after-ages of the world.'[31] Robinson did make some highly significant discoveries – the recognition of Robinson's Arch, named for him, revolutionised understanding of the Temple Mount site – but his most important contribution was to re-conceive the map of Palestine as a modern map of ancient biblical history. The subsequent archaeological search to locate each place mentioned in the Bible, and to find the true site of each religious event or building, was inaugurated by Robinson. It has become a commonplace to think of maps as instruments of imperialism.[32] Robinson's conservative agenda was rather to use modern geographical techniques to oppose challenges to the authority of the Scriptures. In so doing, his work re-conceptualised the image of the eastern province as the proper heritage of the Western Christian tradition, opening the way for the mixture of political and religious ambitions that characterises Christian Victorian Jerusalem.

When Robinson first travelled in Palestine, it was ruled by Mehmet Ali (1827–78) from Egypt. In 1841, the sixteen-year-old new Sultan, Abdul Medjid (1823–61), decided to recapture Palestine and Syria for the Turkish Empire. With the help of British and Austrian fleets, and an uprising of the inhabitants, this was swiftly achieved.[33] In 1839 Britain had been the first Western nation to have a permanent consular presence in Jerusalem.[34] Now, by treaty with the grateful Sultan, France, Prussia, Austria, Spain opened consulates, followed by Italy, America, Russia and others. The combination of a new political openness and the new steamship business brought Jerusalem into the arena of European jostling for power. France claimed the right to protect all Christians in the Holy Land (an ancient authority, now invested with new political purchase). Russia was deeply connected to the dominant Orthodox Church and wished to take over this role – bolstered in its claim by the yearly influx of Russian pilgrims,

---

[31] James Wylie, *The Modern Judea, Ammon, Moab, and Edom, Compared with Ancient Prophecy, with Notes Illustrative of Biblical Subjects* (Glasgow, 1841).

[32] Jeremy Black, *Maps and Politics* (London, 1997).

[33] See Blumberg, *Zion*. The inhabitants revolted in part because the increased efficiency of Mehmet's regime had meant that taxes were collected and bribery became less possible.

[34] See Mordechai Eliav, *Britain and the Holy Land, 1838–1914: Selected Documents from the British Consulate in Jerusalem* (Jerusalem, 1997); M. Vereté, 'Why Was a British Consulate Established in Jerusalem?', *English Historical Review*, 85 (1970), 316–45, who corrects the overly religious reading of Abdul Tibawi, *British Interests in Palestine, 1800–1901: A Study of Religious and Educational Enterprise* (London, 1961).

60,000 a year, which fundamentally altered the precarious economy of Jerusalem. The Crimean War, as Kinglake noted in the first volume of his *Invasion of the Crimea* (1863–87), found its *casus belli* in a row between Orthodox and French Catholic priests in Bethlehem. Italy represented the interests of the Vatican. England needed to protect its trade route to its eastern empire and India in particular; Germany was expanding in influence through its close industrial ties with the Sublime Porte. Austria–Hungary had the largest group of citizens living in Jerusalem, and needed to assert its authority against the Russian and English Empires. From the 1840s until the First World War, Jerusalem became a microcosm of European diplomatic tensions. And it was a microcosm: the British consulate initially operated from the front room of the consul's modest house. The few foreign permanent residents could not easily avoid each other (even when squabbling over a diplomatic crisis), snubs were magnified, and from 1865 the telegraph quickly elevated such snubs to international questions.[35] Robinson arrived as a private citizen, and as an American at a time when the United States had a far less significant public role in the Middle East than in the twentieth century: in 1872 there were only four registered American citizens in Jerusalem, and only thirteen *protégés*.[36] But for the second half of the nineteenth century, archaeology in Jerusalem was implicated with European national interests. The search for biblical truth remained a powerful motivation, but discovering the biblical past functioned as a demonstration of a heritage, which became a claim of justified possession.

This connection between archaeological projects and national interests is well demonstrated by the Palestine Exploration Fund (PEF). The PEF was established in 1867, partly thanks to a benefaction by Angela Burdett Coutts (1814–1906), given in order to improve the water supply of Jerusalem.[37] The committee was manned by a roll-call of the great and good of Victorian society. Like many such Victorian committees, it was not a government agency, but assumed national importance by virtue of its members and role. Its aim was to 'throw light on some of the problems of Biblical History, and of the topography of ancient sites in the Holy city'.

---

[35] Good accounts are James Finn, *Stirring Times* supported by Elizabeth Finn, *Reminiscences of Mrs. Finn, Member of the Royal Asiatic Society* (London, 1929); Estelle Blyth, *When we Lived at Jerusalem* (London, 1927); Vester, *Our Jerusalem*. On American consuls see Ruth Kark, *American Consuls in the Holy Land 1832–1914* (Jerusalem, 1994).

[36] Ibid., p. 201.

[37] On the PEF see Tibawi, *British Interests*, pp. 183–205. Charles Watson, *Fifty Years' Work in the Holy Land: A Record and a Summary, 1865–1915* (London, 1915) is the Fund's own account.

This general statement of purpose, expressive of Robinson's agenda, was tempered by local passions. When George Grove (1820–1900) joined the Fund, he was already part of a heated argument about the holy sites and the potential of archaeological proof. Grove had been a vociferous supporter of the retired indigo planter and gentleman scholar James Fergusson (1808–86) in a quarrel over the authentic site of the Holy Sepulchre. Fergusson's *An Essay on the Ancient Topography of Jerusalem* (1847) had claimed that the Dome of the Rock on the Temple Mount was the original Church of the Holy Sepulchre.[38] He went on to publish his reconstruction of the Temple of Solomon, which looks alarmingly like St Pancras station (Fig. 2.1). Drawing on his authority as a historian of architecture, he declared with paradigmatic Victorian self-confidence that the proportions given in the biblical text led to an aesthetic horror, and must be emended: a glaring example of how the rhetoric of the authority of the past did not prevent the aesthetics – or politics – of the present dominating restoration.[39] Fergusson's apparently bizarre argument about the Dome of the Rock chimed with other attempts to dethrone the existing Church of the Holy Sepulchre, and was authorised by its inclusion in William Smith's *Dictionary of the Bible* in 1858 (to which Grove made significant contributions). However, Fergusson found a worthy adversary in Reverend George Williams (1814–78), formerly a chaplain to the first Anglican bishop in Jerusalem who had published a book on the city in 1845.[40] A man of strong principles and long memory, he despised Fergusson's work.[41] When in the 1860s he came across the work of one Ermete Pierotti, who had enjoyed good access to the Temple Mount, especially its underground crypts, and showed with detailed drawings why Fergusson must be wrong, Williams arranged for publication of his work in a lavish volume. A bitter argument broke out in *The Times*, as Fergusson accused Pierotti of plagiarism. Grove, who had met Fergusson on the Crystal Palace Company board, strongly supported his friend.[42] The public quarrel turned into whispering condemnation, when Fergusson and Grove discovered and privately circulated a document showing that Pierotti had

---

[38] He followed this with James Fergusson, *Collected Opinions on Mr Fergusson's Theory of the Holy Places of Jerusalem* (London, 1865) and *The Temples of the Jews and the Other Buildings in the Haram Area at Jerusalem* (London, 1878): he propagated his theories over thirty-five years.

[39] In Fergusson, *Temples*. See further Goldhill, *The Temple*, pp. 131–4.

[40] Goldhill, *Jerusalem*, pp. 262–3. On the Pierotti affair see Silberman, *Digging*, pp. 73–8.

[41] 'Few who have studied the subject can trust themselves to discuss [Fergusson's work] with entire moderation of temper or language'; George Williams, *Dr Pierotti and his Assailants: Or, a Defence of 'Jerusalem Explored'* (London, 1864), p. 2. See Warren, *Temple or the Tomb* for equally robust rebuttal of Fergusson's arguments and manner.

[42] Williams, *Dr Pierotti*, p. 27.

Figure 2.1 James Fergusson, *Perspective View of Herod's Temple as Restored*

been dismissed from the Sardinian army for embezzlement, and was thus a disreputable character.[43] It is therefore no surprise that the first full-scale project of the Fund's committee was to excavate the Temple Mount and its environs.

They appointed Charles Warren (1840–1927), a captain in the Royal Engineers. It was an inspired choice and the first major step in Warren's starry career. He went on to fight in some of the most famous battles of the Boer War; he rose to become head of the Metropolitan Police Force in London (the case of Jack the Ripper being the most celebrated on his beat); he was a leading Freemason, which underlay his passion for discovering the

---

[43] Williams, *Dr Pierotti*, availed little. It usefully includes thirty pages of published letters on the incident, aimed at showing (33) 'not only how very frivolous but how extremely ungenerous or even malevolent, this attack on Dr Pierotti has been'. On Grove's interests in biblical archaeology (and much else) see Charles Graves, *The Life and Letters of Sir George Grove, CB* (London, 1903).

hidden topography of the Temple; and he retired as General Sir Charles Warren GCMG, KCB, FRS.[44] Warren could have stepped out of central casting for a *Boy's Own* hero. He declared that the only two books a boy needed were the Bible and Baden-Powell's *Scouting for Boys*, and he brought a sense of derring-do to archaeology. As his biographer and grandson notes, he set off for Jerusalem 'somewhat in the *rôle* of a crusader ... for he was stirred by the longing to reveal to the Christian world those Sacred Places which were hidden by the *débris* of many a siege and jealously guarded by the Turkish Mussulmans'.[45] He approached archaeology as a military campaign. When his plans were initially thwarted by the Turkish authorities, who had no desire for a European archaeological project on the Temple Mount or even near it, he calculated that 'I had two courses before me – either to effect my object by stealth or else go straightforward and see if the perseverance of an Englishman would not at last overpower opposition.'[46] There was no question of recognising Turkish sovereignty or any religious scruples of the community.

Both stealth and perseverance in the end worked, in rather different ways. He maintained blunt diplomatic ties with the authorities, which barely concealed deep disdain for Turkish customs. Unlike T. E. Lawrence or Mark Sykes, Warren was dismissive of the lure of the East. He brusquely continued to assert his right and duty to dig, until it became a *fait accompli*. But he also tried stealth. He was finally allowed to dig some distance from the walls; but utilising his engineering background, he simply dug down, then constructed an underground tunnel at right angles to the shaft until he reached his goal. He also bribed the guards of the Temple Mount to be allowed into the innermost sanctuary of the Dome of the Rock (covered by three plucky ladies who talked vociferously to distract any suspicious passer-by) and to start exploring there (the punishment for this would certainly have been death). When the guards became nervous and hustled him away, his response epitomises one strand of imperial cultural and national superiority: 'all these people are like children; if they think over the prospect of anything dangerous, they get frightened and slink out of it'.[47] When de Saulcy, excavating in the name of the French government, claimed

---

[44] On Warren's life, see Watkin Wynn Williams, *The Life of General Sir Charles Warren, etc* (Oxford, 1941).
[45] Williams, *Warren*, p. 41.
[46] Charles Warren, *Underground Jerusalem: An Account of Some of the Principal Difficulties Encountered in its Exploration and the Results Obtained* (London, 1876), p. 11; cf. p. 149: 'I refused to notice the rules he laid down.'
[47] Warren, *Underground*, pp. 402–3.

to have found the Tombs of the Kings – this was the first proper archaeological excavation in Jerusalem, in 1863, which managed to insult the Muslim, Jewish and international community in one botched expedition – *The Times* thundered against the 'shameless profanation' of ancient tombs.[48] But Warren's incursions made him a hero, lauded as 'Jerusalem Warren' by the same paper. Nationalism, as ever, found in archaeology a field for self-aggrandisement. Indeed, Warren himself, direct as ever – and shockingly so to modern sensibilities – puts the case for British imperialism over and against the other empires in the final paragraphs of his book *Underground Jerusalem*: 'Will not those who love Palestine, love freedom, justice, the Bible, learn to look upon the country as one which may shortly be in the market? Will they not look about and make preparations and discuss the question?'[49] That Warren was prescient only emphasises the potent connection in Victorian culture between archaeology and imperial expansion.

Warren did, however, as he himself boasted, 'put the whole subject of topography on a new footing'.[50] He uncovered and explored the underground tunnels and cisterns which are an essential part of the water supply of Jerusalem, completed a relief map of the city at the time of Jesus, and conducted a series of essential surveys. As Walter Besant (1836–1901) commented on behalf of the Fund, 'It was Warren ... who stripped the rubbish from the rocks ... who laid open the valleys now covered up and hidden; he who opened the secret passages, the ancient aqueducts ...'[51] Warren's combination of surveying and adventure changed the image of the city. The preparation of proper maps of Palestine, often funded or at least welcomed by the military, was an integral preparation for British engagement, which ended in the re-drawing of the map of the region. But Warren's maps of Jerusalem achieved something different, despite the imperial ambitions of so many nations towards the Holy City. On the one hand, they brought the city into scientific comprehension. Unlike its medieval or Renaissance counterparts, this was a city now ordered according to contemporary regimes of knowledge: measured in feet and inches, contoured,

---

[48] *The Times*, (1 February 1864), 12, under the heading 'Desecrations at Jerusalem': George Williams (on whom see above) had written in to defend de Saulcy.

[49] Warren, *Underground*, p. 559; cf. pp. 363, 458–9.

[50] Ibid., p. 19. On the history of surveying Palestine, see John Moscrop, *Measuring Jerusalem: The Palestine Exploration Fund and British Interests in the Holy Land* (Leicester, 1999) and the detailed examples of Haim Goren, 'Sacred but not Surveyed: Nineteenth-Century Surveys of Palestine', *Imago Mundi*, 54 (2002), 87–110.

[51] Walter Besant, *Our Work in Palestine: Being an Account of the Different Expeditions Sent out to the Holy Land by the Committee of the Palestine Exploration Fund* (London, 1873), pp. 61–2.

labelled.[52] Jerusalem could appear and be treated like any other city within the purview of the Royal Ordnance Survey.[53] On the other hand, it is telling that Warren made a relief map of Jerusalem *at the time of Jesus*. These maps are still invested with the search for historical vision, an attempt to use scientific geography to discover the truth of the Bible. The map of Jerusalem can never be simply up to date. It is always scored with buried narratives and hidden politics.

Archaeology changed the tourism of Jerusalem. Discovering Jerusalem after 1870 meant travelling with real or metaphorical measuring devices and trowels. The Bible and the archaeological report complemented each other. Individual discoveries were startling: a boy clambering in Hezekiah's tunnel found the oldest extended inscription in Hebrew, recording the completion of the tunnel's construction;[54] de Saulcy may not have uncovered the Tombs of the Kings but he had unearthed the sarcophagus of Queen Helena of Adiabene; the Russians thought they had excavated the Gate of Judgement through which Jesus went to crucifixion, though it turned out to be part of the Constantinian foundation of the Holy Sepulchre site.[55] But perhaps more importantly, not only was archaeology integral to competing European imperial ambitions, it also allowed the religious tourist to bring contemporary scholarship and faith together in a comforting vision, as witnesses of the veracity of the Scriptures. Reading the Bible became a different experience, as the Truth was now enfolded with a historical and archaeological verification. In the illustrated Bibles of the nineteenth century, pictures of archaeological evidence, and photographs of sites enforced this connection – as if the Bible's authority could be bolstered by the drawing of an antique pot, or an olive tree, or a picture of the ruins of a site of Jesus' ministry. As much as art history provided an essential discursive frame for the traveller to Italy's cities, archaeology became embedded in the intellectual expectations of a visitor to Victorian Jerusalem. Pilgrims for centuries had wept and wondered at the Holy Places; now the ground trodden by the figures of biblical times needed to be uncovered by archaeology to be recovered for authentic religious experience.

---

[52] Jerusalem adopted a metric system of weight, length, capacity finally in 1896: Tibawi, *British Interests*, p. 214.

[53] Wilson, with Warren as his assistant, produced the first Ordnance Survey maps of Jerusalem in 1865; further maps were published in 1880. All this work was conducted under the auspices of the PEF. See Tibawi, *British Interests*, pp. 183–205; Moscrop, *Measuring Jerusalem*.

[54] The story is told nicely in Vester, *Our Jerusalem*, pp. 100–3.   [55] Silberman, *Digging*, pp. 66–72.

Realism and the image of a city

New technology and new regimes of knowledge for gaining access to the reality of Palestine as evidenced by archaeology come together in the new technique of photography. Images of the Holy Land are central to the development of the field of photography, and fundamentally changed how Jerusalem and Palestine were represented in the nineteenth century. Where John Murray's first handbook for travellers in the Holy Land recommended the Bible as the best guide for Palestine, in 1876 the Baedeker tellingly could declare in reverse that 'Palestine is the best guide to the Bible'. That is, the reality of Palestine, its landscapes, people, physical impact, will direct a reading of Scripture – reading the Bible is now *grounded* in the real – and photography as a practice played an integral role in this new authorisation of the word from the facts on the ground.[56]

The earliest photographers journeyed with artists and they both made images of the same view.[57] Indeed, many early photographers also doubled as painters. So, Frederick Goupil-Fesquet (1817–1878), probably the first photographer to enter Palestine, travelled in 1839 with the painter Horace Vernet (1789–1863). Goupil-Fesquet also drew and painted. But soon a radical divide opened between painters and photographers. 'The absolute

---

[56] For collections of images, see notably Paul Chevedden, *The Photographic Heritage of the Middle East: An Exhibition of Early Photographs of Egypt, Palestine, Syria, Turkey, Greece & Iran, 1849–1893* (Malibu, CA, 1981); Engin Çizgen, *Photography in the Ottoman Empire, 1839–1919* (Istanbul, 1987); Carney Gavin, ed., *Imperial Self-Portrait: The Ottoman Empire as Revealed in the Sultan Abdul Hamid II's Photographic Albums* (Cambridge, MA, 1988); Shimon Gibson, *Jerusalem in Original Photographs, 1850–1920* (London, 2003); Walid Khalidi, *Before their Diaspora: A Photographic History of the Palestinians, 1876–1948* (Washington, 1984); Jacob Landau, *Abdul-Hamid's Palestine: Rare Century-Old Photographs from the Private Collection of the Ottoman Sultan* (London, 1979); Claire Lyons, John Papadopolous, Lindsey Stewart and Andrew Szegedy-Haszak, *Antiquity and Photography: Early Views of Ancient Mediterranean Sites* (London, 2005); Yeshayahu Nir, *The Bible and the Image: The History of Photography in the Holy Land, 1839–1899* (Philadelphia, PA, 1985); Eyal Onne, *Photographic Heritage of the Holy Land, 1839–1914* (Manchester, 1980); Ely Schiller, *The First Photographs of Jerusalem: The Old City* (Jerusalem, 1978); and for general discussion, see also Kathleen Howe, *Revealing the Holy Land: The Photographic Exploration of Palestine* (Santa Barbara, CA, 1997); Kathleen Howe, 'Mapping a Sacred Geography: Photographic Surveys by the Royal Engineers in the Holy Land, 1864–68', in Joan Schwartz and James Ryan, eds., *Picturing Place: Photography and the Geographical Imagination* (London, 2003), pp. 226–42; Issam Nassar, *Photographing Jerusalem: the Image of the City in Nineteenth-Century Photography* (Boulder, CO, 1997); Vivienne Silver-Brody, *Documentors of the Dream: Pioneer Jewish Photographers in the Land of Israel, 1890–1933* (Jerusalem, 1998); Abigail Solomon-Godeau, *Photography at the Dock* (Minneapolis, MN, 1981). I would never travel in this region without Roland Barthes, *Camera Lucida: Reflections on Photography* (New York, 1981).

[57] See Onne, *Photographic Heritage*, pp. 1–20.

truthfulness which is inseparable from a photograph' was set in opposition to the artistic vision, where 'taste and imagination inevitably modelled reality'.[58] Auguste Salzmann (1824–72), whose photographic album of Jerusalem offered not only scenes but also close-ups of architectural details, offered his images as 'conclusive, brute facts'.[59] As Francis Frith (1822–98) boasted, the 'truthfulness' of the camera is 'unimpeachable'.[60] The English were taken with the new medium: fifty-three English photographers in the Holy Land are attested in the Victorian period (with France next with fifteen, then the Americans with eleven).[61] The circulation of photographs offered to put into the hands of a large public the reality of Jerusalem without the need for visiting, and without the veils of a writer's prose or a painter's brush.

But it is not hard to show that this claim on reality was mediated by a vision of its own. Many photographers were sent out by governmental agencies. The Royal Engineer expeditions of 1864 and 1868, which were so important to the imperial mapping project, were accompanied by McDonald, who kept a photographic record of the projects. The record itself becomes part of the scientific exploration and thus the representational control of the region, which led towards political control.[62] One of the greatest collections of photographs was formed by the American Colony, the well-known religious commune of Swedish and American Christians. They produced huge numbers of pictures, but their commercial sale of a restricted group of scenes produced a repertoire of generic images, which were circulated by tourists back at home, preparing the next travellers for what – how – to see. The scenes that were taken by almost all of the nineteenth-century photographers were, of course, highly selective and recognisably generic.

Religious buildings were of obvious interest – and the static nature of buildings chimed with the limitations of the early technology.[63] Landscapes were framed according to a biblical perspective. Rocky scenes with a single shepherd and some lambs echoed the language of Scripture and the artistic tradition, where the literalisation of the 'lamb' of God and the 'Shepherd of the People' was pervasive. The reality of the photograph's careful

---

[58] *British Journal of Photography* (3 April 1868), 158–9; N-P. Lerebours, *Traité de Photographie, Derniers Perfectionnements Apportés au Daguerréotype* (Paris, 1842).
[59] See Howe, *Revealing*, pp. 20–5.
[60] Frith cited by Carol Armstrong, *Scenes in a Library* (Cambridge, MA, 1998), p. 285, and discussed by her pp. 277–359; see also Nir, *Bible*, pp. 61–84.
[61] Figures from Onne, *Photographic Heritage*. [62] See Howe, *Revealing* and 'Mapping'.
[63] See the discussion of Lyons et al., *Antiquity*.

Jerusalem 89

Figure 2.2 View of Capharnaum, photograph

scenography allowed the viewer to see continuity between the biblical past and contemporary Palestine, creating a religious experience of immediacy, a recognition or determination of the imagination come to life – 'for real'. The selection of buildings and scenes created a vision of a biblical landscape.

Figures 2.2 and 2.3 are contrasting photographs, both taken by the celebrated Bonfils studio in Beirut, the first from around 1870, the second from perhaps a decade or more later. In different ways, each demonstrates the strategies of biblical representation in photography. The first depicts Capharnaum, in Galilee, where Jesus preached at the beginning of his ministry. Foregrounded are the ruins of the synagogue, the very stones of the pillars through which Jesus strode (as archaeology determines). The ruins put us in touch with the reality of the Bible, as the photograph puts us in touch with the reality of the ruins. In the background, a coarse field stretching back towards the fading hills of Galilee, there are two contrasting figures. On one stone sits an Arab youth in a characteristic headdress and carrying a shepherd's stick. He stands in for the continuity of the past in the

Figure 2.3 *Ruth and Boaz*, photograph

locale, the sort of simple shepherd to whom the birth of Jesus was announced. This makes sure that the classical pillars are correctly located in a Middle Eastern context, and provide us with an icon of the witness to Jesus, as if this youth is in a line with 'the shepherds watching in their fields'. But standing, and picked out by his dark robes against the fading background, is a monk or Orthodox priest, dressed in a simple habit, with a skull-cap, apparently carrying a walking-stick or switch. He stands in for an image of the Christianity to emerge from this site: not the grandeur of a papal ceremony or the intellectualism of theological debate, but a single religious figure in a field, a minister reflecting on the site of Jesus' ministry. Even if this figure looks somewhat archaic or even Eastern, he provides a model, a silent injunction, for the tourist's religious experience: a different type of witness to the tradition of Scripture. At very least, the two spectators in the picture, the two witnesses, with their apparently different perspectives, pose the question of 'with what eyes will you look on this place of

Jesus' work?' This photograph, that is, both represents a biblical site, now in ruins, and also positions the viewer in a historical and religious frame.

The second image at first sight appears to be a pastoral, agricultural scene from any part of Palestine. Four figures are cutting wheat in a field with small hand scythes, a fifth bearded man sits and watches. In the foreground, a bearded, turbaned man with a pipe addresses a woman, who is holding a sheaf of wheat, and seems to be smiling, barely, towards the camera. It is, however, titled 'Ruth and Boaz'. That is, the title makes of the picture a *tableau vivant* of a celebrated biblical story. In a standard *tableau vivant*, actors represent a scene or characters from the past. In the living panoramas that were part of the spectacular show-world of London, pygmies, say, were put on display as themselves, exotica from abroad to be stared at as specimens. Here, however, the viewer is asked to see in the realism of the photographed contemporary scene a sort of allegory or icon of the biblical past. These are not 'Ruth and Boaz' themselves, nor actors representing 'Ruth and Boaz'. Rather the realism of the photographic medium allows us to see in the present of Palestine deep continuity with the biblical past. As the Scottish Free Churchman George Adam Smith (1856–1942) wrote in his best-selling *Historical Geography of the Holy Land*, 'You see the landscapes described by Old Testament writers exactly as you will see them today.'[64] What is to be seen is – exactly – a landscape described by the Bible.

The story of Ruth and Boaz leads to the foundation of the house of David, which leads to the birth of Jesus (at least so the genealogy of the Gospel of Luke would have it). These two photographs thus also form part of the same biblical gaze. The connection between the Old and New Testament – as the Christian tradition terms it – embodied in typology, in prophecy and in history, means that the scholars and travellers perceived a continuum between the different periods of archaeological sites or historical memorials that they viewed. Although the Hebrew Bible and the gospels were often subject to separate attack in nineteenth-century criticism, the defence of the veracity of the texts through archaeology and through photography allowed itself to celebrate the continuity of the biblical world, not just in sites like the Temple where Harriet Martineau's recognition of the Temple of David and

---

[64] George Adam Smith, *The Historical Geography of the Holy Land* (London, 1894), p. 99. For Smith's intellectual contribution, see the rather unsatisfactory discussions of Robin Butlin, 'George Adam Smith and the Historical Geography of the Holy Land: Contents, Contexts and Connections', *Journal of Historical Geography*, 14 (1988), 381–404; Aiken, *Scriptural Geography*, pp. 132–85. As the preface to the twenty-fifth edition (1931) makes clear, Allenby used Smith as a field guide, and Smith responded by adding an appendix on Allenby's campaigns.

92   Simon Goldhill

Figure 2.4 Palestinian scene, photograph

Solomon can meld effortlessly into Jesus' overturning of the money-changers' tables and into the prophecy of the new dispensation of Christianity in and through the destruction of the Temple, but also in sites like Capharnaum, where the history evoked by the image is taken to include the deep biblical past. Just as each challenge to the veracity of the biblical texts from criticism challenged the edifice of religious faith, so each act of verification, each recognition of the real, each perception of the link of past and present, contributes to the wholeness of the truth.

Within such a perspective, these biblically charged pictures may not even need a title. Figure 2.4, an untitled and beautifully composed photograph from the American Colony studio in Jerusalem, can hardly fail to recall the young David, facing his Goliath, for any literate viewer. In all of these images, the realism of photography is put in the service of a carefully constructed perspective that encourages the viewer to find the biblical past, his or her continuity with that past – and the realism in turn authorises the religious gaze as seeing what is really there, the truth. Realism is always a profoundly ideological mode of representation.

The images of local people, except for such shepherds, were of much more restricted scope. Exotic portraits of 'Oriental families' were combined with 'backward' labour – ancient styles of threshing, say, or weaving from a pre-industrial age – and street scenes with exotically dressed Bedouins and Turks and always a camel or two. The exoticism of these portraits is both loving and dismissive in the paradigmatic gesture of the Victorian encounter with the domesticity and splendour of the East: 'Eastern costume is one of the blunders of a luxurious but half-civilized state of society,' reflected Frith (who had his picture taken dressed as a Turk).[65] These local pictures testify to a state of society, which can only for Victorians be a less civilised version of the West. In contrast to the 'geopiety' of the landscapes and church-scapes, this easy Orientalism prepared a traveller for the otherness of the East or memorialised it as a souvenir.[66] The photography here seems to fit well with the mix of alienation, disappointment, discomfort and intense religious experience which runs through written responses to Jerusalem.

By the turn of the century, clear lines emerge between different groups. Christians continue to circulate the standard images of holy sites and biblical landscapes, photographs begin to appear in illustrated Bibles as authenticating illustrations of the scriptural narrative, often alongside other artwork. There are some fascinating Jewish postcards advertising the Holy Land as a place to visit and emigrate to.[67] These re-frame landscapes and street scenes not as souvenirs or preparations for the otherness of tourism, but as an image to be completed by the imagination of the viewer as a potential home, a challenge to see yourself in the image in a different way from the biblical scenes. But perhaps the most surprising and interesting change is the active participation of Ottoman and especially Armenian photographers in the production and circulation of photographic representations of Palestine, Jerusalem and the inhabitants of the region.

Although there are some very negative remarks about image making in Haddith, which result in religiously motivated attacks on photography as a form of idolatry or at very least as forbidden figural representation, the Sultan Abdul-Hamid II (1842–1918) as the spiritual head of the Caliphate not only gave permission for photography, but also both sponsored photographers and was a keen photographer himself, with his own darkroom in the harem of his palace. Abdul-Hamid was keenly aware of the negative image of the 'awful Turk' in the West, and how photographs supported the

---

[65] See Armstrong, *Scenes*, p. 302.   [66] Howe, *Revealing*, p. 28.   [67] Silver-Brody, *Documentors*.

pejorative language of political Orientalism.[68] Abdul-Hamid set out to re-address this negativity through image management. It is surprising that this side of the image war is so little discussed or even recognised by modern Western scholarship, intent as it is on proving its past imperialism – and by its silence on this material reproducing one classic strategy of imperial monoculism.

Abdul-Hamid had prepared two sets of forty-one albums of photographs of the modern Ottoman Empire as he wished it to be seen, and had one sent in 1893 to the Library of Congress in Washington, and one sent to the British Museum in London in 1894. These are extraordinary collections, each with 1,824 photographs. There are many more pictures in the collection in Istanbul.[69] The organisation, display and exchange of collections of photographs is described as one of the modernising regimes of knowledge, such as the census, in a conversation between the Sultan and the American Ambassador – who had brought the Sultan an album of photographs of firearms of America, and now encouraged him to undertake a census of his own for the Ottoman Empire.[70] In the albums which the Sultan subsequently produced, we have the unique opportunity to see how some photographs are selected in order to create a specific, politicised portrait of the Ottoman Empire from its political centre, rather than from Western travellers' eyes.

The categories are broad and the examples often assembled at numbing length (modern interest in cadet uniforms or army horses is less developed, I suspect). There are sections on scientific and educational institutions – schools and hospitals; military installations; religious buildings; portraits. It is, however, a riveting document both because of what it puts in and because of what it omits. It is constructed as a 'conscious antidote'[71] to the exotic and Orientalising imagery which is no more than a 'mockery that . . . damage[s] national honour and propriety' – as the Sublime Porte thundered in trying to stop an English showman from collecting boats and exotic Turkish subjects to create a live panorama back in London.[72] So, the street scenes are typically a modern bridge being crossed by men in bowler hats carrying

---

[68] See Gavin, ed., *Imperial Self-Portrait*; and more generally Selim Deringil, *The Well-Protected Domains: Ideology and the Legitimation of Power in the Ottoman Empire, 1876–1909* (Istanbul, 1998), especially pp. 135–66.

[69] See Landau, *Abdul-Hamid's Palestine*.

[70] See Samuel Sullivan Cox, *Diversions of a Diplomat in Turkey* (New York, 1887), pp. 36–46.

[71] William Allen, 'Analysis of Abdul Hamid's Gift Albums', *Journal of Turkish Studies*, 12 (1988), 34.

[72] The story of this grotesque shopping expedition is told with the quotation in Deringil, *Well-Protected*, p. 151.

umbrellas, or an urban scene with tram-lines and fancy shop fronts. The portraits are dignified. The troops are orderly and well armed. The mosques are depicted as elegant works of architectural art; the institutions as replete with cleanliness, order and propriety.

By the same token, there are no odalisques, no harem scenes, nor indeed any sexuality, exotic or otherwise. There are no scenes of backward labour or biblical landscapes. With more political bite, we might also notice that there are no Armenians – this is in the middle of the Armenian massacres – although many of the photographers were Armenians (and Christian rather than Muslim; there were several Muslim photographers too). There are no Jews and no images of Jerusalem, for all that it is the third most holy city of Islam, though there were many fine images of the city in the Sultan's collection, and the Sultan was persuaded to have an Ottoman exhibition including a model of the Dome of the Rock at the World's Fair in St Louis in 1904.[73] Nor are there more than a tiny number of adult women (though there are schoolgirls), which may be part of Muslim propriety, but also part of a patriarchal fantasy. Modernisation has its own idealised imaging too.[74] The irony is that by entering an image war with the West, Abdul-Hamid rehearses the categories of representation by which the East was denigrated: progress, technological development of civilisation, cleanliness, order and so forth. Can the voice of the other speak back and be heard at all, without adopting the tones by which it is constructed as the other in the first place? In a final irony, this multi-volume album was sent to the British Museum in order to change the West's view of the Ottoman Empire in 1894. The packages, wrapped up in brown paper and string, were not opened or catalogued until almost a century later.[75] It is indeed hard for the voice of the Other to get a hearing.

---

[73] See Landau, *Abdul-Hamid's Palestine* – there are also pictures of Armenians and some women. For what the album leaves out see also the comments of Allen, 'Analysis'. This material has not been considered by the works cited in fn. 56, several of which follow are a rather unnuanced approach directed by Edward Said's work. For the World's Fair, see Burke Long, *Imagining the Holy Land: Maps, Models, and Fantasy Travels* (Bloomington, IN, 2003).

[74] On Iranian representations of Western women see Mohamad Tavakoli-Targhi, *Refashioning Iran: Orientalism, Occidentalism and Historiography* (Basingstoke, 2001), pp. 54–76. On Ottoman modernisation, see the standard Roderic H. Davison, *Reform in the Ottoman Empire, 1956–1876* (Princeton, NJ, 1963) and, with different sense of the politics of representation, Zeynep Çelik, *Displaying the Orient: Architecture of Islam at Nineteenth-Century World's Fairs* (Berkeley, CA, 1992); Katherine Fleming, *The Muslim Bonaparte: Diplomacy and Orientalism in Ali Pasha's Greece* (Princeton, NJ, 1999); U. Makdisi, 'Ottoman Orientalism', *American Historical Review*, 107 (2002), 768–96.

[75] As reported in Gavin, ed., *Imperial Self-Portrait*, sadly and even shamefacedly, by the then curator of the photography collection at the British Library.

96   Simon Goldhill

Figure 2.5 C. R. Ashbee, Sketch for the Redevelopment of Jerusalem

The opposition between photography and art became less stark over time and the fictions of the real in photography clearer. Yet the layerings of the imagination that these changing modes of representation produce remain telling. Charlie Ashbee (1863–1942) was the first Civic Advisor in Jerusalem for the British Mandate (to move briefly beyond the nineteenth century).[76] As he travelled around Jerusalem, he joined back together the photographer and the artist, the idealist and the realist. He would take photographs of particular vistas; take them back to his studio and create from them watercolour paintings of designs for the locale. These, on occasion, he would turn into architectural drawings, which then became built objects that were photographed again as part of the report for the Government on his work. Figure 2.5 is one of several of his notebook pages, which have never been

---

[76] On Ashbee see Goldhill (forthcoming); Crawford, *Ashbee*.

published and have only recently come to light.[77] Looking towards Jerusalem across a scrubby, undeveloped landscape, Ashbee imagines in paint a proper road instead of a mule track, with a Middle Eastern-inspired architectural development nestled by the road, and, true to his Garden City principles, an elegant park linking the city and its new suburb. He juxtaposes the photograph of what he saw with the painted vision of what he hopes to see fulfilled. The road is now there, and the whole area is developed, sometimes in a similar architectural style, though without Ashbee's admirable sense of green breathing space. The painting has become realised.

The Victorian discovery of Jerusalem took place through changing images of the city; and photography's medium, with its special claim on the real, produced new strategies of representation for imagining the city – and produced new conflicts over the real in the Holy Land.

Idealism, restoration and the New Jerusalem

General Gordon of Khartoum (1833–85) was a national celebrity. In 1883, he was relaxing in Jerusalem, reading the Bible as usual, on the roof of the American Colony house near the Damascus Gate – this was before they moved out to the current American Colony Hotel. Gordon looked over the wall and saw a small escarpment, which looked to him as if the rocks formed the shape of a skull. Like most Protestants he was deeply dissatisfied with the identification of the Church of the Holy Sepulchre as the site of the crucifixion of Jesus, and he became fixated with the possibility that this escarpment was the true Golgotha: Golgotha means 'skull-place', and it looked like a skull, it was just outside the walls, by a major road, easily visible, as the gospels demanded. He decided to investigate the hill further and as he tramped over the scrubby terrain the General found a tomb. This seemed the clincher: a tomb, in a garden, by a skull-shaped rock. This was Calvary. He wrote articles in support of his theory, and ten years later a letter campaign in *The Times* led to the foundation of the Garden Tomb Association and the purchase of the plot for Protestant posterity. The site became known as 'Gordon's Calvary' and was treated for some years by Protestant pilgrims as the true site of the Passion.[78]

---

[77] They are now in the Modern Archive Centre at the library of King's College, Cambridge.
[78] Charles Gordon, *Reflections in Palestine, 1883* (London, 1884). Vester, *Our Jerusalem*, pp. 107–9 tells the story.

This is the commonly told story of the establishment of the Garden Tomb site.[79] But as with so much in Jerusalem the narrative is far more complicated. First of all, the identification of this site as Golgotha had been made at least forty years earlier by Otto Thenius, as Charles Wilson (1836–1905), the famous explorer and surveyor who discovered and gave the name to Wilson's Arch by the walls of the Temple Mount, attested.[80] Conrad Schick (1822–1901), the leading German archaeologist and architect, says that he had investigated the grave, shortly after it had been discovered and was in the process of being cleared by its owner, in 1867.[81] Gordon knew of the identification before he made his discovery. Second, there was good archaeological evidence available early on that the dating and shape of the grave meant it could not be a newly cut grave of the first century, as demanded by the gospel description of Jesus' tomb; but this evidence was ignored or dismissed by Gordon and other supporters of the claim. Third, the arguments Gordon used were not merely the circumstantial details mentioned above. He also published the most extraordinary claim that the contours of the relief map of Jerusalem at the time of Jesus drawn up by Captain Warren outlined the image of a skeleton – which could not be less than providential. It symbolises, he argued, the victim who abrogated the Old Law. When this skeleton map is overlaid with religious sites, it becomes evident that Gordon's choice of Golgotha was where the skull of the skeleton lay. Thus, argues Gordon, there is a providential topographical proof of the identification. The Dome of the Rock appears in the anus, a slur on Fergusson's identification of the site of the Passion, as well as a childishly offensive joke at the expense of the Muslims (Fig. 2.6).[82] A reflective piece on Gordon by W. H. Mallock (1849–1923), based on unpublished materials he had been given after Gordon's death, captures well Gordon's archaeological gaze: 'Jerusalem on the earth is a spot so sacred, that the configuration of the ground it stands upon is a hieroglyphic designed by God.'[83] Maps may be an instrument of empire, but, for Gordon, Warren's map reveals the world as God's kingdom, inscribed with God's signs. The battle

---

[79] See the works cited in fn. 22 above.
[80] In a letter to *The Times* (1 October 1892) reprinted in *PEFQS* (1893), 88. In *PEFQS* (1890), 125, Captain Churchill is attributed as identifying the site 'twenty years ago'. Conder (*PEFQS* (1881), 202) identifies a different grave on the same hillside as the tomb of Jesus.
[81] *PEFQS* (1892), 120–4.
[82] Reprinted and discussed in Wilson, *Golgotha*, pp. 199–202. See *PEFQS* (1885), 79–82; also Gordon, *Reflections*, pp. 1–18.
[83] William Hurrell Mallock, 'General Gordon's Message', *Fortnightly Review*, 36 (1884), 59, 61. He mischievously suggests that Gordon's linking of the invisible and visible in man's spiritual history is more reminiscent of Catholicism than Protestantism.

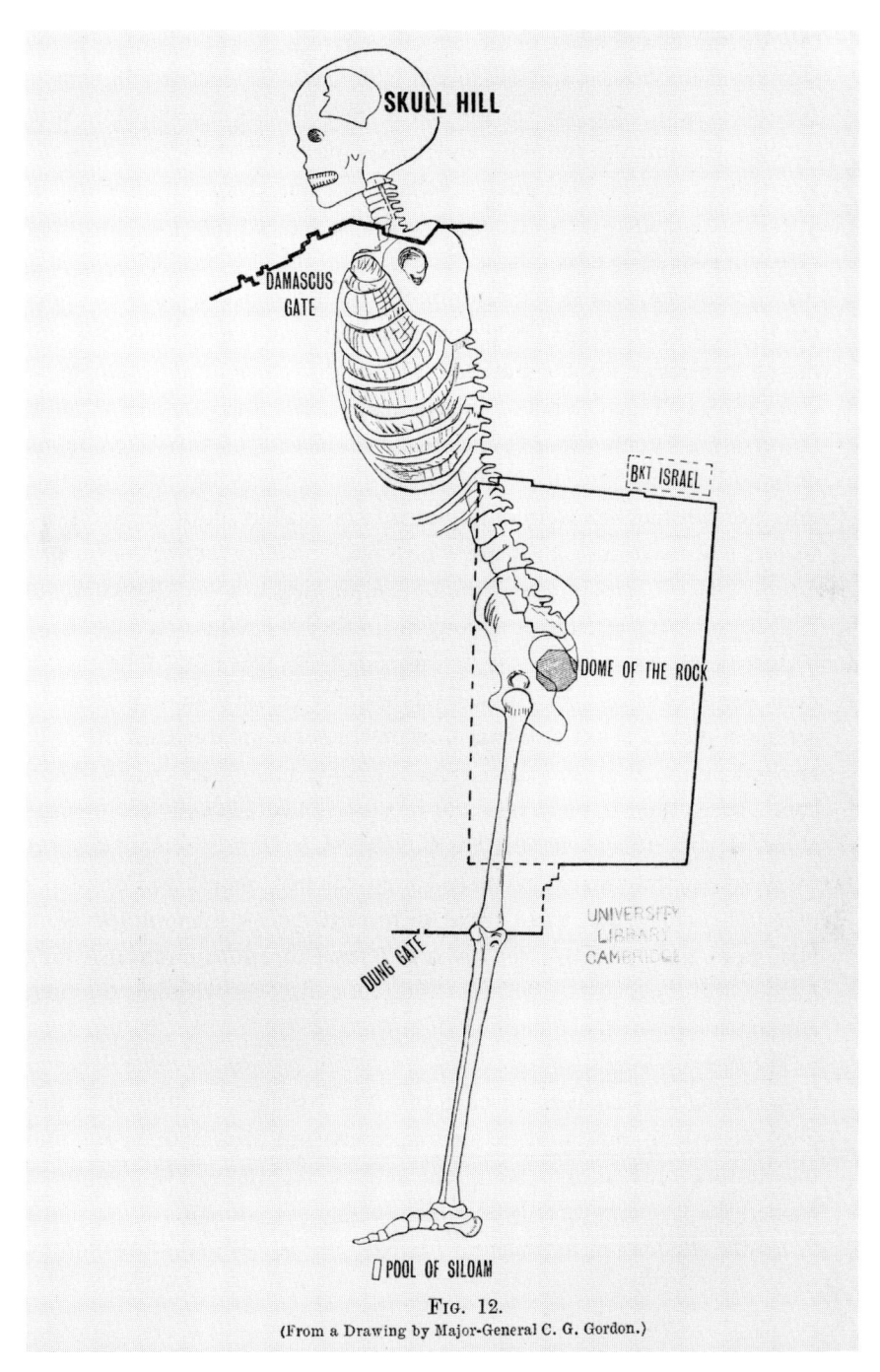

Figure 2.6 *From a Drawing by Major General C. J. Gordon*

over the site of the Church of the Holy Sepulchre, just like the battle over the location of the Temple and its Holy of Holies, was conducted with maps – Fergusson and many others published their historical city-plans, with detailed placements, contours and topographical claims. But Mallock's sympathetic account of Gordon reveals the symbolic value of these charts. These cartographers are pursuing their desire to read and draw 'the hieroglyphic designed by God'.

It is most remarkable that a committee of distinguished men, including the Duke of Argyll (1823–1900) from the PEF, could be led by such arguments to arrange for the purchase of the plot of land, and even more remarkable that the Church of England at first authorised the identification (which it has since rescinded). There can be no doubt that this is not the site of Jesus' death and burial. But the whole story gives a fascinating glimpse into the Victorian discovery of Jerusalem. Above all, it shows the necessary vectors that make such a discovery possible. The discovery of the Garden Tomb needed a hero; it needed the contentiousness over the Church of the Holy Sepulchre, which, however long the history of doubts about it, was fed by specific Protestant antipathy to Catholic ritualism; it needed the growth in the status of archaeology to scaffold the construction of faith; it needed a certain blindness about history and argumentation; and it needed the press to circulate the idea. And these factors together rely on and help create a collective will to see what needs to be seen. As Schick bemusedly wrote about his continuing belief that the Constantinian Church was the best bet for the site of the crucifixion, 'I stand almost alone amongst the Protestants in Jerusalem in holding this view; as the majority believe the so-called "Skull Hill" to be the true Calvary.'[84] Even in Jerusalem, which has such a long history of the search for holy sites and relics, discovery requires the right cultural and historical conditions.

The Garden Tomb is discovery as Protestant re-invention: the desire to discover within Jerusalem another city. The strongest expression of this desire is the long connection between a proselytising mission to the East and the Restorationist movement. From at least the 1840s, the mission to convert the Jews was directly connected with a political and religious plan to resettle the Jews in Jerusalem.[85] In 1840, against the background of the

---

[84] Conrad Schick, *Die Baugeschichte der Stadt Jerusalem in kurzen Umrissen von den ältesten Zeiten bis auf die Gegenwart dargestellt* (Leipzig, 1893), p. 123.

[85] See Donald Lewis, *The Origins of Christian Zionism: Lord Shaftesbury and Evangelical Support for a Jewish Homeland* (Cambridge, 2010); for discussion and as a corrective see James Renton, *The Zionist Masquerade: The Birth of the Anglo-Zionist Alliance 1914–1918* (Basingstoke, 2007), who underplays any religious background. See also William D. Rubinstein and Hilary

blood-libel massacre in Damascus, *The Times* published a series of letters and articles supporting the return of the Jews to Palestine.[86] Warren's later imperialism had the same agenda. His plea that Britain should prepare as Palestine would soon be 'in the market' was made 'with the avowed intention of gradually introducing the Jew, pure and simple, who is eventually to occupy and govern the country'. Restorationism originally combined the biblical prophecy that the Second Coming would take place only after the Jews had returned to a rebuilt Jerusalem and converted, with the imperial willingness to realign populations and boundaries. It was a project passionately supported by leading English politicians, including the Earl of Shaftesbury (1801–85), and constitutes the framework within which the Balfour Declaration has to be seen.[87] The phrase 'a country without a people for a people without a country', or 'a country without a nation for a nation without a country' was coined within this milieu (and not as Zionist propaganda) as early as 1839. It does not mean that Palestine – or Jerusalem – was thought to be uninhabited, as Edward Said (who misattributes, misquotes and misdates the phrase) and others have claimed.[88]

L. Rubinstein, *Philosemitism: Admiration and Support in the English-Speaking World for Jews, 1840–1939* (Basingstoke, 1999).

[86] See in particular *The Times* (17 August 1840), where many columns are given to the issue. See Hugh McNeile, *The Covenants Distinguished, A Sermon on the Restoration of the Jews* (London, 1849); Henry Highton, *A Letter to Sir Moses Montefiore: Containing Observations on the Subject of an Address Lately Presented to him, Signed by nearly 1500 Continental Jews* (London, 1842); Edward Ledwich Mitford, *An Appeal in Behalf of the Jewish Nation, in Connection with British Policy in the Levant* (London, 1845), and the opposition of William Withers Ewbank, *The National Restoration of the Jews to Palestine Repugnant to the Word of God* (London, 1849) and *A Distinction without a Difference: A Letter . . . on a Sermon . . . in Favour of the Restoration of the Jews* (London, 1850), for exemplary pamphlets. Crucial background is the discussion of the Jewish Disability Bill in 1841. In 1841, J. B. Webb published a novel, *Naomi*, with an explicit Restorationist plea in the preface (and a predictable narrative where good Jews convert, and bad Jews get condign punishment).

[87] See Albert Hyamson, *British Projects for the Restoration of the Jews* (London, 1971). General background in Bar-Yosef, *Holy Land*. Lewis, *Origins*, is good on Shaftesbury. Renton, *Zionist Masquerade* is insightful on the misunderstandings that contributed to the Balfour Declaration.

[88] Edward Said, *Orientalism* (New York, 1979), p. 9, who quotes the phrase as 'a land without people . . .' (without the article) as if it meant depopulated, and attributes the phrase to Zangwill. See Adam Garfinkle, *Israel and Jordan in the Shadow of War: Functional Ties and Futile Diplomacy in a Small Place* (London, 1991); Diana Muir, '"A Land Without a People for a People Without a Land"', *Middle East Quarterly* (2008), 55–62, who also criticises Rashid Khalidi, *Palestinian Identity: The Construction of Modern National Consciousness* (New York, 1997). Goldhill, *Jerusalem* (first edition), did not understand this history. There are occasional expressions in Victorian polemic, which could lead to such thoughts. George Gawler, *Tranquillization of Syria and the East, Observations and Practical Suggestions in Furtherance of the Establishment of Jewish Colonies in Palestine* (London, 1845), encouraged the British thus: 'Replenish the deserted towns and fields of Palestine with the energetic people whose warmest affections are rooted in the soil.' But this is a combination of biblical prophetic language of the promise of return – 'The land that was desolate is become like the Garden of Eden, and the waste

Rather, within a Victorian sense of nationalism and the dictates of race, the Jews constitute a people or a race or a nation. Indeed, according to Houston Stewart Chamberlain (1855–1927), in a founding text of German nineteenth-century racial theory, Jews are the only pure race except for the Teutons, with whom they are perpetually at war.[89] A nation depends not only on race and language, as Herder influentially argued, but also on an integral connection to a land. The Restorationists saw Palestine and particularly Jerusalem as the national home of a people, a nation, namely, the Jews. They saw no sense of a national identity among the population of Palestine, and imagined that the population would benefit from and thus welcome the return of the Jews. This project was an integral part of the idealism of Victorian political, theological and intellectual culture – though not for the majority of *Jews*: despite the Zionist tendencies of a leader such as Moses Montefiore (1784–1885), even the foundation of the Zionist Federation and the World Congress of Zionists still represented a minority strand of Jewish political idealism.[90] George Eliot in her novel *Daniel Deronda* (1876) captures the projected ideal beautifully with her hero's commitment to Restoration: 'The idea that I am possessed with is that of restoring a political existence to my people, making them a nation again, giving them a national centre, such as the English have, though they too are scattered over the face of the globe.'[91]

This desire to change Jerusalem into a city of converted Jews motivated the establishment in 1841 of the Anglican bishopric in Jerusalem. It was a joint project of Friedrich Wilhelm IV of Prussia and the British state (much to the disgust of Captain Warren some thirty years later, when the agreement was splitting into Anglo-German rivalry) – and it was from the outset highly contested in some circles: for John Henry Newman, it was the straw that led him to leave the church.[92] The deal was brokered by the Prussian

and desolate and ruined cities are become fenced and are inhabited' [quoted, e.g., by Mitford, *An Appeal*, p. 39] – and the Victorian distaste for lack of industry. Gawler also knows well that Palestine was inhabited. The Bedouins, like most nomads, are regarded with particular disdain by Victorian civic ethnography.

[89] Houston Stewart Chamberlain, *Die Grundlagen des neunzehnten Jahrhunderts* (2 vols., Munich, 1899), with Geoffrey Field, *Evangelist of Race: The Germanic Vision of Houston Stewart Chamberlain* (New York, 1981), and generally Bruce Lincoln, *Theorizing Myth: Narrative, Ideology, and Scholarship* (London, 1999).

[90] On Montefiore see Abigail Green, *Moses Montefiore: Jewish Liberator, Imperial Hero* (Cambridge, MA, 2010). On the misunderstandings of the English establishment about Zionism and the over-confident self-expression of the Zionists see Renton, *Zionist Masquerade*.

[91] *Daniel Deronda* (London, 1876), chapter 72. See Amanda Anderson, 'George Eliot and the Jewish Question', *Yale Journal of Criticism*, 10 (1997), 39–61.

[92] William Henry Hechler, *The Jerusalem Bishopric, 1841: Documents Chiefly Reproduced from a Copy of the Original German Account* (London, 1883), is a hagiographic account, but reproduces

envoy, Christian Karl Josias Bunsen (1791–1860), who envisaged the creation of 'a congregation of Christian proselytes on the sacred hill of Jerusalem' and hailed the plan as 'Zion's revival': it had both a missionary and a Restorationist agenda.[93] The proposal was rushed through Parliament; Bishop Alexander (1799–1845), a converted Jew, a citizen of Prussia who lived in England, was appointed.[94] He arrived in Jerusalem with a small and somewhat motley team and built a church in the Old City – without any visible cross, and with all the inscriptions in Hebrew, to attract a Jewish clientele. The history of the bishopric, however, did not fulfil the fervour with which it was founded. Very few Jews converted; the missionaries found themselves regularly isolated or in conflict with one another; growing tensions between European powers entangled the churches in political arguments.[95] As with so many tourists, the missionaries struggled with the gap between their ideals of a religious city and the realities of religious life in the city. They came in search of a new Jerusalem, and discovered the old Jerusalem, on which they failed to have an impact.

Jews, too, aimed to change the face of Jerusalem. The first extended building project outside the walls of the city, Mishkanot Sha'ananim,

some contemporary documents. He comments (22): 'The adherence to *national characteristics in each Church*, which is not merely an inviolable right, but a sacred duty, was a principle admitted on both sides from the outset.' For an exemplary contribution to the debate on such issues see Frederick Denison Maurice, *Three Letters to the Rev. W. Palmer, Fellow and Tutor of Magdalen College, Oxford* (London, 1842), pp. 39–73. See also Tibawi, *British Interests;* Yaron Perry, *British Missions to the Jews in Nineteenth-Century Palestine* (London, 2003); Lewis, *Origins*; important discussions of the general background in Brian Stanley, *The Bible and the Flag: Protestant Missions and British Imperialism in the Nineteenth and Twentieth Centuries* (Leicester, 1990); Susan Thorne, *Congregational Missions and the Making of an Imperial Culture in Nineteenth-Century England* (Stanford, CA, 1999); Andrew Porter, *Religion versus Empire? British Protestant Missionaries and Overseas Expansion, 1700–1914* (Manchester, 2004).

[93] Quoted in Greaves, 'Jerusalem', 336.
[94] On Alexander, see most recently Kelvin Crombie, *A Jewish Bishop in Jerusalem* (Jerusalem, 2006).
[95] Ferdinand Christian Ewald, *Journal of Missionary Labours in the City of Jerusalem during the Years 1842-3-4* (London, 1846), gives the fullest account of the first years: he was one of Alexander's team, and his book is dedicated to Bunsen. He was frank about his lack of 'glowing enthusiasm' for this 'land full of abominations and desolations!': p. 22. Thomas Halsted, *Our Missions: Being a History of the Principal Missionary Transactions of the London Society for Promoting Christianity amongst the Jews* (London, 1866) and William Gidney, *The History of the London Society for Promoting Christianity amongst the Jews: From 1809 to 1908* (London, 1908) are much more upbeat, but with little cause. On the gap between the missionaries' accounts and the truth, see the outrage of William Holman Hunt, *Jerusalem: Bishop Gobat* in re *Hanna Hadoub* (London, 1858)). For the general history of the bishopric, see P. J. Welch, 'Anglican Churchmen and the Establishment of the Jerusalem Bishopric', *Journal of Ecclesiastical History*, 8 (1957), 193–204; R. W. Greaves, 'The Jerusalem Bishopric, 1841', *English Historical Review*, 64 (1949), 328–52; Eliav, *Britain and the Holy Land;* Tibawi, *British Interests*, 63; Perry, *British Missions*.

marked a sea change in the urban development of Jerusalem. It was directed by the English Jew Moses Montefiore and funded by the American businessman Joseph Touro.[96] Montefiore's aim was to construct cheap, healthy living quarters outside the cramped and disease-ridden Jewish quarter, and to provide reliable work for the inhabitants. By 1860, there were twenty-two houses, a windmill, in a walled compound with cisterns for water and an area for market-gardening. At first, few were willing to risk life outside the walls, and even those who took up residence returned to the Old City at night; but after a cholera epidemic in 1865, when no one in Mishkanot Sha'ananim was infected, the housing became more popular, and by 1896, a further 130 houses had been built in the adjoining area of Yemin Moshe.[97]

The housing project had a rule-book, which paid particular attention to cleanliness.[98] Rule 5 specified that each resident had to clean his home every day and spray the floor with water every day. Rule 6 required residents to use refuse containers. Rule 7 guaranteed that the cisterns would be kept covered. These rules find obvious parallels in the debates in London and other European capitals about the state of the city, where the disposal of sewage, the water supply, and the relation between urban living and the health of the inhabitants were constant concerns. Indeed, the most successful projects of the Christian missionaries in Jerusalem were hospitals, which brought modern Victorian medicine – against some opposition – to the city.[99] The Book of Regulations for Mishkanot Sha'ananim concluded with an injunction not to break the 'fraternal covenant'. It was, in other words, modelled on the idealist communities of industrial philanthropy, such as Robert Owen's New Lanark, where cleanliness, godliness, hard work were the enforced principles of the social reformers committed to improving city life. There had always been small idealist communities in Jerusalem: monasteries, nunneries, *yeshivas*, *madrasas*; but the New City of Jerusalem was a Victorian innovation. The discovery of the biblical city was also the reconstruction of the city on modern principles.

Many other co-operative communities grew up, as rigorous control over land purchase relaxed. The largest of these was Mea She'arim, a housing association founded by five Old City Jews from different countries, which

[96] See Ruth Kark, *Jerusalem Neighborhoods: Planning and By-laws, 1855–1930* (Jerusalem, 1991); for development beyond the walls, see Heike Zaun Goshen, *Beyond the Wall: Chapters on Urban Jerusalem* (Jerusalem, 2006). For Montefiore's project in general see Green, *Montefiore*.
[97] See Eliezer Jaffe, *A Private Foundation Working in Israel: The Doron Foundation for Education and Welfare* (Jerusalem, 1988).
[98] Kark, *Jerusalem*, p. 103 notes that nearly a hundred such books of regulations for different communities were issued, and reproduces several.
[99] See Perry, *British Missions*, pp. 104–7, 133–9, 179–81.

enabled its members to buy houses on easy conditions spread over a long period of time. It is telling that the compound, which by 1881 consisted of 140 houses, arranged in a square so that the backs of the houses formed a wall against the outside world, was designed by Conrad Schick, the German evangelical Christian architect and archaeologist, who was involved in the controversy over the Garden Tomb, and equally telling that the land was purchased through the British Consulate, which had been actively involved in missionary work. Politics, archaeology, religion and social reform overlap in individuals' careers and many a project in Jerusalem.[100] The conditions on which a purchaser could join the community of Mea She'arim were laid down in a book of regulations, which by 1889 had expanded to sixty rules.[101] These rules began, like those of Mishkanot Sha'ananim, with an emphasis on cleanliness and order, but rapidly became an extended statement of the Orthodox Jewish principles of the community. Mea She'arim thus initially resembles an archetypal project of Victorian urban renewal; is rapidly overtaken by longing for a lost style of Eastern European Jewish life; then performs its resistance to modernity with increasingly strong erection of physical and conceptual boundaries. For ultra-religious Jews who came to Mea She'arim, Jerusalem offered the re-invention of the past in the present. This creation of a new Jerusalem turned a progressive Victorian idealism into nostalgic desire to resist change in a fiercely protected self-isolation.

The architecture of imperialism

William Thompson (1819–90), the Archbishop of York, addressed the PEF in 1875 on the principles of the Fund's work: 'Our reason for turning to Palestine', he stated, 'is that Palestine is our country.'[102] Thompson supported the archaeological exploration of the Holy Land, because it was the heritage of Christians. But there is a slippage from recognising the roots of Christianity in Jerusalem to a more forceful determination of sovereignty. Towards the end of the nineteenth century, with the loosening of land purchase regulations in Ottoman-held territories, the increasing European presence in the Holy City, the emergence of the Middle East as a strategic region for the major Western empires, the rise of Arab nationalism and the rise of Zionism, and the major shift of the demographics of the city, the issue

---

[100] For the architecture, see David Kroyanker, *Jerusalem Architecture: Periods and Styles: The Jewish Quarters and Public Buildings outside the Old City Walls 1860–1914* (Jerusalem, 1983), pp. 35–135; see also Ben-Arieh, *Emergence*.
[101] For a reproduction of these laws see *British Missions*, pp. 107–13.   [102] *PEFQ* (1875), 115.

of whose city Jerusalem could be said to be was becoming an insistent question. Unlike the case of Pithom or Sodom or even Ephesus, with Jerusalem possession, or ownership, or jurisdiction over the ancient sites became in the late nineteenth century a profound concern. Crusaders and Saracens had fought pitched battles for the control of Jerusalem. Empires contested Jerusalem at the level of legal and historical and theological discourse; at the level of economic and industrial power; and, above all, with the spectacular, self-promoting construction of nationalist architecture. Outside the Old City walls, gathering like hulking beasts around a victim, a series of large-scale projects was completed by competitive foreign empires.

The Russian Compound was the first.[103] In 1859, the Sultan sold the military training ground, just north of the Jaffa Gate, to the Russians, despite having been at war with them in the Crimea only three years previously, and he even added an extra parcel of land as a gift to the Tsar. Between 1860 and 1864, the Russians built a massive cathedral, surrounded by large hostels for male and female pilgrims, a hospital, a centre for the Russian Delegation and a Russian Consulate, all enclosed by a wall, with huge formal gates that closed at night. A further hostel for noble visitors was added just outside these walls in 1870. The cathedral was quite different from any other building then to be seen in Jerusalem. The large central dome is flanked by four smaller cupolas, and fronted by two towers, topped by small cupolas and Pravoslavic crosses. It is a splendid example of the best of grand contemporary Eastern European architecture, which would grace Vienna or Budapest. The British travellers were shocked by the poor and filthy Russian pilgrims for whose use the compound was intended.[104] For Anthony Trollope (1815–82), they were 'cut-throat looking wretches, with close-shaven heads, dirty beards, and angry eyes; men clothed in skins, or huge skin-like looking cloaks, filthy, foul, alive with vermin, reeking with garlic – abominable to an Englishman'.[105] The Russians had created a city against the city, a Jerusalem over and against the main entrance to the Old City. It made a statement about Russian influence even after the Crimea. In 1888, the Russians changed the skyline of Jerusalem further by building the Church of St Mary Magdalene on the Mount of Olives below

---

[103] See Ben-Arieh, *Emergence*, pp. 70–4; David Kroyanker, *Adrikhalut bi-Yerushalayim* (Jerusalem, 1985–93), III, s.v. for good basic description of the buildings, with plans. Schneller's Orphanage and Finn's farm project at Kerem Avraham (Karm Al Khalil) were scarcely imperial projects and not on the same scale at all.
[104] Fascinating account in Graham, *Russian Pilgrims*.
[105] Anthony Trollope, *The Bertrams* (1859; Oxford, 1991), p. 73.

Gethsemane. This remains one of the most distinctive and visible buildings in the landscape. It has gold, bulbous, onion-shaped domes above glistening white sandstone, topped with Orthodox crosses. Jerusalem architecture was predominantly Muslim and Crusader. This church was designed to stand out, and to make a spectacular statement of Russian presence in the Holy City.

The French and the Italians followed. The Italians built their hospital and church to the north of the Russian Compound – and its tower is a replica of the Palazzo Vecchio in Florence, a small piece of Italy in Jerusalem. The French started their huge hospice in 1884 in the style of a very grand eighteenth-century French church, adding in 1904 on the roof a massive statue of the Virgin Mary, copied from Our Lady of Salvation in Paris. The French were keen to declare their role as protectors of all Christian pilgrims against the Russians, and chose symbolically a site between the Russian Compound and the walls of the Old City, by the New Gate, so that the Russians would see the French hospice every time they looked towards Jerusalem. The British hurried to catch up. St George's Collegiate Church, built to the north of the Italian hospital in East Jerusalem, with its close and attached school, looks startlingly like a cathedral or an Oxford college. (The bell tower, added in 1910, is based on Tewkesbury Abbey in the Cotswolds.) This is where the Anglican bishop now worshipped. In the 1840s, when Bishop Alexander arrived, his simple church in the Old City was designed specifically not to feel unfamiliar or threatening to potential Jewish or Arab worshippers. At the end of the century, worship and its public display through architecture needed to assert a strident national identity. What had been a joint project between Britain and Prussia, was now firmly and solely English.

Kaiser Wilhelm used the money that he would have spent on the bishopric to build the Church of the Holy Redeemer in the Old City. This is a Lutheran church, for German Lutherans, built over the site of an eleventh-century church and cloister. It is archetypically bare, austere and architecturally undistinguished – but it has the tallest tower in Jerusalem.[106] The Kaiser himself may have written in a private letter that he hated 'the race for the highest towers or biggest churches'[107] in Jerusalem, but the German press recognised this was a race worth winning: 'Two German Churches will raise their towers ... Over these towers the Imperial Eagle will henceforth

---

[106] See Jan Stefan Richter, *Die Orientreise Kaiser Wilhelms II. 1898: Eine Studie zur deutschen Außenpolitik an der Wende zum 20. Jahrhundert* (Hamburg, 1997), pp. 145–54.
[107] Grant, ed., *The Kaiser's Letters*, p. 66.

extend its mighty pinions.'[108] The British with customary humour played down the domineering architecture – they called it 'Willy's extinguisher'. But at its opening in 1898 the Kaiser arrived at the church in a parade with his entourage dressed in white as Teutonic knights, accompanied by a band playing Handel's 'See the Conquering Hero Come'. On that occasion, Wilhelm was in Jerusalem also for the dedication of the Dormition Abbey, placed on Mount Zion and on land given by the Sultan, partly in recognition of German industrial assistance in the building of the Anatolian railway line.[109] Shortly before his trip to Jerusalem, the Kaiser had visited the Pope, and he made over the Dormition to the German Catholic community, and promised to support German Christians of all persuasions – a politically loaded attempt to muscle in on the long disagreement between the French and the Russians over rights of protecting pilgrims.[110] The Emperor made a characteristically bombastic speech: 'From Jerusalem there came the light in the splendour of which the German nation has become great...'[111] This is architecture as politics. Architecture – and spectacle: when Wilhelm approached Jerusalem, the wall by the side of the Jaffa Gate had been flattened to allow his wife's car to enter, and to let him ride in on horseback. On his white horse, he entered the city dressed as a Crusader – a piece of pomp which G. K. Chesterton called 'a mixture of madness and vulgarity which literally stops the breath'.[112] *The Times* had no doubt about the import of this trip: 'His pilgrimage to Palestine is invested politically with [the] most significant international character,' it argued. 'The influence of German finance and German commerce in the East has

---

[108] *Cologne Gazette*, quoted in the *The Times* (2 November 1898), 5; the second tower referred to is the Augusta Victoria, not finished till 1910.

[109] See Gregor Schöllgen, *Imperialismus und Gleichgewicht: Deutschland, England und die orientalische Frage 1871–1914* (Munich, 1984), pp. 38–49.

[110] *The Times*, 3 November 1898, 3. More than thirty articles and notices of the Kaiser's trip were published in *The Times* alone in 1898: it was a major political spectacle. *The Times* concluded (23 November [1898], 8): 'the Emperor's visit has brought anything but peace to the Holy City'. Thomas Kohut, *Wilhelm II and the Germans: A Study in Leadership* (Oxford, 1991), p. 145 states that such trips 'were theatrical epics whose political significance was limited to the negative reaction they produced in foreign capitals'; but this underplays Germany's relationship with Turkey.

[111] Speech reported in *The Times*, (2 November 1898), 5. On the speeches see Christopher Clark, *Kaiser Wilhelm II: A Life in Power* (London, 2000) especially pp. 123–85 on foreign policy and self-presentation of the Kaiser. For positive Arabic responses, see Abdel-Raouf Sinno, 'The Emperor's Journey to the East as Reflected in Contemporary Arab Journalism', in Hélène Sader, Thomas Scheffler and Angelika Neuwirth, eds., *Image and Monument: Baalbek 1898–1998* (Beirut, 1998), pp. 115–36.

[112] G. K. Chesterton, *The New Jerusalem* (London, 1920), p. 182 (Chesterton's discussions in this book are marred by some unpleasant anti-Semitism). For pictures of the Kaiser's entrance see Landau, *Abdul-Hamid's Palestine*, pp. 54–7.

mightily increased.' England knew it was watching 'the advance of Teutonic power and influence in the East'.[113] Indeed, at home the Kaiser's welcome was 'like a triumphant return from military campaign'.[114] In 1914, however, a crowd in Constantinople cheered the Kaiser as an 'ally of Islam', and even if German policy in the Middle East remained confused (and the engagement of academics in the process conflicted), the British felt they had good cause to be worried: the Kaiser hoped to 'set the entire Mohammedan world aflame in wild uprising' against the British and French.[115] For the British in particular, the Empire's huge Muslim population made this a significant threat. When General Allenby (1861–1936) walked into Jerusalem in 1917, to take control for the British, it was explicitly seen by the British Government and the newspapers as a counter-gesture to the Kaiser's bombastic entrance on horseback nineteen years earlier – a gesture scripted by Mark Sykes for the cabinet with a careful eye on Muslim response.[116] As the First World War approached, Jerusalem was discovered as a political stage for competition in architecture and spectacle. And as a site for war between the major powers.

Conclusion

Jerusalem is different from the other cities in this book in housing significant, time-honoured Holy Places of three religions, integrated into the fabric of the city, so that the whole city, as a living urban environment, becomes the object of concern. This results in an overlap of archaeological discovery – with its passion to prove the veracity of the biblical narratives – with tourism or pilgrimage, on the one hand, and with the politics of Restorationism and the idealism of Victorian urban planning, on the

---

[113] *The Times* (28 October 1898), 5.
[114] Thomas Scheffler, 'The Kaiser in Baalbek: Tourism, Archaeology, and the Politics of Imagination', in Sader et al., eds., *Image and Monument*, pp. 16–17, 31–32; Sinno, 'The Emperor's Journey', 125.
[115] Gottfried Hagen, 'German Heralds of Holy War: Orientalists and Applied Oriental Studies', *Comparative Studies of South Asia, Africa, and the Middle East*, 24 (2004), 145, 148. See Ulrich Trumpener, *Germany and the Ottoman Empire, 1914–1918* (Princeton, NJ, 1968); Frank Weber, *Eagles on the Crescent: Germany, Austria, and the Diplomacy of the Turkish Alliance, 1914–1918* (Ithaca, NY, 1970); Margaret Lavinia Anderson, '"Down in Turkey, Far Away": Human Rights, the Armenian Massacres, and Orientalism in Wilhelmine Germany', *Journal of Modern History*, 79 (2007), 80–111; and generally Robert Irwin, *Dangerous Knowledge: Orientalism and its Discontents* (New York, 2006) and Suzanne Marchand, *German Orientalism in the Age of Empire: Religion, Race, and Scholarship* (Cambridge, 2009), especially p. 335.
[116] See Bar-Yosef, *Holy Land*.

other. Unlike in other sites, in Jerusalem possession or jurisdiction matters, historically, politically, and religiously – and spiritual and material ownership is often bitterly contested. The long history of warring over Jerusalem, and imagining the Holy City, gives a cultural depth to these struggles, which is lacking in sites which were not discovered until the nineteenth century, such as Pithom and Sodom. In the latter years of the century, the imperialism inherent in biblical archaeology, which always brings together nationalism with the normative claims of heritage, found form in competitive nationalist building projects and political displays, which further reframe the search for biblical history and the expression of religious identity.

For the Victorians, discovering Jerusalem in these different ways, the Holy City insistently highlights the gap between idealism and reality; both between what a city could be and how it painfully turned out to be, and, more sharply perhaps, between what the Holy City of religious hope promised to be and how everyday life in Jerusalem challenged such expectations. As such, Jerusalem vividly focuses the question of how religious and urban life interact. Victorian social and religious thinkers debated how the difficulties of existing in the industrial urban centres of Western Europe threatened the structures and experience of a religious life. Were such debates transferable to the religious centre of Jerusalem? Was Jerusalem a city like any other which could be mapped, improved and re-organised in a more sanitary way? Or was it a city whose historical and religious significance required recognition of how the past informs the present? Negotiating the tensions between these perspectives brought Victorians face to face with the exigencies of a historical and religious self-consciousness. The discovery of Jerusalem was an intense performance of the awkward and contested space between their religious ideals and their ideas of the city.

3 | Nineveh

TIMOTHY LARSEN

In the middle of the nineteenth century, the English adventurer Austen Henry Layard (1817–94) uncovered parts of several ancient, buried Assyrian cities, including the capital, Nineveh, and dragged sizeable bits of them back to the British Museum (Fig. 3.1). His first book on his travels and discoveries, *Nineveh and its Remains: With an Account of a Visit to the Chaldean Christians of Kurdistan, and the Yezidis, or Devil-Worshippers; and an Enquiry into the Manner and Arts of the Ancient Assyrians* (1849), was a Victorian sensation and a triumphant bestseller for many years. The review in *Bentley's Miscellany* can serve to capture the effusiveness of the public response:

It is very rarely – once or twice it may be in a century – that a work of this high character is brought before us ... like a brilliant and unlooked-for comet, it has suddenly burst into view, arousing and astonishing, commanding our attention and claiming our admiration ... Of a book of this description, recounting labours so great, and discoveries so important, it would be difficult to speak in any moderate terms of praise. Its chief subject is one which is in itself of the most exciting interest, and that interest is, if possible, increased by Mr. Layard's lively manner of treating it and all its accessories ... never was any man's triumph over difficulties more complete – never were discoveries made of greater interest and importance, and never were honour and recompense from his countrymen by any one more richly merited ...[1]

Looking back four years later, *Fraser's Magazine* did not think this extraordinary reaction had been overblown: 'we cannot wonder that the rediscovered Nineveh attracted the notice of busy England in a busy time, and that the wondrous tale gained a hearing even among the rumours of external war and the tumults of domestic peace. Everybody read and talked of Layard.'[2] His publisher, John Murray, had his already optimistic view of

---

[1] *Bentley's Miscellany* 25 (1849), 436–9. An earlier version of this article was published as Timothy Larsen, 'Austen Henry Layard's Nineveh: The Bible and Archaeology in Victorian Britain', *Journal of Religious History*, 33 (2009), 66–81.
[2] 'Layard's Second Visit to Nineveh', *Fraser's Magazine*, 47 (1853), 434–44.

Figure 3.1 *Lowering the Great Winged Bull*

the book's prospects greatly exceeded. He wrote to Layard when the book had been in print for almost year:

> Your discoveries & all your proceedings continue to be regarded with the greatest interest in all parts of the Kingdom. I myself last Autumn was one of a numerous congregation assembled in a *Free Kirk* in a small Scotch village called Fairly – on the shore of the Firth of Clyde near Largs – who listened with the greatest interest to a lecture delivered by the minister upon you & your discoveries & the same thing has gone on in countless obscure places. Scharf has lectured on Nineveh at Liverpool & is projecting an itinerant 2ry course in the manufacturing districts.[3]

In March 1850, Layard reported to E. L. Mitford, his original travelling companion on the journey that eventually led to his discoveries: 'Nearly 8000 copies were sold in the year – a new edition is in the press, and Murray anticipates a continual steady demand for the book, which will place it side by side with Mrs Rundell's Cookery.'[4] From this one book, Layard made the

---

[3] John Murray to A. H. Layard, 17 December 1850, Austen Henry Layard Papers, Add. MS 38979, British Library, London.

[4] William N. Bruce, ed., *Sir A. Henry Layard, GCB, DCL, Autobiography and Letters from his Childhood until his Appointment as HM Ambassador at Madrid, with a Chapter on his Parliamentary Career by the Rt. Hon. Sir Arthur Otway* (2 vols., London, 1903), II, p. 91.

extraordinary sum of £1,500 per annum for some years.[5] Moreover, a cheaper, one-volume version entitled *A Popular Account of Discoveries at Nineveh*, came out in 1851 and sold almost 12,000 copies in just over a year. Frederick N. Bohrer has observed, 'Austen Henry Layard's *Nineveh and Its Remains* of 1849 still ranks as the greatest bestseller in the history of its field.'[6] Indeed, it created a genre that continued long after in such volumes as Heinrich Schliemann's *Troy and its Remains* (1875) and M. E. L. Mallowan's *Nimrud and its Remains* (1966).

Nineveh was a city familiar to every literate Briton in an age when the Bible was not just an aid to devotion but a school textbook.[7] As Nineveh was a city that played an important part in the biblical drama, its place in people's minds was not only assured but also frequently reinforced in public and private Bible reading, in sermons and beyond. The Assyrian capital was primarily evoked as an image of God's judgment. Moreover, Nineveh was distinct from other cities that also served this function such as Babylon and Tyre in that the book of Jonah recounted an earlier occasion when this city was granted a reprieve from impending destruction in response to repentance. This more hopeful possibility made Nineveh an apt theme for fast-day sermons.[8] Still, the city's ultimate doom underlined what could happen if repentance was not forthcoming. 'The fall of Nineveh' was a standard theme, expressed not only in explicitly religious contexts, but also cultural ones: Edwin Atherstone's epic poem and *magnum opus* of that title appeared in parts from 1828 until it was published complete in thirty books in 1847.[9] Likewise in 1828, the painter John Martin (1789–1854) produced his most ambitious work on an Old Testament theme, also entitled *The Fall of Nineveh*.

Martin's bravado notwithstanding, most early nineteenth-century Britons could not visualise Nineveh. This set it apart from many other biblical and classical locations, not least cities such as Jerusalem, Athens and Rome. *The Bible Cyclopaedia* (1843) was often able to provide sketches

---

[5] George Paston, *At John Murray's: Records of a Literary Circle, 1843–1892* (London, 1932), p. 78.
[6] Frederick N. Bohrer, 'The Printed Orient: The Production of A. H. Layard's Earliest Works', *Culture and History*, 11 (1992), 85–105. See also Frederick N. Bohrer, *Orientalism and Visual Culture: Imagining Mesopotamia in Nineteenth-Century Europe* (Cambridge, 2003); Julian Reade, 'Layard's *Nineveh and its Remains*', *Antiquity*, 72 (1998), 913–16.
[7] For an exploration of this theme, see Timothy Larsen, *A People of One Book: The Bible and the Victorians* (Oxford, 2011).
[8] See, for examples, George Greig, *God's Expostulation with Nineveh: A Sermon* (London, 1806); John Edward, *The Men of Nineveh and the Men of England: A Sermon* (Oxford, 1855).
[9] Edwin Atherstone, *The Fall of Nineveh: A Poem* (London, 1847).

even of urban areas that had only a minor and fleeting presence in the Scriptures, such as Miletus and Mitylene, but when it came to the entry on 'that great city' it was forced to concede at the outset that the 'exact spot where Nineveh stood cannot now be ascertained' and to offer an illustration which was not one of monumental grandeur but merely a natural landscape.[10] Material remains served a didactic and apologetic purpose in Christian instruction: they could often reinforce the veracity of biblical accounts in people's minds in surprisingly powerful ways. The Unitarian educator, Mary Carpenter (1807–77), for example, recounted that when she taught 'the history of Joseph' to reformatory school boys: 'They all found a difficulty in realizing that this had really occurred.' This scepticism was completely dispelled when she showed them a picture of a pyramid.[11] Before Layard, no accurate illustrations of Nineveh could be produced, giving the city a faint air of unreality.

Moreover, the charge of unreality was being made against the Bible as a whole. The eighteenth-century deists had deemed various parts of the Scriptures unhistorical. This critical discourse culminated in Thomas Paine's *The Age of Reason* (1793), which systematically marched its way through the canon, purportedly discrediting each book in turn. In Germany, a more erudite critical scholarship arose which also challenged the veracity of many parts of the Scriptures. Both British popular radicals and German critics tended to allow grand theories to sweep history clean away. For instance, it was not uncommon for English infidels to deny that Jesus of Nazareth had ever existed, but rather to claim that he was merely a mythological personification of the sun.[12] The self-proclaimed infidel Robert Cooper asserted that there was no nation of Israel in the ancient world, but this was merely a literary fraud perpetrated by later Jews (discoveries at Nineveh would decisively disprove this).[13] Although German scholarship was not usually so extravagant, it often headed in the same direction. In the very year that Layard was excavating Nineveh, 1846, the English translation of David Friedrich Strauss's *Leben Jesu* by Marian Evans appeared, a work that did not deny the existence of a historical Jesus but reinterpreted virtually everything the gospels record that he did or said as mythological rather than historical. In short, by the 1840s the English public had become used to clever theories that denied the veracity of the Bible as a

---

[10] William Goodhugh, *The Bible Cyclopaedia* (2 vols., London, 1841), II, pp. 941–4.
[11] Mary Carpenter, *Reformatory Schools* (London, 1851), p. 96.
[12] A seminal text for this line of reasoning was Robert Taylor, *The Diegesis: Being a Discovery of the Origin, Evidences, and Early History of Christianity* (1829; London, 1834).
[13] Robert Cooper, *The Infidel's Text Book* (Hull, 1846), p. 4.

historical narrative. It was over this horizon that Layard's brilliant, unlooked-for comet came into view.

Before Nineveh, Layard had been a man with scant prospects. His father, who had not been well enough to live in England for most of Layard's childhood, died when Layard was seventeen. Deprived of a university education, Layard, with the aid of his uncle, Benjamin Austen, had trained to be a solicitor in London, but finding himself chafing against such work, had set off on his eastern travels with a vague plan to try again in Ceylon, where another uncle lived. Along the way, he impressed Sir Stratford Canning (1786–1880), the British ambassador in Constantinople, and this led on to Canning privately helping to fund Layard's scheme to dig for antiquities in the large mounds near Mosul. *Nineveh and its Remains* was the turning point. In 1852, Layard began a parliamentary career, being made a privy councillor in 1868, and then going on to serve as British ambassador at Madrid, and later at Constantinople. The honours conferred upon him began with an honorary doctorate (DCL) from Oxford University in 1848 and the Royal Geographical Society's gold medal in 1849, and culminated in his being knighted (GCB) by the Queen in 1878.[14] A wag quipped that actually it was Nineveh that had discovered Layard. The British Library catalogue aptly identifies Sir Austen Henry Layard with the descriptive phrase, 'discoverer of Nineveh, etc.'.

'His hidden testimonies': Nineveh and prophecy

The popular perception that Layard had discovered fresh material to illuminate the Old Testament and perhaps to confirm its veracity is consequently vital in explaining the reception of *Nineveh and its Remains*. Layard fuelled such thinking at specific points in his text. From the very beginning, he was convinced that the images he was seeing on the long-buried walls of an Assyrian palace were ones that had informed the thinking of the prophet Ezekiel. Layard wrote to his mother during his original excavations:

Ezekiel, who wrote from the Hebrew settlements on the banks of the Chebar, either the Khabour of Mesopotamia, [or] another river of the same name which runs into the Tigris at a short distance from Mosul, appears continually to have had the sculptures of the Assyrians or Chaldeans in his eye when he made his prophesies. I am much inclined to suspect that the figures of his vision are suggested to some measure by them. And that various passages in the 23 Chap: (14 & 15) are exact

---

[14] The standard biography is Gordon Waterfield, *Layard of Nineveh* (London, 1963).

descriptions of the bas reliefs of Nimroud. There are many other passages of the same kind in this book. Ezekiel probably saw the Assryo-Chaldean palaces in their glory before their destruction by the combined armies of Media & Bablyonia, and from the remains which exist one need not be surprised at the impression which their vastness and magnificence made upon him.[15]

This argument, and even some of the precise wording, reappeared in *Nineveh and its Remains*.[16] Layard was so impressed with this connection that he quoted Ezekiel 23:14–15 on the title page. Nor was the implication lost on readers. The *British Quarterly Review*, an evangelical nonconformist journal, quoted this passage and then drew the conclusion that the reliability of a biblical author had been decisively established: 'Now, Mr. Layard, having minutely investigated the details, informs his readers that the language of the prophet "illustrates the base-reliefs of Nimroud." What better proof of the trustworthiness of a writer can be desired or found?'[17]

Even more remarkably, Layard argued that the claim in Jonah 3:3 that Nineveh 'was an exceeding great city of three days' journey' was literally accurate. In such a reckoning, the city swells to a fantastical size. In order to make this work, Layard asserted that four separate Assyrian cities were all manifestations of one gargantuan metropolis:

The city had now attained the dimensions assigned to it by the Book of Jonah, and by Diodorus Siculus. If we take the four great mounds of Nimroud, Kouyunjik, Khorsabad, and Karamles, as the corners of a square, it will be found that its four sides correspond pretty accurately with the 480 stadia, or 60 miles of the geographer, which make the three days' journey of the prophet ... Twenty miles is the day's journey of the East, and we have consequently the three days' journey of Jonah for the circumference of the city. The agreement of these measurements is remarkable.[18]

A few years later, the cuneiform script would be deciphered and this speculation would be decisively disproved, but at the time many reviewers reported it hopefully.[19] Henry Hart Milman (1791–1868), writing in the *Quarterly Review*, went so far as to seek to gain credit for having thought of

---

[15] A. H. Layard to his mother, Nimroud, 21 April 1846, Austen Henry Layard Papers, Add. MS 58150, British Library, London.
[16] A. H. Layard, *Nineveh and its Remains: With an Account of a Visit to the Chaldaean Christians of Kurdistan, and the Yezidis, or Devil-Worshippers; and an Enquiry into the Manner and Arts of the Ancient Assyrians* (2 vols., London, 1849), II, pp. 307–9, see also II, pp. 464–5.
[17] [John Relly Beard], 'Nineveh and the Bible', *British Quarterly Review*, 9 (1849), 399–442.
[18] Layard, *Nineveh*, II, p. 247.
[19] For an example of a short review that presented this point, see *Christian Witness*, 6 (1849), 232–4.

this solution himself and to assert that it seemed to be the only hypothesis that accounted for all the facts.[20]

Layard's *Nineveh* was sprinkled with footnotes citing biblical passages and he made numerous connections between the Assyrian objects that he had found and various scriptural texts. Instead of taking a more sceptical approach, as German critical scholars and English freethinkers were doing, his comments on portions of the Old Testament such as the books of Jonah, Esther and Daniel read as if Layard assumed that these biblical characters were historical figures from the places and time periods assigned to them in these stories. His excavations also dramatically brought home the fact that these cities were indeed destroyed just as the prophets had foretold – a point that had profound resonance for many readers. The *General Baptist Repository and Missionary Observer* began its review:

> The great capital of the Assyrian empire, the early history of which appears to be shrouded in impenetrable obscurity, has now slumbered in the dust over two thousand years. The predictions respecting it, uttered by the prophets of Israel, when Nineveh was at the height of its glory, have been literally fulfilled. Twenty-five centuries have proved the Divine origin of those prophecies. Tradition, only, marks the site of the great Assyrian city ...[21]

One might say that Layard dug up Nineveh and confirmed that it was a desolation. For an encore, he went down to Babylon and verified that she had indeed fallen.[22]

For Layard's friend, Miner Kellogg (1814–89), his work was ushering in the millennial reign of Christ:

> You can scarcely *dream* of the importance which your solitary labours may have upon the right understanding of the Historical & Prophetical parts of the Holy Word ... From this state of Idolatry, came forth the Heathen Mythology, which was overthrown by the Christian doctrine, which doctrine is to be fully revealed in the *Second* Coming of the Lord, that is, when the *internal meaning* of His Word will be manifested to every eye. And this last and glorious state of things is to be brought about only by a knowledge of the *true meaning* of the Sacred Scriptures, through this Doctrine of correspondences, agreeable to which they were written, and agreeable in every particular, 'jot and tittle'. To this end John was commanded not to '*seal* the words of the prophecy of this Book,' for the 'time, (of state of the world) was at

---

[20] [Henry Hart Milman], 'Nineveh and its Remains', *Quarterly Review*, 84 (1848), 112.
[21] 'Nineveh and its Remains', *General Baptist Repository and Missionary Observer*, 12 (1850), 360–2.
[22] A. H. Layard, *Discoveries in the Ruins of Nineveh and Babylon: With Travels in Armenia, Kurdistan, and the Desert: Being the Result of a Second Expedition Undertaken for the Trustees of the British Museum* (London, 1853).

hand,' when it would be necessary that it should be opened for the good of mankind. I believe that state *has arrived*, and this is one great reason for the interest I take in what you are doing . . .[23]

The *Quarterly Journal of Prophecy* gave a whole catalogue of ingenious close readings of the Hebrew prophets in the light of Layard's discoveries, concluding triumphantly:

Jehovah is *strengthening faith in the prophetic word*, among His living ones: for if all has so accurately, faithfully, truthfully, literally, come to pass that was foretold of Nineveh, shall any word of His mouth ever fail? If such apparent contradictions as that Nineveh should be 'dry as a wilderness,' 'empty and waste,' yet also a place for 'flocks of the nations to lie down,' are easily seen to be both alike equally true, when the facts are known, shall we not be confident that thus it shall yet be with all obscure portions of unfulfilled prophecy? . . . The Lord himself, unalarmed at the taunts and scoffs of infidels, in His due time brings out to light His hidden testimonies, such as those stirred up from the wreck of Nineveh . . .[24]

The man of science, David Brewster (1781–1868), writing in the *North British Review*, succumbed to the wildest fantasies about what stories from the Bible might be confirmed by the findings of future archaeologists:

The *first* city – the city of Enoch may yet be surveyed, in stone or in dust, beneath some nameless heap, where the Armenian shepherd now feeds his flocks; and the brass and iron utensils of Tubal-cain may yet exhibit to us the infant ingenuity of our race. The planks of Gopher-wood which floated Noah over the universe of waters may yet rise from the flanks or the base of Ararat in lignite or in coal; and the *first* altar – that which Noah 'builded' to his Maker and Preserver, may yet be thrown up from its burying-place by the mighty earthquakes that shake the plain of Araxes.[25]

The *British Quarterly Review* proclaimed enthusiastically that here was proof that 'original German and borrowed English rationalism' had not succeeded in calling into question the truthfulness of the Scriptures: 'Is the Bible wrong? and are Voltaire and his school right? Let Mr. Layard decide.'[26] These quotations will suffice, but they are only a few of the chorus of voices that proclaimed that Layard's findings had given support to the cause of the Bible and the Christian faith.

---

[23] Miner Kellogg to A. H. Layard, Florence, 24 May 1846, Austen Henry Layard Papers, Add. MS 38976, British Library, London.
[24] 'Nineveh and Nahum', *Quarterly Journal of Prophecy*, 2 (1850), 170–83.
[25] [David Brewster], 'Layard's *Nineveh and its Remains*', *North British Review*, 11 (1849), 111–35.
[26] [Beard], 'Nineveh', 414, 417–18.

Figure 3.2 Sculpted relief

Layard's book also led on to numerous other volumes along these lines, one of the most popular being Joseph Bonomi's *Nineveh and its Palaces: The Discoveries of Botta and Layard, Applied to the Elucidation of Holy Writ* (1852).[27] At the top of the first page of the first chapter of this volume was an illustration of one of the lions with wings and a human head that Layard had uncovered (Fig. 3.2). Its caption was simply a verse of Scripture: 'The first was like a lion, and had eagle's wings' (Daniel 7:4). If a picture of a pyramid could reinforce the historicity of the Bible, this kind of astonishing exactitude about such a specific, fantastical image did so tenfold. The story of the discipline of Assyriology is generally told as a long struggle to get out from underneath a preoccupation with the Hebrew Scriptures.[28] P. R. S. Moorey (1937–2004), then Keeper of Antiquities, the Ashmolean Museum, Oxford,

---

[27] Joseph Bonomi, *Nineveh and its Palaces: The Discoveries of Botta and Layard, Applied to the Elucidation of Holy Writ* (London, 1852).

[28] Mogens Trolle Larsen, *The Conquest of Assyria: Excavations in an Antique Land, 1840–1860* (London, 1996), p. xi. See also a thinly researched, highly opinionated, and rather misnamed study, Phillip A. Kildahl, 'British and American Reactions to Layard's Discoveries in Assyria (1845–1860)' (Ph.D. thesis, University of Minnesota, 1959).

observed that 'it is the urge to prove the Bible right that has done so much to compromise Old Testament archaeology for generations'.[29] Although the story of the Bible in the nineteenth century is usually told as one in which confidence in the accuracy of Scripture was eroded by higher criticism, the conviction of many people that archaeological evidence had actually vindicated the Bible is often not given sufficient weight or attention.[30]

'An Arabian tale of wonders'

The fascination that *Nineveh and its Remains* exerted on its readers was not just apologetic but romantic. It delighted them as a tale of travels, adventures and the curious ways of foreigners. The *North British Review* proclaimed that Layard still had enough material for 'an interesting work, even if the ruins of Nineveh had never been mentioned'.[31] While this aspect will not be laboured in this chapter, it looms large in the book. Layard's anecdotes include, for example, the time when he recovered some stolen goods by making a daring raid on a Bedouin encampment. Against overwhelming odds, he and just a few men managed to kidnap the tribe's sheikh and hold him until Layard's property was restored. The appeal of this aspect of the book may be illustrated by a life of Layard written for juvenile readers that was published not long after his death, Alfred E. Lomax, *Sir Henry Layard: His Adventures and Discoveries* (1896).[32] The Sunday School Union being the book's publisher notwithstanding, religious aspects were ignored altogether. Layard's own religion is so disregarded that one cannot even tell whether he was a Christian, and the biblical implications of his discoveries are confined to literally one sentence – a sentence in which it is not claimed that they provided any confirmation or proof, but only that they offered material that gave 'fresh illustrations of Scripture and prophecy'.[33] Moreover, almost the whole book is taken up with Layard's adventures. The book is 144 pages long and Layard does not even start digging until

---

[29] P. R. S. Moorey, *A Century of Biblical Archaeology* (Louisville, KY, 1991), p. 171. See also, Thomas W. Davis, *Shifting Sands: The Rise and Fall of Biblical Archaeology* (Oxford, 2004).

[30] An example of the standard focus on higher criticism is John Rogerson, *Old Testament Criticism in the Nineteenth Century: England and Germany* (London, 1984). For a study set later in the century that explores the perception that archaeology had proved the Bible true, see Barbara Zink MacHaffie, '"Monument Facts and Higher Critical Fancies": Archaeology and the Popularization of Old Testament Criticism in Nineteenth-Century Britain', *Church History*, 50 (1981), 316–28.

[31] [Brewster], 'Layard's *Nineveh*', 132.

[32] Alfred E. Lomax, *Sir Henry Layard: His Adventures and Discoveries* (London, 1896).

[33] Ibid., p. 137.

page 129. The three chapters before the discoveries at Nineveh (which are covered in the penultimate chapter) are entitled, 'The Wild Tribes of Bakhtiyari', 'Adventures among the Mountains', and 'Further Adventures in the Desert'. It is important to bear in mind that the various facets of *Nineveh and its Remains* were often appealing to the same readers – that figures who were specialists in areas of secular knowledge were also fascinated by biblical connections and pious church people also liked to read of the intrepidity of a romantic hero who came dressed up in Byron's romantic garments (Fig. 3.3). The eminent biblical scholar, Edward Robinson (1794–1863), wrote of *Nineveh and its Remains*, 'It has been truly said, that the narrative is like a romance. In its incidents and descriptions it does indeed remind one continually of an Arabian tale of wonders and genii.'[34]

Robinson, however, was an American – as was Layard's enthusiastic friend, Kellogg. In Layard's home country, there was the more specific appeal of national pride. Many people commented that Layard's findings brought glory to Britain – or even that it was a quintessentially British achievement. Lord Ellesmere wrote a private letter praising Layard in February 1849 which was eventually passed along to Lord Palmerston: 'He is one of those men of whom England seems to have a monopoly, who go anywhere, surmount anything and achieve everything without assistance, patronage or fuss of any kind.'[35] *Chambers's Edinburgh Journal* declared that: 'It was reserved for British enterprise, within the last four years, to turn the darkness which had settled on this subject into something like light.'[36]

A specific foil in this context was the nation's historic rival, France. The French Vice-Consul at Mosul, Paolo Emilio Botta (1802–70), had first dug up Assyrian antiquities in 1843, and thus the initial glory went to France. Layard's endeavours, however, met with far greater success. Already in April 1846, Canning, in a letter to Sir Robert Peel, held out this tempting possibility: 'If the excavation keeps its promise to the end there is much reason to hope that Montagu House [the British Museum] will beat the Louvre hollow.'[37] The reviewers were not above gloating about it. The *Christian Observer*, for example, reported in regard to one of Layard's

---

[34] A. H. Layard, *Nineveh and its Remains: With an Account of a Visit to the Chaldaean Christians of Kurdistan, and the Yezidis, or Devil-Worshippers; and an Enquiry into the Manner and Arts of the Ancient Assyrians*, with an introductory note by Edward Robinson (New York, 1852), p. iv.
[35] Waterfield, *Layard*, p. 194.
[36] 'Remains of Nineveh', *Chambers's Edinburgh Journal*, 11 (1849), 56–60.
[37] Stanley Lane-Poole, *The Life of the Right Honourable Stratford Canning Viscount Stratford De Redcliffe* (2 vols., London, 1888), II, p. 149.

Figure 3.3 Henry Phillips, *Austen Henry Layard in Albanian Dress*

most important finds: 'The obelisk, for which the French Government offered £10,000, is deposited in the British Museum.'[38] More generally, Layard's Nineveh Court was a prominent and well-received part of that huge celebration of British achievement, the Crystal Palace, created for the Great Exhibition of 1851.[39] The opening paragraph describing the Nineveh Court in an official guidebook captures well the way that it fused national and religious exuberance:

The Nineveh Court; a restoration of one of the Halls of a Palace of the ancient Assyrian kings. The sudden recovery of these relics of an empire and a civilization long since deemed entirely lost, is one of the most marvellous stories of our time, and, indeed, is equal to a romance for strangeness and interest. It is more than this. That treasures of such incalculable significance in the history of the world should have remained hidden from the rude inhabitants of the country, whose only act, had they known them, would have been to destroy them, and have been discovered in such admirable preservation by those best able to appreciate them, and most keenly desirous to sift to the bottom their precious contents, is indeed more than romantic; it is providential.[40]

There is also much in the reception of *Nineveh and its Remains* that reveals that the British prided themselves in their presumed superiority to the various peoples that Layard encountered in his eastern travels.[41] *Hogg's Instructor* became carried away with a messianic vision for the British race: 'the sun of civilisation shall surely rise again in the east, and the Anglo-Saxon shall yet build his towers where Belshazzar feasted, and shall launch his bark upon the rivers of Eden'.[42] Mogens Trolle Larsen has astutely observed how European studies of these ancient cultures, by privileging themselves as the *telos* of the story of civilization, were the 'stepchildren of imperialism'.[43] Reviewers, moreover, were not always content to leave such realities implicit to be teased out by later scholars. Most notably, *Fraser's Magazine* declared bluntly that 'to recultivate the waste, to repair the havoc of centuries, to succour the oppressed, to civilize the barbarous, to make truth and justice supreme in the place of rapine and fraud – this is an imperial work, and worthy of England. Meanwhile, Mr. Layard and such as he are the *avant-couriers* of the new crusade.'[44]

---

[38] 'Review of Layard's *Nineveh*', *Christian Observer*, 49 (1849), 532–48, 604–15.
[39] A. H. Layard, *The Nineveh Court in the Crystal Palace* (London, 1854).
[40] *The Crystal Palace Penny Guide, By Authority of the Directors* (London, 1864), p. 4.
[41] There is one passing reference to Layard in Edward W. Said, *Orientalism* (1978; New York, 1994), p. 195.
[42] *Hogg's Instructor,* 3 (1849), 92.   [43] M. T. Larsen, *Conquest*, p. xii.
[44] 'Layard's Second Visit', 440.

Layard and his admirers fondly alleged that it had taken the British to value and explicate remains that had baffled Arabs and Turks. Layard, in both his book and his private correspondence, spoke of the 'ridiculous notions' of locals that he was hunting for treasure.[45] Twice in *Nineveh and its Remains*, Layard underlines this point by scenes in which he amazes local authorities with the casual declaration that they can have any gold he finds. These smug self-assessments were not only ethnocentric; they were also overdrawn. Heinrich Schliemann (1822–90), whose exploits at Hisarlik were discussed in Gange and Bryant Davies's chapter, did find gold when excavating Troy and rather than hand it over to the Turkish authorities he smuggled it out of the country. Western minds were not above dreams of treasure. Stewart Erskine Rolland (d. 1881), who worked on Layard's second excavation, alluringly reported in a letter printed in *The Times* regarding Layard's recent finds: 'an immense variety of ivory ornaments, an iron axe-head, and innumerable other articles, which for the present I must forbear to mention, having promised secrecy ... all sorts of buried treasure may lie within his reach'.[46] More broadly, from today's perspective, Layard is seen precisely as what he claimed not to be, a treasure hunter. The extent of his alleged sophistication was that he could think of art treasures – even if made of stone – rather than just precious raw materials such as gold. Archaeologists today can go much further than Layard would have ever imagined: they could boast that all they want is data and documentation, and that therefore the local authorities could keep everything that they find – stones and all. By contrast, in what makes painful reading for archaeologists today, Layard cavalierly ripped through his sites on a single-minded treasure hunt for the best specimens of sculpture to take back to the British Museum. In the early days of the excavation, although he had already had the extraordinary good fortune to find an Assyrian palace, Layard recalled that – from his own vantage point – his hunt had not yet succeeded: 'still no sculptures had been discovered'.[47] *Nineveh and its Remains* recurs with statements that the exploration of buried rooms in a certain area had been stopped because they did not contain art treasures. For example: 'as no more sculptures appeared to exist, I did not think it worth while to incur additional expense in such an examination'.[48] It is safe to conclude that Layard was chiefly interested in the civic and monumental portions of the city, rather than a fully rounded picture of urban life.

---

[45] Layard to his mother, 29 November 1845: Bruce, *Autobiography*, II, p. 161.
[46] *The Times* (6 March 1850), 8.   [47] Layard, *Nineveh*, I, p. 39.   [48] Ibid., II, p. 36.

'A link in the history of art'

The recognition that Layard primarily hoped to contribute to the history of art complicates this volume's account of the biblical city in nineteenth-century culture. Layard aspired to join a world of scholars and aesthetes who did not necessarily share the biblical and apologetic enthusiasms of his broader public. The *Athenaeum* ran a series of articles on Layard's findings years before his book was published and, when it finally was, it found *Nineveh and its Remains* significant enough to continue a review over three separate issues. All of these articles were in the 'Fine Arts' section of the journal. Lord Ellesmere, who praised Layard so highly, approached these discoveries through his interest in fine art. Likewise Joseph Bonomi, although his book spoke of 'the elucidation of Holy Writ' in its very title, was trained in art rather than biblical studies, and the real focus of his book was an examination of these Assyrian objects. Miner Kellogg was also an artist. The very letter that contains his millennial exuberance begins by discussing Layard's findings in terms of 'ancient art' and ends with an account of his current painting, the subject of which was a nude figure of 'a Turkish girl reposing after a bath'.[49] From this perspective, a central question was whether the art of the Assyrians was any good, especially when compared with that of the ancient Greeks. Could the 'Nimroud Marbles' be thought of as in any way comparable to the Elgin Marbles?[50] As steeped as learned British culture was in classics, its reflexive response was against such a possibility.[51]

Layard's initial discoveries led him to concede that Assyrian art could not rival Greek, but he quickly revised this assessment. His writings take on the character of a campaign to establish the artistic merits of his finds. Indeed, Layard's real interest was unquestionably in art rather than the Bible. In order to make this case, it would be useful to begin first with his religious history and views. His family was Church of England. He spent a good part of his childhood in Italy and France and these experiences – especially bullying he received for being a Protestant as a schoolboy – contributed to the decided anti-Catholicism of his adulthood. This is expressed most clearly in *Nineveh and its Remains* through his discussion of the group he

---

[49] Miner Kellogg to A. H. Layard, Florence, 24 May 1846, Austen Henry Layard Papers, Add. MS 38976, British Library, London.
[50] 'The Nimroud Marbles' was the title of an article: *Athenaeum* (19 June 1847), 650.
[51] For these debates in the context of the British Museum, see Ian Jenkins, *Archaeologists and Aesthetes in the Sculpture Galleries of the British Museum, 1800–1939* (London, 1992).

referred to as the 'Chaldean Christians', but had hitherto been generally referred to in the West as 'Nestorians' after a Christological heresy. Layard spoke at length in the book about how this Christian group suffered from 'the persecutions of Popish emissaries' and how their worship was superior to that of the Church of Rome. He even claimed they merited the appellation, 'the Protestants of Asia'.[52] Repeatedly, British reviewers were prompted by this lead to make additional anti-Catholic statements of their own.[53] Indeed, one suspects that they were often misled into imagining that because Layard shared their antipathies he also shared their positive convictions – nothing in fact was more common than for anti-Catholicism to simultaneously serve and mask a critique of all religions.

Layard's heretical views on Christology may have predisposed him to sympathise with the Nestorians. As a young man training to be a solicitor in England, Layard had become a political and religious radical. He later recalled that these convictions were fostered through his friendship with Henry Crabb Robinson (1775–1867),

a Unitarian and what was then called 'a philosophical Radical.' He introduced me to Mr Fox, the celebrated Unitarian preacher, who then had a chapel in the city, which I frequently attended. The eloquence and powerful rhetoric of this remarkable man were a great attraction to me. His discourses and the conversation of my friend Mr Crabb Robinson rapidly undermined the religious opinions in which I had been brought up, and I soon became as independent in my religious as I had already become in my political opinions. My uncle who was supposed to look after me, and to exercise a moral control over me, was little pleased with either, as they both differed so entirely from his own. Being a Tory of the old school and a strict Churchman, he was bound to look upon them with feelings approaching to horror.[54]

William Johnson Fox (1786–1864) was so scandalous in his behaviour and radical in his thought as to be rejected by the main body of Unitarians, and thus Layard had positioned himself on the boundary line where Unitarianism crossed into free thought. Freethinkers openly scoffed at the Bible and sought actively to expose it as false.[55] The value of Holy Scripture

---

[52] Layard, *Nineveh*, I, pp. 236–69.
[53] For example, *Christian Observer*, 49 1849), 545–4; [Milman], 'Nineveh', 120; *Wesleyan Methodist Magazine*, 73 (1850), 75–6. For the wider context of British anti-Catholicism, see John Wolffe, *The Protestant Crusade in Great Britain, 1829–1860* (Oxford, 1991).
[54] Bruce, *Autobiography*, I, p. 56.
[55] See Edward Royle, *Victorian Infidels: The Origins of the British Secularist Movement* (Manchester, 1974); Timothy Larsen, *Contested Christianity: The Political and Social Contexts of Victorian Theology* (Waco, TX, 2004).

for Fox decreased to the point where he 'abandoned biblical texts for his sermons'.[56]

In fact, Layard admitted much later in life that a major prompt for his Eastern travels was that his heterodoxy had caused a rift with his uncle, Benjamin Austen, the head of the family, his employer, and hitherto the main source of his future prospects.[57] Many clues reinforce his detachment from organised, orthodox Christianity during the whole of the Nineveh period. In contrast to respectable and evangelical convention, Layard made a habit of travelling on Sundays during his Eastern sojourn and what is more pointed out that he was doing so.[58] In his unpublished journal, when he wanted to be particularly snide about the bigoted, religious zeal of a mullah, he claimed that it equalled that of 'any Evangelical preacher'.[59]

Nineveh and its Remains also titillated its readers rather than following the straight-and-narrow path of evangelical prudery. It offered a whole series of tales on unabashed public nudity, sexually blissful polygamy, readily apparent homosexuality, and even an 'entertaining' transgender narrative.[60] While some reviewers thought that Layard's findings were so timely and fortuitous as to be providential, Layard was so far removed from this trust in special providences that he called it 'superstitious'.[61] Layard attended public worship when he was with the (Nestorian) Chaldean Christians. His companion received communion, but Layard pointedly declined, explaining to his offended hosts that: 'I did not refuse from any religious prejudice.'[62] We might see in this a radical Unitarian's objection to sacraments of any kind, rather than to the validity of those dispensed by these so-called Nestorians in particular. It would certainly fit with other evidence of his hostility to the sacraments. In 1850, he wrote a letter to Maria Antoinetta Gordon, Countess of Aboyne, declining her invitation to become a godfather to her newborn son. Layard argued that as she took the religious aspect of this function seriously, he would be bound to disappoint her: he was not 'capable of discharging its duties' as 'my opinions on religious subjects differ very materially from those generally professed in England'.[63] This might be contrasted with a passage in *Nineveh and its Remains* on his time among the Yezidis, in which he playfully revealed that

---

[56] H. C. G. Matthew and Brian Harrison, eds., *Oxford Dictionary of National Biography* (60 vols., Oxford, 2004), XX, p. 690.
[57] Bruce, *Autobiography*, I, p. 103. [58] See, for examples, ibid., I, pp. 114, 159.
[59] A. H. Layard, *Nineveh and its Remains*, ed. H. W. F. Saggs (New York, 1970), p. 19.
[60] Ibid., I, pp. 99–100, 218, 280, 364; II, pp. 329–33. [61] Ibid., II, p. 145. [62] Ibid., I, p. 201.
[63] A. H. Layard to Maria Antoinetta Gordon, Countess of Aboyne, Baghdad, 30 December 1850, Austen Henry Layard Papers, Add. MS 38944, British Library, London.

he had consented to stand 'godfather to a devil-worshipping baby'.[64] (The Yezidis apparently had a rather dualistic view of spiritual reality that resulted in endeavours to propitiate the devil.) When he returned to the region in 1849, Layard went so far as playing at conversion to 'devil worship': 'I was allowed to be present at all the ceremonies, made a public confession of faith and was received into the bosom of the Yezidi Church.'[65] In short, Layard was far from being a stodgy Christian on a personal quest to prove the Bible true.

Art, on the other hand, is the thread that runs through every phase of Layard's eventful life. His father had been an art connoisseur, and touring galleries was a major part of Layard's childhood. By the age of twelve, he had developed a precocious ability to identify the artists of Florentine paintings. He also took drawing lessons and considered becoming an artist himself. When he crossed Europe on his way to his Eastern travels, he arranged to see picture galleries along the way. When he settled down into a successful middle age, this lifelong interest found expression in numerous ways. As ambassador in Madrid, Layard studied Spanish painting. He became a trustee not – as the main thrust of this chapter might lead one to predict – of the British Museum, but rather of the National Gallery. Indeed, his place in the world of art was such that he could write in 1865 to Lady Eastlake (1809–93), the wife of the director of the National Gallery, and recount how he had just given the painter John Everett Millais (1829–96) a tour of the Uffizi Gallery, Florence.[66] Layard developed an impressive private collection that was mentioned in travel guides in his own day and which was ultimately donated to the National Gallery. From the 1850s through the 1880s, he wrote substantial articles on art criticism for the *Quarterly Review*. He put much labour into creating a new edition, published in 1891, of Kugler's *Handbook of Painting: The Italian Schools*. He was an animating spirit of the Arundel Society, which sought to make and publish copies of Italian frescos that were in danger of being destroyed. He engaged in this laborious work personally, just as he had done the arduous work of Assyrian excavations, and justified them both in the same way: 'It is very important as a link in the history of Art.'[67]

---

[64] Layard, *Nineveh*, I, p. 274. [65] Waterfield, *Layard*, p. 200.
[66] Bruce, *Autobiography*, II, p. 230. This source is very good on Layard's interest in art and the other facts mentioned in this paragraph may generally be found in it.
[67] Bruce, *Autobiography*, II, p. 221. Layard made this comment about his fresco copying in a letter written in 1858. For his framing of his Assyrian findings in the same terms, see Layard, *Nineveh*, II, p. 288.

Art was Layard's primary intellectual interest in Assyriology. Layard's earliest public voice on this matter – a published letter on Botta's findings – made no mention of any biblical implications, but rather focused enthusiastically on the artistic ones:

To those who have been accustomed to look upon the Greeks as the true perfectors and the only masters of the imitative arts, they will furnish new matter for inquiry and reflection ... they are immeasurably superior to the stiff and ill-proportioned figures of the monuments of the Pharoahs [*sic.*] ... The extreme beauty and elegance of the various objects introduced among the groups are next to be admired ... all designed with the most consummate taste, and rival the productions of the most cultivated period of Greek art.[68]

Conservative biblical scholars today often speak of Assyriology as part of a field that they call 'Ancient Near Eastern Backgrounds' – that is, the Bible is in the foreground and ancient Mesopotamia provides a context for some of its contents. Although Layard refers to biblical passages often in *Nineveh and its Remains*, a careful inspection of these citations reveals that he is actually doing the reverse of Ancient Near East backgrounds. His primary concern is the objects he has found – they are in the foreground – and the Bible is a source that might illuminate them. Thus he writes tellingly: 'Ezekiel, in prophesying the destruction of Tyre by Nebuchadnezzar, has faithfully recorded the events of a siege, and the treatment of the conquered people. His description illustrates the bas-reliefs of Nimroud.'[69] The very same paragraph of his letter to his mother in which he makes the connection to Ezekiel goes on to a discussion of these objects as art. In *Nineveh and its Remains*, the parallel passage likewise comes in the chapter on Assyrian art. It is not insignificant that the subtitle of his book promised not an enquiry into the connections with the Bible but rather into the 'arts of the ancient Assyrians'. In 1846, Layard wrote excitedly to his aunt, Sara Austen, from his excavations:

I wished particularly to trace a lion hunt for you (the bas-relief is among those already sent to England), which is a most remarkable production. It proves that the Assyrians even at this remote period, had acquired sufficient knowledge of and taste for the fine arts to make them no longer subservient to the mere representation of events, but to aim at composition. Of this essential feature in what may properly be termed the fine arts, the Egyptians appear to have been entirely ignorant ... I think the Nimroud bas-reliefs will furnish new ideas on the history of the Arts, and throw great light upon that interesting subject.[70]

---

[68] *The Times* (30 January 1845), 6. [69] Layard, *Nineveh*, II, p. 378.
[70] Bruce, *Autobiography*, II, p. 175.

In *Nineveh and its Remains*, one feels Layard's real agenda when, for example, he argues that the Assyrians rather than the Greeks invented such a key architectural ornament of classical monuments as the Ionic column.[71] If Layard was quietly hoping to prove something, it was not the *bona fides* of the prophets but rather the charms of Assyrian art.

Assyriology and apologetics

Layard's comments on the size of Nineveh in the light of Jonah 3:3 are thus a red herring. It is worth observing that in that passage Layard also based his judgment on a classical source, Diodorus Siculus. Moreover, a hidden factor was probably that the cuneiform script had not yet been deciphered. Most of Layard's original excavations had actually been at Nimrud which, as it turned out, was not Nineveh. His theory on the size of the city enabled him to evoke the resonant name of Nineveh for his book's title without having to also disprove the claims of the traditional site, Kuyunjik (which proved to be the correct one, and where Layard also made some finds that were reported in *Nineveh and its Remains*).

None of the key figures in this crucial phase of recovering a lost culture were zealous Christians seeking to use Assyriology for biblical apologetic purposes. This recovery was primarily the work of Layard and two other men who were both personal friends of his – Paola Botta, who made the initial finds, and Henry Rawlinson (1810–95), who was instrumental in the deciphering of the cuneiform writing and who is sometimes referred to as 'the father of Assyriology'. Botta was an opium addict who unashamedly recommended his drug of choice for general use. Benjamin Disraeli, who knew him intimately and liked him heartily, portrayed Botta as 'a rabid sceptic' and 'an absolute materialist'.[72] Rawlinson was no conservative Christian apologist either. Far from being animated by a desire to prove the Bible true, he wrote to Layard regarding the reception in England of his personal objections to the veracity of the Old Testament:

By the Bye, I find a very much greater degree of religious freedom than I had expected. I have even discussed the probable spuriousness of a great portion of Daniel, with several members of the bench of Bishops without scandalizing them & I

---

[71] Layard, *Nineveh*, II, pp. 293–5.
[72] M. T. Larsen, *Conquest*, p. 18. (Disraeli had created a character in a novel that was modelled on Botta.)

am strongly urged by many people to put forward the arguments against the authenticity of the book in print.[73]

Even Canning, when he sponsored the original excavation, apparently fearing the corrosive power of wishful thinking, had Layard promise in writing that he would 'avoid confidential or frequent intercourse with missionaries, whatever might be their country or religion'.[74]

This study of Layard therefore complicates the picture offered in this volume of the manifold connections between archaeology and the Bible by arguing that the prevailing assumptions regarding mid-century British Assyriology are incorrect. Its practitioners were not much bothered about the authority of the Bible, even if those who read about their researches were. Thus David Gange's excellent account of the religious influences on later nineteenth-century British Egyptology puts the standard view in identifying Layard and Botta as 'first and foremost Christians attempting to tie archaeological records into Old Testament history' and whose work was therefore 'biblically driven'.[75] In fact, far from overselling the biblical value of their archaeological findings, the pioneers of Assyriology ignored it or played it down. Henry Rawlinson was long delayed in his efforts to decipher the cuneiform inscriptions by his inclination to discount biblical references to the Assyrians in favour of those made by Greek authors. Mogen Trolle Larsen notes that Rawlinson 'vehemently denied' that any of the Assyrian kings mentioned in the Bible were referred to in the inscriptions.[76] Instead, he convinced himself that he could read the name of Ninus, an Assyrian king according to the Greeks whose existence has not been confirmed by archaeological evidence and who is now considered to have been entirely mythical. Larsen is repeatedly struck by how 'blocked' Rawlinson was by 'his curious insistence to look for the names of kings and dynasties in the classical writers, avoiding the names from the Bible'.[77] The Rev. Edward Hincks (1792–1866) read some names also recorded in Scripture in the inscriptions earlier, but if anything his status as an obscure Irish clergyman played against him. In the end, the world's knowledge of Assyrian kings long known from the Bible – Tiglath-pileser, Shalmaneser, Sennacherib and Esarhaddon – was vastly expanded through these and subsequent archaeological discoveries, although these connections were

---

[73] Henry Rawlinson to A. H. Layard, 27 March 1850, Austen Henry Layard Papers, Add. MS 38979, British Library, London.
[74] Lane-Poole, *Canning*, II, p. 138.
[75] David Gange, 'Religion and Science in Late Nineteenth-Century British Egyptology', *Historical Journal*, 49 (2006), 1084.
[76] Larsen, *Conquest*, p. 296, see also pp. 217–25, 304, 334.   [77] Ibid., pp. 179–80.

not made in *Nineveh and its Remains* beyond a few, brief speculations – in defiance of Rawlinson –that these palaces might have been from the period of the biblical kings.

Beyond a common cast of characters, specific events recorded in the Bible were also confirmed by Assyrian researches, although this was not known at the time. By mid-1851, Rawlinson had to concede that additional records regarding occurrences mentioned in Scripture had been discovered. He wrote to the *Athenaeum* regarding one Assyrian text:

> Now, this is evidently the campaign which is alluded to in Scripture (2 Kings xviii. vv. 13 to 17) … The agreement, at any rate, between the record of the Sacred Historian and the contemporary chronicle of Sennacherib which I have here copied extends even to the number of the talents of gold and silver which were given as tribute.[78]

Moreover, when Rawlinson's reading of this text seemed 'to point to discrepancies between the biblical and the Assyrian accounts' that unsettled some people at the time, it later turned out that the conflict between the two narratives was not a real one, but only one manufactured by translation errors he had made.[79] Again, although this was not made clear until after *Nineveh and its Remains* was published, Layard had even discovered bas-reliefs depicting a specific biblical event, the siege of Lachish.

The most important object that Layard found in relationship to biblical studies, however, was arguably the black obelisk. He knew it was a great find, was immediately excited about it and gave it prominent coverage, including a full-page illustration, in *Nineveh and its Remains* as 'one of the most remarkable discoveries' he had made.[80] Still, he had no idea what it signified, speculating 'we are naturally led to conjecture, that the monument was erected to celebrate the Indian expedition of one of the early Assyrian monarchs – the Ninus, Semiramis, or Ninyas of history'.[81] This is completely wrongheaded and, led astray by classical sources, the figures he listed are now all thought to belong better in the category of mythology than history. Layard reported in a subsequent footnote that, since he had written this passage about the obelisk, Rawlinson had 'succeeded in deciphering' that it was a record of 'the reign of a son of Ninus'.[82] The obelisk actually records Jehu, king of Israel (who is a character in the Bible), paying tribute to the Assyrian king, Shalmaneser III.

---

[78] *Athenaeum* (23 August 1851), 903. [79] M. T. Larsen, *Conquest*, pp. 303–4.
[80] Layard, *Nineveh*, I, p. 345 (the illustration faced 346). [81] Ibid., II, p. 394. [82] Ibid., II, p. 192.

Later archaeological discoveries would sometimes occasion new controversies regarding the accuracy of biblical passages, but Layard's findings were a moment in the history of nineteenth-century perceptions of the Bible and Christianity when the Scriptures appeared to have been confirmed. Although the standard narrative of the history of the relationship between Assyriology and the Bible is one of results being oversold for pious reasons, a closer examination of Layard's life and work offers a corrective to this presentation: it was the findings themselves that were drawing attention to the historical veracity of the Bible. The exploitation of Nineveh for the vindication of the Bible often went against the assumptions and expectations of the discoverers.

Conclusion

Unable to refute the confirmation of the Bible provided by the uncovering of Nineveh, British sceptics chose to ignore it. The only mention of this extraordinary discovery in the main journal of popular unbelief at that time, the *Reasoner*, was in the record of a debate in which a Christian opponent triumphantly introduced it. His sparring partner, the leading Secularist, G. J. Holyoake (1817–1906), did not deny the import of these findings for the historicity of the Bible, but contented himself with the retort: 'I demanded to know what stone had been turned up in Nineveh or Babylon which established the truth of the many propositions in the Bible which were contrary to our moral sense?'[83] The freethinking *Westminster Review* briefly noticed Bonomi's volume, offering this unsubstantiated grumble:

It would be well if such manuals were confined to abridging or popularizing the narratives of the original explorers, the history of their excavations, and description of the sculptures recovered. To attempt to construct chronology and history out of the material, and so to 'confirm Sacred Writ', can only lead to deception.[84]

Although leading archaeologists came to endorse the argument that the use of archaeology to shore up the authority of religious texts was profoundly problematic, it made relatively little impact on the sensibilities of a broad public. Having the Bible confirmed and illuminated – not least through viewing material remains of the Assyrian capital – became an enduring

---

[83] G. J. Holyoake, 'Incidents in the Nottingham Debate: II', *Reasoner*, 10 (1851), 361.
[84] 'History and Biography', *Westminster Review*, 3 (1858), 620.

reason why some people visited the British Museum.[85] The Christian appropriation of the city of Nineveh as an object lesson in the fidelity of the Bible was universal and tenacious. It was not confined to either popular discourse or to any particular denomination. Thus the Unitarian scholar, Samuel Sharpe (1799–1881), whose heterodox Egyptology is discussed in Gange's chapter on Pithom below, contributed a chapter to Bonomi's *Nineveh and its Palaces* in which he drew heavily on Scripture as an accurate source for the history of the Assyrians.[86] Even the Catholic *Dublin Review*, while warning its readers that Layard was 'one of the most bitter anti-catholic writers we have ever read', nevertheless ran a forty-five-page article that enthused about the ways that the sacred Scriptures were confirmed and illuminated by his findings, offering numerous biblical citations in footnotes and tabulating that the Assyrian monuments refer to 'nearly sixty kings, countries, and cities mentioned in the Old Testament'.[87]

The excavation of Nineveh made an enduring mark on biblical studies in the English-speaking world which tended for generations thereafter to keep a chastened eye on archaeology when developing critical theories. A. H. Sayce (1845–1933), who in 1891 was appointed to Oxford University's first professorial chair in Assyriology, made it a primary theme of his career to declare that archaeology was proving the Scriptures true and overturning the speculations of radical biblical critics. His most important work along these lines was *The 'Higher Criticism' and the Verdict of the Monuments*, but the triumphalist note can be more clearly heard in another title of his, *Monument Facts and Higher Critical Fancies*.[88] Likewise, Edward Bouverie Pusey (1800–82), Oxford University's Regius Professor of Hebrew and a leader of the Tractarians, cited Layard in his 1860 commentary on the Minor Prophets to bolster the assertion that the city of Nineveh had 'exactly the dimensions assigned by Jonah'.[89] What is most telling about Pusey's *Minor Prophets*, however, is that it is primarily intended not as a work of apologetics, but rather to convict people of their sins. Pusey recurrently invites his readers to apply biblical prophetic denunciations of ancient cities specifically to London.[90] Despite Holyoake, he was not

---

[85] A popular volume aided people in this quest: Ada R. Habershon, *The Bible and the British Museum* (London, 1909).
[86] Bonomi, *Nineveh*, pp. 77–88.
[87] [George Crolly], 'Nineveh and Babylon', *Dublin Review*, 35 (1853), 93–138.
[88] A. H. Sayce, *The "Higher Criticism" and the Verdict of the Monuments* (London, 1894); A. H. Sayce, *Monument Facts and Higher Critical Fancies* (London, 1904).
[89] E. B. Pusey, *The Minor Prophets, With a Commentary, Explanatory and Practical, and Introductions to the Several Books* (2 vols., New York, 1885), I, p. 380.
[90] Ibid., I, p. 290; II, pp. 85, 385.

deducing doctrines from the ruins but assuming the doctrines made sense of the remains. The uncovering of the historical reality of Nineveh allowed the traditional use of this city as a warning of divine judgment to be deployed with renewed confidence. Nineveh's fall could now be appropriated as a real, tangible historical event that could be visualised, proving therefore warnings of divine judgment on modern cities were not just flights of poetic fancy but distinct possibilities. Nineveh's past destruction could be the pending future of the modern Victorian metropolis: 'Lo, all our pomp of yesterday / Is one with Nineveh and Tyre! / Judge of the Nations, spare us yet, / Lest we forget – lest we forget!'[91]

---

[91] Rudyard Kipling, 'Recessional' (1897), in M. H. Abrams, *The Norton Anthology of English Literature*, 5th edn (2 vols., New York, 1986), II, pp. 1720–1.

4 | Pithom

DAVID GANGE

As the nineteenth century progressed, Egypt came to be seen as the region most likely to yield dramatic revelations to the archaeologist of the Old Testament. The first fruits of the decipherment of hieroglyphs had been received with disappointment in the 1820s and '30s since they failed to provide answers to the biblical and practical questions asked of them.[1] But dramatic discoveries from the 1860s onwards rapidly raised Egypt's biblical stock. This was especially true after 1881 when the well-preserved mummies of Pharaohs assumed to be those of the Israelite Oppression and Exodus were discovered and displayed in Cairo; after 1886 images of them were reproduced by the hundred. Sites familiar from the Bible narrative were also identified with growing confidence and frequency. As the British Museum antiquarian R. S. Poole (1854–1931) stated in 1882: 'Buried cities have thrown off the grave-clothes which had enwrapped them for thousands of years, and risen to tell us their story ... to fill the ages of oblivion once more with the joy of overflowing life.'[2] Egyptian tombs and temples promised to disclose written and visual material that would elaborate society and events from the age of the patriarchs.

Such promise initially provoked divergent responses from churchmen and public figures. For confident believers in Old Testament authority, this was a glorious opportunity to synchronise biblical chronology and secular history; for the more cautious, it was to be feared as a potential challenge to scriptural authority; to others – especially the Unitarian Egyptologists of the mid-century – investigation of these cities was a duty, both a sociological exercise to discover what model of society could produce such impressive cityscapes and a necessary quest after impartial truth concerning the origins of religion. Most agreed, however, that Egyptology could make the British relationship with the Bible more immediate, if more vexed. As Poole wrote,

---

[1] For instance, Samuel Sharpe, *The Early History of Egypt: From the Old Testament, Herodotus, Manetho, and the Hieroglyphical Inscriptions* (London, 1836), p. 5: 'our disappointment is of course fully equal to our curiosity when we find, from every fresh advance which is made in the reading of hieroglyphics how little the priests thought worth recording ... beyond the titles of their gods and the particulars of the sacred offerings to their shrines'.

[2] R. S. Poole, *Cities of Egypt* (London, 1882), pp. 33–4.

'Egypt obliterates time and brings the present and the past together as by magic art.'³ Egypt's cities 'of all the capitals of the world speak most eloquently of the times that are past, and echo the thoughts of forgotten ages, telling the story of the vicissitudes of earthly fortune as a warning, uttering the cry of human hope and fear for the hereafter as an encouragement'.⁴ The imaginative barriers between modern Europe and the biblical world seemed to be crumbling at unprecedented speed.

Several Egyptian cities stood out. Early in the century, it was 'White-walled' Memphis and Thebes, 'City of Thrones', which were most often evoked. But where Memphis left scant physical remains, Thebes had little biblical context. Memphis soon gathered prominence through dozens of fictional representations set at the time of the Israelite settlement, and through the widely attested attempts of Cairene tour guides to intrude the Exodus into their city itineraries.⁵ Because of the engineering achievement inherent in the pyramids, Memphis was the city that inspired the most comparisons to modern feats of construction. The authors of *Ruined Cities of the Ancient World* (1840) sought to demonstrate that the London to Birmingham railway was a greater achievement than the Great Pyramid. But other cities soon gained parallel importance: On (Heliopolis), predecessor of Alexandria and the 'school of Moses'; Zoan, seat of Joseph; Akhetaten, the first capital of monotheistic religion; and Alexandria, centre of early Christianity and for centuries 'the great mart of the world'.⁶ Each of these could have been treated fruitfully in this volume.

The modest store city of Pithom, however, proved as influential and evocative as any of these great capitals. In 1883, it was the site that opened Egyptology to a broad new British public and established the biblical tone of mainstream British Egyptology for the rest of the century. The large-scale Egyptian excavations of the mid-century had all been carried out by the pioneers of French and German archaeology, and when political conditions and public interest finally became conducive to British activity in the early 1880s it was Pithom – the Hebrew-built 'treasure city' of Exodus – that was the site of the first, dramatic, excavations. The newly founded Egypt Exploration Fund (EEF) made Pithom and its twin city Rameses their pioneering endeavour for several reasons: because these store cities promised to establish fixed points in the disputed question of the Exodus route; because they seemed to promise written evidence of the Israelite presence in Lower Egypt; and because the large mounds of this region of Egypt

---

³ Ibid., p. 63. ⁴ Ibid. ⁵ For instance, ibid., p. 90.
⁶ Charles William Watson, 'Egypt under the Romans', *The Monthly Review*, 3 (1843), 358–65.

contained towns and cities whose monuments had been hidden and preserved for millennia, unlike the more familiar cities of Upper Egypt whose 'noble ruins [were] open to the cloudless sky'.[7]

Pithom also represented a turning-point in biblical history. To many late nineteenth-century commentators, it evoked the moment when the influence of the pastoral Semitic population on Egyptian society (evinced by Hebrew names creeping into use amongst Egyptians as well as by the text of the Old Testament) was finally and dramatically rejected by Rameses II. This most renowned of pharaohs was seen to have jealously guarded the city-based civilisation of Egypt against the less urbanised Hebrew culture, and placed two dramatic statements of his nationalistic intent on the plains shepherded by the Israelites. These symbols of a new despotic Egypt were two formidable civic centres – Rameses and Pithom – built to dominate the region and rising 'to a magnificence' that free cities such as 'Zoan had never known'.[8] They embodied conflict between authority and freedom, between heathenism and monotheism, between ordered city-dwellers and idyllic wandering populations. Their construction was the starting point of Israelite history: while the Hebrew people pursued the happy pastoral life 'they had no history'; only when they were forced to build Pithom 'did their history as a nation begin'.[9] History commences with the founding of a city, just as it does in epics from *Gilgamesh* (Uruk) to the *Aeneid* (Rome).

Pithom is therefore perhaps the best Egyptian site for investigating both the biblical context of the dramatic rise of Egyptology in Britain, and the diverse meanings of the city to the nineteenth-century Bible reader. Before investigating Pithom directly, this chapter will explore the Egyptological context that gave responses to the EEF's excavations their distinctive shape.

Unorthodox Egypt: Egyptology and the Bible in the mid-nineteenth century

Nineteenth-century Egyptology is impossible to comprehend without its theological context, a fact that goes unrecognised in most histories of the discipline. Similarly, the history of biblical criticism needs to acknowledge its connections with the investigation of ancient Egypt: works such as Bunsen's *Aegyptens Stelle in der Weltgeschichte* (1844–57; *Egypt's Place in*

---

[7] Amelia Edwards, *Pharaohs, Fellahs and Explorers* (New York, 1892), p. 40.
[8] Poole, *Cities*, p. 78.   [9] Ibid., p. 41.

World History, 1848–67) deserve to be treated alongside the works of David Friedrich Strauss and Julius Wellhausen. In the 1870s, Egypt still seemed to loom – enigmatic and threatening – over study of the Bible. During this decade expectations for the unfulfilled biblical possibilities of Egyptology mounted to levels unprecedented since the decipherment of the hieroglyphs. In expressing this gathering tension *The Academy* drew on an oracular statement from Ernest Renan (1823–92): 'A curious phenomenon is just now taking place in criticism. Egypt will soon be a beacon in the midst of the deep night of high antiquity.'[10] When Renan wrote, the pressure for organised British excavations – something not yet seen – was increasing. Poole wrote that the British had 'an evil eminence in Europe for our neglect of Egyptian research'; others would describe the situation as a 'national embarrassment'.[11] He identified the problem amongst the decorous educated class who mistakenly regarded Egyptian civilisation as barbaric and distasteful and the excavation of heathendom as un-Christian: 'It may be difficult to raise funds for work in Greece and Turkey, but there is no excuse for the polite indifference of the educated class to a subject which deeply interests the half-educated population, even to the children of the village schools.'[12] Perhaps the most widely read populariser of Egyptology of the period, Amelia Edwards (1831–92), appealed directly to this less dismissive and supposedly more pious domestic constituency. She demanded the attention of 'the church- and chapel- going English people' whose combined influence might usurp the reluctant wealthy.[13]

This manifest reluctance of the great and good to support Egyptology at mid-century is – like most vicissitudes of nineteenth-century interest in ancient Egypt – explicable in theological terms. After the post-Napoleonic enthusiasm for Egypt had died down, the new science of Egyptology was left in unorthodox hands. Two of the three best-selling historians of ancient Egypt in the 1840s – Samuel Sharpe (1799–1881) and John Kenrick (1788–1877) – were leading Unitarians, while the most historically engaged travelogue of the period was written by Harriet Martineau (1802–76), whose Unitarian background coloured her thinking.[14] To many, a Unitarian Egyptology that threatened to play fast and loose with Scripture was a threatening prospect. Even such an erudite enthusiast for ancient history

---

[10] François Lenormant, 'Schliemann's Excavations at Troy', *Academy* (1874), 343.
[11] Poole, *Cities*, p. 87.   [12] Ibid.
[13] Amelia Edwards, 'Cities of Egypt', *Academy* (2 December 1882), 389.
[14] The third writer on Egyptology, John Gardner Wilkinson, produced one of the few influential studies of ancient Egypt before those of Wallis Budge at the end of the century, in which the writer's theological context does not intrude dramatically on the historical narrative.

as George Rawlinson (1812–1902) warned against excavations that came uncomfortably 'close to the Holy Text'.[15] To add to this, Egypt was the heathen oppressor, characterised by 'debasing animal worship suggesting the orgies that accompanied it' and a 'grotesque menagerie' of 'superstition'.[16] It was famously used by figures such as G. R. Gliddon and Josiah Nott (1804–73) in some of the most criticised and alienating defences of the institution of slavery.[17] To the respectable, classically educated intellectual or clergyman there were a host of reasons to regard ancient Egypt with distaste.

Unitarian Egyptology was notorious for its receptiveness to the controversial higher criticism associated with Germany. Kenrick – author of *Ancient Egypt under the Pharaohs* – considered by *The Times* as 'indisputably the greatest non-conformist of our day', had studied at Göttingen, where he embraced the enlightened radicalism of Eichhorn, Semler and Michaelis, though he would always remain distanced from the more sceptical scholarship associated with Tübingen. As intensely religious but heterodox Christians, both Kenrick and Sharpe demonstrated openness to Egyptian thought that was rare in Britain before the 1870s. To these Unitarians, the achievements of the ancient Egyptians in monuments, irrigation, mathematics and astronomy proved that the well-known biblical account of Egyptian despotism traduced this great civilisation. In a pre-Ruskinian assertion that great architecture could only be produced by a free, healthy society, they urged that 'the enquiry into the political condition of any people who have left behind them works worthy of admiration, is of the highest moral importance'.[18] 'That these should have been the works of a people suffering under political disadvantages would contradict all our observations of the human mind and its powers. A tree is known by its fruit.'[19] The Egyptians were free and honest. But in religious terms they were also wrong. Through Alexandria they had an immense influence on Greece, Rome and modern Christianity, but this influence was unwelcome to a Unitarian theologian: Egyptian religion encouraged Trinitarian 'superstition' rather than 'the simple religion which Jesus taught and practiced'.[20] 'Most of the so called Christian doctrines that have no place in the New

---

[15] Sharpe, *Early History*; Harriet Martineau, *Eastern Life, Present and Past* (3 vols., London, 1843); John Kenrick, *Ancient Egypt under the Pharaohs* (2 vols., London, 1852).
[16] Poole, *Cities*, p. 163; A. H. Layard, *The Athenaeum*, 1 (1845), 120.
[17] J. C. Nott and G. R. Gliddon, *Types of Mankind* (Philadelphia, 1854).
[18] Sharpe, *Early History*, p. 7.   [19] Ibid.
[20] Samuel Sharpe, *Egyptian Mythology and Egyptian Christianity: With their Influence on the Opinions of Modern Christendom* (London, 1863), p. vii.

Testament', Sharpe asserted, 'reached Europe from Egypt.'[21] Among the errors learnt from Egypt were 'the Trinity, the two natures of Christ, and the atonement by vicarious sufferings'.[22] Sharpe contended, on these grounds, that only by studying Egyptian religion could the true teachings of Christ be known. But Sharpe's assessment of Egypt was (in true Unitarian fashion) always ameliorated by his recognition that 'the history of religious error is the history of the mind wandering in its search after truth': nothing here was evil or rebarbative.[23]

Figures still more distant from Anglican orthodoxy made even more subversive claims about Egyptian influence on early Christianity. Robert Taylor (1784–1844), renegade cleric and radical deist, spent his years imprisoned for blasphemy in Oakham Gaol developing an anti-Christian rendering of Christian debts to Egypt: 'bind it about thy neck, write it upon the tablet of thy heart: "Everything of Christianity is of Egyptian origin"'.[24] But even in more mainstream evocations of Egyptian civilisation such as Charles Kingsley's novel *Hypatia* (1853), Pharaonic Egypt became a rod with which to beat high-church Christianity.[25] High-church clerics fulminated against Egypt in the words of Moses or the splenetic ejaculations of prophets from Ezekiel to Joel; Edward Bouverie Pusey's *Minor Prophets* (1860) distils this trend.

By the end of the 1870s, when British excavations began to seem imminent, nonconformist Egyptology had lost ground. Just as a generational shift occurred in continental Egyptology – with the deaths of Auguste Mariette (1821–81), François Chabas (1817–82), and Karl Richard Lepsius (1810–84) among others – the three leading representatives of Unitarian interest in Egypt – Sharpe, Kenrick and Martineau – passed away in quick succession between 1876 and 1881. Their approach to the history of religion had preceded them to the grave, and the new generation of British authorities on ancient Egypt rejected higher criticism (indeed their early endeavours were a concerted campaign against it), but retained Sharpe and Kenrick's respect for Egyptian thought and influence. Although almost all major denominations – from Catholicism and the Church of England, to Methodism and the Plymouth Brethren – are represented in the early

---

[21] Ibid., p. viii. [22] Ibid., p. ix, p. 160. [23] Ibid., p. 1.
[24] Robert Taylor, *The Diegesis: Being a Discovery of the Origin, Evidences, and Early History of Christianity* (1829, London, 1834); see also Godfrey Higgins, *Anacalypsis: An Attempt to Draw Aside the Veil of the Saitic Isis or an Enquiry into the Origins of Languages, Nations, and Religions* (2 vols., London, 1836).
[25] Charles Kingsley, *Hypatia* (2 vols., London, 1853): several passages use Pharaonic rather than early Christian Egypt, including the first chapter, I: pp. 1–13.

EEF, founded in 1882, there were no known Unitarians among its initial membership. Favourable estimation of Egyptian achievements had quickly become, it seems, orthodox.

Cities of the living, cities of the dead: Egyptology and the Bible after 1870

Amongst the puzzles in the history of British Egyptology is the question of how a society so frequently derided as barbaric and crude at mid-century could be widely held up as an exemplar of practical and spiritual excellence just twenty or thirty years later. This development is evident in the writings of individual authors: George Rawlinson, who in the 1840s and 1850s had vocally opposed Assyriology and Egyptology, produced a *History of Ancient Egypt* (1881) that celebrated Egyptologists in no uncertain terms. The most significant factor in this transition was that archaeology of Near Eastern sites had uncovered nothing that directly challenged the Bible narrative, and produced evidence that could be turned to the support or illustration of biblical history with remarkable regularity. As the chapter in this book on Troy has argued, the 1870s witnessed dramatic shifts in attitudes to archaeology: ties to radical higher criticism weakened and belief increased in archaeologists' ability to illuminate and fortify the great ancient texts. The fear of Egyptian discoveries was removed, and revisionist writers began to celebrate ancient Egypt with relieved enthusiasm. They distanced themselves from both styles of older scholarship on Egypt: the Unitarian kind that was open to higher criticism, and the more reverent variety that took the Old Testament account of crude despotism and barbaric culture at face value.[26]

This shift is most evident in the extraordinary number of Egyptological articles and reviews published in journals such as the *Academy* at the beginning of the 1880s. Here the new generation of Egyptologists cut their teeth on more traditional approaches to the civilisation. Amelia Edwards' review of her future collaborator, Erasmus Wilson's *Cleopatra's Needle* (1877), is a case in point. Edwards insists that the ancient Egyptians should not be ascribed the vulgar and bombastic character that Wilson gives them: Cleopatra's Needle is not a mere 'triumphal erection' as Wilson claims, but a 'divine symbol', 'the erection of an obelisk was therefore a pious act rather

---

[26] For instance, Poole, *Cities*, p. 32.

than an act of self-commemoration'.[27] At the same time, major works of French and German Egyptology were translated into English for the first time, including those of Johannes Dümichen (1833–94), François Lenormant (1837–83), Lepsius, and Gaston Maspero (1846–1913), revealing a new ancient Egypt that was not barbaric, but an originator of much of the best in modern civilisation.

Key to this change of emphasis was an interrogation of dichotomies between the urban and the desolate, between the civilisation of city-dwellers and the world-denying wisdom of those who wandered the desert. For Poole, the history of 'Janus-faced Egypt' represented a constant battle between the desert – a 'land of oblivion' – and the fertile, civilised valley.[28] Egypt was eternally important because it combined these aspects. The urbane learning of the Egyptians, the transcendent revealed wisdom of the Jews and the rational philosophy of the Alexandrine Greeks were superficially incompatible yet constituted the crucible that forged Christianity. This convergence between complementary aspects of Christian theology began when Moses was 'instructed in the wisdom of the Egyptians'. It came together in the genius of the Egyptian church fathers, Athanasius and Origen. The history of the Egyptian city of On – the supposed school of Moses – was, Poole wrote, the history of the world. It was the first link in a chain of great centres of learning that could be traced ('not a link is wanting') through Alexandria, Baghdad, Cordova, Naples, Bologna and Paris to Oxford and Cambridge. The Egyptian cities began the unbroken history of the 'civilised urban world'.[29]

In 1880, Memphis was the archetypal ancient Egyptian city precisely because it was the most dramatic example of this dichotomy between the urban and the desolate. It demonstrated the fulfilment of Old Testament prophecies assuring the utter destruction of Egyptian cities, and it was the centre from which the great Greek writers on Egypt – Herodotus and Diodorus Siculus – had gathered their intelligence. Memphis embodied the mystery of Egypt. Rising, apparently fully formed, at the supposedly barbaric beginning of history, the city's existence seemed predicated on an immense feat of engineering that changed the course of the Nile. The metropolis described by Herodotus had been wiped from view, yet its appendages – dozens of pyramids and hundreds of less imposing tombs – confirmed this as one of the largest and most sumptuous cities of the ancient

---

[27] Amelia Edwards, 'Cleopatra's Needle: With Brief Notes on Egypt and Egyptian Obelisks', *The Academy* (2 February 1878), 89.
[28] Poole, *Cities*, pp. 9–10.   [29] Ibid., p. 133.

world. The absence of the familiar figures of anthropomorphic gods in Memphite tombs could seem to present a more noble Egyptian religion: 'records of a simple faith' practised by 'high-souled philosophers of that remote age'.[30]

The city of the living has perished, the City of the Dead remains ... We may walk through the silent streets of the City of the Dead, as did the hero of an old Egyptian romance, and read the writings that are engraven on the outer walls of the tombs ... we have discovered the true magic in the recovery of the records of the past, in giving speech to the long silent utterances of the hopes and fears, the joys and sorrows of the fathers of mankind, who return from the underworld and admit us to their company, as having interpreted the title without, we can enter each sepulchral chapel and understand when and why and for whom its pictured reliefs were made in olden time.[31]

The monuments of the dead allow for the reconstruction of the bustling affairs of the living city, yet this is a reconstruction heavy with the expectation of imminent annihilation. This aspect of Memphis is exploited in H. Rider Haggard's most ambitious novel, *Cleopatra* (1892). The tragic hero – Harmachis, a Memphite priest – dreams of the destruction of Alexandria and its Macedonian Queen. The battle fought between the mystical Egyptian religion and the treacherous, worldly Greeks and Romans is represented by the fates of their cities: playing on the reader's knowledge of desolate Memphis, Haggard ironises the hopes the Egyptians attach to their 'eternal' capital. When the crux of the tale comes, Harmachis plans to assassinate Cleopatra, but his commitment to the spirituality of Memphis fails as he is beguiled by the sensuality of the more graceful but less substantial city. In this momentary lapse of faith he realises that for the love of 'a city of the infernal gods – a sink of corruption ... a home of false faith springing from false hearts' he has caused the collapse of his temple at Abouthis and of white-walled Memphis, city of wonders: 'the day comes when the desert sands shall fill thy secret places ... new faiths shall make a mock of all thy Holies ... Centurion shall call upon Centurion across thy fortress walls'.[32] The reader is drawn to mourn the fact that the wind sweeps across the wrecks of Abouthis and Memphis rather than Alexandria, and that a world of spiritual grandeur has fallen to worldly vice. The dual

---

[30] Ibid., p. 162; here Poole assures his readers that this popular view is not entirely supported by the contents of the newly translated hieroglyphs in these tombs.
[31] Ibid., p. 17.
[32] H. Rider Haggard, *Cleopatra: Being an Account of the Fall and Vengeance of Harmachis, the Royal Egyptian, as Set Forth by his Own Hand* (London, 1892), p. 35.

conceptions of the city – corrupt Babylon and the holy New Jerusalem are both present. Haggard's literary recreations of Memphis (here and in a string of other books including *Morning Star* and *Moon of Israel*) were intended to serve as popular introductions to Egyptology. He swathed his narrative in archaeological detail, so that 'the long dead past be made to live again before the reader's eyes with all its accessories of faded pomp and forgotten mystery'.[33] Most dramatically, he instructed 'such students as seek a story only, and are not interested in the faith, ceremonies, or customs of the Mother of Religion and Civilisation, ancient Egypt' to skip the first of the novel's three books since this substantial section was not intended as narrative.[34] Haggard became so obsessed with the landscape of Memphis in ancient times that in questioning a medium known to embark on 'spiritual wanderings' he wrote, 'I suppose there isn't any method for getting oneself back to old Egypt. How do you do it? I should like to go.'[35] He eventually procured a hallucinogenic substance for the purpose, the desired effects of which are fictionalised in *The Ancient Allan* (1920).

Dozens of literary figures, from Marie Corelli (*Ziska: Or the Problem of a Wicked Soul* (1897)) to James Joyce ('The Sisters' (1904)), would play on Memphis' dual association with desolation and spiritual wisdom. Joyce traced Irish Druidism and the origin of Dublin back to ancient Memphis, but reminded his audience that heroic Ireland was as dead as the white-walled city.[36] Others exploited the dichotomy from the other side of Egypt's decline, contrasting the early Christian city with both monk-scattered deserts and abandoned ruins. This was a genre dominated by Kingsley's *Hypatia*, Anatole France's powerfully anti-clerical *Thaïs* (1890) (alongside Massenet's notorious operatic adaptation) and Gustave Flaubert's *La Tentation de Saint Antoine* (1874).

The Egyptologists of the 1870s and '80s were more orthodox in drawing a spiritual message from the stark desolation of Memphis. Their reading of the monuments to the Memphite dead expressed exactly the message of personal piety and religious vision that Edwards drew from Cleopatra's Needle. The pyramids were not symbols of crude arrogance as they had been to William Makepeace Thackeray, Mark Twain and William Holman Hunt; the Egyptians were not morbidly obsessed with death as countless

---

[33] Ibid., p. ix [34] Ibid.
[35] H. Rider Haggard to W. T. Horton, 14 December 1910: Norfolk Record Office, MC 31/12.
[36] The 1907 lecture in which Joyce laid these ideas out most fully can be found in Ellsworth Mason and Richard Ellmann, *The Critical Writings of James Joyce* (London, 1959), pp. 162–89; see also Susan Swartzlander, 'James Joyce's "The Sisters": Chalices and Umbrellas, Ptolemaic Memphis and Victorian Dublin', *Studies in Short Fiction*, 32 (1995), 295–306.

earlier travellers had seen them. Poole interpreted the City of the Dead as a monument to

> a vital belief in the future state ... The Egyptian tomb was due to no mere convention; faith raised its mighty mass above the rock or cut its hidden halls beneath. Those who accuse this great nation of a vain ostentation in these costly sepulchres, cannot conceive the delight of lavishing gold and silver without return in the consecration of a noble idea. The Egyptians raised monuments that have defied time, to show to all who should come after them that they believed in the immortality of the soul.[37]

Despite these intensely positive readings the fascination of Memphite desolation prevented this archetypal Egyptian city gaining any identity as an urban site. Memphis was not just another ruined city: as the only great city of the ancient world to have 'so utterly disappeared' this was a desert space where 'more than even in the midst of the ocean man feels conscious of the Divine Presence'.[38] The desert was the rosy-hued spiritual idyll of the painter David Roberts (1796–1864) rather than the scorched 'void sand' of Alexander Kinglake, but desert – not city – it was.[39] Although essential to the formulation of new respect for Egyptian achievements after 1880, Memphis was not seen as a fruitful site for British archaeology of the city: it remained a symbol of destruction rather than a vital site whose remains could be elaborated into historical reconstructions. Pithom, by contrast, was imagined as a fortified site with walls, overlooked by prophecy, which would echo Egyptian power and Israelite toil through the ages.

'The positive philosophy of pick and spade': Pithom, the Exodus and the Egypt Exploration Fund

In a manner familiar to nineteenth-century readers of Egyptian history, Pithom was a city with two names: 'Pithom' described the sacred site with its temple to the divinity Tum – 'god of the setting sun' – while 'Succoth' denoted the secular city that enclosed it. This city recurs under both names throughout the first fifteen chapters of Exodus. In chapter one, Pharaoh realises the potential power of the increasingly numerous Israelites and sets taskmasters over them 'to afflict them with their burdens. And they built for Pharaoh treasure cities, Pithom and Ramses'. Later – chapter five – Pharaoh

---

[37] Poole, *Cities*, pp. 27–8.   [38] Ibid., pp. 14–15.
[39] Alexander Kinglake, *Eothen: Or, Traces of Travel Brought Home from the East* (London, 1844), p. 190.

responds to Moses and Aaron's demands for Israel's deliverance by intensifying their oppression. The taskmasters carry this message to the builders of Pithom: 'Ye shall no more give the people straw to make their brick, as heretofore: let them go and gather straw for themselves. And the tale of the bricks which they did make heretofore, ye shall lay upon them ... So the people were scattered abroad throughout all the land of Egypt to gather stubble instead of straw.' The plagues ensue, until in chapter twelve 'the Egyptians were urgent upon the people, that they may send them out of the land in haste; for they said, We *be* all dead *men* ... And the children of Israel journeyed from Rameses to Succoth about six hundred thousand on foot that were men beside children'. In chapter 13, 'God led the people about, through the way of the wilderness of the Red Sea ... And they took their journey from Succoth, and encamped in Etham in the edge of the wilderness'. Then, in one of the most familiar Old Testament passages, the Israelites, led by pillars of fire and cloud, reach the Red Sea. The miraculous crossing ensues: Pharaoh's hosts are drowned, and the chosen people are delivered out of bondage. Pithom has been both site of enslavement and gateway to freedom, beginning and ending the period of harshest oppression.

In the 1830s, the locality of Pithom-Succoth was a matter for regular speculation. Prevailing opinion used linguistic evidence to argue that On, Heliopolis and Pithom were one and the same site, while Rameses and Zoan might be identical.[40] At this point, the Exodus was considered crucial in defining Egyptian chronology: this and the Trojan War were the two 'transnational' events capable of interleaving the mistrusted chronologies of Manetho with the chronological records of other peoples.[41] As the century progressed, French and German scholars such as Emmanuel de Rougé (1811–72) and Lepsius showed increasing interest in defining the actual route of the Exodus and so began to consider other possible locations for Pithom and Rameses. Thanks to the wealth of Egyptian sites available to the excavator, however, the mounds of the Wadi Tumilat – between the presumed starting point of the Exodus and the Red Sea – remained largely untouched when Edwards and Poole began to plan their excavating organisation. The established archaeologists of France and Germany jealously discouraged British excavation of the better-preserved sites of Upper Egypt, but were prepared to cede rights to the less spectacular Delta which

---

[40] Sharpe, *Early History*, p. 13; the latter identification persisted into the 1870s thanks to its use by Emanuel De Rougé from 1867 onwards.
[41] Ibid., p. v, pp. 158–66.

contained almost all the sites with biblical resonance (largely because of its geographical accessibility from Palestine). In the agreement that Edwards made with Gaston Maspero, the French Director of Antiquities, the unusual prominence of biblical concerns in British Egyptology was formalised. The organisation based its initial appeal on almost purely biblical concerns, promising to investigate the route of the Exodus and the land of Goshen: 'here must undoubtedly lie concealed the documents of a lost period of Bible history – documents which we may confidently hope will furnish the key to a whole series of perplexing problems'; under the mounds of the Wadi Tumilat 'are to be found the missing records of those four centuries of the Hebrew sojourn in Egypt which are passed over in a few verses of the Bible, so that the history of the Israelites during that age is almost blank'.[42] Indeed, M. L. Herbert, an active publicist for the Fund (and translator of major French and German works), emphasised that the organisation of which he was an honorary secretary was not really engaged in Egyptian archaeology at all, but Hebrew archaeology: 'the cultivators of the Eastern Delta were the Israelites; for three-hundred years the pastures of Goshen had been as much a fatherland to the descendants of Jacob as Normandy was to Rolf'.[43] Hoping that Heinrich Schliemann might repeat his sensational success with the *Iliad* for the Old Testament, the organisation approached him to conduct their excavations. Maspero, however, vetoed the appointment of so notorious a manipulator of the press. The 'intensely religious' Swiss philologist Edouard Naville (1844–1926) was employed instead and dispatched to investigate locations for the Hebrew store cities.

All the major cities of Egypt were given distinctive identities in the nineteenth century: where Memphis was accepted as a symbol of desolation, Thebes stood for royal grandeur and Bubastis evoked the superstitious 'lower elements' of Egyptian cult. But the store cities of Rameses and Pithom were dramatically different in meaning from all the others. Constructed not by Egyptians but by Israelites, their very walls were the handiwork of the chosen people. They were not a mere backdrop to the biblical narrative; their conception was a biblical event, engineered to awe the cowed Israelite population. Bricks from these sites might have been fashioned by companions of Moses, and the name of the Hebrew law-giver might be recorded in the ruins. Few sites anywhere could compete with such intense evocation of biblical history. But more than this, these cities offered

---

[42] 'Egyptian Antiquities', *The Times* (30 March 1882), 8; Poole to Naville, 28 April 1882: EES, box XIX, c.2–3 contains information on the drafting of the memorandum and a list of the journals and newspapers in which it was published.

[43] M. L. Herbert, 'Recent Excavations in Egypt', 17 July 1888: EES, box XVIII, 75.

an unrivalled opportunity to establish the relationship between biblical and Egyptian chronologies once and for all. The identity of the Exodus Pharaoh could finally be proved, and the Old Testament's worth as history demonstrated in the process.

Before Naville began his excavations, Edwards and Poole set about instructing the British public on the meaning of these cities and the importance of excavating them. By this point, the authority of Lepsius and Georg Ebers (1837–98) led Edwards to be confident that the site of Tel el Maskutah housed the remains of the city of Rameses. In a long series of articles in the popular science periodical *Knowledge*, 'Was Rameses II the Pharaoh of the Oppression?', she combined romantic depictions of the modern landscape of the Wadi Tumilat with evocations of biblical treasures lying in their midst. She asserted that the name of the city of Goshen survived in the Arabic Fa-Koos, 'a miserable mud village, close to the Aboo-Kebeer station on the line between Zagazig and Salaheeyeh' that 'nestles at the foot of some ancient rubbish-mounds, beyond which lie undulating hillocks, covered in spring with waving corn-crops. These mounds and hillocks mark the site of that city of Goshen to which Joseph (being in attendance upon the Pharaoh at Zoan) hastened in his chariot "to meet Israel his father"'. Such blending of biblical events and modern scenery was a staple of her highly coloured style. Even contemporary military events were put to use, with two 'tells' where Pithom and Rameses might be found being identified as bases of operations for Sir Garnet Wolseley (1833–1913) in the battles preceding the 1882 occupation.[44]

Once the biblical scene and its modern setting were well and truly set, Edwards presented *Knowledge*'s (purported) twenty thousand readers with ancient descriptions of the 'twin cities', Rameses and Pithom, culled from texts such as the Anastasi papyri. Each city is a 'beautiful outpost', as 'stable as Memphis . . . all men hasten to remove from their own cities that they may live within its boundaries'.[45] The scribe Amen-em-apt announced the arrival of Menephthah, son of Rameses II, at the store-cities with lists of assets indicative of military purpose: 'the tower adorned with lapis and turquoise; the exercise-ground of the cavalry; the parade ground of the archers'.[46] Versified descriptions count the cities 'peerless, like the foundation of Thebes where to live is happiness'.[47]

Edwards describes the discovery of the mummy of Rameses II as having raised more public excitement than any previous archaeological event,

---

[44] Amelia Edwards, 'Was Rameses II the Pharaoh of the Oppression?', *Knowledge*, 2 (1882), 260.
[45] Ibid., 292. [46] Ibid., 293. [47] Ibid., 324.

rivalled only by the decipherment of the Deluge Tablets by the late George Smith.[48] The claim was typical of the 1880s and 1890s: George St Clair's 1892 survey of Near Eastern archaeology calls the recovery of this mummy 'the most important archaeological discovery of modern times', implying that, for a while at least, it overshadowed the ruins of Pompeii, Nineveh and even the Rosetta stone.[49] Edwards raises her audience's curiosity by insisting that only by exploring these cities will they get a conclusive answer to the question 'was this man that you see before you the Bible Pharaoh or not?'. Never mind the potent issues of biblical chronology, here was a tangible object with ready-made celebrity to which public interest could be attached. *The Times, Academy, Standard* and *Athenaeum* were among many periodicals to feature discursions on the importance of the store cities and their imminent excavation. As a result, the EEF garnered the support of public figures, ranging from Gladstone and Ruskin to Edward White Benson (1829–96), Archbishop of Canterbury, who named the family cat Ra and stood a statue of Horus on his desk in combined homage to the biblical potency of Egyptology and England's imperial mission (this was the man who, decades earlier, had responded to the establishment of an Anglo-Prussian bishop at Jerusalem by celebrating the idea that all the East would soon be English).

Naville's excavations were already widely known when the notices of imminent endeavour turned into descriptions of work underway. The press recounted buildings excavated and a long submerged city re-emerging brick by Israelite brick. One of the first reports delivered to journalists was of an object that seemed decisive in the Exodus debate. 'The Pithom Stele' recorded the foundation of a city by Rameses II and suggested that where the EEF looked for the city of Rameses, they had found its twin. Poole called this 'a document of the class of the Rosetta stone' since it 'revolutionises all recent theories of the place of the passage of the Red Sea by the Israelites'.[50] Edwards was no less ebullient:

to discover the site of Pithom-Succoth is actually a matter of far greater importance than to discover Rameses. To have adopted a certain hypothesis; to have backed that hypothesis by a mass of evidence laboriously accumulated, sifted and compared; to be presently proved entirely mistaken, and yet to be, therefore, more rejoiced than if shown to be absolutely right, is, I venture to think, an entirely unique position.[51]

---

[48] Ibid., 2. [49] George St Clair, *Buried Cities and Bible Countries* (London, 1892), p. 19.
[50] R. S. Poole, 'The Progress of Discovery in Egypt', *Academy*, 23 (1883), 193.
[51] Edwards, *Academy*, 23 (1883), 140.

This was 'final proof' that Rameses II was the great oppressor, 'a new proof of the accuracy of the book of Exodus' and a discovery that would '"make an epoch" in biblical criticism, for the Egyptian and biblical history can now be synchronised'.[52] Strangely, suggestions that, while Rameses had been the oppressor, his son Meneptah might be the calamitous Pharaoh of the Exodus were welcomed by some as partial exoneration of a ruler who seems to have maintained something of a personality cult. The African-Canadian artist Edward Bannister (1828–1901) wrote to Edwards to insist that the real identity of the Pharaoh of the Exodus had been obvious to him all along since Rameses the Great 'was too sensible a monarch to use excessive measures towards the Israelites and it is far more likely that this course was followed by his son'.[53]

By April 1884, Naville had excavated the central enclosure containing a temple and a large number of two-storey buildings. This he described as the sacred area, Pithom, as opposed to its civic site Succoth. Despite its modest size, this enclosure was surrounded by walls twenty-two feet thick; the partitions of the buildings inside had breadths of ten feet or more. These were imposing structures that matched the military purpose of biblical Pithom. Naville described the lower levels of the two-storey buildings as 'storage cellars' unconnected except by the rooms above, and intended to hold grain: the identity of this site as a 'store city' seemed irrefutable. To make the picture still more vivid, three types of brick were evident. Those making up the highest layers of construction were held together by neither mortar nor straw. There soon ensued a series of extensive re-imaginings of Hebrew slaves at work on these structures, with Pharaoh's harsh decree falling two-thirds of the way through construction:

So here we have the whole pathetic Bible narrative surviving in solid evidence to the present time. We go down to the bottom of one of these cellars. We see the good bricks for which the straw was provided. Some few feet higher we see those for which the wretched Hebrews had to seek reeds, or stubble. We hear them cry aloud 'Can we make bricks without straw?' Lastly, we see the bricks which they had to make, and did make, without straw, while their hands were bleeding and their hearts were breaking. Shakespeare, in one of his most familiar passages, tells us of 'sermons in stones;' but here we have a sermon in *bricks*, and not only a

---

[52] Ibid., 176; EES, box XIX contains a string of press clippings relating to this find running from 1883 right up to 1888.
[53] Edward M. Bannister to Amelia Edwards, 20 May 1887: EES, box XVI, e.4.

sermon, but a practical historical commentary of the highest importance and interest.[54]

Where mid-century literary treatments of Exodus, including Edwin Atherstone's *Israel in Egypt* (1861), had neglected Pithom and Rameses completely, later literature gave them extensive treatment:

Sunrise on the uncompleted city tipped the raw lines of her half-built walls with broken fire and gilded the gear of gigantic hoisting cranes. Scaffolding, clinging to bald facades, seemed frail and cobwebby at great height, and slabs of stone, drawn and held by cables near the summit of chutes, looked like dice on the giddy slide. Below in the still shadowy passages and interiors, speckled with fallen mortar, lay chains, rubble of brick and chipped stone; splinters, flinders and odd ends of timber; scraps of metal, broken implements and the what-not that litters the path of construction . . . Roadways, beaten in the dust by a multitude of bare feet, led in a hundred directions, all merging in one great track toward the camp of the labouring Israelites.[55]

Elizabeth Miller's description is a heady conflation of modern industrial construction with the one famous painting of 'Ramses and Pithom', Edward Poynter's *Israel in Egypt* (Fig. 4.1).

Unfortunately this site of Pithom was not as picturesque as Edwards' emotive word-painting, or as grand as Miller and Poynter's construction sites. Walls were buried deep in rubble rather than standing proud against the horizon, so were hardly an inspiration for new, Poynter-like grand and theatrical Pithoms. But less prestigious images were produced in large numbers, including photographs for the stereoscope (Fig. 4.2), miniature water-colours and engravings (Fig. 4.3). None revealed much about the site; but all that was needed to feed public demand was depiction of the famous bricks. Poole and Edwards jumped at the chance to reward their subscribers with genuine biblical relics and each independently demanded that Naville dismantle his site and ship the bricks to Britain to be dispersed among interested parties. Poole demanded 500 such items while Edwards requested 1,000. However evocative the excavator's reports had been, they seemed not to have conveyed the scale of the task of transporting these large objects or the logistical and legal challenge their export would have raised. Most historians of Egyptology have sought to characterise Edwards as driven by a forward-thinking impulse to preserve ancient sites, more or less aloof to biblical concerns. Her response to the discovery of Pithom

[54] Edwards, *Pharaohs*, p. 50.
[55] Elizabeth Miller, *The Yoke: A Romance of the Days when the Lord Redeemed the Children of Israel from the Bondage of Egypt* (Indianapolis, IN, 1904), p. 2.

Figure 4.1 Edward Poynter, *Israel in Egypt*, engraving [detail]

demonstrates that enthusiasm for the Old Testament easily overrode her sympathy for the incipient heritage movement.

'Men are in all likelihood coming closer to the fact about God's making the world': interpreting the Pithom excavations

When Naville prepared the Pithom excavation report he favoured the established conventions that limited interpretation and presented hard facts to be used for popular and theological purposes elsewhere. Many of the EEF's members regarded this as a terrible miscalculation: this report was the one

LAST EXHIBITION OF THE ROYAL ACADEMY

Figure 4.1 (cont.)

document that subscribers received in return for their investment, and to force them to look elsewhere for their interpretative material seemed perverse. Letters of complaint soon began to arrive at the EEF and the newspapers. These could be remarkably revealing of the meanings attached to Pithom and the new Egyptology:

The bricks of Pithom were a discovery of thrilling interest to many people to whom the Bondage in Egypt and the Exodus represent typically the greatest events in their own spiritual lives. I have found that believers in the Bible tend to care more about that detail than for the discovery of the place itself! Moreover

Figure 4.2 The brick store-chambers of Hebrew bondsmen

the verification in this particular of a Bible story is valued as showing that such narratives cannot lightly be put aside as mere legends. The Bondage and the deliverance from it are cardinal facts in their history, and in their, and our, religion. The Sabbath (Deut v.15) and, by inference, the Passover commemorate them; and they are frequently referred to not merely in the Pentateuch, but in other parts of the Old Testament ... The bricks show conclusively that these references are not to a legend, but to a fact. Further, the Oppression being now by the aid of the bricks an established fact, so also is the liberation – and *that* without a successful revolt, or the books would have mentioned it. That an enslaved oppressed nation should have been allowed freedom to commence their journey is a *marvel* to be accounted for somehow. Spontaneous emancipation of their slaves by the Egyptians would have been a moral wonder, comparable to the physical one of water running up hill, or to any of the miracles of Moses. Thus the bricks are evidential in various ways. In these views I am not alone: I express them in order to show that there is a class of people represented among the subscribers to the Fund, which highly appreciates the discovery of the bricks. To such the absence of all mention of them in the Quarto is a felt loss, reducing the value of the book.[56]

But there was no shortage of those prepared to take up the task of interpretation declined by Naville. Popular lecturers wove great rhetorical turns around discoveries at Pithom:

---

[56] J. O. Corrie to Amelia Edwards, 17 May 1887: EES, box XVI, e.23.

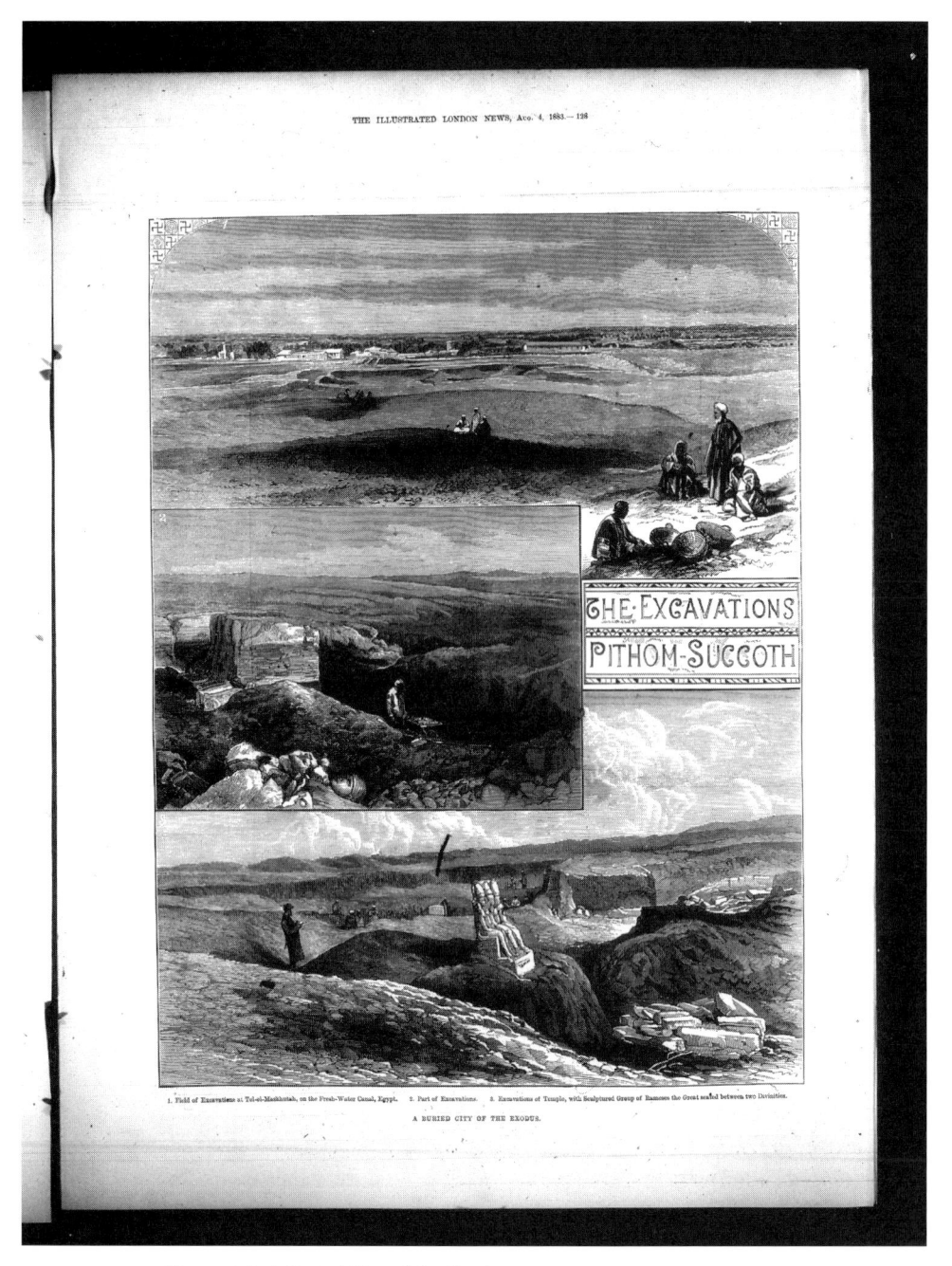

Figure 4.3 *A Buried City of the Exodus*

You will go with me so far, when I affirm that all written history is debatable unless it be confirmed by monuments or documents contemporary with the period of which it treats . . . Had you asked, seven years ago, what contemporary confirmation there was for the statement in the first chapter of Exodus that the Israelites built military store cities, Pithom and Ramses, for Pharaoh, your query would have been met with silence:

It is my privilege tonight to break that silence.[57]

M. L. Herbert then asked his audience 'How does this city practically affect our individual thought or action at the present day?' and answered: 'these historical discoveries are of the most vital importance in establishing beyond the power of question the truth and authenticity of the statements of Holy Scripture, and at a time like the present, contemporary confirmation is doubly valuable'.[58]

Where Edwards had evoked Shakespeare's 'sermons in stones' some popular lecturers preferred the Epistle to the Hebrews:

God had a purpose in hiding [Egypt's confirmation of the Bible] beneath the accumulation of ages. When in our day infidelity has become rampant, when the Old Testament has with great confidence been pronounced a mass of fables, the very stones have risen from the ground to verify in baked brick and tablet and rock and cylinder what of the sacred records had been fiercely assailed by a sceptical criticism.[59]

Those who believed Moses to have been an accurate chronicler of ancient events could thank the EEF for the historical evidence that allowed them to hold their own against 'the repeated derision of ribald sceptics' who produced works with titles such as 'Moses demolished' and 'The authority of Moses defied by history'.[60]

Inspired by such rhetoric, travellers added Pithom to their itineraries. In reporting their experience they were still more sensitive than their predecessors to the biblical associations of the region: fishermen on nearby Lake Timsah were described in the words of Matthew 4:18–22; buffaloes induced reference to Genesis 41:19; desert sands recalled Psalm 63:1; and local customs evoked verses from Judges, 1 Kings, Hosea, Acts and Ezekiel.[61] A museum was soon founded at Ismailia to cater for these new tourists (many of whom combined biblical itineraries with 'the trail of the army of 1882'). It

---

[57] M. L. Herbert, 'Recent Excavations in Egypt', 17 July 1888: EES, box XVIII, 75.   [58] Ibid.
[59] Andrew Archibald, *The Bible Verified* (New York, 1893), p. 234.
[60] Charles Robinson, *The Pharaohs of the Bondage and the Exodus* (London, 1888), p. 17.
[61] For instance, Joseph Pollard, *The Land of the Monuments: Notes of Egyptian Travel* (London, 1896), pp. 15–33.

housed Naville's discoveries alongside spent shells which 'may or may not have been originally picked up off the battlefield'.[62] The first features noted by almost all those who recorded their visit to the site were 'those bricks made and laid in their present position by the Children of Israel during their oppression'.[63] Travellers seemed not to visit the city itself, but to make pilgrimages to 'the bricks of Pithom': the visible patches of brick wall began to be treated with the reverence accorded to shrines. Stereoscopic images of these walls were published in collections that otherwise consisted of imposing monuments. Images like Figure 4.3, in which the *Illustrated London News* presented an elaborate collage of these shapeless muddy undulations, also demonstrate the extent to which a superficially un-photogenic scene gained a grand aura through its association with biblical events.

The EEF's first endeavour proved successful enough for them to expand their operations in the following seasons: an excavator was quickly found who shared their biblical concerns. This was William Matthew Flinders Petrie (1853–1942), the son of a Plymouth Brethren preacher who delivered sermons on the Giza pyramids.[64] Over the following years Naville and Petrie excavated extensively around the Delta, focusing on 'the Land of Goshen' and sites such as Zoan, Tahpanhes (the city to which Jeremiah fled with Zedekiah's daughters when Nebuchadnezzar invaded Judaea) and Tel el Yahoudeh, 'Egypt's Jerusalem', built on its own artificial mound in imitation of the Holy City by the exiled Jewish priest Onias.[65] At Tahpanhes, Petrie hoped to rival the coup caused by the discovery of the bricks of Pithom by finding the stones placed by Jeremiah in the foundations of 'Pharaoh's house' but found that 'Unhappily, the great denudation which has gone on has swept away most of this platform, and we could not expect to find the stones whose hiding is described by Jeremiah'.[66] Tel el Yahoudeh was chosen by Petrie because 'if any considerable remains of the temple can be found, they may assist ... the understanding of the descriptions which have come down to us of the more important structure on Mount Moriah'.[67] This was, of course, the structure that was supposed to be a microcosm of the whole universe, a role that Petrie and his father had earlier ascribed to the Great Pyramid. At Zoan, Naville discovered the head of a black granite

---

[62] Stanley Lane-Poole, 'Discovery of Pithom Succoth', *British Quarterly Review*, 78 (1883), 108.
[63] Pollard, *Land*, p. 25.
[64] For material on the Petries and Pyramid Metrology, see E. M. Reisenauer, 'The Battle of the Standards: Great Pyramid Metrology and British Identity, 1859–90', *Historian*, 65 (2003), 931–78.
[65] Herbert, 'Recent Excavations', 11.
[66] William Flinders Petrie, *Tanis* (London, 1888), IV, p. 51.   [67] Pollard, *Land*, p. 71.

statue which was briefly celebrated as 'a portrait of the Hyksos Pharaoh who raised Joseph to the highest position in the land' before it was identified as Orsokon I of the 22nd dynasty.[68] In keeping with this insistent Hebrew focus, the title 'Joseph's pharaoh' would soon be attached to another statue found at Bubastis. These biblical identifications were frequent until after the turn of the century. Biblical importance would also be attached to sites such as Tel el Amarna because of the insights they offered in terms of comparative religion. These finds were enough for M. L. Herbert to state that each excavation by the EEF had been 'a fresh nail' in the coffin of higher criticism.[69]

Equally dramatically, in the 1890s the EEF would be responsible for the discovery of vast collections of papyri at Oxyrhynchus, including sayings of Christ, and biblical and apocryphal manuscripts. But their success at exciting the 'church and chapel going public' with discoveries at Pithom was never quite repeated. After two decades, disappointment at the limited success of archaeology in uncovering dramatic biblical evidence began to parallel that which had ensued when the hieroglyphs proved not to recount the actions of Joseph and Moses. The Pithom excavations had come at a moment of extraordinary confidence in the potential of archaeology to recover specific locations and events, and so the bricks of Pithom had been embraced with an enthusiasm usually reserved for excavations at the most spectacular of ancient monuments. The find also came at the moment when Egyptologists were at their most successful in attracting an extraordinarily broad public. Over the following decades, tensions evident in Naville's reluctance to tailor excavation reports to public taste became increasingly significant. Techniques and disciplinary conventions developed by Petrie and others established professional/amateur, scholarly/popular distinctions in Egyptology that were barely evident in 1883.

The EEF's first subscribers had shown little interest in chronologies or dynastic successions: instead they obtained satisfaction from elaboration or confirmation of the most intricate details of the urban environments of the Old Testament era. This unusual emphasis is symptomatic of the organisation's emergence at an equivocal moment in the history of archaeology. Earlier, comparable groups such as the Palestine Exploration Fund (PEF) and the Society of Biblical Archaeology had conformed reasonably well to the traditional model of the learned society. They consisted of male antiquarians from the upper social orders, typically holders of public office with university educations. Like Naville they shied away from free expression of

---

[68] Ibid., p. 30.   [69] Herbert, 'Recent Excavations', 11.

their religious commitments and focused on philology and surveying rather than explicit biblical interpretation. Excavation itself was considered 'unbecoming' of a scholar, and many never visited the regions they studied.[70] Authors who allowed biblical illustration to become their central theme were condemned as practitioners of 'sentimental archaeology'.[71] The EEF broke all these conventions and made certain that 1880s and 1890s British Egyptology rarely fitted this mould. More than half those who ran local EEF branches in the late 1880s were women, while 1897 saw the first excavation in Egypt run by British women. Few Egyptologists had university educations, while many were from more modest social backgrounds than their antiquarian predecessors.

At least as interesting as any of these factors, however, is the denominational diversity of those involved with the EEF. Biblical concerns united the organisation, but those who drove and funded this new Egyptological movement were from backgrounds as diverse as Anglicanism, Catholicism, Presbyterianism, the Plymouth Brethren and Quakerism. This implies a vast and potentially divisive range of attitudes to the biblical text, yet there is no record of theological dispute within the organisation. These Egyptologists were perhaps defined by what they stood against. All of them could subscribe, it seems, to condemnation of higher criticism and, in the 1880s, most even to opposition to Darwinian evolution. They were helped by the fact that some of their noisiest opponents were among the most intolerant and under-researched proponents of the 'Huxley, Tyndall, Darwin and Herbert Spencer school'.[72] Amicable debates among EEF members over the crossing of the Red Sea – focusing on whether it had been achieved by supernatural means or by the 'well-known ... action of the East wind' at a spot liable to unusual natural phenomena – demonstrate that there was much room for manoeuvre on sensitive theological issues within the group. The early years of the EEF, before Petrie and Poole fell out irreconcilably, were characterised by such enthusiastic confidence in the social and theological power of archaeology that common ambitions were a more powerful force for unity than sectarian differences were for instability. Only when success began to look less dramatic and biblical evidence more problematic, did cracks begin to show.

---

[70] Walter de Gray Birch, *Biographical Notices of Dr. Samuel Birch* (London, 1886), p. viii.
[71] Ibid.
[72] See for instance Gerald Massey, *Natural Genesis* (2 vols., London, 1883), II, p. 7; in 1883 Huxley mocked the biblical schemes of the EEF in correspondence with his daughter; he claimed that they 'want all their money to find out the pawnbrokers shops that Israel kept in Pithom and Ramses and then went off with all the pledges'.

Pithom's bricks also provided an unusual model of how the ancient city might be conceived. Re-imaginings of other cities – such as Edward Bulwer Lytton's *Last Days of Pompeii* – created spaces to be navigated and viewed from the perspective of their inhabitants, contrasted with the thorn and briar of the wilderness without. Pithom was a city to be laboriously constructed. No nineteenth-century author writes of the lives of the Egyptians who lived in Pithom, except when quoting the Anastasi papyri. It is a labour camp, rather than a pleasure-ground or civic centre, viewed from the perspective of the powerless staring up at its imposing fortifications, not conducting business within. Beyond the city is the pastoral home of the Hebrews, not a barren, forbidding wilderness. Pithom has no famous thoroughfares, no municipal facilities, no great governor or renowned general. Instead, it is a gambit in the contest played out between Moses and Pharaoh, stamped by the contrasting characters of hero and anti-hero. It is the catalyst for a new stage in Hebrew history: a physical symbol of the meaning of the Exodus for the diverse Christians and Jews in the EEF. As such it had an extraordinary, monolithic power. Just as it had for Sharpe, it embodied questions: What could the Chosen People learn from the city-dwelling Egyptians? What could the Egyptians learn from these wanderers? Why, once accustomed to a civilised, almost 'modern' way of life did the Israelites reject the ideals of the city and revert to an apparently less developed mode of living? Most importantly of all, what impact did these two ways of life have on the subsequent development of civilisation: what debt did moderns owe to the cultures whose histories were forced apart at Pithom? Poole reminded his audience that modern urban life wasn't the only valid model for the progressive society:

Some may hesitate to believe that the Egyptians, nourished by centuries of culture, had aught to learn from wandering shepherds or serfs, who scarcely held even their lives secure. But these are shallow doubts, common enough to modern dwellers in great cities, surrounded by the neglected wealth of ancient literatures. Let them ask whether either Homer, or the writers of the sagas, or Llywarch Hen and Taliesin . . . or the Arabs before Mohammad . . . lived as we do. Were they not all wanderers? Did most of them even write? How many poets may have sung before Moses we know not; but the Egyptians heard the songs of their captivity and learnt melodies unknown before.[73]

Petrie would later turn this principle of the constructive clash of cultures into a eugenicist trope, but until the turn of the century this collision

---

[73] Poole, *Cities*, p. 77.

between two great societies was seen more straightforwardly, as the driving force behind the birth of the Christian West.[74] Egyptian civilisation, as Acts 7:22 claimed, had much to teach Moses; but at Pithom and Zoan Christians could 'contrast the enduring spiritual work of Moses with the shattered material trophies of the great oppressor of his people'.[75] Pithom was the site of conflict or compromise between urban pragmatism and an emphatically non-urban spirituality: the city was a place for practical action, not spiritual insight. Alexandrine ascetics were criticised for complete withdrawal from the cities; the ideal model was identified in Abraham, Moses, Elijah and John the Baptist. Each of these celebrated figures left mankind to be alone with God in the desert, but returned to civilisation armed with divine wisdom applicable to practical tasks. Like George Dawson (1821–76) in his call for a Brummagem 'civic gospel' and Henry Drummond (1851–1927), in *The City Without a Church* (1893), Poole argued that the city was the necessary sphere of action for the true Christian: 'the perfect saint' for Poole and Drummond 'is the perfect *citizen*'.[76] Christianity infused cities with a spirituality that was alien to their nature – a notion as applicable to the ancient world as the modern. Ruskin celebrated the balance between action and mysticism as characteristic of the Egyptian priesthood; in several works he explored the combination of scientific and spiritual competence behind Pharaonic monuments, hoping to discover how far the Egyptians 'knew God'.[77] This idea also inflected attempts to rediscover spiritual–practical balance in the *fin-de-siècle* flowering of Hermetic occultism. Hermes Trismegistus, mythical originator of the Hermetic wisdom texts, was presented as a colleague of Moses at the school of Heliopolis; or Moses himself; or a disciple handpicked by the Messiah to perpetuate the learning of the priests of Memphis.[78]

Several of these conceptions of history could be tinged with anti-Semitism, with those of Rider Haggard being notable examples: Poole's assertions of Hebrew superiority over the Egyptians were frequently undercut by others. The civilising role of Egyptian cities sometimes became a means of explaining how a people so 'uncivilised' as the Jews had produced the greatest work of pre-classical literature. In this model, the Hebrews contributed no particular abilities to the world, only a revealed knowledge

---

[74] For instance William Flinders Petrie, *Janus in Modern Life* (London, 1907); but especially *The Revolutions of Civilisation* (London, 1911).

[75] Poole, *Cities*, p. 87.   [76] Drummond, *City*, p. 13.

[77] Ruskin, *Praeterita* (London, 1885–9), pp. xviii, xxxiv; see also, Francis O'Gorman, 'To See the Finger of God in the Dimensions of the Pyramid', *Modern Language Review*, 98 (2003), 563–73.

[78] See, e.g., David Duguid, *Hermes: Disciple of Jesus* (London, 1893).

which they were incapable of using without first being civilised in Egyptian cities. Moses himself could be considered Egyptian in racial as well as cultural terms. But most of the literature produced by writers on ancient Egypt during these decades was a twin celebration of the Israelite 'chosen people' and spectacular Egyptian discoveries, in which the interface of sacred and secular history at cities such as Pithom justified study and celebration of previously disparaged Egyptian achievements. As chapter one demonstrated, Homeric scholars went through elaborate contortions to avoid charges of impiety in their commitment to Greek legend and philosophy. The fact that Moses had been schooled in Egyptian wisdom when 'he prepared to be the leader and lawgiver' meant that similar charges could not be directed at enthusiasts for Egyptian civilisation.

Pithom epitomises some of the roles the Bible played in ancient history in the late nineteenth century. It demonstrates the extent to which biblical ideas suffused more areas of nineteenth-century culture than is often recognised. The EEF were not practising a marginal biblical archaeology: this scripturally informed excavation was mainstream, almost monopolistic, in the 1880s and 1890s. These decades stood between the sidelining of antiquarian interests and the emergence of a formalised university Egyptology. Between 1840 and 1890, Near Eastern excavation reports were developed from extended discursive travelogues into records of archaeological process. This transition has led historians of archaeology to see a discipline undergoing secularisation. This is illusory: where reports such as Layard's *Nineveh and its Remains* were intended as stand-alone documents, the Egyptologist of the 1880s produced dozens of supporting works suffused with biblical material. Their choice of excavation sites like Pithom was driven by biblical concerns, and their relationships with readers were predicated on a common interest in Old Testament texts.

5 | Babylon

MICHAEL SEYMOUR

Babylon on the map

At the end of the eighteenth century, the Danish explorer Carsten Niebuhr (1733–1815) gave accurate measurements of longitude and latitude for the city of Babylon. The strangeness of this piece of recording may not be immediately apparent; it was, after all, an act in keeping with its own time and with ours. Babylon, however, was possessed of an unusual geography. For the previous two thousand years, it had been known not so much as a physical place as a moral condition. The few visitors who had sought to observe its physical ruins did so at many different sites, including the correct one, and once there had sought more than anything else to observe an absence: the prophets had foretold the city's destruction and it had come to pass.

In his account, the twelfth-century traveller Rabbi Benjamin of Tudela records the physical marks of divine destruction in the vitrification of part of the ruins of the Tower of Babel.[1] The mound he took for the Tower was actually the ziggurat at Birs Nimrud, ancient Borsippa, a city located several miles from Babylon itself, but the impression that a large part of the mound had been exposed to great heat was remarked upon by other visitors. Other candidates were suggested for the Tower, including one of the mounds, still known as Babil, at Babylon itself and the remains of the ziggurat at 'Aqar Quf, much nearer to Baghdad and probably seen by many more foreign travellers than relatively inaccessible Birs Nimrud.

The debate over the Tower's location continued into the nineteenth century, when attempts were made, particularly by the French Assyriologist Jules Oppert (1825–1905), to explain Birs Nimrud's distance from the main Babylon site with reference to the vast dimensions for the city and its walls given by classical authorities.[2] The likely inspiration for the biblical Tower, the ziggurat Etemenanki, had long since vanished, many of

---

[1] Michael Signer, ed., *The Itinerary of Rabbi Benjamin of Tudela* (Malibu, 1983), p. 103.
[2] Julian Reade, 'Early Travellers on the Wonders: Suggested Sites', in Irving Finkel and Michael Seymour, eds., *Babylon: Myth and Reality* (London, 2008), pp. 112–17.

its bricks having been extracted and re-used over the centuries, with the result that none of the nineteenth-century visitors were able to hit on precisely the right location.

A more detailed description of the ruins at Babylon is given by the Roman nobleman Pietro della Valle (1586–1652), who in 1616 visited the site, documented what he saw in a series of letters edited by his friend Mario Schipano, and had an artist produce two illustrations of what he took to be the ruins of the Tower of Babel.[3] The mound, Tell Babil, did not contain the remains of the ziggurat, but was part of the city of Babylon, making the drawings the earliest to reach Europe of the site itself. They and della Valle's description, with Latin translation, were included in Athanasius Kircher's monumental *Turris Babel*, alongside many fantastic images of the biblical Tower.[4] Finally, della Valle takes the opportunity to correct another long-standing source of confusion regarding Baghdad:

> Now, to start talking about the city, which, during the time I have been here, I have looked at very closely and diligently, including the outskirts, let me state first of all that those who think Baghdad is the ancient Babylon (as the common people call it) are mistaken. First, because the old Babylon (which everyone knows about) has always been described as being on the Euphrates, and not on the Tigris, where Baghdad is. Secondly, because from its buildings, architecture, the Arabic inscriptions cut or sculpted in many places, or made in stucco, and all the other circumstances, Baghdad is clearly seen to be a work of modern times. And doubtless it was built by Mohammedans, according to what (as I understand) is written in their histories.[5]

Other travellers followed, including eventually Niebuhr, whose achievement may be better understood in the light of the unusual circumstances of his mission. He was part of – indeed the sole survivor of – a six-man scientific

---

[3] Pietro della Valle, *Viaggi di P. della Valle il Pellegrino: Descritti da lui medesimo in lettere familiari all'erudito suo amico Mario Schipano* (1650–3; Brighton, 1843); for modern edition and commentary see Antonio Invernizzi, ed., *Pietro della Valle, In Viaggio per l'Oriente: le Mummie, Babilonia, Persepoli* (Alexandria, 2001). For an English edition of selected parts of the account, including the description of Babylon, see George Bull, *The Pilgrim: The Journeys of Pietro della Valle* (London, 1989); Antonio Invernizzi, 'Discovering Babylon with Pietro della Valle', in P. Matthiae, A. Enea, L. Peyronel and F. Pinnock, eds., *Proceedings of the First International Congress on the Archaeology of the Ancient Near East (Rome, May 18th–23rd 1998)* (Rome, 2000), pp. 643–9.

[4] Athanasius Kircher, *Turris Babel, Sive Archontologia Qua Primo Priscorum post Diluvium Hominum Vita, Mores Rerumque Gestarum Magnitudo, Secundo Turris Fabrica Civitatumque Exstructio, Confusio Linguarum, et Inde Gentium Transmigrationis, cum Principalium Inde Enatorum Idiomatum Historia, Multiplici Eruditione Describuntur et Explicantur* (3 vols., Amsterdam, 1679).

[5] Bull, *The Pilgrim*, p. 102.

expedition to Arabia by Frederick V of Denmark, inspired by the ideas of Johann David Michaelis (1717–91). A towering figure in the biblical scholarship of the eighteenth century, Michaelis had a great impact on the nature and scope of biblical scholarship, one aspect of which was to influence profoundly the treatment of the physical remains of the past. Broadening his enquiries from the philological concerns of biblical scholars to far broader historical questions, not only philological but ethnographic and archaeological, Michaelis produced a Bible translation based on principles markedly different from any predecessor. Michaelis' translation was more concerned with the historical distance, even strangeness, of the world of the Old Testament, and with historical particulars extending from the minutiae of daily life to decisive political events.[6] Wishing to bring new breadth and a fresh scholarly eye to his subject, Michaelis 'sought consciously to avoid traditional constraints on interpretation in order to create the conditions for a neo-humanistic encounter with ancient Israel, one characterized by philological rigor, philosophical interest, and aesthetic insight'.[7] The very idea that the study of Middle Eastern geography, ethnography and ancient sites might conceivably inform a better understanding of Scripture was to some extent dependent on Michaelis' new outlook; certainly it is hard to identify travellers' observations earlier than the Danish expedition that suggest any such ambitious goals. That the Danish mission did indeed aim at serious scholarly discovery was in no doubt: an original ambition to send a single individual somehow trained in all the disciplines Michaelis deemed relevant – possible perhaps for the polymath Michaelis himself – led eventually to the more plausible solution of a team of six: a philologist, a botanist, an engineer (Niebuhr), a doctor, an illustrator and a servant.[8] This selection, based on expertise and funded with the intention of discovery and information-gathering, was in itself novel: previous accounts of the Middle East had largely been the by-products of pilgrimages and mercantile journeys, their authors' suitability for and interest in recording what they saw almost entirely as a matter of luck.

  The Danish mission was ill-fated, but Niebuhr, its only surviving member, was still able to produce an account of his travels that recorded much detail of a kind unseen in earlier travel writing, including detailed physical descriptions of topography and of ancient sites. The approach taken by Niebuhr, and to some extent by the Abbé de Beauchamp, who visited

---

[6] Jonathan Sheehan, *The Enlightenment Bible: Translation, Scholarship, Culture* (Princeton, NJ, 2005), pp. 184–6.
[7] Michael Legaspi, *The Death of Scripture and the Rise of Biblical Studies* (Oxford, 2010), p. 100.
[8] Ibid., p. 187.

Babylon at around the same time and confirmed Niebuhr's measurements, does represent a significant departure from that of their predecessors.[9] Overall, however, European knowledge of Babylon's geography had made only modest headway. Much of the cartographical confusion found in medieval accounts remained even in the eighteenth century: an uncertainty regarding the relationship between ancient Babylon and modern Baghdad, conflicting accounts of the location of the former and especially of the biblical Tower of Babel, and confusion between the two great rivers Tigris and Euphrates continued to puzzle Europeans reliant on travellers' accounts for their knowledge of Mesopotamia.[10]

Claudius Rich and explorations in the early nineteenth century

The turning point in Babylon's physical exploration really came in 1811 when Claudius James Rich (1787–1821), then East India Company Resident at Baghdad, made his own survey of the ruins. His *Memoir on the Ruins of Babylon*, first published in the Viennese journal *Mines de l'Orient / Fundgruben des Orients* and subsequently as an individual volume, is remarkable on three counts.[11] First, the volume contains the first detailed plan of the site of Babylon to become available in Europe (Fig. 5.1). Second, the author brings a thorough knowledge of the classical sources on the ancient city to bear. Finally, and most importantly, Rich was prepared to test the ancient Greek sources – and indeed the accounts of more recent European travellers – against his own observations. Niebuhr's co-ordinates and Rich's preparedness to supplement and contradict the textual sources on the basis of what he saw amounted to a significant shift in what it meant to visit and observe Babylon's ruins. It was in these acts and others like them that what we now classify as archaeology really begins. For this reason Babylon's incorporation into modern cartography is stranger than the rediscovery of a place more completely lost, and its consequences more significant. It opens new channels for understanding the past while

---

[9] Joseph de Beauchamp, *Itinéraire du Voyage fait par le Citoyen Beauchamp, Astronome et Correspondent de la Cidevant Académie de Sciences, Depuis le Mois de Mars de l'année 1781 Jusqu'en Décembre, 1789*. 1790–1800, Cartographic Items Add. MS 15,331.2, British Library.

[10] A. Invernizzi, 'Les Premiers Voyageurs', in Béatrice André-Salvini, ed., *Babylone* (Paris, 2008), pp. 505–7.

[11] Claudius James Rich, 'Memoir on the Ruins of Babylon', *Mines de l'Orient / Fundgruben des Orients*, 3 (1813), 129–62, 197–200; *Memoir on the Ruins of Babylon* (London, 1815).

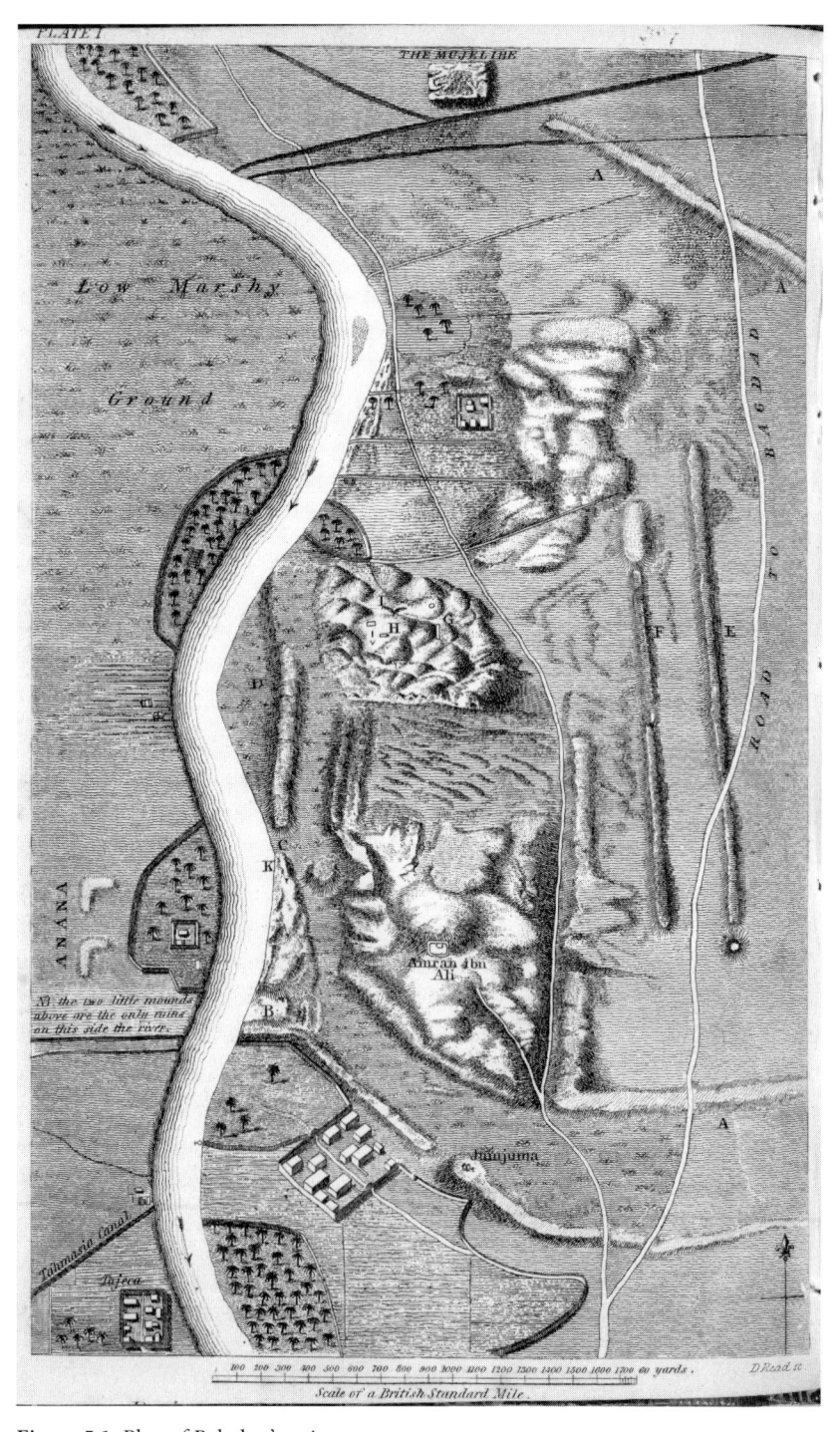

Figure 5.1 Plan of Babylon's ruins

potentially threatening others. This transformation is certainly not an event particular to Babylon. Other chapters in this volume note similar changes as distant locations rich in legend were pinned down, classified and brought within the reach of empirical study.[12]

Rich's motivations were not religious but more broadly antiquarian. As for any European, the Bible played a large part in structuring his picture of ancient history and of the significance of cities like Babylon and Nineveh (of which he also produced an important description), but his writing does not dwell unduly on biblical connections, nor does he attempt to draw religious or moral conclusions, though the opportunity presented itself: for the pious, Babylon's ruins could act as much as a warning against sin and corruption as a proof of the Bible's historicity and the fulfilment of prophecy.[13] Largely eschewing such concerns, Rich's discussion is framed firmly in the context of classical accounts, principally Herodotus and Diodorus, which offer physical description of a kind absent in the biblical accounts and that might be compared with the city's remains as he found them. The final edition of Rich's work on Babylon contains a variety of related material, including extracts from earlier travellers' accounts and the debate between Rich and Major James Rennell (1742–1830), but nothing relating to its religious impact or utility. If in England there was some popular application for his discoveries, Rich himself was concerned instead with a community and discourse that was scholarly, exclusive and pan-European – the latter reflecting a cosmopolitan openness that would be eroded later in the century, not least by the nationalist character of competition for antiquities.[14]

The changing character of travel accounts and increasing detail over time seen in descriptions of Babylon is a good example of epistemological change driving changes in observation and recording. The development of antiquarian studies in the Near East and eventually of archaeological reports was not provoked by changes to the physical landscape that travellers saw. Accumulation of information and the incorporation of material from earlier travellers were visible and significant in the process, but ultimately do little

---

[12] In this volume see Gange and Bryant Davis; Goldhill; Ledger-Lomas. See also Holger Hoock, *Empires of the Imagination: Politics, War and the Arts in the British World, 1750–1850* (London, 2010), pp. 213–14, who notes similar developments in the study of the classical world in the topographical work of William Gell and William Martin Leake.

[13] Claudius James Rich, *Narrative of a Residence in Koordistan, and on the Site of Ancient Nineveh ... Edited by his Widow* (2 vols., London, 1836).

[14] For a striking example of English popular usage of Rich's account, see George Stanley Faber, *Horæ Mosaicæ: Or, a Dissertation on the Credibility and Theology of the Pentateuch* (2 vols., London, 1818), I, pp. 169–75.

to help us understand the differences between the accounts of Benjamin of Tudela and Claudius Rich, nor any particular reason why a description comparable to that of Rich was not produced by any earlier visitor. Rather, Rich's *Memoir* is witness to an improved status for observations on the ground relative to the textual sources: there is no point in producing a detailed topographical account of a site unless one believes that the information can be of some use in expanding or improving the knowledge of that site that can be derived from existing texts. The emphasis of earlier visitors on identifying sites and features known from the textual sources had, by the early nineteenth century, become a broader and more ambitious attempt to understand the ruins using a combination of textual sources and empirical observation.

Rich himself became involved in a debate with Major James Rennell on his interpretation of Herodotus and the site, questions raised in which contributed to the publication of a *Second Memoir*.[15] This debate turned to some degree on the status of Herodotus as a canonical, authoritative account, and on the degree to which Rich's method was considered plausible. Both sides of the argument were included in a posthumous publication of Rich's work.[16] That Rich's major antagonist was another Englishman is perhaps slightly unrepresentative of the cosmopolitan context of his work; the fact that Rennell himself was a scholar who had taken an ambitious new approach to the geography of Herodotus, however, is entirely fitting. Though engaged in a debate in which Rich as the antiquary on the ground challenged the authority of the more text-dependent Rennell, the two men were fundamentally engaged in the same transformative approach to ancient texts, ancient sites and the pursuit of knowledge about the past. Rennell's *Geographical System of Herodotus* (1800) was based upon modern advances in cartography and the mapping of the Middle East (Rennell had himself already been responsible for surveying and mapping large parts of India for the first time), as well as the still relatively novel view that the connection between text and physical remains could lead to a richer understanding of both.[17] Rennell's expertise and his geographical work were part of British imperial expansion; the same, to only a slightly lesser extent, could

---

[15] Claudius James Rich, *Second Memoir on Babylon, Containing an Inquiry into the Correspondence Between the Ancient Description of Babylon and the Remains Still Visible on the Site* (London, 1818).

[16] Claudius James Rich, *Narrative of a Journey to the Site of Babylon ... Edited by his Widow* (London, 1839). Rich's health suffered badly in the Middle East, sickness repeatedly thwarting both his professional duties and antiquarian ambitions. He died of cholera in Shiraz in 1821.

[17] See James Rennell, *The Geographical System of Herodotus Examined and Explained, by a Comparison with those of Other Ancient Authors, and with Modern Geography* (London, 1800).

be said of Rich's antiquarian researches in Mesopotamia. Though Rich largely prevailed regarding Babylon, due to his personal familiarity with the site, more generally his own and Rennell's work were similarly indicative of the direction of scholarship.

A succession of mainly English travellers in the decades following Rich's work supplied detailed accounts of their visits to Babylon. These visits tended to include some minor excavation, and thus the accounts of Robert Ker Porter (1777–1842), James Silk Buckingham (1786–1855), George Keppel (1799–1891) and Robert Mignan (d. 1852) occasionally add to or help to clarify the thorough description given by Rich, but are also useful for their incidental records of local traditions and folklore relating to the site and descriptions of life in Ottoman Iraq.[18] It should be mentioned that none of these are dedicated studies of the site on the model of that produced by Rich. Instead they are travel memoirs, so that in each case visits to Babylon and other ancient sites form part of general narratives encompassing all aspects of the travellers' journeys through the Middle East.

To talk first of the exploration of the site itself, however, is perhaps an unfortunate projection of a contemporary archaeologist's perspective onto the Victorian cultural and intellectual landscape. One might equally begin an exploration with the Babylon that was far better known and understood: that of the Bible.

Cities of sin ancient and modern

Babylon's biblical identity is defined above all else by Nebuchadnezzar's sack of Jerusalem and deportation of Judaeans to his capital, and it is unsurprising that the symbolic role of the Judaean Exile in Victorian culture was considerable. Nebuchadnezzar's campaigns against Jerusalem in 597 and 587/6 BC followed, in Mesopotamian terms, quite normal military and imperial procedure. The deportation of a large part of the Judaean population to Babylon was partly a policy directed at imperial integration, and it is ironic that it should ultimately have been the single greatest contributor to Babylon's permanently blackened reputation. Emotive language attends

---

[18] Robert Ker Porter, *Travels in Georgia, Persia, Armenia, Ancient Babylonia, &c. &c. During the Years 1817, 1818, 1819 and 1820* (2 vols., London, 1821); James Silk Buckingham, *Travels in Mesopotamia* (2 vols., London, 1827); George Keppel, *Personal Narrative of a Journey from India to England* (London, 1827); Robert Mignan, *Travels in Chaldaea Including a Journey from Bussorah to Bagdad, Hillah, and Babylon, Performed on Foot* (London, 1829).

both the anger felt against Babylon and the plight of the Judaean exiles. Terrible retribution is promised:

> Whoever is captured will be thrust through;
>   all who are caught will fall by the sword.
> Their infants will be dashed to pieces before their eyes;
>   their houses will be looted and their wives ravished.
> See, I will stir up against them the Medes,
>   who do not care for silver
>   and have no delight in gold.
> Their bows will strike down the young men;
>   they will have no mercy on infants
>   nor will they look with compassion on children.
> Babylon, the jewel of kingdoms,
>   the glory of the Babylonians' pride,
>   will be overthrown by God
>   like Sodom and Gomorrah.
> She will never be inhabited
>   or lived in through all generations;
>   no Arab will pitch his tent there,
>   no shepherd will rest his flocks there.[19]

But the defining text here is that of Psalm 137, 'By the rivers of Babylon we sat down and wept'.

> By the rivers of Babylon we sat and wept
>   when we remembered Zion.
> There on the poplars
>   we hung our harps,
> for there our captors asked us for songs,
>   our tormentors demanded songs of joy;
>   they said, 'Sing us one of the songs of Zion!'
> How can we sing the songs of the Lord
>   while in a foreign land?
> If I forget you, O Jerusalem,
>   may my right hand forget its skill.
> May my tongue cling to the roof of my mouth
>   if I do not remember you,
>   if I do not consider Jerusalem
>   my highest joy.
> Remember, O Lord, what the Edomites did
>   on the day Jerusalem fell.

---

[19] Isaiah 13:15–20.

> 'Tear it down,' they cried,
> 'tear it down to its foundations!'
> O Daughter of Babylon, doomed to destruction,
> happy is he who repays you
> for what you have done to us–
> he who seizes your infants
> and dashes them against the rocks.[20]

The Psalm is usually invoked in relation to the image of a people suffering stoically. The final lines and their angry desire for Babylon's violent destruction are often forgotten; the text has been treated so as to resonate with Christian pacifism, and it is naturally the earlier verses that are represented in nineteenth-century artists' visions of a captive people in desolation and despair (Fig. 5.2). Nonetheless, the knowledge that their oppression will not last forever is crucial. More than simply a people oppressed, the biblical Judaeans are a people with a special destiny. This sense of historic purpose is an important aspect of the role of religion in European nationalism at large, but perhaps also goes some way towards explaining specifically how such empathy with unwilling imperial subjects could flourish without apparent conflict in the high culture of the world's greatest imperial power. Imperial culture usually – perhaps necessarily – involves some idea of a special destiny, and the particular nature of this sense of historical significance in nineteenth-century England has been the topic of much discussion. There were of course multiple imperial models on which to draw; Richard Hingley's *Roman Officers and English Gentlemen* (2000) has explored perhaps the most important of these.[21] Another significant facet of the notion of destiny, however, is rooted in a history seen from the other side of the imperial coin: that of ancient Israel and Judah. This history, as known through the Old Testament, presented a spiritual problem. In the Bible, the great earthly powers of Egypt, Assyria and Babylonia are emphatically not God's chosen people; they are doomed. What fate then for England, the greatest earthly power of all?

Alongside the triumphalism, there was also a strong apocalyptic strand in Victorian culture, which is where Babylon and Jerusalem come in. The formula applied was itself ancient, inherited from St Augustine: all cities contain both the earthly and the heavenly city, sinful Babylon and the seeds

---

[20] Psalm 137:1–9.
[21] Richard Hingley, *Roman Officers and English Gentlemen: The Imperial Origins of Roman Archaeology* (London and New York, 2000).

Figure 5.2 Dalziel brothers after Edward John Poynter, *By the Waters of Babylon*, woodcut

of the New Jerusalem. This is not to say that some millenarians did not take a more literal view: Richard Brothers (1757–1824), calling himself 'Prince of the Hebrews', offered prophecies including French conquest of England and London's destruction, and led a popular movement promising to save both real Jews and the 'invisible' Jews of England: he and his followers, Gentiles included by virtue of their spirit of liberty.[22]

In the early nineteenth century, the most important exponent of the Babylon/Jerusalem metaphor is William Blake. Blake's Babylon consisted of all worldly trappings, from conventional vices to more cherished institutions such as law and even organised religion. The coming of the New Jerusalem would necessarily involve the destruction of Babylon. Quite how this would manifest itself in human terms is not clear, but violent revolution seems necessary, and indeed Blake was initially a supporter of the revolution in France. The removal of society's constraints on human energy would bring about the New Jerusalem, and a state in which law was simply unnecessary, but the process by which this was achieved would not necessarily be benign. The French Revolution signalled for many the beginning of the End Times and heralded the coming of the Antichrist.[23] For some that Antichrist was Napoleon himself, and prophecies of Daniel and Revelation were seen to be fulfilled with his deposing of Pope Pius VI in 1798. The sharp rise in the production of millenarian works and prophecies in England at the beginning of the nineteenth century seems either directly linked to this belief or at the very least a consequence of the broader European sense of turmoil and uncertainty that France's turbulent politics had created.[24]

Blake, as a poet, artist and celebrated eccentric, had more latitude to explore the Apocalypse than most. A more sober counterpart, however, can be seen in the actions of those who saw the improvement of urban life in Britain as a religious mission as well as a practical problem. Here the language of Babylon and Jerusalem was frequently invoked: Benjamin Disraeli himself famously referred to London as a 'modern Babylon'.[25] The influential writer and editor Robert Mudie (d. 1842), to take one example, produced two moralising books bearing the title *Babylon the Great* (1825; 1829), in which London's many 'Babylonian' faults were held up to criticism and scrutiny.[26] Mudie's works had nothing to do with an

---

[22] Richard Brothers, *A Revealed Knowledge of the Prophecies and Times* (London, 1797); Ian McCalman, 'New Jerusalems: Prophecy, Dissent and Radical Culture in England, 1786–1830', in Knud Haakonssen, ed., *Enlightenment and Religion: Rational Dissent in Eighteenth-Century Britain* (Cambridge, 1996), pp. 322–4.

[23] C. D. A. Leighton, 'Antichrist's Revolution: Some Anglican Apocalypticists in the Age of the French Wars', *Journal of Religious History*, 24 (2000), 125–42.

[24] David Hempton, 'Evangelism and Eschatology', *Journal of Ecclesiastical History*, 31 (1996), 182–3.

[25] Benjamin Disraeli, *Tancred, Or, the New Crusade* (London, 1847), book 5, chapter 5.

[26] Robert Mudie, *Babylon the Great: A Dissection and Demonstration of Men and Things in the British Capital* (2 vols., London, 1825), Robert Mudie, *London and Londoners: Or, a Second Judgement of 'Babylon the Great'* (2 vols., London, 1829).

apocalypse or New Jerusalem in the future, and everything with calls to reform in the present. Similar sentiments are sometimes expressed in the form of disapproval from visitors or of social investigations revealing the great city's many iniquities.[27] For the Babylon reference to have force in this context, it was not necessary to imagine a great cataclysm; the quest was surely to achieve redemption in the form of a more just society without the horrors of revolution. But these municipal efforts to bring the earthly city closer to its heavenly counterpart were nonetheless attempts to purge the sinful 'Babylon' that naturally formed a part of the Victorian city.

Some, inevitably, did see the parallel in full, with London suffering Babylon's supposed fate.[28] 'Supposed' because, powerful though the language of the prophets has been in culture, the fall to which they refer is the 539 BC conquest of the city by Cyrus, following which the city continued as the largest of the Achaemenid Persian royal capitals for another two hundred years before that empire in its turn fell to Alexander. The latter planned to make Babylon the capital of his empire, but that empire as a unified whole was so short-lived that the dream was effectively never realised. Gradually marginalised by Seleucia on the Tigris (founded by Seleucus Nicator at the end of the fourth century BC), Babylon faded rather than fell, and its exact end as a city is not well documented. The cataclysmic fall associated with Babylon in Western culture results from several factors: first, the destruction and desertion foretold by Jeremiah and Isaiah; second, the transference of this language and Babylon as a metaphor to the Apocalypse in the Book of Revelation; and finally by a moral, narrative need. The impious act of eating and drinking from the gold of the Jerusalem Temple at Belshazzar's Feast deserves the most severe divine punishment, and so that punishment enters into our understanding of the narrative despite its absence from the biblical account, which contains only the statement that 'In that night was Belshazzar the king of the Chaldeans slain. And Darius the Median took the kingdom, being about threescore and two years old'.[29]

What ultimately became of this statement can be seen in the apocalyptic images produced by John Martin (1789–1854). His *Belshazzar's Feast*

---

[27] E.g. Harry Hawthorn (pseudonym), *A Visit to Babylon; with Observations, Moral and Political* (London, 1829); 'M. L. C.', *The New-Zealander on London Bridge: Or, Moral Ruins of the Modern Babylon* (London, 1878); James Greenwood, *Unsentimental Journeys, or, Byways of the Modern Babylon* (London, 1867). For the genre see also Lodewijk Brunt, 'The Ethnography of "Babylon": The Rhetoric of Fear and the Study of London, 1850–1914', *City and Society*, 4 (1990), 77–87.

[28] The titles of pamphlets such as *London: The Babylon of the Apocalypse* (London, 1836) leave little room for ambiguity.

[29] Daniel 5:30–1.

Figure 5.3 John Martin, *Belshazzar's Feast*

(Fig. 5.3) and *Fall of Babylon*, depicting scenes separated by only a few hours, the latter featuring both the invading army that the ancient sources concur never rampaged through Babylon and the most tumultuous and unnatural of skies. This is a destruction that makes deliberate reference to the apocalypse, but also, it seems, to London. The argument that 'mad' Martin, a millenarian, saw something of his contemporary society's impending destruction in his biblical subjects is supported by the interpretation of his brother Jonathan, who while held at Bedlam (rabidly anti-clerical, he had tried to burn down York Minster) produced a drawing of London's destruction closely modelled on his brother's *Fall of Nineveh*.[30] Martin is a good example of the Victorian ability to connect salvation with the most practical of civic works: his concern with a looming apocalypse did not prevent his taking a passionate interest in sewerage and municipal planning. Others, however, took a more fatalistic view, leading many millenarians to doubt the value of another great Victorian endeavour to bring about the New Jerusalem: the missionary endeavours and evangelism that over the course of the century would come to sweep the British Empire. 'What the evangelicals were trying to do with Bibles, tracts and missionaries,' Hempton observes, 'the millenarians believed could only be achieved through Christ's personal return.'[31]

London was not the only Babylon towards which religious fervour and fear were directed in Victorian England. Another prominent target was the Catholic Church, explicitly likened to Babylon from the beginnings of the Reformation and in nineteenth-century English Protestant culture strongly associated with sin and corruption. A paranoid and highly sexualised vision

---

[30] David Bindman, 'The English Apocalypse', in F. Carey, ed., *The Apocalypse and the Shape of Things to Come* (London, 1999), p. 268.
[31] Hempton, 'Evangelism and Eschatology', 188.

of Catholicism earned it the moniker of 'Babylon' in the eyes of many Protestants.[32]

Discovery and decipherment

In the mid-nineteenth century, a revolution occurred in knowledge of ancient Mesopotamia.[33] From 1842 Paolo Emilio Botta (1802–70) and Austen Henry Layard (1817–94) found and excavated the ancient Assyrian capitals in northern Iraq, including Nineveh itself. The sight of biblical cities rising from the ground excited huge interest, particularly in England, where the *Illustrated London News* played an important role in disseminating information about the discoveries and, subsequently, the arrival of huge stone sculptures and reliefs in London, where they were displayed at the British Museum. Layard's own account of the discoveries, *Nineveh and its Remains*, was published in 1849 to great public interest, becoming arguably the first ever archaeological best-seller.[34] Its content was of course far from purely archaeological: the author's travels in Iraq and observations of contemporary life make up a large proportion of the book, which is not a formal report but a travel account in the same vein as those produced by Buckingham and Ker Porter earlier in the century. It has been observed that the French reception of Assyrian antiquities differs substantially from the English case, most strikingly in the absence of a popular work playing a role parallel to *Nineveh and its Remains*.[35] One might also argue that the tradition of popular writing on the ancient Near East engendered by this development from travel accounts can still be seen in the popular work of some twentieth-century British archaeologists, particularly Leonard Woolley (1880–1960) and Max Mallowan (1904–78).

At the same time as these momentous discoveries were taking place the decipherment of the cuneiform script and the languages of the ancient Near East also progressed rapidly. In 1821 Wordsworth could still write that,

---

[32] Michael E. Schiefelbein, *The Lure of Babylon: Seven Protestant Novelists and Britain's Roman Catholic Revival* (Macon, CA, 2001), p. 2.

[33] For an excellent account of developments over this period see Mogens Trolle Larsen, *The Conquest of Assyria: Excavations in an Antique Land, 1840–1860* (London and New York, 1996).

[34] A. H. Layard, *Nineveh and its Remains: With an Account of a Visit to the Chaldæan Christians of the Kurdistan, and the Yezidis, or Devil-Worshippers; and an Inquiry into the Manners and Arts of the Ancient Assyrians* (2 vols., London, 1849).

[35] See especially Frederick Bohrer, 'Inventing Assyria: Exoticism and Reception in Nineteenth-Century England and France', *Art Bulletin*, 80 (1998), 336–56.

> Babylon,
> Learnèd and wise, hath perished utterly,
> Nor leaves her Speech one word to aid the sigh
> That would lament her.[36]

Yet by the turn of the twentieth century, a wealth of ancient Mesopotamian documents had been read and even published. The key to decipherment, a monumental trilingual inscription produced by Darius the Great at Bisitun in western Iran, was copied by Henry Rawlinson (1810–95) in stages from 1835 to 1837. Rawlinson himself played a great role in the decipherment, although he has perhaps been given too much credit at the expense of Edward Hincks (1792–1866), whose most important advances seem to have been made slightly ahead of Rawlinson's own.[37] The process was a very gradual one, but a safe date for effective decipherment is given by a challenge set by the Royal Asiatic Society at the suggestion of Henry Fox Talbot (1800–77) in 1857. Given the same cuneiform inscription to translate, Rawlinson, Hincks, Jules Oppert (1825–1905) and Talbot independently produced translations whose similarity was too great to admit of much further doubt that decipherment had been achieved. From here, the work moved to the gradual translation of texts and the rediscovery of ancient Mesopotamian literature. In 1872 London would witness the *cause célèbre* of George Smith's discovery of the 'Flood Tablet' containing a Babylonian version of the biblical Deluge. The intersection of the new discoveries and the Bible raised theological questions but also great excitement. News of Smith's discovery was widely publicised and money given by the *Daily Telegraph* for Smith to travel to Iraq to find the rest of the account. This, incredibly, he did, and the whole story, the *Epic of Gilgamesh*, has gone on to become perhaps the only ancient Mesopotamian text to secure a wide general readership and recognition in the canon of world literature. Although he did not excavate there, Smith did also visit Babylon. Following Rawlinson's identification of the tell as the ruined lower levels of a ziggurat, he felt that Birs Nimrud was the most likely candidate for the Genesis Tower of Babel, while realising that the city in which it was actually located was Borsippa.[38]

---

[36] William Wordsworth, 'Missions and Travels', in Abbie Findlay Potts, ed., *The Ecclesiastical Sonnets of William Wordsworth* (London, 1922), p. 132.

[37] Julian Reade, 'Tablets at Babylon and the British Museum', in Irving Finkel and Michael Seymour, eds., *Babylon: Myth and Reality* (London, 2008), p. 76.

[38] George Adam Smith, *Assyrian Discoveries: An Account of Explorations and Discoveries on the Site of Nineveh During 1873 and 1874* (New York, 1875), p. 59.

The result of these achievements was that by the end of the 1840s some vision of the material culture of ancient Assyria was available to all, to be followed quickly by translations of ancient texts. The Sydenham Crystal Palace, opened in 1854, featured a spectacular Nineveh Court, and for the first time in over two thousand years at least one ancient Mesopotamian society could be known to some extent on its own terms and in its own voice.[39] Quite how great the immediate impact of this change was in the European imagination is however far from clear. Frederick Bohrer's study of the aesthetic reception of the Assyrian material in Britain demonstrates its apparently low status in the eyes of many at the British Museum.[40] Henry Rawlinson, keenly aware of the value of the texts discovered, could not agree with Layard that there was anything aesthetically to justify the sculptures of Nimrud being housed in the Museum. He made the case instead on the basis of their historical value, a hint of the Museum's changing role and identity. In an 1846 letter to Stratford Canning, the British Ambassador to the Sublime Porte in Constantinople, Rawlinson writes that

[M]odern art cannot desire instruction from the marbles of Nineveh, and ... the mere connoisseur of statuary will be offended at the inelegant (sometimes grotesque) forms. But far be it from me to declare the marbles valueless on this account. I am rather afraid of erring on the other side – afraid that my antiquarian predilections may cause me to overestimate their importance, to regard them with an undue reservation.

... The marbles of Nimrud will be, in my opinion, an honour to England, not in the exclusive department of art, but in that more worthy field, a general knowledge of the early world; and I should indeed be disappointed to find after your Excellency's zealous exertions in the cause that a mere inferiority in their design and execution had led to an abandonment of such extraordinary relics ...[41]

A strong bias towards classical art characterises the mid-nineteenth-century British Museum, a significant part of whose role was considered to be the presentation of humanity's very finest artistic achievements to connoisseurs and students of fine art. How non-classical sculpture might fit into this

---

[39] For a brief description with illustration, see J. M. Russell, *From Nineveh to New York: The Strange Story of the Assyrian Reliefs in the Metropolitan Museum and the Hidden Masterpiece at Canford School* (New Haven, CT and London, 1997), pp. 117–18.

[40] Bohrer, 'Inventing Assyria'; Frederick Bohrer, *Orientalism and Visual Culture: Imagining Mesopotamia in Nineteenth-Century Europe* (Cambridge, 2003), pp. 98–223.

[41] Quoted in Ian Jenkins, *Archaeologists and Aesthetes in the Sculpture Galleries of the British Museum, 1800–1939* (London, 1992), p. 156.

Figure 5.4 Edwin Long, *The Babylonian Marriage Market* (1875)

scheme was a long-running problem Mesopotamia shared with ancient Egypt, whose sculptures were accorded similarly doubtful status.[42]

The Assyrian discoveries and fine art

In art, the Assyrian discoveries of the 1840s supplied new iconography for painters but not necessarily new narratives. The latter continued to be drawn from biblical and ancient Greek accounts, resulting in the appearance of material from Assyrian reliefs in scenes such as Daniel in the lion's den or the sorrowing exiles by the rivers of Babylon. The most extreme instance is that of the Babylonian marriage market described by Herodotus. For his 1875 interpretation of the scene, Edwin Long (1829–91) studied the Assyrian sculptures of the British Museum in great detail, with exact copies of many elements appearing in the final painting (Fig. 5.4).[43] If the theme itself was an innovation in fine art, however, this had far less to do with recent Mesopotamian discoveries than with the suitability of the Herodotus story to Orientalist painting as a genre. Strange customs, exoticism, sexual power relations and transgression of established social norms are all to be found here, or, to take a dimmer view, the painting simply appealed because it constituted 'a piece of respectable pornography depicting sexually available girls for sale'.[44] The Assyrian discoveries of mid-century would have given Long special incentives to attempt the subject, both by fuelling great interest in ancient Mesopotamia and by supplying wonderful sources for

---

[42] Jenkins, *Archaeologists and Aesthetes*; Stephanie Moser, *Wondrous Curiosities: Ancient Egypt at the British Museum* (Chicago, IL, 2006).

[43] See Martha Cowling, ed., *The Price of Beauty: Edwin Long's Babylonian Marriage Market (1875)* (London, 2004).

[44] Michael Rogin, 'The Great Mother Domesticated: Sexual Difference and Sexual Indifference in D. W. Griffith's *Intolerance*', *Critical Inquiry*, 15 (1989), 527.

authentic detail. Such incentives, however, are a very different thing from a discovery that enables or directly causes the artist to treat the subject. The story had been available to European painters for at least the past several centuries and in a source that certainly was used for other purposes: some sixteenth- and seventeenth-century images of Babylon's monuments reflect a familiarity with the topographical information given by Herodotus. The coincidence of the theme's appeal and the discovery of Assyrian antiquities in the nineteenth century is in part just that.

The Babylonian Marriage Market epitomises a genre, and presents in sharp outline the limits of the impact that Assyrian art could make upon the image of ancient Mesopotamia in European culture. That a great part of the Victorian engagement with the discoveries of mid-century was primarily aesthetic is highlighted by the wealth of Assyrian revival material to be found in the decorative arts.[45] In one respect, however, Long's image is peripheral to the nineteenth-century English reception of Assyrian antiquities. Its subject is drawn from an ancient Greek source, whereas the most urgent issues generated by Layard and Botta's discoveries at Mosul concerned the Bible.

Orientalism and exoticism

The City of Sin was therefore made for voyeurism. Nonetheless Babylon is not a major subject in Orientalist painting generally, where the contemporary Ottoman and Persian worlds are the focus. Opera and theatre seem to have been the important media in which the sexually degenerate, luxurious Babylon could be seen. Certainly it is in this context that the name of Babylon's legendary queen Semiramis resonated most strongly. A wealth of Semiramis stories exist in the classical sources, the fullest and most important of which was given by Diodorus Siculus in the first century BC, based principally on the fourth-century sources of Ctesias and Cleitarchus. This account presents an ambitious and warlike figure who disguises herself as a man in order to fight alongside her beloved Ninus, the founding king of all Asia. Having married and survived Ninus (some versions have Semiramis tricking her husband out of the throne) she founds Babylon

---

[45] See Henrietta McCall, 'Rediscovery and Aftermath', in S. M. Dalley, ed., *The Legacy of Mesopotamia* (Oxford, 1998), pp. 183–213; 'Reinventing Babylon: Victorian Design in the Assyrian Style', in Cowling, ed., *The Price of Beauty*, pp. 44–9.

among many other cities and building projects before embarking upon a series of incredible military adventures in distant lands. Diodorus' image of a warrior queen doing battle in India against armies with elephants is very distant from real Assyrian history. That the account is not a straightforward historical biography is clear to any reader: Semiramis is the daughter of the goddess Derceto, her infancy parallels the story of Moses in the bulrushes, and at the end of the account she does not die but is transformed into a dove. Here the account refers to traditions of worshipping the dove and thus to the other probable origin of the name Semiramis: Syrian folklore.[46]

The Diodorus account is filled with adventure, and with ideal material for Orientalist fantasy. In order to retain her sovereign power, Semiramis does not marry, but instead chooses soldiers from her army to sleep with before having them beheaded the following morning. It is the same account from which Sardanapalus (ruling from Nineveh and conceived as a corrupted and depraved descendant of Semiramis) provided the model for Byron's famous play *Sardanapalus* (1822). The latter spawned further plays and operatic productions, as well as Delacroix's iconic large-format 1827 painting *La Mort de Sardanapale*. For the Victorian audience, as for the ancient Greeks, the empires of Assyria and Babylonia were not distinct: the whole of Mesopotamia is frequently referred to as Assyria in the classical sources, and the Greek impression that the Neo-Babylonian dynasty simply inherits the Assyrian empire (and thus that Babylon replaces Nineveh as the capital of 'Assyria') has seen the two states conflated ever since. Within this fluid geography, Sardanapalus fulfils some of the role for a necessary last king of Babylon: for Diodorus he is the result of thirty generations of degeneration in the Babylonian monarchy, and thus Semiramis, standing at the beginning of this dynasty, is vastly superior and in some ways heroic. Nonetheless she is an exotic ancient Oriental queen who transgresses Victorian norms for gender and sexuality at every step. In terms of her place in culture, one approximate measure is the identification of the powerful, successful but brutal Catherine II 'the Great' of Russia as the 'Semiramis of the North'. The basis of the parallel is clear enough: the two figures play aggressive, masculine roles, and are generally presented as impressive rather than admirable, fearsome rather than contemptible.

Just as Byron supplies the definitive nineteenth-century vision of Sardanapalus, so Voltaire is responsible for the Semiramis of stage and

---

[46] Moshe Weinfeld, 'Semiramis: Her Name and Origin', in Mordechai Cogan and Israel Eph'al, eds., *Ah, Assyria . . . Studies in History and Ancient Near Eastern Historiography Presented to Hayim Tadmor* (Jerusalem, 1991), pp. 99–103.

music. Voltaire saw the classical sources as a resource to use for fantasy and play. His play *Sémiramis* (first performed 1748) is based on the Greek descriptions and Armenian legend, but fuses elements of them together to produce an original story revolving around confused identities. The story culminates in the murder of Semiramis by her own son. This account, a modern composite from the classical sources, is the template for, among others, Rossini's opera *Semiramide* (first performed 1823).

The most famous use of Babylon in opera is Verdi's *Nabucco* (first performed 1842).[47] In this case the stories from which the plot is adapted are primarily biblical, though classical elements are involved and the result is very different from anything in the Bible. King Nabucco (Nebuchadnezzar) is the victim of an intrigue and usurped by Abigaille, a character created for the purpose. His madness, drawn from the Book of Daniel, also features. The Judaean exiles in Babylon are present throughout, oppressed but virtuous. Nonetheless, the content differed sufficiently from biblical material to be performed in London in 1847 under the name *Nino*, avoiding the problem of representing biblical figures on the London stage with a single name change to the principal character. Abigaille seems to combine elements of Salome, Lilith and Semiramis. She is an Eastern seductress but also an active and power-hungry anti-heroine. More importantly, perhaps, she is the product of a convergence between two separate, biblical and classical, traditions associating Babylon with female sexuality and female transgression.

Late nineteenth-century excavations and the career of Hormuzd Rassam

All of the above discoveries were made in and related primarily to Assyria: its palaces, its libraries, its kings. Babylon and Babylonia remained buried. Efforts to excavate in southern Iraq were made in the later nineteenth century, many of these under the general direction of Hormuzd Rassam (1826–1910) (Fig. 5.5) on behalf of the British Museum, whose primary interest was in the recovery of cuneiform tablets. Among many other sites Rassam excavated both at Babylon and at nearby Borsippa, but for these and other researches has never received the credit his work deserved. The

---

[47] Michael Seymour, 'Power and Seduction in Babylon: Verdi's *Nabucco*', in Silke Knippschild and Marta Garcia Morcillo, eds., *Seduction and Power: Antiquity in the Visual and Performing Arts* (London, in press).

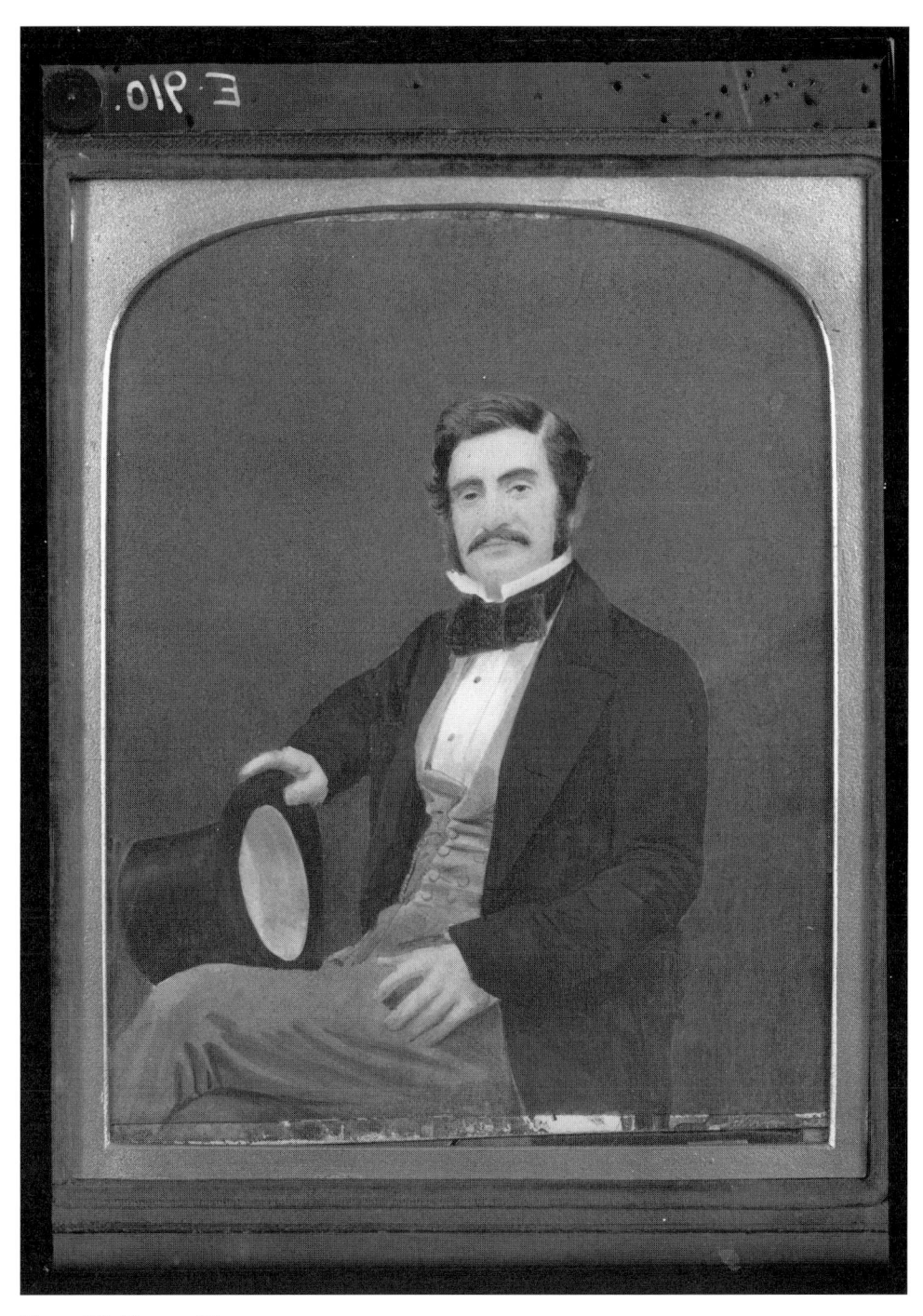

Figure 5.5 Hormuzd Rassam

responsibility for this omission lies largely with staff and agents of the British Museum in the later nineteenth century. Julian Reade has recently endeavoured to restore Rassam's reputation, arguing that

> he is condemned for not recording and publishing his excavations properly, and for being a treasure-hunter rather than a seeker after truth, when such criticisms might more reasonably be directed at the people who were giving him his orders, or rather at the entire climate of opinion, concerning archaeology and Biblical antiquities, in Victorian England.[48]

There are then two categories of accusation levelled at Rassam, both significant in terms of the culture within which he worked. The first is methodological, and as Reade notes the censure here is both anachronistic and misdirected. The second is personal, and since Hormuzd Rassam was both the first Iraqi archaeologist and an Anglophile who moved to England, his fortunes in nineteenth-century British society are of particular interest.

Rassam rose to prominence through his work as Austen Henry Layard's assistant at Nimrud. Here he is generally agreed to have made an indispensable contribution to Layard's success, particularly in handling logistical and political matters that required local knowledge. The two men formed a lasting friendship, characterised on Rassam's side by explicit gratitude, admiration and loyalty, most strongly felt in the dedication of Rassam's memoir.[49] Layard left archaeology to begin a political career (he was elected Liberal member for Aylesbury in 1852), after which Rassam's work fell under the supervision of Henry Rawlinson as British consul in Baghdad, to whom some of his Assyrian discoveries would later be wrongly attributed.[50]

Problems began in the second half of Rassam's career, when from 1878 he somewhat reluctantly returned to the field to supervise numerous excavations, including those at Babylon and Borsippa. After his return to England in 1882 he was subject to accusations of dishonesty and corruption in his dealings in Iraq from E. A. Wallis Budge (1857–1943).[51] Rassam brought a successful libel action against Budge, but his reputation was shattered. Budge went on to become Keeper of Egyptian and Assyrian Antiquities from 1894; Rassam was largely forgotten. Despite a loyalty to and enthusiasm for Britain expressed in the Anglicisation of his dress, language and manner, he nonetheless suffered as an outsider and was easily sidelined. A final contributor to Rassam's poor reputation, at least in France, was his

---

[48] Julian Reade, 'Hormuzd Rassam and his Discoveries', *Iraq*, 55 (1993), 39–62.
[49] Hormuzd Rassam, *Ashhur and the Land of Nimrod* (New York, 1897), p. iv.
[50] Reade, 'Hormuzd Rassam', 50. [51] Ibid., 59–60.

excavation of a 'French' area of the Kuyunjik mound at Nineveh, thus breaking the terms of an informal agreement made between Rawlinson and the French consul Victor Place.[52] That the results of Rassam's excavation included the great lion-hunt reliefs of Ashurbanipal (r. 669–631 BC), widely considered the finest of all Assyrian sculpture, made the transgression doubly offensive to France. The story is worth mentioning because it is exceptional: although sometimes ferocious in its rhetoric, imperial competition over antiquities in Mesopotamia was commonly tempered by gentlemen's agreements, friendship between excavators of different nationalities and some sense of shared endeavour, as seems to have been the case with Layard and Botta.[53] For Rassam this diplomacy proved less important than his responsibility to British interests or, just as important, his own curiosity about this promising but unexcavated area of the Kuyunjik mound.

A large part of Rassam's work in southern Iraq revolved around acquiring tablets for the British Museum.[54] The most famous text he discovered is surely the Cyrus Cylinder, found at Babylon. The document presents the conquering Cyrus as a good Babylonian king, restoring order and the cult of Marduk, the city's chief deity, and pouring scorn on the city's previous king, Nabonidus, who had failed to fulfil his cultic responsibilities. The text refers to the return of peoples to their home cities and the restoration of their own cults, thus offering a strong link to the biblical text of Ezra 1:1–4 in which Cyrus allows those of the Judaean exiles who so chose to return to Jerusalem and rebuild the Temple. The excitement with which this discovery was greeted in late Victorian Britain – its content and significance were explained by Rawlinson to the Royal Asiatic Society in 1879 – is only the beginning of a remarkable afterlife in which the Cylinder has transcended the limits of ancient Near Eastern studies to become a politically significant document in the present, popularly – if anachronistically – associated with the modern concept of human rights.[55] For Rawlinson, the significance had not so much to do with the verification of Scripture – in which, as Larsen's chapter notes, he showed little interest – as with the validation of his field as one able to enrich and bring new perspectives to those grand historical narratives for so long accessible only through biblical or classical sources. Most cuneiform documents record minutiae of daily economic life; even

---

[52] Ibid., 48.   [53] Larsen, *Conquest of Assyria*, pp. 134–40.
[54] Reade, 'Tablets at Babylon'; for a more detailed account see Julian Reade, 'Rassam's Babylonian Collection: The Excavations and the Archives', in E. Leichty, ed., *Catalogue of the Babylonian Tablets in the British Museum* 6 (London, 1986), pp. xii–xxxvi.
[55] Henry Rawlinson, 'Notes on a Newly Discovered Cylinder of Cyrus the Great', *Journal of the Royal Asiatic Society*, 12 (1880), 70–97.

royal chronicles are relatively dry and their Mesopotamian focus makes direct connections with the biblically and classically derived metanarratives of Western history rare. Most of the cuneiformists' work was only of interest to their fellow Mesopotamian scholars, whereas texts such as the Cyrus Cylinder, the Flood Tablet and the Bisitun inscriptions – all of which tied in with and were seen to affirm well-known biblical and classical texts – afforded the cuneiformists the chance to figure on a grander stage. For a man like Rawlinson, used to the spotlight and proud of his achievements as grandee of the new scholarly field, such opportunities had an obvious value. Not that connections to the Old Testament texts were unimportant from a scholarly perspective. The Cyrus Cylinder could seem to stand as a vivid proof of the divinely sanctioned destruction of Babylon, the Judaeans' deliverance by Cyrus and of the restoration of the Temple (none of which events, it should be noted, the Cylinder directly records); and to those engaged in the study of cuneiform texts it was another step towards the developing understanding of Near Eastern history in which the Old Testament, cuneiform texts and archaeology informed and bolstered one another. The idea that the result might be less supportive than challenging to some parts of the biblical account was occasionally raised – including by the young Canon George Rawlinson (1812–1902), brother of Sir Henry. But in general the mood in Britain between the 1850s and 1890s was one of robust confidence that such fears were ill-founded. The situation was quite different in Germany, where the rise of the higher criticism and particularly the influence of Julius Wellhausen (1844–1918) had already laid the foundations for a more fractious engagement with cuneiform texts, discussed below.

Rassam also attempted to make some survey of building plans at Babylon and Borsippa, but this was not the work he had been sent to do, nor was it at all straightforward: the difficulties involved in accurately tracing mud-brick walls were only successfully addressed some years later by a German excavation whose focus was architectural. Although Layard, Rassam and others searched, Babylon contained no monumental stone architecture of the kind found at Nineveh, Nimrud and Khorsabad (ancient Dur Kurigalzu), the Assyrian capitals. The mud-brick architecture that did exist was difficult to identify and trace, and more importantly held apparently limited value: scholarly interest was focused on art and texts. Nonetheless Rassam did produce some architectural plans, including a detailed plan of the Nabu Temple at Borsippa.[56] He was certain that

---

[56] Rassam, *Asshur*, pl. facing 224; Julian Reade, 'Rassam's Excavations at Borsippa and Kutha', *Iraq*, 48 (1986), pl. XIII.

Borsippa / Birs Nimrud was entirely separate from the city of Babylon, but nonetheless felt unable to establish even approximately the extent or edges of the latter city.[57] He laments that, 'Had it not been for my scruple not to waste public money on such an object, which is of no material benefit to the British Museum, I should certainly have gone about differently to discover some clue to the positions of the important parts of the old city'.[58]

Unlike Layard, Rassam was highly religious.[59] A devoted adherent of the Church of England from an early age, his religious conviction is perhaps impossible to separate from the ardent Anglophilia which was ultimately so poorly rewarded. Where Layard or Rawlinson would use the relationship of their discoveries to the Bible principally for poetic effect or popular appeal, Rassam was not aloof from the endorsement of providential history, proof of biblical events and, in general, the application of work in his young field to questions in which a large and devout late Victorian public were most interested. The published text of a lecture to the Victoria Institute (a conservative organisation explicitly dedicated to reconciling Christian faith and scientific discovery) is perhaps the strongest example of this engagement and reflects not only the strength of his belief but also its literalism: he believed in the Genesis confusion of tongues and in linguistic theories endorsing it, while in the fates of ancient empires he certainly saw a divine hand at work:

There is another striking proof of the fulfilment of prophecy in the utter destruction and annihilation of the Assyrian and Babylonian monarchies for their rebellion and pride. God, through his omnipotent power, left no remnant of their sovereignty nor a vestige of their grandeur ... But the Persians whom God raised to chastise the rebellious nations have held their own up to day [sic], because it was divinely decreed that they should conquer and be victorious; and in return for the victories which God bestowed upon them, they ordered the rebuilding of His temple at Jerusalem, and thus Persia has remained an independent monarchy as it was then, and where God Jehovah is acknowledged as the only Lord and King with the revealed religion of the Jews and Christians at the base of their belief in Mohammed.[60]

Babylon in the history of human progress

One defining feature of the Victorian vision of the ancient past, and indeed one still prevalent in our popular culture, is a desire to structure a history of

---

[57] Rassam, *Asshur*, p. 360.   [58] Ibid., p. 363.
[59] For whose religious beliefs see Larsen, this volume.
[60] Hormuzd Rassam, *Babylonian Cities: Being a Paper read Before the Victoria Institute, or Philosophical Society of Great Britain* (London, 1894), pp. 17, 19–20.

human progress in which nations hold sway in the world in linear succession and in which each contributes something to civilisation. The quotation from Rassam above is just one example of a history based on such a succession of powers and on a grand scheme that is ultimately providential and just. The ancient Middle East in general has suffered in such models, since the achievements of European culture have traditionally been seen as rooted in those of ancient Greece. Egypt, Mesopotamia and Persia were never accorded the same status as the classical world, as their antiquities' ambiguous status on arrival at the British Museum demonstrates. The prices paid for antiquities from Iraq were relatively low, and their usefulness to a collection of man's great artistic achievements (the rationale by which the Parthenon marbles became so central to the Museum's collection and identity) was questioned. Layard championed the artistic merit of the Assyrian sculptures but, as we have seen above, without support.

Aside from their defining role as oppressors of the Judaeans, the Babylonians were remembered – accurately, as it later turned out – as astronomers whose knowledge had informed that of the ancient Greeks. In his account of Babylon's fall, the American poet C. W. Everest (1814–77) can spare a stanza for the achievements of Babylonian science:

> And Science came, a pilgrim, to her walls,
> And learned Magi, from the distant shore;
> There the Chaldean, in her nursing halls,
> Delved o'er his mystic, astrologic lore;
> And wealth to genius oped her glittering store;
> In learning's, honor's, grandeur's varying scene,
> She brooked no rival, no companion bore;
> But peerless, lone, in proud, imperial mien,
> Like mighty Juno, swayed – Earth's universal queen.[61]

Nonetheless, the Babylonian achievement is tempered by mysticism and superstition: the Babylonians worship idols (entirely true: the temples of Babylon contained cult statues of the gods; bodies which, in ways still not well understood, the deity actually inhabited) and the Book of Daniel as well as the story of Daniel, Bel and the Serpent give a picture of a people in thrall to superstition and the cheap conjuring tricks of a greedy priesthood. That Babylon is seen as misguided in its religion is no small matter in terms of its placement within nineteenth-century models of history: the model of linear progress itself is to some extent rooted in a Christian idea of the world's

---

[61] C. W. Everest, *Babylon: A Poem* (Hartford, CT, 1838), vi.

history leading, eventually, to the Second Coming, and the progress of the human spirit is more important in this sense than social or scientific achievements. Ancient Greece was also polytheist, but because it is not the religion of ancient Athens that is opposed to that of Jerusalem in the Bible – and because classical literature found its own permanent place at the heart of European culture – it is Babylon that is associated forever with idol worship and false gods.

This perception of Babylon, in common with other ancient cities of the Middle East, as a place whose time had come and gone in large part due to its innate religious and moral shortcomings, can be seen in Victorian travel literature and popular histories. Its divinely sanctioned fate is stressed, destroyed by God for its sins like Sodom and Gomorrah.[62] Whatever Babylon's virtues, its vices and their consequences were well known. Perhaps this is why few of the city's nineteenth-century explorers appeared to take their interest in the site for religious reasons: antiquarian interest and curiosity regarding the classical sources were motives that might be rewarded by careful exploration of the site, whereas for the pious, the bare fact of the city's desolation was the most vivid confirmation that observation on the ground could ever offer. The discoveries of explorers and antiquaries might be interesting, even spiritually resonant, but the one salient point about Babylon – its desertion – required no close examination.

As for antiquarian curiosity, this had yet to be fully rewarded. Though by the end of the nineteenth century many texts had been recovered from Babylon, in understanding the physical form of the city little advance had been made on the pioneering survey of Claudius Rich. Religious convictions or no, for antiquarians too Babylon remained to some extent a series of formless ruined mounds. This was to change, however, with the arrival of new actors and a new approach to the city's remains.

Babylon recovered: the German excavations

At the very end of the nineteenth century, Babylon finally became the focus of major archaeological excavations. These were neither English nor French but German, the first significant project conducted under the auspices of the newly formed Deutsche Orient-Gesellschaft. In the spring of 1899 a team led by Robert Koldewey (1855–1925) began uncovering and planning the

---

[62] E.g., Theodore Buckley, *The Great Cities of the Ancient World, in their Glory and in their Desolation* (London, 1852), p. 23.

Figure 5.6 The reconstructed Ishtar Gate in Berlin

very centre of Nebuchadnezzar's city. Today visitors to Berlin's Vorderasiatisches Museum can even walk through the Ishtar Gate, Babylon's grandest entrance (Fig. 5.6). Koldewey and his assistants paid great attention to architecture, and in the tracing and recording of excavated buildings their work had a significant methodological impact on excavations in Iraq thereafter. Koldewey did not by any means ignore the biblical and classical background to his work at Babylon. The character of his research, however, was a study of the physical remains in which links to texts – his proposal of a site for the Hanging Gardens, for example – tended to play a secondary role. A process that began with Rich's comparison of Herodotus' description with his own observations had come to fruition. The most authoritative descriptions of ancient Babylon's physical appearance were now those of the Deutsche Orient-Gesellschaft, and based more on examination of the city's physical remains than on textual sources.

The Deutsche Orient-Gesellschaft excavations were innovative in several ways. First and foremost, the quality of recording was extremely high, but alongside the sheer detail and precision of the descriptions and architectural plans was also a new model for both study and publication. This is arguably the first antiquarian or archaeological work to be conducted in Mesopotamia that resembled a modern, professional excavation: it was a key moment in the process whereby the conventions and aims of the natural sciences began to predominate over those of the travel account or antiquarian study. Even the focus of Koldewey's main, semi-popular publication was almost exclusively upon the site itself, with little room for anecdotes or asides.[63] The contrast with Layard's *Nineveh and its Remains* is striking: the latter is a personal travelogue incorporating – in more or less equal measure – descriptions of the Assyrian discoveries, of Layard's journey, of local customs and folklore, and of the local politics with which the author had to engage in order to conduct his excavations and export finds to England. Some of these observations are still present in Koldewey's work, but increasingly they fall into a separate category. In the case of the German archaeologists' experience in Mesopotamia, the memoir of Koldewey's colleague Walter Andrae provides the background that in the accounts of Victorian explorers might have appeared in the same volume as the description of the excavations themselves.[64]

If the German excavations involved significant departures in method, their *raison d'être* was a matter of conscious continuity with British and French predecessors. Germany came late to this sphere of imperial cultural competition, but with grand designs, including economic and territorial ambitions in the form of the planned Baghdad railway. The Deutsche-Orient Gesellschaft was founded with the intention of acquiring antiquities for Germany to match those of the other European powers, and the Society's composition reveals an admixture of imperial, nationalist, commercial, theological and scholarly interests not wholly different from that which, albeit less formally, had made Layard's work in Assyria a matter of national interest in Britain half a century before.[65]

A second, almost entirely separate, aspect of the German experience bearing on that of their English predecessors comes in the form of the notorious 'Babel–Bibel' crisis that engulfed the Assyriologist Friedrich Delitzsch and the Deutsche-Orient Gesellschaft at the beginning of the twentieth century. The son of the theologian Franz Delitzsch (1813–90), Friedrich Delitzsch (1850–1922) had always taken seriously the potential for material found in cuneiform texts to bear on the interpretation of the Old Testament; the discoveries of the late nineteenth century confirmed this view and had a major impact on his own view of Scripture. When, as Professor of Assyriology in Berlin, Delitzsch was invited to deliver a series of high-profile lectures, he chose the interface between Babel and Bible as his

---

[63] Robert Koldewey, *Das Wiedererstehende Babylon* (Leipzig, 1913).
[64] Walter Andrae, *Lebenserrinerungen eines Ausgräbers*, ed. K. Bittel and E. Heinrich (Berlin, 1961).
[65] Bohrer, *Orientalism*, p. 280.

theme.[66] Although the lectures were publicly associated with Germany's entry into the field, the German excavations then in progress at Babylon and Ashur hardly bore on the content of the lectures and certainly not on his central arguments, rooted largely in material – such as the Flood Tablet and the *Epic of Gilgamesh* – translated in Britain some years earlier. What made Delitzsch's treatment different was an attempt to take on a role as moral adjudicator, in which capacity he put forward the controversial view that the religion of ancient Mesopotamia was if anything morally superior to that of the Old Testament. In the furore that ensued, Assyriologists' ability to read the tablets was not in serious dispute as it had been in the mid-nineteenth century. Here the argument centred on Delitzsch's right and ability to undermine the special status of the Old Testament. His position, unsurprisingly, was deeply unpopular, but he did not significantly rescind it. Later he would take an explicitly anti-Semitic position, denying entirely the status of the Old Testament as Scripture.[67] Despite its extremism this was a position in which he was far from alone, and indeed his views chimed perfectly with those of radical pastors pushing for the creation of a new German Christianity in which the Old Testament was rejected entirely, its place substituted by tales of Germanic virtue.[68]

British reaction to the Babel and Bible affair was muted, characterised by a feeling that Delitzsch's views would not have excited the same controversy if expressed in England, where 'we have long known how much Hebrew thought and expression owe to Babylonia'.[69] It is quite true that the existence of cuneiform texts with strong biblical connections had been well known since George Smith's discovery of the Flood Tablet, but the cool reaction and its implicit superiority are disingenuous: if the content of Delitzsch's lectures did not seem as radical in an English context this was

---

[66] Friedrich Delitzsch, *Babel und Bibel: Ein Vortrag* (Leipzig, 1902), *Zweiter Vortrag über Babel und Bibel* (Stuttgart, 1903), *Babel und Bibel. Dritter (Schluss-) Vortrag* (Stuttgart, 1905); collected and translated as Friedrich Delitzsch, *Babel and Bible: Three Lectures on the Significance of Assyriological Research for Religion, Embodying the most Important Criticisms and the Author's Replies*, trans. Thomas J. McCormack and W. H. Carruth (Chicago, IL, 1906). For discussion of the lectures and the crisis see esp. Reinhard G. Lehmann, *Friedrich Delitzsch und der Babel-Bibel-Streit* (Fribourg, 1994); Bill T. Arnold and David. B. Weisberg, 'A Centennial Review of Friedrich Delitzsch's "Babel and Bibel" Lectures', *Journal of Biblical Literature* 121 (2002), 441–57.

[67] Friedrich Delitzsch, *Die grosse Täuschung* vol. I (Stuttgart, 1920); *Die grosse Täuschung* vol. II (Württemberg, 1921).

[68] Delitzsch, *Die grosse Täuschung* II, 97, specifically advocates Wilhelm Schwaner's *Germanen Bibel. Aus heiligen Schriften germanischer Völker herausgegeben von W. Schwaner* (Schlachtensee, 1905).

[69] Review of *Babel and Bible . . . Translated from the German by T. J. McCormack* (Chicago, IL and London, 1902), *Saturday Review*, 95 (1902), 366.

partly because confidence in the moral authority of the Old Testament had not already been significantly shaken, as it had in Germany, by Wellhausen.[70] A recognition that the cuneiform texts existed was a long way from preparedness to imagine they would affect the moral authority of Scripture, the really contentious part of Delitzsch's argument. What was highly controversial in Germany remained more or less unthinkable in Britain, with the strange result that the Babel and Bible lectures were perceived as somewhat less radical than they actually were and provoked correspondingly less anxiety and debate.

Conclusion

The journey from the survey of Claudius Rich to the excavations of Robert Koldewey at Babylon is an important one in the history of archaeology. Over the course of the nineteenth century, Babylon became accessible to archaeology, but other ways of knowing and understanding the city continued to flourish. Mid-century concerns surrounding the decipherment of cuneiform proved well founded, in the sense that the predicted controversies over the text of Scripture did ensue, and unfounded, in the sense that the development of the modern discipline of archaeology finally resulted in a remit that did not, after all, extend to interventions in theology or morality. George Smith's reservations about crossing into these difficult waters served him well; in the early twentieth century, the enthusiasm of Friedrich Delitzsch to do so would leave him ostracised.

The development of archaeology in the nineteenth century is as much a matter of setting disciplinary boundaries as improving methods or accumulating accurate data. Through the same process, the role of art in our relationship to the human past was also changed. Perhaps at no time does this latter role come so close to the accurate representation of scenes from the past or to archaeological reconstruction as in mid–late nineteenth-century English painting, yet the very qualities of naturalism and inclusion of objects from real antique contexts produced a great tension: between very different categories of knowledge, between moral purpose in the present and interest in the past for its own sake, and finally between the creative and narrative needs of the artist and the increasing circumspection and

---

[70] For an excellent treatment of the history of German biblical and oriental scholarship, including the rise of the higher criticism, the impact of Wellhausen and the intellectual context of the Babel–Bibel affair, see Suzanne Marchand, *German Orientalism in the Age of Empire: Race, Religion, Scholarship* (Cambridge, 2009).

recognition of fragmentary data of the archaeologist. If Edwin Long's *Babylonian Marriage Market* represents a remarkable confluence of the artistic and the archaeological, it is because it catches a moment in the intellectual balance that, by the early twentieth century, had already tipped decisively towards a strong separation. Twentieth- and twenty-first-century works of art involving Babylon tend to return to the theme of Babel, and to iconographic sources in fine art rather than in archaeology.[71] Appropriately, since the subjects they treat – identity and displacement in the contemporary world – are not themes that archaeology as practised by Koldewey and by archaeologists ever after is in a strong position to inform. There is a meaningful separation of purpose. Babylon as the City of Sin has lost some resonance, and here we may look to the close of the nineteenth century and to the permissive values of *fin-de-siècle* artists and writers for the early stages of this change. The New Jerusalem did not come about, but perhaps a better accommodation was reached with Babylon.

Today, it is interesting to note an emerging body of contemporary Iraqi art that does draw on the iconography of ancient Mesopotamia itself.[72] This material is very distant in tone, style and meaning from the nineteenth-century European canvases incorporating Assyrian reliefs. Here the archaeology of Babylon begins to take on an iconic meaning with its own role in art, often strongly tied to the emotive contemporary issue of the destruction of cultural heritage. At the same time archaeology as an academic discipline in the twentieth century has gone through stages of positivism to emerge less confident of the objectivity and universal relevance of its methods and approaches. New attempts by archaeologists to engage with contemporary creative work on the past do not constitute a return to an earlier phase in the history of the field, but they do go to show that the discipline's boundaries have never been fixed once and for all.[73] The problem of establishing an intellectual framework for the study of the past is quite rightly a perennial one, and archaeology, like art, depends and grows on its own continual reinvention.

---

[71] Michael Seymour, 'Babylon in Contemporary Art and Culture', in Irving Finkel and Michael Seymour, eds., *Babylon: Myth and Reality* (London, 2008), pp. 203–12.
[72] Venetia Porter, *Iraq's Past Speaks to the Present* (exhibition guide booklet, London, 2008).
[73] John H. Jameson Jr, John E. Ehrenhard and Christine A. Finn, eds., *Ancient Muses: Archaeology and the Arts* (Tuscaloosa, AL, 2003).

6 | Sodom

ASTRID SWENSON

'Remember Sodom?'[1]

'Go where we will, at every time and place Sodom confronts, and stares us in the face,' complained the poet Charles Churchill (1732–64) about sinful practices that should have disappeared with the destruction of the cities of the plain. Famously lauded by Lord Rochester and the Marquis de Sade but condemned by many more, few biblical cities had such an evocative power as Sodom and Gomorrah.[2] Many a place was identified as a modern city of the plain: Queen Victoria called Paris 'Sodom and Gomorrah'; the French returned the favour identifying the English as modern descendants of Sodom and found their views shared by Americans worried about the 'sins of Sodom ... committed in England'.[3] Oxford and Cambridge were the 'Two Famous Universities of S-d-m and G-m-rr-h' in an eighteenth-century poem on paedophilic dons, while London became Sodom on the Thames in Oscar Wilde's time.[4] Even humble Barking in Essex earned the epithet: Hensley Henson (1863–1947) attracted reporters from London after preaching that 'The appeal of sensuality is clamorous and they yield – from end to end of Barking they yield – until the streets of this ancient Christian town have become as the highways of the cities of the plain'.[5] The Victorians identified many Sodoms beyond the shores of their island. Trollope applied the label to the United States 'prospering in

---

[1] Laurent Gaudé, *Sodome, ma douce* (Arles, 2009), p. 6.
[2] Charles Churchill, '*The Times* (1764)', in Paul Hallam, ed., *The Book of Sodom* (London, 1993), pp. 131–4. See also Paul Hallam, 'Sodom: A Circuit-Walk' in Paul Hallam, ed., *The Book of Sodom* (London, 1993), p. 15; John Wilmot, Earl of Rochester, *Sodom, or the Quintessence of Debauchery* (1684); Marquis de Sade, *Les 120 Journées de Sodome* (1785; Paris, 1931–5).
[3] 'Sodom', *Oxford English Dictionary online*, 2nd edn (1989); 'French Views of Things in England', *The Times* (22 December 1847), 3; George Burder, *Village Sermons* (1798; 3 vols., Philadelphia, 1817), II, p. 281.
[4] Anon., *College-Wit Sharpen'd: or, the Head of a House, with a Sting in the Tail ... Address'd to the Two Famous Universities of S-d-m and G-m-rr-h*, qu. in A. D. Harvey, *Sex in Georgian England: Attitudes and Prejudices from the 1720s to the 1820s* (London, 2001), p. 128; Morris B. Kaplan, *Sodom on the Thames: Sex, Love and Scandal in Wilde Times* (Ithaca, NY, 2005).
[5] Owen Chadwick, *Hensley Henson* (Oxford, 1983).

wickedness'.[6] A mid-Victorian musical comedy based on Lord Byron found Venice to be on the 'Sea of Sodom', echoing a long tradition that portrayed Italy as the place where young Englishmen were trained in 'the art of whoring, the art of poisoning, the art of sodomy'. Wherever a city was destroyed Sodom was present, from Sebastopol to Miramichi.[7] Beyond giving a name to specific cities, Sodom was a constant presence in the language. 'Fire and brimstone', 'becoming a pillar of salt' and of course 'sodomy' were common expressions. The wicked 'sodomite' as well as the 'poor sod' populated the earth long after the fall of the cities.[8]

The Story of Sodom as told in Genesis 18–19 repulsed and inspired. These verses provided material for psalters and church walls, edifying and pornographic tracts alike: Abraham's haggle with God to save the city if at least ten righteous men could be found; the arrival of two angels disguised as strangers to test the inhabitants; the demand of the Sodomites 'to know' the strangers; Lot's offering of his virgin daughters as an alternative; God's decision to destroy the cities and spare only Lot and his family; Lot's flight; his wife's disobedience in ignoring God's command by looking back and being turned into a pillar of salt; the destruction of the city by fire and brimstone; and the seduction of Lot by his daughters in the following nights. The biblical passage framed debates over 'that detestable and abominable crime (among Christians not to be named) called buggary', and was the justification for capital punishment in sodomy trials.[9] Yet the story also had a more general application as a warning against living among sin.[10] Many commentators interpreted Sodom's sins as crimes against faith, charity or nature.[11] Its fate provoked reflections on urban conditions in Victorian Britain. Often named in one breath with Babylon, Sodom outmatched it in

---

[6] 'Sodom', *Oxford English Dictionary Online*, 2nd edn (1989).

[7] 'Scene from the Doge of Venice', *Illustrated London News* (23 November 1867), 560; Thomas Nashe, *The Unfortunate Traveller* (1594), qu. in Hallam, 'Sodom', p. 38; 'The Fire at Miramichi, *The Times* (16 November 1825), 2; 'The Church in the Crimea', *The Times* (20 October 1855), 10. See, generally, Rolf Engelsing, '*Wie Sodom und Gomorrha . . .' Die Zerstörung der Städte* (Berlin, 1979).

[8] Gomorrah was less prolific, only engendering the now obsolete word 'Gomorrh(h)ean' that remained closely tied to analysis of the biblical story, *Oxford English Dictionary Online*, 2nd edn (1989).

[9] Old Bailey Proceedings Online (www.oldbaileyonline.org), December 1776, Thomas Burrows qu. in Julie Peakman, 'Sexual Perversion in History: An Introduction', in Julie Peakman, ed., *Sexual Perversions, 1670–1890* (Basingstoke, 2009), p. 14; Harry Cocks, 'The Discovery of Sodom, 1851', *Representations*, 112 (2010), 12; Jeffrey Weeks, *Sex, Politics and Society* (2nd edn, London, 1989).

[10] Cocks, 'Discovery', 10.

[11] See Weston W. Fields, *Sodom and Gomorrah: History and Motif in Biblical Narrative* (Sheffield, 1997); J. A. Loader, *A Tale of Two Cities: Sodom and Gomorrah in the Old Testament, Early Jewish and Early Christian Traditions* (Kampen, 1990); Michael Carden, *Sodomy: History of a*

sinfulness, but also in epitomising total, irreversible destruction. Invoked by Jesus to warn other cities in the Bible itself and as a model for the Apocalypse, Sodom was as no other city a template for the destruction of modern cities.

In the nineteenth century, rapid progress in technology made it possible to try and match these images with real ruins. Steam and the expansion of European influence in the Ottoman Empire facilitated travel to the Dead Sea and the disinterment of other biblical cities, kindling hopes that Sodom could be found. The 'idea of these living monuments of Divine vengeance yet remaining, after six- and thirty centuries, with the actual marks of the instrument of their overthrow still visible upon their blasted ruins' was a 'strangely awful' prospect. The discovery of Sodom and Gomorrah would be, its more optimistic publicists claimed, 'the most striking within the whole range of Biblical antiquity. The disinterment of Nineveh is, as a matter of feeling, a small matter, compared with the discovery of Sodom and Gomorrah'.[12]

This chapter examines how the archaeological search for Sodom and her 'daughters' meshed with the older imaginings. Sodom both echoes and complicates the account of the biblical city's reception offered in this book. Although different chapters of the archaeological search for Sodom and Gomorrah have received scholarly attention, the question of how imaginary and archaeological Sodoms interacted remains particularly unclear.[13] Was it a unique preoccupation with Sodom's sin that drove the investigations of archaeologists, as Harry Cocks has suggested, or was the case of Sodom just a colourful example of a preoccupation with lost cities equally evident in the case of Pithom, Babylon or Troy? Sodom, moreover, enables us to ask whether the synthesis between archaeology, travel, scholarship and imagination insisted on in this book worked without spectacular, or indeed any, remains. Sodom's supposedly total destruction by fire and brimstone rendered it impossible for investigators to bring home the remains demanded by the public. A few pillars of salt that even their

---

Christian Myth (London, 2004); Mark D. Jordan, *The Invention of Sodomy in Christian Theology* (Chicago, IL, 1997).

[12] Advertisement for de Saulcy's book, *The Times* (24 October 1853), 10.

[13] For some key episodes see Neil Asher Silberman, *Digging for God and Country: Exploration, Archaeology and the Secret Struggle for the Holy Land, 1799–1917* (New York, 1982); Andrew C. A. Jampoler, *Sailors in the Holy Land: The 1848 American Expedition to the Dead Sea and the Search for Sodom and Gomorrah* (Annapolis, 2005); Cocks, 'Discovery' and Harry Cocks, 'Sodom and Gomorrah, 14th January 1851', *Victorian Review*, 36 (2010), 27–30; Hallam, ed., *Sodom* offers a rich anthology of sources on learned and popular culture.

discoverers thought not to be authentic were as good as it got.[14] Finally, the search for the cities of the plain allows us to think about the relation between national and international factors in the exploration and reception of a cultural icon: the major expeditions were led by the French and Americans rather than the British, even though the British public took the keenest interest in their discoveries.

Sunken Sodom

What was to be found after 'the Lord rained upon Sodom and upon Gomorrah brimstone and fire from the Lord out of heaven: And he overthrew those cities, and all the plain, and all the inhabitants of the cities and that which grew upon the ground'?[15] A visit to Sodom and Gomorrah, as well as to the other three cities of the Pentapolis – Admah, Zeboiim and Bela, which was sometimes also named Zoar – had long been worth a detour for pilgrims and travellers to the Holy Land.[16] It was believed that the Dead Sea resulted from the destruction of the cities, and that their remains were on its shores, or under its waters. Travellers brought home precise ideas about their locations: maps placed Sodom and Gomorrah at the bottom of a much enlarged Dead Sea, Zeboim in the north and Bela/Zoar on the north western shore.[17] Palestine's geography was rendered familiar by likening distances from Jerusalem to distances of English towns in relation to London, so that 'the Lake of Sodom and Gomorrah is from Jerusalem, as Gravesend is from London'.[18] The properties of the salty, oily and thick sea and the impossibility of getting 'their Bodies under Water', however, seemed to satisfy the desire for 'curiosities and rarities' of many early-modern travellers more than 'the Ruins of one of the cities that were destroy'd for Sodomy' lying a good part out of the Water, and supposed to be Zeboim.[19]

---

[14] 'The Destroyed Cities of the Plain', *Good Words*, 1 (1860), 220. For a geological deconstruction of the 'Pillar of Salt' see B. K. Emerson, 'Geological Myths', *Science*, 4 (1896), 328–44.

[15] Genesis 19:24, 25.

[16] See Barbara Krieger, *The Dead Sea: Myth, History, and Politics* (Hanover, 1988), pp. 18–26 and Joan Taylor, 'The Dead Sea in Western Travellers' Accounts from the Byzantine to the Modern Period', *Strata: Bulletin of the Anglo-Israel Archaeological Society*, 27 (2009), 9–29.

[17] Most prominently in Thomas Fuller, *A Pisgah-Sight of Palestine and the Confines Thereof* (London, 1650).

[18] *A Strange and True Account of the Travels of Two English Pilgrims Some Years Since*, in Nathaniel Crouch, ed., *Two Journies to Jerusalem* (London, 1738), pp. 75–6.

[19] *The Travels of Fourteen Englishmen in 1669 to Jerusalem, Bethlem, Jericho, the River Jordan, the Lake of Sodom and Gomorrah, &c.* in Nathaniel Crouch, ed., *Two Journies to Jerusalem* (London, 1738), pp. 104–5.

Despite a long tradition of travel and travel writing about the area, Voltaire could still complain that 'the curious have but little information about anything concerning the Asphaltic Lake' and its capital city.

Not one of our travellers has yet thought fit to examine the soil of Sodom, with its asphaltus, its salt, its trees and their fruits, to weight the water of the lake, to analyze it, to ascertain whether bodies of greater specific gravity than common water float upon its surface, and to give us a faithful account of the natural history of the country.

Regrettably, 'pilgrims to Jerusalem do not care to go and make these researches', as the desert was supposed to be 'infested by wandering Arabs' far from the authority of the pasha of Damascus.[20] For François-René de Chateaubriand, who travelled to the area in 1806 having rediscovered his Christian faith, 'the ancients were much better acquainted with it than we, as may be seen, by Aristotle, Strabo, Diodorus Siculus, Pliny, Tacitus, Solinus, Josephus, Galen, Dioscorides, and Stephen of Byzantium. Our old maps also trace the figure of this lake in a much more satisfactory manner than the modern ones.'[21]

The first nineteenth-century voyages that 'furnished us with any notion whatever of this capital city' were American rather than European.[22] When the American travellers Edward Robinson and Eli Smith – whose pioneering contributions to scriptural geography have been noted in Goldhill's chapter – reached the Jordan Valley, they explored En-gedi and Masada and identified probable sites for Sodom and Gomorrah.[23] Their research brought a wave of travellers to Palestine, intent on discovering the biblical past, but interest was also driven by a desire to develop trade routes, with the Sea of Galilee, the Jordan River and the Dead Sea promising a route from Syria to the Gulf of Arabia and the Red Sea to ship goods from the Mediterranean to the Indian Ocean. Early attempts to establish whether the Dead Sea was navigable proved fatal. A gravestone in the Protestant cemetery in Jerusalem was all that remained of the Irish adventurer Christopher Costigan (1810–35), who together with a Maltese sailor attempted to sail on the surface of the Dead Sea in midsummer 1835, but failed to take enough fresh water and died of sunstroke. In 1847, a contingent of the British Navy under the command of Lieutenant William

---

[20] Voltaire, 'Asphaltus, Asphaltic Lake – Sodom', in Paul Hallam, ed., *The Book of Sodom* (London, 1993), p. 187.

[21] François-René de Chateaubriand, *Travels in Greece, Palestine, Egypt and Barbary*, trans. F. Shoberl (1812; New York, 1814), p. 266.

[22] Voltaire, 'Asphaltus', p. 187.   [23] Silberman, *God*, p. 44.

Molyneux, supported by the Royal Geographical Society, was decimated by thirst, sunstroke, marauding Bedouins and malaria before having shed light on the properties of the Dead Sea.[24]

Some of these mysteries were lifted by a forty-six-year-old American navy lieutenant.[25] With the Mexican–American War coming to an end and no other prospects in sight, William Francis Lynch (1801–65) applied for permission to undertake an expedition to the Holy Land. Besides allowing him to get away from a protracted divorce and the death of his oldest child and only daughter, Lynch professed two motives: to open up a new trade route and to prove the veracity of the Bible.[26] Unlike his predecessors, Lynch survived. Although his first objective to establish an American trade route did not come off, he returned from the expedition believing that he had identified the site of Sodom on the southern sea floor. 'Everything', he concluded, 'said in the Bible about the sea and the Jordan, we believe to be fully verified by our observations.'[27] Some of his fellow travellers, especially Henry Anderson, who produced the geological survey in the official report, felt uncomfortable about the lack of proof, given that 'with few exceptions the actual phenomena of deposit and denudation belong to a period incontestably long anterior to all annals of our race', but contended that stories of the destruction had not been proved false.[28] For Lynch no such reservations were necessary:

> We entered upon this sea with conflicting opinions. One of the party was sceptical, and another, I think a professed unbeliever of the Mosaic account. After twenty-two days close observation, if I am not mistaken, we are unanimous in the conviction of the truth of the Scriptural account of the destruction of the Cities of the Plain. I record with diffidence the conclusions we have reached, simply as a protest against the shallow deductions of would-be unbelievers.[29]

Lynch was unwilling to endorse either a pillar of salt as the remains of Lot's wife (as expounded by an unofficial report by one of his crew members), or a few tumbled stones branded by Royal Navy captains Charles Irby

---

[24] Ibid., p. 53; E. W. G. Masterman, 'Three Early Explorers in the Dead Sea Valley', *Palestine Exploration Fund Quarterly Statement* (1911), 12–27; Haim Goren, *Dead Sea Level: Science, Exploration and Imperial Interests in the Near East* (New York, 2011).

[25] William Francis Lynch, *Narrative of the United States Expedition to the River Jordan and the Dead Sea* (Philadelphia, 1849); Yehoshua Ben-Arieh, 'William F. Lynch's Expedition to the River Jordan and the Dead Sea, 1847–8', *Prologue*, 5 (1973), 15–21.

[26] Jampoler, *Sailors*, pp. xiii–xvii; Silberman, *God*, p. 54.   [27] Lynch, *Narrative*, p. 318.

[28] *Official Report of the United States' Expedition to the River Jordan and the Dead Sea* (Baltimore, MO, 1852), p. 78.

[29] Lynch, *Narrative*, p. 380; also Jampoler, *Sailors*, p. 193.

(1789–1845) and James Mangles (1786–1867) during their trip around the southern Dead Sea in 1817–21 as the ruins of Zoar, or the collapsed walls of a building identified by Costigan as the ruins of Gomorrah. Yet as far as the broader biblical account was concerned, he needed no remains.[30] Instead he followed the tradition of the sublime derived from Thomas Burnet's *Theory of the Earth* (1684): the landscape was proof enough of God's wrath and for Scripture's account of its effects. For Burnet, the earth had been a smooth sphere, so that mountains and seas were created after the deluge as symbols of human sin. Sodom and Gomorrah figured in this theory as their story combined theological with naturalistic reasoning: first destroyed by fire then submerged by water after an earthquake, they were the ultimate example of God's diluvian and apocalyptical wrath.[31] Lynch, like many before him, therefore took the appearance of the landscape as proof of the biblical account.[32]

Yet many pilgrims, travellers and armchair archaeologists still wanted tangible evidence. Shortly after Lynch returned to America, the French *savant* Louis Félicien Joseph Caignart de Saulcy (1807–80) claimed to supply it. Like Lynch, de Saulcy was motivated to explore the Dead Sea by 'a severe domestic bereavement'.[33] After the death of his wife in 1850, de Saulcy took his son on a tour of Greece, Syria and Asia Minor to complete his education and to collect material for his *Académie des Inscriptions et Belles Lettres*. He avoided 'the beaten paths already traced by hundreds of other tourists' and decided 'to attempt to visit countries still unexplored.'[34] As some of his critics mocked, the field of research was already cramped. 'Europe was thoroughly used up. Nineveh seemed to be the perquisite of M. Botta and Dr. Layard. Where could he go?'[35] Making a virtue of necessity, he convinced the French Ministry of Public Instruction to send him together with a priest and three other young men, on a scientific mission to the Dead Sea; 'the perils awaiting the traveller who might be bold enough to venture on those mysterious shores' added to the attraction. 'Mystery and danger' fixed his resolution.[36]

---

[30] Edward Montague, *Narrative of the Late Expedition to the Dead Sea* (Philadelphia, 1849); Jampoler, *Sailors*, pp. 180–2; Lynch, *Narrative*, p. 304.

[31] On the sublime see Cocks, 'Discovery'.

[32] For a similar statement see Chateaubriand, *Travels*, p. 265.

[33] Louis Félicien Joseph Caignart de Saulcy, *Voyages Autour de la Mer Morte et dans les Terres Bibliques* (2 vols., Paris, 1853), I, p. 1. Translated as *Narrative of a Journey round the Dead Sea and in Bible Lands*, ed. Edward de Warren (2 vols., London, 1853). Quotes are taken from the 1854 Philadelphia edn, p. 1.

[34] Ibid., p. 1. The original is more emphatic: 'visiter des contrées encore closes pour la science'.

[35] 'The Dead Sea', *The Times*, (29 December 1853), 9.   [36] De Saulcy, *Narrative*, p. 1.

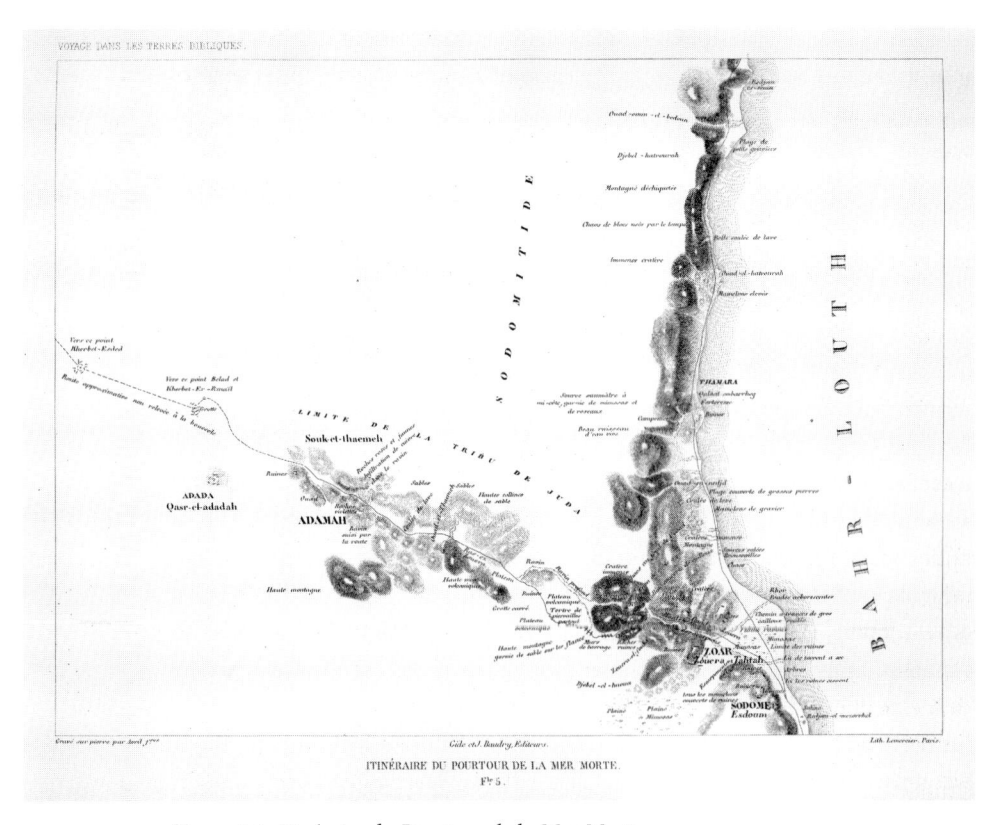

Figure 6.1 *Itinéraire du Pourtour de la Mer Morte*

After surviving many adventures – described in over a thousand pages of his book – and bribing his way through tribal territory de Saulcy finally arrived at the Dead Sea, where he discovered burned ruins at a place called Kharbet-Esdoum, which he translated as the 'Ruins of Sodom'.[37] He contested the established opinion that the sites of the lost cities were covered by water. Drawing on the notion established by American and German scholars such as Robinson, Smith, Seetzen and Burckhardt that biblical Hebrew names could be derived from modern Arabic ones, de Saulcy used his Arabic, Greek and Latin to identify ruins at various sites as the five cities of the plain. (Fig. 6.1). The publication of *Voyages autour de la mer Morte et dans les terres bibliques* (1853) by the Ministry for Public Instruction was greeted with international acclaim and published in translation as *Narrative of a Journey round the Dead Seas and in The Bible Lands in 1850 and 1851* (1853). As the Cambridge scholar and missionary to the Jews the Rev. Albert

---

[37] H. B. Tristram, *The Land of Israel: A Journal of Travels in Palestine* (London, 1865), p. 193.

Augustus Isaacs pointed out, 'There was perhaps no feature in these researches that called forth such interest as the professed discovery of the sites of the five cities of the plain.'[38] Editors seized upon this fact and the book was reprinted in popular editions that focused on the discovery of Sodom and Gomorrah. The book was included in Mudie's Select Library and immediately reissued in a cheaper edition, enticingly titled *Discovery of the Sites of Sodom and Gomorrah*. The evangelical William Elfe Tayler produced an even racier shorter version within a year, the *Vestiges of Divine Vengeance, or the Dead Sea and the Cities of the Plain*.[39] Nothing in biblical archaeology had ever been 'more thrilling' – not even Nineveh and the arrival of the Bulls at the British Museum the year of de Saulcy's voyage.[40] Even if it might appear surprising that the visible vestiges of the Pentapolis 'should have escaped the attention of travellers for so long a period, and that it should have been left for a French savant, in the middle of the nineteenth century, to reveal their existence to the antiquarian and the religious worlds', the same had held for 'Nineveh and other eastern cities'.

However, de Saulcy's identifications soon 'dwindled into nothing but a collection' of 'burnt stones'.[41] The Dutch cartographer Carl Wilhelm Van de Velde (1818–98), having heard de Saulcy in Paris, set out on a journey of his own, but could not find any basis for his claims.[42] He concluded that it was only because 'most people are inclined too readily to accept whatever is strange and wonderful' in scriptural geography that de Saulcy's book was such a hit.[43] In Britain, Isaacs, who had at first had been so enthusiastic about the discoveries, felt compelled to question de Saulcy's findings after meeting travellers who had returned from Palestine in a sceptical mood.[44] Isaacs was keen to move the debate from story-telling to scientific objectivity with the help of modern technology,

> supplying those who could not personally visit the localities with the best materials for judging of the soundness or unsoundness of that writer's inductions: We well know how often the pencil is proved to be treacherous and deceptive: while on the

---

[38] Albert Augustus Isaacs, *The Dead Sea: Or, Notes and Observations Made During a Journey to Palestine in 1856–7, on M. de Saulcy's Supposed Discovery of the Cities of the Plain* (London, 1857), p. 1.

[39] W. E. Tayler, *Vestiges of Divine Vengeance* (London, 1854). 'Discovery of Vestiges of Sodom and Gomorrah', *Sunday at Home*, 11 (1854), 173.

[40] Advertisement, *The Times* (24 October 1853), 10.

[41] 'The Destroyed Cities of the Plain', *Good Words*, 1 (1860), 221.

[42] C. W. M. Van de Velde, *Narrative of a Journey through Syria and Palestine in 1851 and 1852* (2 vols., Edinburgh, 1854).

[43] C. W. M. Van de Velde, 'M. De Saulcy's Discoveries', *Literary Gazette* (April 1854), 377.

[44] Isaacs, *Dead Sea*, p. 3.

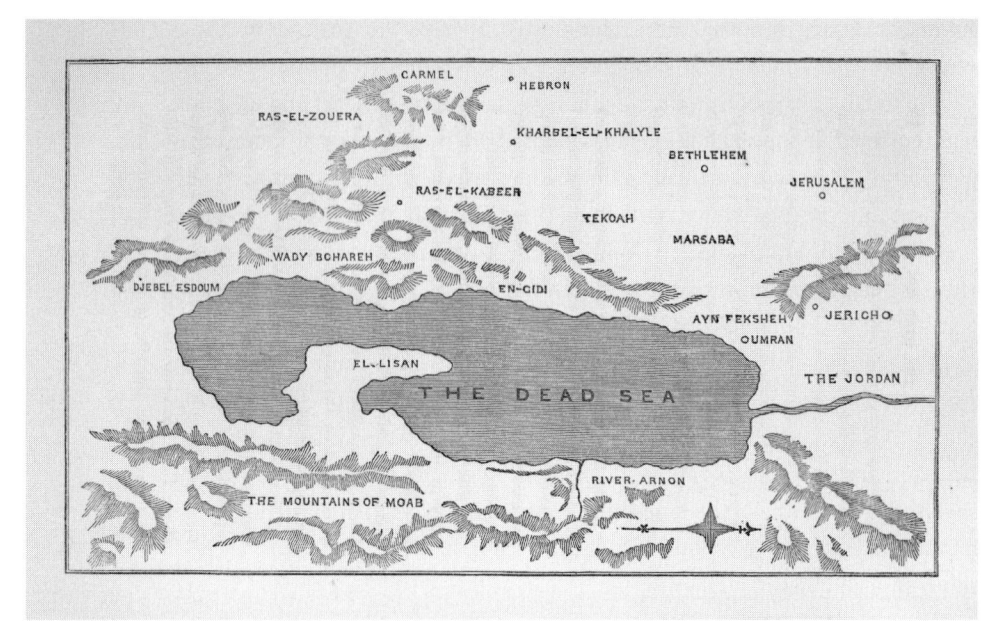

Figure 6.2 *Map of the Dead Sea and Surrounds*

other hand the fac simile of the scene must be given by the aid of the photograph. This consideration induced me to determine that . . . I would visit these places, and not only judge for myself, but endeavour likewise to give the public the best means of arriving at a just conclusion.[45]

Although he promised his readers that it was not his intention to occupy their time by any account of his 'deeply interesting travels' in this now overly familiar region, they got their fair share of the usual tales of rain, Bedouins and peril, plus a number of illustrations and no conclusions as to the place of Sodom and Gomorrah (Fig. 6.2).[46] While no alternative sites were provided, de Saulcy's 'discovery' was soon seen merely as 'information obtained from a wandering Arab, whom the French count liberally encouraged by baksheesh to point out every object of interest and who had thus a strong temptation to multiply his stock of traditional marvels'. For some, he was a Baron Munchhausen.[47] The Rev. Henry Baker Tristram (1822–1906) politely blamed his excesses on overactive erudition:

M de Saulcy has imagined that he can discover ruins in the heaped rocks which form the island. Those who can detect these will, doubtless, be equally ready to recognise the foundations of Gomorrah and Sodom, as revealed by the learned

---

[45] Ibid., p. 4.   [46] Ibid., pp. 4–5.   [47] 'Destroyed Cities', 222–3.

antiquarian. To our unlearned eyes, there were no traces either of tools on the stone or of design in their arrangement.[48]

Armchair travellers pitched in, arguing that 'every fireside traveller' could recognise that the 'alleged places' did not match the geographical descriptions in the Bible.[49]

Yet finding Sodom and Gomorrah remained high on the agenda and not only of biblical scholars and archaeologists. In 1855, the naval captain William Allen (1793–1864) drew on biblical geography to promote a canal scheme from Acre, down the Jordan to the Red Sea. He claimed that the cities were on the shores and not destroyed by a volcano and then submerged by the sea: fear of seismic disruption, he worried, might have endangered his canal scheme.[50] While William Smith's *Dictionary of the Bible* (1863) stated that 'no satisfactory solution' to the 'situation of Sodom' was likely, two years later, at its founding meeting, the Palestine Exploration Fund (PEF) named the identification of Sodom and Gomorrah as an important aim.[51] It hoped that a study of the geology of the Dead Sea 'may throw a new aspect over the whole narrative of the destruction of Sodom and Gomorrah, which had hitherto been interpreted almost wholly without reference to the geological evidence of the ground'. Likewise, the American school of biblical archaeology, founded at the end of the nineteenth century, saw the investigation of the area around the Dead Sea as one of its main tasks.[52] The discovery of other destroyed cities kindled hopes of finding Sodom and Gomorrah, for 'although destroyed by fire, they may not have been utterly annihilated, any more than Pompeii'.

However, while in Pompeii a graffito of 'Sodom and Gomorrah' was found scribbled on a wall, American archaeologists were to learn that, if the 'remains are hiding beneath the dust' in Palestine, 'the dust keeps its secret well'.[53] Despite increased travel to the Dead Sea, and the professionalisation of archaeology, the evidence consisted not so much of archaeological data (with no actual excavations undertaken during the nineteenth century), as

---

[48] Tristram, *Israel*, p. 247. [49] 'Destroyed Cities', 223.
[50] William Allen, *The Dead Sea, A New Route to India* (London, 1855), p. 247.
[51] William Smith, *A Dictionary of the Bible* (3 vols., London 1860–3), III, p. 1340; 'Palestine Exploration Fund', *The Times* (22 April 1865), 9.
[52] Melvin Grove Kyle, *Explorations at Sodom: The Story of Ancient Sodom in the Light of Modern Research* (London, 1928). On recent developments see, e.g., David Neev, *The Destruction of Sodom, Gomorrah, and Jericho: Geological, Climatological, and Archaeological Background* (Oxford, 1995); Neil A. Silberman, 'Visions of the Future: Albright in Jerusalem, 1919–1929', *The Biblical Archaeologist*, 56(1) (1993), 8–16.
[53] Mary Beard, *Pompeii: The Life of a Roman Town* (London, 2008), p. 25; George St Clair, *Buried Cities and Bible Countries* (London, 1892), p. 105.

of a reshuffling of textual sources from the Old and New Testament, Josephus and Strabo, Arabic toponymy and geological evidence. While the search for the cities of the plain continued, some archaeologists came to feel that the location of Sodom and Gomorrah might be an insoluble riddle. Members of the American Geological Society stated as early as 1877 that 'there are some points that can never be settled beyond a mere conjecture, such as the site of the Holy Sepulchre, Calvary, the grave of Moses, or the cities of Sodom and Gomorrah'.[54] Although travellers in the north of Afghanistan learned that its inhabitants believed they were living with the ruins of Sodom and Gomorrah, this new variable hardly affected the bigger picture.[55] Biblical and general dictionaries reflected growing scepticism. The Rev. Josiah Porter's entry in the 1877 edition of the *Encyclopaedia Britannica* concluded that 'the ruins of Sodom and Gomorrah have entirely disappeared' and that 'their site is disputed'.[56] The 1893 edition of Smith's *Dictionary of the Bible* affirmed that 'we are not at present in possession of sufficient knowledge of the topography and of the names attached to the sites of this remarkable region to enable any profitable conclusion to be arrived at' about the location or destruction of the five cities.[57]

Free-floating Sodom

Driven by motives ranging from personal grief to evangelical fervour, the pursuit of trade and sheer adventurism, the search for Sodom and Gomorrah had thus been inconclusive. A few lumps of bitumen and a piece from one of the various pillars of Salt identified as Lot's wife, which made it back to America onboard Lynch's ship, were the only treasures of note.[58] An American satirical magazine's feature on an artefact found at the bottom of the Dead Sea in the second-floor rooms of the house of the biblical dead – a small pot marked 'THISISANURINAL'– pretty much summed up the findings.[59] And yet public interest in the discoveries was

---

[54] A. L. Rawson, 'Palestine', *Journal of the American Geographical Society of New York*, 7 (1875), 108.
[55] 'Geographical Notes', *Proceedings of the Royal Geographical Society*, 3 (1881), 737–8.
[56] Josiah L. Porter, 'The Dead Sea', *Encyclopaedia Britannica* (1771; 25 vols., 1877–88), VII.
[57] 'Sodom', in William Smith, ed., *A Dictionary of the Bible: Comprising its Antiquities, Biography, Geography and Natural History* (3 vols., London, 1893), III.
[58] Crouch, *Two Journies*, pp. 75–6l; *Scientific American* (23 December 1848); Jampoler, *Sailors*, p. 182.
[59] *John-Donkey*, 15 July 1848, quoted in Jampoler, *Sailors*, p. 193.

enormous. The German geologist Leopold von Buch (1774–1853) had not been wrong to guess in 1839 that revelations about Sodom's fate would 'interest all the world'.[60] While the reports by Lynch and his crew were widely discussed on both sides of the Atlantic, de Saulcy 'electrified' all Europe. The 'extraordinary discovery' struck a chord 'in the hearts of Christian people': 'the idea of seeing the remains of inhabited places which had undergone so terrible a fate seemed to drive the minds of people out of their propriety'.[61] Such statements were not limited to narrowly religious publications.[62] The Whiggish *Morning Post* saw de Saulcy's work as equal to Layard's and 'of the deepest interest even to the general reader'; the *New Monthly Magazine* labelled it 'one of the most remarkable events in the history of research in Holy Land' (*sic*).[63] *The Times* devoted a long review to the book, even if it was less ecstatic about the religious meaning and ironical about de Saulcy's self-fashioning.[64] The debate about the discoveries only heightened the excitement: 'Never was there greater discrepancy in the statements of travellers!' The question 'Which is in the right? What are the true bearings of the question?' made sure that 'everything that can be told of the Dead Sea and the lost cities of the plain' remained of 'universal interest'.[65]

This phenomenon tapped the interest in biblical archaeology outlined in this book and refreshed it by taking the reader to new sites. The timing of de Saulcy's announcement was also vital. It followed the exhibition of Layard's discoveries from Nineveh at the British Museum in 1851, which (as Larsen's chapter argues) was a spectacular demonstration that hitherto lost biblical cities could be recovered.[66] The magnitude of Sodom's destruction ranked

---

[60] Leopold von Buch to Edward Robinson, 20 April 1839, quoted in Edward Robinson and Eli Smith, *Biblical Researches in Palestine, and the Adjacent Regions: A Journal of Travels in the Year 1838* (1841; 2 vols., London, 1856), II, p. 192. See Cocks, 'Discovery', 2

[61] 'Destroyed Cities', 221.

[62] Norman Macleod, 'Note by the Editor', *Good Words*, 1 (1860), 796. See also 'Discovery of Vestiges of Sodom and Gomorrah', *Sunday at Home*, 11 (1854), 172; 12 (1854), 189–91; 13 (1854), 284–6.

[63] Quoted in advertisement for 'The Bible Lands, Narrative of a Journey Round the Dead Sea', *The Guardian* (30 July 1853), 4 quoted in Cocks, 'Discovery', 9; [William Francis Ainsworth] 'The Sites of the Doomed Cities', *New Monthly Magazine*, 102 (1854), 1.

[64] 'The Dead Sea', 9. For American reports see E. C. Mitchell, 'The Bibliography of Exploration: A List of American Writers upon Biblical Archaeology and the Work of Exploration in Bible Lands', *The Old Testament Student*, 6 (1887), 303–15.

[65] 'The Sites of the Doomed Cities', 1; 'The Holy Land', *The Guardian* (9 May 1865), 3.

[66] A. H. Layard, *Nineveh and its Remains: With an Account of a Visit to the Chaldaean Christians of Kurdistan, and the Yezidis, or Devil-Worshippers; and an Enquiry into the Manner and Arts of the Ancient Assyrians* (2 vols., London, 1849); Mogens Trolle Larsen, *The Conquest of Assyria: Excavations in an Antique Land, 1840–1860* (London, 1996); Tim Larsen, 'Nineveh', *infra*.

the discovery high despite the lack of any artefacts. For most accounts in the press, 'the confirmation of the Scriptural account' in an age of growing scepticism about the literal veracity of Scripture, providing 'sermons in stone': 'vestiges' which 'still proclaim to the wide world, from the solitudes of the Judean desert, the vengeance of the Divine Being against all ungodliness in men'.[67]

De Saulcy's discoveries 'opened up a diverse market in popular religious interpretation in which many different voices and opinions – radical and mainstream, orthodox and sceptical – could be expressed and presented to new audiences'. Cocks argues that evangelical writers popularised his work to emphasise the consequences of sin and homoerotic lust. However, the link between discovery and appropriation was surely less straightforward than this. Rather than 'sparking' the imagination, the discoveries came at a moment when political, literary and artistic interpretations of the cities already abounded. The main crowd-pleasers, from dioramas, to theatre plays or Turner's and John Martin's paintings were produced before the publication of the discoveries. Rather than allowing 'his readers to discover anew' the tradition of the 'Apocalyptic sublime', the discoveries tapped into an existing boom that needs explaining.[68] The Victorian public encountered Sodom in many guises, beyond the Bible and the travel report. The cities of the plain featured in sermons, pamphlets, caricatures, paintings, photographs, panoramas, postcards, plays, poems, pornography and even children's stories.[69] The cities were used not just to intervene in debates about the veracity of the Bible or the geological origins of the earth, but in debates about faith, sin, hospitality, homosexuality, urban development, poverty, reform movements from Chartism to Mazzini's Young Italy, penal colonies, the workhouse, the death penalty, wartime destruction, cholera and a variety of carnal pleasures, mentionable and unmentionable. Interpreting the interaction of archaeology and imagination involves surveying the sheer range of formats in which the public encountered Sodom – from sermons, homosexuality trials, to social and political reform and literary and artistic life – before analysing how an increasing number of travellers appropriated the city for themselves.

[67] 'Discovery of Vestiges [II]', 189, 191.
[68] Cocks, 'Discovery', 3, 4, 9. Cocks claims that the interest in de Saulcy sparked revival in religious entertainment for a middle-class public. However, most of the dioramas and panoramas were constructed before the discovery and unless visitor figures are available there is no proof for this revival.
[69] 'Scripture Illustrations No 1: History of Abraham', *The Child at Home*, 1 (1841), 19; 'Lot', *The Children's Friend* (1 August1855), 180–6.

Sunday Sodoms

There was no place more natural to discuss the meaning of Sodom's discovery than the pulpit. However, sermons about Sodom, either before or after the wave of exploration, paid little attention to the city proper. A sermon by George Burder (1752–1832), a Congregational minister in the urban Midlands during the early nineteenth century, was a rare exception in briefly mentioning that the ruins were visible during the time of Josephus, but he did not speculate about their location or aspect, merely suggesting that their hinterland was once as fertile as Egypt and therefore that their fate offered lessons about the evils of urban affluence.[70] Sodom and Gomorrah provoked dark reflections from clerics on Britain's mushrooming cities. Genesis 18–19 provided reasons to increase inner-city missionary effort to prevent similar calamities and was quoted during campaigning and fund-raising.[71] This was all the more important in time of cholera, with Charles Kingsley (1819–75) adverting to the fate of Sodom during one epidemic.[72]

Kingsley was rather exceptional in taking as the moral of Sodom the need to reform cities. For most writers of sermons, the fate or even the character of the city mattered less than the individual duty to avoid divine wrath. Lot and Lot's wife incited modern Christians to flee from sin without casting a parting glance. The same lesson was drawn by men of the cloth working in urban Britain, from Congregationalists such as Burder, to Charles Girdlestone (1797–1881), a high churchman of a firmly Protestant bent with experience of poor urban parishes, the Claphamite evangelical Francis Goode (1797–1842), the Anglican John Henry Newman (1801–90) and Robert Murray M'Cheyne (1813–43), a popular evangelical Church of Scotland minister.[73] Newman's colleague Edward Bouverie Pusey (1800–82) took a different tack, arguing that the destruction of Sodom (and of cities such as Tyre, Nineveh, Babylon and Jerusalem) exemplified God's power in punishing the wicked, thus proving the existence of hell. For Pusey too

---

[70] Burder, *Village Sermons*, III: 'Sermon on Lot's Deliverance', pp. 273, 275.
[71] See Cocks, 'Discovery' on a collection issued to help with the construction of a church in the new London suburb of Kensal Green in 1850, which invoked 'God's fearful judgements upon Sodom, and the other polluted cities of the plain'.
[72] Charles Kingsley, *Sermons on National Subjects* (London, 1890), p. 149.
[73] Charles Girdlestone, *Twenty Parochial Sermons* (Oxford, 1832), pp. 275–90; Francis Goode, *Sermons on Various Topics of Doctrine, Practice and Experience* (London, 1838), p. 259; John Henry Newman, *Parochial and Plain Sermons* (8 vols., London 1868), III, pp. 1–15; Robert Murray M'Cheyne, *The Sermons of the Rev. Robert Murray M'Cheyne* (New York, 1861), pp. 355–62. The sermon on Lot's Wife was given in 1837.

though, the city sites were barely relevant.[74] The emphasis on repulsion and flight changed little after the putative discoveries. The Tractarian poet Isaac Williams (1802–65), writing at the height of de Saulcy's fame, told his parishioners that 'you are not as they of Sodom ... you must be either as Lot or as Lot's wife; in a state of uncertainty of good or evil, and one in which faith may be strengthened or weakened'.[75] For Goode, the wickedness of the Sodomites was general rather than specific, let alone sexual: they were 'a type of mankind in general' in their open rebellion against God.[76] Later in the century, the Baptist Charles Haddon Spurgeon (1834–92) paid more attention to goings-on in the city, worried not so much about unnatural sexuality (that 'gross part of Sodom life, that Lot could not bear' and which 'made Mistress Lot uncomfortable at times'), but the 'very sweet city life', 'the liberal spirit', 'the fine free bearing of the people, their gaiety and artistic culture', which were quite to her mind. He drew the familiar conclusions about the necessity to stand fast against urban temptations, but also gave fathers and husbands a patriarchal warning to shelter their wives from them.[77]

For sermon writers, Sodom was less a material city than a symbol of Christ's teachings, which was approached through a cluster of New Testament texts. Christ's injunction to 'Remember Lot's wife / Whosoever shall seek to save his life shall lose it; and whosoever shall lose his life shall preserve it' (Luke 17:32–33) was a common sermon text. Modern Christians enjoyed greater privileges through Christ's sacrifice than Sodom ever possessed, 'and our sins are consequently more aggravated than theirs ... "It shall be more tolerable for Sodom and Gomorrah in the day of judgement" than for those who hear the Gospel, but reject its evidences, and neglect its salvation.'[78] Equally forbidding were the words of Christ in Capharnaum: 'And thou, Capernaum, which art exalted unto heaven, shalt be brought down to hell: for if the mighty works, which have been done in thee, had been done in Sodom, it would have remained until this day' (Matthew 11:23). Interestingly enough, this text provoked a debate about Capharnaum which paralleled that about Sodom. Although no one could agree which, if any, ruins were those of Capharnaum, the difficulty of

---

[74] E. B. Pusey, *A Course of Sermons on Solemn Subjects Chiefly Bearing on Repentance* (London, 1847), pp. 96–8.
[75] Isaac Williams, *Sermons on the Characters of the Old Testament* (London, 1856), pp. 58–9.
[76] Goode, *Sermons*, p. 248.
[77] Charles Haddon Spurgeon, *Spurgeon's Sermons on Old Testament Women: Book One* (1960, Grand Rapids, MI, 1994), chapter 6, 'Remember Lot's Wife', p. 78.
[78] Burder, *Village Sermons*, II, pp. 272–81.

tracking them down verified Christ's warning that disbelief entailed obliteration. Henry Baker Tristram's *The Land of Israel* (1865) made explicit the point about the 'erasure from the face of the earth ... Capernaum in its oblivion preaches to Christendom a sermon more forcible than the columns of Tyre or the stone of Jerusalem'.[79] It was to his mind captious and counter-productive for Christians to posit or hope for evidence of the 'destruction of Sodom and Gomorrah'. If one demanded such proof, then the 'whole question of miraculous intervention has been surrendered to the enemy, and modern scientific knowledge not legitimate criticism, is made the test of Scriptural authenticity' and 'we may as well at once refuse all credence to the miraculous as beyond our own experience, and reduce the world of God to the level of the tales of Egyptian priests, or the traditions of Livy'.[80]

Sodom and sodomy

According to Cocks, the discoveries fuelled a homophobic discourse in evangelical circles that built upon the traditions in Protestant theology and the criminal law identifying Sodom's sin with homoerotic desire.[81] While late antique and medieval readings were ambiguous about the city's sins, the interpretation of Sodom's sin as homoerotic lust may have increased in response to the rising number of sodomy trials since the 1720s and the debates about effeminacy in eighteenth-century political discourse.[82] It found its way into biblical commentaries and family Bibles. Albeit reserved for 'closet reading' by senior family members, they described the sins committed against the angels in clear terms.[83] Cocks suggests that the interpretation left a mark on travel writing and retellings of biblical stories, linking the sins of Sodom to the characteristics of the geography of the Dead Sea area. For instance, J. A. Wylie followed the success of his novelistic *Scenes From the Bible* (1844) in which he described how Sodom's male population set out to commit the 'most unnatural and horrid crimes' with a book collating ancient prophecies with modern Judaea in which he

---

[79] Tristram, *Israel*, p. 444.
[80] Ibid., pp. 356–8. This did not however prevent Tristram imagining that he might have found 'physical evidence' of the 'catastrophe which destroyed Sodom and Gomorrah'.
[81] Cocks, 'Discovery', 12.
[82] Loader, *Two Cities*; Carden, *Sodom*; Peakman, 'Sexual Perversion', p. 14 and Randolph Trumbach, 'Modern Sodomy: The Origins of Homosexuality, 1700–1800', in Matt Cook, Robert Mills, Randolph Trumbach and H. G. Cocks, eds., *A Gay History of Britain: Love and Sex between Men Since the Middle Ages* (London 2007), pp. 77–106.
[83] Mary Carpenter, *Imperial Bibles, Domestic Bodies* (Athens, OH, 2003), p. 21.

warned of what would happened to those who emulated the inhabitants of the cities.[84] Holy Land travellers confirmed these prophecies. De Saulcy's reception might have been motivated by homophobic fears and might have informed, as Cocks proposes, the popular edition of de Saulcy by the anti-Catholic polemicist William Elfe Tayler, which recalled God's 'righteous anger against sin'.[85] However, this was a tradition enhanced rather than established by discoveries. Overall, the sermon literature was strikingly free from allusions to unnatural desire. In most travel writing too, the link was implicit at best. In debates about homosexuality and in sodomy trials the biblical passage was invoked to justify measures against 'contamination', but the archaeology seems to have been no more mentioned than it was from the pulpit.[86]

The only figure who explicitly used the discoveries as part of an attempt to change established sexual politics was John Frost (1784–1877), a Chartist who was transported to Australia for his part in the Newport Rising of 1839.[87] While there he was shocked to encounter 'unrestrained indulgence of unnatural lust' that had no equal 'even in the worst days of the Canaanites'. As Cocks has discussed, from the 1830s onwards, the story of Sodom had played a prominent part in radical and Chartist attacks on the Australian penal colonies, which criticised transportation for encouraging the commission of unnatural acts in a formerly virginal land. At roughly the same time, a copy of the *Guardian* fell into Frost's hand, reporting on de Saulcy's discovery.[88] It proved that there was 'no fact in history sustained by stronger evidence than the destruction of the Cities of the Plain and the causes which produced that destruction' and that action needed to be taken to prevent Britain and her Empire from similar consequences. To prevent the innocent from being destroyed with the guilty, Frost advocated not just a reform of colonial transportation but of the whole British political system. Upon his return to Britain in 1855, he tried to revive Chartist attacks on political corruption through revelations about the convict colonies delivered in lectures across the country.[89]

---

[84] J. A. Wylie, *Scenes from the Bible* (Glasgow, 1844), p. 112; J. A. Wylie, *The Modern Judea, Compared with Ancient Prophecy* (2nd edn, Glasgow 1850), p. 260.

[85] Tayler, *Vestiges*, p. 137.

[86] Sam Brady, *Masculinity and Male Homosexuality in Britain, 1861–1913* (Basingstoke, 2005).

[87] On the following discussion see Cocks, 'Discovery', 15–17. See also Kirsty Reid, 'The Horrors of Convict Life: British Radical Visions of the Australian Penal Colonies', *Cultural and Social History*, 5 (2008), 481–95.

[88] John Frost, *Horrors of Convict Life* (London, 1856), pp. 35–7.

[89] See Cocks, 'Discovery', 15, 17.

Sodom on stage

Beyond shaping theological arguments, the cities sparked the literary and visual imagination. Sodom appeared frequently in literature and on stage, yet again one is hard pressed to find much engagement with the archaeological researches. *The Destruction of Sodom: A Dramatic Poem*, one of several *Hebrew Dramas Founded on Incidents of Bible History* by William Tennant (1784–1848), Professor of Oriental Languages in the University of St Andrews, was part of the 1840s Sodom mania and deployed the same linguistic and textual methods used to find the cities. The *dramatis personae* consisted of the Angels, Abraham, Lot and his family members, who received new doom-ridden names, thanks to Tennant's linguistic expertise. The city's location was established through the same combination of textual sources that guided explorers: 'The Scene is laid at the Gates, or in the Town of Sodom, – the heights of Hebron, and Carmel, on the west of the Dead Sea, and commanding, from many points, a full view of the Lake, and of the Pentapolis, or Five Cities of the Plain.' But as it was written before the discoveries, the 'confines of her slime-concocted walls' could be filled from Tennant's imagination. The other main dramatic poem based on the biblical account, James Glover, *The Destruction of the Cities of the Plain: A Poem* also predated the discoveries, as did Benjamin Disraeli's allegorical discussion in *Tancred*, where Britain becomes Sodom and can only be saved by an angelic visit.[90] The discovery of the cities did not trigger new literary renditions in Britain.[91] Older Sodoms re-emerged in re-editions, but apart from the medieval poem *Cleanness*, the biblical account was of little interest to the exploration of Sodom's streets.[92] The *Sodom* attributed to the Earl of Rochester and edited by the Victorian collector of pornography H. S. Ashbee had as little concern with the Dead Sea as John Saul's *The Sins of the Cities of the Plain: Or the Recollections of a Mary-Ann with Short Essays on Sodomy and Tribalism* (1881), a rare piece of Victorian gay pornography.[93] This trend was further enhanced through the incorporation of

---

[90] William Tennant, *The Destruction of Sodom: A Dramatic Poem* (London, 1845); James Glover, *The Destruction of the Cities of the Plain: A Poem* (Edinburgh, 1850); Benjamin Disraeli, *Tancred: Or, The New Crusade* (3 vols., London, 1847), I, chapter 7.

[91] The story, however, provided the plot for a later German Drama by Hermann Sudermann, *Sodoms Ende: Drama in fünf Akten* (1891, Stuttgart, 1894). It was known in England – or at least made it into the Cambridge University Library. For American fiction see Janis P. Stout, *Sodoms in Eden: The City in American Fiction before 1860* (Westport, CT, 1976).

[92] Israel Gollancz, ed., *Cleanness: An Alliterative Tripartite Poem on the Deluge, the Destruction of Sodom, and the Death of Belshazzar* (Oxford, 1921).

[93] See Matt Cook, *London and the Culture of Homosexuality, 1885–1914* (Cambridge, 2003).

French Sodoms into the British canon. The Marquis de Sade's *100 Days of Sodom* was finally translated into English at the end of the nineteenth century while Marcel Proust's *Sodom and Gomorrah* foreshadowed the symbolic appropriation of the city by the emerging gay movement, building upon an old libertine tradition rather than newer archaeological insights.[94]

The iconography of Sodom

The force of artistic over archaeological tradition was stronger still in visual renderings. Depicting the destruction of Sodom was not for the fainthearted, as M. Woolmer, an 'acceptable painter' known for his 'fanciful, though not forcible colouring' and appreciated for the recreational value of his 'dream like scenes' found out when in 1849 he 'made a sad mistake in quitting those cool grottos and Oriental retreats in which he is so much at home, and attempting the "Destruction of Sodom and Gomorrah"' for an exhibition of the Society of British Artists. Nothing, sighed a critic for *The Times*, 'can be less sublime than those lumps of red which are hurled upon the devoted cities, sparkling with all sorts of amazing hues'.[95]

The iconography of the destruction of Sodom was enduring.[96] Focusing on Sodom, rather than the entire Pentapolis, the earliest occurrences are in the Catacomba Nuova and on a sarcophagus in San Sebastiano in Rome from the fourth century. Since early Christian times, the city was usually depicted on the left side, devoured by flames falling from the sky. Often, but not always, the city was on the border of the sea or a lake. In the foreground, Lot was usually shown fleeing towards the right with his two daughters, while his wife was shown turning around and becoming a pillar of salt. Mostly she was portrayed as a shadowy figure in a pale dress, or from the fourteenth century onwards occasionally as a pillar from which a human head emerges. Sometimes one or two angels were shown above Sodom. Occasionally the destroyed city was shown without Lot and his family, with the destruction sometimes portrayed as a cycle presenting the destruction and Lot's flight separately. Having become a popular scene in illustrated Bibles, sculpture cycles and frescos during the Renaissance, the traditional iconography was maintained, but the city's background

---

[94] Throughout the nineteenth century, de Sade was only available to a few British readers in partial translations or in the original. On his influence, Peakman, 'Sexual Perversion', pp. 27–31.
[95] 'Suffolk-Street Exhibition', *The Times* (4 April 1849), 8.
[96] On most of the following examples, see C. M. Kaufmann, 'Lot', in Wolfgang Braunfels, ed., *Lexikon der christlichen Ikonographie* (8 vols., Freiburg, 1968–76), III: cols. 107–12.

became more naturalistic, resembling an Italian city – as in Benozzo Gozzoli's fresco in Pisa's Campo Santo (1468–84). In the Vatican Loggias, Raffael showed Lot holding his daughter's hand in the manner seen in the early Christian depictions. Later images, such as Veronese's version now in the Louvre, increasingly depicted the angel guiding the daughters. The fire was rendered bigger for increased effect, while the characters became smaller, such as in the paintings attributed to Dürer or Matthäus Merian, the Elder (1625–30). Often Lot's wife became a smaller figure in the background or disappeared entirely. Sometimes the flight before the punishment of Lot's wife was shown, as in Peter Paul Rubens' painting of 1625 (also now in the Louvre) and a number of Rembrandt's etchings (executed between 1655 and 1660 now in the Bibliothèque nationale and the British Museum), but during the seventeenth century, the scene was rarer than the portrayal of Lot's seduction by his daughters.

While the incestuous scenes became less frequent in the nineteenth century, other trends were enhanced. The iconography of Lot's flight was maintained in French paintings such as in Camille Corot's *The Burning of Sodom*, but the two most popular nineteenth-century British paintings of the destruction, Turner's *The Destruction of Sodom*, first exhibited in 1805, and John Martin's *The Destruction of Sodom and Gomorrah* (Fig. 6.3) exhibited in 1832 emphasised the destruction of the city over the flight.[97] Turner's painting no longer shows the city from afar, but from within. The darkness of the image contrasts with the bright flames devouring the buildings. In the shady foreground fallen Sodomites lie, while on the left Lot and his family are turning away to leave. Martin increased the glow of the burning city. The painting is dominated by the red flames over the city on the right; separated from the inferno are the small figures of Lot and his daughters after his wife has turned to salt. The burning sky has much in common with Martin's other paintings of biblical disasters, including *The Deluge*, *The Days of the Lord*, *The Destruction of Babylon* and *The Fall of Nineveh* but is arguably the most dramatic. While he painted Babylon and Nineveh in meticulous architectural detail, the buildings of Sodom are vague, resembling ruined medieval structures rather than an eastern townscape.

Both Turner and Martin's paintings were completed before any debate about discoveries.[98] The only prominent image explicitly influenced by the archaeological discoveries did not depict the destruction of Sodom, but the

---

[97] William Feaver, *The Art of John Martin* (Oxford, 1975).
[98] See, e.g., *The Great Original Grand Moving Diorama of the Holy Land* (Glasgow, n.d., c. 1850); *A Pilgrimage through the Holy Land, Explanatory of the Diorama of Jerusalem and the Holy Land* (London, 1851). An image of the Dead Sea was shown, the exhibition catalogue described the

Figure 6.3 John Martin, *The Destruction of Sodom and Gomorrah* (1852)

expulsion of the Scapegoat. William Holman Hunt (1827–1910) felt inspired by de Saulcy to camp on the shores of the Dead Sea to paint a realistic scene of utter desolation. Those who depicted the burning of the cities did not feel the need to capture the site *en plein air*. Nor did they make any allusions to the archaeological writings. However, the detailed depictions of medieval and Renaissance cities often recede in favour of generic architecture and Dead Sea landscape, perhaps reflecting some knowledge of the uncertainty about the city sites and the increased availability of descriptions and photographs of Holy Land geography and architecture. There had been an interest in the appearance of the holy places from the days of early pilgrimage, but it was the circulation of images and in particular photographs since the 1850s that left a widespread mark on nineteenth-century art.[99] Jean-Baptiste Corot's *The Burning of Sodom*, executed between 1843 and 1857, shows a more Orientalised landscape and architecture than earlier paintings. Gustave Doré's *The Flight of Lot* from *La Sainte Bible* (1865) and his *Flight of Lot* from *The Holy Bible containing the Old and New Testaments* (1872–6) maintained the iconography of the burning city in the background with the group around Lot at the front, but minimised architectural details, emphasising the flaming sky over a landscape that resembles photographs of the Dead Sea. The same applies for less remembered artists. While the burning city of Sodom by Alexandre Bida (1813–95) is more reminiscent of the burning castle of Heidelberg, the landscape is that of the Dead Sea.[100] *The Destruction of Sodom* by Edward Armitage

scene and the cities as submerged by water; on panoramas see Ralph Hyde, *Panoramania! The Art and Entertainment of the 'All Embracing View'* (London, 1988).

[99] See R. S. R. Boase, 'Biblical Illustration in Nineteenth-Century English Art', *Journal of the Warburg and Courtauld Institutes*, 29 (1966), 351.

[100] Edward Egglestone, *Christ in Art: The Story of the Words and Acts of Jesus Christ as Related in the Language of the Four Evangelists, Arranged in One Continuous Narrative* (New York, 1875).

(1817–96) also emphasised the mountains surrounding the Dead Sea, while the city is virtually invisible.[101] However, other late nineteenth-century depictions betray vague Orientalism rather than specific knowledge: *Abraham Sees Sodom in Flames* (1896–1900) by James Tissot (1836–1902) shows an Oriental Abraham in front of an unidentifiable city in flames; *The Angels of Sodom*, circa 1890 by Gustave Moreau (1826–98), shows the angels over a city in a gorge more evocative of Petra than Sodom.

Most Bible readers would have encountered images depicting the destruction of the Cities of the Plain in a mixture of formats. Old images were reprinted, redrawn and redistributed as Bible cards. Illustrated Bibles borrowed international images, mixing old with new, and paintings with photographs. *The Bible and Its Story Taught by One Thousand Picture Lessons* (1908) is characteristic in its combination of canonical painters, lesser works and photographs, illustrating Genesis 14:3 with a photograph of the Dead Sea, Genesis 19:28 with *Sodom is Destroyed* by Armitage, Genesis 19:15 'Lot Flees from Sodom' with Rubens and Genesis 19:26 'Lot's Wife turns into a Pillar of Salt' with Corot.[102]

While the city of Sodom did not look much different over the period, the background certainly did. This did not mean that viewers preferred a naturalistic rendering. The attempt by Holman Hunt to 'reenact a sense of lived biblical experience' in the Holy Land had mixed results.[103] Preoccupied with Christianity's relation to its Judaic origins, he chose to depict the goat driven from the Temple on the Day of Atonement, carrying the sins of the community and representing a type of Christ and his relationship with Judaism.[104] Inspired by de Saulcy, Hunt chose the site as Sodom for this painting on sin and redemption.[105] Having found a 'suitably wretched starved goat' to paint, he narrowly escaped disaster during his

---

[101] Reproduced in Charles Horne and Julius Bewer, eds., *The Bible and Its Story Taught by One Thousand Picture Lessons* (10 vols., New York, 1908), I.

[102] Ibid.

[103] Albert Boime, 'William Holman Hunt's *The Scapegoat*: Rite of Forgiveness/Transference of Blame', *The Art Bulletin*, 84 (2002), 94; Carol Jacobi, *William Holman Hunt: Painter, Painting, Paint* (Manchester, 2006), pp. 41–60 (see photograph of William Holman Hunt re-enacting Painting at the Dead Sea in 1894, p. 41); on re-enactment see also Simon Coleman, 'A Tale of Two Centres? Representing Palestine to the British in the Nineteenth Century', *Mobilities*, 2 (2007), 331–45.

[104] Boime, '*Scapegoat*', 94.

[105] Ibid., 107, note 91. On references to de Saulcy see George P. Landow, 'William Holman Hunt's Letters to Thomas Seddon', *Bulletin of the John Rylands University Library of Manchester*, 66 (1983), 139–72 and for a retrospective view William Holman Hunt, 'Painting "The Scapegoat"', *Contemporary Review*, 52 (1887), 29; also William Beamont, *A Diary of a Journey to the East in the Autumn of 1854* (2 vols., 1855; London, 1856), II, 41, 91, 208, 229.

trips to the site in search of the right light conditions.[106] To portray the topography as accurately as possible was a noble, self-sacrificial duty, one that elided the disparity between secular and sacred time.[107] Hunt and his friend Thomas Seddon (1821–56) had been bitterly disappointed by the errors in illustrations in the books published by the Society for the Promotion of Christian Knowledge and complained that the photographs circulated by the London Jews' Society Mission in Jerusalem were inadequate: greens and yellows appeared so dark that it was impossible to distinguish between grass and shadows. It mattered little that Hunt doubted the accuracy of de Saulcy's findings. In his retrospective account, he admitted that his local guides knew nothing of de Saulcy's ruins. Whether this was to cleanse himself of having believed an impostor is not clear, but by concluding that both he and de Saulcy must have been so taken in by the landscape that imagination filled the gaps, Hunt revealed a lot about his belief in the sublime.[108] De Saulcy might have been 'mendacious', but ruins mattered little in comparison with the imprint of God's wrath on the landscape. The vivid sunburnt colours that Hunt observed and which startled critics used to sombre, monochrome images of the site gave the lie to images of utter desolation.[109] Neither Hunt's first painting nor the landscape clad in a 'livery of crimson and gold' that his travel companion remembered evoked a 'desolate space' but rather 'God's covenant of mercy above the most memorable scene of his wrath'.[110] Though Hunt eliminated an overly cheering rainbow from the final version of his picture, the image was still too colourful for many artists and critics.[111] The Dead Sea should not be painted in all the colours of the rainbow, but 'gloomy and terrible, full of clouds and darkness, with only lurid lights about it to make the blackness more impressive' to reflect the darkness of the Sodom story (Fig. 6.4).[112]

---

[106] The consul James Finn, quoted in Boime, 'Scapegoat', 103.

[107] The feeling of continuity is explicitly captured in Seddon's observations upon arriving in Jerusalem, quoted in Boime, 'Scapegoat', 104. See also John Davis, *The Landscape of Belief: Encountering the Holy Land in Nineteenth-Century American Art and Culture* (Princeton, NJ, 1996), pp. 127–48 and Nick Tromans, ed., *The Lure of the East: British Orientalist Painting* (London, 2008).

[108] William Holman Hunt, *Pre-Raphaelitism and the Pre-Raphaelite Brotherhood* (2 vols., London, 1905), I, p. 481.

[109] 'Fine Arts: Royal Academy', *Athenaeum* (10 May 1856), 589–90.

[110] Beamont, *Diary*, I, pp. 198–9; II, pp. 42–3. See also a longer analysis of the conflict between his readings and his eyes in Hunt's journal in Jacobi, *Hunt*, p. 51.

[111] See Leslie Parris, *The Pre-Raphaelites* (London, 1984), pp. 153–5, no. 84. Hunt did allude to the rainbow theme in the frame of the final work with the relief of the dove and its olive branch. See Kenneth P. Bendiner, 'William Holman Hunt's "The Scapegoat"', *Pantheon* 45 (1987), 124–8.

[112] 'Painting "The Scapegoat"', 21–39 and *Contemporary Review* (August 1887), 219.

Figure 6.4 William Holman Hunt, *The Scapegoat* (1854–6)

Daytrips to Sodom

Holman Hunt's removal of the rainbow from the final version of *The Scapegoat* is representative of how for many visitors impressions at the Dead Sea still fitted a biblical mould. The iconography of Sodom has had more influence on the perception, or at least writings, of travellers, than the landscape had on representations.[113] While artefacts of Sodom were scant, tales and images were aplenty.[114] Many early accounts seemed fascinated with the bathing qualities of the water, and with the strange beauty that Holman Hunt observed, but their authors still made the obligatory references to 'utter desolation'.[115] The imprint of the biblical account had to be demonstrated in the landscape. For Chateaubriand, the 'dismal sound' of the 'waves, charged with salt' resembled the 'stifled clamours of the people

---

[113] Montague's account of Lynch's expedition almost reads like a description of John Martin's painting.
[114] Frank DeHass, *Buried Cities Recovered: Or, Explorations in Bible Lands* (1882; Philadelphia, PA, 1884), p. 8.
[115] Ibid., pp. 296, 303.

ingulphed in its waters'.[116] The continuity of imagery is striking, from seventeenth-century accounts of 'a most cursed barren place', a 'filthy lake' and 'barren desolation'[117] to late nineteenth-century travel accounts written as 'humble contribution[s] to Biblical archaeology for the home circle'.[118] The author of one such account, former United States Consul in Palestine and Member of the American Geographical Society Frank S. De Hass (b. 1823) echoed Lynch's apologetic use of Scriptures or de Saulcy's erasure of the difference between biblical time and the present, noting that

> a person visiting this region who had never heard of the destruction of Sodom and Gomorrah, would infer from the sterility and death-like solitude which prevail, that nothing but some great judgement from the Almighty could ever have produced such utter desolation. We find here 'a waste land that smoketh, and a fruitful land turned into saltness for the wickedness of them that dwelt therein'; (Psalm cvii 34; Jeremiah xlix, 18) so that 'no man shall abide there, neither shall a son of man dwell in it; and the stranger that shall come from a far land shall say . . . Wherefore hath the Lord done thus unto this land? What meaneth the heat of this great anger? . . . The whole land is brimstone, and salt, and burning' (Deuteronomy xxix, 22, 24).[119]

Towards the end of the nineteenth century, greater ease in travel demystified the Dead Sea. It was imagined that a canal would soon allow one to 'pass through the Dead Sea, under the shadow of the mountains of Moab, and over the buried cities of the Plain, without disturbing the dead of Sodom and Gomorrah'.[120] Members of the American Colony in Jerusalem used a motorboat to explore the region, reporting on a pleasant week in which every night was spent upon the boat, away from mosquitoes or sandflies (Fig. 6.5).[121] While the idea that Sodom and Gomorrah would make the ideal holiday place (if it were not for the guilt) or that an 'an ingenious travel agency could organize fairly passable day-trips to Sodom on behalf of gay tourists' was still a long way away, in the 1860s it was safe enough for the Prince of Wales to visit.[122] His party noted that the Dead Sea 'is not near so dead nor so desolate as it has pleased travellers to describe it. The water, though not very limpid, was at all events sufficiently pure and cool to invite

---

[116] Chateaubriand, *Travels*, p. 264.
[117] *The Travels of Fourteen Englishmen in 1669*, pp. 104–5; Chateaubriand also describes how 'The Dead Sea, and the valley of the Jordan, glowed with an admirable tint; but this rich appearance served only to heighten the desolation of the scene', *Travels*, p. 264.
[118] DeHass, *Buried Cities*, pp. 7, 8.
[119] De Saulcy, *Narrative*, p. 418; DeHass, *Buried Cities*, p. 303.
[120] 'A Projected Railway in Palestine', *The Old Testament Student*, 3 (1884), 355.
[121] Jacob E. Spafford, 'Around the Dead Sea by Motor Boat', *Geographical Journal*, 39 (1912), 37–40.
[122] Andrew Lumsden, 'A Day-trip to Sodom', *Gay News*, 252 (1982), in Hallam, *Sodom*, pp. 176–8.

LOOKING SOUTH, ON WEST SIDE OF DEAD SEA, FROM AM JIDDY (ENGEDI), WITH JEBUL USDUM IN THE FAR DISTANCE.

Figure 6.5 *Looking South, on West Side of Dead Sea, from Am Jiddy (Engedi) with Jebul Usdum in the Far Distance*

one to a dip, and the majority of the company, including the Prince, responded to the invitation.'[123] Playfulness entered in, with postcards of the colourful Dead Sea, next to the flight of Lot sent with pre-printed 'Greetings from Sodom and Gomorrah'.[124] While popular religious accounts still endorsed the view that the landscape reflected the Almighty's punishment, they also pointed out that 'the impression that this sea is always a dead calm, sending forth poisonous vapors, with the angel of death brooding over it, is erroneous' and that 'instead of the exhalations from the sea being injurious, as has been supposed, they seem to . . . impart new life to the whole physical system'. Hence 'a steamer on this sea for excursion, and a good hotel near its shores, would make this a most charming winter resort for invalids, nature's own sanatorium for suffering mortals'.[125]

---

[123] 'The Prince of Wales in the Holy Land', *Illustrated London News* (3 May 1862), 448.
[124] Postcard titled 'Gruss aus Sodom and Gomorrah', dated 1898, Wikimedia Commons, upload. wikimedia.org/wikipedia/commons/9/9a/Sodoma_-_Cartolina.jpg, accessed 20 June 2011.
[125] DeHass, *Buried Cities*, p. 304.

For a long time, the Lake of Sodom had remained the 'blessed dark corner of the imagination, wherein the terrible yet peeps out at us', yet the 'disenchanting processes of rationality and science' had evidently damaged its aura.[126] While mid-century travel guides such as the *Handbook for Travellers in Syria and Palestine* (1858) not only occluded the separation between ancient and modern landscapes but also transferred the sins of the ancients to the modern inhabitants, describing them as 'licentious', 'cowardly' and 'degenerate', by the turn of the century, refuting the received dreariness of the place was itself a topos.[127] For instance, *Half Hours in the Holy Land, a Tale of Travel, Nature and Science for Young Readers* skimmed over the punishment of the cities because 'one must draw upon fancy more than on what is seen by the eye to make the Dead Sea so very dreadful as it is generally supposed to be'.[128] The exultation of floating in the sea, the sensation of salty water on lips and bodies now outstripped any interest in the biblical cities.

There was then a noticeable change between Lynch's, de Saulcy's or Holman Hunt's scriptural landscape and the less spiritually charged travel accounts of the late nineteenth century. But multiple visions continued to coexist. In the land of Sodom's first 'discoverer', as late as 1890 an official history and geography secondary-school textbook offered in its history section a sanitised retelling of Genesis without homosexuality, rape, incest or any allusion to actual geography, illustrated not by a photograph but by Raphael's *Destruction of Sodom*. In the next chapter on geography, a description of the river Jordan and the Dead Sea was given without any allusion to the biblical background or any reflection on the origins of this landscape.[129]

Conclusion

In the international search for the location of Sodom and Gomorrah, the British played only a secondary role, interpreting material produced by French and American explorers rather than stomping around the Dead Sea with excavation tools. Its exploration was marked by commercial competition, but mostly by scholarly collaboration. De Saulcy might have provoked snide remarks about his scholarship, but had staunch defenders

---

[126] Francis Power Cobbe, *The Cities of the Past* (London, 1864), p. 109; Cocks, 'Discovery', 20.
[127] *Handbook for Travellers in Syria and Palestine* (London, 1858), p. 202.
[128] *Half Hours in the Holy Land* (London, 1898), pp. 203–5.
[129] Victor Duruy, *Histoire de l'Orient* (Paris, 1890), pp. 136–7, 170–1.

in Britain.[130] A few grumblings about the growing presence of the Germans around the Dead Sea could be heard during the naval race preceding the Great War, but although an image of the *Mountain of Rock Salt by the Sea of Lot: Sodom* was used to illustrate the worry that the Holy Land 'is gradually being Germanised', the concern was less with Scripture than with German plans to secure the mineral wealth of the Dead Sea basin.[131] Otherwise, collaboration was exemplary in the area. No remains of note could provoke rival claims. Instead, members of different nations were free to interpret the meaning of the findings according to their own domestic needs.

The archaeological search for the cities as well as the wider interest in biblical archaeology and biblical cities fed the craze for Sodom and Gomorrah, but did not trigger it. In Britain, the allusions to Sodom in art, in sermons and the like, although continuous throughout the century, reached a peak in the 1840s, just before the 'discoveries', at a moment of urban turmoil and faith in crisis. It would be tempting to see the search for the cities as a result rather than the cause of this presence. Alas, the international dimension and the entanglement of personal, commercial and learned motives, the 'mystery and danger' animating the search, rule out such a conclusion. It was the strong presence of Sodom in the mind of various audiences that explains the extraordinary reception of de Saulcy's discovery and the continuing interest in the site of the cities thereafter. And yet, the discoveries left little mark in the wider imagination. Imaginary Sodoms continued to be built without much reference to historical accuracy. As other chapters in this book also suggest, if the imagination did not have to follow the discovery of artefacts, the absence of artefacts did not prevent the free exercise of the imagination. Virtually no accounts actually imagined what the cities of the plain must have looked like. A rare description concluded that

these towns doubtless exhibited the same features in common with all the ancient and many of the modern towns in the East, the houses would probably stand apart, with gardens and orchards interspersed between, and the ground in the outskirts would be laid out in cultivated fields, as traces of furrows are still distinctly discernible about Zoar, or would stretch out to a greater distance in extensive commons.[132]

---

[130] When de Saulcy was accused of having desecrated the Tombs of the Kings, several prominent Cambridge scholars came to the defence of the 'distinguished antiquary' and 'friend', see Ermete Pierotti, 'A Word for M. de Saulcy: Letter to the Editor of *The Times*', *The Times* (3 February 1863), 10; George Williams, 'M de Saulcy at Jerusalem: Letter to the Editor of *The Times*', *The Times* (26 January 1864), 10.
[131] 'Does Germany Covet the Dead Sea?' *Illustrated London News* (9 September 1911), 394, 408.
[132] 'Destroyed Cities', 219.

Otherwise, the imagination focused on what happened in the city, not on how it looked.

Much of Sodom's lure lies in its elusiveness. Although scholarly orthodoxy today sees the 'real challenge for biblical archaeologists' as not so much the 'search for long-lost cities, but to understand why the ancient Israelites formulated these powerful myths', the desire to lift the secrets of the destruction of Sodom and Gomorrah continues to animate travel writers,[133] geologists and evangelical biblical scholars and regularly receives media coverage.[134] The question whether there is 'any evidence for the Biblical story of Sodom and Gomorrah's destruction by fire and brimstone' remains live for some: christiananswers.net replies in English, Dutch, French and Indonesian in truly Victorian terms.[135] More generally, Sodom and Gomorrah remain important cultural signifiers. Detailed allusions to the biblical passage became less prevalent over the course of the twentieth century, but other Victorian tropes have an afterlife. References to Sodom and Gomorrah continued to frame debates about the righteous destruction of cities during the First and Second World War, when 'aviators' became 'agents of Sodom and Gomorrah'.[136] Gomorrah also appeared powerfully evocative of urban decay in the title of Roberto Saviano's 2006 account of the Camorra.[137] While some popular Sodom images became forgotten after the First World War, Sodom conquered the screen,[138] and many twentieth-century luminaries from Salvador Dali to

---

[133] 'As a challenge to the more adventurous traveller', the preface to J. Wellard, *The Search for Lost Cities* (London, 1980) starts with 'SODOM AND GOMORRAH; Air to Amman, Bus to Kerak, Taxi down to the Dead Sea'.

[134] Willem C. van Hattem 'Once Again: Sodom and Gomorrah', *The Biblical Archaeologist*, 44 (1981), 87–92. More recently, Bryant G. Wood, 'The Discovery of the Sin Cities of Sodom and Gomorrah', Part 1 of 2, www.ankerberg.org/Articles/_PDFArchives/science/SC3W0903.pdf and Tall el-Hammam Excavation Project, College of Archaeology, Trinity Southwest University and Department of Antiquities of the Hashemite Kingdom of Jordan, www.tallelhammam.com/ , does not rule out the cities might not be found, but believes in the need to follow leads provided by the Bible. The project's director 'noted that the legitimate discovery of the Cities of the Plain, as Sodom and Gomorrah are called in the Bible, would be compelling evidence that the historical information in Genesis is factual'. See Michelle Vu, 'Sodom and Gomorrah Archaeologist Discusses Importance of Discovery', www.christianpost.com/article/20060213/sodom-and-gomorrah-archaeologist-discusses-importance-of-discovery.htm.

[135] www.christiananswers.net/q-abr/abr-a007.html, 14 July 2008.

[136] Charles Lowe, 'The Duration of Great Wars', *Illustrated London News* (25 January 1918), 94; Gordon Musgrove, *Operation Gomorrah, The Hamburg Firestorm Raids* (London, New York, Sydney, 1981).

[137] Roberto Saviano, *Gomorrah*, trans. Virginia Jewiss (London, 2007).

[138] *The Dawn of the World* pictured Lot's escape, see 'The Old Testament Filmed: Wonderful Scenes from a £1,500,000 Picture, "The Dawn of the World"', *Illustrated London News* (2 April 1921), 438–9; Alan Dent, 'The World of the Cinema: From Sodom to Notting Hill', *Illustrated London News* (22 December 1962), 1030.

Nikos Kazantzakis continued to develop the city's place in the artistic canon.[139] Sodom retains a place in popular culture, from Death Metal band Undercroft's song 'Sodom and Gomorrah', to its use in Rastafarian culture, where in tandem with Babylon it refers to white subjugation.[140] While Sodom was more and more used to protest against racial and sexual oppression, appropriation also became increasingly playful and satirical: George Bernard Shaw's play, *Lot's Wife* staged in 1938 at the Whitehall Theatre sees Lot and his daughters 'take refuge on a mountain-top' with a 'picnic hamper with all the forty-seven varieties of a well-known tinned-food firm ... Mrs Lot runs back to answer the telephone. Instead of being turned into a pillar of salt, she finds happiness eventually with a lover'.[141] Freeing itself from the threat of destruction, Sodom has become ever more linked to the emerging gay rights movement and the ancient town is symbolically appropriated, without worrying too much about its archaeology: the nineteenth-century trend to identify Sodom with sex, not the city, persists.

---

[139] Salvador Dali, *Uxnor Lot in Satuam Salis Conversa*, c. 1964–7 published in *Biblia Sacra* (Rome, 1969); Nikos Kazantzakis, *Two Plays: Sodom and Gomorrah; and Comedy, a Tragedy in One Act*, trans. Kimon Friar (St Paul, MN, 1982).

[140] Michael Seymour, 'Babylon in Contemporary Art and Culture', in I. Finkel and Michael Seymour, eds., *Babylon: Myth and Reality*. (London, 2008), pp. 203–12; Ruth Rosenberg, 'Spacemen Destroy Sodom and Gomorrah', *Western Folklore*, 21 (1962), 1151–6.

[141] '"Lot's Wife" at the Whitehall', *The Illustrated London News* (18 June 1938).

7 | Bethlehem

EITAN BAR-YOSEF

Leaving Jerusalem before dawn, anxious to reach Sinai and to discover the Semitic origins of his Christian faith, Tancred – the protagonist of Benjamin Disraeli's 1847 novel – approaches Bethlehem just as the sun is about to rise:

> At this moment, Tancred and his escort are in sight of Bethlehem, with the population of a village but the walls of a town, situate on an eminence overlooking a valley, which seems fertile after passing the stony plain of Rephaim. The first beams of the sun, too, were rising from the mountains of Arabia and resting on the noble convent of the Nativity.

Tancred does not have time to tour the convent: he is off 'to penetrate the great Asian mystery'.[1] Still, even this brief description captures the tensions evoked by the encounter with Bethlehem, a locale marked by a sense of relativity and flux. Defined by a geographical schism (eminence/valley), which, in turn, could only be appreciated when compared to the adjoining landscape (fertile/lush), here was a perplexing urban formation. The 'City of David' was a town with the population of a village, or a village with the walls of a town.

Of course, perplexing experiences were part and parcel of the journey to the Holy Land in the first decades of the nineteenth century. Setting out to discover the realities of Palestine – or rather '*re*discover' them, as the title of Yehoshua Ben-Arieh's influential book has insisted – Western travellers were unsettled by the physical appearance of the land, dotted with small, dirty villages that carried the names of great biblical cities.[2] They were expecting something quite different: after all, for centuries, the European Great Masters had depicted scriptural scenes in the settings of their native lands, with Jerusalem painted overlooking a sea, a lake or the green Roman countryside, while the patriarchs and the Israelite kings were seen dressed in contemporary European clothes.[3] With the Reformation, and the renewed

---

[1] Benjamin Disraeli, *Tancred: Or the New Crusade* (3 vols., London, 1847), II, pp. 114–15.
[2] Yehoshua Ben-Arieh, *The Rediscovery of the Holy Land in the Nineteenth Century* (Jerusalem, 1979).
[3] Naomi Shepherd, *The Zealous Intruders: The Western Rediscovery of Palestine* (London, 1987), pp. 17–18.

emphasis on the authority of the sacred text, Protestant popular culture perfected this internalisation and domestication of the biblical geography: a range of works, from allegories such as *The Pilgrim's Progress* to hymns such as 'Jerusalem, My Happy Home', encouraged English believers to think of themselves as the elect Israelites, expecting Jerusalem to be built, imminently, in England's green and pleasant land. These texts, assisted by the decline of the earthly pilgrimage and the new geo-political conditions in Palestine following the Ottoman conquest, shifted the believers' attention from the geographical Holy Land to its metaphorical double, a Canaan of pure delight that could be imagined in, or as, one's own vicinity. The 'Holy Land' thus became an integral part of English imagination, identity and culture, associated with the foremost institutions of popular Protestant piety: the English churchyard, the Sunday school, the family Bible, home. Little wonder that early nineteenth-century travellers were unprepared for the hard, exotic, Oriental features of the landscape that welcomed them in the Holy Land.[4]

Yet the encounter with the land, from the early 1800s onwards, soon reshaped its representation in Western culture: Palestine was gradually Orientalised, with stock images of the picturesque East – bare hills, minarets, camels, palm trees, Bedouins – replacing the previous, vernacular, images. And because these images, in turn, were often disseminated through the same popular religious channels (from Sunday school prize-books to magic-lantern presentations at the local chapel), these new images, too, were internalised and domesticated, intimately associated with the idea of an English 'home'.

Of all the cities, towns and villages in Palestine, it was Bethlehem, this chapter will argue, that was most commonly imagined in these intimate terms. Always overshadowed by *the* holy city – the Holy City, Jerusalem – Bethlehem did not evoke the same sense of awe and reverence. Nevertheless, it was precisely the town's complex history and its compact dimensions that made it so suitable for further cultural compression. If, as Simon Goldhill claims in his chapter, Jerusalem was always the great type of a biblical city but also the great exception, Bethlehem offered a much more nuanced case, easier to grasp, manage, imagine and re-imagine. Unlike some of the cities described in this collection, Bethlehem was not excavated until the twentieth century (in the mid-1930s, by the Mandatory Department of Antiquities), and even then, the archaeological findings were extremely

---

[4] Eitan Bar-Yosef, *The Holy Land in English Culture: Palestine and the Question of Orientalism* (Oxford, 2005), esp. pp. 74–94.

limited.[5] Consequently, and notwithstanding the existence of the Grotto in the Church of the Nativity, Bethlehem never offered that fascinating shift, from surface to buried depth and back again: to paraphrase the title of Charles Warren's successful 1876 memoir, there was never really an *Underground Bethlehem*. However, as we shall see, the town's topographical, architectural and human features made it possible for Western – and particularly Protestant – travellers to think about it in ambiguous, fluent and liminal terms, exchanging the vertical hierarchy (overground/underground) with a sort of horizontal spectrum which complicated and ultimately challenged the strict division between city and village, 'home' and 'elsewhere', past and present, East and West.

Town, village, city

Even before it was gazed at, surveyed, or experienced directly, Bethlehem was associated with a sense of liminality, shaped by the town's geographical location and its position in the nineteenth-century travel circuit. Peripheral, though only six miles from Jerusalem, Bethlehem was almost always the first stop just after, or just before, the much longer visit to the Holy City. This was in stark contrast to another sacred town, Nazareth, which demanded a much longer and more elaborate journey: not all travellers to the Holy Land made their way to Galilee, but none failed to explore Jerusalem and its environs.

Bethlehem's Church of the Nativity, one of the oldest Christian monuments in the world (the first basilica on the site was built by Helena, mother of Constantine), offered visitors a range of subterranean wonders – among them the Chapel of the Nativity (where a silver star proclaimed 'Here Jesus Christ was born of the Virgin Mary'), the Altar of the Innocents (marking the spot where the twenty thousand babies slaughtered by Herod were allegedly buried) and the tomb of St Jerome. All these were administered by and carefully divided between the Roman Catholics, Greek Orthodox and Armenian Apostolic monks, who lived in the three convents on the site. Other important locales in Bethlehem included the Milk Grotto, situated in the side of the rocky ridge below the church. According to tradition, this is where Mary and Jesus hid from the fury of Herod; the white chalky stone, made whiter after a few drops of the virgin's milk fell on it, could

---

[5] Michael Avi-Yonah, 'Bethlehem', in Ephraim Stern, ed., *The Encyclopedia of Archaeological Excavations in the Holy Land* (4 vols., Jerusalem, 1993), I, esp. pp. 205–8.

miraculously increase a woman's milk. A mile or so from the church was a grotto in a field, marking the place where the shepherds, 'keeping watch over their flock by night' (Luke 2:8), were approached by the angels. Other important sites close by included the Tomb of Rachel, with its iconic Oriental dome; the traditional Well of David, for whose water he yearned when hiding in the cave of Adullam; Solomon's Pools, part of an ancient aqueduct system which carried water to Jerusalem; and the Convent of St Elias.[6]

To see all this did not require more than a one-day excursion. Some travellers stopped in Bethlehem on their way from Jerusalem to the Mar-Saba convent, from which they continued down to the Dead Sea and Jericho (or, like Disraeli's Tancred, to Sinai). Others took the opposite route. John Murray's *Handbook for Travellers in Syria and Palestine* (1858) advised those journeying from Mar-Saba to Jerusalem to make an early start and stop at Bethlehem: 'the traveller will have sufficient time to visit all the places of interest there, and to return to Jerusalem in the evening. Thus a day may be saved'.[7] Travelling to Palestine from Sinai, via Petra, Harriet Martineau obtained her first view of Jerusalem shortly after quitting Bethlehem. 'Soon after, we saw, on the opposite northern ridge, a line of walls which looked so insignificant that some of our company were unaware at first what it was,' Martineau recalled in *Eastern Life, Present and Past* (1848): 'Mr. E. said to me, "You know that is Jerusalem".'[8] Interestingly, visited by this order – travelling northward, that is, and reaching the destination towards dusk – both cities offered, according to Martineau, an unremarkable first sighting. Perhaps that is why Martineau eventually performed the opposite (and certainly more common) route: trying their new horses, which were to take them from Jerusalem to Damascus, she and her fellow-travellers 'were glad to have one more view of Bethlehem, which we had not expected to see again. We rode as far south as the convent of St. Elias; and thence Bethlehem looked well on its hill promontory, commanding the plain towards Moab'.[9] The result was a double 'first' view of Bethlehem, or rather a 'final' view that complemented (and thus corrected) the original impression.

Bethlehem's pastoral surroundings reinforced its liminality. Evoking the memory of David, keeper of the sheep, Ruth's wheat harvest and Luke's

---

[6] Josiah L. Porter, *A Handbook for Travellers in Syria and Palestine* (2 vols., London, 1858), I, pp. 209–11.
[7] Ibid., I, p. 206.
[8] Harriet Martineau, *Eastern Life, Present and Past* (3 vols., London, 1848), III, p. 77.
[9] Ibid., III, p. 181.

shepherds, abiding in the field, Bethlehem – 'the house of bread' in Hebrew – presented a rather hazy spatial formation, in which city and country were fused together. It is telling that the first chapter of the best-selling *Life of Christ* (1874) by Frederic William Farrar (1831–1903) opens in that hallowed spot on the margins of the town: 'One mile from Bethlehem is a little plain, in which, under a grove of olives, stands the bare and neglected chapel known by the name of "the Angel to the Shepherds".'[10] An intermediate space, empty and inhabited at the same time, the Shepherds' Plain anticipates and mimics Bethlehem itself, 'with the population of a village but the walls of a town', as Disraeli observed in *Tancred*. This ambiguous description could be said to reflect broader Victorian anxieties regarding the nature of urban space, in the ancient Bible Lands but also in nineteenth-century Britain: is it defined by the presence of people or edifices? When does a village become a town, and a town – a city? Where exactly does the city end, and the countryside begin? And, more specifically, to what extent were the biblical cities, towns or villages worthy of their respective titles?

Edwin Paxton Hood (1820–85), author of *The Villages of the Bible* (1874), agreed that 'some difficulty may be apprehended as to what the Bible means by a village'. Nevertheless, he reminded his readers that 'this is a difficulty which is felt not merely in dealing with the villages of the Bible; . . . We have cities of only a few hundreds of inhabitants, and we have what technically may be called villages, having neither cathedral nor corporation, neither bishop nor high bailiff, numbering ten or twenty thousand in population'. Hood does not offer a clear-cut definition of a biblical village or even of a village in general: 'We feel the idea we attach to the term village better than we can accurately or exactly define it,' he observes. Still, Bethlehem certainly seems to exhibit many of the features listed by Hood as characteristic of the biblical village, 'a spot where human beings were very few, where society was primitive and unconventional, where nature held an almost absolute sway over the mind and the senses, . . . where streets and architecture, huge fanes and fabrics, had not gathered in the swarming crowds of people'.[11]

Like the other locales recorded in *The Villages of the Bible*, from Mamre to Bethany, Hood's description of Bethlehem sets out to focus on the reality of biblical life. To do so, however, the author must first eradicate the more modern architectural sites that have been established to commemorate the

---

[10] Frederic W. Farrar, *Life of Christ* (1874; London, 1963), p. 1.
[11] Edwin Paxton Hood, *The Villages of the Bible: Descriptive, Traditional, and Memorable: Sabbath Evening Lectures in Brighton* (London, 1874), pp. 2–3.

sacred significance of the place. In Jerusalem, the 'real' city seems to lie underground: 'the hills, the valleys, the springs of old Jerusalem lie thirty or forty feet below the surface,' explained the clergyman and scriptural geographer Arthur Penrhyn Stanley (1815–81) in an article in *Good Words*: 'we can still, if we go deep enough, arrive at the streets where David trod'. In Bethlehem, in comparison, the division is horizontal, spread out across the ridge.[12] 'Picture to yourself two hills, and the abrupt valley between,' Hood instructs his readers: 'now on the one hill stands a convent with a cluster of buildings around it, but all that is of these later ages. Formerly the village stood only on the one hill, – a little cluster of homesteads on the hill and hillside'.[13] Hood makes no reference to the curious fact that his reading of the landscape locates the manger, on which the Church of the Nativity was allegedly built, outside the boundaries of the original Bethlehem.[14] Typically, rather than dwell on the 'original' village that could be said to lie underneath the Convent, Hood prefers to focus on the visible evidence alone. The question, nevertheless, remains: if the 'village' stood 'formerly' on one hill only, did the addition of another hill, and with such prominent buildings, transform Bethlehem into a town?

This question, which shaped the uneasy ambiguity captured in *Tancred*, could often be traced in various nineteenth-century images of Bethlehem, which sought to define the relationship between the two sections. J. M. W. Turner's illustration in *The Biblical Keepsake; Or, Landscape Illustrations of the Most Remarkable Places Mentioned in the Holy Scriptures* (1835) offers a complex representation of Bethlehem as viewed from the north (Fig. 7.1): showing a panorama of the two summits on the ridge, the image is divided almost equally between the Church and the older section of the town.[15] Nevertheless, the imposing, fortified Church spills over the middle of the

---

[12] Arthur Penrhyn Stanley, 'Palestine Exploration', *Good Words* (1 March 1868), 175.
[13] Hood, *Villages*, p. 286.
[14] The tradition which locates the cave outside Bethlehem could be traced back to Justin, who notes in *Dialogue with Trypho* that 'when Joseph could not find any lodgings in the village, he went to a nearby cave'. Justin's geography, however, is extremely vague: as Joan Taylor observes, his identification of the site 'implies a place further away than the Tomb of Rachel which, according to Justin is "*in* Bethlehem"'. The writings of Origen, Eusebius and Jerome, in contrast, suggest that 'by the end of the third century, the famous cave where the mysteries of Tammuz-Adonis were celebrated was identified with the birthplace of Jesus; these do not continue the tradition of Justin, in which the cave is located outside the town, but rather demonstrate a blending of pagan and Christian traditions'. The pagan site, which was taken to prove the antiquity of the Christian veneration, was decidedly *inside* Bethlehem, probably near the western border of the ancient village. See Joan E. Taylor, *Christians and the Holy Places: The Myth of Jewish-Christian Origins* (New York, 1993), pp. 100–1, 112.
[15] The image in the book is an engraving of Turner's watercolour drawing, based on sketches made on the spot by Barry and Master.

Figure 7.1 J. M. W. Turner, *Bethlehem*

illustration, overshadowing the much smaller residential quarters. This shift is reinforced by the presence of the couple in front: the pious woman (holding a baby, it seems) is situated slightly past the middle, aligned with the entrance to the Church compound behind her, while the man and his horse, in much darker colours, are pushed towards the margins of the picture. The shining star above the Church – a reference, of course, to the Star of the East mentioned in Matthew 2 – emphasises the unsettlingly ahistorical quality of the picture, which projects the architectural framework of the modern Bethlehem back onto the biblical 'village' and shows Mary and Joseph (or are these merely their types?) with the majestic Church of the Nativity behind them.

Many nineteenth-century images of Bethlehem focused on the Convent compound alone, with its huge dramatic walls, as depicted from the middle of the ridge. Other visual representations, however, preferred to follow Hood's cue by recoiling from the holy sites altogether. The engraving of Bethlehem in *Pictorial Journey through the Holy Land: or, Scenes in Palestine* (1863), published by the Religious Tract Society, turned its gaze from the Convent and centred on the 'village' section, situated on a rather bare hill. A grimly built setting, brightened by the trees in the foreground,

Figure 7.2 *Bethlehem*

the illustration is entitled *Bethlehem as It Is*, although the artist had clearly set out to portray Bethlehem as it was. The engraving in Henry Baker Tristram's *Scenes in the East* (1884) goes even further: viewed from a rooftop within Bethlehem itself, it depicts a crowded assemblage of two- and even three-storey houses, lined up on the slope of the hill (Fig. 7.2). There are some short trees in front and a valley that separates these dwellings from another inhabited, though less crowded hill. Nevertheless, the appearance of this 'village' is almost urban – very different, certainly, from the pastoral descriptions of *The Villages of the Bible*.

Indeed, fusing his account of biblical rustic life with a nostalgia for rural old England and an abhorrence of the modern metropolis, Hood neatly overlooks the fact that the Bible often designates Bethlehem a city: 'And Joseph also went up from Galilee, out of the city of Nazareth, into Judaea, unto the city of David, which is called Bethlehem' (Luke 2:4).[16] While this

---

[16] In the Old Testament (2 Samuel 5:7 and henceforth) the 'city of David' is of course Jerusalem.

raises the broader subject of biblical spatial nomenclature, it is significant to note that the New Testament often complicates further the nature of Bethlehem (a 'town', according to John 7:42). The two accounts of Jesus' birth construct a careful dichotomy between the cataclysmic event and its humble earthly manifestation, but the implications for Bethlehem's 'municipal' character are radically different. Led by the Star of the East, the wise men described in Matthew 2 naturally travel to the city of Jerusalem, only to learn that their real destination is the smaller and much more marginal Bethlehem.[17] In Luke 2, by comparison, the marginality is created by the manger – a lowly space within the 'city of David'. Although the environment is undoubtedly bucolic – with the shepherds abiding in the field – Luke constructs a distinct separation between the city and the country, reflected by the shepherds' response ('Let us now go even unto Bethlehem') as they make their way 'with haste' to witness the miracle heralded by the angels (Luke 2:15).

So important and yet so small, situated both inside and outside the rural setting, the tensions that mark the spatial depiction of Bethlehem in the Bible still resonate, I argue, in nineteenth-century accounts of the place. '"Little among the thousands of Judah", Bethlehem has never claimed pre-eminence from its position, its buildings, or its wealth,' wrote the clerical naturalist and traveller Henry Baker Tristram (1822–1906) in *Scenes in the East* (1884):

Like many other spots of hallowed or ennobled memory, it owes its fame to its history and associations alone ... But, as it stands on the summit of the chalky limestone range, where the white ridge culminates in a rounded mound higher than the rest, it is an exact type – almost the only specimen left to us intact – of the cities of the hill-country of Judah. Take away the Church of the Nativity and the conventual buildings, and what the cities of Judah were, Bethlehem is: probably little, if at all changed, in its streets, in its architecture, in the arrangement of the houses, from any 'fenced town' through which the chariots of David or Solomon may have rolled.

Lacking pre-eminence (yet standing on the summit, 'higher than the rest'), Bethlehem is in fact a typical 'city' of the tribe of Judah – not a 'village', as Hood insisted (although Tristram, too, must imagine a Bethlehem devoid of

---

[17] The ironic discrepancy between the small dimensions of the place and its vast importance is already anticipated in Micah 5:2: 'But thou, Bethlehem Ephratah, though thou be little among the thousands of Judah, yet out of thee shall he come forth unto me that is to be ruler in Israel.' Rephrasing the prophecy, the version in Matthew 2:6 magnifies the 'little' Bethlehem: 'And thou Bethlehem, in the land of Juda, *art not the least* among the princes of Juda: for out of thee shall come a Governor, that shall rule my people Israel' (my emphasis).

the Church and the convents). Spared the fate of the 'desolate heaps which mark the often nameless sites of the cities of Judah, to which David resorted during his residence at Ziklag,' Tristram writes, Bethlehem is thus significant for its insignificance.[18] Perhaps that is why travellers seldom professed disappointment at Bethlehem's proportions, as they so often did in other Holy Land sites: here was a village/town/city which resisted clear-cut categorisations.

Sacred sites, holy landscape

The liminality which characterised, for nineteenth-century travellers, Bethlehem's topographical features, its geographical position *vis-à-vis* Jerusalem and its urban nature could also be attributed to the town's most sacred site, the Church of the Nativity, a space associated, after all, with a *temporal* transition – the birth that was to change the course of history. 'Here the Saviour was born in a stable and cradled in a manger,' mused Murray's *Handbook*: 'What a mighty influence for good has gone forth from this spot over the human family!'[19] This was the event that proclaimed a new dawn for the world: no wonder that Disraeli's account in *Tancred* colours the Church of the Nativity with the 'first beams of the sun'.

Similar language appears elsewhere in Victorian descriptions of Bethlehem, suggesting how the conventions of travel (in this case, departing from Jerusalem before daybreak) could merge with the poetic association between the sunrise and the rise of the son. Consider, for example, Emily Beaufort's *Egyptian Sepulchres and Syrian Shrines* (1861). Having spent Christmas in Bethlehem – characteristically defined as 'one of the brightest villages in Palestine', which 'is in truth a town of considerable extent' – Beaufort offers her own variation on the daybreak theme:

> the night was gone, the beautiful stars had vanished back into heaven, and the sunlight in vast tides of brightness had come in – . . . it lit up the hill tops, and brightened the terraces and the little meadows, while all the distant mountains of the Dead Sea deepened into hues of blood-red and deep purple. Then I looked back to Bethlehem, all white and radiant like a pearl of great price, as the bright beams shone on the Convent walls where many hearts were then bowed in prayer: the vines and

---

[18] Henry Baker Tristram, *Scenes in the East: Consisting of 12 Views of Places Mentioned in the Bible* (London, 1884), pp. 2–3.
[19] Porter, *Handbook*, I, p. 207.

the corn around it soon lightened up, and I thought of Ruth – the gentle, bravehearted girl.[20]

Like the Church of the Nativity – whose symbolic significance, as we have seen, is often enmeshed in these texts with Bethlehem's spatial, topographical and geographical features – the reference to Ruth the Moabite is yet another reminder of Bethlehem's association with a transformation – in this case, the shift from Judaism to Christianity. Indeed, more than any other biblical site in the Holy Land, Bethlehem dramatises the shift from the Old Testament to the New Testament through a wide array of episodes: the early reference to the death of Rachel, who was buried by Jacob 'in the way to Ephrath, which is Bethlehem' (Genesis 35:19); David's lineage and his rise to prominence (Bethlehem as the 'city of David'); and, of course, the story of Ruth and Boaz, which links the Davidic dynasty to the birth of Jesus (prophesied, it was believed, in Micah 5:2). By visiting Bethlehem, one could experience the spatial equivalent of reading the genealogy 'of Jesus Christ the son of David, the son of Abraham', detailed in Matthew 1.

For Victorian Protestant travellers, in particular, the inscription of this typology onto the landscape meant that Bethlehem became 'the ultimate place of conversion', as Billie Melman has observed.[21] This conversion could relate to several contexts and projects: Ruth's adoption of the Israelite faith; the Nativity and the shift from Jewish history to Christian history; or, more topically, the nineteenth-century Evangelical mission of proselytising the indigenous Palestinian population. In all these cases, Bethlehem's sanctity was continuously associated with a liminal phase, a movement – that is, a *conversion* – from one stage to the other, culminating with the triumph of Christianity.

Needless to say, 'Christianity' was not monolithic; and for Protestants, at least, the representation of Bethlehem as a liminal space was inseparable from the problematic status of the holy sites within it. On the one hand, time-honoured traditions, some of them dating back to the mid-second century AD, seemed to corroborate the identification of these locales. 'The tradition respecting the Cave of the Nativity seems so well authenticated, as hardly to admit of dispute,' the classicist and traveller Edward Daniel Clarke (1769–1822) was forced to admit in 1812: 'Having been always held in veneration, the oratory established there by the first Christians attracted the

---

[20] Emily Beaufort, *Egyptian Sepulchres and Syrian Shrines* (1861; 2 vols., London, 1862), II, pp. 124, 191.
[21] Billie Melman, *Women's Orients: English Women and the Middle East, 1718–1918* (1992; London, 1995), p. 225.

notice and indignation of the Heathens so early as the time of Adrian, who ordered it to be demolished, and the place to be set apart for the rites of Adonis.'[22] On the other hand, the encounter with the ostentatious rites and rituals of the Roman and Orthodox Catholics often shocked and dismayed Protestant travellers. 'We were entertained by the Superior of the Greek Convent, in a fine refectory, with ceremonies and hospitalities that pilgrims of the middle ages might have witnessed,' wrote William Makepeace Thackeray (1811–63) in *Notes of a Journey from Cornhill to Grand Cairo* (1846): 'We were shown over the magnificent Barbaric Church, visited of course the Grotto where the Blessed Nativity is said to have taken place, and the rest of the idols set up for worship by the clumsy legend.'[23]

The fact that the dispute between Latins and Greeks about access to the various sites of the Church – and particularly about the presence of the silver star in the grotto – was seen as one of the causes for the Crimean War, offered a topical variation on the theme. British commentators were appalled by the astounding discrepancy between the triviality of the star (for Protestants, that is) and the immensity of the war – between the peace and goodwill associated with the birth of Christ and the need to solve this religious dispute 'by the advance of armies and the threatening movement of fleets', as Alexander Kinglake (1809–91) wrote in his history of the Crimean War.[24]

Still, so many Protestants yearned to believe. On visiting the Grotto of the Nativity, Walter, the pious young protagonist of Daniel Eddy's *Walter's Tour in Jerusalem* (1863), is distressed to learn that according to Edward Robinson – the importance of whose *Biblical Researches in Palestine* (1841) has been outlined in earlier chapters – 'it would hardly seem consistent with a love of simple historic truth to attach to this tradition any much higher degree of credit than we have shown to belong to the parallel tradition respecting the place of our Lord's Ascension'. 'That takes away half my pleasure!' moans Walter, to which his teacher responds, 'It need not; for other biblical critics, of as much judgment as Robinson, take the other view, and tell us there can be no doubt of the place.'[25] 'Tradition is in its favour,

---

[22] Edward Daniel Clarke, *Travels in Various Countries of Europe, Asia, and Africa* (1810–23; 6 vols., London, 1817), IV, p. 415. On the pagan tradition see note 14 above. See Gange and Bryant Davies, *supra*, for Clarke's pursuit of Troy.

[23] William Makepeace Thackeray, *Notes of a Journey from Cornhill to Grand Cairo* (London, 1846), p. 222.

[24] Alexander William Kinglake, *The Invasion of the Crimea* (8 vols., London, 1863–87), I, p. 51.

[25] Daniel C. Eddy, *Walter's Tour in the East: Walter in Jerusalem* (New York, 1863), p. 155. Eddy is quoting from Edward Robinson, *Biblical Researches in Palestine, and in the Adjacent Regions: A Journey of Travels in the Year 1838* (1841; 2 vols., London, 1856), I, p. 417.

but facts and probabilities are against it,' concluded John Kitto (1804–54), the author of popularising guides to biblical criticism.[26] As Ruth and Thomas Hummel have observed,

> Bethlehem was an ambiguous site. Many found the Grotto of the Nativity a likely location for the manger and the grotto itself iconographically acceptable. Others dismissed it as a fraud, finding inspiration in the nearby 'authentic' grotto of St Jerome, whose presence gave sanctity to the complex. The other sites, like the Milk Grotto, were rejected out of hand as tourist traps. The Shepherd's Field in the outskirts of the town, although lacking any definite proof for its appellation, did give the Protestant imagination a vision of the landscape of the events surrounding the nativity and was, therefore, suitably appreciated.[27]

The Protestants' gaze, then, was naturally drawn from the holy places themselves to the larger town around them, and from there to the open landscape. 'Just about here this message must have been delivered,' pondered Helen Balkwill Harris as she was sitting 'on the height of the Bethlehem plateau', producing a loving drawing of the Shepherds' Field beneath her (Fig. 7.3), and gazing at the rustic little church at its centre. 'A little farther off from Bethlehem, or a little nearer, makes no difference,' she cheerfully stated: 'It was on this plain that the announcement to the simple shepherds was made, and the blue sky overhead was once peopled with the angelic host.'[28]

The turn to the sacred landscape becomes particularly evident when we juxtapose Roman Catholic and Protestant responses. 'Nothing can be more pleasing, or better calculated to excite sentiments of devotion, than this subterranean church,' wrote François-René de Chateaubriand, recalling his visit to the Church of the Nativity:

> on quitting the crypt, where you have met with the riches, the arts, the religion, of civilized nations, you find yourself in a profound solitude, amidst wretched Arab huts, among half naked savages and faithless Mussulmans. The place is, nevertheless, the same where so many miracles were displayed; but this sacred land dares no longer express its joy, and locks within its bosom the recollections of its glory.[29]

---

[26] John Kitto, *The Popular Cyclopedia of Biblical Literature* (Boston, 1854), p. 150.
[27] Ruth and Thomas Hummel, *Patterns of the Sacred: English Protestant and Russian Orthodox Pilgrims of the Nineteenth Century* (London, 1995), p. 14.
[28] Helen B. Harris, *Pictures of the East: Sketches of Biblical Scenes in Palestine and Greece* (London, 1897), p. 46.
[29] François-René de Chateaubriand, *Travels to Jerusalem and the Holy Land Through Egypt* (1810–11), trans. Fredric Shoberl (1811; 2 vols., London, 1835), II, pp. 331–2.

THE PLAINS OF BETHLEHEM

Figure 7.3 *The Plains of Bethlehem*

Arthur Penrhyn Stanley, in comparison, was only too happy to turn away from the shrine to the open landscape surrounding it:

> I have said one is reminded of the Nativity by the convent. But, in truth, I almost think it distracts one from it. From the first moment that those towers, and hills, and valleys burst upon you, there enters the one prevailing thought that now, at last, we are indeed in the 'Holy Land.' It pervades the whole atmosphere – even David and Ruth wax faint in its presence.[30]

This process, in which the Protestant gaze consecrates the natural landscape rather than the traditional holy places, was not limited to Bethlehem: it marks the entire nineteenth-century British project of touring and surveying the Bible Lands (as Goldhill describes in his chapter, this is how the Protestants 'invented' the Garden Tomb, conveniently situated outside the walls of Jerusalem). Nevertheless, this effortless shift from towers and terraces to hills to valleys – this fusion, in other words, of the urban elements with the green features outside it, as terraces become 'gigantic stairs' – is

---

[30] Arthur Penrhyn Stanley, *Sinai and Palestine* (1856; London, 1896), pp. 104–5.

acutely visible in Bethlehem, a place already associated with such an array of tensions and ambiguities.[31] If Ernest Renan (1823–92), in his *Vie de Jésus* (1864), creates a clear division between Christ's rustic Galilee and a corrupt Jerusalem, Bethlehem seems to strike an intriguing balance between these two extremes, the pastoral scenery that confirms the truth of Scripture – 'The sky, the hills, the vales, the rocks of Bethlehem saw these things come to pass' – and the corrupt religiosity of the so-called 'sacred' sites (merging the New Testament's critique of the Sanhedrin's reign in Jerusalem with the superstition associated by the Protestants with the contemporary Roman Catholic and Eastern Orthodox churches).[32]

For Protestants, moreover, turning to the open, unmarred landscape was a way of authenticating the truth of Scripture, of challenging the sceptical higher criticism using its own tools. As Naomi Shepherd has noted, 'Protestant clergymen who had tried to authenticate scriptural miracles in terms of Palestine's flora and fauna had more than a little in common with Renan, a rational Christian who saw Jesus as a social revolutionary and moralist.'[33] At the same time, Protestants simply could not accept Renan's assertion that 'Jesus was born at Nazareth, a small town in Galilee, which before him had no celebrity. All his life he was designated by the name of "Nazarene", and it is only by an awkward detour that the legends succeed in fixing his birth at Bethlehem'.[34] 'Awkward or not,' stormed John Stebbinsee in *Sacred Cities: Narrative, Descriptive, Historical* (1878), 'the fact is as well authenticated as any other event in ancient history, and as Rénan [*sic*] gives us no valid reason for rejecting the statements of Luke and John, we must accept them as well as the universal testimony of the Christian world for the last eighteen hundred years and locate the place of his birth at Bethlehem.'[35]

Indeed, the opening of Farrar's *Life of Christ*, which makes great play of his own visit to the scenes of the nativity (Lee, too, begins his account of Bethlehem in the Shepherds' Field), exemplifies this powerfully Protestant desire to employ the landscape to lend verisimilitude to narratives of Christ's life, a tradition that stretches from popular accounts for children (*Walter's Tour in Jerusalem*) to scholarly studies such as William Ramsay's *Was Christ Born at Bethlehem?* (1898).[36] Nevertheless, affirming the

---

[31] Norman Macleod, *Eastward* (London, 1866), p. 216.
[32] *Pictorial Journey Through the Holy Land: Or, Scenes in Palestine* (London, 1863), p. 135.
[33] Shepherd, *Zealous Intruders*, p. 98.
[34] Ernest Renan, *The Life of Jesus*, trans. Charles Edwin Wilbour (New York, 1864), p. 65.
[35] John S. Lee, *Sacred Cities: Narrative, Descriptive, Historical* (Cincinnati, OH, 1877), p. 32.
[36] See Jennifer Stevens, *The Historical Jesus and the Literary Imagination 1860–1920* (Liverpool, 2010), esp. pp. 34–138.

authenticity of Luke the historian was one thing; defining more specifically how the landscape of Bethlehem and the surrounding area could serve to verify the truth of the New Testament was another, more complex issue. Hood made a point of calling Nazareth, not Bethlehem, 'the Village of the Incarnation; and you may say "Jesus of Nazareth", with more propriety than "Jesus of Bethlehem", because, although He was born in Bethlehem, in Nazareth He spent the first thirty years of His life, and even the life of His public ministration was passed in its neighbourhood'. Hood did not go as far as Renan – whose *Vie de Jésus*, he observed, was merely a 'romance' – but his account of Nazareth, 'the most honoured of all the villages of the Bible', seems to reinforce the marginalisation of Bethlehem.[37] Murray's *Handbook* was of the same opinion, noting that 'to the simple Christian', Nazareth's setting and environs 'possesses a far greater charm, a far more intense interest, than the Annunciation could have ever given it. In this respect it far surpasses Bethlehem'.[38]

Christians, crusaders, coquettes

The construction of Bethlehem as a quintessentially Christian space blended with the cultural politics of nineteenth-century Orientalism: Bethlehem's role in the biblical narrative and its association with the shift from Jewish to Christian eschatologies meant that the Muslims were often relegated to the background or omitted from the scenery. True, the great majority of the town's population throughout the nineteenth century (estimations varied from 3,000 to 5,000) was indeed Christian, mostly Greek Orthodox.[39] Nevertheless, the Western erasure of Muslims from the landscape was also a fantasy that corresponded to the image of Bethlehem as a symbol of a new dawn, a fresh start. 'The contrast between Bethlehem and Hebron is very striking,' noted Claude Reignier Conder (1848–1910),

---

[37] Hood, *Villages*, pp. 315, 316, 314.   [38] Porter, *Handbook*, II, p. 344.
[39] The Greek Orthodox Church was the largest Christian sect in nineteenth-century Palestine. There are no specific figures for Bethlehem, but it is indicative that, according to Ottoman records, 26,337 Christians lived in the Jerusalem *sanjak* (district) in 1886–7, of whom 17,264 (65 per cent) were Greek Orthodox and 7,724 (30 per cent) were Roman Catholics; in 1911–12, when the overall Christian population rose to 43,934, the figures were 27,990 (63 per cent) and 10,622 (24 per cent), respectively. Specific and reliable sources are available from the Mandate period onwards: according to the 1931 census, 10,628 Christians lived in the Bethlehem sub-district, of whom 7,052 (66 per cent) were Greek Orthodox and 2,774 (26 per cent) were Roman Catholics. Other sects included Syrian Orthodox (291), Armenians (105), Anglicans (9) and Maronites (4). See Justin McCarthy, *The Population of Palestine: Population History and Statistics of the Late Ottoman Period and the Mandate* (New York, 1990), pp. 12, 78–9.

a Royal Engineer employed by the Palestine Exploration Fund: 'it is the contrast between Christianity and Islam, between the vitality of the religion of progress and civilisation and the hopeless stagnation of a fantastic creed'. Thus, while 'Hebron is a city of the past', Bethlehem 'is a thriving modern town – the birthplace of a faith that looks forward rather than back'.[40] Modernity and faith go hand in hand (even if this faith happens to be Greek Orthodox and not Protestant), making the city appear cleaner and brighter, an intermediate space between Western and Oriental standards. 'Bethlehem is a small city,' notes Lee in *Sacred Cities*: 'Compared with western cities, the streets are narrow, but wider and cleaner than those of Hebron, Nablous, and Tiberias.'[41]

Anticipating twentieth-century Zionist/Israeli historiography, which has often overplayed the role of Crusading heritage in the Holy Land, nineteenth-century British accounts of Bethlehem stressed the town's history during the Crusades: some believed that the present inhabitants were actually descendants of the Crusaders. By doing so, they minimised and even obliterated the many centuries of Muslim rule. The violent events which followed the Egyptian occupation of Palestine in the early 1830s – in 1834, following a local insurgency, Ibrahim Pasha (1789–1848) all but destroyed the Muslim quarter of Bethlehem – allowed British writers to expand further their fantasies of a Christian (albeit non-Protestant), Muslim-free sphere. As Alexander Kinglake noted in *Eothen* (1844),

By a strange chance in these latter days it happened that, alone of all the places in the land, this Bethlehem, the native village of our Lord, escaped the moral yoke of the Mussulmans, and heard again, after ages of dull oppression, the cheering clatter of social freedom, and the voices of laughing girls. It was after an insurrection which had been raised against the authority of Mehemet Ali, that Bethlehem was freed from the hateful laws of Asiatic decorum. The Mussulmans of the village had taken an active part in the movement, and when Ibrahim had quelled it, his wrath was still so hot, that he put to death every one of the few Mahometans of Bethlehem who had not already fled. The effect produced upon the Christian inhabitants, by the sudden removal of this restraint, was immense. The village smiled once more.[42]

Free from the 'Asiatic' yoke, the village could once again 'smile', an enlightened (though perhaps temporary) Western enclave within the Oriental sea

---

[40] Claude Reignier Conder, *Tent Work in Palestine: A Record of Discovery and Adventure* (London, 1878), p. 283.
[41] Lee, *Sacred Cities*, p. 31.
[42] Alexander Kinglake, *Eothen: Or, Traces of Travel Brought Home from the East* (London, 1844), p. 235.

of ignorance and despotism. At the same time, however, the fact that these Bethlehemite Christians were, after all, Palestinians (and hence Oriental) explains their representation in nineteenth-century travel literature as hybrids of sorts. The 'people, who are all Christians,' writes Emily Beaufort,

> are a race apart, marrying chiefly among themselves, and taking much pride in their origin, – they are the descendants of the Crusaders and the beautiful women of Bethlehem, *then* degraded and despised, but now proud and haughty: they are excessively quarrelsome and unruly, but also very industrious, and a handsome, bold-looking, blue-eyed people – the children especially are, many of them, remarkable for their beauty, which is set off by the scarlet or crimson mash'lahs they *all* wear, neat and clean of their kind.[43]

The idea that the people of Bethlehem are a 'restless race, given to quarrelling and sedition' (as Murray's *Handbook* notes) could be traced back to Robinson's observations in his *Biblical Researches* ('a restless race, prone to tumult and rebellion'), and perhaps even earlier.[44] Like their town, Bethlehemites – 'quarrelsome and unruly', but also 'very industrious' and 'handsome' – seemed to fuse the polite 'Western' (that is, Christian) features with the well-known wicked characteristics of the East. Spatially, racially and culturally, then, Bethlehem is defined by a sense of intermediacy and relativity. 'I imagine that to ninety-nine travellers out of a hundred, Bethlehem is just one more ill-paved, unkempt, unsanitary Oriental city, noisy with the shouts of an unintelligible jargon and crowded with strangely garbed, fierce-looking "Arabs",' writes Lewis Gaston Leary in *The Real Palestine of Today* (1911): 'But after you have become somewhat acquainted with modern Palestine, that same Bethlehem appears noteworthy for its tone of prosperous self-respect; its inhabitants possess unusual dignity; the men are sturdy and handsome and the women are graceful and attractive.'[45]

Few writers failed to comment on the beauty of Bethlehem's women, attractive no doubt because their appearance adhered to Western ideals ('blue-eyed'). 'The Bethlehemites are admitted to be the most handsome of all the inhabitants of Palestine, and the women (who do not veil) recall the type of Raffaello's Madonnas more exactly than any others in the world,' explained Tristram: 'Their beauty is popularly ascribed to the fact of the Bethlehemites being the descendants of the Crusaders, who have never mingled with any of the surrounding tribes, and have thus preserved intact

---

[43] Beaufort, *Egyptian Sepulchres*, II, p. 124.
[44] Porter, *Handbook*, I, p. 208; Robinson, *Biblical Researches*, I, p. 472.
[45] Lewis Gaston Leary, *The Real Palestine of Today* (New York, 1911), pp. 39–40.

the noblest blood of Europe.'[46] The racial 'purity' of the women was often fused in these accounts with an assessment of their moral purity, which was complicated, in turn, by the Oriental setting and the traveller's own anxieties, both denominational and gendered. Carefully balancing nineteenth-century conceptions of femininity, domesticity and motherhood, Evangelical women tended to see Bethlehem and the surrounding landscape as projections of Ruth and the Virgin Mary, 'fertile' yet pure. Mary Eliza Rogers' *Domestic Life in Palestine* (1862), for example, depicts a visit to the house of a Bethlehem carver, whose wife – naturally named Miriam – has recently given birth to a baby boy. This present-day nativity scene rests on a delicate balance between the carver's 'rosaries, crucifixes, cups, and crosses, of olive-wood', associated with the New Testament, and the presence of the Palestinian women, whose appearance evokes the Old Testament: 'In such a vail as this Ruth, the young Moabitish widow, who three thousand years ago gleaned in the fertile fields of the broad valley below, may have carried away the six measures of barley.'[47]

In other accounts, the masculine, libidinous perspective exposes the frailty of this Evangelical fantasy. Kinglake's *Eothen* offers a particularly disconcerting description of the 'free innocent girls' of Bethlehem who are drawn towards the male Western traveller, exploring his appearance, first 'the wondrous formation that you call a hat', then 'your stately height, and your nut-brown hair, and the ruddy glow of your English cheeks', and finally, catching 'a glimpse of your ungloved fingers, then again will they make the air ring with their sweet screams of delight and amazement, as they compare the fairness of your hand with the hues of your sunburnt face, or with their own warmer tints'. The lengthy and intricate scene culminates when the girls, who go on to caress the naked English hand, force 'the fairest, and the sweetest of all, [who] is yet the most timid' girl among them to advance towards the Westerner 'and marry her hand to yours. The quick pulse springs from her fingers, and throbs like a whisper up your listening palm'. This strangely erotic scene constructs Bethlehem's Christian girls as both innocent and flirtatious, neglecting their Christian duties but only because they are true to a non-Muslim (that is, non-Oriental) straightforward simplicity. This duality is replicated in Kinglake's narration, in which the unusual usage of the second-person voice ('your hand'), so different from the traveller's customary first-person eye/I, is later developed into a

---

[46] Tristram, *Scenes*, p. 5.
[47] Melman, *Women's Orients*, pp. 226–7; Mary Eliza Rogers, *Domestic Life in Palestine* (London, 1862), pp. 61, 63.

full-fledged schizophrenic performance, which concludes Kinglake's account of Bethlehem:

'I regret to observe that the removal of the moral restraint imposed by the presence of the Mahometan inhabitants has led to a certain degree of boisterous, though innocent levity, in the bearing of the Christians, and more especially in the demeanour of those who belong to the young portion of the female population; but I feel assured that a more thorough knowledge of the principles of their own pure religion will speedily restore these young people to habits of propriety, even more strict than those which were imposed upon them by the authority of their Mahometan brethren.' Bah! Thus you might chant, if you choose; but loving the truth, you will not so disown sweet Bethlehem – you will not disown nor dissemble your right good hearty delight, when you find, as though in a desert, this gushing spring of fresh and joyous girlhood.[48]

Domesticated, miniaturised, internalised

The representation of Bethlehem's population follows, in other words, the same logic we have identified so far in its geographical and theological construction as a place of in-betweenness, a liminal space which resists clear-cut distinctions and allows a flow of temporal, topographical and national categories – including, as we have just seen, an internal schism within the Western psyche itself. Small, compact, easy to gaze at and take in, identified with the motherly care of Rachel, Ruth and Mary, it was easy for Bethlehem to become domesticated, domesticised, carried off, as it were, back to Britain in various shapes and forms. To be sure, the imperative significance of Jerusalem meant that miniaturised versions of the Holy City were also imagined and distributed throughout the nineteenth century, from postcards and Sunday-school prize-books to travelling models and panoramas, culminating with the Jerusalem bazaar constructed in the itinerant 'Palestine Exhibition' of the 1890s.[49] Nevertheless, Bethlehem seems to have been the only other Holy Land locale – city, town, or village – similarly domesticated, compressed, and conveyed back home.

---

[48] Kinglake, *Eothen*, pp. 238–9.
[49] Eitan Bar-Yosef, 'Jerusalem, My Happy Home: The Palestine Exhibition and the Limits of the Orientalist Imagination', in Jim Buzard, Joseph Childers and Eileen Gillooly, eds., *Victorian Prism: Refractions of the Crystal Palace* (Charlottesville, VI, 2007), pp. 186–202. On the domestication of the Holy Land, especially in the US, see also Burke Long, *Imagining the Holy Land: Maps, Models, and Fantasy Travels* (Bloomington, IN, 2003); Annabel Jane Wharton, *Selling Jerusalem: Relics, Replicas, Theme Parks* (Chicago, 2006).

But how was this done? We can begin, perhaps, by noting that, long before the nineteenth century, sacred sites from the Holy Land were reproduced in Europe. The best-known English example was the tradition associated with Walsingham, Norfolk. In 1061, Lady Richeldis de Faverches was taken, in a vision, to Nazareth; on her return, she instructed carpenters to build an exact replica of Mary's house, which came to be known as England's Nazareth. Visitors to the site were called palmers, just like the pilgrims to the Holy Land.[50]

Bethlehem's holy sites were not carried to medieval England in a similar fashion, but among the numerous spoils, customs and institutions brought by the Crusaders from Palestine was the order of Bethlehem: the small priory founded in London in 1247 to cater for the exiled bishop of Bethlehem and members of the order during their visits to England eventually became the Hospital of St Mary of Bethlehem, used, from the early sixteenth century onwards, as an asylum for the mentally ill. The founders of the priory, Nicholas Vincent has written, 'would no doubt have been surprised to learn of the subsequent fate of their institution, intended in origin not as a mad-house but as a link between England and the Holy Land, part of a wider movement in which the cathedral church of the Nativity at Bethlehem and its bishops sought land, alms and hospitality in western Europe'.[51] The Bethlehem Hospital was soon known as 'Bedlam' – the *OED* dates the earliest reference to 1528 – but the small town in Judaea was also known for centuries as Bedlam, at least until 1601.[52] During the sixteenth century, then, the name 'Bedlam' could be used, interchangeably, to refer to two, radically different, spheres and realities. There is no evidence that Victorian travellers to Palestine recalled Bedlam when they visited Bethlehem. Nevertheless, the historical, cultural and etymological processes that positioned 'Bethlehem' at the heart of early-modern London testify to the complex affinity between East and West, 'here' and 'elsewhere'.

This affinity is also visible, in miniature, in the nineteenth century. While numerous images of the town – textual, visual, popular, academic – were disseminated in Victorian Christian and Orientalist culture, it is telling that Bethlehem was particularly well known for its souvenir industry.[53] As

---

[50] Elizabeth Ruth Obbard, *The History and Spirituality of Walsingham* (Norwich, 1995).

[51] Nicholas Vincent, 'Goffredo de Prefetti and the Church of Bethlehem in England', *Journal of Ecclesiastical History*, 49 (1998), 213.

[52] 'bedlam, *n.*', *OED Online*. November 2010. Oxford University Press, www.oed.com/view/Entry/16879?redirectedFrom=bedlam, accessed 30 November 2010. See also Catharine Arnold, *Bedlam: London and Its Mad* (2008; London, 2009), esp. pp. 9–11.

[53] Giries Nicola Elali, *Bethlehem, The Immortal Town*, trans. Issa Massou (Jerusalem, 1991), pp. 146–8.

Edward Robinson noted, the people of Bethlehem, 'besides their agriculture, employ themselves in carving beads, crucifixes, models of the Holy Sepulchre, and other similar articles, in olive wood, the fruit of the Dôm palm, mother of pearl, and the like, in the same manner as the Christians of Jerusalem. Indeed the neatest and most skilfully wrought specimens of all these little articles, come from Bethlehem'.[54] One visitor to the town reported in 1897 that 'there are said to be ninety different establishments manufacturing souvenirs'.[55] The mother-of-pearl workers, both men and women, became well-known figures, often depicted in illustrations of travel to Bethlehem (Fig. 7.4).

This was no novelty – Bethlehemites had been carving mementoes for pilgrims from as early as the fourteenth century – but with the rise of travel and tourism in the nineteenth century, the industry developed considerably, fusing piety, commerce and commodification on an increasing scale. Elaborate models of the Church of the Nativity and the Church of the Holy Sepulchre were still considered the most expensive and prestigious products of the souvenir trade; artisans were compelled to reconcile the demands of mass production and the desire for self-expression.[56] 'The carver showed us, with especial pride, some large flat shells, on which he had sculptured pictures of sacred subjects and holy places', recalled Mary Eliza Rogers: 'During the past Easter he had reaped a goodly harvest, for the pilgrims eagerly buy these objects, and, when they are blessed by the priests, preserve them as relics'. Carried back home, these tiny tokens of remembrance allowed travellers to take an authentic piece of Bethlehem with them. Nevertheless, the claim for authentication is given an interesting twist by Rogers, who notes that it was her brother, Edward Thomas Rogers, the British Vice Consul to Haifa, who had initiated the carver's career in the first place: 'He had once been in my brother's service, and during that time showed decided taste for carving, which my brother encouraged by giving him a little instruction in the art, and some English tools'. And not only tools: the carver proudly informs them that English travellers 'had bought a great number of paper knives, bracelets, and brooches, made at my brother's suggestion – the original sketches for which the carver had preserved with loving care, and with new expressions of gratitude he showed them to me, saying, "Peace be on his hands"'.[57]

---

[54] Robinson, *Biblical Researches*, I, p. 472.
[55] Shailer Mathews, 'Bethlehem: City of Children', *The Biblical World*, 10 (1897), 474.
[56] Rehav Rubin, 'Relief Maps and Models in the Archives of the Palestine Exploration Fund in London', *Palestine Exploration Quarterly*, 138 (2006), 43–4.
[57] Rogers, *Domestic Life*, p. 61.

MOTHER-OF-PEARL WORKERS OF BETHLEHEM,
Making beads for rosaries.

Figure 7.4 *Mother-of-pearl Workers of Bethlehem*

Made by a Palestinian carver, yet shaped by an Englishman to cater for the English taste, the souvenir becomes an emblem of Bethlehem's geographical and cultural fusion.

While Bethlehem's souvenirs offered a tiny, symbolic slice of Palestine, ideal for exhibiting in the domestic British space, the story of the Montefiore mausoleum in Ramsgate suggests how Bethlehem could be replicated and re-imagined in Britain on a much grander magnitude. In 1827, the renowned

Anglo-Jewish philanthropic entrepreneur, Sir Moses Montefiore (1784–1885), made his first pilgrimage to Palestine with his beloved wife, Lady Judith. The couple was childless, and Judith Montefiore was deeply moved by her visit to the Tomb of Rachel: the biblical account of the barren Rachel who finally gave birth made the tomb a favourite site of religious pilgrimage for infertile Jewish women and an iconic image of motherhood and domesticity. In 1841, Montefiore secured the Ottoman authorities' consent to renovate the tomb, repair the familiar cupola and complete an adjacent vestibule, which became a place of prayer for Muslims.[58] Following Judith's death in 1862, Montefiore contemplated burying her in Jerusalem; instead, he decided to erect an exact replica of the Tomb of Rachel over his wife's grave in their Ramsgate estate.[59]

A Victorian Anglo-Jewish version of England's Nazareth, the mausoleum was in many ways a reflection of Montefiore's complex status in nineteenth-century British culture – a pivotal, yet in some ways peripheral figure. Replicating a site which stood at the outskirts of (the already marginal) Bethlehem, revered by a marginal group within British society, situated in a seaside town remote from the metropolis, and celebrating the memory of a barren woman who was nevertheless seen as a great matriarch of the Anglo-Jewish community, 'Ramsgate's Bethlehem' redefined and reworked the fluidity identified in this chapter.

The final and most enduring example of Bethlehem's domestication is the popular revival of the nativity play, with children at schools, churches and chapels throughout the Anglo-American world dressing up as the shepherds of Bethlehem or as Kings of the East. To be sure, this is how vernacular medieval drama had functioned for centuries, on the Continent and in Britain alike. Opening with the shepherds' complaints about the bleak weather, the heavy taxes and the gentry's treatment, *The Wakefield Second Shepherds' Play*, for example, reallocates Bethlehem at the time of Christ's birth to the fifteenth-century Yorkshire moors. Mystery plays reached the height of their popularity following the decline of the Crusades and the closing up of Palestine to the West; the modern Protestant revival of the genre, in comparison, took place just as the Western presence in the Holy Land was ever-increasing.

---

[58] Frederick M. Strickert, *Rachel Weeping: Jews, Christians, and Muslims at the Fortress Tomb* (Minnesota, 2007), pp. 111–17; Abigail Green, *Moses Montefiore: Jewish Liberator, Imperial Hero* (Cambridge, MA, 2010), pp. 78–80. See also Susan Starr Sered, 'Rachel's Tomb and the Milk Grotto of the Virgin Mary: Two Women's Shrines in Bethlehem', *Journal of Feminist Studies in Religion*, 2 (1986), 7–22.

[59] Green, *Imperial Hero*, pp. 1, 298, 359–60.

Theological and dramaturgical conventions slowed this process down. The Theatres Act of 1843 was only a limited liberalisation of the conventions that prohibited dramas adapted from Scripture. It upheld, for instance, the outright ban on the depiction of Christ on stage. The original mystery and morality plays were allowed, but playwrights who wished to perform new work were forced to find creative solutions: Lawrence Housman established a private theatre society to stage *Bethlehem: A Nativity Play* (1902) after it was denied a licence by the Examiner of plays.[60] The legislation did not apply to school productions, of course, but the suspicion towards religious drama meant that it was only after the First World War that nativity plays became a truly popular phenomenon: changes in the cultural climate, experience with pageantry in marking the 1916 tercentenary of Shakespeare's death, and a growing interest in the use of drama in education led to the appearance of the Christmas pageant in schools and churches, in both Britain and North America.[61] With Palestine under British control since 1917, the actual Bethlehem was more accessible than ever before; souvenirs from Bethlehem were displayed at the Palestine Pavilion during the British Empire Exhibition of 1924, and relays from the Church of the Nativity were broadcast in Christmas Day programmes on the BBC from the 1930s onwards.[62] Just at the same time, however, children all over Britain were busy imagining a rustic Bethlehem, where angels and shepherds meet, in the familiar setting of their churches or schools.

This annual re-enactment of the birth of Christ fused several elements together: the vernacular medieval play, and perhaps also the Mummers' play which survived in some rural communities; the Orientalist cliché of the never-changing East, where present-day Bedouin shepherds still wear the garb of biblical peasants; the Victorian invention of a Christmas which stood at the heart of Protestant biblical culture; but also – and most relevant for this chapter – the domestic role assigned to Bethlehem as a bridge between East and West. With the church or school masquerading as Judaea, and tea-towels serving to protect the little English shepherds from the scorching Middle Eastern sun, the nativity play continued and continues still to imagine Bethlehem in transitory, ambiguous, domesticated terms.

---

[60] Stevens, *Historical Jesus*, pp. 217–18.
[61] J. A. R. Pimlott, *The Englishman's Christmas: A Social History* (Hassocks, 1978), p. 151; Katharine Lambert Richards, *How Christmas Came to the Sunday-Schools: The Observance of Christmas in the Protestant Church Schools of the U.S., an Historical Study* (New York, 1935), pp. 192–3. I am grateful to Gerry Bowler for alerting me to Richards' study.
[62] *British Empire Exhibition 1924 – Official Guide* (London, 1924), pp. 87–8; John M. MacKenzie, '"In touch with the infinite": The BBC and the Empire, 1923–53', in John M. MacKenzie, ed., *Imperialism and Popular Culture* (Manchester, 1986), p. 181.

This image of Bethlehem at home, as home, is beautifully encapsulated in Thackeray's final verdict of his visit:

> The picturesque crowds, and the Arabs and the horsemen, in the sunshine; the noble old convent, and the grey bearded priests, with their feast; and the church, and its pictures, and columns, and incense; the wide brown hills spreading round the village; with the accidents of the road, – flocks and shepherds, wells, and funerals, and camel-trains, – have left on my mind a brilliant, romantic, and cheerful picture. But you, Dear M –, without visiting the place, have imagined one far finer; and Bethlehem, where the Holy Child was born, and the angels sang, 'Glory to God in the highest, and peace and good-will on earth', is the most sacred and beautiful spot in the earth to you.[63]

---

[63] Thackeray, *Notes*, p. 223.

8 | Ephesus

MICHAEL LEDGER-LOMAS

'In the present day of strange combinations and extraordinary associations,' mused the *Eclectic Review* in 1865, 'few things surpass the announcement of a RAILWAY FROM SMYRNA TO EPHESUS.'[1] Ephesus had never really been a lost city. Since the later seventeenth century, a number of Europeans had reached its impressive remains near the village of Ayasalouk, a few hours' ride from Smyrna. They had stood in the Great Theatre and recalled the riot that had taken place there against St Paul, searched for Christian antiquities and speculated on the location of the Temple of Artemis. Yet the coming of the Smyrna to Aidin railway, with a stop at Ayasalouk, triggered a new phase in the exploration of the city, making it easier to visit than ever before and challenging explorers and archaeologists to match their discoveries with the accounts of the city provided by classical and biblical writers. Built by an influx of British capital after the Crimean Wars, the railway enabled pilgrims to shuttle to Ephesus and back within a day. It was an architect formerly employed by the railway, John Turtle Wood (1821–90), who conducted the first major excavations at the city (1863–74) and located the temple. Wood ran out of initiative and then funds, but Ephesus later became among the most thoroughly explored of ancient cities. David Hogarth (1862–1927) completed the excavation of Wood's temple plot on behalf of the British Museum, unearthing thousands of artefacts that are now in the archaeological museum at Istanbul.[2] The Austrians had acquired a large plot nearby in 1895, beginning a comprehensive excavation and reconstruction that continues up to the present.[3]

The discovery of Ephesus fits into a historiography that has emphasised classical archaeology's transition from a hunt for treasure to big digs superintended by professionals now intent on mapping cities.[4] Yet histories of

---

[1] 'Recent Books of Travel', *Eclectic Review*, 8 (1865), 239.
[2] David Hogarth, *Excavations at Ephesus: The Archaic Artemisia* (London, 1908).
[3] For an overview, see Traute Wohle-Scharf, *Die Forschungsgeschichte von Ephesos: Entdeckungen, Grabungen und Persönlichkeiten* (Frankfurt, 1995).
[4] See, e.g., Richard Stoneman, *The Land of Lost Gods: The Search for Classical Greece* (London, 1987); Eve Gran-Aymeric, *La Naissance de l'archéologie moderne, 1798–1945* (Paris, 1998), chapters 3–6; Stephen Dyson, *In Pursuit of Ancient Pasts: A History of Classical Archaeology in the*

classical archaeology largely ignore the manifold connections at sites such as Ephesus between archaeology and the study of the New Testament.[5] Conversely, the history of biblical archaeology is centred on the Holy Land and on the identification of Old Testament sites in Egypt and elsewhere.[6] Yet the Acts of the Apostles, Paul's Epistles and the Apocalypse had always transported pious readers to cities across Europe, Asia Minor and the Near East; from Tarsus and Antioch to Athens and Corinth, Lystra and Smyrna, Ephesus and Rome. Like Egyptologists or archaeologists in the Holy Land, discoverers or excavators of such cities turned up *realia* that illustrated and seemingly vindicated biblical books, even though they often had varied motives: to resurrect Hellas, to fill museums or to burnish national pride.[7] It is a truism of the scholarship that a symbiosis between literary texts, artefacts and inscriptions governed the practice of classical archaeology, with the desire to corroborate classical literature influencing which cities were unearthed and how their remains were explained.[8] Yet the revolution in biblical criticism during the eighteenth and nineteenth centuries meant that the archaeologists were also profoundly involved with the New Testament, which was increasingly regarded as a series of discrete texts to be explicated and corroborated by material evidence.[9] This chapter shows how the exploration of Ephesus and its reception was shaped by the Protestant public's anxiety to prove the truth of the New Testament. In reconstructing the urban and multi-racial crucible of apostolic Christianity, discoverers of Ephesus also promised to furnish theologians and ministers in the late-Victorian period with guidance about how to adapt the gospel to an increasingly urban and global world.

It is of course misleading to posit just one relationship between Ephesus and the New Testament, for the city was mentioned in many of its books, each of which was read differently by Protestants who were themselves divided in their theological and sectarian commitments. The questions that they hoped explorers or archaeologists might answer for them thus depended on which biblical verses were under review. For many writers,

---

Nineteenth and Twentieth Centuries (London, 2006), chapters 2–5; Suzanne Marchand, *Down from Olympus: Archaeology and Philhellenism in Germany, 1750–1970* (London, 1996).

[5] For exceptions, see Stephen L. Dyson, *Ancient Marbles to American Shores* (Pennsylvania, 1998), pp. 85–7 on Corinth and Debbie Challis, *From the Harpy Tomb to the Wonders of Ephesus: British Archaeologists in the Ottoman Empire, 1840–1880* (London, 2008), chapter 6 on Ephesus.

[6] See Thomas W. Davis, *Shifting Sands: The Rise and Fall of Biblical Archaeology* (Oxford, 2004), which does not mention Ephesus or other New Testament sites such as Antioch or Corinth.

[7] Ibid., p. viii and chapters 1–3.

[8] Bruce Trigger, *A History of Archaeological Thought*, 2nd edn (Cambridge, 1996), pp. 61–7.

[9] Jonathan Sheehan, *The Enlightenment Bible: Translation, Scholarship, Culture* (Princeton, NJ, 2005); Michael Legaspi, *The Death of Scripture and the Rise of Biblical Studies* (Oxford, 2011).

the 'chief religious interest' of Ephesus was as one of the 'seven churches which are in Asia' that had received John's epistles in the Apocalypse.[10] Ephesus was admonished by Christ for falling away from its first love and threatened with having its candlestick moved out of place if it did not repent (2:1–7). For others, Ephesus was more redolent of Paul. The Acts of the Apostles described a first visit by Paul to the city and then a longer visit of three years, during which time his preaching provoked a riot in the Great Theatre. It was orchestrated by the silversmith Demetrius, whose trade in making shrines to Artemis was threatened by Paul (Acts 19). After leaving Ephesus, Paul later returned as far as Miletus to bid farewell to the Elders of Ephesus, before making sail for Jerusalem (Acts 20:17–38). The first Epistle to the Corinthians gave an unhappy glimpse of Paul's experiences at Ephesus, mentioning his fight with 'beasts' there (15:32), while the Epistle to the Ephesians provided yet another perspective on Paul's relationship with the city, although biblical critics could not agree whether Paul had even written it or addressed it to Ephesus. Ephesus had also supposedly harboured other New Testament writers and figures, such as Paul's allies Prisca, Aquila and Timothy. The author of John's Gospel – whose identity with the apostle and with the author of Apocalypse came to be controversial – was supposed to have lived in Ephesus and Mary was said by tradition to have died there.

This chapter nonetheless shows that the relationship between the ruins of Ephesus and the New Testament fell into phases. The Apocalypse dominated early nineteenth-century interest in Ephesus, not least because the still indecipherable ruins confirmed to an evangelical British public the truth of their punitive theology. 'No ruins,' pronounced the *Wesleyan-Methodist Magazine*, 'yield a clearer testimony than these to the truth of the handwriting on the wall that predicted their doom.'[11] The careful mapping of Ephesus that began with Edward Falkener (1777–1864) and ended with Wood shifted the public's attention from the destruction of Ephesus to the restoration of its vanished life. Their work struck a chord with apologists for the New Testament, who were seeking to counteract the challenge to Acts posed by the higher critics of Tübingen, then popularised in such works as W. R. Cassels' *Supernatural Religion* (1874). For leading apologists such as Joseph Barber Lightfoot (1828–89) and William Ramsay (1851–1939), the more archaeological evidence about the apostolic cities they could gather,

---

[10] John Saul Howson, 'The Seven Churches of Asia', *Contemporary Review*, 10 (1869), 317.
[11] 'The Seven Churches in Asia', *Wesleyan-Methodist Magazine*, 8 (1862), 320. Note the echo of Daniel 5:1–31.

the more Acts became a credible historical narrative of events within those cities. The inscriptions in which Ephesus was rich offered a particularly powerful way of protecting Scripture from the sharp scalpels of the German critics. Yet archaeological reconstruction arguably came to matter less as a tool of polemical verification and more in helping to understand the crucible in which apostolical Christianity was forged. This had consequences for the present. The bad cosmopolitanism of later nineteenth-century cities could foster anti-urban sentiments, as Protestant, Ruskinian dreams of building provincial Jerusalems turned into nightmares about Babylonian and imperial London.[12] Ephesus suggested more cheering parallels. If it was akin to the 'great cities' of the present in the wealth and heterogeneity of its large population, then Paul's success in preaching the gospel there was all the more educative. Ephesus had become a beacon of Christianity because it was a commercial centre on the highway from Asia to Europe and integrated into the Roman Empire's networks of power. If Christians feared that the globalisation of commerce and the expansion of imperial power was crowding people into cities and threatened their faith, then archaeology suggested that Christianity had survived and could thrive in such conditions.

The 'city of change': Ephesus and the Apocalypse

Nineteenth-century visitors to the sites of the seven churches of Asia – Ephesus, Smyrna, Pergamum, Thyatira, Sardis, Laodicea and Philadelphia – followed a beaten track. The nonjuring clergyman Thomas Smith (1638–1710) had toured the sites and published a widely noticed English account as early as 1678. He was then followed by a number of others, such as Richard Pococke (1704–65) and Richard Chandler (1737–1810) of the Dilettanti.[13] The Navy's dominance of the Mediterranean in the period following the defeat of Napoleon, the development of Smyrna as an entrepôt for European traders and the weakening hold of the Ottoman Empire opened up the sites of the seven churches to a new wave of travellers.[14] From 1836, they could follow the Navy's chart of the region in doing so. Visiting Ephesus became in time a tourist jaunt, a mere two and a

---

[12] Tristram Hunt, *Building Jerusalem: The Rise and Fall of the Victorian City* (London, 2004), chapter 6.
[13] W. H. C. Frend, *The Archaeology of Early Christianity: A History* (London, 1996), chapter 3.
[14] Holger Hoock, 'The British State and the Anglo-French Wars over Antiquities, 1798–1858', *Historical Journal*, 50 (2007), 49–72.

half hour ride from Smyrna. The photographer Alexander Svoboda advised travellers that they could see all seven churches in twenty-four days, fuelled on brandy, preserves and boiled hams.[15] Many early nineteenth-century travellers were clergymen who packed the Greek Testament alongside their Pliny and Pausanias, but the ground was also covered by such avowedly scientific travellers as William Martin Leake (1777–1860), William John Hamilton (1805–67) of the Geographical Society, Charles Fellows (1799–1860) and the Frenchmen Léon de Laborde (1807–69) and Charles Texier (1802–71).[16] Primarily intent on producing an accurate topography of Asia Minor through comparison between classical writers and the landscape, rather than on recovering Christian antiquities, they were often critical of the roving clerics who had preceded them. Nonetheless, their works also provided fodder for sermon writers and biblical commentators. Recycled in biblical commentaries and homiletic works, often citing each other and their predecessors, most early travellers hit a note of edifying gloom on confronting Ephesus. 'The traveller cannot hear the jackal's cry in the loneliness of Ephesus', keened Charles Macfarlane (1799–1858) in a lament that can stand for many, 'without asking where are the thousands and thousands that thronged its streets and issued from its gates.'[17]

Macfarlane's ears pricked up at the jackal's cry because the Apocalypse had conditioned his reaction to Ephesus: he traced in 'the dread prediction of eighteen centuries ago, the very picture of the present desolation'. Many early nineteenth-century Protestants, especially evangelicals, believed that the Apocalypse resembled the Old Testament in making definite predictions about the doom of cities, whose fulfilment could be tested in detail.[18] Fulfilled prophecy had become central to Anglican apologetics in Georgian England because it offered a plain test of the Bible's truth and inspiration. Rather than being an epitome of the seven ages of the church, a universal history or a mystical treatise on Christian virtues, the letters to the seven churches were read as frank messages to particular churches, whose 'promissory and threatening part' had evidently been realised.[19] For the Rev.

---

[15] Alexander Svoboda, *The Seven Churches of Asia* (London, 1869), p. 61.
[16] See, e.g., Stoneman, *Lost Gods*, pp. 155–62; J. M. Wagstaff, 'Colonel Leake: Traveller and Scholar', in Sarah Searight and Malcolm Wagstaff, eds., *Travellers in the Levant: Voyagers and Visionaries* (Durham, 2001), pp. 3–16.
[17] Charles Macfarlane, *The Seven Apocalyptic Churches* (London, 1832), p. 3.
[18] See Harry Cocks, 'The Discovery of Sodom, 1851', *Representations*, 112 (2010), 3, 7 on the persistent search for material evidence of God's wrath.
[19] Thomas Newton, *Dissertations on the Prophecies, Which Have Remarkably Been Fulfilled and at This Time are Fulfilling in the World* (1758; London, 1832), pp. 450–2; Neil Hitchin, 'The Evidence of Things Seen: Georgian Churchmen and Biblical Prophecy', in Bertrand Taithe and

Thomas Milner (d. 1882), there could be no 'more striking illustration of the *sure* word of prophecy', than the history of the Asian churches – 'once, brilliant with light, but now, in consequence of a predicted apostasy, the subjects of predicted ruin and desolation'.[20] Although the letters of the Apocalypse had been addressed to the heads of the churches, Milner and the Scottish Presbyterian Alexander Keith (1792–1880) – a shameless plagiarist of his Georgian predecessors – fudged the spiritual doom of these churches with the material destruction of their host cities. Ruined by Goths and pillaged by Byzantine Emperors and Seljuk Turks, razed by Tamerlane and then disappearing beneath the marshes of the River Cayster, Ephesus fulfilled the prediction that its 'candlestick' would be moved from its place if it did not 'repent' for forgetting its 'first love'. Contemplating the malarial marshes of the Cayster, the clerical naturalist Henry Baker Tristram (1822–1906) – an expert on biblical fauna, already encountered visiting the Dead Sea in Astrid Swenson's chapter and Bethlehem in Eitan Bar-Yosef's – reached not just for the Apocalypse but for Isaiah's condemnation of Babylon: 'I will also make it a possession for the bittern, and pools of water: and I will sweep it with the besom of destruction, saith the LORD of hosts.'[21]

The prophecy's fulfilment did not require the disappearance of human life, but only the extinction of Christianity. This was happening under the eyes of British travellers. While Chandler had found a reasonable number of Greek Christians in the neighbouring hamlet of Ayasalouk, by the time the Rev. Francis Arundell (1780–1846) reached Ephesus only one was left, with the tents of Turcoman nomads the only other sign of human life. At Sardis, Arundell similarly found only two Christians – living counterparts to the tottering pillars of the city's famous Temple of Cybele.[22] As Edward Gibbon (1737–94) had noted, Smyrna and Philadelphia's prosperity and their robust Christian communities contrasted with these scenes of desolation. If anything, that contrast further illustrated the truth of prophecy, given the milder tone of John's messages to the churches of Smyrna and Philadelphia. If some travellers felt that misrule by the Ottomans rather than direct intervention by God had destroyed the prosperity of Asia Minor, then the Ottomans could nonetheless be

---

Tim Thornton, eds., *Prophecy: The Power of Inspired Language in History, 1300–2000* (Stroud, 1997), pp. 119–42.

[20] Thomas Milner, *History of the Seven Churches of Asia … Designed to Show the Fulfilment of Scripture Prophecy* (London, 1832); Macfarlane, *Churches*, p. 7.

[21] Henry Baker Tristram, *The Seven Golden Candlesticks* (London, 1869), p. 25.

[22] Francis Arundell, *A Visit to the Seven Churches of Asia* (London, 1828), pp. 26, 56, 179.

Figure 8.1 Thomas Allom, *Ephesus*

presented as agents of the prophecy's fulfilment, especially given their habit of plundering ruins for building materials.[23]

Early visual representations of Ephesus reinforced the message of rolling dilapidation. In the popular engravings after the sketches by Thomas Allom (1804–72) (Fig. 8.1), scattered ruins merge with the 'dismal swamp' and 'extensive jungle of low bushes' described in the accompanying letterpress by the Rev. Robert Walsh (1772–1852), with nomads the only sign of life.[24] Rather than offering a more objective record of Ephesus, photography actually strengthened the prophetic mode. Keith had welcomed the daguerreotype as a 'mode of demonstration that could neither be questioned nor surpassed', for the very 'rays of the sun would depict what the prophets saw', bringing a 'still deeper conviction of the defined precision of the *sure word of prophecy*'.[25] While the panorama in Alexander Svoboda's photographic guide to the seven cities lacks the picturesque flourishes of Allom's

[23] Charles Texier, *Description de L'Asie Mineure* (3 vols., Paris, 1839–49), I, p. iii.
[24] Thomas Allom, *Constantinople and the Scenery of the Seven Churches of Asia Minor* (London, 1838), pp. 63–4.
[25] See Eitan Bar-Yosef, *The Holy Land in English Culture 1799–1917: Palestine and the Question of Orientalism* (Oxford, 2005) and Claire Lyons, 'The Art and Science of Antiquity in Nineteenth-Century Photography', in Clare Lyons, John Papadopolous, Lindsey Stewart and Andrew

Figure 8.2 *Ephesus*, photographic plate

image, the cluttering of the visual field with a chaotic jumble of stones heightens the impression of total destruction (Fig. 8.2).[26]

The fate of Ephesus not only demonstrated Scripture's predictive accuracy, but was quoted by preachers to steel congregations against becoming 'formal religionists' whose zeal dissolved into urban frivolity. Evangelicals read the letter to Ephesus as a 'warning voice' against apostasy, one that touched a masochistic streak in believers whose stern god was 'no respecter of persons' (Acts 10:34).[27] In 1850, the Scottish Presbyterian John Cumming (1807–81) reminded his London congregation that Christ's warning was 'God's prescription for human kind'. Once the Christians of Ephesus abandoned love, 'her ships [had] left her harbours,

Szegedy-Haszak, *Antiquity and Photography: Early Views of Ancient Mediterranean Sites* (London, 2005) for photography's impact on the biblical and classical imagination.

[26] Svoboda, *Seven Churches*.

[27] Alexander Keith, *Evidence of the Truth of the Christian Religion, Derived from the Literal Fulfilment of Prophecy* (1826; London, 1859), pp. 254–5, 519; Henry Blunt, *A Practical Exposition of the Epistles to the Seven Churches of Asia* (London, 1838), pp. 55–7; Augustus William West, *The Spiritual Condition of the Seven Churches of Asia Minor* (London, 1846).

her soldiers deserted her standard, her ancient and illustrious buildings stumbled into ruins'. The English were similarly doomed if they abandoned their first love and the secret of their greatness, the gospel. Cumming's definition of apostasy would have struck many Protestants as ludicrously narrow, including as it did reading chemistry or palaeontology instead of missionary reports, keeping a playhouse box, rubbing shoulders with Unitarians or gadding about in Paris.[28] Yet long into the nineteenth century, preachers of various stripes offered up the judgment on Ephesus as a glass of seltzer water to city dwellers who had over-indulged in the 'fascinations and attractions of social life'.[29]

The materialising interpretation of ruins encountered increasing criticism. Critics had always questioned whether it was right to equate the spiritual downfall of the churches with the material destruction of cities. The more travellers learnt about the Mediterranean and Near East, the clearer it was that ruined cities were not cooling lava left by God's volcanic anger, but evidence of a secular pattern of sedimentary composition and decay. City after city had been founded near and using stones from ruined predecessors and in turn they supplied materials for new cities. For liberal Anglicans such as the scriptural geographer and ecclesiastical historian Arthur Penrhyn Stanley (1815–81), this realisation strengthened their conviction that prophecy did not entail snatched glimpses of the future distribution of 'stocks and stones', but rather insight into the eternal laws of 'souls and sins' that conditioned the rise and fall of civilisations.[30] Stanley's admirer and biographer E. H. Plumptre (1821–91) applied this approach to the Apocalypse, noting how difficult it was to square the vicissitudes of Ephesus in the post-apostolic centuries with the belief that Christ had menaced it with imminent destruction. If the 'present desolate condition of the town of *Agio-soluk*' demonstrated anything, it was the 'working of the law' that no community thrived without charity.[31] By the later nineteenth century, many commentators handled the letters as descriptions of the seven churches in John's day rather than as predictions of what the future had in store for their host cities. Once the 'special dangers' of unhistorical readings were eliminated, Protestant readers could treat these portraits

---

[28] John Cumming, *Apocalyptic Sketches* (1848; London, 1850), p. 153.
[29] James Culross, *'Thy First Love': Christ's Message to Ephesus* (London, 1878); Andrew Tait, *The Message to the Seven Churches* (London, 1884), pp. 149–50.
[30] Arthur Penrhyn Stanley, *Sinai and Palestine in Connexion with their History* (London, 1856), preface.
[31] Edward Hayes Plumptre, *Popular Exposition of the Epistles to the Seven Churches of Asia* (London, 1877), p. 172.

as typological 'mirrors' for their own spiritual life.[32] In 1892, the Congregational minister Alexander Mackennal (1835–1904) noted that although 'the geographer and the explorer, have ... [created] mental images of Ephesus and Thyatira, for instance, as vivid as of Edinburgh and Macclesfield', his interest lay in finding 'types of humanity in the story of bygone life'. As a Congregational dissenter instinctively averse to the idea that the Christian church could be bounded by or tied to place, he was less interested in the cities than in the small congregations they harboured and in their struggle to master a culture whose 'ethical conditioning' resembled his own *fin de siècle*. For Mackennal, Ephesus was the 'strenuous church', whose contempt for immorality bore the 'charm of manliness', but degenerated when not informed by love. For this cultivated minister to a smart suburban congregation just outside Manchester, Congregationalists should heed this lesson, because their nonconformity left them prone to the 'Puritan temper'.[33]

Yet the ruins of Ephesus still spoke of the Apocalypse. The archaeologist and topographer William Ramsay (1851–1939) could still present John as a prophetic commentator on the city's fate in his *Letters to the Seven Churches* (1904). John did not forecast the city's imminent destruction, but he was a hawk-eyed analyst of its failings. He understood that the fickle Ephesians would not retain their civic grandeur or episcopal status for long. Wood, Hogarth and the Austrians' excavations had revealed the truth of this 'milder denunciation', showing that the city's skittish inhabitants had repeatedly shifted its position in pre-Christian times, from plain to hilltop and back again, before the silting up of the Cayster rendered it uninhabitable. Like all Asiatic cities – but unlike Ramsay's hometown of Glasgow, whose burghers regularly dredged its harbour to keep it navigable – it was a passive victim of its natural environment.[34] Biblical scholars demurred from Ramsay's portrayal of John as a Hellenised thinker whose mind had been shaped by life in Greek cities, sensing that it derived less from close criticism of texts than from Ramsay's intuitive bond with sites that he had personally explored.[35] It was, after all, when sitting on the heights above Ephesus and

---

[32] John Hutchinson, *Messages of our Lord to the Seven Churches of Asia* (London, 1882), p. 13.

[33] Alexander Mackennal, *The Seven Churches in Asia Considered as Types of the Religious Life of Today* (London, 1895), p. x; Dugald Macfadyen, *Alexander Mackennal, BA, DD: Life and Letters* (London, 1905).

[34] William Ramsay, *The Letters to the Seven Churches of Asia and their Place in the Plan of the Apocalypse* (London, 1904), p. 245.

[35] 'Ramsay's *Letters*', *The Interpreter*, 1 (1905), 451–5. Ramsay's argument for Greek modes of thought in John was firmly opposed by Henry Barclay Swete, *The Apocalypse of St John: The Greek Text with Introduction, Notes and Indices* (London, 1906).

listening to the reeds whisper in the silted-up harbour that he had first seen the truth of John's indictment: Ephesus was the 'city of change'.[36]

A 'running commentary': Ephesus and Paul

The initial emphasis on the obliteration of Ephesus reflected not only theological priorities but the limitations of early travellers. Moving rapidly over the ground, intent on surveying monuments or inscriptions and lacking manpower or money for major excavations, they had not delved far below the surface of apostolic sites in Asia Minor. The problem was acute in the malarial marshes around Ayasalouk, which discouraged a long stay. Even diligent travellers such as Charles Texier quailed at deciphering the remains.[37] Fanciful travellers certainly claimed to have found material traces of apostolic or sub-apostolic church building in Ephesus and elsewhere. Yet such identifications required naive acceptance of local traditions and ignored the fact that apostolic Christians were too few and secretive to have built anything, least of all in stone.[38] Even credulous visitors had to recognise that such traditional sites as 'Paul's prison' were post-apostolic remains that could have had little to do with the apostle. The first English book to offer a comprehensive account of Ephesus, Edward Falkener's *Ephesus and the Temple of Diana* (1863), sought to explode the belief of even 'intelligent persons' that it was actually possible to *see* the seven churches.[39]

Falkener, an architect and traveller who had dug at Pompeii and who wrote prolifically on classical architecture, first visited the site during a prolonged European tour (1842–9). He swept away the few vestiges of the temple supposedly found by previous travellers. Many had claimed that the remains of the Gymnasium must be those of the temple – a speculation endorsed in 1842 by the geologist William Hamilton and then in William Smith's *Dictionary of the Bible* (1860–3).[40] It was pooh-poohed by Falkener,

---

[36] Ramsay, *Letters*, p. 245.   [37] Texier, *Asie*, pp. 269–80.
[38] Charles Fellows, *Travels and Researches in Asia Minor* (London, 1852), p. 205 faulted predecessors with 'indulg[ing] too freely their imagination whilst contemplating the few silent walls which remain'.
[39] See Edward Falkener, *Ephesus and the Temple of Diana* (London, 1862), pp. 5, 19, 95.
[40] John Saul Howson, 'Ephesus', in William Smith, ed., *Dictionary of the Bible* (1860–3; 2 vols., London, 1861), I, p. 562; William John Hamilton, *Researches in Asia Minor, Pontus, and*

who insisted in his book on the city that the temple had vanished altogether: after its destruction by the Goths and pillaging by Justinian, every last stone had disappeared beneath the marsh.[41] Yet few readers were content to think that the 'temple of ice' had melted away completely.[42] It loomed large in the Protestant imagination as the fortress of idolatry against which Paul had triumphed.[43] For gentlemen familiar with Pliny and Philostratus, there were also secular motives to resurrect the temple. It was a wonder of the world and supposedly a treasure house of Hellenistic art, a missing link between Greek sculpture and imperial Rome and thus in the developing history of art.[44] The praise lavished on Falkener's 'sumptuous volume' and its princely plates hint at these preoccupations. It was significant that Falkener sited his temple at the head of the inland port, where it would have been the most striking feature of a truly monumental city (Fig. 8.3). For the *Saturday Review*, Falkener's Ephesus surpassed Rome or Athens and would have matched modern-day New York or Cincinnati in the graceful rationality of its planning.[45] If aesthetic and biblical interests thus supplied powerful motives to search for the temple's remains, so did national pride. Falkener's reviewers recalled the acquisition of works of art for the British Museum from Nineveh, Lycia and Halicarnassus and urged that it was high time for a corresponding expedition to Ephesus.[46]

John Turtle Wood may have been an unexpected answer to these prayers, but he was nonetheless representative of the Britons roaming Asia Minor. He was introduced to Ephesus and the hunt for the temple while working as an architect for the Smyrna to Aidin railway. Wood had been so depressed by 'continuous rain' on his return to London and was so stirred by reading Falkener's recently published book that he decided to return in search of the temple.[47] In December 1869, after several seasons of digging, he hit upon the pavement of the last Temple of Artemis. His enterprise illustrates the partnership between adventurers and the state that stocked the British Museum in this period.[48] He initially contacted the

---

Armenia: With Some Account of their Antiquities and Geology (2 vols., London, 1842), II, pp. 25–6.
[41] Falkener, *Diana*, chapters 5 and 8.
[42] Texier *Asie*; James Emerson, *Letters from the Aegean* (London, 1829), p. 140.
[43] J. M. Bellew, 'The Church at Ephesus', *Art Journal*, 3 (1864), 10.
[44] 'Diana of the Ephesians', *Critic* (28 June 1862), 627.
[45] *Saturday Review* (23 August 1862), 224.
[46] *Art Journal*, 8 (1862), 17; 'Ephesus and the Temple of Diana', *Athenaeum* (6 September 1862), 312.
[47] John Turtle Wood, 'Ephesus, and the Temple of Diana', *Sunday at Home* (24 March 1877), 181.
[48] See Holger Hoock, *Empires of the Imagination: Politics, War, and the Arts in the British World, 1750–1850* (London, 2010), part II.

Figure 8.3 *Ephesus*

Museum for help in obtaining a firman from Constantinople but used early finds to lure the trustees into funding work on the site and chivvied them for additional funds thereafter.[49] Wood also enjoyed help from the Navy, which shipped crates of inscriptions and fragments of sculpture back to London. Even Robert Lowe (1811–92), a notoriously stingy chancellor, moved a vote of £6,000 towards completing the excavation in the Commons, which was granted *nem con*. By the time Wood's ally Charles Newton had inspected the site and called time on further funding in 1874, he had received about £12,000 towards finding and excavating the temple, with the total cost of all his excavations amounting to £16,000.[50] Nor did Wood's demands on officialdom stop there, for he brassily requested an appointment as architect to the Museum with the plea that he was

---

[49] John Turtle Wood papers, British Museum (hereafter W) 1 1240 Wood to John Winton Jones, 5 February 1863; W4 103457 Wood to Newton, 20 November 1863.

[50] John Turtle Wood, *Discoveries at Ephesus, Including the Site and Remains of the Great Temple of Diana* (London, 1877), p. viii.

otherwise unfit to resume his profession; he was later awarded a pension by the crown.[51]

Wood may have been good at extracting money from the state but he failed to win a lasting footing in the history of archaeology, a failure that has obscured his contribution to the study of the New Testament. His cavalier approach to recording finds has caused him to be remembered as an inept precursor to Hogarth and the Austrians. He groused about theft by workers and pillage by tourists who turned up at Ephesus armed with chisels, but did little to prevent it. Indeed, he used 'antiquities' to whet the appetites of the British Museum's trustees and to placate Ottoman contacts. He held back coins to make a necklace for Mrs Wood – his helpmate and occasional viceroy for much of the dig – and a statue for a friend.[52] Moreover, even at the time his discoveries made at best a muted sensation. Wood's *Discoveries at Ephesus: Including the Site and Remains of the Great Temple of Diana* (1877) was partly to blame. While the book convinced reviewers of his pluck, including as it did vignettes of Wood dining with a loaded revolver on his table to discourage robbers, investigating deadly feuds among his workforce and surviving a stabbing, his pedestrian prose failed to establish him as a second Layard, while its sludgy photographs of 'malarious mudholes' (Fig. 8.4) and its high price of three guineas worked against its popularity.[53] Scholarly readers delighted in undermining Wood's scholarship. His sharpest critic was Hyde Clarke (1815–95), whose knowledge of Ephesus likewise originated in employment on the railway.[54] Clarke accused Wood of passing off the northern location of the temple as his own idea when it had already been suggested in Ernst Guhl's *Ephesiaca* (1843). Although Newton shielded Wood from the charges, Clarke's sneers went home. Thus he reported the philologist and biblical critic Ernest Renan's contempt for Wood's procedures and wobbly command of Greek and Latin.[55] Clarke's animus was extreme, but other commentators, including the architectural historian James Fergusson (1806–86), who was as Simon Goldhill's chapter above demonstrates no stranger to controversy, lamented Wood's slapdash

---

[51] W213 Wood to Museum, 28 February 1874; W222 12 May 1874 2125.
[52] Wood, *Discoveries*, pp. 63–4; W122 10543 Wood to Museum, 2 September 1871; W186 2050 Wood to Museum, 1 May 1873.
[53] 'Diana of the Ephesians', *The Examiner* (16 December 1876), 1412–13.
[54] Hyde Clarke, *The Imperial Ottoman Smyrna and Aidin Railway, its Position and Prospects* (Constantinople, 1861); Hyde Clarke, *Ephesus. Being a Lecture Delivered at the Smyrna Literary and Scientific Institution* (Smyrna, 1863).
[55] *Athenaeum* (12 August 1871), 219; (7 October 1871), 469; (14 October 1871), 502; (28 October 1871), 566; (4 November 1871), 599; (11 November 1871), 630; (18 November 1871), 661; (16 March 1872), 341; (30 March 1872), 406.

Figure 8.4 *View of Excavation on the Site of the Temple, looking East, December 1871*

recording of his finds and the liberties he took with Pliny's words in his proposed reconstruction of the temple.[56]

Wood's finds were not spectacular enough to shroud him in Layard's glamour. Reviewers cooed over the *columna caetala* or sculptured drum that was his best find, recognising it as a valuable example of Hellenistic sculpture, which proved against purist admirers of classical architecture that the temple's columns must have been heavily decorated.[57] Yet one 'relic of witching beauty' could not compensate for the 'mournful wrecks of many others once as beautiful'.[58] The Museum did not display these fragmentary sculptures and inscriptions with any great enthusiasm. Bank Holiday crowds passed them by, along with George Smith's cuneiform tablets.[59] Many went into the basement, the 'Hades of the establishment'.[60] Not until 1884 were the best finds united in an 'Ephesian Gallery', a modest adjunct to the Halicarnassus gallery. There was no guide to the room and the inscriptions remained in the basement.[61] Wood's critics argued that this was insufficient compensation for his despoliation of the site, which had robbed it of romantic and biblical interest. The merciless Clarke was the first to lay

[56] Percy Gardner, 'Fine Art', *Academy* (9 December 1876), 572; [Charles Newton], 'Discoveries at Ephesus', *Edinburgh Review*, 145 (1877), 224; James Fergusson, *Temple of Diana at Ephesus: With Especial Reference to Mr. Wood's Discoveries of its Remains* (London, 1883).
[57] 'The Sculptures from Ephesus', *Saturday Review* (11 January 1873), 50.
[58] 'Diana of the Ephesians', 1412.
[59] 'The British Museum', *The Times* (30 March 1875), 6 col. b.
[60] 'Buried treasure at the British Museum', *Pall Mall Gazette* (28 January 1880).
[61] John Turtle Wood, 'The Ephesian Gallery: British Museum', *The Times* (10 September 1884), 8, col. d; A Further Inquirer, 'British Museum Catalogues', *The Times* (1 September 1885), 8 col. b.

the charge, arguing that it was rich to accuse the Ottomans of destroying monuments when the combined efforts of the railwaymen and Wood had reduced Ephesus to 'a mass of bats and fragments under the auspices of the British Museum'.[62] In 1882, when Wood was fundraising to resume digging, J. Russell Endean (b. 1826) protested in *The Times* that any additional funds should be spent on preserving the exposed monuments in co-operation with the local authorities.[63]

Yet Wood was able to mobilise patriotism and religion as arguments for the resumption of his work. His book coincided with and was reviewed alongside the spectacular finds at Hissarlik by Schliemann – a visitor to Wood's excavation – and was followed by the lavishly funded German excavation of Olympia.[64] The contrast between the penny-pinching British state and munificent Germany was a painful one. Newton condemned the sums wasted on 'trivial and ignoble objects' and asked, 'Why has England no Schliemanns?'[65] After the trustees of the Museum declined Wood's overtures to resume the dig or to apply for a treasury grant on his behalf (1878–80), a committee was formed in 1882 under the presidency of the Lord Mayor of London to raise funds for him.[66] Its committee included the Archbishop of Canterbury; Joseph Barber Lightfoot (1828–89), the Bishop of Durham; Frederic William Farrar (1831–1903), the Dean of Westminster, and Charles Newton. Sir John Lubbock (1834–1913), the politician and writer on prehistory, was its honorary treasurer. At its inaugural meeting, Newton spoke once more of the lack of Schliemanns and urged the need to match the Germans.[67] Enough money was raised to support Wood for two more stints in 1883–4, although the rationale for a return visit was weak. Having exhausted the temple site, Wood claimed that excavating the remainder of the plot purchased by the British Museum might turn up any portions of the frieze that had been projected outwards when the temple collapsed. The meagre haul that resulted from his return trip seems to have killed off the enthusiasm of his subscribers.

[62] Hyde Clarke, 'Destruction of Monuments in Turkey', *Athenaeum* (8 January 1870), 63.
[63] J. Russell Endean, 'Ephesus In September', *The Times* (11 October 1882), 4 col. f; T. Hayter Lewis and John Turtle Wood, 'Ephesus', *The Times* (18 October 1882), 4 col. g; J. Russell Endean, 'Ephesus', *The Times* (21 October, 1882), 4 col. g; John Turtle Wood, 'The Ruins Of Ephesus', *The Times* (18 April 1883), 5 col. e; Endean, *The Times* (18 April 1883), 5 col. e.
[64] Wood, *Discoveries*, p. 176; W. F. Wilkinson, 'Trojan Antiquities', *Leisure Hour* (11 July 1874), 438; Charles Newton, 'The Discoveries at Olympia', *Edinburgh Review*, 149 (1879), 243.
[65] See also J. Mahaffy, 'Modern Excavations', *Contemporary Review*, 29 (1877), 893; A. S. Murray, 'Exploration in Greece', *Nineteenth Century*, 12 (1882), 382–3.
[66] BM papers: C 13447, C 16893.4, C 17137.d.
[67] John Leighton, 'The Explorations at Ephesus', *The Times* (15 September 1884), 6, col. e. Even this artefact was thought by many to be a biblical artefact, the 'Satan's seat' of Apocalypse 2:13.

The presence of influential churchmen on Wood's committee shows that, while he was no Schliemann, he was a plausible friend to the Bible. Speaking at the committee's inaugural meeting, Lightfoot praised Wood for creating a 'running commentary' on the Acts, enabling us to understand and to trust its account of Paul's struggles 'with a stubborn heathendom'.[68] Whereas Larsen's chapter in this volume argues that Layard was cool about the religious implications of his work, Wood emphasised the value of his discoveries to the New Testament. In 1878, he attended a meeting of the Society of Biblical Archaeology to extol the relevance of his work to the study of the New Testament. He dwelt on the inscriptions he had discovered and airily claimed that on his return to Ephesus he expected to find a copy of a decree issued after the riot in the Theatre, forbidding Paul to preach Christianity. More audaciously still, he repeated a claim from the *Discoveries* that an ancient tomb marked with engravings of a bull and a cross must have been the resting place of St Luke, who had died in or near Ephesus, if a tradition passed on to him by the Greek Archbishop of Smyrna was to be believed.[69]

These claims copped withering fire from other scholars. In discussion after his paper and in papers subsequently submitted to the Society's transactions, scholars pitched into his slipshod thinking. No less a visitor to the Society than Ernest Renan scratched his head at the legerdemain involved in turning a pagan monument marked with some ambiguous symbols into an apostolic shrine. Writing to the Society from Carmarthenshire, the elderly Edward Falkener marvelled that

[Wood] not only discovers that St Luke went to Ephesus! that he died and was buried there! and that his bones were removed 300 years afterwards to another place, and a pagan-looking monument built over them! but having discovered all this, he wishes an annual service to be held over this so-happily-discovered spot!

Worse, he alleged that the contested site was already marked on his own plan of Ephesus.[70] Wood was soon embroiled in a cross correspondence in the *Academy* about his findings.[71] Yet Wood could speak over the scholars to less critical audiences, informing the young readers of the *Girl's Own Paper* that he had probably found the tomb of Luke.[72] The notes he contributed to a Sunday School textbook on Paul sounded a pious note,

---

[68] *The Times* (13 June 1885), 13 col. f. [69] Wood, *Discoveries*, pp. 58–9.
[70] 'Letter from Edward Falkener upon the so-called Tomb of St Luke at Ephesus', *Proceedings of the Society of Biblical Archaeology*, II, 1879.
[71] See the intemperate exchanges in the *Academy* (10 August 1878), 143; (17 August 1878), 170; (6 April 1880), 293; (1 May 1880), 574; (5 June 1880), 73; (24 July 1880), 63.
[72] 'The Temple of Diana at Ephesus', *Girl's Own Paper* (12 August 1895), 137–41.

imagining the apostle gazing 'sorrowfully' on the temple and using even minor incidents during the dig to evoke Scripture: when he saw bullocks kicking against the prick of a whip, it brought to mind the words of Jesus to Paul on the road to Damascus; the sight of an ox and ass harnessed together in pulling a cart illustrated Paul's command: 'Be ye not unequally yoked together with unbelievers' (2 Cor. 6:14).[73] If the ox's bellows are the sound of a scraped barrel, then Wood presented still more such material in his posthumous *Modern Discoveries on the Site of Ancient Ephesus* (1890), part of a Religious Tract Society series on *By-paths of Biblical Knowledge*.[74]

Wood fed the appetite for the reconstruction of New Testament locations nourished by such works as Thomas Lewin's *Life and Epistles of Saint Paul* (1851), William John Conybeare and John Saul Howson's *The Life and Epistles of Saint Paul* (1852) and Frederic Farrar's *Life and Work of Saint Paul* (1879). These collages of antiquarian and archaeological information were apologetic as well as devotional, for their authors hoped that if they could prove the New Testament to be a 'mental photograph of the life which then surrounded the Mediterranean Sea, in its breadth and its depth, from the palace to the dungeon, and from the east to the west' then its veracity would be established against Straussian higher criticism. Wood's book created potent reality effects. Newton revelled in floating above Ephesus with 'the key to its topography which we have now obtained', spotting the mob in the theatre and worshippers of Artemis wending their way to the temple.[75] The railway and Wood made it fashionable for Holy Land travellers – including Cook's tourists – to 'do' Ephesus while staying in Smyrna. There was 'no place more attractive to the Christian pilgrim', who could stand in the theatre to conjure up the riot against Paul.[76] Those who could not reach Paul's Ephesus could visit it in London. Readers of Ada Habershon's *The Bible and the British Museum* (1909) were directed to enter the Ephesus Room and 'stand among the ruins of that very building which the Apostle Paul saw when he visited that city' (Fig. 8.5).[77]

---

[73] B. P. Pask, *The Apostle of the Gentiles: A Handbook on the Life of St. Paul* (London, 1877), pp. 270–82.
[74] John Turtle Wood, *Modern Discoveries on the Site of Ancient Ephesus* (London, 1890).
[75] Charles Newton, 'Discoveries at Ephesos', [*Edinburgh Review*, 1876] in his *Essays on Art and Archaeology* (London, 1886), p. 241.
[76] 'Two Months in Palestine', *Leisure Hour* (31 July 1869), 492; Josias Leslie Porter, 'A Visit to Ephesus', *Good Words*, 22 (1881), 822; R.I.P., 'A Visit to Ephesus', *Sunday at Home* (3 October 1885), 632; Thomas Cook, 'Travelling Experiences', *Leisure Hour* (29 June 1878), 414.
[77] Ada Habershon, *The Bible and the British Museum* (London, 1909), pp. 10, 15. Inevitably, the archaeology of Ephesus made it a popular setting for Christian fiction, much of it American: J. E. Copus, *Andros of Ephesus* (New York, 1910); Richard Short, *Saronia: A Romance of Ancient*

THE EPHESUS ROOM.

Figure 8.5 *The Ephesus Room*

Beyond this broad appeal to the imagination, the remains of Paul's Ephesus had a more detailed use in the defence of the New Testament. What mattered were not so much the stones Wood found as the words inscribed on them.[78] Inscriptions found in the Theatre and Odeon had put Wood on the track that led to the temple, while an inscription found at the peribolus wall established that he had hit upon its precincts.[79] The most impressive find was the series of decrees Wood had uncovered in the theatre, recording the endowment by the Roman knight C. Vibius Salutaris in AD 104 of a procession of statues to the temple in honour of Artemis. Though the poor reproduction of the inscriptions in the appendix to Wood's books attracted much criticism, the clerical epigrapher Edward

Ephesus (London, 1900); Russell Carter Kelso, *Amor Victor: A Novel of Ephesus and Rome, 95–105 AD* (New York, 1902).

[78] Arthur Cayley Headlam, 'The Authority of Christianity', in David George Hogarth, ed., *Authority and Archaeology: Sacred and Profane: Essays on the Relation of Monuments to Biblical and Classical Literature with an Introductory Chapter on the Nature of Archaeology by the Editor* (London, 1899), p. 527.

[79] See Wood to Jones and copy of Waddington's letter to Wood, British Museum MSS 8249 (11–12).

Lee Hicks (1843–1919) established their importance by editing them for the British Museum.

Inscriptions mattered to apologists who sought to refute the claim of Ferdinand Christian Baur (1792–1860) and other critics such as Eduard Zeller (1814–1908) and Albert Schwegler (1819–57) that the narrative portions of Acts were fundamentally unhistorical.[80] Baur had dismissed Acts 19 as a fictionalised rendition of Paul's impact on the town (*ein idealistisches Gemälde der erfolgreichen Wirksamkeit des Apostels*). 'One knows not which to admire more,' wrote one early British student of the Tübingen school, 'the imagination which called [the scenes from Acts] into being, and threw around them the vesture of seeming truth, or that rough magic which has conjured them back into nothingness.'[81] The Tübingen school partly based the claim that Acts was a second-century fabrication on the observation that its account of cities made numerous slips about their location and governance. As William Ramsay put it, scholars adopting this approach should no more call the Acts writer a historian than they would a person who described travelling from London into England.[82] British clerics believed that, if the civic and religious world revealed by inscriptions tallied with the account of that world in Acts, then its credit was restored. They resembled the Egyptologists described in David Gange's chapter above who backed 'monument facts' against 'higher critical fancies'. As Lightfoot told the Ephesus committee, biblical critics had exhausted all the 'extant literature' relevant to the New Testament, but had not realised the worth of inscriptions. Lightfoot was the best-known English critic of Baur and of his English epigone Cassels and was keen to exploit the potential of archaeology.[83] As well as serving on Wood's committee, he became a vice-president of the Society of Biblical Archaeology and was the president of the Hellenic Society.[84] In an 1878 article, he had lingered over the seamless fit between Acts and Wood's inscriptions. The Salutaris inscription in particular was evidence that the portrait in Acts of the Ephesians as fanatical devotees of

---

[80] See generally W. Ward Gasque, *A History of the Criticism of the Acts of the Apostles* (Tübingen, 1975).

[81] Robert Blackley Drummond, 'The Acts of the Apostles: How Far Historical?' *National Review*, 10 (1860), 404.

[82] William Ramsay, *The Bearing of Recent Discovery on the Trustworthiness of the New Testament* (London, 1915), p. 40.

[83] A. H. Sayce, *Monument Facts and Higher Critical Fancies* (London, 1902); [W. R. Cassels], *Supernatural Religion: An Inquiry into the Reality of Divine Revelation* (London, 1874). See generally Geoffrey Treloar, *Lightfoot the Historian* (Tübingen, 1998), chapter 12.

[84] 'Fine-Art Gossip', *Athenaeum* (13 June 1885), 767.

Artemis was true to life.[85] Numerous late nineteenth-century and early twentieth-century apologetic works emulated Lightfoot's approach, claiming that the stones of Ephesus were 'crying out to vindicate and illustrate . . . the Acts of the Apostles'.[86] The discovery of many other inscriptions devoted to the Ephesian Artemis throughout Asia Minor confirmed at once the power of her cult, Paul's gumption in challenging it and the credibility of Acts in asserting that he had provoked her worshippers to riot against him.[87]

William Ramsay emerged as the leading champion and practitioner of this method. His early fieldwork was funded by Lightfoot's Hellenic Society and then the Asia Minor Exploration Fund, his admirers presenting him as a 'methodical collector of evidence', whose systematic procedures elevated him above the 'random hunter for treasure'.[88] Yet the more Ramsay discovered about the buried cities of Asia Minor, the more he was willing to lend his scholarly prestige to defend the accuracy of the New Testament and specifically of Luke, the putative author of Acts. By the later nineties, Ramsay had lost his respect for Tübingen, whose books he had studied in student days at Göttingen, and returned to the convictions of his Presbyterian youth, when he had read Conybeare and Howson at his mother's knee. For the mature Ramsay, Acts accurately reproduced the location and the distinctive forms of governance of the cities of Asia Minor.[89] Every year in the field yielded new evidence that Luke, whom Ramsay now accepted as the author of Acts, used correct terms to describe the variety of municipal government Paul and the other apostles had encountered.[90] Ramsay's *Trustworthiness of the New Testament* (1915) was a definitive statement of his trust in Acts as an accurate

---

[85] Joseph Barber Lightfoot, 'Illustrations of the Acts from Recent Discoveries', *Contemporary Review*, 32 (1878), 288–96. See too George T. Stokes, 'Modern Discoveries and the Christian Faith: St Paul at Ephesus II', *The Sunday at Home* (2 July 1892), 555–8 for a popularising insistence on the inscription's importance. Guy Rogers, *The Sacred Identity of Ephesus: Foundation Myths of a Roman City* (London, 1991), is a good modern study.

[86] W. S. W. Vaux, *Ancient History from the Monuments: Greek Cities and Islands of Asia Minor* (London, 1877), chapter 5; Thomas Nichol, *Recent Archaeology and the Bible: Croall Lectures for 1898* (London, 1898); Frederick Henry Chase, *The Credibility of the Acts of the Apostles* (London, 1902).

[87] Stokes, 'Modern Discoveries', 488.

[88] David George Hogarth, 'Introduction', in David George Hogarth, ed., *Authority and Archaeology: Sacred and Profane: Essays on the Relation of Monuments to Biblical and Classical Literature with an Introductory Chapter on the Nature of Archaeology by the Editor* (London,1899), p. x.

[89] Ramsay, *Bearing*, chapter 2. For a similar argument, drawing on Lightfoot, see George Salmon, *A Historical Introduction to the Study of the Books of the New Testament* (London, 1885), pp. 403–5.

[90] In 1910 for instance, Ramsay excavated a site in ancient Iconium for the first time, turning up Phrygian inscriptions apparently proving that Luke was correct in locating the city in Phrygia.

history. He marvelled that in Acts 'every person is found just where he ought to be: proconsuls in senatorial provinces, asiarchs in Ephesus, strategoi in Philippi, politarchs in Thessalonica, magicians and soothsayers everywhere'.[91]

Yet this method could do no more than establish the general verisimilitude of the scriptural narrative. It could not identify individuals mentioned in Scripture and prove that they had acted as Acts said they did – or that they had even existed. Epigraphers emphasised that it was vain to try and find proof that famous people had done the things history attested of them: their 'democratic science' generalised from classes of facts, but could not scent smoking guns.[92] Hicks thought he had found such an exception when he found a priest named Demetrius thanked in one of Wood's inscriptions for services to Artemis. Surely this was 'Demetrius, a silversmith' (Acts 19:24), who had provoked the riot against Paul? If the identification stuck, it would both prove the latter's existence and implicate the temple's servants in the opposition to Christianity. Yet it was Ramsay who exposed his wishful thinking, for the proof was no more compelling than assuming that two 'John Smiths' mentioned in two documents of their own time must be identical.[93]

The idea that archaeology could prove the New Testament to be true was thus a narrower claim than its advocates hoped. Biblical scholars of both conservative and radical inclinations had differing reasons to dislike surrendering the Bible to archaeologists for use as a list of factual assertions to be checked against history.[94] Ramsay was criticised for his simple-minded approach to the questions posed in his volume of essays, *Was Christ Born at Bethlehem?* (1898). For biblical critics, the value and interests of texts was settled by inquiries into their form and the intrinsic probability of the events they described. By 1914, archaeologists knew much more about Ephesus but had little to contribute to such old problems as what Paul meant by his fight with 'beasts' there. Although the stock of Acts as a source in both Britain and

---

[91] Ramsay, *Bearing*, pp. 97–8.
[92] Francis Haverfield, 'The Roman World', in David George Hogarth, ed., *Authority and Archaeology: Sacred and Profane: Essays on the Relation of Monuments to Biblical and Classical Literature with an Introductory Chapter on the Nature of Archaeology by the Editor* (London, 1899), p. 313.
[93] 'Demetrius the Silversmith: An Ephesian Study', *Expositor*, 1 (1890), 401–22; 'Ephesus: A Postscript', *Expositor*, 2 (1890), 144–9; William Ramsay, 'Saint Paul at Ephesus', *Expositor*, 2 (1890), 2–22. The question is revisited in Guy Rogers, 'Demetrios of Ephesos: Silversmith and Neopoios?' *Belleten* (1987), 877–82.
[94] Davis, *Shifting Sands*, pp. 45–6.

Germany rose in line with the exploration of Asia Minor, authoritative commentators on Acts did not share the view that it was literally true.[95]

'Centres of unity': Greek cities and the future of Christianity

If the reconstruction of Ephesus could not vindicate the letter of the New Testament, then in the eyes of many later nineteenth-century theologians and Protestant writers it could nonetheless make a vital contribution to understanding the evolution and survival prospects of Christianity. It was a fashionable assumption of scholars at this time that the message of the New Testament had to be not only historicised but also localised; placed in cultural and geographical space, as well as in historical time. If the later nineteenth century saw a growing appreciation of what both Jesus and Paul owed to Palestinian Judaism, then the works of the Oxford theologian Edwin Hatch (1835–89) among others reflected an increased interest in how Greek thought and culture had coloured the gospel. Although modern scholars feel they are just starting to ask what the archaeology of Ephesus and other cities reveals about the Christianity of the New Testament, these questions were being posed at the end of the nineteenth century.[96] Nor were the answers purely academic. For biblical critics, archaeologists and classical scholars who wrote popular religious works, Ephesus and the other cities of Paul not only revealed the sources of his thought but also symbolised Christianity's status as a religion that had always thrived in urban settings. They detected parallels between the cosmopolitan metropolises of their own time and the racially and culturally mixed cities of the first century, hoping that a religion that had thrived in the latter could prosper in the former.

The heterogeneous character of Ephesus was a scholarly commonplace. It had long been argued that commerce had brought Greeks to found cities on the coasts of Asia Minor and then lured them up along the rivers into the hinterland. In the cities they had founded or remodelled, their Greek culture was diluted by Asiatic locals or Jewish colonists. What was seen as the Orientalising or mongrelisation of the cities in Asia Minor had also often

---

[95] See, e.g,. Carl Weizsäcker, *The Apostolic Age of the Christian Church* (London, 1895), pp. 390–1; Arthur Cushman McGiffert, *A History of Christianity in the Apostolic Age* (New York, 1897), pp. 283–6.

[96] See, e.g., G. H. R. Horsley, 'The Inscriptions of Ephesos and the New Testament', *Novum Testamentum*, 34 (1992), 105–68; Rick Strelan, *Paul, Artemis and the Jews* (Berlin, 1996); Paul Treblico, *The Early Christians in Ephesus from Paul to Ignatius* (Tübingen, 2007); Jerome Murphy O'Connor, *Ephesus: Texts and Archaeology* (London, 2008).

been lamented. For Frederic William Farrar, Ephesus was 'more Hellenic than Antioch, more Oriental than Corinth, more populous than Athens . . . the corruptress of Ionia – the favourite scene of her most voluptuous love-tales, the lighted theatre of her most ostentatious sins'.[97] Farrar's clerical flannelling was a close paraphrase of his hero Renan, whose *Saint Paul* (1869) had described Ephesus as one of those 'nondescript towns [*villes banales*] that the Roman Empire had multiplied, towns placed beyond nationality, foreign to love of country, dominated by all kinds of races and religions'. It was characterised by 'something light, passionate and mobile; the vain curiosity of frivolous people . . . an easy ability to follow fashion, without ever being able to set it'.[98] If Second Empire Paris perhaps served here as the model for ancient Ephesus, then Renan also insisted that its vices were those of luxurious Asia. The Temple of Artemis was the dark Asiatic heart of a '*ville théocratique*'.[99] A lecture by the German Hellenist Ernest Curtius (1814–96) agreed, describing Ephesus as a place in which the municipal culture of free Greek seafarers had succumbed to the poison of Asiatic civilisation [*Gift asiatischer Gesittung*]. Their failure was legible in the constant shifting of the city's centre from temple complex to walled city and back again.[100] Other scholars read this lesson into the city's coinage, which alternately featured images of an Asiatic nature goddess and the graceful human form of the Greek Diana.[101]

When British authors wrote of the temple's statue of Artemis, 'the image which fell down from Jupiter' (Acts 19:35), they drew on their memories of trips to continental Catholic churches or on their exposure to missionary stories of Hindu superstition. Farrar insisted that it was a 'hideous fetish . . . covered with monstrous breasts', resembling the 'hideous dolls' of folk Catholicism or Indian temple statues and compared the chanting of her angry worshippers to the screeching of Indian 'yoghis'.[102] Seeking to evoke Paul's loneliness in Ephesus, the Baptist minister and social gospeller Frederick Meyer (1847–1929) invoked the missionary 'in the midst of Benares, surrounded by that vast heathen population, worshipping on the

---

[97] Frederic W. Farrar, *The Life and Work of Saint Paul* (1879; London, 1890), pp. 356–7.
[98] Ernest Renan, *Saint Paul* [1869], in *Histoire des origines du Christianisme* (2 vols., Paris, 1995), I, pp. 671–2. Chandler, Falkener and Svoboda were Renan's main sources for his portrait of Ephesus.
[99] Ibid., p. 673.
[100] Ernest Curtius, *Ephesos: ein Vortrag gehalten im wissenschaftlichen Verein zu Berlin am 7 Februar 1874* (1874), p. 3.
[101] Barclay Head, *On the Chronological Sequence of the Coins of Ephesus* (London, 1880).
[102] Farrar, *Paul*, pp. 358–9. See similarly, 'One of the Seven Wonders of the World', *Quiver* (March 1862), 452–3.

banks of the brown and muddy Ganges, or ascending the thousand stairs of the marble temples which extend along the river side'.[103] The ubiquity of magic was another mark of the city's bad syncretism. If Paul had jousted with philosophers in Athens, wrote Farrar, then in the shadow of the 'acropolis of Paganism ... the stronghold of Eastern fanaticism and Grecian vice' he tangled with exorcists and conjurers.[104] The most resonant mark of Paul's victory was the burning of magical books (Acts 19:18–19) by penitent Ephesians, a bonfire represented in the Gustave Doré engraving that adorned many a late Victorian Bible (Fig. 8.6). The celebration of this 'condensed Christian triumph' was the more fervent because many Victorian clerics worried about the challenges posed to Christian belief and practice by the fashionable 'necromancy' of the spiritualists.[105]

The vision of Ephesus as a city in thrall to a 'grotesque and archaic idol' denied any reality or virtue to its civic religion and indulged the notion that Paul's teaching must have readily precipitated its collapse there and then across Asia Minor.[106] For Farrar, Paul prevailed over Artemis because he confronted paganism as a Hebrew of the Hebrews, who met Hellenism's debased polish with 'holy philistinism'. For Farrar, Paul's mind was narrowly Jewish, his upbringing in Hellenistic Tarsus making little impact on his culture or thought. He thus moralised Renan's ironic portrait of Paul as an innocent abroad in sophisticated Greek cities. The notion of Paul as an oppositional figure was very attractive to nonconformists struggling to preserve a crusading identity in the worldly metropolis. For Joseph Parker (1830–1902), the rebarbative Congregational minister of the City Temple in Holborn, Demetrius the silversmith symbolised not just the civic religion of Ephesus but the metropolitan cynicism that inhibited the energy of Christians in the 'thoroughfares of the capital cities of the world': they should ignore his sneers and press on with crusades against drink and dirty books.[107]

Farrar's view of Paul as a hostile outsider to Asia Minor's debauched cities did not convince all his readers and was changing at the century's close.[108]

---

[103] F. B. Meyer, *Paul, a Servant of Jesus Christ* (London, 1897), p. 146.
[104] Farrar, *Paul*, p. 364; Renan, *Saint Paul*, pp. 676–7.
[105] Joseph Parker, *Apostolic Life as Revealed in the Acts of the Apostles* (2 vols., London, 1884), II, pp. 282–4.
[106] Robert William Dale, *The Epistle to the Ephesians* (London, 1882), pp. 6–9; Charles Gore, *The Epistle to the Ephesians* (London, 1898), pp. 36–7. Strelan, *Paul*, pp. 128–31, 153–62 notes the persistence of this view in the literature.
[107] Parker, *Apostolic Life*, pp. 297–8. On the crusading Puritanism of Parker and other late nineteenth-century nonconformists, see Dominic Erdozain, 'The Secularization of Sin', *Journal of Ecclesiastical History*, 62 (2011), 59–88.
[108] See, e.g., 'Canon Farrar's *Life and Work of Saint Paul*', *Examiner* (11 October 1879), 1313.

Figure 8.6 Gustave Doré, *St Paul at Ephesus*

This shift owed much to the recovery of further inscriptions as well as papyri from the Hellenistic cities of Egypt. For scholars such as the widely read Gustav Adolf Deissmann (1866–1937), such findings narrowed the gap between the ordinary inhabitants of Hellenistic cities such as

Ephesus and the apostles.[109] Paul was a member of the hardworking urban middle classes, who had spoken and written their language. He was after all a consummate writer of letters, which connected apostolic cities just as the telegraph did modern ones.[110] Edward Lee Hicks argued from the Ephesus inscriptions that Paul was an organic product of Hellenistic city life. His travels, which took him from one great city to another, evinced his urban mentality, as too did his imagery. While Jesus dealt in lost sheep and sown corn, Paul's metaphors were drawn from civic games and temples.[111]

This emphasis reflected more than the pressure of evidence. Scholars who now shuttled around the Mediterranean by steamer and railway during university vacations were tempted to regard first-century Asia Minor as a network of cities whose levels of urbanisation and quality of communications mirrored their own international world.[112] The breeziest statement of the convergence across centuries came in Harold Morton's *In the Steps of Saint Paul* (1936), a best-seller which encapsulates many features of Victorian religious tourism. Morton felt it strangely appropriate to enter Paul's Turkey aboard a carriage of the Compagnie International des Wagons-Lits, whose staff in their identical 'chocolate-coloured uniform[s]' reproduced the transnational mobility of the apostolic age and the 'magnificent standardisation of the Roman road'.[113]

Paul had exploited openings and diagnosed problems that existed wherever big cities had developed. For theorists of Christian missions in towns, this ensured the eternal relevance of his message. As Ramsay's friend the slum parson Hensley Henson (1863–1947) told the working men of Barking in 1898, the most archaic age of Christianity was the most immediately relevant to them, because 'two millenniums of Christianity have not altered the inveterate characteristics of modern cities'. The 'frivolity, cynical scepticism [and] sensuality' against which Paul battled were eternal 'notes of

---

[109] Adolf Deissmann, *Saint Paul: A Study in Social and Religious History*, trans. Lionel Strachan (London, 1912), p. 47; Adolf Deissmann, *New Light on the New Testament from the Records of the Graeco-Roman Period*, trans. Lionel Strachan (London, 1907), pp. 7–8.

[110] Adolf Deissmann, *Bible Studies: Contributions Chiefly from Papyri and Inscriptions to the History of the Language, the Literature, and the Religion of Hellenistic Judaism and Primitive Christianity*, trans. Alexander Grieve (London, 1909), chapter 1; William Ramsay, *The Church in the Roman Empire before AD 170* (London, 1893), chapter 3.

[111] Edward Lee Hicks, 'St Paul and Hellenism', in *Studia Biblica, Essays Chiefly in Biblical and Patristic Criticism, by Members of the University of Oxford: IV* (Oxford, 1896), pp. 1–14. See too Deissmann, *Saint Paul*, p. 74.

[112] Ramsay, *Letters*, chapter 2; Deissmann, *Paul*, p. 199.

[113] H. V. Morton, *In the Steps of Saint Paul* (London, 1936), p. 46.

urban life'.[114] Hicks was equally determined to show that primitive Christianity had the resources to heal the wounds of modern urbanisation, having been deeply marked by his move from Oxford and the British Museum to an Anglican living in Manchester, where he had become an ally of the social reformer T. C. Horsfall (1841–1932) and worried about the problems of 'life in great cities'.[115]

The imagined cosmopolitanism of the apostolic city explains its appeal to many commentators. The blend of Jew, Greek and Asiatic in Paul's Ephesus came close to materialising the difficult idea of Christian universality, in which, as Brooke Foss Westcott (1825–1901) wrote, the church at once realised the 'brotherhood of men' and was the 'abiding pledge of that truth in the face of present separations and rivalries of nations'.[116] As Renan had observed, Ephesus released its inhabitants from their origins, encouraging a degree of cosmopolitanism unmatched until recent times. The stress in British writing on Pauline Christianity's chameleonic adaptation to urban cultures was also informed by the changing attitudes to missionary enterprise in the East. Advocates of missions had always presented it as doing Paul's work, but definitions of what made for successful mission were changing. In India, missionaries sought an improving accommodation with Hindu traditions, while in China missionary societies adopted a strategy of settling small parties of missionaries in large cities, where they were to blend in with the locals and act as a leaven in conscious imitation of Paul's discretion in Athens and Ephesus.[117] Roland Allen (1868–1947), a former China missionary, explained how Paul's urban strategy could reform *Missionary Methods* (1912). Paul had singled out cities that blended Greek culture with large Jewish populations and were 'great marts where the material and intellectual wealth of the world was exchanged'. Modern missionaries must similarly abandon 'racial and religious pride' and seek out 'points in the circumference of a larger unity'.[118]

William Ramsay was central to advancing this evolving interpretation of Pauline cities and undertaking the research on which it was based. He used his investigations into and publications on Phrygian cities to make the

---

[114] Hensley Henson, *Apostolic Christianity: Notes and Inferences Based Mainly on Saint Paul's Epistles to the Corinthians* (London, 1898), p. xv.

[115] J. H. Fowler, *The Life and Letters of Edward Lee Hicks* (London, 1922), pp. 95–6. See generally Graham Neville, *Radical Churchman: Edward Lee Hicks and the New Liberalism* (Oxford, 1998).

[116] Brooke Foss Westcott, *Social Aspects of Christianity* (London, 1887), p. 68.

[117] Grace Stott, *Twenty-six Years of Missionary Work in China* (London, 1897), p. 316 and Geraldine Guinness, *The Story of the China Inland Mission* (2 vols., London, 1893), I, p. 321.

[118] Roland Allen, *Missionary Methods: Saint Paul's or Ours* (London, 1912), pp. 23–4, 94–7, 191.

argument that in Paul's teaching the 'Eastern mind and the Hellenic ... intermingled in the closest union, like two elements which have undergone a chemical mixture' and that cities were the crucible and symbol of that union.[119] As an instinctive defender of the Turkish state against insensitive Westernisation, Ramsay revelled in identifying 'Asianic elements in Greek civilisation'. He argued that cities in Asia Minor were 'an experiment in the amalgamation of Asiatic and European in a social organism'.[120] They were political and religious entities that had united Greek colonists, Jewish settlers and Persian kings in civilising native peasant populations. Having then been integrated into a Roman Empire that universalised their understandings of citizenship, they had known nothing of the 'race hatred and colour hatred', which was 'the most dangerous symptom of degeneration in modern civilisation'. The colour bar of the Southern United States would have been absurd in Anatolia, the 'highway of nations', where 'real mixing of blood and stock' had always taken place.[121]

For Ramsay, Paul had come not to destroy but to fulfil the civic religion of Asia Minor. He regarded the cult of Artemis not as a type of Catholic idolatry but as a codification of a benign natural religion.[122] Paul's arrival at Ephesus coincided though with a crisis of civic religion, in which the laudable syncretism of Hellenistic cities was lapsing into 'philosophic speculation' or giving way to the 'sham' deification of Roman emperors.[123] No wonder that the tradesmen of Ephesus had rioted against Paul, or that its priestly elite the Asiarchs had welcomed his teaching.[124] With its watchwords of orderly freedom and universal education, Pauline Christianity could have put urban culture on a sounder footing. Its failure to do so reflected the hostility of Roman emperors from Nero onwards, who had persecuted the infant church as a 'political party' whose reforms would have shaken their illegitimate power.[125] The influence of Ramsay's interpretation is evident in the entry for 'Ephesus' in the *Dictionary of the Apostolic Church* (1915), an authoritative if conservative summary of scholarship. 'Oriental' in its religion, 'Greek' in its culture and 'Roman' in its governance, Ephesus was the 'gateway of Asia ... as Bombay is the portal of India today'. On the

---

[119] William Ramsay, *The Cities of Saint Paul: Their Influence on his Life and Thought* (London, 1908), p. 7.
[120] William Ramsay, *Asianic Elements in Greek Civilisation* (London, 1915); Ramsay *Cities*, p. v.
[121] Ramsay, *Cities*, p. 45; 'The Intermixture of Races in Asia Minor: Some of its Causes and Effects', *British Academy* (1915–16), pp. 359–422.
[122] Ramsay, *Cities*, p. 28; Ramsay, *Letters*, chapter 10, p. 17; Ramsay *Asianic Elements*, chapter 3.
[123] Ibid., pp. 135, 140.   [124] Ramsay, *Roman Empire*, p. 135.   [125] Ibid., pp. 10, 361.

eve of Paul's arrival the 'best mind of the age was wistfully awaiting a new order of things', hence his ready embrace by the Asiarchs.[126]

Ramsay's intimation of positive connections between the civic gospel and Paul's gospel was reproduced in the growing body of research into 'Oriental' and mystery religions, which not only rescued them from imputations of superstition and immorality, but pointed out that Paul appropriated their sacramental language.[127] For Protestant modernists such as the Oxford classicist and Anglican layman Percy Gardner (1846–1937), the first editor of the Hellenic Society's *Journal* and Ramsay's successor at Oxford, the result subverted conventional readings of the Bible. Early Christianity was continuous with the evolving religious life of the pagan world and especially with the Oriental cults that flourished in places such as Ephesus.[128] For Gardner, the New Testament did not introduce new doctrines or beliefs into the world but baptised those that had already evolved into the spirit of Christ. He believed that the New Testament would survive if presented not in isolation but as 'a set of textbooks of religion, and classics for all time ... [that] embodied all that was best in the religions of previous ages, and of all nations'. As classics they would not just speak to but improve the populations of 'our great cities, where dwell multitudes cut off from all tradition and from the daily influences which act like sea and air and earth, multitudes engaged in a never-ceasing struggle for existence'.[129]

By the beginning of the twentieth century therefore, Ephesus had multiple meanings for British Protestants. It was no longer a spectacle of God's judgment and it was both more and less than a quarry for proofs of the truth of the New Testament. It encouraged theologians to develop new ideas about how Christianity had developed and could be diffused in the future. If sensitive Victorians had winced to hear the 'shriek of the steam whistle' during quiet Sundays in Ephesus, then it was the railway age that took them there. If rail and steam assisted in bringing bits of the city to London, then it was great cities such as London that generated the anxieties that archaeology helped to answer. If Ephesus is now the preserve

---

[126] Alexander Souter and James Strahan, 'Ephesus', in James Hastings, ed., *Dictionary of the Apostolic Church* (2 vols., London, 1915), I, p. 350.
[127] See, e.g., Franz Cumont, *Les Religions orientales dans le paganisme romain* (Paris, 1906) and Kirsopp Lake, *The Earlier Epistles of Saint Paul: Their Motive and Origin* (London, 1911).
[128] Percy Gardner, *Exploratio Evangelica* (London, 1899), chapter 26; see too *The Religious Experience of Saint Paul* (London, 1896) and *The Ephesian Gospel* (London, 1915).
[129] Gardner, *Exploratio*, pp. 476, 500.

of professional archaeologists, then it also continues to draw in devout readers of Scripture. For the American Christians who have replaced Victorian explorers in the ruins and who make their pilgrimage by plane, coach or cruise ship rather than under steam, it is undoubtedly still a city of God.[130]

[130] Dieter Knibbe, *Ephesus – ΕΦΕΣΟΣ: Geschichte einer bedeutenden antiken Stadt und Portrait einer modernen Großgrabung* (Frankfurt, 1998), pp. 16–17.

9 | Rome

JANE GARNETT AND ANNE BUSH

> 'I have also thought of a model city from which I deduce all the others,' Marco answered. 'It is a city made only of exceptions, exclusions, incongruities, contradictions. If such a city is the most improbable, by reducing this number of abnormal elements, we increase the probability that the city really exists. So I have only to subtract exceptions from my model, and in whatever direction I proceed, I will arrive at one of the cities which, always as an exception, exist. But I cannot force my operation beyond a certain limit: I would achieve cities too probable to be real.'
> (Italo Calvino, *Invisible Cities*)

In the nineteenth century, no road to Rome offered the approaching traveller a view of the city as a whole. It was the church rather than the monuments of ancient Rome that provided most travellers with the initial evidence of the larger city to come. In his diary for 1802, Walter Scott's friend James Skene (1775–1864) recorded not only his first view of St Peter's as he neared Rome, but how its 'mountainous Dome ... rose like a huge pillar of mist in the distance'.[1] Extolling the transporting effects of such a vision, he went on to explain how the sight made him insensible to the roughness of his immediate surroundings at the same time that it encouraged his imaginary musings. 'When in bed,' he wrote, 'the image still continued to dance before my eyes, whether asleep or awake, attended with a thousand fanciful forms of the long expected wonder of Rome ...'[2] Writing in 1814, Samuel Rogers (1763–1855) described a similarly ethereal and evocative view. Seen from approximately fifteen miles along the Appian Way, the dome of St Peter's stood out against the sky of the Campagna. Surrounded by the morning smoke that obscured the outline of the remaining city, the cupola rose above an almost angelic haze – one which separated the dome from the city below and made the smoke appear as a 'light over the rest of the line'.[3] For the Catholic priest John

---

[1] *Italian Journey. Being Excerpts from the pre-Victorian Diary of James Skene of Rubislaw* (London, 1930), p. 30.
[2] Ibid.
[3] J. R. Hale, *The Italian Journey of Samuel Rogers, Edited with an Account of Rogers's Life and of Travel in Italy in 1814–1821* (London, 1956), p. 207.

Chetwode Eustace (1761–1815), the view was more clearly metaphorical. The dome marked the pinnacle of Christianity as well as classical Rome. It introduced the 'Eternal City' – a Rome, sacred and secular, hidden from view and revealed only by degree – a Rome rising from the ground as the traveller approached.[4] By synecdoche, he went on to link Rome, Jerusalem and Mount Sion in this vision of the city. Catherine Taylor, whose account of a journey to Rome in the 1830s was published by the Society for the Promotion of Christian Knowledge in 1849, commented that:

> It is difficult, nay, impossible, to describe the various feelings that pressed upon us, when we first saw the dome of St Peter's rising in the distance over the Campagna di Roma. Perhaps the most distinct sensation I experienced was that for the first time I was going actually to set my foot in a place mentioned in the Bible: a place of which St Paul had said, 'I must also see Rome' (Acts xix.21) and in which he had 'dwelt two whole years' (Acts xxviii.30).[5]

In the ground out of which Rome rose were the roots of many cities, full of contradictions: the city of the early Christian church, the medieval and modern Roman Catholic Church and Western civilisation as a whole. These overlapping, conflicting and confusing inheritances were increasingly contested in the nineteenth century.[6] Onto Rome was mapped both literally and metaphorically an ideological battle for the possession of symbolic capital and the construction of memory. Rome was a mythical city and a real one; one to which travellers journeyed with preconceptions formed by literature, by religious prejudice and aspiration, and by political standpoint; and which carried potent resonances for those who would never go there but would imagine it or invoke it. From the post-Napoleonic period, when papal rule was restored, and ideas of Risorgimento developed, to the debates about the city at and after the unification of Italy, Rome was the subject of intense focus for British commentators. An important facet of this heightened attention was its status as a biblical city. More than the seat of the Roman Republic, the throne of the Caesars and the destination of Mazzini and Garibaldi, it was a cradle of apostolic Christianity and the supposed resting place of St Paul and St Peter. This biblical focus was stimulated by the archaeological works being carried out under the aegis of successive popes

---

[4] John Chetwode Eustace, *A Tour through Italy: Exhibiting a View of its Scenery, its Antiquities, and its Monuments* (2 vols., London, 1813), I, p. 193.
[5] Catherine Taylor, *My Journey to Italy Ten Years Ago: Or Extracts from Letters to a Younger Sister* (London, 1849), pp. 96–8.
[6] For Victorian attitudes to ancient Rome in general, see Norman Vance, *The Victorians and Ancient Rome* (Oxford, 1997).

from the late eighteenth century – British responses to which were complicated by religious controversy in the early nineteenth century, and by related debate about the definitions of history and archaeology as scholarly disciplines.

The Times published regular bulletins on the progress of excavations in Rome from the early 1860s. An article in 1869, referring to the appeal for funds to all nations, commented that 'Rome being the natural centre of all archaeology' a spirit of emulation was developing as to who could do the most to 'ascertain the real history of the city'.[7] Such a positivistic notion of reality belied the plurality of Romes at issue. Throughout this period, the drive towards a heightened scientific basis for Rome's history – and through it for an authoritative history of the early church – was in tension with the different religious and secular narratives which the archaeology could tell. In Rome itself, polarised interpretations of archaeology formed a key component of the debate between the papacy and its republican opponents throughout the early and mid-nineteenth century.[8] The Colosseum became symbolic of this contest over the lines of continuity from the antique past – as the Stations of the Cross (initially placed there by Benedict XIV to reclaim the site as one of Christian martyrdom) were moved in and out of it under different regimes up to the 1870s (Fig. 9.1).

The presence of the past

British perspectives were nuanced ones. By the 1840s and 1850s, there was a shift of emphasis from the elegiac romanticisation of ruins as signifiers of absence, of a glorious past irrevocably past – 'Rome and her Ruin past Redemption's skill'[9] – to a greater preoccupation with engaging the past with the present. On the one hand, views of Rome were inflected by rising church party tension in the Anglican Church, and wider fears of Tractarianism as crypto-Catholicism: the idea of Rome as the fount of corruption was intensified at a time of revived Protestant preoccupation with prophetic interpretation of the Book of Daniel and Revelation, in which Rome was figured as Babylon and the Pope as Antichrist.[10] Rising

---

[7] *The Times* (17 February 1869).
[8] C. Springer, *The Marble Wilderness: Ruins and Representation in Italian Romanticism, 1775–1850* (Cambridge, 1987).
[9] G. G. Byron, *Childe Harold's Pilgrimage: Canto the Fourth* (London, 1818), pp. v 145.
[10] See, especially, Edward Bishop Elliott, *Horae Apocalypticae* (3 vols., London, 1844); John Cumming, *Lectures for the Times, Or, an Exposition of Tridentine and Tractarian Popery*

Figure 9.1 Robert Macpherson, *Portion of the Interior Wall of the Coliseum, c. 1860*, albumen print from collodian negative

Catholic confidence, symbolised by the papal restoration of the episcopal hierarchy in England, gave rise to a torrent of anti-Catholic sentiment in 1850–1. The very topography of Rome was re-identified forcibly with the papal threat, as Nicholas Wiseman (1802–65), newly appointed Cardinal Archbishop of Westminster, gloried in the change with his combative letter 'Out of the Flaminian Gate'. The reference to the northern gate of Rome facing towards England was the more pointed as the Anglican community in Rome had been obliged from 1826 to worship beyond the city in a barn outside the same gate. The barrister Joseph Beldam (1795–1866) stood for many anti-Catholic critics in 1851 when he ridiculed the Christmas ceremonies at Rome, which many British visitors attended, as exhibiting 'a religion at which a Protestant may well blush, and which a Mahommedan

(London, 1844); cf. also the conservative High Church Christopher Wordsworth, *Lectures on the Apocalypse* (London, 1847).

consistently condemns' – and paralleled the decadence of Catholicism with late-imperial Rome.[11] But others were already keen to challenge this association, and continued to do so. An anonymous English resident in 1846 contrasted his first dreamy, awe-struck and abstracted impression of Rome as Eternal City with his later awareness of the 'glorious realities of the place ... the influence of the *genius loci*'. This he characterised specifically in terms of popular religiosity – the shrines on every street corner and in every shop signifying a touching intermingling of religion with the everyday (his point of contrast being 'gay, thoughtless Paris'). Acknowledging British prejudices against devotion to images in such shrines, he emphasised the real religious sentiment revealed, and pointed to a common religious spirit underlying different forms of worship and transcending institutional frameworks (such as the papacy).[12]

Others again sought to redeem the ruins of Rome as part of the ancestry not just of universal but specifically either Anglo-Saxon or British Christianity. The development of such genealogies formed a key point of division between Catholics and Protestants. In his introduction to *Rome Ancient and Modern* (1842), the greater part of which focused on a systematic guide to its three hundred churches, the Catholic priest Rev. Jeremiah Donovan used strong terms in describing Christian Rome as 'the parent of our Religion ... In her fertile soil were sown by Apostolic hands the precious seeds of the Gospel, which, irrigated with the blood of martyrs, produced fruit an hundred-fold'.[13] Monsignor Baggs (1806–45), writing as Vice-Rector of the English College at Rome in 1839 (with many subsequent editions) on the ceremonies of Holy Week to justify and dignify them to a sceptical or anti-Catholic British readership, had been careful to argue in more moderate language that Catholic seasons of devotion were taken from apostolic usage and to emphasise English Christian links with Rome – that it was from Rome that the Saxons had received Christianity in the first place.[14] Although Baggs' eirenic purpose made his book popular with British travellers to Rome from across the religious spectrum, it had a partisan underpinning. Its gentle and reasonable tone was regarded as all the more seductive and dangerous by the anonymous author of 'The Spiritual Peril

---

[11] Joseph Beldam, *Recollections of Scenes and Institutions in Italy and the East* (2 vols., London, 1851), I, chapter 3.

[12] *Rome, Pagan and Papal; by an English Resident in the City* (London, 1846), pp. 1–8.

[13] Jeremiah Donovan, *Rome Ancient and Modern, and its Environs* (4 vols., Rome, 1842–44), I, p. xix.

[14] Charles Baggs, *The Ceremonies of Holy Week at the Vatican and St John Lateran Described* (1839; Rome, 1859), pp. 38, 1.

of British Travellers' in 1845.[15] The argument that Saxon Christianity derived from papal Rome was contested by the liberal Anglican R. W. Morgan (1813–89). In *St Paul in Britain* (1861), he preferred to trace the pre-existing links between British Christianity and the apostolic Christians of first-century Rome. The seven-year exile of Caractacus in Rome and the marriage of his daughter to Pudens, a supposed Christian whose house was thought to have been the home of St Paul and St Peter, provided the link between Britain and the New Testament. From this close connection between British royalty and St Paul (who might even have come to Britain), Morgan constructed a Protestant appropriation of early Christian Rome and derived an apology for the Anglican union of church and state with a sovereign at its head (as opposed to either papal or dissenting models of their separation).[16] This narrative was to be rearticulated as a specific contribution to debates about the disestablishment of the church in Wales, where the Church of England claimed authority by descent from the original British church.[17] Meanwhile Paul's Christian mission within the Roman empire would be figured in a later nineteenth-century context as a prototype for Britain's Christian imperial mission.[18]

From 1860, and after the unification of a large part of northern and central Italy, intensified attention was paid to the relationship between Rome and the Papal States and the liberated parts of the peninsula, and perspectives were achieved through a biblical lens. The Liberal journalist Edward Dicey (1832–1911) went to Rome in 1860 and, a year later, published his observations. His first chapter – entitled 'The Rome of Real Life' – set out how hard it was 'for anyone at any time to judge of Rome fairly'. He deprecated the 'glamour' which stole over every visitor to Rome – who arrived already with an idea of the Eternal City: 'Here above all places in God's earth it is hard to forget the past and think only of the present. This, however, is what I want now to do.' After painting a vivid picture of the desolation of the Campagna, the dismal nature of contemporary Rome, its immorality and tawdriness and the tedium of its rituals, as he travelled from Rome to Tuscany (part of the newly unified north), he launched with purple prose into a section called 'The Promised Land':

---

[15] [John Cumming?], 'The Spiritual Peril of British Travellers', *Fraser's Magazine*, 32 (1845), 62–71.

[16] Richard William Morgan, *St. Paul in Britain: Or, The Origin of British Christianity as Opposed to Papal Christianity* (Oxford and London, 1861).

[17] S. Russell Forbes, *The Footsteps of St Paul in Rome: An Historical Memoir from the Apostle's Landing at Puteoli to his Death, AD 62–64* (1882; London, 1888), pp. 88–90.

[18] Walter Lock, *St Paul the Master-Builder* (London, 1899).

out of chill clouds and dull gloom, I passed into summer sunshine ... into a rich garden-country, studded with thriving towns swarming with life, and watered with endless streams, I came into a land such as the children of Israel never looked upon from over Jordan, after their weary wanderings in the wilderness ... This, indeed, is the true Italy ... I saw her free, and rejoicing in her freedom.[19]

To a conventional association of papal rule with disease and decay, Dicey added the biblical language of liberation, arguing – as the political economist Nassau Senior had in 1851 – that real Catholicism could only flourish in a free Italy.[20] The Methodist minister William Arthur (1819–1901), who also visited Italy including Rome in 1860 with a comparable interest in the developing political situation, presented a strikingly more measured account. He was careful always to make distinctions between sincere faith and institutional corruption – even whilst naturally believing Catholics to be misguided – and punctured many British myths about Catholicism (for example, that only women went to church). Constant references were made to the early church, and to the potential to invoke it, despite the overlay of later and less pure religious forms. He argued that if the Italians were to have opportunities to read the Bible, they would be able to go directly back to St Paul, who planted the first church in Italy, rather than looking to Britain or America for models. Drawing on two Catholic guides to Rome – Monsignor Baggs and Charles Isidore Hemans (1817–76) – he reflected on the scope for Italy to restore its links with its original indigenous religious culture, which was by extension part of the original mission of the primitive Christian church. In contemplating the ruins of the ancient city, instead of focusing on decline, he mused on the persistence of biblical principles, and thought optimistically about the future:

How strange that among all the historic ruins of Pagan times, the idea now represented by living men is always a Bible one! Among the Pyramids, Moses, – in Nineveh, the Hebrew Kings, – at Athens, the preaching Paul, – here in Rome, the golden candlesticks of the temple, the unrecorded martyrs of the Colosseum. What they believed in lives, and yearly grows younger and stronger; but the beliefs against which they stood up have passed away.[21]

From 1860 there was an enhanced incentive for nonconformists and liberal-minded Anglicans as well as liberal Catholics to construct an approach to

---

[19] Edward Dicey, *Rome in 1860* (Cambridge and London, 1861), pp. 1ff, 257.
[20] M. C. M. Simpson, ed., *Journals Kept in France and Italy from 1848 to 1852 by the Late Nassau William Senior* (2 vols., London, 1871), II, pp. 93–168.
[21] William Arthur, *Italy in Transition: Public Scenes and Private Opinions in 1860* (London, 1860), *passim* and p. 312.

the archaeology and antiquities of Rome which would deepen the universal Christian status of the city in the present, through a dynamic dialogue with a past which was not the possession of any one religious or political group. In his enthusiastic characterisation of archaeology as an inherently Christian pursuit (insofar as a deeply felt interest in humanity was the offspring of Christianity), Charles Isidore Hemans, a liberal universalist, briefly a convert to Catholicism, who started the first English newspaper in Rome in 1846 and helped to set up the British Archaeological Society there in 1865, invoked Niebuhr's use of the imagination. Where Niebuhr in introducing his *History of Rome* had argued that 'Roman heroes and patriots [needed] to appear before us, not like Milton's angels, but as beings of our flesh and blood', Hemans saw communing with dead heroes in Rome as a way to recover the simplicity of Christ.[22] Arguing passionately against an antiquarian interpretation of archaeology, he praised Madame de Staël for trying to find the human interest in all things, and saw the contemplation of the pictures in the catacombs as a key to engagement with the earliest Christians.

It is melancholy to observe ... how much fruit of toil and learning has been forgotten – owing ... to the failure, on the part of many writers, to concentrate regards on general and permanent interests in their antiquarian pursuits. As other Sciences seek the vestiges of creation in the cosmic universe, the Archaeological should seek, as its permanent aim, the traces of moral and intellectual life in the relics of the far-off Past.[23]

Here the past could speak to the present in a resounding reinforcement of the evolution of Christian history – a conversation enabled by the work of archaeology, just as the scientific study of geology and biology underlined the divine presence in physical creation. Writing originally in 1865, and revising his work in the 1870s, Hemans took a magisterially overarching view of the evidence of the Christian monuments in Rome. His somewhat detached stance in relation to the details of critical method made fitting his allusion to the controversial *Vestiges of Creation*, which had made such a sensational impact on the British public in 1844.[24] Feeling it unnecessary to engage in debate about the historical status of Peter's and Paul's imprisonment in the Mamertine prisons, and expressing scepticism about Paul's

---

[22] Barthold Georg Niebuhr, *History of Rome*, trans. Julius Charles Hare and Connop Thirlwall (2 vols., Cambridge and London, 1828–32), I, p. 4.
[23] Charles Isidore Hemans, *Historical and Monumental Rome: A Handbook for the Students of Classical and Christian Antiquity in the Italian Capital* (London, 1874), p. 32; cf. his earlier *The Story of Monuments in Rome and its Environs* (2 vols., Florence, 1865).
[24] On which see James A. Secord, *Victorian Sensation: The Extraordinary Publication, Reception and Secret Authorship of* Vestiges of the Natural History of Creation (Chicago, 2000).

and Luke's stay beneath Santa Maria in Via Lata, he rose loftily above the issues raised by the study of the catacombs, observing that, 'where such high and deeply-felt interests are at stake, it is difficult to attain the intellectual independence requisite for impartial, clear, incisive and strictly just decision'. Everything none the less served to illustrate the 'Divine character and office of Christ'.[25] Archaeology was serving a resoundingly Christian end, and was not just an antiquarian means.

The probable and the improbable

Archaeology in Rome had been fraught by religious controversy from its beginnings in the sixteenth century, when the rediscovery of the catacombs provided material especially for conflicting interpretations of the role of images in the primitive church.[26] Only really in the early nineteenth century did a more consciously scientific archaeology develop – no less religiously inspired, but now concerned to base itself on the most modern and authoritative methodology – and to differentiate itself sharply from the apologetic work of the past. This development continued to take place under the aegis of the papacy – first with Padre de Marchi, SJ (d. 1860), who was appointed custodian of the Christian antiquities in 1841, and who worked on a huge project on the monuments of early Christian art, and then with Giovanni Battista de Rossi (1822–94), his pupil, who was one of the most energetic members of the Commission of Sacred Archaeology, set up by Pius IX in 1851. De Rossi worked closely with Wilhelm Henzen (1816–87), long-standing secretary of the German archaeological institute in Rome (from 1856), and with Theodor Mommsen (1817–1903), who directed the *Corpus Inscriptionum Latinarum* from 1853. He thus had impeccable Protestant connections, as well as links with German Catholic scholars, and with the distinguished French historian and palaeographer Léopold Delisle (1826–1910), for many years head of the Bibliothèque nationale. There were international celebrations on his sixtieth and seventieth birthdays in 1882 and 1892. His English translators and interpreters – James Spencer Northcote (1821–1907) and William Brownlow (1830–1901), both prominent Catholic converts – devoted considerable attention to establishing his

---

[25] Hemans, *Monumental Rome*, p. 365.
[26] See Simon Ditchfield, 'Reading Rome as a Sacred Landscape, ca.1586–1635', in W. Coster and A. Spicer, eds., *Sacred Space in Early Modern Europe* (Cambridge, 2005), pp. 167–92.

credentials, commenting that readers needed to have confidence in their guide because the subject was religiously so controversial. In support of his scholarly impartiality, they cited Henzen and Mommsen (emphasising his impeccable critical status by reminding readers that he had attacked the historical veracity of St Luke), alongside the High Churchman John William Burgon (1813–88), whose approach to the authority of Scripture was at the opposite end of the spectrum, and the distinctly anti-Catholic antiquarian and biblical scholar Wharton Marriott (1823–71). De Rossi's scholarly method of relating the critical study of texts to that of the material evidence (using also his brother's geological expertise) meant that, in Northcote's and Brownlow's view,

> this branch of Christian archaeology has now been brought so completely within the domain of science, that at this moment there is hardly any group of ancient monuments which can be classified so exactly and their history established so perfectly as the Roman Catacombs.[27]

De Rossi published his work (in successive volumes in 1864, 1867 and 1877) under the same title – *Roma Sotterranea* – as that of Antonio Bosio's pioneering book published posthumously in Rome in 1632. Northcote's and Brownlow's comment that 'The desire to have new light thrown on the beginning of Christianity was then [i.e. in the mid-seventeenth century] felt in the interests of science and religion' implicitly underlined this dual and interrelated significance in the mid-nineteenth century.[28] Whilst stressing the honesty and scrupulousness of Bosio, it was rhetorically crucial for them to underscore the greater historical sophistication and inductive power of de Rossi.[29] This was the more important for English readers, given Northcote's own reputation as a liberal Catholic who had been involved in controversy since the early 1850s about the status of the phials deemed by the Catholic Church to contain the blood of early Christian martyrs (a position reiterated by the Vatican in 1863).[30] In confronting this issue, Northcote had ultimately equivocated, on the one hand not wanting the church to stand or fall on such an issue, on the other being concerned about the potential spiritual

---

[27] James Spencer Northcote and William Brownlow, *Roma Sotterranea: Or An Account of the Roman Catacombs Especially of the Cemetery of St Callixtus Compiled from the Works of Commendatore de Rossi with the Consent of the Author*, new edn (2 vols., London, 1879), I, p. 50.
[28] Ibid., I, pp. vi–vii.   [29] Cf. ibid., II, p. 11.
[30] W. Meyer, 'The Phial of Blood Controversy and the Decline of the Liberal Catholic Movement', *Journal of Ecclesiastical History*, 46 (1995), 75–94. Meyer overstates the liberal Catholic decline in the context of debates about Christian archaeology in Rome.

side-effects of publishing chemical analysis of the phials. In this case distinct bounds had been put on the domain of science.

Despite Northcote's and Brownlow's rhetorical care – itself indicative of the on-going difficulties of establishing an approach which was not tainted by suspicions of partisanship – controversy continued. In their 1879 compilation of de Rossi's work, in arguing that the high antiquity of some of the remaining specimens of Christian painting in the catacombs was generally agreed, they referred to the opposing views of John Henry Parker, erstwhile Oxford bookseller and writer on historical architecture. Parker had founded the British Archaeological Society in Rome in 1865, was currently supervising many important excavations in Rome, including those of the house of Pudens and the Porta Capena (Figs. 9.2, 9.3), and had been working on an extraordinary and ambitious *Catalogue of 3,300 Historical Photographs of Antiquities in Rome and Italy*, which he published in several series between 1867 and 1879. His work on the catacombs had led him to argue that many of the paintings were later restorations of various periods from the fourth to the ninth centuries, and that the early paintings were of pagan subjects.[31] Before moving to Rome for his health, Parker had been an active member of the Oxford Architectural and Historical Society, where he was seen along with the historian Edward Freeman (1823–92) as a mediator between ecclesiology and science. The Society's emphasis was on the practical direction of church building and restoration in the present, based on systematic and on-site historical analysis; the latter methodology was to be carried by Parker to Rome.[32] The publisher of the *Tracts for the Times* in the 1830s and 1840s, he remained a friend of John Henry Newman, and perhaps in part because of his formative experience in a period of intense and bitter religious contention, he was the more concerned to establish and proclaim his historical objectivity. In his *Archaeology*, part XI, he remarked that:

As there is some delicacy required from an Anglo-Catholic in touching on such subjects in Rome, the centre of the Roman Catholic system, it has been thought better to give exact translations of what the monsignor [Barbier de Montault] has written, lest any charge of tampering with them should be brought. They are, in fact, works belonging to the History of Art, which is Archaeology, and have nothing to do with religious tenets; but it is known that great jealousy exists on the subject, and every care has been taken to avoid giving any just cause of offence.[33]

---

[31] Northcote, *Roma Sotterranea*, pp. 7–11.
[32] W. A. Pantin, *The Oxford Architectural and Historical Society, 1839–1939* (Oxford, 1939).
[33] J. H. Parker, *The Archaeology of Rome, Part XI: Church and Altar Decoration and Mosaic Pictures* (Oxford, 1876), p. 76.

Figure 9.2 Unknown photographer, *Recent Excavations – Chamber of the House of Pudens of the First Century, Excavated in March 1870, in front of the Church of S. Pudentiana, West Side*, 1870, Parker catalogue no. 1733, albumen print from collodian negative

This disclaimer may have been in part for the benefit of his reputation with the Catholic authorities in Rome, as much as for his English readers. The *Saturday Review*, reviewing Parker's *Mosaic Pictures of Rome* in 1877, commented indeed that it could not conceive why Mr Parker should have twice put in an odd kind of protest or apology about delicacy, or something of the kind, between 'a Roman Catholic prelate and an Anglo-Catholic layman'. Why on earth should not 'a Roman Catholic prelate and an Anglo-Catholic layman', or any other two people of any two persuasions on earth, work together about plain facts and dates?[34] But 'facts' and 'dates' were never that plain, as the bluster of the *Saturday Reviewer* (maybe Freeman himself) half-revealed.

[34] 'Parker's Mosaic Pictures of Rome', *Saturday Review* (31 March 1877), 390.

Figure 9.3 Unknown photographer, *Excavations 1871 – View of the Ruins of the Porta Capena, with the Gardener's Cottage, to Shew the Exact Site of It*, 1871, Parker catalogue no. 2222, albumen print from collodian negative

Parker's friend, the Rev. Richard St John Tyrwhitt (1827–95), who wrote extensively on Christian art and its pedagogical value, was invited by Parker to compare his photographs of the frescoes in the catacombs with those of the various mosaic series in Rome. Tyrwhitt referred to the tendency of both Catholics and Anglicans 'on the specially Protestant side' to distort their interpretative lens and to be partial in their datings. He felt that it was 'his duty to say what he observe[d], suppressing comment and even inference'. This led him to a middle way, acknowledging (with Parker) the later re-touchings, and some but not all of Parker's criticisms of Northcote (here he cited Marriott to argue against Northcote), but commending de Rossi's work, and pointing to the early evidence which did survive for the existence of the martyrs, and for early Christian adoption of pagan ornament. He went on to argue that the limits of representation and symbolism apparent in the first Christian centuries ought to content his own contemporaries; and to recommend mosaic and fresco as especially Christian art forms, which should be revived in the present.[35] Here he was making a point not just about the appropriate media for a revived Christian art – on which there had been much contemporary debate, itself stirring religious partisanship[36] – but also about the role of history in the present. A history rooted in agreed evidence could provoke creative re-engagement with the realities witnessed by the material remains. In this respect he followed the emphasis of Henry Reeve (1813–95), who had reviewed a number of works on the catacombs in 1859, emphasising that the growth of the church in Rome was 'the most important event in the propagation of the gospel amongst the gentiles'. Books by de Marchi, Louis Perret, Charles Maitland and Northcote were addressed by him alongside Wiseman's anonymously published popular novel *Fabiola* (1855), which traced the practices of the modern Catholic Church to the church of the catacombs. Reeve had been equally critical of all for their partiality, and looked forward to the publication of de Rossi's findings, but pointed out that they themselves would simply provide the basis for further interpretative analysis. His position was that, whatever the different meanings ascribed, it was important to emphasise the truths 'on which all Christians agree, as in the primitive faith', the most fundamental and resonant of which was that 'the very dust in these vaults is the dust of men who carried with them the faith of the New Testament to their

---

[35] Richard St J. Tyrwhitt, *The Art Teaching of the Primitive Church* (London, n.d.), pp. 101–37, 300–1.
[36] See Michaela Giebelhausen, *Painting the Bible: Representation and Belief in Mid-Victorian Britain* (Aldershot, 2006).

graves'.[37] The priority for Reeve, no less than for Tyrwhitt, had been to enable early Christian Rome to recover the significance which had been undermined by the overlay of ecclesiastical controversy.[38] Such controversy was not so easily removed, but whilst denominational differences remained, the interlinked stress on reputable historical method and on historical authenticity opened up a more complex discursive space within which Rome could be reconceived as a biblical city.

In this context, Parker's *Catalogue* was praised for offering a way of cutting through the theological disputes that had plagued the study of the catacombs. The historian Charles William Boase (1828–95) commended it both for its facts and specifically for the photographs which captured them.[39] Boase echoed others who, as early as 1868, lauded the 'absolute truthfulness' of the photographic image and, as a result, its utility as an aid to archaeological research.[40] History, at last, could be directly observed, documented and stored. One reviewer drew parallels between Parker's work and the Indian government commission to photograph all the ancient monuments of India; the Ordnance Survey of Jerusalem; Lord Lyndhurst's photographs of Sinai; and Piazzi Smyth's images of the pyramids; most of which, it was emphasised, were taken 'solely with a view to procuring aids to scientific enquiry'.[41] Parker himself was quick to distinguish his larger body of 'historical' photographs from those that merely represented the 'hack subjects' of Rome. 'Archaeology', Parker claimed, was 'true history applied to the existing remains of ancient buildings, it explained them and at the same time test[ed] the truth of history by them'.[42] His project was intended to be at once comprehensive and open to customisation – images could be used individually and in selected sets. This had a practical aspect: the photographs were both a resource for study and a vehicle to raise funds for his excavations. But they also constituted an approach to history, which was both self-consciously scientific and also imaginative – their sheer volume recognising the challenges of seizing the city, and the integrity of each and every selective view. Readers of Murray's 1875 *Handbook* – which significantly appealed to 'artistic and archaeological' visitors and specifically

---

[37] [Henry Reeve], 'The Roman Catacombs', *Edinburgh Review*, 109 (1859), 86–121, at 87, 88.

[38] Cf. Arthur Cayley Headlam, 'Christian Authority', in David George Hogarth, ed., *Authority and Archaeology Sacred and Profane. Essays on the Relation of Monuments to Biblical and Classical Literature* (London, 1899), pp. 408, 421.

[39] Charles William Boase, 'Roman Archaeology', *Academy*, 12 (1877), 255.

[40] J. Henderson, 'Photography as an Aid to Archaeology', *Photographic Journal* (18 April, 1868), 37.

[41] Ibid., 38–9.

[42] John Henry Parker, letter to John Murray III, 10 May 1874. MS, John Murray Archive, National Library of Scotland, Edinburgh, UK.

affirmed its eschewal of archaeological controversy – were directed to establishments in Rome and London where they could assemble their own selection of images.

Cheap to create, durable and reproducible, Parker's photographs simultaneously preserved the evidence of Rome's past and extended its reach. In a lecture at Oxford in 1870, Parker explained that his catalogue, at the time consisting of two thousand photographs, allowed the student to observe, at once, 'all the existing remains in Rome' without visiting the city.[43] Self-consciously disregarding his own interpretative lens, Parker worked tenaciously to ensure such verisimilitude, often having a site photographed multiple times to achieve optimum clarity and detail. Photographs were more than 'silent witnesses' to literary truths, and 'a building shewn in a photograph [was] as well seen as on the spot, sometimes better ....'[44] Photographs, unlike evidence *in situ*, could be examined at leisure. Fragments in one place could be compared against different examples, and students could base their evaluations on the visible remains rather than memory or written description. Such evidence could also assist in the understanding of other branches of history. Archaeology, especially that of Rome, according to Parker, was necessarily 'cosmopolitan', and had a wide cultural and geographical reach.[45] At a point when the new government's focus on Rome's national and secular role as the Italian capital was putting its cosmopolitan status under threat, Parker was the more keen to stress its universal significance. His archaeological principles needed to be the more forcefully defended against the politically driven and destructive 'restoration to make a display' that had begun under the French occupation and was proceeding apace in the early 1870s.[46]

Parker's photographic project was widely acknowledged as making a significant contribution to archaeology, even though reactions to his historical conclusions were mixed. Criticised by many for his erroneous translations of ancient authors, Parker was praised for his 'careful observation [and] critical comparison'[47] – an approach which many equated with the scientific essence of archaeology, in making history visible. His project was compiled at the high point of confidence in the medium's potential to

---

[43] John Henry Parker, *The Ashmolean Museum: Its History, Present State, and Prospects* (Oxford, 1870), p. 15.
[44] John Henry Parker, *The Archaeology of Rome, Part I: The Primitive Fortifications* (1874; London, 1878), p. vi; John Henry Parker, *Ashmolean Museum*, p. 14.
[45] John Henry Parker, *Ashmolean Museum*, p. 12.
[46] John Henry Parker, 'Excavations in Rome During the Winter 1870–71', *Archaeological Journal*, 28 (1871), 229.
[47] Charles Isidore Hemans, 'The Archaeology of Rome', *The Academy* (4 April 1874), 379.

capture details neither visible to the naked eye nor recordable by the human hand.[48] Certainly in the catacombs, where tight spaces, poor light, distractions from visitors, and preconceptions could alter what was seen or documented, the objective eye of the camera had a particular advantage. The Catholic convert and founder of the liberal periodical *The Rambler*, John Moore Capes (1813–89), asserted in 1873 that, *pace* theological controversy and resistance by 'extreme' Catholics, such visual 'transcripts' introduced observers to the 'actual realities' of history – to the 'literal truth' of the past rather than the exaggeration of legendary records.[49] In 1877, the writer and long-standing resident of Rome, William Davies, would argue that Parker's documentary project, which ultimately included plans and diagrams as well as photographs, was valuable because it was 'purely archaeological' – a practical illustration of the structural history of Rome rather than a treasure-hunt for valuable objects.[50] Parker associated archaeology with such practicality and therefore with conscious neutrality. Archaeology, he claimed, 'had nothing to do with Politics or Polemics'.[51] He was determined to present himself, in what were becoming rather old-fashioned terms, as a scientist, not an antiquarian.[52] Thus, regardless (and because) of the necessary subjectivity embedded in his representational project, he worked incessantly to insulate his photographic project from religious and intellectual debates. Archaeological observation and documentation, for Parker, had an immediate and intrinsic truth – one which the photograph could capture and preserve.

In 1879, the year in which Parker completed his larger photographic project, the historian Charles Merivale (1808–93) noted the importance of studying Rome's past (as those of Egypt, Troy and Mycenae) through her material monuments – including the primitive fortifications. The history of early Rome was still and would always be 'un grand peut-être'. The legends would always remain 'unsusceptible of reasonable proof ... They will, however, assume an air of greater probability if we become accustomed to people the long periods of time which preceded accredited history with generations of human beings who built themselves dwellings, and protected

---

[48] 'Stillman's Photographs of Athens', *Saturday Review* (2 November 1872), 575.
[49] [J. M. Capes], 'Historical Photographs of Old Rome', *Cornhill Magazine*, 28 (1873), 671–4. It is worth noting that, by the early twentieth century, more conservative Catholic scholars in Rome were once more emphasising that the skilful artist could record what the camera did not see: J. Wilpert, *Die Malereien der Katakomben Roms* (2 vols., Freiburg im Breisgau, 1903).
[50] [William Davies], 'Recent Discoveries in Art and Archaeology in Rome', *Quarterly Review*, 144 (1877), 80–1.
[51] Parker, *Ashmolean*, p. 11.   [52] Ibid., pp. 11–12.

their social life with regular and well-planned defensive works'.[53] Even if some of Parker's inferences went too far, this was better than the excessive scepticism of Niebuhr, Arnold and George Lewis, who discounted the possibility of history without literary evidence. Here the imaginative and novel potential of Parker's work was clearly recognised. Ironically, as someone who, despite a lifetime's commitment to the study of ancient Rome, only visited the city once (in 1845), Merivale went on to commend Jean-Jacques Ampère, author of *L'Histoire romaine à Rome* (2nd edn, Paris, 1865), when he extolled the benefits of contemplating history *in situ*. Ampère believed that he had caught the history of the Roman people in a new light by contemplating it from Rome itself: 'Events considered on the spot are ... rendered more distinct and life-like. Our recollection of them acquires a precision and a reality which make them present ... as if [they] were visible to us ...'[54]

For Christian travellers to Rome, and indeed for those who would never visit the city, the promise of such immediacy could be realised both through the provision of minute detail and by drawing attention to the differences between the Rome of the present and of the past. These approaches, often adopted in the same works, responded to a demand for realism at different levels. This was a complex realism, which embraced subjectivity. William John Conybeare and John Saul Howson presented their two-volume work on St Paul, which was to become a standard point of reference, as grounded in different dimensions of reality. The recreation of the unfamiliar historical context of the scriptural narrative was fundamental to understanding Paul's life and work: following in the footsteps of Paul, entering Rome 'by the same Appian Road, through the same Capenian gate' brought communion with him and the possibility of '[imagining] to themselves the feelings with which he must have looked upon the objects before him'.[55] Acknowledging that Paul's prospect of the city was very different from that of modern Rome – indeed more like modern London 'with all its miseries, vices, and follies exaggerated' – Conybeare and Howson nonetheless gave the precise distances from Paul's landing-place at Puteoli to Rome, and evoked timeless qualities of the landscape and season.[56] Thus the reader was encouraged to ponder both the physical reality of Paul's journey and the spiritual challenge he faced, which could be likened to nineteenth-century Christian urban mission. S. Russell Forbes' *The Footsteps of St Paul in Rome*, first published

---

[53] [Charles Merivale], 'Recent Excavations in Rome', *Edinburgh Review*, 149 (1879), 344.
[54] Ibid., 345.
[55] William John Conybeare and John Saul Howson, *The Life and Epistles of St Paul* (2 vols., London, 1856), I, pp. x–xiv.
[56] Ibid., II, pp. 440–1, 445–53.

in 1882, was self-consciously distinguished from previous works which had proceeded 'from a sentimental point of view'.[57] The need to stimulate the imagination was underlined, but within the framework of a 'rational and probable account' rooted in the latest archaeological, topographical and biblical research (a second edition in 1888 was produced in the light of 'new facts', also about the dating of the epistles). This precise form of probability was specifically differentiated from the much more speculative notions of the popular evangelical writer John MacDuff, who had evoked in the vaguest of romanticised probabilities contested moments of Peter's and Paul's supposed life in Rome.[58]

In terms of artistic visualisation too, Conybeare and Howson had called for 'real' representations – depictions 'of nature and reality' produced on the spot being preferable to the idealisations of Raphael (Fig. 9.4).[59] J. M. Wilson's 1852 volumes of scriptural landscapes had followed the same principle, claiming, somewhat implausibly, that topography was the least controversial aspect of biblical illustration. Whilst an engraving of the lower chamber of the Mamertine prison taken from a 'recent drawing' was reproduced as part of the record of biblical sites (one of only two Roman images), the text denied the historicity of the legend of Peter's or Paul's imprisonment there.[60] Inspiration was nonetheless to be drawn from the legendary context, perhaps the more so from the lack of rhetorical excess in the image (Fig. 9.5). In all these cases the emphasis on producing images 'on the spot' signalled various sorts of authenticity, but did not preclude an enduring picturesque sensibility, as is also apparent in some of the more composed of Parker's photographs (Fig. 9.6). Forbes in turn advertised a set of forty-three 'historical photographs' to accompany his book, 'illustrating the Footsteps of St Paul in Rome, places he actually saw, or connections with the early church'.[61] History could thus make the Bible live.[62]

---

[57] S. Russell Forbes, *Footsteps* (1882 edn), preface.

[58] Ibid., p. 74. John MacDuff, *The Footsteps of St Paul* (London, 1855); John MacDuff, *The Footsteps of St Peter* (London, 1877). Cf. Thomas Lewin, *The Life and Epistles of St Paul* (2 vols., London, 1851), a breathy narrative taking no account of interpretative controversy.

[59] Conybeare and Howson, *Life*, I, p. xiv.

[60] J. M. Wilson, *Landscapes of Interesting Localities Mentioned in the Holy Scriptures* (2 vols., Edinburgh, 1852), I, pp. iii–vi; II, pp. 280–1.

[61] Forbes, *Footsteps*, p. 90.

[62] And in so doing continue to serve a profoundly moral purpose. Cf. Elizabeth Prettejohn, 'Recreating Rome in Victorian Painting: From History to Genre', in Michael Liversidge and Catherine Edwards, eds., *Imagining Rome: British Artists and Rome in the Nineteenth Century* (London, 1996), pp. 54 ff, on the shift to historical genre in later-Victorian painting of Roman subjects, although (principally focusing on figurative subjects) she argues for the general repudiation of earlier-nineteenth-century moral themes.

The Palace of the Cæsars.[1]

Figure 9.4 *Palace of the Caesars*

Figure 9.5 *The Mamertine Prison, Rome.* Drawn by W. Linton on the spot. Engraved by E. Finden

Reconstituting Rome

The use of documentary photography in supporting the role of archaeology in keeping the past visible also drew attention to change over time – to the often day-by-day transience of perspective on the remains of the past and their relationship with the present. This was at one and the same time characteristic of the experience of modernity in a city undergoing rapid transformation and a critique of what modernisation was doing to Rome, the capital of a new Italy. Henry James observed in the 1870s that in various respects Rome had become vulgar and somehow more provincial as a result. Not only were ancient sites destroyed by urban development, but even those which were preserved were stripped of their former life.[63] Writing in 1877, William Davies lamented the changes to the Colosseum and the 'blank

---

[63] H. James, 'The After-Season at Rome', *Nation*, 16 (1873), 399–400; H. James, 'A Roman Holiday', *Atlantic Monthly*, 32 (1873), 1–11; '"Very Modern Rome" [London 188?], Henry James previously unpublished manuscript', *Harvard Library Bulletin*, 8 (1954), 128–40.

Figure 9.6 Charles Smeaton, *Catacomb of S. Domitilla – Brickwork at the Entrance, c. AD 100, Taken with Magnesian Light*, c. 1864–6, Parker catalogue no. 620, albumen print from collodian negative

monotony' that was the result.[64] The removal of the exotic vegetation which adorned the arena along with the Stations of the Cross erected inside destroyed what had kept the past intact and alive. In 1855, Richard Deakin had already precisely itemised the plants in the Colosseum, noting that they were threatened by the restoration and cleaning of the ruins. He hoped that his work (reissued in 1873) would help to discourage this practice. His invocation of the power of plants to recall 'to the memory time and place, and especially that of generations long passed way' was not simply the expression of romantic regret. To him flowers could 'form a link in the memory, and teach us hopeful and soothing lessons ... [and] tell of that regenerating power which reanimates the dust of mouldering greatness' (Fig. 9.7).[65] His rigorous catalogue was meant to give them objective and

---

[64] [Davies], 'Recent Discoveries', 47.
[65] Richard Deakin, *Flora of the Colosseum of Rome: Or, Illustrations and Descriptions of Four Hundred and Twenty Plants Growing Spontaneously upon the Ruins of the Colosseum of Rome* (London, 1855), pp. vi–vii.

Figure 9.7 *Interior of Colosseum*

tangible status – and to mark a very specific moment in time. By 1877 their absence had reduced the Colosseum to an empty signifier, which could neither conjure up the past nor act as an inspiration for the future. John Ruskin, for whom the relationship of plants and architecture was so fundamental a mark of vitality, wrote in 1874 to Joan Severn (1846–1924) that he needed to be busy in his last days in Rome, drawing a ruined cloister or a sarcophagus or rose thicket – all of which might have been cleared away or altered by the time he returned.[66] The monuments and the rose were given an equivalent significance in a task that evoked Parker's photographic project – with which he was sympathetic, and probably used to illustrate his lectures in 1873.[67] He wrote also to his cousin about a visit to the basilica of San Paolo where he painted the roses, before going to kneel by St Paul's grave: 'I got thinking – more rightly, I believe, than ever before – of St Paul's work, and what the power of it had been; and how what had been most put to evil use in it was only corrupted by evil men. How still his work was perhaps to be done – in great part.'[68] Here again the flowers both trigger reflection on the relationship between past and present and act as a metaphor for that relationship.

For Ruskin, the changing landscape of Rome in the 1870s symbolised not just modernisation but a form of religious corruption, to which early Christian Rome – the Rome of St Paul – could be counterpoised. The pope's new tobacco factory was now more prominent in the views from the west of the city than either the Palatine or the Capitol; and the 'documents of Egyptian religion – obelisks – [were] entirely eclipsed by the obelisks of our English religion, lately elevated, in full view from the Pincian and the Montorio, with smoke coming out of the top of them'.[69] In his writings throughout the 1870s and 1880s, Ruskin returned to focus on Rome as an emblem of intrinsic Christianity and as a foil to Protestant hypocrisy. His 1884 Slade Lectures notably presented Rome – one of the five cities whose history 'every fairly educated European boy or girl' should learn – as symbolic of Christianity's triumph over paganism.[70] In his autobiography, Ruskin recalled with contempt how 'zealous, pugnacious, and self-sure a Protestant' he had been on his first visit to Rome in December 1840, when he had parroted received opinions about the disease and idleness of the city, and in a blinkered way commented favourably on the causal relationship between Protestantism and both

---

[66] E. T. Cook and A. Wedderburn, eds., *The Works of John Ruskin* (39 vols., London, 1903–12), XXXVII, pp. 97–8: letter to Mrs Arthur Severn, 5 May 1874.
[67] Ibid., XXIII, p. 99.   [68] Ibid., XXIII, pp. xxxvii–xxxviii: letter of June 1874.
[69] Ibid., XXVIII, pp. 125–6: John Ruskin, *Fors Clavigera*, in E. T. Cook and A. Wedderburn, eds., *Works of John Ruskin* (39 vols, London, 1903–12) Letter 44 (June 1874).
[70] Ibid., XXXIII, p. 423.

industry and cleanliness in Switzerland. The association of dirt with Rome was already a well-established *topos* at that point, and one which was to persist, acting both as a sign of idleness and degradation and – insofar as it was juxtaposed to the extravagant spectacle of Catholic religious practice – as a sign of moral corruption.[71] The older Ruskin's intensely critical stance towards this sort of Protestant complacency – with which by inversion he associated the corruptions of modern industrial and commercial culture – led him to treat Rome as the metaphorical embodiment of values which the modern Protestant commercial world had lost.[72] Dirt itself was inverted in its significance: likening both evangelicalism and 'papal sects' to the pardoner, in *Fors Clavigera* in 1872 he observed:

Strange, too, how these two great pardoning religions agree in the accompaniment of physical filth. I have never been hindered from drawing street subjects by pure human stench but in two cities, – Edinburgh and Rome. There are some things, however, which Edinburgh and London pardon nowadays, which Rome would not. Penitent thieves by all means, but not impenitent; still less impenitent peculators.[73]

Direct engagement with the monuments of early Christianity was one way of figuring Rome as a deposit of fundamental Christian principles. In *Fors* again, in 1874, he wrote of standing by St Paul's grave, and being asked by a peasant where Paul was. When Ruskin replied that he was under the ground – or at least his body was, his head being at the Lateran – the peasant then asked where his statue was. Ruskin immediately undercut the anticipated scorn of the British reader for superstitious Catholic image-worship by making a savagely ironic reference to the notorious recent case of George Hudson, the railway speculator and swindler, designated idolatrously the 'railway king', who had been the toast of London society before being disgraced for fraud and dying after a long eclipse in 1871:

Such a wicked thing to ask for that! Wasn't it, my Evangelical friend? You would so much rather have had him ask for Hudson's![74]

---

[71] Cf. R. McTear, *Notes of a Continental Tour, and a Visit to Caprera by a Glasgow Gentleman* (Glasgow, reprinted from the *Glasgow Herald* for private circulation, 1865), pp. 66–8. See also Mark Bradley and Kenneth Stow, eds., *Rome, Pollution and Propriety: Dirt, Disease and Hygiene in the Eternal City from Antiquity to Modernity* (Cambridge, 2012).

[72] Cf. the imagery used by Cardinal Wiseman in his *A Few Flowers from the Roman Campagna Offered to the Immaculate Conception Charity* (London, 1861), preface: 'May the sneer, with which some may glance over the withered flowers of now almost plague-stricken Rome, relax before this symbol of evils nearer home, – of thousands of blanched cheeks – cursing lips at starving Coventry.'

[73] Cook and Wedderburn, *Works of John Ruskin*, XXVII, p. 312: Ruskin *Fors Clavigera*, Letter 18 (April 1872).

[74] Ibid., XXVIII, pp. 119–20.

Ruskin's use of Rome for critical purposes went deliberately and powerfully against the grain in a hegemonic Protestant culture. From a very different vantage-point, the Ultramontane Catholic Archbishop of Westminster Henry Manning (1808–92) preached an eloquent and polemical sermon in 1870 against the reduction of the capital of the Christian world to the capital of a nation. Pointing to the lack of 'public, domestic and personal commonwealth' in contemporary England – citing Lord Shaftesbury (1801–85), and James Greenwood's *The Seven Curses of London* (1869) – he generalised what had happened in Rome to signify a more pervasive neglect of Christian moral law.[75] As it moved into a new political identity, Rome continued to be a battleground for competing religious conceptions of value. As many liberals had predicted – indeed hoped for – the separation of the temporal and spiritual power of the Catholic Church created opportunities for the reclamation of elements of the religious past; even more conservative Catholics were to adapt to a different but no less controversial context. In this process, discussion of immediate political and religious issues continued to be interleaved with debate on the authority of the biblical city. *The Times* correspondence columns in May and early June 1871 – seven months or so after the annexation of Rome to Italy and the suspension of the First Vatican Council – published a heated interchange on the plausibility of the historical evidence for St Peter's having been in Rome.[76] The status of historical method – itself defined in different ways – took on a new relevance in the new political context. But Rome continued to refract the multiple projections of those who visited it or contemplated it. Frances Elliott (1820–98) wrote in 1872 of the imaginative resonances of the Mamertine, and of her ability – unaffected by historical scepticism – to picture the sufferings of St Peter through 'glanc[ing] round on the very walls where his eyes had rested'. Her wonder at Rome flowed in a stream of consciousness:

It is only at Rome one can spend such days, where the present and past meet, clash or harmonise, as the case may be; where one may rush from the catacombs to the marionettes, or from an appointment with the Holy Father to the hurdle-races ridden by real English jockeys. New phases of life open out with the passing hour ... and the spirit grows well-nigh paralysed under the overwhelming sense of its utter inability to grasp even a portion of the mighty whole which unfolds in all its excellence before it.[77]

---

[75] H. E. Manning, *Rome the Capital of Christendom* (London, 1870), pp. 9–10, 18–25.
[76] *The Times* (31 May, 5 and 7 June 1871).
[77] Frances Elliott, *Diary of an Idle Woman in Italy* (2 vols., Leipzig, 1872), I, pp. 317–18, 290–1.

With the publication of the first instalment of Rodolfo Lanciani's *Forma Urbis Romae* (a new map of ancient Rome) in 1893 came the prospect that such a comprehensive view of Rome, past and present, could actually be visualised.[78] Begun in 1867, the map (which ultimately included forty-six sheets) was intended to supply a cohesive graphic view of the city's historical transformation over time and include not only the monuments of the city (with their age distinguished by colour), but also the discovery of artistic objects and inscriptions useful for the study of Rome's history. Depicting only what was known from a half-century of excavation (and avoiding imaginative reconstruction), the map represented what the Roman historian, Ugo Balzani, would claim was not only a clear idea of the city's transformation, but one which (because of its long development and publication at the end of the first major period of excavation after unification, 1871–89) could 'furnish sufficient certainty' of Rome's history.[79] Certainly the fact that new building and archaeology had slowed considerably for most of the 1890s reinforced such a notion. Yet, by the late 1890s, fresh excavations renewed scepticism about whether archaeology could ever provide more than a partial view of the past. According to the historian and archaeologist Francis John Haverfield (1860–1910), Rome would always remain the central feature of one's personal landscape, although as a destination of pilgrimage it was 'in some sense a strange centre, a goal which when we reach it does not seem altogether what we expected'. Recent research in this respect had thrown very limited light on the early history of Christianity; ruins abounded, but most remained 'shapeless and enigmatic', their increased volume far from reducing the force of imaginative effort required to vitalise them.[80] Writing in 1899, the archaeologist and traveller David Hogarth (1862–1927) compared modern archaeology with conceptions of archaeology in the past. Engaging more than aesthetic sensibilities, contemporary archaeology had distinguished itself from antiquarianism. Yet, in its focus on strictly material remains, it had also distinguished itself from Sir Charles Newton's 'greater archaeology' – one that could encompass the entire breadth of the human past. According to Hogarth, the 'lesser archaeology' of the present day was a science 'clearly outlined but not unduly extensive' – one that depended on literary documents as well as material evidence and worked with history in the 'reconstitution of the picture'. The archaeologist's work of 'seeking, examining and ordering' had become

[78] R. Lanciani, *Forma Urbis Romae* (Milan, 1893–1901).
[79] U. Balzani, 'A New Map of Ancient Rome', *Academy* (5 August 1893), 117.
[80] [Francis John Haverfield], 'Ancient Rome in 1900', *Edinburgh Review*, 191 (1900), 106–7.

methodologically more rigorous, but neither literary nor material evidence was inherently more objective or subjective than the other.[81] Lanciani himself, as the secretary of the Commissione Archeologica set up in 1871 to supervise the archaeology of Rome, and well known to English readers for his eye-witness accounts of archaeological activity published in *The Athenaeum* from 1876 to 1913, as well as for his many popular works on Rome, had a clear sense of the crucial but delimited role of archaeology, not least in its symbiotic relationship with modern building in the city, which further complicated the acquisition of a sense of place. Like others, he missed in modern Rome 'the aged ilexes, forming as it were the frame of the picture'.[82] Yet, in response to those who bemoaned change, he invoked the history of archaeology to point out that Rome had 'always lived, and lived at the expense of the past'.[83] More sanguine than Ruskin or Henry James about modernisation, he emphasised that the 'process of destruction and transformation' (including the re-use of ruins, which had preserved them) was 'as old as the history of Rome itself'.[84] Although Rome was 'no more the Rome of our dreams', and was looking more like a modern capital, improvements were necessary, and 'in every great undertaking there [was] a period of transition'.[85]

By the turn of the century, the old claim that most English travellers entered Rome the 'wrong way' had an ironic resonance (not least as most travellers were 'shot into' the city by train from Civitavecchia).[86] Although the excitement associated with the first view of the city had not waned, there was a much more diverse sense of what such seeing encompassed. The objectification of the city, once anticipated from a distant prospect, had given way to a more consciously hybrid view – one that not only accommodated the subjective eye, but championed such individual seeing as the only way to arrive at a truthful understanding of Rome's history. Already in 1863, the American Protestant traveller and long-standing resident in Rome William Wetmore Story (1819–95) had ridiculed 'Englishmen carrying a Murray for information and a Byron for sentiment . . . finding out from them what he is to know and feel at every step'.[87] His own focus on the everyday in Rome, especially local Catholic traditions, albeit somewhat

---

[81] Hogarth, ed., *Authority*, pp. v–viii.
[82] R. Lanciani, *Ancient Rome in the Light of Recent Discoveries* (London, 1888), p. xxiv.
[83] Ibid., p. xii.   [84] Ibid., pp. xiv and xvii.   [85] Ibid., pp. xxv, xxviii.
[86] Originally suggested by Rev. Edward Burton in *A Description of the Antiquities and Other Curiosities of Rome* (London, 1828), pp. 4–6 and later cited by Henry Hart Milman in 'Via Appia dalla Porta Capena a Boville', *Quarterly Review*, 118 (1865), 34, 36.
[87] W. W. Story, *Roba di Roma* (2 vols., London, 1863), I, p. 7.

folkloric in tone, had been intended to serve a serious intellectual purpose in drawing the attention of a Protestant readership to the earnest lived quality of modern religious culture in the city. Moreover, it represented to him a more coherent way of capturing the identity of the place than ticking off monuments in a guidebook: '[t]he soil has been almost overworked by antiquarians and scholars, to whom the modern flower was nothing, but the antique brick a prize'.[88] A Catholic writer in 1864 had criticised sightseers (and Protestant ones in particular) for being so preoccupied with tangible proof that they saw Rome in narrow and disconnected ways. From his (partisan) perspective only a Christian traveller who approached Rome 'spiritually as well as geographically' could obtain a larger and more objective view of its historical significance. The New Testament scholar Arthur Cayley Headlam (1862–1947) emphasised that Christian monuments did not 'prove the fact but the belief': they could not provide evidence to solve points of theological controversy, but were valuable for showing 'the intense reality with which the earliest Christians held the most transcendent doctrines of their faith'.[89] Such views expressed from across the religious spectrum were only reinforced by the proliferation of archaeological discoveries that raised rather than solved difficult questions about the location of early Christian sites, as well as being co-dependent on the modernisation of the city, with all its increased challenges to legibility, whether topographical, political or moral. Such uncertainties coexisted with a range of contemporary approaches to scriptural analysis. The two most popular Protestant biblical encyclopaedias in Britain at the turn of the twentieth century were at opposite poles in their interpretation of the material evidence as they were about the historicity of the relevant biblical texts for the founding of the church in Rome.[90] For the individual Christian traveller reflecting on Rome from the perspective of the New Testament, the role of place could thus readily continue to map onto different conceptions of Scripture and tradition. The aperture of the lens had become wider, though. In 1875, Cook's travel agency (which had opened an office in Rome the year before) organised a Baptist pilgrimage to Rome, which was welcomed by Garibaldi.[91] In 1901 Lanciani could look back dismissively (as distinctly of another age) at Benjamin Jowett's attempt 'forty years ago to demolish blind and undiscriminating admiration for St Paul'. Archaeological and

---

[88] Ibid., I, p.7. [89] Headlam, 'Christian Authority', pp. 408, 422.
[90] T. K. Cheyne and J. S. Black, *Encyclopaedia Biblica* (4 vols., London, 1899–1903); James Hastings, ed., *A Dictionary of the Bible* (5 vols., Edinburgh, 1898–1904).
[91] J. Champ, *The English Pilgrimage to Rome: A Dwelling for the Soul* (Leominster, 2000), p. 192; cf. Piers Brendon, *Thomas Cook. 150 Years of Popular Tourism* (London, 1991; 1992), pp. 168, 172.

biblical evidence needed to be sifted from pious tradition, but the figure of St Paul 'appeals to us more forcibly than any other in the history of the propagation of the gospel in Rome'.[92] And even if St Peter had never set foot in Rome, his basilica could still be reddened inspirationally at twilight with an 'internal fire'.[93]

[92] R. Lanciani, *New Tales of Old Rome* (London, 1901), pp. 153–6.
[93] Story, *Roba di Roma*, I, p. 107.

Bibliography

Primary manuscript sources

Ancient Near East Department correspondence archives, British Museum, London, 1884/23–4.
Ashbee Papers, Modern Archive Centre, King's College, Cambridge.
Austen Henry Layard Papers, Add. MS 38979, British Library, London.
British Museum papers: C 13447, C 16893.4, C 17137.d.
de Beauchamp, J., *Itinéraire du Voyage fait par le Citoyen Beauchamp, Astronome et Correspondent de la cidevant Académie de Sciences, Depuis le Mois de Mars de L'Année 1781 jusqu'en Décembre, 1789*. 1790–1800, Cartographic Items Add. MS 15,331.2, British Library.
Egypt Exploration Society Archive, London.
John Murray Archive, National Library of Scotland, Edinburgh.
John Turtle Wood papers, British Museum, London.
Norfolk Record Office, MC 31/12.

Newspapers and journals

Academy
Antiquary
Archaeologia
Art Journal
Athenaeum
British Journal of Photography
British Quarterly Review
Christian Observer
Christian Witness
Contemporary Review
Cornhill Magazine
Critic
Dublin Review
Dublin University Magazine
Edinburgh Review
English Review

Examiner
Fraser's Magazine
General Baptist Depository
Girl's Own Paper
Good Words
Graphic
Hansard
Hogg's Instructor
Illustrated London News
John Bull
La Belle Assemblée
Leisure Hour
Manchester Times
Morning Chronicle
North British Review
Old Testament Student
Pall Mall Gazette
Proceedings of the Royal Geographical Society
Proceedings of the Society of Biblical Archaeology
Quarterly Journal of Prophecy
Quarterly Review
Quiver
Saturday Review
Sunday at Home
The Times
Transactions of the Society for Biblical Archaeology
Wesleyan Methodist Magazine

Primary printed sources

Acland, Henry, *The Plains of Troy* (Oxford, 1839).
[Ainsworth, William Francis], 'The Sites of the Doomed Cities', *New Monthly Magazine*, 102 (1854), 1–18.
Allen, Roland, *Missionary Methods: Saint Paul's or Ours?* (London, 1912).
Allen, William, *The Dead Sea, A New Route to India* (London, 1855).
Allom, Thomas, *Constantinople and the Scenery of the Seven Churches of Asia Minor* (London, 1838).
Andrae, Walter, *Lebenserrinerungen eines Ausgräbers*, ed. K. Bittel and E. Heinrich (Berlin, 1961).
'Archaeology for Girls', *Girl's Own Paper* (16 February 1895), 315–19.
Archibald, Andrew, *The Bible Verified* (New York, 1893).
Arthur, William, *Italy in Transition: Public Scenes and Private Opinions in 1860* (London, 1860).

Arundell, Francis Jago, *A Visit to the Seven Churches of Asia* (London, 1828).
Asher, Adolf, *The Itinerary of Rabbi Benjamin of Tudela* (New York, 1841).
Atherstone, Edwin, *The Fall of Nineveh: A Poem* (London, 1847).
Baggs, Charles, *The Ceremonies of Holy Week at the Vatican and St John Lateran Described* (1839; Rome, 1859).
Bain, Alexander, ed., *George Grote: Minor Works* (London, 1873).
Balzani, Ugo, 'A New Map of Ancient Rome', *Academy* (5 August 1893), 117.
Barrett Browning, Elizabeth, *Aurora Leigh* (London, 1857).
Bartlett, William Henry, *Footsteps of the Lord and his Apostles in Syria, Greece, and Italy: a Succession of Visits to the Scenes of New Testament Narrative* (London, 1851).
Barton, George Aaron, *A Year's Wandering in Bible Lands* (Philadelphia, 1904).
Beamont, William, *A Diary of a Journey from Warrington to the East in the Autumn of 1854* (1855; 2 vols., London, 1856).
[Beard, John Relly], 'Nineveh and the Bible', *British Quarterly Review*, 9 (1849), 399–442.
Beaufort, Emily, *Egypt Sepulchres and Syrian Shrines* (1861; 2 vols., London, 1892).
Beaufort, Francis, *Karamania: Or, A Brief Description of the South Coast of Asia-Minor* (London, 1817).
Beldam, Joseph, *Recollections of Scenes and Institutions in Italy and the East* (2 vols., London, 1851).
Bellew, J. M., 'The Church at Ephesus', *Art Journal*, 3 (1864), 10–11.
Besant, Walter, *Our Work in Palestine: Being an Account of the Different Expeditions Sent out to the Holy Land by the Committee of the Palestine Exploration Fund* (London, 1873).
Birch, Walter de Gray, *Biographical Notices of Dr. Samuel Birch* (London, 1886).
Blind, Karl, 'Troy Found Again', *The Antiquary* (9 May 1884), 197–203.
Bliss, Frederick, *The Development of Palestine Exploration* (London, 1906).
Blunt, Henry, *A Practical Exposition of the Epistles to the Seven Churches of Asia* (London, 1838).
Blyth, Estelle, *When We Lived at Jerusalem* (London, 1927).
Boase, Charles William, 'Roman Archaeology', *Academy*, 12 (1877), 255.
Bonomi, Joseph, *Nineveh and its Palaces: The Discoveries of Botta and Layard, Applied to the Elucidation of Holy Writ* (London, 1852).
Borlase, William, 'A Visit to Dr. Schliemann's Troy', *Fraser's Magazine*, 17 (1878), 228–39.
Box, John, *The Deluge* (3 vols., London, 1882).
[Brewster, David], 'Layard's *Nineveh and its Remains*', *North British Review*, 11 (1849), 111–35.
Brierley, Jonathan, *Our City of God* (London, 1907).
British Empire Exhibition, 1924 – Official Guide (London, 1924).
Brooke, Stopford, 'Theology in the English Poets', *Dublin University Magazine*, 84 (1874), 89–103.

Brothers, Richard, *A Revealed Knowledge of the Prophecies and Times* (London, 1797).
Browne, Henry, *Handbook of Homeric Study* (London, 1908).
Browning, Robert, 'Development', in John Pettigrew, ed., *Poems* (2 vols., London, 1981).
Bruce, William, ed., *Sir A. Henry Layard, G.C.B., D.C.L., Autobiography and Letters from his Childhood until his Appointment as H.M. Ambassador at Madrid* (2 vols., London, 1903).
Bryant, Jacob, *Dissertation Concerning the War of Troy* (1796; London, 1799).
Buckingham, James Silk, *Travels in Mesopotamia* (2 vols., London, 1827).
Buckley, Theodore, *The Great Cities of the Ancient World, in their Glory and in their Desolation* (London, 1852).
Bull, George, trans. and ed., *The Pilgrim: The Journeys of Pietro Della Valle* (London, 1989).
Bunbury, Edward Herbert, 'Anatolica', *Academy* (2 January 1875), 2–4.
 'Dr Schliemann's Trojan Antiquities', *Edinburgh Review*, 139 (1874), 506–44.
Bunsen, C. C. J., *Egypt's Place in Universal History* (5 vols., London, 1848–67).
Burder, George, *Village Sermons* (1798; 3 vols., Philadelphia, 1817).
Burton, Edward, *A Description of the Antiquities and Other Curiosities of Rome* (London, 1828).
Byron, George Gordon, *Childe Harold's Pilgrimage: Canto the Fourth* (London, 1818).
'Canon Farrar's Life and Work of Saint Paul', *Examiner*, 11 October 1879, 1313.
[Capes, J. M.], 'Historical Photographs of Old Rome', *Cornhill Magazine* 28 (1873), 671–4.
Carpenter, Mary, *Reformatory Schools* (London, 1851).
[Cassels, W. R.], *Supernatural Religion: An Inquiry into the Reality of Divine Revelation* (London, 1874).
Chalmers, Thomas, *On the Christian and Civic Economy of Large Towns* (3 vols., London, 1821).
Chamberlain, Houston Stewart, *Die Grundlagen des neunzehnten Jahrhunderts* (2 vols., Munich, 1899).
Champney, Elizabeth, *Three Vassar Girls in the Holy Land* (Boston: MA, 1892).
Chandler, Richard, *Travels in Asia Minor and Greece: Or, An Account of a Tour Made at the Expense of the Society of Dilettanti* (London, 1776).
Charles, Elizabeth Rundle, *Wanderings over Bible Lands and Seas* (1862; New York, 1866), p. 12.
Chase, Frederick Henry, *The Credibility of the Acts of the Apostles* (London, 1902).
Chateaubriand, François-René de, *Itinéraire de Paris à Jerusalem* (1811; Paris, 2005).
 Travels in Greece, Palestine, Egypt and Barbary: during the years 1806 and 1807, trans. Frederic Shoberl (1812; New York, 1814).
 Travels to Jerusalem and the Holy Land Through Egypt (1810–11), trans. Frederic Schober (1811; 2 vols., London, 1835).

Chesterton, G. K., *The New Jerusalem* (London, 1920).
Cheyne, T. K. and J. Sutherland Black, *Encyclopaedia Biblica* (4 vols., London, 1899–1903).
  'Pressing Needs of the Old Testament Study', *Hibbert Journal*, 1 (1902–3), 747–62.
The City and the Land: A Course of Seven Lectures on the Work of the Society, Delivered in Hanover Square in May and June, 1892 (London, 1892).
Clark, Francis, *In the Footsteps of St Paul: His Life and Labors in the Light of a Personal Journey to the Cities Visited by the Apostle* (New York, 1917).
Clarke, Edward Daniel, *Travels in Various Countries of Europe, Asia and Africa* (2 vols., Cambridge, 1810).
Clarke, Hyde, 'Destruction of Monuments in Turkey', *Athenaeum* (8 January 1870), 63.
  Ephesus: Being a Lecture Delivered at the Smyrna Literary and Scientific Institution (Smyrna, 1863).
  The Imperial Ottoman Smyrna and Aidin Railway, its Position and Prospects (Constantinople, 1861).
Clifford, John, *The New City of God: Or, The Primitive Christian Faith as a Social Gospel* (London, 1888).
Clifford, William Kingdon, 'The Ethics of Belief', *Contemporary Review*, 29 (1877), 289–309.
Cobbe, Frances Power, *The Cities of the Past* (London, 1864).
[Coleridge, Hartley Nelson], 'Acland's Plains of Troy', *Quarterly Review*, 66 (1840), 355–74.
Conder, Claude Reignier, 'Ancient Palestine and Modern Exploration', *Contemporary Review*, 46 (1884), 856–69.
  The City of Jerusalem (London, 1909).
  Tent Work in Palestine: A Record of Discovery and Adventure (London, 1878).
Conybeare, William John and John Saul Howson, *The Life and Epistles of St Paul* (2 vols., London, 1852).
Cook's Cruise to the Mediterranean, the Orient and Bible Lands (New York, 1903).
Cook, E. T. and A. Wedderburn, eds., *Works of John Ruskin* (31 vols., London, 1903–12).
Cook, Thomas, 'Travelling Experiences', *The Leisure Hour* (29 June 1878), 414–15.
Cooper, Robert, *The Infidel's Text Book* (Hull, 1846).
Copping, Arthur, *A Journalist in the Holy Land: Glimpses of Egypt and Palestine* (London, 1911).
Copus, J. E., *Andros of Ephesus* (New York, 1910).
Cox, Samuel Sullivan, *Diversions of a Diplomat in Turkey* (New York, 1887).
[Crolly, George], 'Nineveh and Babylon', *Dublin Review*, 35 (1853), 93–138.
Crouch, Nathaniel, ed., *Two Journies to Jerusalem: Containing, I. A Strange and True Account of the Travels of Two English Pilgrims Some Year Since . . . II. The Travels of Fourteen Englishmen in 1669 to Jerusalem, Bethlem, Jericho, the River Jordan, the Lake of Sodom and Gomorrah, &c. To which are Prefixed*

Memorable Remarks upon the Ancient and Modern State of the Jewish Nation (London, 1738).
The Crystal Palace Penny Guide: By Authority of the Directors (London, 1864).
Culross, James, *'Thy First Love': Christ's Message to Ephesus* (London, 1878).
Cumming, John, *Apocalyptic Sketches* (1848; London, 1850).
    Lectures for the Times, or, an Exposition of Tridentine and Tractarian Popery (London, 1844).
[Cumming, John?], 'The Spiritual Peril of British Travellers', *Fraser's Magazine*, 32 (1845), 62–71.
Cumont, Franz, *Les Religions orientales dans le paganisme romain* (Paris, 1906).
Curtis, George, *The Wanderer in Syria* (London, 1852).
Curtius, Ernest, *Ephesos: ein Vortrag gehalten im wissenschaftlichen Verein zu Berlin am 7 Februar 1874* (Berlin, 1874).
Curzon, Robert, *Visits to the Monasteries of the Levant* (London, 1849).
Dale, Robert William, *The Epistle to the Ephesians* (London, 1882).
    The Laws of Christ for Common Life (London, 1884).
Dali, Salvador, *Biblia Sacra* (Rome, 1969).
Dalziels' Bible Gallery: Illustrations from the Old Testament: From Original Drawings by Sir F. Leighton [etc.] (London, 1881).
[Davies, William], 'Recent Discoveries in Art and Archaeology in Rome', *Quarterly Review*, 144 (1877), 46–81.
Deakin, Richard, *Flora of the Colosseum of Rome: Or, Illustrations and Descriptions of Four Hundred and Twenty Plants Growing Spontaneously upon the Ruins of the Colosseum of Rome* (London, 1855).
DeHass, Frank, *Buried Cities Recovered: Or, Explorations in Bible Lands* (1882; Philadelphia, 1884).
Deissmann, Adolf, *Bible Studies: Contributions Chiefly from Papyri and Inscriptions to the History of the Language, the Literature, and the Religion of Hellenistic Judaism and Primitive Christianity*, trans. Alexander Grieve (London, 1909).
    Light from the Ancient East (London, 1910).
    New Light on the New Testament from the Records of the Graeco-Roman Period, trans. Lionel Strachan (London, 1907).
    Saint Paul: A Study in Social and Religious History, trans. Lionel Strachan (London, 1912).
Delitzsch, Friedrich, *Babel and Bible: Three Lectures on the Significance of Assyriological Research for Religion, Embodying the most Important Criticisms and the Author's Replies*, trans. Thomas J. McCormack and W. H. Carruth (Chicago, IL, 1906).
    Babel und Bibel. Dritter (Schluss-) Vortrag (Stuttgart, 1905).
    Babel und Bibel: Ein Vortrag (Leipzig, 1902).
    Die grosse Täuschung vol. I (Stuttgart, 1920).
    Die grosse Täuschung vol. II (Württemberg, 1921).
    Zweiter Vortrag über Babel und Bibel (Stuttgart, 1903).

Della Valle, Pietro, *Viaggi di P. della Valle il Pellegrino: Descritti da lui medesimo in lettere familiari all'erudito suo amico Mario Schipano* (1650–3; Brighton, 1843).
De Saulcy, Louis Félicien Joseph Caignart, *Narrative of a Journey Round the Dead Sea and in Bible lands*, ed. Edward de Warren (2 vols., London, 1853).
  Voyages Autour de la Mer Morte et dans les Terres Bibliques (2 vols., Paris, 1853).
'Description of the Plain of Troy', *English Review* (21 May 1793), 321–6.
'The Destroyed Cities of the Plain', *Good Words*, 1 (1860), 218–23.
'Diana of the Ephesians', *Critic* (28 June 1862), 627–28.
'Diana of the Ephesians', *The Examiner* (16 December 1876), 1412–13.
Dicey, Edward, *Rome in 1860* (Cambridge and London, 1861).
'Discovery of Vestiges of Sodom and Gomorrah', *Sunday at Home*, 11 (1854), 172; 12 (1854), 189–91; 13 (1854), 284–6.
Disraeli, Benjamin, *Tancred: Or, the New Crusade* (3 vols., London, 1847).
Donovan, Jeremiah, *Rome Ancient and Modern, and its Environs* (4 vols., Rome, 1842–4).
'Dr and Madame Schliemann', *Graphic* (20 January 1877), 62.
Drews, Arthur, *Die Christusmythe* (Jena, 1909).
Driver, Samuel R., *Modern Research as Illustrating the Bible* (London, 1909).
Drummond, Henry, *The City Without a Church* (London, 1893).
Drummond, Robert Blackley, 'The Acts of the Apostles: How Far Historical?' *National Review*, 10 (1860), 392–421.
Duguid, David, *Hermes: Disciple of Jesus* (London, 1893).
Duruy, Victor, *Histoire de l'Orient* (Paris, 1890).
Eddy, Daniel C., *Walter's Tour in the East: Walter in Jerusalem* (New York, 1863).
Edward, John, *The Men of Nineveh and the Men of England: A Sermon* (Oxford, 1855).
Edwards, Amelia, 'Cities of Egypt', *Academy*, 22 (1882), 389–90.
  'Cleopatra's Needle: With Brief Notes on Egypt and Egyptian Obelisks', *The Academy* (2 February 1878), 89.
  Pharaohs, Fellahs and Explorers (New York, 1892)
  'Was Rameses II the Pharaoh of the Oppression?', *Knowledge*, 2 (1882).
Egglestone, Edward, *Christ in Art: The Story of the Words and Acts of Jesus Chirst as Related in the Language of the Four Evangelists, Arranged in One Continuous Narrative* (New York, 1875).
Eliot, George, *Daniel Deronda* (3 vols., London, 1876)
Ellicott, Charles John, *Story of The Trojan War: An Epitome (From Classic Writers) of Incidents, Actions and Events which Occurred Before, at and After the Siege of Troy* (London, 1875).
Elliott, Edward Bishop, *Horae Apocalypticae* (3 vols., London, 1844).
Elliott, Frances, *Diary of an Idle Woman in Italy* (2 vols., Leipzig, 1872).
Emerson, B. K., 'Geological Myths', *Science*, 4 (1896), 328–44.
Emerson, James, *Letters from the Aegean* (London, 1829).

Engelmann, Richard and William Anderson, *Pictorial Atlas to Homer's Iliad and Odyssey* (London, 1892).
'Ephesus', *Sunday at Home* (16 August 1855), 517–20.
'Ephesus and the Temple of Diana', *Athenaeum* (6 September 1862), 312–14.
Essays and Reviews (London, 1860).
Eustace, John Chetwode, *A Tour through Italy: Exhibiting a View of its Scenery, its Antiquities, and its Monuments* (2 vols., London, 1813).
Evans, Arthur, 'Introduction', in Emil Ludwig, *Schliemann of Troy*, trans. D. F. Tait (London, 1931).
Everest, C. W., *Babylon: A Poem* (Hartford, CT, 1838).
Ewald, Ferdinand Christian, *Journal of Missionary Labours in the City of Jerusalem during the Years 1842-3-4* (London, 1846).
Ewbank, William Withers, *A Distinction Without a Difference: A Letter ... on a Sermon ... in Favour of the Restoration of the Jews* (London, 1850).
 The National Restoration of the Jews to Palestine Repugnant to the Word of God (London, 1849).
Faber, George Stanley, *Horæ Mosaicæ: Or, a Dissertation on the Credibility and Theology of the Pentateuch* (2 vols., London, 1818).
Fairbairn, Andrew, *'The City of God': A Series of Discussions in Religion* (London, 1882).
Falkener, Edward, *Ephesus and the Temple of Diana* (London, 1862).
Farrar, Frederic W., *Life of Christ* (1874; London, 1963).
 The Life and Work of St. Paul (1879; London, 1890).
Fellows, Charles, *Travels and Researches in Asia Minor* (London, 1852).
Fergusson, James, *Collected Opinions on Mr Fergusson's Theory of the Holy Places of Jerusalem* (London, 1865).
 An Essay on the Ancient Topography of Jerusalem, with Restored Plans of the Temple (London, 1847).
 Temple of Diana at Ephesus: With Especial Reference to Mr. Wood's Discoveries of its Remains (London, 1883).
 The Temples of the Jews and the Other Buildings in the Haram Area at Jerusalem (London, 1878).
'Fine-Art Gossip', *Athenaeum* (13 June 1885), 767.
Finn, Elizabeth, *Reminiscences of Mrs. Finn, Member of the Royal Asiatic Society* (London, 1929).
Finn, James, *Stirring Times, Or: Records from Jerusalem Consular Chronicles of 1853 to 1856* (2 vols., London, 1878).
Foot, M. R. D. and Colin Matthew, eds., *The Gladstone Diaries* (14 vols., Oxford, 1968–94).
Forbes, S. Russell, *The Footsteps of St. Paul in Rome: An Historical Memoir from the Apostle's Landing at Puteoli to his Death, AD 62–64* (1882; London, 1888).
Forchhammer, P. W., 'Observations on the Topography of Troy', *Journal of the Royal Geographical Society of London*, 12 (1845), 28–44.

Fowler, J. H., *The Life and Letters of Edward Lee Hicks* (London, 1922).
Frost, John, *Horrors of Convict Life* (London, 1856).
Froude, James Anthony, 'A Plea for the Free Discussion of Theological Difficulties', in James Anthony Froude, ed., *Short Studies on Great Subjects* (1867–83; 4 vols., London, 1898), I, pp. 202–40.
Fuller, Thomas, *A Pisgah-Sight of Palestine and the Confines Thereof* (London, 1650).
Gardner, M., 'A Walk in Athens', *Good Words* (January 1897), 31–7.
Gardner, Percy, *The Ephesian Gospel* (London, 1915).
  Exploratio Evangelica (London, 1899).
  'Fine Art', *Academy* (9 December 1876), 72.
  'Lay Liberalism', in *Anglican Liberalism: By Twelve Churchmen* (London, 1908), pp. 135–66.
  The Religious Experience of Saint Paul (London, 1896).
Gawler, George, *Tranquillization of Syria and the East, Observations and Practical Suggestions in Furtherance of the Establishment of Jewish Colonies in Palestine* (London, 1845).
Gell, William, *The Topography of Troy, and its Vicinity* (London, 1804).
'Geographical Notes', *Proceedings of the Royal Geographical Society*, 3 (1881), 737–8.
Gidney, William, *The History of the London Society for Promoting Christianity Amongst the Jews: From 1809 to 1908* (London 1908).
Girdlestone, Charles, *Twenty Parochial Sermons* (Oxford, 1832).
Gladstone, William Ewart, *Homeric Synchronism* (London, 1875).
  'The Place of Homer in History and in Egyptian Chronology', *Contemporary Review*, 24 (1874), 1–22.
  Studies on Homer (3 vols., London, 1858).
Glover, James, *The Destruction of the Cities of the Plain: A Poem* (Edinburgh, 1850).
Gollancz, Israel, ed., *Cleanness: An Alliterative Tripartite Poem on the Deluge, the Destruction of Sodom, and the Death of Belshazzar* (Oxford, 1921).
Goode, Francis, *Sermons on Various Topics of Doctrine, Practice and Experience*, (London 1838).
Goodhugh, William, *The Bible Cyclopaedia* (2 vols., London, 1841).
Gordon, Charles, *Reflections in Palestine, 1883* (London, 1884).
Gore, Arthur, 'A Walk through Athens', *Quiver*, 18 (1883), 735–8.
Gore, Charles, *The Epistle to the Ephesians* (London, 1898).
Gorst, John, 'Introduction: Settlements in England and America', in Arthur Winnington Ingram, ed., *The Universities and the Social Problem: An Account of the University Settlements in East London* (London, 1895).
Graham, Stephen, *With the Russian Pilgrims to Jerusalem* (London, 1913).
Grant, Neil, ed., *The Kaiser's Letters to the Tsar: Copied from Government Archives in Petrograd* (London, 1921).
Graves, Charles, *The Life and Letters of Sir George Grove, CB* (London, 1903).

The Great Original Grand Moving Diorama of the Holy Land (Glasgow, n.d., c. 1850).

Greenwood, James, *Unsentimental Journeys, or, Byways of the Modern Babylon* (London, 1867).

Greig, George, *God's Expostulation with Nineveh: A Sermon* (London, 1806).

Guinness, Geraldine, *The Story of the China Inland Mission* (2 vols., London, 1893).

Habershon, Ada, *The Bible and the British Museum* (London, 1904).

—— *A Gatherer of Fresh Spoil: An Autobiography and Memoir* (London, 1918).

Haggard, H. Rider, *The Ancient Allan* (London, 1920).

—— *Cleopatra: Being an Account of the Fall and Vengeance of Harmachis, the Royal Egyptian, as Set Forth by his Own Hand* (London, 1892).

Hale, J. R., ed., *The Italian Journey of Samuel Rogers, Edited with an Account of Rogers's Life and of Travel in Italy in 1814–1821* (London, 1956).

Halsted, Thomas, *Our Missions: Being a History of the Principal Missionary Transactions of the London Society for Promoting Christianity amongst the Jews* (London, 1866).

Hamilton, William John, *Researches in Asia Minor, Pontus, and Armenia: With Some Account of their Antiquities and Geology* (2 vols., London, 1842).

Handbook for Travellers in Syria and Palestine (London, 1858)

Harris, Helen B., *Pictures of the East: Sketches of Biblical Scenes in Palestine and Greece* (London, 1897).

Hartley, John British, *Researches in Greece, and the Levant* (1831; London, 1833).

Hastings, James, ed., *A Dictionary of the Bible* (5 vols., Edinburgh, 1898–1904).

[Haverfield, Francis John], 'Ancient Rome in 1900', *Edinburgh Review*, 191 (1900), 106–22.

—— 'The Roman World', in David George Hogarth, ed., *Authority and Archaeology: Sacred and Profane: Essays on the Relation of Monuments to Biblical and Classical Literature with an Introductory Chapter on the Nature of Archaeology by the Editor* (London, 1899).

Hawthorn, Harry (pseudonym), *A Visit to Babylon: With Observations, Moral and Political* (London, 1829).

Head, Barclay, *On the Chronological Sequence of the Coins of Ephesus* (London, 1880).

Headlam, Arthur Cayley, 'Christian Authority', in David G. Hogarth, ed., *Authority and Archaeology: Sacred and Profare: Essays on the Relation of Monuments to Biblical and Classical Literature: With an Introductory Chapter on the Nature of Archaeology by the Editor* (London, 1899), pp. 333–422.

Hechler, William Henry, ed., *The Jerusalem Bishopric, 1841: Documents Chiefly Reproduced from a Copy of the Original German Account* (London, 1883).

Hemans, Charles Isidore, 'The Archaeology of Rome', *Academy* (4 April 1874), 379–81.

—— *Historical and Monumental Rome: A Handbook for the Students of Classical and Christian Antiquity in the Italian Capital* (London, 1874).

The Story of Monuments in Rome and its Environs (2 vols., Florence, 1865).

Henderson, 'Photography as an Aid to Archaeology', *Photographic Journal* (18 April 1868), 37.

Henson, Hensley, *Apostolic Christianity: Notes and Inferences Based Mainly on Saint Paul's Epistles to the Corinthians* (London, 1898).

Herbert, Sydney, *Egyptian Art and its Influence* (Cheltenham, 1884).

Hicks, Edward Lee, 'Demetrius the Silversmith: An Ephesian Study', *Expositor*, 1 (1890), 401–22.

'Ephesus: A Postscript', *Expositor*, 2 (1890), 144–9.

'St Paul and Hellenism', in *Studia Biblica, Essays Chiefly in Biblical and Patristic Criticism, by Members of the University of Oxford: IV* (Oxford, 1896), pp. 1–14.

Higgins, Godfrey, *Anacalypsis: An Attempt to Draw Aside the Veil of the Saitic Isis or an Enquiry into the Origins of Languages, Nations, and Religions* (2 vols., London, 1836).

Highton, Henry, *A Letter to Sir Moses Montefiore: Containing Observations on the Subject of an Address Lately Presented to Him, Signed by Nearly 1500 Continental Jews* (London, 1842).

'History and Biography', *Westminster Review*, 3 (1858), 603–21.

Hobhouse, John Cam, *A Journey through Albania and Other Provinces of Turkey in Europe and Asia* (London, 1817).

Hodges, Richmond, ed., *Cory's Ancient Fragments: A Manual for the Chronologist and Mythological Antiquarian, Revised Edition* (London, 1876).

Hogarth, David G., ed., *Authority and Archaeology: Sacred and Profane: Essays on the Relation of Monuments to Biblical and Classical Literature: With an Introductory Chapter on the Nature of Archaeology by the Editor* (London, 1899).

ed., *Excavations at Ephesus: The Archaic Artemisia* (London, 1908).

Holland, Henry Scott, *God's City and the Coming of the Kingdom* (London, 1897).

The Holy Bible, Containing the Old and New Testaments, With Introductory Remarks to Each Book, Parallel Passages, Critical, Explanatory, and Practical Notes, Illustrated with Photographs by Frith (Glasgow, 1862).

The Holy Bible: Containing the Old and New Testaments, According to the Authorised Version, With Illustrations by Gustave Doré (3 vols., London, 1889–91).

Holyoake, G. J., 'Incidents in the Nottingham Debate: II', *Reasoner*, 10 (1851), 361–3.

Horne, Charles and Julius Bewer, eds., *The Bible and Its Story Taught by One Thousand Picture Lessons* (10 vols., New York, 1908).

Howson, John Saul, 'Ephesus', in William Smith, ed., *Dictionary of the Bible* (1860–3; 2 vols., London, 1861).

'The Seven Churches of Asia', *Contemporary Review*, 10 (1869), 317–19.

Hunt, William Holman, *Jerusalem: Bishop Gobat in re Hanna Hadoub: With Original Documents Detailing the Case* (London, 1858).

'Painting "The Scapegoat"', *Contemporary Review*, 52 (1887), 21–38; 206–20.

Pre-Raphaelitism and the Pre-Raphaelite Brotherhood (2 vols., London 1905).

Hutchinson, John, *Messages of our Lord to the Seven Churches of Asia* (London, 1882).

'The Intermixture of Races in Asia Minor: Some of its Causes and Effects', *British Academy* (1915–16).

Invernizzi, Antonio, ed., *Pietro della Valle, In Viaggio per l'Orente: le Mummie, Babilonia Persepoli* (Alexandria, 2007).

Irby, Charles Leonard and James Mangles, *Travels in Egypt and Nubia, Syria, and Asia Minor, During the Years 1817 and 1818* (London, 1823).

Isaacs, Albert Augustus, *The Dead Sea: Or, Notes and Observations Made During a Journey to Palestine in 1856-7, on M. de Saulcy's Supposed Discovery of the Cities of the Plain* (London, 1857).

Italian Journey: Being Excerpts from the Pre-Victorian Diary of James Skene of Rubislaw (London, 1930).

James, Henry, 'The After-Season at Rome', *Nation*, 16 (1873), 399–400.

'A Roman Holiday', *Atlantic Monthly*, 32 (1873), 1–11.

'"Very Modern Rome" [London 188?], Henry James Previously Unpublished Manuscript', *Harvard Library Bulletin*, 8 (1954), 128–40.

Jebb, Richard, 'Homeric Troy', *Fortnightly Review*, 41 (1884), 433–52.

'A Tour in the Troad', *Fortnightly Review*, 39 (1883), 514–29.

Keith, Alexander, *Evidence of the Truth of the Christian Religion, Derived from the Literal Fulfilment of Prophecy* (1823; Edinburgh, 1847).

Kelso, Russell Carter, *Amor Victor: A Novel of Ephesus and Rome, 95–105 A.D.* (New York, 1902).

Kenrick, John, *Ancient Egypt under the Pharaohs* (2 vols., London, 1852).

Keppel, George, *Personal Narrative of a Journey from India to England* (London, 1827).

Kinglake, Alexander, *Eothen: Or, Traces of Travel Brought Home from the East* (London, 1844).

The Invasion of the Crimea (8 vols., London, 1863–87).

Kingsford, Anna and Edward Maitland, *The Perfect Way: Or, the Finding of Christ* (London, 1909).

Kingsley, Charles, 'Great Cities and their Influence for Good and Evil', in *The Works of Charles Kingsley: Volume 13: Sanitary and Social Essays* (London, 1880), pp. 187–225

Hypatia: Or, New Foes with an Old Face (2 vols., London, 1853).

Sermons on National Subjects (London, 1890).

Kipling, Rudyard, 'Recessional', in M. H. Abrams, ed., *The Norton Anthology of English Literature* (1962; 2 vols., New York, 1986), II, pp. 1720–1.

Kircher, Athanasius, *Turris Babel, Sive Archontologia Qua Primo Priscorum Post Diluvium Hominum Vita, Mores Rerumque Gestarum Magnitudo, Secundo Turris Fabrica Civitatumque Exstructio, Confusio Linguarum, et inde Gentium*

Transmigrationis, cum Principalium inde Enatorum Idiomatum Historia, Multiplici Eruditione Describuntur et Explicantur (3 vols., Amsterdam, 1679).

Kitto, John, *The Popular Cyclopeida of Biblical Literature* (Boston, 1854).

Koldewey, Robert, *Das Wiedererstehende Babylon* (Leipzig, 1913).

Lagerlöf, Selma, *Jerusalem*, trans. Jessie Bröckner (London, 1903).

Lake, Kirsopp, *The Earlier Epistles of Saint Paul: Their Motive and Origin* (London, 1911).

Lanciani, R., *Ancient Rome in the Light of Recent Discoveries* (London, 1888).
  Forma Urbis Romae (Milan, 1893–1901).
  New Tales of Old Rome (London, 1901).

Landow, George, ed., 'William Holman Hunt's Letters to Thomas Seddon', *Bulletin of the John Rylands University Library of Manchester*, 66 (1983), 139–72.

Lane-Poole, Stanley, 'Discovery of Pithom Succoth', *British Quarterly*, 78 (1883), 108–19.
  The Life of the Right Honourable Stratford Canning Viscount Stratford De Redcliffe (2 vols., London, 1888).

Lang, Andrew and H. Rider Haggard, *The World's Desire* (London, 1892).

Layard, A. H., *Discoveries in the Ruins of Nineveh and Babylon: With Travels in Armenia, Kurdistan, and the Desert: Being the Result of a Second Expedition Undertaken for the Trustees of the British Museum* (London, 1853).
  Nineveh and its Remains: With an Account of a Visit to the Chaldaean Christians of Kurdistan, and the Yezidis, or Devil-Worshippers; and an Enquiry into the Manner and Arts of the Ancient Assyrians (2 vols., London, 1849).
  Nineveh and its Remains: With an Account of a Visit to the Chaldaean Christians of Kurdistan, and the Yezidis, or Devil-Worshippers; and an Enquiry into the Manner and Arts of the Ancient Assyrians (New York, 1852).
  Nineveh and its Remains, ed. H. W. F. Saggs (New York, 1970).
  The Nineveh Court in the Crystal Palace (London, 1854).

'Layard's Second Visit to Nineveh', *Fraser's Magazine*, 47 (1853), 434–44.

Leaf, Walter, *Homer and History* (London, 1915).
  'Introduction', in Carl Schuchardt, ed., *Schliemann's Excavations: An Archaeological and Historical Study*, trans. Eugenie Sellers (London, 1891).

Leake, William Martin, *Journal of a Tour in Asia Minor, with Comparative Remarks on the Ancient and Modern Geography of that Country* (London, 1824).

Leary, Lewis Gaston, *The Real Palestine of Today* (New York, 1911).

Leathes, Stanley, *The Cities Visited by Saint Paul* (London, 1878).

Lee, John Stebbins, *Sacred Cities: Narrative, Descriptive, Historical* (Cincinnati, 1877).

Lenormant, François, 'Dr Schliemann's Discoveries in the Troad', *Academy* (21 March 1874), 314–16.

Lerebours, N. P., *Traité de Photographie, Derniers Perfectionnements Apportés au Daguerréotype* (Paris, 1842).

Lewin, Thomas, *The Life and Epistles of Saint Paul* (2 vols., London, 1851).

Lewis, George Cornewall, *Suggestions for the Application of the Egyptological Method to Modern History* (London, 1862).

Lightfoot, Joseph Barber, 'Illustrations of the Acts from Recent Discoveries', *Contemporary Review*, 32 (1878), 288–96.

Lock, Walter, *St Paul the Master-Builder* (London, 1899).

Lomax, Alfred E., *Sir Henry Layard: His Adventures and Discoveries* (London, 1896).

London: The Babylon of the Apocalypse (London, 1836).

'Lot', *The Children's Friend* (1 August 1855), 180–6.

Lynch, William Francis, *Narrative of the United States Expedition to the River Jordan and the Dead Sea* (Philadelphia, 1849).

M'Cheyne, Robert Murray, *The Sermons of the Rev. Robert Murray M'Cheyne* (New York, 1861).

MacDuff, J. R., *The Footsteps of St Paul* (London, 1855).

The Footsteps of St Peter (London, 1877).

Macfadyen, Dugald, *Alexander Mackennal, BA, DD: Life and Letters* (London, 1905).

McGiffert, Arthur Cushman, *A History of Christianity in the Apostolic Age* (New York, 1897).

Mackennal, Alexander, *The Seven Churches in Asia Considered as Types of the Religious Life of Today* (London, 1895).

Maclaren, Charles, *The Plain of Troy Described: And the Identity of the Ilium of Homer with the New Ilium of Strabo Proved* (1822; Edinburgh, 1863).

Macleod, Norman, *Eastward* (London, 1866).

Half Hours in the Holy Land: Travels in Egypt, Palestine, Syria (1884; London, 1896).

'Note by the Editor', *Good Words*, 1 (1860), 796.

McNeile, Hugh, *The Covenants Distinguished: A Sermon on the Restoration of the Jews* (London, 1849).

Macpherson, John, *Apologetics* (3 vols., London, 1888).

McTear, R., *Notes of a Continental Tour, and a Visit to Caprera by a Glasgow Gentleman* (Glasgow, 1865).

Mahaffy, J. P., 'Modern Excavations', *Contemporary Review*, 29 (1877), 888–900.

Mallock, William Hurrell, 'General Gordon's Message', *Fortnightly Review*, 36 (1884), 57–74.

Mallowan, M. E. L., *Nimrud and its Remains* (London, 1966).

Manning, Henry, *Rome the Capital of Christendom* (London, 1870).

Martineau, Harriet, *Eastern Life, Present and Past* (3 vols., London, 1848).

Mason, Ellsworth and Richard Ellmann, eds., *The Critical Writings of James Joyce* (London, 1959).

Mason, W. H., 'Homer and Dr. Schliemann', *Macmillan's Magazine*, 34 (1876), 448–56.

Massey, Gerald, *Natural Genesis* (2 vols., London, 1883).

Masterman, Charles, 'Realities at Home', in Charles Masterman, ed., *The Heart of the Empire: Discussions of Problems of Modern City Life in England, With an Essay on Imperialism* (London, 1901), pp. 1–52.

Mathews, Shailer, 'Bethlehem: City of Children', *The Biblical World*, 10 (1897), 474.

Maurice, Frederick Denison, *Three Letters to the Rev. W. Palmer, Fellow and Tutor of Magdalen College, Oxford: On the Name 'Protestant', on the Seemingly Ambiguous Character of the English Church, and on the Bishopric at Jerusalem* (London, 1842).

Melville, Herman, *Clarel, A Poem and Pilgrimage in the Holy Land* (1876; London, 1960).

[Merivale, Charles], 'Recent Excavations in Rome', *Edinburgh Review*, 149 (1879), 321–54.

Meyer, Ernst, ed., *Heinrich Schliemann: Briefwechsel*, (2 vols., Berlin, 1953).

Meyer, Frederick, *Paul: A Servant of Jesus Christ* (London, 1897).

Mignan, Robert, *Travels in Chaldaea including a Journey from Bussorah to Bagdad, Hillah, and Babylon, Performed on Foot* (London, 1829).

[Milman, Henry Hart], 'The Appian Way: Pagan and Christian Sepulchres', *Quarterly Review*, 118 (1865), 34–77.

'Nineveh and its Remains', *Quarterly Review* 84 (1848), 106–53.

Milner, Thomas, *History of the Seven Churches of Asia ... Designed to Show the Fulfilment of Scripture Prophecy* (London, 1832).

Miller, Elizabeth, *The Yoke: A Romance of the Days when the Lord Redeemed the Children of Israel from the Bondage of Egypt* (Indianapolis, IN, 1904).

Mitchell, E., 'The Bibliography of Exploration: A List of American Writers upon Biblical Archaeology and the Work of Exploration in Bible Lands', *The Old Testament Student*, 6 (1887), 303–15.

Mitford, Edward Ledwich, *An Appeal in Behalf of the Jewish Nation, in Connection with British Policy in the Levant* (London, 1845).

'M. L. C.', *The New-Zealander on London Bridge: Or, Moral Ruins of the Modern Babylon* (London, 1878).

Montague, Edward, *Narrative of the Late Expedition to the Dead Sea* (Philadelphia, PA, 1849).

Moore, Thomas, ed., *Letters and Journals of Lord Byron, with Notices of his Life* (2 vols., London, 1830).

Morgan, Richard William, *St. Paul in Britain: Or, the Origin of British Christianity as Opposed to Papal Christianity* (Oxford and London, 1861).

Morton, H. V., *In the Steps of Saint Paul* (London, 1936).

Moulton, James Hope, 'New Testament Greek in the Light of Modern Discovery', in Henry Barclay Swete, ed., *Essays on Some Biblical Questions of the Day* (London, 1909), pp. 461–500.

Mudie, Robert, *Babylon the Great: A Dissection and Demonstration of Men and Things in the British Capital* (2 vols., 1825, London, 1829).

London and Londoners: Or, a Second Judgement of 'Babylon the Great' (2 vols., London, 1829).

Murray, Alexander S., 'Exploration in Greece', *Nineteenth Century*, 12 (1882), 381–90.

Newman, John Henry, *Parochial and Plain Sermons* (8 vols., London 1868).

[Newton, Charles], 'Discoveries at Ephesus', *Edinburgh Review*, 145 (January 1877), 204–28.

'The Discoveries at Olympia', *Edinburgh Review*, 149 (1879), 211–43.

Essays on Art and Archaeology (London, 1886).

Newton, Thomas, *Dissertations on the Prophecies, Which Have Remarkably Been Fulfilled and at This Time are Fulfilling in the World* (1758; London, 1832).

Nichol, Thomas, *Recent Archaeology and the Bible: Croall Lectures for 1898* (London, 1898).

Niebuhr, Barthold Georg, *History of Rome*, trans. Julius Hare and Connop Thirlwall (2 vols., Cambridge and London, 1828–32).

'Nineveh and Nahum', *Quarterly Journal of Prophecy*, 2 (1850), 170–82.

'Nineveh and its Remains', *General Baptist Repository and Missionary Observer*, 12 (1850), 360–2.

Northcote, James Spencer and William Brownlow, *Roma Sotterranea: Or an Account of the Roman Catacombs especially of the Cemetery of St Callixtus Compiled from the Works of Commendatore de Rossi with the Consent of the Author*, new edn (2 vols., London, 1879).

Nott, Josiah and G. R. Gliddon, *Types of Mankind* (Philadelphia, PA, 1854).

Official Report of the United States' Expedition to the River Jordan and the Dead Sea (Baltimore, MD, 1852).

Old, William Watkins, *New Readings of Homer* (London, 1860).

Oliphant, Laurence, *The Land of Gilead: With Excursions in the Lebanon* (London, 1880).

'One of the Seven Wonders of the World', *Quiver* (March 1862), 452–53.

Paget, Stephen, *Henry Scott Holland: Memoir and Letters* (London, 1921).

Paine, Thomas, *The Age of Reason* (Paris, 1793).

Parker, John Henry, *The Archaeology of Rome, Part I: The Primitive Fortifications* (1874; London, 1878).

The Archaeology of Rome, Part XI: Church and Altar Decoration and Mosaic Pictures (Oxford, 1876).

The Ashmolean Museum: Its History, Present State and Prospects (Oxford, 1870).

'Excavations in Rome during the Winter 1870–71', *Archaeological Journal*, 28 (1871), 229.

Parker, Joseph, *Apostolic Life as Revealed in the Acts of the Apostles* (2 vols., London, 1884).

'Parker's Mosaic Pictures of Rome', *Saturday Review* (31 March 1877), 389–1.

Pask, B. P., *The Apostle of the Gentiles: A Handbook on the Life of St. Paul* (London, 1877).

Paul, Charles Kegan, 'The Recovery of Jerusalem', *Theological Review*, 8 (1871), 407–14.

[Paxton Hood, Edwin], 'Recent Books of Travel', *Eclectic Review*, 8 (1865), 237–53.
  The Villages of the Bible: Descriptive, Traditional, and Memorable: Sabbath Evening Lectures in Brighton (London, 1874).

Peake, A. S., *The Bible: Its Origin, its Significance and its Abiding Worth* (London, 1913).

Petrie, William Flinders, *Janus in Modern Life* (London, 1907).
  The Revolutions of Civilisation (London, 1911).
  Tanis (London, 1888)

A Pilgrimage through the Holy Land, Explanatory of the Diorama of Jerusalem and the Holy Land, (London, 1851).

Pictorial Journey Through The Holy Land: Or, Scenes in Palestine (London, 1863).

Plumptre, Edward Hayes, *Popular Exposition of the Epistles to the Seven Churches of Asia* (London, 1877).

Pollard, Joseph, *The Land of the Monuments: Notes of Egyptian Travel* (London, 1896).

Poole, R. S., *The Cities of Egypt* (London, 1882).
  'The Progress of Discovery in Egypt', *Academy*, 23 (1883), 193–4.

Porter, Josias Leslie, 'The Dead Sea', *Encyclopaedia Britannica* (1771; 25 vols., 1877–88), VII.
  The Giant Cities of Bashan: And Syria's Holy Places (London, 1865).
  Handbook for Travellers in Syria and Palestine (London 1858).
  'A Recent Journey East of the Jordan', *The Sunday at Home* (18 August 1877), 522–4.
  'A Visit to Ephesus', *Good Words*, 22 (1881), 781–6.

Porter, Robert Ker, *Travels in Georgia, Persia, Armenia, Ancient Babylonia, &c. &c. During the Years 1817, 1818, 1819 and 1820* (2 vols., London, 1821).

Potts, Abbie Findlay, ed., *The Ecclesiastical Sonnets of William Wordsworth* (London, 1922).

Poynter, Mary Mason, 'A Day at Old Troy', *Athenaeum* (20 March 1915), 271.

'A Projected Railway in Palestine', *The Old Testament Student*, 3 (1884), 354–5.

Pusey, Edward Bouverie, *A Cause of Sermon on Solemn Subjects Chiefly Bearing on Repentance* (London, 1847).
  The Minor Prophets: With a Commentary, Explanatory and Practical, and Introductions to the Several Books (2 vols., New York, 1885).

Ramsay, William, *Asianic Elements in Greek Civilisation* (London, 1915).
  The Bearing of Recent Discovery on the Trustworthiness of the New Testament (London, 1915).
  The Church in the Roman Empire before AD 170 (London, 1893).
  The Cities of Saint Paul: Their Influence on his Life and Thought (London, 1908).
  'The Intermixture of Races in Asia Minor: Some of its Causes and Effects', *British Academy (1915–1916)*, 359–422.

The Letters to the Seven Churches of Asia: and their Place in the Plan of the Apocalypse (London, 1904).

'Saint Paul at Ephesus', *Expositor*, 2 (1890), 2–22.

'Ramsay's Letters', *The Interpreter*, 1 (1905), 451–5.

Rassam, Hormuzd, *Ashhur and the Land of Nimrod* (New York, 1897).

Babylonian Cities: Being a Paper Read before the Victoria Institute, or Philosophical Society of Great Britain (London, 1894).

Rawlinson, George, *History of Ancient Egypt* (2 vols., London, 1881).

Rawlinson, Henry, 'Notes on a Newly Discovered Cylinder of Cyrus the Great', *Journal of the Royal Asiatic Society* 12 (1880), 70–97.

Rawson, A. L., 'Palestine', *Journal of the American Geographical Society of New York*, 7 (1878), 101–13.

'Recent Books of Travel', *Eclectic Review*, 8 (1865). 239.

[Reeve, Henry], 'The Roman Catacombs' *Edinburgh Review*, 86–121.

'Remains of Nineveh', *Chambers's Edinburgh Journal* 11 (1849), 56–60.

Renan, Ernest, *The Life of Jesus*, trans. Charles Edwin Wilbour (New York, 1864).

Saint Paul [1869], in *Histoire des Origines du Christianisme* (2 vols., Paris, 1995).

Rennell, James, 'Concerning the Identity of the Architectural Remains at Jerash, and Whether They are Those of Gerasa, or of Pella', *Archaeologia*, 21 (1827), 138–47.

The Geographical System of Herodotus Examined and Explained, by a Comparison with those of other Ancient Authors, and with Modern Geography (London, 1800).

'On the Topography of Ancient Babylon: Suggested by the Recent Observations and Discoveries of Claudius James Rich, Esq.', *Archaeologia*, 18 (1817), 244–62.

'On the Voyage, and Place of Shipwreck, of Saint Paul, AD 62', *Archaeologia*, 21 (1827), 92–108.

Renouf, Peter Le Page, *Lectures on the Origin and Growth of Religion as Illustrated by the Religion of Ancient Egypt* (London, 1880).

'Review of Layard's Nineveh', *Christian Observer*, 49 (1849), 604–15.

Rich, Claudius James, *Memoir on the Ruins of Babylon* (London, 1815).

'Memoir on the Ruins of Babylon', *Mines de l'Orient / Fundgruben des Orients*, 3 (1813), 129–62, 197–200.

Narrative of a Journey to the Site of Babylon . . . Edited by his Widow (London, 1839).

Narrative of a Residence in Koordistan, and on the Site of Ancient Nineveh . . . Edited by his Widow (2 vols., London, 1836).

Second Memoir on Babylon, Containing an Inquiry into the Correspondence between the Ancient Description of Babylon and the Remains still Visible on the Site (London, 1818).

Richardson, Robert, *Travels Along the Mediterranean and Parts Adjacent: In Company with the Earl of Belmore* (2 vols., London, 1822).

R.I.P., 'A Visit to Ephesus', *Sunday at Home* (3 October 1885), 632–6.

Robinson, Charles, *The Pharaohs of the Bondage and the Exodus* (London, 1888).
Robinson, Edward and Eli Smith, *Biblical Researches in Palestine, and the Adjacent Regions: A Journal of Travels in the Year 1838* (1841; 2 vols., London, 1856).
　Later Biblical Researches in Palestine, and in the Adjacent Regions: A Journal of Travels in the Year 1852 (London, 1856).
Rogers, Mary Eliza, *Domestic Life in Palestine* (London, 1862).
Rome, Pagan and Papal; by an English Resident in the City (London, 1846).
Ruskin, John, *Fors Clavigera*, in E. T. Cook and A. Wedderburn, eds., *Works of John Ruskin* (39 vols., London, 1903–12), XXVII.
　Praeterita (London, 1885–9).
　The Stones of Venice (1851; 2 vols., London, 1880).
Russell, William Howard, *A Diary in the East during the Tour of the Prince and Princess of Wales* (London, 1869).
Sade, Marquis de, *Les 120 Journées de Sodome* (1785; Paris, 1931–5).
Salmon, George, *An Historical Introduction to the Study of the Books of the New Testament* (London, 1885).
St Clair, George, *Buried Cities and Bible Countries* (London 1892).
Saul, John, *The Sins of the Cities of the Plains: Or the Recollections of a Mary-Ann with Short Essays on Sodomy and Tribalism* (London, 1881).
Sayce, Archibald Henry, *Fresh Light from the Ancient Monuments* (London, 1893).
　The 'Higher Criticism' and the Verdict of the Monuments (London, 1894).
　Monument Facts and Higher Critical Fancies (London, 1902).
　Reminiscences (London, 1923).
'The Sculptures from Ephesus', *Saturday Review* (11 January 1873), 50.
Schick, Conrad, *Die Baugeschichte der Stadt Jerusalem in kurzen Umrissen von den ältesten Zeiten bis auf die Gegenwart dargestellt* (Leipzig, 1893).
Schliemann, Heinrich, *Troy and its Remains* (London, 1875).
Schwaner, Wilhelm, *Germanen-Bibel. Aus heiligen Schriften germanischer Völker herausgegeben von W. Schwaner* (Schlachtensee, 1905).
'Scripture Illustrations No 1: History of Abraham', *The Child at Home*, 1 (1841), 19.
'The Seven Churches in Asia', *Wesleyan-Methodist Magazine*, 8 (1862), 320–2.
Seymour, Thomas Day, *Life in the Homeric Age* (London, 1907).
Sharp, William, 'The Eternal City', *Good Words*, 40 (1899), 267–70.
Sharpe, Samuel, *The Early History of Egypt from the Old Testament, Herodotus, Manetho, and the Hieroglyphical Inscriptions* (London, 1836).
　Egyptian Mythology and Egyptian Christianity: With their Influence on the Opinions of Modern Christendom (London, 1863).
Short, Richard, *Saronia: A Romance of Ancient Ephesus* (London, 1900).
Simpson, M. C. M., ed., *Journals Kept in France and Italy from 1848 to 1852 by the Late Nassau William Senior* (2 vols., London, 1871).
Simpson, William, 'The Schliemannic Ilium', *Fraser's Magazine* 96 (1877), 1–16.
Smith, George Adam, *Assyrian Discoveries: An Account of Explorations and Discoveries on the Site of Nineveh during 1873 and 1874* (New York, 1875).

The Historical Geography of the Holy Land (London, 1894).

The Legacy of Israel: Essays by George Adam Smith with an Introduction by A.D. Lindsay (Oxford, 1944).

Smith, Henry and Roswell Hitchcock, *The Life, Writings and Character of Edward Robinson, DD, LL.D* (New York, 1863).

[Smith, Philip and William Ewart Gladstone], 'Discoveries at Troy', *Quarterly Review*, 136 (1874), 526–56.

[Smith, William], 'Bunsen's Egypt and the Chronology of the Bible', *Quarterly Review*, 105 (1859), 382–421.

ed., *Dictionary of the Bible* (3 vols., London 1860–3).

ed., *A Dictionary of the Bible: Comprising its Antiquities, Biography, Geography and Natural History* (3 vols., London, 1893).

[Smith, William Henry], 'Gladstone's Homer', *Blackwood's Magazine*, 84 (1858), 127–48.

Souter, Alexander and James Strahan, 'Ephesus', in James Hastings, ed., *Dictionary of the Apostolic Church* (2 vols., London 1915), I, p. 350.

Spurgeon, Charles Haddon, *Spurgeon's Sermons on Old Testament Women: Book One* (1960; Grand Rapids, MI, 1994).

Stanley, Arthur Penrhyn, 'Christ on Earth and Christ in Heaven', in Arthur Penrhyn Stanley, ed., *The Unity of Apostolical and Evangelical Preaching: Sermons Preached Mostly in Canterbury Cathedral* (London, 1859), pp. 350–60.

'Palestine Exploration', *Good Words* (1 March 1868), 173–6.

Sinai and Palestine in Connexion with their History (1856; London 1896).

[Stillman, W. J.], 'Homer's Troy and Schliemann's', *Cornhill Magazine*, 29 (1874), 663–74.

'Stillman's Photographs of Athens', *Saturday Review* (2 November 1872), 575.

Stokes, George, 'Recent Discoveries and the Christian Faith', *Sunday at Home* (4 June 1892), 485–8.

Story, William Wetmore, *Roba di Roma* (2 vols., London, 1863).

Stott, Grace, *Twenty-six Years of Missionary Work in China* (London, 1897).

A Strange and True Account of the Travels of Two English Pilgrims some Years Since., in Nathaniel Crouch, ed., *Two Journies to Jerusalem: Containing, I. A Strange and Time Account of the Travels of Two English Pilgrims some year since . . . II, The Travels of Fourteen Englishmen in 1669 to Jerusalem, Bethlem, Jericho, the River Jordan, the Lake of Sodom and Gomorrah, To which are Prefixed Memorable Remarks upon the Ancient and Modern state of the Jewish Nation* (London, 1738).

Sudermann, Hermann, *Sodoms Ende: Drama in fünf Akten* (1891; Stuttgart, 1894).

Svoboda, Alexander, *The Seven Churches of Asia* (London, 1869).

Swete, Henry Barclay, ed., *The Apocalypse of St John: The Greek Text with Introduction, Notes and Indices* (London, 1906).

Symons, Arthur, *Cities* (London, 1903).

Tait, Andrew, *The Message to the Seven Churches* (London, 1884).

Tayler, William Elfe, *Vestiges of Divine Vengeance* (London, 1854).
Taylor, Catherine, *My Journey to Italy Ten Years Ago: Or Extracts from Letters to a Younger Sister* (London, 1849).
Taylor, Robert, *The Diegesis: Being a Discovery of the Origin, Evidences, and Early History of Christianity* (1829; London, 1834).
Tennant, James, *The Destruction of Sodom: A Dramatic Poem* (London, 1845).
Tertullian, *De Praescriptione Haereticorum*, ed. Pierre de Labriolle (Paris, 1907).
Texier, Charles, *Description de L'Asie Mineure* (3 vols., Paris, 1839–49).
Thackeray, William Makepeace, *Notes of a Journey from Cornhill to Grand Cairo* (London, 1846).
Thomson, William McClure, *The Land and the Book* (1859; 2 vols., New York, 1874).
'Travels in Albania', *Morning Post* (11 December 1855), 3.
Tristram, Henry Baker, *The Land of Israel: A Journal of Travels in Palestine* (London, 1865).
  Scenes in the East: Consisting of 12 Views of Places Mentioned in the Bible (London, 1884).
  The Seven Golden Candlesticks (London, 1869).
Trollope, Anthony, *The Bertrams* (1859; Oxford, 1991).
Twain, Mark, *The Innocents Abroad, or, the New Pilgrim's Progress: Being Some Account of the Steamship Quaker City's Pleasure Excursion to Europe and the Holy Land* (1869; Charlottesville, VI, 2002).
'Two Months in Palestine', *Leisure Hour* (31 July 1869), 492–6.
Tyrwhitt, Richard St John, *The Art Teaching of the Primitive Church* (London, n.d.).
Van de Velde, Carel Willem Meredith, 'M. De Saulcy's Discoveries', *Literary Gazette* (22 April 1854), 377–8.
  Narrative of a Journey through Syria and Palestine in 1851 and 1852 (2 vols., Edinburgh, 1854).
Vaughan, Robert, *The Age of Great Cities: Or, Modern Society Viewed in its Relation to Intelligence, Morals, and Religion* (London, 1843).
Vaux, W. S. W., *Ancient History from the Monuments: Greek Cities and Islands of Asia Minor* (London, 1877).
V.E.G., *The Homeric Birthday Book* (London, 1890).
Vester, Bertha, *Our Jerusalem: An American family in the Holy City, 1881–1949* (Garden City, NY, 1951).
Wakefield, Gilbert, *A Letter to Jacob Bryant, Esq: Concerning his Dissertation on the War of Troy* (London, 1797).
Ward, John, *The Sacred Beetle* (London, 1902).
Warren, Charles, *The Temple or the Tomb, Giving Further Evidence in Favour of the Authenticity of the Present Site of the Holy Sepulchre* (London, 1880).
  Underground Jerusalem: An Account of Some of the Principal Difficulties Encountered in its Exploration and the Results Obtained (London, 1876).

Washington, George, 'A Day in the Troad', *The Monthly Packet of Evening Readings for Members of the English Church* (1 July 1881), 83.

Watson, Charles William, 'Egypt under the Romans', *The Monthly Review*, 3 (1843), 358–65.

Watson, Charles, *Fifty Years' Work in the Holy Land: A Record and a Summary, 1865-1915* (London, 1915).

Weizsäcker, Carl, *The Apostolic Age of the Christian Church* (London, 1895).

West, William, *The Spiritual Condition of the Seven Churches of Asia Minor* (London, 1846).

Westcott, Brooke Foss, *Social Aspects of Christianity* (London, 1887).

Westropp, Hodder M., *The Age of Homer* (London, 1884).

White, Arnold, *The Problems of a Great City* (London, 1886).

Wilberforce, Robert Isaac, *The Five Empires: An Outline of Ancient History* (London, 1840).

Wilkinson, W. F., 'Trojan Antiquities', *Leisure Hour* (11 July 1874), 438–45.

Willcocks, William, *From the Garden of Eden to the Crossing of the Jordan* (Cairo, 1919).

Restoration of the Ancient Irrigation Works on the Tigris: Or, the Recreation of Chaldea (Cambridge, MA, 1903).

Sixty Years in the East (London, 1935).

Williams, George, *Dr. Pierotti and his Assailants: Or, a Defence of 'Jerusalem Explored'* (London, 1864).

The Holy City: Or, Historical and Topographical Notices of Jerusalem (London, 1845).

Williams, Isaac, *Sermons on the Characters of the Old Testament* (London, 1856).

[Williams, Rowland], 'Rawlinson's Bampton Lectures for 1859', *Westminster Review*, 18 (1860), 33–49.

Wilmot, John, *Sodom, or the Quintessence of Debauchery* (London, 1684).

Wilpert, J., *Die Malereien der Katakomben Roms* (2 vols., Freiburg im Breisgau, 1903).

Wilson, Charles, *Golgotha and the Holy Sepulchre* (London, 1906).

Wilson, Charles, and Charles Warren, *The Recovery of Jerusalem: A Narrative of Exploration and Discovery in the City and the Holy Land* (London, 1871).

Wilson, J. M., *Landscapes of Interesting Localities Mentioned in the Holy Scriptures* (2 vols., Edinburgh, 1852).

Wiseman, Nicholas, *A Few Flowers from the Roman Campagna Offered to the Immaculate Conception Charity* (London, 1861).

Wood, John Turtle, *Discoveries at Ephesus, Including the Site and Remains of the Great Temple of Diana* (London, 1877).

'Ephesus, and the Temple of Diana', *Sunday at Home* (24 March 1877), 180–3.

Modern Discoveries on the Site of Ancient Ephesus (London, 1890).

'The Temple of Diana at Ephesus', *Girl's Own Paper* (12 August 1895), 137–41.

Wood, Robert, *An Essay on the Genius and Writings of Homer: With a Comparative View of the Ancient and Present State of the Troade* (London, 1775).
Woods, Robert Archey, ed., *The City Wilderness: A Settlement Study* (New York, 1898).
Wordsworth, Christopher, *Lectures on the Apocalypse* (London, 1847).
Wordsworth, William, 'Missions and Travels', in Abbie Findlay Potts, ed., *The Ecclesiastical Sonnets of William Wordsworth* (London, 1922).
Wright William, B., *Ancient Cities from the Dawn to the Daylight* (New York, 1899).
Cities of Saint Paul: Beacons of the Past Rekindled for the Present (London, 1905).
'The Land of the Giant Cities', *Leisure Hour* (13 June 1874), 379–83; (25 July 1874), 475–8; (15 August 1874), 521–4; (19 September 1874), 597–600; (17 October 1874), 661–4; (28 November 1874), 760–4; (19 December 1874), 806–11.
Wylie, James, *The Modern Judea, Ammon, Moab, and Edom, Compared with Ancient Prophecy with Notes Illustrative of Biblical Subjects* (Glasgow, 1841; 1850).
Scenes from the Bible (Glasgow, 1844).

Secondary unpublished

Bryant Davies, Rachel, 'Imaginary Cities: Troy and Carthage in the Long Nineteenth Century' (unpublished thesis: University of Cambridge, 2011).
Kildahl, Phillip A., 'British and American Reactions to Layard's Discoveries in Assyria (1845–1860)' (Ph.D. thesis, University of Minnesota, 1959).

Secondary

Aiken, Edward, *Scriptural Geography: Portraying the Holy Land* (London, 2010).
Allan, Susan Heuck, *Finding the Walls of Troy* (Berkeley, CA, 1998).
Allen, William, 'Analysis of Abdul Hamid's Gift Albums', *Journal of Turkish Studies*, 12 (1988), 33–7.
Anderson, Amanda, 'George Eliot and the Jewish Question', *Yale Journal of Criticism*, 10 (1997), 39–61.
Anderson, Margaret Lavinia, '"Down in Turkey, Far Away": Human Rights, the Armenian Massacres, and Orientalism in Wilhelmine Germany', *Journal of Modern History*, 79 (2007), 80–111.
Anderson, Patricia, *The Printed Image and the Transformation of Popular Culture, 1790–1860* (Oxford, 1994).
Armstrong, Carol, *Scenes in a Library* (Cambridge, MA, 1998).
Arnold, Bill T. and David. B. Weisberg, 'A Centennial Review of Friedrich Delitzsch's "Babel and Bibel" Lectures', *Journal of Biblical Literature*, 121 (2002), 441–57.
Arnold, Catherine, *Bedlam: London and its Mad* (2008; London, 2009).

Arscott, Caroline, 'The Representation of the City in the Visual Arts', in Martin Daunton, ed., *The Cambridge Urban History of Britain 1840–1950* (Cambridge, 2000), pp. 811–32.

Aston, Nigel, 'Horne and Heterodoxy: The Defence of Anglican Beliefs in Late Enlightenment,' *English Historical Review*, 108 (1993), 895–919.

Attenborough, John, *A Living Memory: Hodder and Stoughton Publishers 1868–1975* (London, 1975).

Barr, James, *Fundamentalism* (1978; London, 1981).

Bar-Yosef, Eitan, *The Holy Land in English Culture 1799–1917: Palestine and the Question of Orientalism* (Oxford, 2005).

'Jerusalem, My Happy Home: The Palestine Exhibition and the Limits of the Orientalist Imagination', in Jim Buzard, Joseph Childers and Eileen Gillooly, eds., *Victorian Prism: Refractions of the Crystal Palace* (Charlottesville, VI, 2007)

Barthes, Roland, *Camera Lucida: Reflections on Photography* (New York, 1981).

Bartlett, John R., 'What has Archaeology to Do with the Bible: or Vice Versa?' in John R. Bartlett, ed., *Archaeology and Biblical Interpretation* (London, 1997), pp. 1–19.

Beard, Mary, *Pompeii: The Life of a Roman Town* (London 2008).

Bebbington, David, 'The City, the Countryside, and the Social Gospel in Late Victorian Nonconformity', in Derek Baker, ed., *The Church in Town and Countryside* (Oxford, 1979), pp. 415–26.

The Mind of Gladstone (Oxford, 2004).

Bell, Duncan, 'From Ancient to Modern in Victorian Imperial Thought', *Historical Journal*, 49 (2006), 735–59.

Ben-Arieh, Yehoshua and Moshe Davis, eds., *Jerusalem in the Mind of the Western World, 1800–1948* (Westport, CT, 1997).

Jerusalem in the Nineteenth Century (Tel Aviv, 1989).

Jerusalem in the Nineteenth Century: Emergence of the New City (Jerusalem, 1986).

Jerusalem in the Nineteenth Century: The Old City (Jerusalem, 1984).

Painting the Holy Land in the Nineteenth Century (Jerusalem, 1997).

The Rediscovery of the Holy Land in the Nineteenth Century (Jerusalem, 1979)

'William F. Lynch's Expedition to the River Jordan and the Dead Sea, 1847-8', *Prologue*, 5 (1973), 15–21.

Bendiner, Kenneth, 'William Holman Hunt's "The Scapegoat"', *Pantheon*, 45 (1987), 124–8.

Bindman, David, 'The English Apocalypse', in F. Carey, ed., *The Apocalypse and the Shape of Things to Come* (London, 1999), pp. 208–69.

Black, Jeremy, *Maps and Politics* (London, 1997).

Blumberg, Arnold, *Zion before Zionism, 1838–1880* (Syracuse, NY, 1985).

Boase, R. S., 'Biblical Illustration in Nineteenth-Century English Art', *Journal of the Warburg and Courtauld Institutes*, 29 (1966), 349–67.

Bohrer, Frederick, 'Inventing Assyria: Exoticism and Reception in Nineteenth-Century England and France', *Art Bulletin*, 80 (1998), 336–56.
  Orientalism and Visual Culture: Imagining Mesopotamia in Nineteenth-Century Europe (Cambridge, 2003).
  'The Printed Orient: The Production of A. H. Layard's Earliest Works', *Culture and History*, 11 (1992), 85–105.
Boime, Albert, 'William Holman Hunt's *The Scapegoat*: Rite of Forgiveness/Transference of Blame', *The Art Bulletin*, 84 (2002), 94–114.
Bradley, Mark and Kenneth Stow, eds., *Rome, Pollution and Propriety: Dirt, Disease and Hygiene in the Eternal City from Antiquity to Modernity* (Cambridge, 2012).
Brady, Sam, *Masculinity and Male Homosexuality in Britain 1861–1913* (Basingstoke, 2005).
Braunfels, Wolfgang, ed., *Lexikon der christlichen Ikonographie* (8 vols., Freiburg, 1968–76).
Brendon, Piers, *Thomas Cook: 150 Years of Popular Tourism* (1991; London, 1992).
Briggs, Asa, *Victorian Cities* (London, 1963).
Brown, Callum, 'Did Urbanization Secularize Britain?' *Urban History Yearbook* (1988), 1–14.
  Religion and Society in Scotland since 1707 (London, 1997).
Brown, Stewart J., *Thomas Chalmers and the Godly Commonwealth in Scotland* (Oxford, 1982).
Brunt, Lodewijk, 'The Ethnography of "Babylon": The Rhetoric of Fear and the Study of London, 1850–1914', *City and Society*, 4 (1990), 77–87.
Butlin, Robin, 'George Adam Smith and the Historical Geography of the Holy Land: Contents, Contexts and Connections', *Journal of Historical Geography*, 14 (1988), 381–404.
Buzard, James, *The Beaten Track: European Tourism, Literature, and the Ways to Culture, 1800–1918* (Oxford, 1993).
Campbell, Iain, *Fixing the Indemnity: The Life and Work of George Adam Smith* (Carlisle, 2004).
Carden, Michael, *Sodomy: History of a Christian Myth* (London, 2004).
Carhart, Michael, *The Science of Culture in Enlightenment Germany* (Cambridge, MA, 2005).
Carpenter, Mary, *Imperial Bibles, Domestic Bodies* (Athens, OH, 2003).
Çelik, Zeynep, *Displaying the Orient: Architecture of Islam at Nineteenth-Century World's Fairs* (Berkeley, CA, 1992).
Chadwick, Owen, *Hensley Henson* (Oxford, 1983).
  The Victorian Church (2 vols., London, 1966–70).
Challis, Debbie, *From the Harpy Tomb to the Wonders of Ephesus: British Archaeologists in the Ottoman Empire, 1840–1880* (London, 2008).
Champ, J. *The English Pilgrimage to Rome: A Dwelling for the Soul* (Leominster, 2000).

Chapman, Mark, *The Coming Crisis: The Impact of Eschatology on Theology in Edwardian England* (Sheffield, 2001).

Chevedden, Paul, *The Photographic Heritage of the Middle East: An Exhibition of Early Photographs of Egypt, Palestine, Syria, Turkey, Greece & Iran, 1849–1893* (Malibu, CA, 1981).

Churchill, Charles, 'The Times (1764)', in Paul Hallam, ed., *The Book of Sodom* (London, 1993).

Çizgen, Engin, *Photography in the Ottoman Empire, 1839–1919* (Istanbul, 1987).

Clark, Christopher, *Kaiser Wilhelm II: A Life in Power* (London, 2000).

Cline, Eric, *Jerusalem Besieged: From Ancient Canaan to Modern Israel* (Ann Arbor, MI, 2004).

Cocks, Harry, 'The Discovery of Sodom, 1851', *Representations*, 112 (2010), 1–26.
 'Sodom and Gomorrah, 14th January 1851', *Victorian Review*, 36 (2010), 27–30

Coleman, Simon, 'A Tale of Two Centres? Representing Palestine to the British in the Nineteenth Century', *Mobilities*, 2 (2007), 331–45.

Coltman, Viccy, *Classical Sculpture and the Culture of Collecting in Britain since 1760* (Oxford, 2009).

Cook, Matt, *London and the Culture of Homosexuality, 1885–1914* (Cambridge, 2003).

Cowling, Martha, ed., *The Price of Beauty: Edwin Long's Babylonian Marriage Market (1875)* (London, 2004).

Crawford, Alan, *C. R. Ashbee: Architect, Designer and Romantic Socialist* (London, 1985).

Crombie, Kelvin, *A Jewish Bishop in Jerusalem* (Jerusalem, 2006).

Crook, J. M., *The Greek Revival: Neo-Classical Attitudes in British Architecture 1760–1870* (London, 1972).

Daunton, Martin, ed., *The Cambridge Urban History of Britain: vol. III, 1840–1950* (Cambridge, 2000).

Davis, John, *The Landscape of Belief: Encountering the Holy Land in Nineteenth-Century American Art and Culture* (Princeton, NJ, 1996).

Davis, Thomas, *Shifting Sands: The Rise and Fall of Biblical Archaeology* (Oxford, 2004).

Davison, Roderic, *Reform in the Ottoman Empire, 1856–1876* (Princeton, NJ, 1963).

DeLaura, David, *Hebrew and Hellene in Victorian Britain* (Austin, TX, 1970).

Deringil, Selim, *The Well-Protected Domains: Ideology and the Legitimation of Power in the Ottoman Empire, 1876–1909* (Istanbul, 1998).

Ditchfield, Simon, 'Reading Rome as a Sacred Landscape, ca. 1586–1635', in W. Coster and A. Spicer, eds., *Sacred Space in Early Modern Europe* (Cambridge, 2005), pp. 167–92.

Drower, Margaret, *Flinders Petrie: A Life in Archaeology* (London, 1985).

Dyson, Stephen, *Ancient Marbles to American Shores* (Pennsylvania, PA, 1998).
 In Pursuit of Ancient Pasts: A History of Classical Archaeology in the Nineteenth and Twentieth Centuries (London, 2006).

Edwards, Catharine, ed., *Roman Presences: Receptions of Rome in European Culture, 1789–1945* (Cambridge, 1999).

Elali, Giries Nicola, *Bethlehem, the Immortal Town*, trans. Issa Masson (Jerusalem, 1991).

Eliav, Mordechai, *Britain and the Holy Land, 1838–1914: Selected Documents from the British Consulate in Jerusalem* (Jerusalem, 1997).

Elsner, Jas and Ian Rutherford, eds., *Pilgrimage in Greco-Roman and Early Christian Antiquity: Seeing the Gods* (Oxford, 2007).

Engelsing, Rolf, '*Wie Sodom und Gomorrha . . .*' *Die Zerstörung der Städte* (Berlin, 1979).

Erdozain, Dominic, 'The Secularization of Sin', *Journal of Ecclesiastical History*, 62 (2011), 59–88.

Feaver, William, *The Art of John Martin* (Oxford, 1975).

Field, Geoffrey, *Evangelist of Race: The Germanic Vision of Houston Stewart Chamberlain* (New York, 1981).

Fields, Weston W., *Sodom and Gomorrah: History and Motif in Biblical Narrative* (Sheffield, 1997).

Finkel, Israel and Michael Seymour, eds., *Babylon: Myth and Reality* (London, 2008).

Fleming, Katherine, *The Muslim Bonaparte: Diplomacy and Orientalism in Ali Pasha's Greece* (Princeton, NJ, 1999).

Flint, Kate, *The Victorians and the Visual Imagination* (Cambridge, 2000).

Foot, M. R. D. and Colin Matthews, eds., *The Gladstone Diaries* (14 vols., Oxford, 1986–94).

Frei, Hans, *The Eclipse of Biblical Narrative* (London, 1974).

Frend, W. H. C., *The Archaeology of Early Christianity: A History* (London, 1996).

From Dogma to History: How our Understanding of the Early Church Developed (London, 2003).

Gange, David, *Dialogues with the Dead: Egyptology in British Culture and Religion* (Oxford, 2013).

'Religion and Science in Late Nineteenth-Century British Egyptology', *Historical Journal*, 49 (2006), 1083–103.

Gardner, Brian, *Allenby* (London, 1965).

Garfinkle, Adam, *Israel and Jordan in the Shadow of War: Functional Ties and Futile Diplomacy in a Small Place* (London, 1991).

Gascoigne, John, 'Anglican Latitudinarianism, Rational Dissent and Political Radicalism in the Late Eighteenth Century', in Knud Haakonssen, ed., *Enlightenment and Religion* (Cambridge, 1996), pp. 219–40.

Cambridge in the Age of the Enlightenment: Science, Religion and Politics from the Restoration to the French Revolution (Cambridge, 1986).

Gasque, W. Ward, *A History of the Criticism of the Acts of the Apostles* (Tübingen, 1975).

Gaudé, Laurent, *Sodome, ma douce* (Arles, 2009).

Gavin, Carney, ed., *Imperial Self-Portrait: The Ottoman Empire as Revealed in the Sultan Abdul Hamid II's Photographic Albums, Presented as Gifts to the Library of Congress (1893) and the British Museum (1894)* (Cambridge: MA, 1988).

Gibson, Shimon, *Jerusalem in Original Photographs, 1850–1920* (London, 2003).

Giebelhausen, Michaela, *Painting the Bible: Representation and Belief in Mid-Victorian Britain* (Aldershot, 2006).

Girouard, Mark, *Cities and People: A Social and Architectural Survey* (London, 1987).

Glover, T. Willis, *Evangelical Nonconformists and Higher Criticism in the Nineteenth Century* (London, 1954).

Goldhill, Simon, *Jerusalem: City of Longing* (Cambridge, MA, 2008).

The Temple of Jerusalem (Cambridge, MA, 2005).

Goren, Haim, *Dead Sea Level: Science, Exploration and Imperial Interests in the Near East* (New York, 2011).

'Sacred but not Surveyed: Nineteenth-Century Surveys of Palestine', *Imago Mundi*, 54 (2002), 87–110.

Gorst, John, 'Introduction: Settlements in England and America', in Arthur Winnington-Ingram, ed., *The Universities and the Social Problem: An Account of the University Settlements in East London* (London, 1895), pp. 1–30.

Goshen, Heike Zaun, *Beyond the Wall: Chapters on Urban Jerusalem* (Jerusalem, 2006).

Grafton, Anthony, *Worlds Made by Words: Scholarship and Community in the Modern West* (Cambridge, MA, 2009).

Gran-Aymeric, Eve, *La Naissance de l'archéologie moderne, 1798–1945* (Paris, 1998).

Greaves, R. W., 'The Jerusalem Bishopric, 1841', *English Historical Review*, 64 (1949), 328–52.

Green, Abigail, *Moses Montefiore: Jewish Liberator, Imperial Hero* (Cambrige, MA, 2010).

Green, S. J. D., 'Church and City Revisited: New Evidence from the North of England, c.1815–1914', *Northern History*, 43 (2006), 345–60.

The Passing of Protestant England: Secularisation and Social Change, c.1920–1960 (Cambridge, 2011).

'In Search of Bourgeois Civilisation: Institutions and Ideals in Nineteenth-Century Britain', *Northern History*, 28 (1992), 228–47.

Gregory, Frederick, *Nature Lost? Natural Science and the German Theological Traditions of the Nineteenth Century* (Cambridge, MA, 1992).

Haakonssen, Knud, ed., *Enlightenment and Religion: Rational Dissent in Eighteenth-Century Britain* (Cambridge, 1996).

Hagen, Gottfried, 'German Heralds of Holy War: Orientalists and Applied Oriental Studies', *Comparative Studies of South Asia, Africa, and the Middle East*, 24 (2004), 145–62.

Hallam, Paul, 'Sodom: A Circuit Walk', in Paul Hallam, ed., *The Book of Sodom* (London, 1993).
Harris, Harriet, *Fundamentalism and Evangelicals* (Oxford, 1998), chapters 3 and 4.
Harrison, Peter, *'Religion' and the Religions in the English Enlightenment* (Cambridge, 1990).
Harvey, A. D., *Sex in Georgian England: Attitudes and Prejudices from the 1720s to the 1820s* (London, 2001).
Hempton, David, 'Evangelism and Eschatology', *Journal of Ecclesiastical History* 31 (1996), 179–94.
  Religion and Political Culture in Britain and Ireland: From the Glorious Revolution to the Decline of Empire (Cambridge, 1996).
Hennock, E. P., *Fit and Proper Persons: Ideal and Reality in Nineteenth-Century Urban Government* (London, 1968).
Hillenbrand, Carole, *The Crusades: Islamic Perspectives* (Edinburgh, 1999).
Hilton, Boyd, *The Age of Atonement: The Influence of Evangelicalism on Social and Economic Thought, 1785–1865* (Oxford, 1986).
Hingley, Richard, *Roman Officers and English Gentlemen: The Imperial Origins of Roman Archaeology* (London and New York, 2000).
Hitchin, Neil, 'The Evidence of Things Seen: Georgian Churchmen and Biblical Prophecy', in Bertrand Taithe and Tim Thornton, eds., *Prophecy: The Power of Inspired Language in History 1300–2000* (Stroud, 1997), pp. 119–42.
Hoock, Holger, 'The British State and the Anglo-French Wars over Antiquities, 1798–1858', *Historical Journal*, 50 (2007), 49–72.
  Empires of the Imagination: Politics, War, and the Arts in the British World, 1750–1850 (London, 2010).
Hopwood, Derek, *The Russian Presence in Syria and Palestine, 1843–1914: Church and Politics in the Near East* (Oxford, 1969).
Horsley, G. H., 'The Inscriptions of Ephesos and the New Testament', *Novum Testamentum*, 34 (1992), 105–68.
Howard, Thomas, *Religion and the Rise of Historicism: W. M. L. de Wette, Jacob Burckhardt, and the Theological Origins of Nineteenth-Century Historical Consciousness* (Cambridge, 2000).
Howe, Kathleen, 'Mapping a Sacred Geography: Photographic Surveys by the Royal Engineers in the Holy Land, 1864–68', in Joan Schwartz and James Ryan, eds., *Picturing Place: Photography and the Geographical Imagination* (London, 2003), pp. 226–42.
  ed., *Revealing the Holy Land: The Photographic Exploration of Palestine* (Berkeley, CA, 1997).
Hummel, Ruth and Thomas Hummel, *Patterns of the Sacred: English Protestant and Russian Orthodox Pilgrims of the Nineteenth Century* (London, 1995).
Hunt, E. D., *Holy Land Pilgrimage in the Later Roman Empire AD 312–460* (Oxford, 1982).

Hunt, Tristram, *Building Jerusalem: The Rise and Fall of the Victorian City* (London, 2004).
Hyamson, Albert, *British Projects for the Restoration of the Jews* (London, 1971).
Hyde, Ralph, *Panoramania! The Art and Entertainment of the 'All Embracing View'* (London, 1988).
Invernizzi, A., 'Discovering Babylon with Pietro della Valle', in P. Matthiae, A. Enea, L. Peyronel and F. Pinnock, eds., *Proceedings of the First International Congress on the Archaeology of the Ancient Near East (Rome, May 18th–23rd 1998)* (Rome, 2000), pp. 643–49.
  'Les Premiers Voyageurs', in Béatrice André-Salvini, ed., *Babylone* (Paris, 2008), pp. 505–7.
Irwin, Robert, *Dangerous Knowledge: Orientalism and its Discontents* (New York, 2006).
Jacobi, Carol, *William Holman Hunt: Painter, Painting, Paint* (Manchester, 2006).
Jaffe, Eliezer, *A Private Foundation Working in Israel: The Doron Foundation for Education and Welfare* (Jerusalem, 1988).
Jameson, John H., John E. Ehrenhard and Christine A. Finn, eds., *Ancient Muses: Archaeology and the Arts* (Tuscaloosa, AL, 2003).
Jampoler, Andrew, *Sailors in the Holy Land: The 1848 American Expedition to the Dead Sea and the Search for Sodom and Gomorrah* (Annapolis, 2005).
Jenkins, Ian, *Archaeologists and Aesthetes in the Sculpture Galleries of the British Museum, 1800–1939* (London, 1992).
Jenkyns, Richard, *The Victorians and Ancient Greece* (Oxford, 1980).
Jeremias, Joachim, *Jerusalem in the Time of Jesus* (London, 1969).
Jordan, Mark, *The Invention of Sodomy in Christian Theology* (Chicago, IL, 1997).
Joyce, Patrick, *Liberalism and the Rule of Freedom* (London, 2004).
Kark, Ruth, *American Consuls in the Holy Land, 1832–1914* (Jerusalem, 1994).
  Jerusalem Neighborhoods: Planning and By-laws, 1855–1930 (Jerusalem, 1991).
Katz, David, *God's Last Words: Reading the English Bible from the Reformation to Fundamentalism* (London, 2004).
Kazantzakis, Nikos, *Two Plays: Sodom and Gomorrah; and Comedy, a Tragedy in One Act*, trans. Kimon Friar (St Paul, MN, 1982).
Kendall, Harry, *Jerusalem: The City Plan: Preservation and Development During the British Mandate, 1918–1948* (London, 1948).
Khalidi, Rashid, *Palestinian Identity: The Construction of Modern National Consciousness* (New York, 1997).
Khalidi, Walid, *Before their Diaspora: A Photographic History of the Palestinians, 1876–1948* (Washington, 1984).
Knibbe, Dieter, *Ephesus–ΕΦΕΣΟΣ: Geschichte einer bedeutenden antiken Stadt und Portrait einer modernen Großgrabung* (Frankfurt, 1998).
Kochav, Sara, 'The Search for a Protestant Holy Sepulchre: the Garden Tomb in Nineteenth-Century Jerusalem', *Journal of Ecclesiastical History*, 46 (1995), 278–301.

Kohut, Thomas, *Wilhelm II and the Germans: A Study in Leadership* (Oxford, 1991).
Kokkonen, Lars, 'The Prophet Motive? John Martin as a Civil Engineer', in Martin Myrone, ed., *John Martin: Apocalypse* (London, 2011), pp. 35–42.
Koven, Seth, *Slumming: Sexual and Social Politics in Victorian London* (London, 2004).
Krieger, Barbara, *The Dead Sea: Myth, History, and Politics* (Hanover, 1988).
Kroyanker, David, *Adrikhalut bi-Yerushalayim* (Jerusalem, 1985–93).
 Jerusalem Architecture: Periods and Styles: The Jewish Quarters and Public Buildings Outside the Old City Walls 1860–1914 (Jerusalem, 1983).
Kyle, Melvin Grove, *Explorations at Sodom: The Story of Ancient Sodom in the Light of Modern Research* (London, 1928).
Landau, Jacob, *Abdul-Hamid's Palestine: Rare Century-Old Photographs from the Private Collection of the Ottoman Sultan Now Published for the First Time* (London, 1979).
Laplanche, François, *La Bible en France: entre mythe et critique, 16ème–19ème siècles* (Paris, 1994).
Larsen, Mogens Trolle, *The Conquest of Assyria: Excavations in an Antique Land, 1840–1860* (London, 1996).
Larsen, Tim, 'Austen Henry Layard's Nineveh: The Bible and Archaeology in Victorian Britain', *Journal of Religious History*, 33 (2009), 66–81.
 Contested Christianity: The Political and Social Context of Victorian Theology (Waco, TX, 2004).
 A People of One Book: The Bible and the Victorians (Oxford, 2011).
 'Thomas Cook, Holy Land Pilgrims and the Dawn of the Modern Tourist Industry', in R. N. Swanson, ed., *Holy Land, Holy Lands, and Christian History* (Woodbridge, 2000), pp. 459–73.
Lascarides, A. C., *The Search for Troy, 1553–1874* (Bloomington, IN, 1977).
Leask, Nigel, *Curiosity and the Aesthetics of Travel Writing, 1770–1840* (Oxford, 2002).
Ledger-Lomas, Michael, 'Mass Markets: Religion', in David McKitterick, ed., *The Cambridge History of the Book in Nineteenth-Century Britain, 1830–1914* (Cambridge, 2009), pp. 324–58.
 'Shipwrecked: James Smith and the Defence of Biblical Narrative in Victorian Britain', *Angermion*, 1 (2008), 83–110.
Lees, Andrew, *Cities Perceived: Urban Society in European and American Thought* (Manchester, 1985).
Lees, Lynne, 'Urban Networks', in Martin Daunton, ed., *The Cambridge Urban History of Britain: 1840–1950* (Cambridge, 2000), pp. 68–9.
Legaspi, Michael, *The Death of Scripture and the Rise of Biblical Studies* (Oxford, 2010).
Lehmann, Reinhard G., *Friedrich Delitzsch und der Babel-Bibel-Streit* (Fribourg, 1994).

Leighton, C. D. A., 'Antichrist's Revolution: Some Anglican Apocalypticists in the Age of the French Wars', *Journal of Religious History*, 24 (2000), 125–42.

Le Strange, Guy, *Palestine under the Moslems: A Description of Syria and the Holy Land from AD 650 to 1500* (1890; Beirut, 1965).

Levine, Lee, ed., *Jerusalem: Its Sanctity and Centrality to Judaism, Christianity, and Islam* (Philadelphia, PA, 1999)

Levitin, Dmitri, 'From Sacred History to the History of Religion', *Historical Journal* 52 (2013) 1117–60.

Lewis, Donald, *The Origins of Christian Zionism: Lord Shaftesbury and Evangelical Support for a Jewish Homeland* (Cambridge, 2010).

Lincoln, Bruce, *Theorizing Myth: Narrative, Ideology, and Scholarship* (London, 1999).

Loader, J. A., *A Tale of Two Cities: Sodom and Gomorrah in the Old Testament, Early Jewish and Early Christian Traditions* (Kampen, 1990).

Lockley, Philip, 'Millenarians in the Pennines, 1800–1830: Building and Believing Jerusalem', *Northern History*, 47 (2010), 297–317.

Long, Burke, *Imagining the Holy Land: Maps, Models, and Fantasy Travels* (Bloomington, IN, 2003).

Ludwig, Emil, *Schliemann of Troy*, trans. D. F. Tait (London, 1931).

Lyons, Claire, 'The Art and Science of Antiquity in Nineteenth-Century Photography', in Claire Lyons, John Papadopolous, Lindsey Stewart and Andrew Szegedy-Haszak, *Antiquity and Photography: Early Views of Ancient Mediterranean Sites* (London, 2005), pp. 22–65.

Lyons, Claire, John Papadopolous, Lindsey Stewart and Andrew Szegedy-Maszak, *Antiquity and Photography: Early Views of Ancient Mediterranean Sites* (London, 2005).

McBirnie, William Steuart, *The Search for the Authentic Tomb of Jesus* (London, 1975).

McCall, Henrietta, 'Rediscovery and Aftermath', in S. M. Dalley, ed., *The Legacy of Mesopotamia* (Oxford, 1998), pp. 183–213.

  'Reinventing Babylon: Victorian Design in the Assyrian Style', in Martha Cowling, ed., *The Price of Beauty: Edwin Long's Babylonian Marriage Market (1875)* (London, 2004), pp. 44–9.

McCalman, Iain, 'New Jerusalems: Prophecy, Dissent and Radical Culture in England, 1786–1830', in Knud Haakonssen, ed., *Enlightenment and Religion: Rational Dissent in Eighteenth Century Britain* (Cambridge, 1996), pp. 312–35.

McCarthy, Justin, *The Population of Palestine: Population History and Statistics of the Late Ottoman Period and the New Mandate* (New York, 1990).

Macfarlane, Charles, *The Seven Apocalyptic Churches* (London, 1832).

MacHaffie, Barbara Zink, '"Monument Facts and Higher Critical Fancies": Archaeology and the Popularization of Old Testament Criticism in Nineteenth-Century Britain', *Church History*, 50 (1981), 316–28.

Mackenzie, John M., '"In Touch With the Infinite": The BBC and the Empire, 1923–53', in John M. Mackenzie, ed., *Imperialism and Popular Culture* (Manchester, 1986).

McLeod, Hugh, *Piety and Poverty: Working-Class Religion in Berlin, London and New York 1870–1914* (New York, 1996).

Makdisi, U., 'Ottoman Orientalism', *American Historical Review*, 107 (2002), 768–96.

Mandelbrote, Scott, 'Biblical Hermeneutics and the Sciences, 1700–1900: An Overview', in Jitse van der Meer and Scott Mandelbrote, eds., *Nature and Scripture in the Abrahamic Religions: To 1700* (Leiden, 2009), pp. 1–37.

'Early Modern Biblical Interpretation and the Emergence of Science', *Science and Christian Belief*, 23 (2011), 105–10.

'Early Modern Natural Theologies', in Russell Manning, ed., *Oxford Handbook to Natural Theology* (Oxford, 2013).

Mandler, Peter, 'Against "Englishness": English Culture and the Limits to Rural Nostalgia, 1850–1940', *Transactions of the Royal Historical Society*, 7 (1997), 155–75.

Marchand, Suzanne, *Down from Olympus: Archaeology and Philhellenism in Germany, 1750–1970* (London, 1996).

German Orientalism in the Age of Empire: Religion, Race, and Scholarship (Cambridge, 2009).

Markus, R. A., *The End of Ancient Christianity* (Cambridge, 1991).

Marsden, George, *Fundamentalism and American Culture* (1980; London, 2006).

Masterman, E. W. G., 'Three Early Explorers in the Dead Sea Valley', *Palestine Exploration Fund Quarterly Statement* (1911), 12–27.

Mather, James, *Pashas: Traders and Travellers in the Islamic World* (London, 2009).

Meacham, Standish, *Toynbee Hall and Social Reform, 1880–1914: The Search for Community* (New Haven, CT, 1987).

Melman, Billie, *The Culture of History: English Uses of the Past 1800–1953* (Oxford, 2006).

Women's Orients: English Women and the Middle East, 1718–1918 (1992; London, 1995).

Meyer, Wendell, 'The Phial of Blood Controversy and the Decline of the Liberal Catholic Movement', *Journal of Ecclesiastical History*, 46 (1995), 75–94.

Moorey, P., *A Century of Biblical Archaeology* (Louisville, KY, 1991).

Morris, Ian, *Archaeology as Cultural History* (Oxford, 2000).

Moscrop, James, *Measuring Jerusalem: The Palestine Exploration Fund and British Interests in the Holy Land* (Leicester, 1999).

Moser, Stephanie, *Wondrous Curiosities: Ancient Egypt at the British Museum* (Chicago, 2006).

Muir, Diana, '"A Land Without a People for a People Without a Land"', *Middle East Quarterly* (2008), 55–62.

Mullin, Bruce, *Miracles and the Modern Religious Imagination* (London, 1996).

Muree-van Den Berg, Heleen, 'William McClure Thomson's *The Land and the Book* (1859): Pilgrimage and Mission in Palestine', in Heleen Muree-van Den Berg, ed., *New Faith in Ancient Lands: Western Missions in the Middle East in the Nineteenth and Early Twentieth Centuries* (Leiden, 2006), pp. 43–64.

Myrone, Martin, ed., *John Martin: Apocalypse* (London, 2011).

Nassar, Issam, *Photographing Jerusalem: The Image of the City in Nineteenth-Century Photography* (Boulder, CO, 1997).

Nead, Lynda, *Victorian Babylon: People, Streets and Images in Nineteenth-Century London* (London, 2005).

Neev, David, *The Destruction of Sodom, Gomorrah, and Jericho: Geological, Climatological, and Archaeological Background* (Oxford, 1995).

Neville, Graham, *Radical Churchman: Edward Lee Hicks and the New Liberalism* (Oxford, 1998).

Newsome, David, 'The Assault on Mammon: Charles Gore and John Neville Figgis', *Journal of Ecclesiastical History*, 17 (1966), 227–41.

Nickel, Douglas, *Francis Frith in Egypt and Palestine: A Victorian Photographer Abroad* (Oxford, 2005).

Nir, Yeshayahu, *The Bible and the Image: The History of Photography in the Holy Land, 1839–1899* (Philadelphia, PA, 1985).

Norton, Rictor, 'Sodom on the Thames: Sex, Love, and Scandal in Wilde Times', *English Historical Review*, 122 (2007), 1104–5.

O'Connor, Jerome Murphy, *Ephesus: Texts and Archaeology* (London, 2008).

O'Connor, Ralph, *The Earth on Show: Fossils and the Poetics of Popular Science, 1802–1856* (Chicago, 2008).

O'Gorman, Francis, 'To See the Finger of God in the Dimensions of the Pyramid', *Modern Language Review*, 98 (2003), 563–73.

Obbard, Elizabeth Ruth, *The History and Spirituality of Walsingham* (Norwich, 1995).

Onne, Eyal, *Photographic Heritage of the Holy Land, 1839–1914* (Manchester, 1980).

Oren, Michael, *Power, Faith, and Fantasy: America in the Middle East, 1776 to the Present* (London, 2007).

Osterhammel, Jürgen, *Die Verwandlung der Welt: Eine Geschichte des 19. Jahrhunderts* (Munich, 2009).

Oxford English Dictionary Online, 2nd edn, 1989.

Paley, Morton, *The Apocalyptic Sublime* (London, 1986).

Pals, Daniel, *Victorian 'Lives' of Jesus* (San Antonio, TX, 1980).

Pantin, W. A., *The Oxford Architectural and Historical Society, 1839–1939* (Oxford, 1939).

Parfitt, Tudor, *The Jews in Palestine, 1800–1882* (Woodbridge, 1987).

Parris, Leslie, *The Pre-Raphaelites* (London, 1984).

Parrott, André, *The Temple of Jerusalem* (London, 1957).

Parry, Jon, 'The Impact of Napoleon III on British Politics, 1851–1880', *Transactions of the Royal Historical Society*, 11 (2001), 147–75.

Paston, George, *At John Murray's: Records of a Literary Circle, 1843–1892* (London, 1932).

Paz, D. G., *Popular Anti-Catholicism in Mid-Victorian England* (Stanford, CA, 1992).

Peakman, Julie, 'Sexual Perversion in History: An Introduction', in Julie Peakman, ed., *Sexual Perversions, 1670–1890* (Basingstoke, 2009), pp. 1–49.

Perry, Yaron, *British Missions to the Jews in Nineteenth-Century Palestine* (London, 2003).

Peters, F. E., *Jerusalem: The Holy City in the Eyes of Chroniclers, Pilgrims and Prophets from the Days of Abraham to the Beginnings of Modern Times* (Princeton, NJ, 1985).

Pike, David, *Subterranean Cities: The World Beneath Paris and London, 1800–1945* (Ithaca, NY, 2005).

Pimlott, J. A. R., *The Englishman's Christmas: A Social History* (Hassocks, 1978).

Pocock, J. G. A., *Barbarism and Religion: Volume 5, Religion: The First Triumph* (Cambridge, 2011).

Porter, Andrew, *Religion versus Empire? British Protestant Missionaries and Overseas Expansion, 1700–1914* (Manchester, 2004).

Porter, Venetia, *Iraq's Past Speaks to the Present* (London, 2008).

Prettejohn, Elizabeth, 'Recreating Rome in Victorian Painting: From History to Genre', in Michael Liversidge and Catherine Edwards, eds., *Imagining Rome: British Artists and Rome in the Nineteenth Century* (Bristol, 1996), pp. 54–69.

Prickett, Stephen, 'Introduction', in Stephen Prickett, ed., *Reading the Text: Biblical Criticism and Literary Theory* (London, 1991).

Prochaska, Frank, *The Disinherited Spirit: Christianity and Social Service in Modern Britain* (London, 2006).

Reade, Julian, 'Early Travellers on the Wonders: Suggested Sites', in Irving Finkel and Michael Seymour, eds., *Babylon: Myth and Reality* (London, 2008), pp. 112–17.

'Hormuzd Rassam and his Discoveries', *Iraq*, 55 (1993), 39–62.

'Layard's Nineveh and its Remains', *Antiquity*, 72 (1998), 913–16.

'Rassam's Babylonian Collection: The Excavations and the Archives', in E. Leichty, ed., *Catalogue of the Babylonian Tablets in the British Museum* 6 (London, 1986), pp. xii–xxxvi.

'Rassam's Excavations at Borsippa and Kutha', *Iraq*, 48 (1986), 105–16.

'Tablets at Babylon and the British Museum', in Irving Finkel and Michael Seymour, eds., *Babylon: Myth and Reality* (London, 2008), pp. 74–80.

Redford, Bruce, 'The Measure of Ruins: Dilettanti in the Levant, 1750–1770', *Harvard Library Bulletin*, 13 (2002), 5–36.

Reid, Kirsty, 'The Horrors of Convict Life: British Radical Visions of the Australian Penal Colonies', *Cultural and Social History*, 5 (2008), 481–95.

Reisenauer, E. M., 'The Battle of the Standards: Great Pyramid Metrology and British Identity, 1859–90', *Historian*, 65 (2003), 931–78.

Renton, James, *The Zionist Masquerade: The Birth of the Anglo-Zionist Alliance 1914–1918* (Basingstoke, 2007).

Richards, Katharine Lambert, *How Christmas Came to the Sunday-Schools: The Observance of Christmas in the Protestant Church Schools of the US, an Historical Study* (New York, 1935).

Richter, Jan Stefan, *Die Orientreise Kaiser Wilhelms II. 1898: Eine Studie zur deutschen Außenpolitik an der Wende zum 20. Jahrhundert* (Hamburg, 1997).

Riley-Smith, Jonathan, ed., *The Oxford History of the Crusades* (Oxford, 1999).

Rogers, Guy, 'Demetrios of Ephesos: Silversmith and Neopoios?' *Belleten* (1987), 877–82.

The Sacred Identity of Ephesus: Foundation Myths of a Roman City (London, 1991).

Rogerson, John, *The Bible and Criticism in Victorian Britain: Profiles of F. D. Maurice and William Robertson Smith* (Sheffield, 1995).

Old Testament Criticism in the Nineteenth Century: England and Germany (London, 1984).

Rogin, Michael, 'The Great Mother Domesticated: Sexual Difference and Sexual Indifference in D. W. Griffith's Intolerance', *Critical Inquiry*, 15 (1989), 510–55.

Röhricht, Reinhold, *Bibliotheca Geographica Palaestinae: Chronologisches Verzeichnis der von 333 bis 1878 verfassten Literatur über das Heilige Land* (London, 1989).

Rosenau, Helen, *Vision of the Temple: The Image of the Temple of Jerusalem in Judaism and Christianity* (London, 1979).

Rosenberg, Ruth, 'Spacemen Destroy Sodom and Gomorrah', *Western Folklore*, 21 (1962), 115–16.

Rosovsky, Nitza, ed., *City of the Great King: Jerusalem from David to the Present* (Cambridge, MA, 1996).

Royle, Edward, *Victorian Infidels: The Origins of the British Secularist Movement* (Manchester, 1974).

Rubin, Rehav, 'Relief Maps and Models in the Archives of the Palestinian Exploration Fund in London', *Palestine Exploration Quarterly*, 138 (2006), 43–4.

Rubinstein, William D. and Hilary L. Rubinstein, *Rubinstein, Philosemitism: Admiration and Support in the English-Speaking World for Jews, 1840–1939* (Basingstoke, 1999).

Russell, J. M., *From Nineveh to New York: The Strange Story of the Assyrian Reliefs in the Metropolitan Museum and the Hidden Masterpiece at Canford School* (New Haven, CT, and London, 1997).

Sader, Hélène, Thomas Scheffler and Angelika Neuwirth, eds., *Image and Monument: Baalbek 1898–1998* (Beirut, 1998).

Said, Edward, *Orientalism* (New York, 1979).

St Clair, William, *The Reading Nation in the Romantic Period* (Cambridge, 2004).

Scafi, Alessandro, *Mapping Paradise: A History of Heaven on Earth* (Chicago, IL, 2006).

Scheffler, Thomas, 'The Kaiser in Baalbek: Tourism, Archaeology, and the Politics of Imagination', in Hélène Sader, Thomas Scheffler and Angelika Neuwirth, eds., *Image and Monument: Baalbek 1898–1998* (Beirut, 1998), pp. 51–88.

Schiefelbein, M. E., *The Lure of Babylon: Seven Protestant Novelists and Britain's Roman Catholic Revival* (Macon, CA, 2001).

Schiller, Ely, *The First Photographs of Jerusalem, the Old City* (Jerusalem, 1978).

Schöllgen, Gregor, *Imperialismus und Gleichgewicht: Deutschland, England und die orientalische Frage 1871–1914* (Munich, 1984).

Secord, James, *Victorian Sensation: The Extraordinary Publication, Reception and Secret Authorship of Vestiges of the Natural History of Creation* (Chicago, IL, 2000).

Sered, Susan Starr, 'Rachel's Tomb and the Milk Grotto of the Virgin Mary: Two Women's Shrines in Bethlehem', *Journal of Feminist Studies in Religion*, 2 (1986), 7–22.

Seymour, Michael, 'Babylon in Contemporary Art and Culture', in Irving Finkel and Michael Seymour, eds., *Babylon: Myth and Reality* (London, 2008), pp. 203–12.

  'Powers and Seduction in Babylon: Verdi's *Nabucco*', in Silke Knippschild and Marta Garcia Morcillo, eds., *Seduction and Power: Antiquity in the Visual and Performing Arts* (London, in press).

Sheehan, Jonathan, *The Enlightenment Bible: Translation, Scholarship, Culture* (Princeton, 2005).

Shepherd, Naomi, *The Zealous Intruders: The Western Rediscovery of Palestine* (London, 1987).

Shuger, Debora, *The Renaissance Bible: Scholarship, Sacrifice and Subjectivity* (London, 1998).

Silberman, Neil Asher, *Digging for God and Country: Exploration in the Holy Land, 1799–1917* (London, 1982).

  'Visions of the Future: Albright in Jerusalem, 1919–1929', *The Biblical Archaeologist*, 56 (1993), 8–16.

Silver-Brody, Vivienne, *Documentors of the Dream: Pioneer Jewish Photographers in the Land of Israel, 1890–1933* (Jerusalem, 1998).

Singer, Michael, ed., *The Itinerary of Rabbi Benjamin of Tudela* (Malibu, 1983)

Sinno, Abdel-Raouf, 'The Emperor's Journey to the East as Reflected in Contemporary Arab Journalism', in Hélène Sader, Thomas Scheffler and Angelika Neuwirth, eds., *Image and Monument: Baalbek 1898–1998* (Beirut, 1998), pp. 115–36.

Small, Helen, 'Science, Liberalism and the Ethics of Belief', in Geoffrey Cantor and Sally Shuttleworth, eds., *Science Serialized: Representations of the Sciences in Nineteenth-Century Periodicals* (Cambridge, MA, 2004), pp. 239–58.

Smith, Wilfred Cantwell, *Islam in Modern History* (Princeton, NJ, 1957).

Solomon-Godeau, Abigail, *Photography at the Dock* (Minneapolis, MN, 1981).

Sorkin, David, *The Religious Enlightenment: Protestants, Jews, and Catholics from London to Vienna* (Princeton, NJ, 2008).

Southworth, Edmund, 'The Ince Blundell Collection: Collecting Behaviour in the Eighteenth Century', *Journal of the History of Collections*, 3 (1991), 219–34.

Spafford, Jacob, 'Around the Dead Sea by Motor Boat', *Geographical Journal*, 39 (1912), 37–40.

Spencer, Terence, 'Robert Wood and the Problem of Troy in the Eighteenth Century', *Journal of the Warburg and Courtauld Institutes*, 20 (1957), 75–105.

Springer, C., *The Marble Wilderness: Ruins and Representation in Italian Romanticism, 1775–1850* (Cambridge, 1987).

Stanley, Brian, *The Bible and the Flag: Protestant Missions and British Imperialism in the Nineteenth and Twentieth Centuries* (Leicester, 1990).

Stern, Ephraim, ed., *The Encyclopedia of Archaeological Excavations in the Holy Land* (4 vols., Jerusalem, 1993).

Stevens, Jennifer, *The Historical Jesus and the Literary Imagination 1860–1920* (Liverpool, 2010).

Stoneman, Richard, *The Land of Lost Gods: The Search for Classical Greece* (London, 1987).

Stout, Janis P., *Sodoms in Eden: The City in American Fiction before 1860* (Westport, CT, 1976).

Strelan, Rick, *Paul, Artemis and the Jews* (Berlin, 1996).

Strickert, Frederick M., *Rachel Weeping: Jews, Christians, and Muslims at the Fortress Tomb* (Minnesota, 2007).

Swartzlander, Susan, 'James Joyce's "The Sisters": Chalices and Umbrellas, Ptolemaic Memphis and Victorian Dublin', *Studies in Short Fiction*, 32 (1995), 295–306.

Tavakoli-Targhi, Mohamad, *Refashioning Iran: Orientalism, Occidentalism and Historiography* (Basingstoke, 2001).

Taylor, Joan, *Christians and the Holy Places: The Myth of Jewish-Christian Origins* (New York, 1993).

  'The Dead Sea in Western Travellers' Accounts from the Byzantine to the Modern Period', *Strata: Bulletin of the Anglo-Israel Archaeological Society*, 27 (2009), 9–29.

Taylor, Nicholas, 'The Awful Sublimity of the Victorian City', in Jim Dyos and Michael Wolff, eds., *The Victorian City* (2 vols., London, 1973), II, pp. 431–48.

Thorne, Susan, *Congregational Missions and the Making of an Imperial Culture in Nineteenth-Century England* (Stanford, CA, 1999).

Tibawi, Abdul, *British Interests in Palestine, 1800–1901: A Study of Religions and Educational Enterprise* (London, 1961).

Todd, David, 'A French Imperial Meridian, 1814–1870', *Past and Present*, 210 (2011), 155–86.

Treblico, Paul, *The Early Christians in Ephesus from Paul to Ignatius* (Tübingen, 2007).

Treloar, Geoffrey, *Lightfoot the Historian* (Tübingen, 1998).

Trigger, Bruce, *A History of Archaeological Thought*, 2nd edn (Cambridge, 1996).

Tromans, Nicholas, ed., *The Lure of the East: British Orientalist Painting* (London, 2008).
Trumbach, Randolph, 'Modern Sodomy: The Origins of Homosexuality, 1700–1800', in Matt Cook, Robert Mills, Randolph Trumbach and H. G. Cocks, eds., *A Gay History of Britain: Love and Sex Between Men Since the Middle Ages* (London 2007), pp. 77–106.
Trumpener, Ulrich, *Germany and the Ottoman Empire, 1914–1918* (Princeton, NJ, 1968).
Turner, Frank, *The Greek Heritage in Victorian Britain* (New Haven, CT, 1981).
Vaio, John, 'Gladstone and the Early Reception of Schliemann in England', in William M Calder III and Justus Cobert, eds., *Heinrich Schliemann nach hundert Jahren* (Frankfurt, 1990), pp. 415–30.
Van Hattem, Willem, 'Once Again: Sodom and Gomorrah', *The Biblical Archaeologist*, 44 (1981), 87–92.
Vance, Norman, *The Victorians and Ancient Rome* (Oxford, 1997).
Vereté, M., 'Why Was a British Consulate Established in Jerusalem?' *English Historical Review*, 85 (1970), 316–45.
Vincent, Nicholas, 'Goffredo de Prefetti and the Church of Bethlehem in England', *Journal of Ecclescastical History*, 49 (1998), 213.
Von Reventlow, Henning Graf, *The Authority of the Bible and the Rise of the Modern World* (London, 1985).
Wagstaff, J. M., 'Colonel Leake and the Historical Geography of Greece', in James Moore, Ian Morris and Andrew Bayliss, eds., *Reinventing History: The Enlightenment Origins of Ancient History* (London, 2008), pp. 169–83.
  'Colonel Leake: Traveller and Scholar', in Sarah Searight and Malcolm Wagstaff, eds., *Travellers in the Levant: Voyagers and Visionaries* (Durham, 2001), pp. 3–15.
Walker, Franklin, *Irreverent Pilgrims: Melville, Browne, and Mark Twain in the Holy Land* (Seattle, 1974).
Wallace, Jennifer, *Digging the Dirt: The Archaeological Imagination* (London, 2004).
  'Digging for Homer: Literary Authenticity and Romantic Archaeology', *Romanticism*, 7 (2001), 73–87.
Walsh, Cheryl, 'The Incarnation and the Christian Socialist Conscience in the Victorian Church of England', *Journal of British Studies*, 34 (1995), 351–74.
Waterfield, Gordon, *Layard of Nineveh* (London, 1963).
Weber, Frank, *Eagles on the Crescent: Germany, Austria, and the Diplomacy of the Turkish Alliance, 1914–1918* (Ithaca, NY, 1970).
Weeks, Jeffrey, *Sex, Politics and Society*, 2nd edn (London, 1989).
Weinfeld, M., 'Semiramis: Her Name and Origin', in Mordechai Cogan and I. Eph'al, eds., *Ah, Assyria . . . Studies in History and Ancient Near Eastern Historiography Presented to Hayim Tadmor* (Jerusalem, 1991), pp. 99–103.
Welch, P. J., 'Anglican Churchmen and the Establishment of the Jerusalem Bishopric', *Journal of Ecclesiastical History*, 8 (1957), 193–204.
Wellard, J., *The Search for Lost Cities* (London, 1980).

Wharton, Annabel Jane, *Selling Jerusalem: Relics, Replicas, Theme Parks* (Chicago, 2006).

White, Bill, *A Special Place: A Wide Angle View of the Garden Tomb, Jerusalem* (Stanborough, 1989).

Wigley, John, *The Rise and Fall of the Victorian Sunday* (Manchester, 1980).

Williams, Watkin Wynn, *The Life of General Sir Charles Warren, etc* (Oxford, 1941).

Wohle-Scharf, Traute, *Die Forschungsgeschichte von Ephesos: Entdeckungen, Grabungen und Persönlichkeiten* (Frankfurt, 1995).

Wolffe, John, *The Protestant Crusade in Great Britain, 1829–1860* (Oxford, 1991).

Wrigley, E. A., *Energy and the English Industrial Revolution* (Cambridge, 2010).

Young, Brian, *Religion and the Enlightenment in Eighteenth-Century England: Theological Debate from Locke to Burke* (Oxford, 1994).

Ziter, Edward, *The Orient on the Victorian Stage* (Cambridge, 2006).

Index

'Aqar Quf, 164
Abdul Hamid II, 93–5
Acland, Henry, 41, 44
Albright, William Foxwell, 35
Alexander, 44, 176
Alexandria, 144
Alexandria Troas, 44, 50
Ali, Mehmet, 10, 80
Allen, Roland, 281
Allen, William, 207
Allenby, Edmund, 109
Allom, Thomas, 15, 260
American Geographical Society, 222
American Geological Society, 208
American School of Biblical
    Archaeology, 207
Ampère, Jean-Jacques, 302
Anastasi papyri, 149, 161
Anderson, Henry, 202
Andrae, Walter, 193
anti-Catholicism, 4, 8, 10, 100, 125, 126, 177, 214, 288
Antichrist, 175
Antinoë, 19
Antioch, 30
apologetics, 4, 9, 13, 20, 22, 23, 45, 58, 61, 130–3, 159, 273, 274
Argyll, eighth Duke of, 100
Aristotle, 56, 58
Armenian Church, 74
Armitage, Edward, 218, 219
Arnold, Matthew, 44
Arthur, William, 291
Arundel Society, 128
Arundell, Francis, 259, 264
Ashbee, C. R., 96, 97
Ashbee, H. S., 215
Ashton-under-Lyne, 8
Ashurbanipal, 187
Aswan dam, 1
Athens, 21, 41
Atherstone, Edwin, 113, 152
Augustine, Saint, 173

Austen, Benjamin, 115, 127
Austen, Sara, 129

Baalbec, 29, 50
Babel und Bibel Streit, 24, 193, 194, 195
Babylon, 7, 25, 27, 28, 37, 69, 117, 164–96
    Hanging Gardens, 192
    Ishtar Gate, 192
Baden-Powell, Robert, 84
Baedeker
    Jerusalem, 87
Baggs, Monsignor, 289, 291
Baghdad, 165, 167
Balzani, Ugo, 311
Bannister, Edward, 151
Baptist, 212, 313
Barking, 37, 197
Barnes, Joshua, 68
Barnett, Samuel, 33
Bartlett, William Henry, 15, 30
Barton, George, 21
Bashan, 13
Baur, Ferdinand Christian, 9, 273
Beauchamp, Abbé de, 166
Beaufort, Emily, 237, 245
Beldam, Joseph, 288, 289
Belmore, Countess, 73, 77
Ben-Arieh, Yehoshua, 228
Benjamin of Tudela, 164, 170
Benson, Edward White, 150
Besant, Walter, 85
Bethlehem, 30, 81, 228–53
    Altar of the Innocents, 230
    Church of the Nativity, 230, 233, 234, 236, 237, 238, 240, 248, 252
    Convent of St Elias, 231
    Grotto of St Jerome, 240
    Hospital of St Mary of Bethlehem, 248
    Milk Grotto, 230, 240
    Shepherd's Field, 240, 242
    Solomon's Pools, 231
    souvenir industry, 248, 249, 250
    Tomb of Rachel, 231

355

Bethlehem (cont.)
  Tomb of St Jerome, 230
  Well of David, 231
Bethlehem Hospital, 248
Bida, Alexandre, 218
Birch, Samuel, 19, 22, 46
Birs Nimrud, 164, 179, 189
Bisitun, 179, 188
Blake, William, 175
Blind, Karl, 70
Blundell, Henry, 10
Boase, Charles William, 299
Boer War, 83
Bohrer, Frederick, 113, 180
Bonfils studio, Beirut, 89
Bonomi, Joseph, 119, 125, 133, 134
Borlase, William Copeland, 64
Borsippa, 164, 179, 184, 186, 188, 189
Bosio, Antonio, 294
Botta, Paolo Emilio, 49, 121, 130, 131, 178, 182, 187
Box, John, 43
Brewster, David, 118
Bristol, 27
British and Foreign Bible Society, 14
British Empire Exhibition, 1924, 252
British Mandate of Palestine, 35, 96
British Museum, 19, 29, 35, 94, 95, 111, 121, 123, 134, 178, 180, 181, 184, 187, 190, 209, 254, 266, 267, 268, 269, 273
Brooke, Stopford, 57
Brothers, Richard, 174
Browne, Henry, 67
Browning, Elizabeth Barrett, 40
Browning, Robert, 40, 41
Brownlow, William, 293, 294, 295
Bryant, Jacob, 51, 52, 53, 60, 61, 65
Bubastis, 148
Buckingham, James Silk, 171
Budge, E. A. T. Wallis, 186
Bunarbashi, 49, 50, 52, 53, 58
Bunsen, Christian Carl Josias, 42, 46, 103, 138
Burder, George, 211
Burdett Coutts, Angela, 81
Burgon, John William, 53, 294
Burnet, Thomas, 203
Butler, Bishop, 58
Byron, 29, 42, 52, 63, 183, 198, 312

Calvert, Frank, 53
Calvino, Italo, 285
Canning, Stratford, 18, 115, 121, 131, 180
Capes, John Moore, 301

Caractacus, 290
Carlyle, Joseph Dacre, 41
Carlyle, Thomas, 25, 42
Carpenter, Mary, 114
Cassels, W. R., 42, 47, 48, 256, 273
Chabas, François, 141
Chaldean Christians, 126, 127
Chalmers, Thomas, 9, 26
Chamberlain, Houston Stewart, 102
Chandler, Richard, 257, 259
Charles, Elizabeth Rundle, 31
Chartism, 214
Chase, Frederick Henry, 23
Chateaubriand, François-René de, 14, 74, 201, 221, 240
Chesterton, G. K., 108
Cheyne, Thomas Kelly, 23
Choiseul-Gouffier, Comte, 50, 52, 59
Christian Israelites, 8
Christian Socialism, 27, 32
Churchill, Charles, 197
civic gospel, 32, 33, 37, 162
Clarke, Edward Daniel, 11, 41, 42, 238
Clarke, Hyde, 267, 268
Classical Association, 67
Cleitarchus, 182
Cleopatra's Needle, 142, 145
Clifford, William Kingdon, 40
Cocks, Harry, 199, 210, 213, 214
Conder, Claude Reignier, 29, 243
Congregationalism, 24, 25, 31, 79, 211, 263, 278
Conybeare, William John, 271, 302, 303
Cook, Thomas, 21
Cook's tours, 271, 313
Cooper, Robert, 114
Corelli, Marie, 145
Corinth, 14, 19, 21, 27
Corot, Camille, 217, 219
Corot, Jean Baptiste, 218
Cory's Ancient Fragments, 20, 62
Costigan, Christopher, 201
Crimean War, 81, 239
Crusades, 244, 245, 248
Crystal Palace Company, 82
Ctesias, 182
Cumming, John, 261
Curtis, George, 75
Curtius, Ernest, 277
Curzon, Robert, 75
Cyrus, 176, 187, 188
Cyrus Cylinder, 187, 188

daguerreotype, 16
Damascus, 101
Darius the Great, 179
Darwin, Charles, 39, 47
Davies, William, 301, 305
Davis, Thomas, 35
Dawson, George, 162
de Faverches, Lady Richeldis, 248
de Laborde, Léon, 10, 258
de Marchi, Padre, 293
de Montault, Barbier, 295
de Rossi, Giovanni Battista, 293, 294, 295, 298
de Rougé, Emmanuel, 147
de Sade, Marquis, 197, 216
de Saulcy, Louis Félicien, 84, 86, 203, 204, 205, 206, 209, 210, 214, 218, 219, 220, 222, 224, 225
de Vogüé, Comte, 11
Deakin, Rome, 306
DeHass, Frank, 222
deism, 7, 114, 141
Deissmann, Gustav Adolf, 279
Delacroix, F. D. E., 183
Delisle, Léopold, 293
Delitzsch, Franz, 193
Delitzsch, Friedrich, 193, 194, 195
della Valle, Pietro, 165
Deutsche Orient-Gesellschaft, 191, 192, 193
Dicey, Edward, 290, 291
Dilettanti, Society of, 7
Diodorus Siculus, 116, 130, 143, 169, 182, 183
diorama, 210
Disraeli, Benjamin, 69, 130, 175, 215, 228, 232, 237
Donovan, Jeremiah, 289
Doré, Gustave, 218, 278
Dörpfeld, Wilhelm, 67
Driver, Samuel, 22, 23
Drummond, Henry, 5, 32, 38, 162
Dümichen, Johannes, 143
Dürer, Albrecht, 217

Eastern Orthodox Church, 80
Eastern Question, 44
Eastlake, Lady, 128
Ebers, Georg, 149
Eddy, Daniel, 239
Eden, Garden of, 1
Edwards, Amelia, 20, 139, 142, 145, 147, 148, 149, 150, 153
Egypt Exploration Fund, 18, 34, 70, 137, 138, 142, 148, 150, 153, 155, 157, 158, 159, 160, 161, 163

Eichhorn, Johann Gottfried, 41
Eliot, George, 48, 102
Ellesmere, Lord, 121, 125
Ellicott, Charles John, 68, 69
Elliott, Frances, 310
Emerson, Ralph Waldo, 28
Endean, J. Russell, 269
England's Nazareth, Walsingham, 248
Ephesus, 19, 21, 29, 254–84
    Great Gymnasium, 264
    Great Theatre, 256, 272
    Odeon, 272
    Salutaris inscription, 273
    Temple of Artemis, 254, 265, 272, 277
Essays and Reviews, 17, 42, 47, 68
Etemenanki, 164
Euripides, 56
Eustace, John Chetwode, 286
evangelical, 17, 36, 38, 211, 213, 238
evangelicalism, 8, 105, 116, 127, 211, 303
Evans, Arthur, 60
Evans, Marian, 114
Everest, C. W., 190
Exodus, 136, 137, 153, 157
exoticism, 93, 94, 184
Ezekiel, 115, 116, 129

Fairbairn, Andrew, 31
Falkener, Edward, 256, 264, 265, 270
Farrar, Frederic William, 232, 242, 269, 271, 277, 278
Fellows, Charles, 258
Fergusson, James, 29, 82, 98, 100, 267
Finn, James, 75
First World War, 34, 35, 109
Flaubert, Gustave, 145
Flood Tablet, 20, 43, 59, 61, 150, 179, 188, 194
Forbes, Edward, 10
Forbes, S. Russell, 302, 303
Fox, William Johnson, 126, 127
France, Anatole, 145
Franciscan Church, 74
Frederick V of Denmark, 166
Free Church, 13, 16
Freeman, Edward, 295
freethinkers, 25, 117, 126, 133
French Revolution, 175
Friedrich Wilhelm IV, 102
Frith, Francis, 16, 88, 93
Frost, John, 214

Galilee, 242
    Capharnaum/Capernaum, 89, 92, 212, 213

Garden of Eden, 43, 44, 58
Garden Tomb Association, 97
Gardner, Mary, 15
Gardner, Percy, 22, 24, 33, 283
Garibaldi, Giuseppi, 313
Garstang, John, 35
Gell, William, 52
Geographical Society, 258
Gerasa/Jerash, 29
Gibbon, Edward, 259
Gilead, 20
Gilgamesh, Epic of, 179, 194
Girdlestone, Charles, 211
Gladstone, William Ewart, 42, 46, 47, 54, 55, 56, 57, 58, 59, 60, 61, 65, 67, 68, 69, 70, 150
Gliddon, George, 140
Glover, James, 215
Gomorrah, 197–227
Goode, Francis, 211, 212
Goodwin, Charles Wycliffe, 42
Gordon, General Charles, 76, 97, 98, 100
Gordon, Maria Antoinetta, 127
Gore, Arthur, 21
Goshen, 148, 149
Göttingen, 7, 47, 140, 274
Goupil-Fesquet, Frederic, 16, 87
Gozzoli, Benozzo, 217
Graham, Stephen, 72
Grand Tour, 7
Greek Orthodox Church, 74, 243
Greenwood, James, 310
Grote, George, 41, 52, 59
Grove, George, 82
Guhl, Ernst, 267

Habershon, Ada, 20, 35, 271
Haggard, Henry Rider, 68, 144, 145, 162
half-tone reproductions, 16
Hamilton, William John, 258, 264
Harnack, Adolf, 23
Hartley, John British, 14
Hatch, Edwin, 276
Haverfield, Francis John, 311
Headlam, Arthur Cayley, 313
Hebron, 243, 244
Helena of Adiabene, 86
Hellenic Society, The, 67, 273, 274
Hemans, Charles Isidore, 291, 292
Hempton, David, 177
Henson, Hensley, 25, 37, 197, 280
Henzen, William, 293
Herbert, M. L., 148, 157, 159
Herder, Johann Gottfried, 102

Hermes Trismegistus, 162
Herodotus, 143, 169, 170, 181, 182, 192
Heth, 49
Heyne, Christian Gottlob, 47
Hicks, Edward Lee, 273, 275, 280, 281
Higgins, Godfrey, 55
higher criticism, 4, 9, 13, 17, 23, 39, 41, 47, 48, 91, 92, 114, 117, 120, 138, 140, 141, 142, 159, 160, 188, 256, 271
Hincks, Edward, 131, 179
Hisarlik, 39, 42, 49, 53, 63, 64, 67, 68, 70, 124, 269
Hittite, 70
Hobhouse, John Cam, 52
Hogarth, David, 254, 263, 267, 311
Holland, Henry Scott, 32
Holyoake, G. J., 133
Homer, 13
Homeric Birthday Book, 57
Hood, Edwin Paxton, 25, 232, 233, 234, 236, 243
Horsfall, T. C., 281
Housman, Lawrence, 252
Howson, John Saul, 215, 271, 302, 303
Hudson, George, 309
Hummel, Ruth, 240
Hummel, Thomas, 240
Hunt, Philip, 41, 42
Hunt, William Holman, 145, 218, 219, 220, 221
Huxley, Thomas Henry, 39, 47

Ibrahim Pasha, 244
Irby, Charles, 202
Isaacs, Albert Augustus, 205, 206
Isaiah, 28, 69, 176
Ismailia, 157
Istanbul
 archaeological museum, 254

Jaffa, 14
James, Henry, 305
Jebb, Richard, 50, 65
Jeremiah, 158, 176
Jericho, 38
Jerusalem, 2, 5, 8, 23, 30, 31, 32, 33, 36, 41, 71–110, 220, 228, 229, 230, 236, 242
 American Colony, 88, 92, 97, 222
 Anglican bishopric, 102
 Anglo-Prussian bishopric, 10, 103, 107, 150
 British Consulate, 105
 Church of St Mary Magdalene, 106
 Church of the Holy Redeemer, 107
 Church of the Holy Sepulchre, 74, 75, 76, 77, 82, 97, 100

Damascus Gate, 97
Dome of the Rock, 82, 84, 95, 98
French hospice, 107
Garden Tomb, 98, 100, 105
Gate of Judgement, 86
Gethsemane, 77
Golgotha, 76, 97, 98
Gordon's Calvary, 97
Hezekiah's tunnel, 86
Italian hospital, 107
Kaiser Wilhelm's entry to, 108
Mea She'arim, 104, 105
Mishkanot Sha'ananim, 103, 104, 105
Nebuchadnezzar's sack of, 171
New City, 104
Robinson's Arch, 80
Russian Compound, 106
St George's Collegiate Church, 107
Temple Mount, 80, 82, 83, 84, 98
Temple of Solomon, 71, 78, 82, 84, 91, 100, 176, 187, 188
Tombs of the Kings, 86
Warren's map of, 98
Wilson's Arch, 98
Yemin Moshe, 104
Jesus Christ, 9, 24, 25, 34, 36, 48, 86, 89, 90, 92, 100, 114, 140, 199, 230, 236, 238, 242, 243, 271, 276, 280
John, St, 5, 24, 32, 117, 263
Jonah, 14, 43, 113, 116, 134
Joseph, 114, 137, 149, 159
Josephus, 7, 72
Jowett, Benjamin, 313
Joyce, James, 145

Kean, Charles, 29
Keith, Alexander, 16, 259, 260
Keith, George, 16
Keller, Werner, 36
Kellogg, Miner, 117, 121, 125
Kenrick, John, 47, 139, 140, 141, 326
Keppel, George, 171
Kharbet-Esdoum, 204
Khorsabad, 188
Kinglake, Alexander, 44, 45, 52, 57, 58, 63, 78, 81, 146, 239, 244, 246, 247
Kingsford, Anna, 25
Kingsley, Charles, 27, 141, 145, 211
Kircher, Athanasius, 165
Kitto, John, 240
Koldewey, Robert, 191, 192, 193, 195, 196
Kuyunjik, 130, 187

Lachish, 132
Lagerlöf, Selma, 74
Lake, Kirsopp, 24
Lanciani, Rodolfo, 311, 312, 313
Lang, Andrew, 68
Lardner, Nathaniel, 9
Layard, Austen Henry, 16, 18, 20, 28, 29, 35, 49, 50, 59, 111–35, 178, 180, 182, 186, 187, 188, 189, 190, 193, 209
Leaf, Walter, 67
Leake, William Martin, 11, 258
Leary, Lewis Gaston, 245
Lechevalier, Jean Baptiste, 50, 51, 52, 53, 59, 67
Lee, John Stebbins, 244
Legh, Thomas, 14
Lenormant, François, 57, 143
Lepsius, Karl Richard, 141, 143, 147, 149
Lewin, Thomas, 271
Lewis, George Cornewall, 46
Lightfoot, Joseph Barber, 23, 256, 269, 273, 274
Liverpool, 2, 33
Livy, 13, 46, 47
Lomax, Alfred, 120
London, 27, 28, 31, 33, 34, 37
London Jews' Society, 220
Long, Edwin, 181, 182, 196
Louis, St, 14
Lowe, Robert, 266
Lubbock, John, 269
Lucretius, 40, 56
Luke, St, 21, 243, 270, 293
Lynch, William François, 202, 203, 208, 209, 222
Lytton, Edward Bulwer, 161

Macaulay, Thomas Babbington, 58
Maccabeus, Judas, 14
McCheyne, Robert Murray, 211
MacDuff, John, 303
Macfarlane, Charles, 258
Mackennal, Alexander, 263
Macleod, Norman, 30, 31
Maitland, Edward, 25
Mallock, W. H., 98, 100
Mallowan, Max, 113, 178
Mandatory Department of Antiquities, 229
Manetho, 147
Mangles, James, 203
Manning, Henry, 310
Mariette, Auguste, 141
Marriott, Wharton, 294
Mar-Saba, 231
Martin, John, 27, 28, 113, 176, 177, 210, 217
Martin, Jonathan, 177

Martineau, Harriet, 17, 75, 77, 78, 91, 139, 141, 231
Mason, W. H., 65
Maspero, Gaston, 143, 148
Massenet, Jules, 145
Masterman, Charles, 38
Medjid, Abdul, 80
Melman, Billie, 238
Melville, Herman, 75
Memphis, 137, 143, 144, 145, 146, 148, 149
Merian, Matthäus, 217
Merivale, Charles, 301, 302
Methodism, 141, 291
Meyer, Frederick, 277
Michaelis, Johann David, 7, 47, 166
Mignan, Robert, 171
Miletus, 256
Millais, John Everett, 128
Miller, Elizabeth, 152
Milman, Henry Hart, 116
Milner, Thomas, 259
Milton, John, 44
Mitford, E. L., 112
Molyneux, William, 202
Mommsen, Theodore, 293
Montefiore, Judith, 251
Montefiore, Moses, 102, 104, 251
Moorey, P. R. S., 119
Moreau, Gustave, 219
Morgan, R. W., 290
Morton, Harold, 280
Moses, 30, 137, 143, 147, 148, 154, 157, 161, 162, 163, 208, 291
Mosul, 59, 115, 182
Mudie, Robert, 175
Müller, Friedrich Max, 55
Murray, John, 111, 112
Mycenae, 65, 67

Napoleon, 14, 53, 175
Napoleon III, 11
Napoleonic Wars, 8, 10, 14
National Gallery, 128
nativity play, 251, 252
Naville, Edouard, 148, 149, 150, 151, 153, 158, 159
Nazareth, 230, 235, 243, 248
Nestorians, 126, 127
New Jerusalem, 32, 33, 38, 58, 175, 177
New Lanark, 104
Newman, Francis William, 48
Newman, John Henry, 102, 211, 295
Newton, Charles, 266, 267, 269, 311

Niebuhr, Carsten, 7, 164, 165, 166, 167, 292
Nimrud, 186, 188
Nineveh, 17, 20, 28, 29, 49, 50, 62, 111–35, 178, 180, 188, 199, 205, 209
  Black Obelisk, 123, 132
Northcote, James Spencer, 293, 294, 295
Nott, Josiah, 140

Old, William Watkins, 44, 56, 57
Oliphant, Laurence, 21
Olympia, 269
Oppert, Jules, 164, 179
Orientalism, 93, 94, 184, 229, 252
Orientalist painting, 181, 182, 196, 216, 218, 219
Ottoman Empire, 7, 10, 35, 72, 94, 95, 199, 257, 259
Owen, Robert, 104
Oxford, 58
Oxford Architectural and Historical Society, 295
Oxford Declaration, 42
Oxhyrhynchus, 159

Paine, Thomas, 114
Palestine Exploration Fund, 16, 18, 20, 22, 29, 34, 38, 70, 81, 82, 83, 85, 100, 105, 159, 207, 244
Paley, F. A., 65
Paley, William, 9
Palmerston, Lord, 121
Palmyra, 29, 50
panorama, 28
  living, 94
Paris, 197
Parker, John Henry, 295, 296, 298, 299, 300, 301, 302, 303, 308
Parker, Joseph, 278
Parnassus, 14
Patmos, 32
Paul, Charles Kegan, 18
Paul, St, 14, 15, 21, 24, 30, 44, 254, 255, 256, 257, 286, 290, 291, 293, 302, 303, 308, 314
Peake, Arthur, 23
Peel, Robert, 121
Peloponnesian War, 40
Peter, St, 14, 286, 303, 310, 314
Petrie, William Matthew Flinders, 19, 22, 59, 62, 158, 160, 161
Philadelphia, 259
Philostratus, 65, 265

photography, 5, 16, 54, 86, 87, 88, 89, 91, 93, 95, 96, 97, 218, 219, 220, 258, 260, 298, 299, 300, 301, 305, 308
    Armenians, 74, 93–5
    Ottoman, 93, 94, 95
Pierotti, Ermete, 82
Pisa
    Campo Santo, 217
Pithom, 17, 23, 163
Pithom Stele, 150
Pius IX, 293
Place, Victor, 187
Plato, 56
Pliny, 265, 268
Plumptre, E. H., 262
Plymouth Brethren, 141, 158
Pococke, Richard, 257
Pompeii, 19, 207
Poole, Reginald Stuart, 12, 13, 30, 68, 136, 139, 143, 146, 147, 149, 150, 153, 161, 162
Pope, Alexander, 50, 57
Porter, Josias Leslie, 13, 17, 208
Porter, Robert Kerr, 171
postcards
    Bethlehem, 247
    Dead Sea, 223
Poynter, Edward, 152
Presbyterianism, 259, 261, 274
prophecy, 7, 8, 17, 27, 69, 115, 117, 129, 141, 164, 172, 174, 175, 176, 258, 259, 260, 263
Proust, Marcel, 216
Pusey, Edward Bouverie, 22, 134, 141, 211

Quaker, 16
Queen's Bible, 16

Rameses (city), 137, 138, 147, 148, 149, 150, 152, 157
Rameses II, 138, 149, 150, 151
Ramsay, William, 22, 23, 242, 256, 263, 273, 274, 275, 281, 282, 283
Ramsgate
    Montefiore mausoleum, 250, 251
    'Ramsgate's Bethlehem', 251
Raphael, 217, 224, 245, 303
Rassam, Hormuzd, 195
Rawlinson, George, 17, 140, 142, 188
Rawlinson, Henry, 17, 18, 49, 130, 131, 179, 180, 186, 187, 188, 189
Reade, Julian, 186
Reeve, Henry, 298, 299
Religious Tract Society, 36, 69, 234, 271
Rembrandt, 217

Renan, Ernest, 11, 139, 242, 243, 267, 270, 277, 278, 281
Rennell, James, 11, 169, 170, 171
Restorationism, 101, 102, 103, 110
Rich, Claudius, 171, 191, 192, 195
Richardson, Robert, 73, 77
Roberts, David, 146
Robinson, Edward, 12, 75, 76, 79, 80, 81, 82, 121, 201, 239, 245, 249
Robinson, Henry Crabb, 126
Rochester, Earl of, 197, 215
Rogers, Edward Thomas, 249
Rogers, Mary Eliza, 246, 249
Rogers, Samuel, 285
Rolland, Stewart Erskine, 124
Rome, 8, 16, 28, 30, 33, 34, 285–314
    Appian Road, 302
    Basilica of San Paolo, 308
    British Archaeological Society, 292, 295
    Capernian Gate, 302
    Catacomba Nuova, 216
    catacombs, 292, 293, 298, 299, 301
    Colosseum, 287, 305, 308
    Commisione Archaeologica, 312
    Commission of Sacred Archaeology, 293
    English College, 289
    Flaminian Gate, 288
    German Archaeological Institute, 293
    Mamertine prison, 303, 310
    San Sebastiano, 216
    St Peter's, 285, 286, 310
Rossini, Gioacchino, 184
Royal Asiatic Society, 179, 187
Royal Engineers, 88
Royal Geographical Society, 202
Royal Navy, 10, 201, 202, 257, 266
Royal Ordnance Survey, 86
Royal Society, Edinburgh, 51
Rubens, Peter Paul, 217, 219
Ruskin, John, 27, 41, 42, 150, 162, 308, 309, 310

Said, Edward, 101
Salzmann, Auguste, 16, 88
Sandys, George, 50
Sardanapalus, 183
Sardis, 259
Saviano, Roberto, 226
Sayce, Archibald Henry, 22, 48, 49, 60, 67, 70, 134
Schick, Conrad, 98, 100, 105
Schipano, Mario, 165
Schliemann, Heinrich, 13, 39, 43, 44, 46, 49, 53, 54, 55, 113, 124, 148, 269

Schwegler, Albert, 273
Scottish Free Church, 91
secularisation, 26
Seddon, Thomas, 220
Semiramis, 182, 183
Senior, Nassau, 291
Severn, Joan, 308
Seymour, Thomas Day, 68
Shaftesbury, Earl of, 101, 310
Shapira, Moses, 64
Sharp, William, 33
Sharpe, Samuel, 134, 139, 140, 141
Shaw, George Bernard, 227
Shepherd, Naomi, 242
Sinai, 228
Skene, James, 285
slum settlement, 33, 34
Smith, Eli, 12, 79, 201
Smith, George, 13, 20, 43, 46, 59, 62, 91, 150, 179, 194, 195, 268
Smith, Thomas, 257
Smith, William, 46, 47, 82, 207, 264
Smyrna, 7, 257, 258, 259
Smyrna to Aidin railway, 254, 265, 271
Society for the Promotion of Christian Knowledge, 220, 286
Society of Biblical Archaeology, 19, 159, 270, 273
Society of Biblical Literature, 70
Society of British Artists, 216
Society of Dilettanti, 257
Sodom, 27, 32, 37, 42, 48, 197–227
Solomon, 68
South Kensington Museum, 53
Spinoza, Baruch, 48
Spratt, Thomas, 10
Springs of Amatha, 21
Spurgeon, Charles Haddon, 212
St Clair, George, 31, 150
Stanley, Arthur Penrhyn, 13, 17, 233, 241, 262
steamship, 5, 71, 72, 199, 223
Stebbins, John, 242
Stillman, W. J., 63, 64
Story, William Wetmore, 312
Strauss, David Friedrich, 9, 48, 114, 139
Stuart, Moses, 79
suburbanisation, 37
Sunday School Union, 120
Svoboda, Alexander, 258, 260
Sydenham Crystal Palace, 29
    Nineveh Court, 123, 180
Sykes, Mark, 109

Tahpanhes, 158
Talbot, William Henry Fox, 179
Tarshish, 43
Tarsus, 30
Tayler, William Elfe, 205, 214
Taylor, Catherine, 286
Taylor, Robert, 141
Tel el Yahoudeh, 158
telegraph, 81
Tennant, William, 215
Tertullian, 39
Texier, Charles, 10, 258, 264
Thackeray, William Makepeace, 145, 239, 253
Thebes, 137, 148, 149
Thenius, Otto, 98
Thompson, William, 105
Thomson, William McClure, 12, 25
Thucydides, 40
Tiryns, 65
Tissot, James, 219
topography, 45, 50, 51, 70, 80, 85, 86, 88, 98, 100, 110, 164, 170, 200, 201, 254, 256, 286, 311, 313
Touro, Joseph, 104
Townley, Charles, 10
Toynbee Hall, 33, 34
Tractarianism, 212
Tristram, Henry Baker, 206, 213, 235, 236, 237, 259
Trollope, Anthony, 106, 197
Troy, 3, 13, 39–70
    as classical Jerusalem, 39, 42, 58
Tübingen, 23, 140, 256, 273, 274
Turner, J. M. W., 210, 217, 233
Twain, Mark, 74, 145
Tyndall, John, 39, 47
typology, 6–8, 27, 238, 263
Tyre, 27, 129, 135
Tyrwhitt, Richard St John, 298

undercroft, 227
Unitarianism, 4, 18, 47, 114, 126, 127, 136, 139, 140, 141, 142
Ur, 1
urbanisation, 2, 5, 25, 26, 73

Van de Velde, Carl Wilhelm, 205
Vaughan, Robert, 24, 26, 27, 28
Verdi, Giuseppi, 184
Vernet, Horace, 87
Veronese, 217
Victoria, 197
Vincent, Nicholas, 248

Virgil, 50
Voltaire, 183, 201
von Buch, Leopold, 209
Vorderasiatisches Museum, Berlin, 192

Waddington, William, 11
Wadi Tumilat, 147, 148, 149
Walsh, Robert, 260
Warren, Charles, 38, 83, 84, 85, 86, 98, 101, 102, 230
Wellhausen, Julius, 139, 188, 195
Westcott, Brooke Foss, 281
Westropp, H. M., 64, 65
Wilberforce, Robert, 20
Wilberforce, Samuel, 47
Wilhelm, Kaiser, 75, 107, 108, 109
Wilkinson, John Gardner, 20
Willcocks, William, 1, 38
Williams, George, 82
Williams, Isaac, 212
Williams, Raymond, 18
Williams, Rowland, 17, 42
Wilson, Charles, 98
Wilson, Erasmus, 142
Wilson, J. M., 303
Wiseman, Nicholas, 288, 298

Wolf, Friedrich August, 40, 41, 48, 52, 67
Wolseley, Garnet, 149
Wood, John Turtle, 254, 256, 263, 265, 267, 268, 269, 270, 271, 272, 273, 275
Wood, Robert, 50
Woolley, Leonard, 178
Woolmer, Alfred, 216
Wordsworth, William, 178
World's Fair
   St Louis, 1904, 95
Wroe, John, 8
Wylie, J. A., 213

Xanthus marbles, 10

Yezidis, 127, 128

Zeboim, 200
Zeller, Eduard, 273
Zion, 71
Zionism, 101, 102, 103, 105
Zionist Federation, 102
Zionists, World Congress of, 102
Zoan, 158
Zoar, 225